AN INQUIRY INTO WELL-BEING
AND DESTITUTION

Praise for *An Inquiry into Well-Being and Destitution*

'Although he is himself a theoretical economist, his models start in political philosophy, and go beyond what most economists think of as economics into the real conditions of life in the South. An Inquiry into Well-Being and Destitution is in many ways as impressive as Hume, Smith and Marx themselves. . . . No one, however, has gone so far beyond the generalities and brought so much of the many bits of available information together. No one, certainly, has thought it through so hard.'

London Review of Books

'a rich, unusual and wide-ranging work . . . When one reads the whole book, one is forced to jettison incorrect impressions of simple-mindedness. Without doubt, this is mandatory reading for every social scientist anywhere in the world'

Indian Express

'An excellent survey of the literature.'

Social & Behavioural Sciences

'It is a characteristic work: philosophically sophisticated, empirically well-informed, ambitious and lively. I think that there can be few people as able as he is to write the book.'

James Griffin

'a valiant and valuable effort which is much needed . . . I am amazed at the thoroughness with which Dasgupta has mastered the nutrition literature'

John Waterlow

'Dasgupta has produced a *tour de force*, a book which is a model of good economics. He has addressed a set of questions which are of central importance, questions for which we really do care what the answers are. To answer these questions he has marshalled an array of evidence, empirical studies drawn from a wide range of sources. And he has brought some simple, but deep, theories and ideas to bear on these questions. The book will be a must for every development economist, but its reach should go well beyond that: every economist should be concerned with the questions it raises, and as a model of how good economics should be done, it should be required reading for every graduate student.'

Joseph Stiglitz

'Dasgupta's book on resource allocation in poor countries covers a remarkably wide range of material, including work by anthropologists, nutritionists, political scientists, and others. At the same time as making this data available to economists interested in economic development, he raises important issues that are relevant to anthropologists, especially those dealing with the household, with poverty, and with gender differences. This is a cross disciplinary study of great importance to the various disciplines it engages.'

Jack Goody

An Inquiry into Well-Being and Destitution

Partha Dasgupta

CLARENDON PRESS · OXFORD

Oxford University Press, Walton Street, Oxford OX2 6DP

Oxford New York

Athens Auckland Bangkok Bombay
Calcutta Cape Town Dar es Salaam Delhi
Florence Hong Kong Istanbul Karachi
Kuala Lumpur Madras Madrid Melbourne
Mexico City Nairobi Paris Singapore
Taipei Tokyo Toronto
and associated companies in
Berlin Ibadan

Oxford is a trade mark of Oxford University Press

Published in the United States
by Oxford University Press Inc., New York

British Library Cataloguing in Publication Data

Data available

Library of Congress Cataloging in Publication Data

An inquiry into well-being and destitution / Partha Dasgupta.
Includes bibliographical references and index.
1. Poverty—Developing countries. 2. Quality of life—Developing countries.
3. Resource allocation. 4. Income distribution—Developing countries.
5. Households—Developing countries. 6. Malnutrition—Developing countries
I. Title.
HC59.72.P6D37 1993 330.9172'4—dc20 92–43313
ISBN 0–19–828835–2 (Pbk)

Printed in Great Britain
on acid-free paper by
Bookcraft (Bath) Ltd., Midsomer Norton, Avon

To the memory of my father,
Amiya Dasgupta

This book was meant for my father. He knew it, and he read the first draft of the early chapters in the summer of 1989 when my mother and he were visiting my family in Cambridge. In February 1990 he became ill, and for the first time I had the sense that one's parents can't be expected to be there always. His recovery must have been slow, for he responded to subsequent drafts only intermittently, and his letters became infrequent. I was teaching at Stanford then, and sometime in the spring of 1990 it came to me that I had all along been writing this book *to* him. For me it was a sense of profound well-being, the realization that I had been participating in a dialogue he had initiated many years ago, that this book was my response. But it wasn't meant to teach him anything. What I was trying to say to my father instead was, 'Look, this is what I think I know to be important, this is what I now believe, these are my values, this is how I *think*'.

The line of Dasguptas I belong to comes from Gaila, a village in the district of Barisal in what is now Bangladesh. As far as the records show, we had been there since the middle of the seventeenth century. My father was born and raised there. Ours was a lineage of scribes, and therefore of somewhat poor means. Along the way a few had attained a measure of scholarly eminence, but when my father was born our line was financially impoverished. In his early years, as I understand it, my father displayed no exceptional intellectual talents, and no special attention was given to him by his teachers. There was no patron to assist him when he sought higher education, and he pursued it by means of token scholarships and massive loans, and encouragement from his eldest brother. My father told me many times over the years that the only thing he ever consciously desired was a university teaching post. That he even entertained this thought, let alone managed to lift himself out of what was a totally unpromising rural background to become the founder of modern economics in India, reflects a commitment to learning I have seen in no one else. We were close, and even as a schoolboy I knew he was a wholly admirable person.

At the time I got to know my father properly, which was round about 1956, he used to devote his intellectual energy entirely to economics. Because he never talked of it, I did not know that he had a deep knowledge of Sanskrit and Bengali literature. I had just entered my teens then and had begun emulating my sister by reading late nineteenth- and early twentieth-century novels and plays. We found that our father had read only a bit of Shaw, not much else. This made me think he had no interest in literature. What I found him reading instead were the classics of economics, which were of no interest to me. So we talked of other things. He had a passion for reason and honesty, and convinced me by means of examples that almost all the world's politicians were either mentally deficient or hypocritical, or both. Among political leaders the one person he admired absolutely was Mahatma Gandhi, and he explained to me why it was correct to think of Gandhi as a Mahatma.

While I admired my father, I knew we were temperamentally different. For example, my mother used to say that my father's notion of perfection was a world in which the only thing anyone ever did was read. She and I agreed this couldn't be a perfect world, because in terms of goodness it would be surpassed by one where everyone read only some of the time. But if my father was Socratic in his approach to life, he was also innocent of the irrational drives which influence even the most rational of persons, and of the complexities which surround both personal and social behaviour. For example, he once told me that academics must inevitably be liberals in their politics because intellectual endeavour can thrive only in a liberal environment. I imagine this is why communism and narrow nationalism held no attractions for him. He felt if only the poor in India were to cease admiring the rich and were instead to laugh at their conspicuous consumption, the rich would be embarrassed into doing something worthwhile with their personal wealth. My father thoroughly distrusted revolutions.

In the autumn of 1991 I could see that my father did not have much time left. The book was still unfinished and I knew he wouldn't live to read it. So in an autobiographical essay I had been asked to prepare I tried to convey to him a sense of what I was attempting to do in the book.[1] My father was now very frail, and was slow to read the essay, but he told me several times as I accompanied him and my mother back to their home in Santiniketan from my sister's home in Baroda in late December that he liked it. He said the way I do economics wasn't his way, but he also said he liked my way, that I should stick to it. This was his benediction, but I didn't ask what he meant by it. In his presence there was never any sense of rush, and I didn't wish to tire him. Instead, I worked on my book in his study, and this seemed to please him. In any case, my wife and I were planning to bring our children to Santiniketan to visit their grandparents in the spring. At a conscious level I do not suppose we can ever admit that our parents aren't immortal. I left Santiniketan on 29 December, saying hardly a goodbye.

My father died on 14 January 1992.

P.D.

Cambridge
June 1992

[1] 'Population, Resources, Knowledge and Destitution: The Making of an Economist', in Arnold Heertje (ed.), *The Makers of Modern Economics* (Hemel Hempstead, Herts.: Harvester Wheatsheaf), 1993.

PREFACE

Technical economists, like people in other disciplines, write mainly for one another. They communicate their findings in journals without indulging much in the way of preliminaries about the motivation behind their inquiry and their chosen line of analysis. In part it is to save resources; but in part it reflects something larger and common to all human interchange. I still find it revelatory that all communication is predicated on something like a common conception of the world. It presumes a background of shared experience. What is uttered makes no sense unless we have an understanding of what has not been spoken.

Something of this shared experience would seem to be missing in economics. Consider, for example, the widely held belief that the subject is in a crisis, at a time when anyone who works in the field knows that it has for quite some while been enjoying a supremely productive phase, during which any number of social phenomena that earlier made no sense have come within its orbit. In any event, evaluating a subject by its weaknesses is not very useful (none would pass the test by this criterion). It seems to me far more fruitful to judge it by its successes.

This absence of shared experience has been costly. It has retarded progress in the subject because people misunderstand what others try to say, and this prolongs debates that should have, for the time being, been put to rest. The debating style of discourse continues to hold an attraction among economists. In places it has its merits (for example, it is effective in economic journalism); but I have come to believe increasingly that on the whole it is a hindrance. At its worst, it blunts our capacity to distinguish explanation from description; at its least bad, it dulls our ability to recognize the difference between deep and shallow explanations, and between vital and inessential distinctions.

I say this with feeling. As an economic theorist, I have from time to time worked on the economics of poor countries, and have read a good bit of what has been written. It is a field in which the style I speak of is often practised in its most unbridled form. It is also a field in which some of the deepest advances in the social sciences have occurred over the past dozen years or so. The subject resembles the streets of my home town of Varanasi, where pedestrians, animals, and half a dozen forms of transport all compete for room at their respective cruising speeds. It is an unfortunate state of affairs.

This book is both an analytical and an empirical inquiry into human well-being. In order to make progress, I study it largely by inquiring into the phenomenon of destitution, which is an extreme condition of ill-being. Destitution is first and foremost a personal calamity; and, although not self-evident, it is usually seen also as a grave weakness of any society that harbours it. However, while modern political and moral philosophers have enriched our understanding of the reasons why it is correct to view it as a social tragedy, there has been no real attempt to get this reasoning to face the phenomenon as it occurs in the world we have come to know. For example, the most comprehensive exploration in political philosophy to have been undertaken in modern times, John Rawls's *A Theory of Justice*, was expressly limited by the author to relatively wealthy societies. But the bulk of the world's destitutes live in Asia, Africa, and Latin America. So the theory would not seem to speak directly to them.

It is important that we try to establish a political philosophy that includes these societies, and that we do so with the care that is now standard among modern political philosophers. To leave unexamined so central a feature of living as the link between the private and public realms is to leave economic policies in poor countries exposed to the possibility of tragic errors. By the same token, not to force the abstract reasonings of moral and political philosophy to work on so sharp a phenomenon as destitution is to take no advantage of an essential method by which we can test their general validity. The laboratories where moral and political philosophers usually work are the Classics, but there is no reason why this restrictive practice should continue. We have now in hand a vast quantity of data on the conditions of living among the poorest of the poor. We have also much accumulated knowledge about the essential features of the various resource —allocation mechanisms that have prevailed over the years in different countries. There is every reason to put these findings to work on those considerations about the human condition that have been shown by modern philosophers to possess universal validity.

This book is an attempt to do each of these things. To begin with, I am trying to understand something about the common core of the circumstances in which people are born, and the manner in which they live and die in rural communities of poor countries. I seek a common language in which to discuss the lives of rural people in Asia, Africa, and Latin America. But even at the crudest level of classification (namely, resource endowments and agrarian structure) these regions differ considerably. For example, the pressure of rural population on land is striking in Asia, whereas it is the low and deteriorating quality of land and the environmental resource base that stands out when we study Africa; while the feature that most distinctly characterizes Latin America is the stark inequality in the distribution of land. This means that I have to avoid case-studies: they will not get me far. On the other hand, cross-country data cannot be trusted beyond an early point, because, among other things, the methods by which they are obtained are often non-comparable. So I am forced to experiment in a number of ways. I make use of ideas and information culled from a number of disciplines: anthropology, demography, ecology, economics, epidemiology, geography, moral and political philosophy, and the environmental, nutrition and political sciences. We will discover that their findings reinforce one another and help in the building of composite pictures of peoples, communities, and societies. Unfortunately, I am less than familiar with data on Latin America. So, in the main, the illustrations we will rely on will be from Asia and sub-Saharan Africa. For my purposes here, this will suffice.

The idea of a 'composite characterization' is vital to the research strategy I follow in this book. For example, I often lift material from widely different sources (from different regions even, when I require it) to construct composite households (not to be confused with 'representative households' in economic models). But it may be an uncommon household that has all the features I sometimes attribute to it. Similarly, the composite person I draw may also be difficult to locate. My notion of a composite person is a bit like the physician's concept of 'normal health': there aren't too many people who can pass the test, but it is an invaluable construction all the same. On occasion I hazard to make predictions about what the data will tell us about matters that haven't yet been explored on an empirical basis; and I report on several studies that have successfully made such predictions. This is risky business, but if a theory is any good, it had better do more than merely provide *ex post* explanations.

In this book I am also much involved with prescriptions, on matters concerning the relationships between individuals, households, communities, and the State. It is useful to distinguish generalized prescriptions from specific policy recommendations. I am concerned with the former, because we will be exploring foundational matters here. But even within the class of generalized prescriptions, there are two tiers: the first concerns the duties of the State (a central topic in political philosophy), while the second concerns an identification of the nature of those resource allocation mechanisms through which these duties can be best discharged (the business of political economy). Since the State can shape the resource allocation that prevails, the second tier is an essential part of any inquiry into well-being and destitution. Part I of this work addresses the first tier; Parts II–IV are concerned with the second. I develop a unified approach to social analysis and illustrate it with examples, taken from various sources. Detailed recommendations must, of course, be country-specific. Since I do not have the means or ability to arrive at them, I limit myself to the over-arching basis on which such recommendations ought to be founded, and on the types of institutions that can best deliver them.

The viewpoint I arrive at eventually is a pluralist one, but I reach it through a mode of analysis that reflects my own specialized training. I adopt what can be called a resource allocation point of view of the circumstances of living. Repeatedly, we will explore the instrumental worth of rules and institutions. No doubt we will miss something from adopting this perspective; but as we will see, there is much to be gained.

I have found this book hard to write, and my guess is that it is also hard to read. This is because the issues we will study here are complex, and are at the frontiers of a number of disciplines. The subject is of interest to people with widely differing backgrounds. So I have tried to make the book self-contained. This has meant that the level of exposition varies considerably even within each chapter. The specialist reader will find some passages most elementary and others very technical and advanced. However, what is obvious to, say, an economist is often novel to a nutritionist (and vice versa), and I had no wish to prejudge the matter. The level of exposition will no doubt strike the reader as jagged; but I have persisted with it, because I have in mind readers from a number of disciplines. For this same reason, I have been extensive with citations. Often, I refer to several publications (sometimes by the same author) on the same theme. I think this diversification will be of help. I have found libraries round the world to differ in their coverage: some are strong on journals but not so strong on books, while others provide wide-ranging publications from international organizations, but are weak on periodicals, and so forth. Seen from this perspective, it is a very good thing that academics often publish the same paper in several guises, a practice I had earlier thought was confined to economists.

A preliminary set of a few of the ideas to be found here, mainly connected with the epidemiological and nutrition side of things, was developed in the E. S. Woodward Memorial Lectures that I delivered at the University of British Columbia in 1986. I kept postponing the preparation of the manuscript for publication, because I needed to do more work on the subject. Some of this additional work was developed in a set of lectures on the economics of poverty that I gave later that year at the University of Texas (Austin), and subsequently at Harvard University in 1987 and Princeton University in 1988, and then summarized in my Walras-Bowley Lecture to the Econometric Society in 1989. The outlines of the book were even then something resembling what could have become a treatise on the economics of destitution. But in the Spring of 1989, while preparing the Frank Paish Memorial Lecture of the Royal Economic Society and the Association of University Teachers of Economics in the UK (on civil and political liberties, and their link with economic performance in poor countries), I knew that I was going to write an altogether different sort of book. In this I was greatly encouraged by Andrew Schuller of Oxford University Press, who thought that the risk of writing the sort of book I was planning was worth taking.

This work has not been supported by any grant. I have had no research assistant to help me in its preparation. But I have had the privilege of something far better: the guidance and advice of people belonging to the invisible college that makes up academic life. The bulk of the work was completed during 1989–1991, while I was teaching at Stanford University, an institution uncommonly good for collaborative work, among many other things. Portions of the manuscript (mainly those concerned with the more philosophical issues, Part I) were discussed at a seminar on social ethics that I conducted, successively, with Rachel Cohon and Julius Moravcsik in the Philosophy Department. Much of the material in Parts II–IV was developed in a graduate course on development economics in the Economics Department. My understanding of the epidemiological and environmental sides of things was helped greatly from a workshop on poverty that I conducted with Julie Anderson; from the Environmental Studies Forum at the Institute for International Studies, conducted by Walter Falcon and Roz Naylor; and from a workshop on population and environment at the Morrison Institute for Population and Resources, conducted by Marc Feldman. This book would not have been written but for the intellectual atmosphere I was privileged to enjoy at Stanford.

Other than Sue Hughes, who did the copy-editing with understanding and efficiency, I have not inflicted the entire typescript on anyone. Instead, I asked a number of people from different disciplines to read those chapters that required their scrutiny. Peter Bauer, Frank Hahn, Sheila Ryan Johansson, Reynaldo Martorell, John Rawls, Robert Solow, and John Waterlow provided me with comments so extensive, that I was obliged to rewrite the chapters entirely. The present version reflects the impact of their thoughts.

On several of the themes covered in this book, I have collaborated over the years with Ken Binmore, Charles Blitzer, Paul David, Peter Hammond, Geoffrey Heal, Karl-Göran Mäler, Stephen Marglin, Eric Maskin, Debraj Ray, Amartya Sen, Joseph Stiglitz, and Martin Weale. Many of the ideas expressed here were given to me by them, and they will recognize this fact.

During the process of writing a book one invariably accumulates debts for having things explained, and for suggestions on how one should ask questions. For me it is a fact of life that my friends are better at understanding things than I am, and I have learnt a great deal while writing this book from the many conversations and correspondences I have had with Irma Adelman, Anil Agarwal, Julie Anderson, Kenneth Arrow, Surjit Bhalla, Donald Brown, Patrick Byrne, Susan Cochrane, Rachel

Cohon, Carol Dasgupta, Angus Deaton, William Durham, Paul Ehrlich, Walter Falcon, Andrew Feldman, Marc Feldman, Victor Fuchs, Madhav Gadgil, Diego Gambetta, Jack Goody, Avner Greif, James Griffin, Bronwyn Hall, John Harsanyi, Geoffrey Hawthorn, Stephen Howes, Ramaswamy Iyer, Lal Jaywardena, Ray Jobling, Laurence Lau, Youngjae Lim, Michael Lipton, Paul Milgrom, James Mirrlees, Julius Moravcsik, Mohan Munasinghe, Roz Naylor, Sheilagh Ogilvie, Raylynn Oliver, Alaknanda Patel, Alex Rawls, Ashok Rudra, Hamid Sabourian, Paul Seabright, Pronab Sen, Shekhar Shah, Prakash Shetty, Nicholas Stern, Paul Streeten, Vinod Thomas, Pan Yotopoulos, and Stefano Zamagni; and from the comments of numerous members of the seminars and workshops at which I have aired the ideas in this book. Louise Cross has been most generous with her time and care in preparing large numbers of drafts of the chapters during the final stages of the book's preparation. To all these good people, I am most grateful.

Partha Dasgupta

St John's College
Cambridge.
26 October 1992

CONTENTS

PART I: WELL-BEING: THEORY AND REALIZATION

1. THE COMMODITY BASIS OF WELL-BEING   3

   1.1 Welfare and Freedoms   3
   1.2 Facts and Values in the Phenomenon of Destitution   5
   1.3 Destitution as a Resource Allocation Problem   9
   1.4 The Effects of Ill-Health   11
   1.5 Institutions and Agency Roles   15
   1.6 Theory and Policy   19

2. POLITICAL MORALITY AND THE STATE   22

   2.1 The Government as an Agency   22
   2.2 Acts and their Consequences   27
   2.3 Utility and Rights: Public Judgements and Aggregative
       Evaluations of Well-Being   32
   2.4 Commodity Needs   36
   2.5 Freedom and Rights: Positive and Negative   40
   2.6 Impersonality and the Public Sphere   46

3. THE OBJECTS OF SOCIAL CONTRACTS   50

   3.1 Rules versus Discretion   50
   3.2 Outcome- versus Resource-Based Evaluative Principles   53
   3.3 Political Competition and Civil Liberties   56
   3.4 Motivation and Choice   58
   3.5 Social Systems: A Formulation   60
   3.6 Contractual and Optimization Theories   64
   3.7 *Ex Post* Equilibria and *Ex Ante* Contracts   65
   3.8 Measures of Freedom   68
   3.9 Social Well-Being Functions   70
   3.10 Efficiency, Equality, and the Problem of Implementation   72

4. WELL-BEING: FROM THEORY TO MEASUREMENT   75

   4.1 Constituents and Determinants of Well-Being   75
   4.2 Income   78
   4.3 Health, 1: Anthropometric Measures   81
   4.4 Health, 2: Mortality Indices   87

4.5 Health, 3: Morbidity   90
4.6 Education: Numeracy and Literacy   97

5. THE REALIZATION OF WELL-BEING   104
5.1 Citizenship: Civil, Political, and Socio-Economic   104
5.2 Inter-Country Comparison of the Quality of Life   108
5.3 Political and Civil Liberties versus Economic Progress:
     Is There a Trade-Off?   116
5.4 Wars and Strife   121
5.5 Inequalities   125
5.6 The Point of Cross-Country Studies   127
Appendix   Political and Civil Rights Indices   129

PART II: ALLOCATION OF RESOURCES AMONG
HOUSEHOLDS: THE STANDARD THEORY

6. RESOURCE ALLOCATION MECHANISMS   135
6.1 Resources and Property Rights   135
6.2 Markets and Market Mechanisms   137
6.3 Culture and Market Transactions   140
6.4 Externalities: Public Goods and Common Property
     Resources   143
6.5 Infrastructure and Fixed Costs   147
6.6 Private and Public Realms, and Private and Collective
     Goods   149
6.7 Knowledge, Organization, and Economic Growth   151

*6. PUBLIC GOODS AND COMMON-PROPERTY RESOURCES
*6.1 The Theory of Public Goods   159
*6.2 The Problem of the Commons   161

7. DECENTRALIZATION AND CENTRAL GUIDANCE   165
7.1 Competitive Mechanisms in the Private Realm   165
7.2 Existence of Competitive Equilibrium   169
7.3 Competitive Markets and Efficiency   170
7.4 The Implementation of Just Allocations in the Private
     Realm   171
7.5 Pluralism and Exchange Restrictions in the Public Realm   173
7.6 Producer versus Consumer Taxation   176
7.7 National Income in a Pluralist Society   182

*7. REAL NATIONAL INCOME AS A MEASURE OF
GENERAL WELL-BEING   184

8. UNCERTAINTY, INSURANCE, AND SOCIAL NORMS   189
8.1 Environmental Uncertainty   189
8.2 Choice under Uncertainty and Risk Aversion   193

8.3   Avoiding Disasters   199
8.4   Trading in Risks: Pooling and Spreading   201
8.5   Correlated Risks in Agriculture   204
8.6   Reciprocity as a Social Norm in Stationary
      Environments   208
8.7   Overlapping Generations and the Transmission of
      Resources   212

        PART III: THE HOUSEHOLD AND ITS SETTING:
        EXTENSIONS OF THE STANDARD THEORY

9.   LAND, LABOUR, SAVINGS, AND CREDIT   221

9.1   The Peasant Household   221
9.2   Credit Constraints and the Organization of Production 224
9.3   Moral Hazard, Wage Labour, and Tenancy   229
9.4   Village Enclaves as Production Units   234
9.5   Land, Labour, and Credit Markets: Observations
      on Rural India   238
9.6   Agrarian Relations in Sub-Saharan Africa   243
9.7   Consumption as Investment   245
9.8   Lack of Credit among the Assetless   249
9.9   Consumption Smoothing   252
9.10 Unemployment   254

*9.   HOUSEHOLDS AND CREDIT CONSTRAINTS   257

*9.1 Model of the Peasant Household   257
*9.2 Precautionary Motive for Saving   260
*9.3 Credit, Insurance, and Agricultural Investment   264
*9.4 Why May Credit be Rationed?   265

10.   POVERTY AND THE ENVIRONMENTAL RESOURCE
      BASE   269

10.1 The Resource Basis of Rural Production   269
10.2 What Are Environmental Resources?   274
10.3 Needs, Stress, and Carrying Capacity: Land
      and Water   278
10.4 Environmental Shadow Prices, Project Evaluation,
      and Net National Product   280
10.5 Markets and their Failure: Unidirectional and Reciprocal
      Externalities   284
10.6 Property Rights on Land   288
10.7 Public Failure and the Erosion of Local Commons   290
10.8 Work Allocation among Women and Children and the
      Desirable Locus of Environmental Decisions   294

*10.   NET NATIONAL PRODUCT IN A DYNAMIC ECONOMY   297

       *10.1 The Economics of Optimal Control   297
       *10.2 NNP in a Deterministic Environment   298
       *10.3 The Hamiltonian and Sustainable Well-Being   302
       *10.4 Future Uncertainty   303

 11.   FOOD, CARE, AND WORK: THE HOUSEHOLD AS AN
       ALLOCATION MECHANISM   305

       11.1 Gender Differentials among Adults   305
       11.2 Allocations among Girls and Boys   309
       11.3 Bridewealth and Dowry   311
       11.4 Regional Patterns of Household Allocations:
             The Case of India   313
       11.5 Marriage and Inheritance in India   322
       11.6 Bargaining Theory as a Framework for Household
             Choice   324
       11.7 The Nash Programme: A Formalization   330
       11.8 Bargaining vs. Well-Being Maximization within the
             Household   333

*11.   AXIOMATIC BARGAINING THEORY   337

       *11.1 Nash Bargaining Solution   337
       *11.2 The Kalai–Smorodinsky Bargaining Solution   340

 12.   FERTILITY AND RESOURCES: THE HOUSEHOLD AS
       A REPRODUCTIVE UNIT   343

       12.1 Income, Fertility, and Food: The Environmentalist's
             Argument   343
       12.2 The Population Problem   346
       12.3 Population Externalities: Household versus Societal
             Reasoning   349
       12.4 Birth Control and Female Education   353
       12.5 Children as Consumer and Insurance Goods   356
       12.6 Environmental Degradation, and Children as Producer
             Goods   358
       12.7 Some Special Features of Sub-Saharan Africa   361
       12.8 Modelling Fertility Decisions   363
       12.9 Allocation Failure and Public Policy   368

*12.   STRATEGIC COMPLEMENTARITIES IN FERTILITY
       DECISIONS   371

       *12.1 Atmospheric Externalities   371
       *12.2 Why Nash Equilibria?   376

13. POPULATION AND SAVINGS: NORMATIVE
    CONSIDERATIONS   377

    13.1 Parental Concerns   377
    13.2 The Genesis Problem and the Repugnant Conclusion   379
    13.3 Is the Repugnant Conclusion Repugnant?   383
    13.4 Actual Problems and an Underlying Asymmetry   385
    13.5 Rational Ends   392

*13. CLASSICAL UTILITARIANISM IN A LIMITED WORLD   395

    *13.1 The Model   395
    *13.2 The Solution   396

         PART IV: UNDERNOURISHMENT AND DESTITUTION

14. FOOD NEEDS AND WORK CAPACITY   401

    14.1 Complementarities among Nutrients   401
    14.2 Nutrition and Infection   405
    14.3 Energy Conservation   408
    14.4 Energy Requirements, Nutritional Status, and
         Productivity   412
    14.5 Basal Metabolic Rates and Maintenance Requirements 423
    14.6 Special Requirements, 1: Growth and Development   426
    14.7 Special Requirements, 2: Pregnancy and Lactation   431
    14.8 Determinants of Work Capacity and Endurance   432

15. ADAPTATION TO UNDERNOURISHMENT   437
    15.1 The International Incidence of Calorie Deficiency   437
    15.2 Adaptation: Genetic, Physiological, and Behavioural 441
    15.3 Short-Term Adjustment, or Homeostasis   443
    15.4 Homeostasis and the Magnitude of Undernourishment 448
    15.5 Long-Term Adaptation   452
    15.6 Metabolic Disequilibrium   458
    15.7 Food Intake, Efficient Productivity, and Stature   461
    15.8 Activity Possibility Sets   466

16. INEQUALITY, MALNUTRITION, AND THE
    DISFRANCHISED   473

    16.1 Asset Ownership, Maintenance Costs, and Labour
         Power   473
    16.2 The Labour Market and Involuntary Unemployment   477
    16.3 Efficiency Wages and Piece-Rates   483
    16.4 Competitive Market Allocations   486
    16.5 Development Regimes   490
    16.6 Growth with Redistribution   494

16.7 Robustness and Extensions   498
16.8 Involuntary Unemployment and Surplus Labour   505
16.9 Who Resists Wage Cuts?   509
16.10 The Appeal of Nutrition-Based Theories of the Labour
      Market   511

*16. ANALYSIS OF ALLOCATION MECHANISMS WHEN
     NUTRITION AFFECTS PRODUCTIVITY   512

     *16.1 Characteristics of Equilibrium Allocations in the Timeless
           World: Proofs   512
     *16.2 A Two-Class Example   515
     *16.3 The Speed of 'Trickle-Down'   517
     *16.4 The Coexistence of Casual and Permanent Labour   518
     *16.5 Food Distribution within Poor Households   523

17. INCENTIVES AND DEVELOPMENT POLICIES   525

     17.1 Agrarian Reform   525
     17.2 Food Subsidies   528
     17.3 Employment Guarantee Schemes and Rural
          Infrastructure   533
     17.4 Community Participation and Credit Facilities   535
     17.5 Health and Education   539
     17.6 Envoi   542

References   546

Index of Names   627

Index of Subjects   640

PART I

Well-Being: Theory and Realization

1

The Commodity Basis of Well-Being

1.1 *Welfare and Freedoms*

Two aspects of personhood have alternated in dominating the thinking of social philosophers over the centuries, each true in itself, but each quite incomplete without the other. One sees us capable of deliberation, having the potential capacity to do things. It details agency, choice, independence, and self-determination, and thereby that aspect of our selves which fashions projects and pursues goals. The other views us as a seat of utility or satisfaction; as loci of possible states of mind, described by the extent to which desires are fulfilled, by the activities that are undertaken and the relationships that are enjoyed. If one vision sees us *doing* things, the other sees us residing in states of *being*. Where the former leads one to the language of freedom and rights, the latter directs one to a concern with welfare and happiness.

These are related aspects, of course, in fact so closely related that they have often been conflated into one without it having caused any obvious damage. But they are not the same, and there is no guarantee that fusing them does not lead to errors in the choice of policy, especially public economic policy. For this reason much has been written in recent years on the dangers of regarding the two as essentially the same, and we will study the force of such concerns later in this book (see Chapters 2–7).

In a great many instances, this conflation has been made possible by the practice of allowing each aspect in turn to usurp the other. Consider, for example, that ethical justifications of the Welfare State, at least those often provided by social philosophers, are undertaken in a language quite different from the one most common among economists debating public policy. The idea of socio-economic rights (that is, rights to certain scarce resources), liberally used by social philosophers, is rarely to be found in discourses on welfare economics, where instead the rationale for public choice is most often grounded on some aggregate measure of utility or, more generally, on some measure of aggregate welfare.[1] Now, the languages

---

[1] Contrast the styles in two classics, T. H. Marshall (1964) and Graaff (1962), and in more recent commentaries, such as Rimlinger (1983) on the one hand, and Atkinson and Stiglitz (1980), Boadway and Bruce (1984), Barr (1987), and Starrett (1988) on the other. I shall

may be different, but their recommendations are usually the same. Each
type of justification is allied to a substantive theory of public policy, and
it involves the establishment of resource allocation mechanisms in which
citizens are assured of an access to primary health care, legal aid, potable
water, sanitation facilities, shelter, primary and secondary education, and,
more generally, income sufficient for essential food and clothing. Putting
it in a more aggregative manner, and somewhat loosely and crudely, both
sets of justifications inform the State to provide guarantees of a 'basic
minimum' living standard or, if this proves to be infeasible in the
immediate future, to pursue policies that will make it feasible in reasonably
short time.[2]

To give an instance, consider that people often appeal to a category of
socio-economic rights when advocating policies that have an impact on the
extent of absolute poverty in a society. It is possible to use instead some
notion of aggregate welfare and reach similar conclusions. We may, for
example, be considering the desirability of a nutrition-guarantee scheme.
We could advocate it by invoking people's interests, for example certain
types of 'positive' rights (see Chapter 2). We could also commend it on
grounds of general welfare in the sense of the classical utilitarians. We
could do this by noting first that nutrition intake is a determinant of
individual welfare, that at low levels of intake it is a critical determinant,
and that in the absence of such a scheme a sizeable fraction of the
population would be vulnerable to food deprivation. We could thus argue
that the level of aggregate welfare that would be expected to be achieved
could be increased by the establishment of a policy of food guarantees, for
example by the issue of means-tested food stamps, an income maintenance
programme, a food- or cash-for-public-work scheme, unemployment benefits, targeted food subsidies, or whatever.[3] In other words, it is not
immediate if the language of socio-economic rights has any greater cutting
power over aggregate-welfare reasoning, at least not when we come to
discuss the rationale behind the Welfare State, its appropriate limits, and
its mode of operation. Current social philosophers who use the language
of positive rights and are critical of the narrowness of utilitarianism overlook
that the philosophical foundations of the Welfare State in Britain rested
originally on utilitarian calculations (see Gutmann, 1980; Phelps-Brown,

refer to a number of technical terms, such as 'rights', 'utility', and 'resource allocations
mechanisms', even before explaining them in subsequent chapters. They are in frequent use
in the social sciences and so will be familiar, at least in a loose sense. Furthermore, for the
moment I shall follow the literature and use the terms 'utility' and 'welfare' interchangeably.

[2] I am referring to the extra reach of the Welfare State. The protection and promotion of a
wide range of freedoms are taken for granted not only in it, but even in the Minimal State
(see Nozick, 1974).

[3] These instruments are not equally effective; I am merely listing a few which have been
tried in a number of countries. See Ch. 17 for further discussion.

1988). It isn't enough to attack utilitarian theories merely by asserting that they glide over the claims of individual rights, and to produce hypothetical examples in which they move us in different ethical directions. Rights themselves need to be justified, and it would be remarkable if they could be justified in ways other than by an appeal to the human interests their recognition protects and promotes. This, as has been noted elsewhere (see Scanlon, 1978: 93), was the incontrovertible insight of the classical utilitarians.

Nevertheless, there are differences between these two broad outlooks, for example in the design of economic institutions they recommend within the Welfare State for the sharing of benefits and burdens. Later in this book we will study this more closely (see also Dasgupta, 1986a). But for the moment it will prove useful to concentrate on the similarity between the outlooks and note that their resemblance has emerged not only because rights and utility have over the years acquired elastic meanings, but also because of the plain truth that they *are* closely related, even when the terms assume their classical nuances. Something that is in a person's interest can hardly fail to influence his state of mind. What a person does, what he achieves—more generally, what he is capable of achieving—are things that, while plainly not the sole determinant of his welfare, are clearly one set of ingredients of his welfare. This points to a close connection, and it has helped obfuscate their differences.

1.2 *Facts and Values in the Phenomenon of Destitution*

There is another, related reason why utilitarian considerations tend to point at the same set of obligations on the part of the State as do those founded on the notion of rights. It is that states of mind are notoriously difficult to monitor. It isn't merely the problem of utility measurement, difficult though that is: there is also the question of how one may go about making interpersonal welfare comparisons. This is not to say that we do not constantly make such comparisons. We do. But we do so by comparing what we believe are the major ingredients of welfare.[4]

What are they? They are easy enough to identify in those regions of the human circumstance where a person's welfare is consonant with her interests. This is because the principal ingredients of a person's interests

---

[4] I am deliberately stating the matter in the way it is customarily put; that the ingredients which result in various experiential states are a mere surrogate for what we are ultimately after, namely, the interpersonal comparison of experiential states. This is a wrong way of stating the matter. D. Davidson (1986) has made the powerful claim that it isn't a mere surrogate; he has argued that the meaning we attach to the idea of such comparisons involves our own judgements on the value of such ingredients. See below in the text for further discussion. See also Scanlon (1992).

are immediate. They are, for example, her state of health and the number of years she expects to live, her command over commodities and services, and the use she is capable of making of such commodities and services. Plainly, also, they consist of the degree to which she is free to form associations and friendships, to speak her mind, to do what she rationally desires to do, the access she has to information about others and the world, and so forth—in fact, precisely those items that loom prominently in right-based ethical theories. There is then the agreeable fact that these determinants of a person's good *are* measurable and comparable, and that this is so irrespective of what a person's conception of her good happens to be. This itself is symptomatic of the objectivity of ethical truth, and it provides a reason why the shop-worn distinction between facts and values is far less sharp than it has typically been taken to be.

Economists stress that people differ in their judgement on what are appropriate rates of trade-off among competing social goals. Political differences among people are to be traced to this, or so the assertion goes.[5] My own understanding is otherwise. Divergences in people's opinions about how the world "works" assume importance in political debates long before differences in ethical views manifest themselves. I have yet to meet anyone who does not wish to see unemployment reduced, or destitution a thing of the past. I have also heard many disagreements on what are the most effective means of bringing them about. (In Section 1.8, I will provide an illustration of this.) As Putnam (1989:7) puts it:

It is all well and good to describe hypothetical cases in which two people 'agree on the facts and disagree about values', but in the world in which I grew up such cases are unreal. When and where did a Nazi and an anti-Nazi, a communist and a social democrat, a fundamentalist and a liberal . . . agree on the facts? . . . There is weird discrepancy between the way philosophers who subscribe to a sharp fact–value distinction *make* ethical arguments sound and the way ethical arguments *actually* sound.

It will be out of place to try and explicate the entanglement between facts and values in any depth here. But, as it will influence the way I will throughout argue in this book, it is essential I offer a sketch of what the claim amounts to.[6]

Concepts like *undernourishment* and *disease* and *destitution* on the face of it have only a descriptive content. In fact, there is an evaluative content as well, in that there is no way of saying what our ethical evaluation of the state of undernourishment, or disease, or destitution should be, or can be, without our having to use words *like* undernourishment, or disease, or

---

[5] Among the most prominent expositions of this view are Samuelson (1947), Graaff (1962), and J. Robinson (1964).
[6] The influence of Putnam (1981, 1989) will be evident. See also McDowell (1978).

destitution. To give an example, suppose it is an appropriate description that a full 15 per cent of a nation's population suffers from chronic undernourishment. In evaluating this state of affairs, there is no role for an additional sentence like: 'It is a bad state of affairs where 15 per cent of a population are undernourished.' This is because, in answering why it is bad, we would be forced merely to provide a description of undernourishment, or something very much like it; that is, we would be obliged to describe the physical and mental consequences of an inadequate diet. The 'descriptive' and 'evaluative' components of concepts like destitution cannot be separated. They are entangled.

There are then two distinct, but related, sets of issues in both utilitarian and rights-based ethical theories: what are the indices that go to reflect a person's utility or interest, and how should the indices of different persons be weighted and aggregated to fashion public judgements on social and economic policies? A great deal of recent political philosophy and welfare economic theory has been concerned with these questions. So too has development economics, but, as I will argue subsequently, most development economists, when studying international data on these matters, have addressed the issues from an unnecessarily restricted point of view. One group (albeit a small group) has on the whole judged states of affairs primarily in terms of the extent to which individuals and groups enjoy negative rights, and thereby negative freedom (e.g. Bauer, 1971, 1984); the other, primarily in terms of positive rights, and thus positive freedom (e.g. Drewnowsky and Scott, 1966; Amiya Dasgupta, 1975; Streeten, 1977; Streeten and Burki, 1978; Hicks and Streeten, 1979; M. D. Morris, 1979; Streeten et al., 1981; Sen, 1981a, 1988a; Silber, 1983; UNDP, 1990; World Bank, 1990). And they are not the same (see Chapter 2).[7]

The notion of rights is central to the present study, and one of my aims here is to develop the idea in a way that may prove useful to social scientists. I say this with feeling; the philosophical literature on freedom and rights, even while voluminous, isn't transparent. It isn't always clear how certain distinguished kinds of freedoms are related to one another and how they are in turn related to welfare and preference satisfaction. It will prove helpful to discuss these matters in a language social scientists are

---

[7] I am not suggesting that these authors aren't sensitive to the distinction between these two broad categories of freedom, which we will study in Ch. 2. A number have written extensively on liberties and rights (see e.g. Sen, 1985, 1988b). It is only that in their applied work they have usually concentrated on one at the exclusion of the other. To take an example, Sen (1988a), in asking what (sub-Saharan) Africa and India have to learn from each other, concentrates on gender biases in survival chance (Africa beats India) and on the occurrence of famines (India wins hands down). There is no mention that the African record on civil and political rights is appalling, not only absolutely, but also in comparison with those in India (see Ch. 5).

used to, because the idea of rights and interests prompts us to consider an ethical conception of life more pluralist in reach than the ones on offer in much of the literature on welfare economics. It is such a pluralist conception of a person's good that I shall call her *well-being*.

This book is an inquiry into the idea of a person's well-being and, thereby, into the still broader notion of *social well-being*. I will argue that in evaluating public policies one must show that they protect or promote some such object as this. But the concept is an elusive one, and it is hard to identify it accurately. So my strategy will be to explore a starker notion, that of *destitution*. My idea is that by studying an extreme form of ill-being we can obtain an understanding of well-being itself. In our study, we will not only inquire into what constitutes destitution, we will try and see what it is like to *be* a destitute. This will take us into an extensive empirical literature into the nature and extent of the phenomenon in the world as we know it. But description isn't explanation, and no account of destitution can get off the ground unless it includes an analysis of the forces that bring about states of affairs where a large proportion of people can be destitutes, or at the very least come perilously close to being so. Therefore, much of this book will be devoted to the development of a resource allocation theory which accommodates the phenomenon.

It is usual, it is certainly correct, to insist from the distinctness of every human being that each person is different; that needs differ, that talents differ, that aspirations differ, and that each person's conception of her own good differs from those of others. Both political philosophy, and welfare and development economics have made much of this in recent years. But when we inquire into well-being and destitution, it is it seems to me illuminating to notice the commonality of the human experience: that for example we all have similar needs—for food and care and shelter, for friendship and love and a communal life, and for freedom to develop our talents and to pursue our ends. That this commonality will nevertheless lead to differences in cultural norms and social practices is not a paradox: it is to be expected. Differences in the social sphere are not merely an outcome of historical accidents: they arise also from ecological differences across communities. It is a common failing of modern social commentators to regard differences in cultural practices as reflecting differences in primary ethical values. My earlier remarks imply that as a research strategy this is bad practice. Since norms are often internalized by people, it is also dangerous, if recent experiences in poor countries is any guide. Anthropological evidence informs us that much of what are called cultural values have an instrumental basis. (Systems of belief play a role here, and are entangled with values.) It seems to me that there is less danger of an eventual error in ethical reasoning were we to start from the commonality of the human experience and to then show how and why people and societies differ, than to start from an assumption of complete differences and to then narrow them down by admitting commonalities. For all these reasons, the sense of the many commonly shared features of human life will influence much of what follows in this book.

1.3 *Destitution as a Resource Allocation Problem*

These are no mere academic matters. If welfare and development economics, more generally political philosophy, are not about the circumstances in which people are born and the manner in which they are able to live and die, they are about nothing. In asking the question what sorts of lives are well-lived, we at once ask what things are necessary for persons to be able to live such lives. When we inquire into a person's state of destitution we simultaneously seek to know what precisely he is bereft of. Towards this end we will look at fundamental commodity needs (sometimes called *basic needs*), and the claim-rights that may follow from them. We will wish to know what they are, what they amount to, why prominence must be given to them, and what is the magnitude of destitution among men, women, and children in the modern world (see Chapters 4, 5, 10–12, and 14–15). We will also wish to know what the role of the State is in the allocation of benefits and burdens and, more generally, in the protection and promotion of human interests (see Chapters 3, 6–8, 10, and 17). The incidence of extreme commodity deprivation occurs everywhere, of course, but it isn't endemic everywhere. When studying the evidence, we will for this reason look closely at poor nations, where the overwhelming bulk of the incidence occurs. These are predominently agrarian and pastoral societies, where over a long period communal support systems have developed to cope with the twin facts of poverty and uncertainties in personal fortunes.[8] There are often considerable inequities in such 'solidarity' systems (see S. L. Popkin, 1979; Beteille, 1983; Commander, 1983; Iliffe, 1984); nevertheless, they can be seen as an imperfect version of what we today call social security.

A good portion of 'household' incomes in such economies is derived from communally owned natural resource endowments (see Chapter 10). The economic theory of common property resources informs us that an elaborate network of mutual controls on resource use needs to be in force. Otherwise, human well-being will not be served. (See Dasgupta and Heal, 1979: chapter 3, for a classification of alternative institutional arrangements which can support equitable and efficient use.) Recent anthropological work has reconfirmed the presence of community-based controls

[8] See e.g. Wiser (1936), K. Polanyi (1957a, 1977), Epstein (1967), Goody (1973), J. C. Scott (1976), J. Cohen (1980), Wynne (1980), Chambers, Longhurst and Pacey (1981), Das Gupta (1987b), Cashdan (1989), B. Agarwal (1990), Platteau (1991), and Chs. 8–9.

on such resources.[9] This work has also recorded a growing erosion of such controls and support systems in the face of technological change, population growth and migration, and the opening of new markets. Modernization benefits many. In the long run it can benefit all. But in the process of modernization a great many get trampled upon, the vast majority of whom are women, children, the old, and the infirm.[10] This suggests a central role for government action. But at the level of economic policy, the duties of government cannot be identified unless we know something about the nature and extent of household, or kinship, or religious, or community support systems. These themes will be studied in Chapters 10–11 and 16–17.

We will find it necessary to offer an account of the analytical economics of commodity deprivation. This will allow us to identify resource allocation mechanisms in which fundamental needs can go unfulfilled for an entire class of people. We will wish to identify those categories of people in a society who are particularly vulnerable to chronic destitution, and we will try to find an explanation for why such people are vulnerable; why in particular they are bereft of resources (see Chapters 9–11, and 16). This is essential if we are to understand the phenomenon; but it is also necessary if we are to identify prescriptions. The point, as always, is that one should not be asked to locate commendable policies if there isn't an understanding of the environment in which policies are put into effect; otherwise, it isn't possible to know what the effects of a policy will be. Now, even though much has been written in recent years on poverty and destitution, the analytical economics of chronic, or even of sharp and fatal, deprivation has remained an underdeveloped subject. What is currently on offer is mostly policy without the backing of theory. The literature consists largely of commentaries on food security programmes implemented by governments and international organizations over the years (see Underwood, 1983; Biswas and Pinstrup-Anderson, 1985; Reutlinger and Pellekaan, 1986; Berg, 1987; Bell and Reich, 1988; Dreze and Sen, 1990; UNDP, 1990; World Bank, 1990; Alamgir and Arora, 1991).

Now, narratives without an underlying theory can inform, but they do not necessarily illuminate. I shall therefore try to construct the beginnings of such a theory. This will require work, because the standard theory of resource allocation (as presented in, say, Debreu, 1959; Arrow and Hahn,

[9] See Howe (1986), Wade (1987), Agarwal and Narain (1989), Chopra, Kadekodi and Murty (1989), Falconer and Arnold (1989), Falconer (1990), and Ensminger (1990). Historical societies in Europe had similar support systems. This has been studied in Reynolds (1984).

[10] Ch. 16 will present a formal account of a process by which the disadvantaged can become destitutes even while the economy on average grows. This is not to deny the possibility of increased wealth along the growth process trickling down to the poorest of the poor even over the short run. For a fine, empirical study of the spread of the benefits of the Asian Green Revolution in agriculture to the rural poor, see Singh (1990).

1971; Malinvaud, 1972a; Bliss, 1975; Layard and Walters, 1978; and Varian, 1984) does not make any essential use of the idea of basic commodity needs. For concreteness, we will make a study of the most fundamental of needs: those that are necessary for sheer survival, best exemplified by nutrition, shelter, sanitation, and health care. We will study what happens when such needs are not met. This will require us to review an extensive biomedical literature on food deprivation, and the ways in which individuals try to adapt in such circumstances. We will explore how costly it is for people to so adapt. We will also investigate what effect this has on their ability to work and to produce commodities which would enable them to obtain the food and care necessary for good health. Put differently, we will confront a basic circularity in living: that people need food and care in order to be able to be in a position to produce food and care. And we will confirm that the standard theory of resource allocation does not accommodate the notion of basic physiological needs. Because of this, without modification it is incapable of absorbing an allied concept: destitution. These issues will be pursued in Chapters 14–17.

Given that modern resource allocation theory has nothing direct to offer on the matter of destitution, we may ask if there is some other source one can turn to. It might be thought that classical political economy would have a good deal to offer. If the idea of physiological needs is to be found anywhere in the economics literature, it has surely got to be here. In fact, the picture portrayed there is woefully inadequate. For example, in his famous chapter on wages, David Ricardo begins by saying: 'the natural price of labour is that price which is necessary to enable the labourers, one with another, to *subsist* and to perpetuate their race, without increase or diminution' (Ricardo, 1911: 52; emphasis added). This suggests a demographic principle of the following sort: population growth is dependent on the wage rate, and there is a critical wage at which population growth is nil; anything else, and the system adjusts to return to this stationary state. Viewing the matter over the long run, this is the subsistence wage. Any wage below this spells reduction for the labour force, and so for the population. But over the short and medium run, the theory says nothing. It doesn't say anything about a person's capacities for work and reflection and play. It is mostly a theory concerning a person's capability and propensity to breed.[11]

1.4 *The Effects of Ill-Health*

When we come to study the biomedical evidence in Chapters 4, 14 and 15 on one critical set of needs, namely calories, we will also touch upon a few

[11] For an illuminating account of the role of the concept of a subsistence wage in classical political economy, see Amiya Dasgupta (1985).

allied, complementary needs, such as protein and micro-nutrients, potable water, basic medical care, and sanitation; and we will see that the matter is more complex than might be thought at first blush. Survival, and not just short-run survival, does not on its own say much about a person's raw productive capacity. A person can be *malnourished* (or *undernourished*; I will use these terms interchangably here) and continue to exist. Malnourishment is not usually the immediate cause of death even among the very poor. There is much evidence that relatively low mortality rates can co-exist with a high incidence of malnutrition and morbidity.

Malnourishment isn't the same as undernourishment: a malnourished person can be obese. Since the context will always be clear, there will be no risk in my using the terms interchangeably. The general effects of persistent undernourishment and infections vary widely, but they all result in an impaired life. In expectant mothers it affects the growth of the foetus, and therefore its health status (e.g. weight) at birth.[12] In extreme cases it affects the lactation peformance of nursing mothers (Gopalan, 1958; Jelliffe and Jelliffe, 1978; Whitehead *et al.*, 1976; Prentice, 1984; Martorell and Habicht, 1986; Waterlow, 1992b; Chapter 14). Nutritional anaemia, common among expectant mothers in poor countries, causes fatigue, and lowers resistence to infections. (This is analysed in Royston, 1982; Scrimshaw and Wallerstein, 1982; Scrimshaw, 1984; H. M. Levin, 1986; Whitehead, 1989.) In sub-Saharan Africa, some two-thirds of pregnant women and over half of all women of reproductive age are estimated to suffer from this (see Chapters 4 and 14; World Bank, 1989b). In children, chronic malnutrition causes muscle wastage and growth retardation, and thus future capability (see Spurr, Barac-Nieto and Maksud, 1978; Blaxter and Waterlow, 1985; Falkner and Tanner, 1986; Spurr, 1988; Martorell, 1990), and it increases morbidity and their vulnerability to infections. (The classic is Scrimshaw, Taylor and Gordon, 1968. See also Scrimshaw, 1970; Chen and Scrimshaw, 1983.) There is evidence that, just as with the foetus, severe malnutrition can affect brain growth and development (see Monckeberg, 1968; Brockman and Ricciuti, 1971; Pollitt, 1980). It influences mental capacities through damages to the nervous system during the period when the brain is growing.[13] It also affects future capabilities by reducing the

[12] See Lechtig *et al.* (1975), Read *et al.* (1975), Klein *et al.* (1976), Morgane *et al.* (1979), Johnston *et al.* (1980), Prentice (1980), Harmish and Munroe (1981), Prentice *et al.* (1981), Adair (1984), and Mueller and Pollitt (1982). Some 20 million infants are born underweight (less than 2.5 kg) each year, and over 20% of children under 5 years of age in poor countries are below 90% of normal weight-for-height. This translates to well over 100 million children under 5. See Chs. 4 and 14.

[13] See Dodge, Prensky and Feigin (1975) and Winick (1976). Damages caused by mild to moderate undernourishment probably represent a retardation and not permanent injury. They would appear to be reversible. See Balazs *et al.* (1986), Cravioto and Arrieto (1986), and Waterlow (1992a).

energy that children have available for learning through interacting with their environment; for example, their motor development is impeded (Scrimshaw and Gordon, 1968; Rutihauser and Whitehead, 1972; Graves, 1976; A. Kumar, Ghai and Singh, 1977; McKay *et al.*, 1978; Chavez and Martinez, 1979, 1984; Satyanarayana, Naidu and Rao, 1979; Colombo and Lopez, 1980; Malina, 1980a, b, 1984; Viteri and Torun, 1981; Raina and Spurr, 1984; Jamison, 1986; Moock and Leslie, 1986; Spurr, 1988; Chapter 14). Chronic malnutrition among adults diminishes their muscular strength, their capacity to do physical work, and their protection against a wide range of infectious diseases (see Chapters 14–15).[14] It also brings in its wake marked psychological changes, manifested by mental apathy, depression, introversion, and lower intellectual capacity and concentration (M. S. Read, 1977; Basta *et al.*, 1979; Caliendo, 1979). Life expectancy among the malnourished is low. Undernourishment increases the chance of immediate death, although it doesn't enforce it. Malnutrition is on this side of starvation. For this reason the world can, and does, carry a stock of undernourished people, living and breeding in impaired circumstances. Computations by the Food and Agriculture Organization of the United Nations (FAO) suggest a figure for the world's undernourished in the early 1980s, based solely on calorie deficiency, to be around 500 million persons (FAO, 1987). When I comment on this estimate in Chapter 15 we will see that it is a conservative figure. The science of nutrition and health is a difficult one. But none of the complexity should obscure the fact that, provided we are careful in its use (for example, by bearing in mind that freedom from infections plays a complementary role to nutrition; see Chapter 14), the concept of a food adequacy standard is not only meaningful, but also useful. In particular, long-run nutrition intake falling short of requirements implies impairment in a person's capacity to live and work owing to forced inactivity, or to illness or plain weakness.

A person's nutrition needs and her ability to satisfy them depend not only on biological factors. Communities in sub-Saharan Africa, to give an example, frequently live miles away from permanent water sources. Surveys in East Africa have shown that individuals (mainly women and children) spend up to five hours a day collecting water during the dry season. Anything between 10 and 25 per cent of daytime energy expenditure is required for the purposes of collecting water each day (see e.g. White, Bradley and White, 1972; Chen, 1983). Surveys in India have shown that fuelwood collection for a family in the drylands can require more than five hours each day, involving over 5 km of walking (see B. Agarwal, 1989). And to cite a different sort of example, the seasonal peaks

---

[14] It isn't so much that malnourished persons are more prone to catching infections: rather, it is that they suffer from longer bouts when they do catch infections. See Martorell (1985).

of malaria, the diarrhoeas, and guinea worm coincide with the hungry, rainy season, when agriculture's demand for work is at a peak. A person struck by such a disease is constrained that much more in her ability to acquire food.

We will find it useful to think of a person's health as an output, and the commodities and services and the background environment that go to determine a person's health as inputs, and thereby to think of this socio-biological transformation process qualitatively in the same way we think of the production of material commodities by means of commodities and resources.[15] When we come to discuss nutrition needs in Chapters 14–17, we will pay close attention to this analogy. We will also study the consequences to a person of not having such needs fulfilled.

The analogy with commodity production can be carried further. We will see that there is a wide penumbra between a person dying quickly through commodity deprivation and her being in a physical and mental state which enables her to pursue what the medical profession quaintly refers to as a 'normal' life. This continuum is missing in current economic modelling, and it will force us to make certain theoretical explorations into resource allocation mechanisms in decentralized private property-owning economies. (These are otherwise known as market economies.) We will find that the resulting construct is not the one in standard use among economists, for a number of technical reasons which the biomedical evidence urges upon us. We will then wish to ask what class of people in market economies are particularly vulnerable to acute nutritional (and more generally commodity) deprivation, and we will ask what this implies by way of the role the State ought to adopt. When we come to study destitution in this book, we will for the most part look at persistent destitution, not the acute, transitory type. We will study chronic undernourishment, not starvation.[16] But we will see that, with a suitable reinterpretation of quantitative variables, our analysis of the economics of undernourishment can be translated into the analytics of the processes of transitory but terminal destitution, such as famines.

---

[15] I should emphasize the qualification, because biological processes are mostly ill-understood but are known to be complex and highly non-linear. The analogy with commodity production processes is offered because the analogy sticks, and not because experts understand the link between a person's nutritional status and her ability to fight infections as well as experts do about the right mix of inputs in the production of stainless steel.

[16] A landmark empirical study of the causes of sudden, acute forms of deprivation, namely famines, is Sen (1981b). Other important studies include Alamgir (1980), McAlpin (1983), Ravallion (1987a,b), de Waal (1989), Dreze and Sen (1990), Newman (1990), and World Bank (1990). A vivid account of the forces that have caused and sustained the most recent famine in the Sudan is provided by Bonner (1988).

1.5 Institutions and Agency Roles

In developing a language for evaluating public policy, we will be much concerned with the agency role of government. At a level removed, we will assess social institutions, such as markets, by their instrumental value. By 'instrumental' here I mean that they are a means of furthering general well-being.[17] From such a perspective, it isn't possible to delineate the appropriate role of any one class of institutions in a society (the government, family, the village community, the producing firm, the temple or mosque or church, charities, and so on) without studying the variety of other organizations that coexist in this same society (charities, the temple or mosque or church, the producing firm, the village community, the family, government, and so forth). In Chapters 2 and 3 I will develop the concepts of utility and freedom and the claim-rights associated with them, and will arrive at the idea of well-being, which embraces them both.[18] I will then use them to develop the agency role of the State as an institution. The treatment will be analytical. Attention will be paid to a distinction between negative and positive freedom, and from there to a distinction between negative and positive rights, which are rights *to* these freedoms. I will argue that their protection and promotion are among the vital responsibilities of government. In Chapter 4 I will move beyond this abstract discussion and see how general well-being might be measured, and will explicate a set of measures much in use in the literature on living standards. This will be a transition chapter: from theory to measurement. In Chapter 5 I will bring together the ideas explored in Chapters 2–4 and use them on international data to compare the quality of life in today's poorest nations. What I shall do is provide a ranking of the world's poorest countries in terms of an aggregative measure of well-being, one that includes as its ingredients not only the standard of living, but also indices of political and civil liberties. I will then ask whether, as is often claimed, there is as a matter of fact a conflict in poor countries between the claims of socio-economic liberties and of political and civil liberties; and will arrive at some tentative, and what I think are encouraging, conclusions on this.

The observation that societies differ enormously by way of their institutions is today a sheer banality. It is, however, not a banality to reiterate that they are similar in many respects, and that they are similar because

---

[17] This isn't to say that markets can't be advocated for non-instrumental reasons. (We will go into this in Chs. 6–8.) It is only to say that for the most part we will seek their instrumental value.

[18] I am usurping the term 'well-being' from the philosophical literature, where it has been used for many years under various guises. See in particular Williams (1985) and J. Griffin (1986).

human motivation regarding survival and maintenance is universal. Of all resource allocation mechanisms, the one driven by markets has received the greatest attention from economists and modern political philosophers. The 'market' has been much admired for its ability to allocate resources efficiently and has been much criticized for its inability to allocate them equitably. Putting it in near-vulgar terms, the 'market' has most often been seen as having an eye on the aggregate output of an economy and as displaying no sensitivity to its distribution. In Chapter 6–9 we will study the analytical properties of the institution of markets. We will develop our arguments along the lines that modern economic analysis has made possible. This will enable us to identify the kinds of resource allocation mechanisms needed to be put into operation by a society guided by a pluralist social ethic.

Recent writings on the economics of poor countries have alternated between an emphasis on the failure of many such economies to increase sufficiently their production of basic goods and services, and on their inability to eliminate 'absolute' poverty (see Bauer, 1971, 1984; Amiya Dasgupta, 1975, 1976; Stewart and Streeten, 1976; Lipton, 1976; Sen, 1981b, 1985; Streeten et al., 1981; Little, 1982; Stewart, 1985; World Bank, 1986, 1990; Bhagwati, 1988b; Dreze and Sen, 1990; UNDP, 1990). If one were to attempt to summarize a large and contentious debate on the mechanism of economic development, it would have to be along some such line as this. Reading this literature, one would be forgiven for thinking that the twin goals of growth in average income and poverty eradication in poor countries are always in conflict with each other.[19] In many instances they may well be, but little is known of the circumstances where they are not. One of my aims in this book will be to identify states of affairs where they do come together, and are consonant with each other. We will discover that they often come together in those circumstances where large groups of people find themselves disfranchised from the resource allocation mechanism characterizing the economy (see Chapter 16).

As always, it helps not to concentrate upon one item at the expense of all others. If we are currently witnessing a massive curtailment of liberties in sub-Saharan Africa, we are also observing an erosion of its resource base. Sub-Saharan destitution cannot be traced to any single source. Chapter 10 will develop the analysis of a central form of modern resource allocation failure: that occasioned by the erosion of long-established social norms mediating the use of local common property resources. We will take note of government policies that have exacerbated such problems. And we will discover that these circumstances provide another class of cases where

---

[19] I am exaggerating, of course. The writings of Irma Adelman were quite explicit on the possible synergism between the two; see e.g. Adelman (1979).

policies can be fashioned so as to sustain an increase in aggregate output, and simultaneously to reduce the magnitude of destitution.

Modern resource allocation theory for the most part sees the household as the unit of analysis. This is partly because markets mediate *inter*-household transactions. It is partly also because data on the lives and deaths of people are based usually on household surveys. Development economics has customarily assumed government policies to be directed at resource allocation among households. The family is a black box.[20] Recent studies on fertility behaviour, and on the health, education, and work status of different categories of persons in families, direct us to look at resource and work allocation mechanisms within the household, where there are inequalities in food and health-care allocations, and in education and work: between men and women, between the young and the old, between male and female children, and between lower- and higher-birth-order female children. Data that do not penetrate the household are incapable of exposing this kind of inequality. Measures of inequality that are based on such data are, therefore, biased: they display less inequality among people than is actually the case. This is a simple implication of the analytical structure underlying all inequality measures of import (see Atkinson, 1970; Rothschild and Stiglitz, 1970). Haddad and Kanbur (1990) have shown that the resulting bias can be large: in many parts of the world inequality among people would be some 30–40 per cent higher were household inequality to be included.

These empirical findings are also suggestive of the determinants of family size. It is a tragedy in recent intellectual history that economic demography should not have found an integrated place in the economics of poor countries. For the moment we have to live with it. This, and issues connected with food, work, and health-care allocations within households, will be addressed briefly and, as befits current understanding, inadequately, in Chapters 4, 11, and 12.

Attaining something of an understanding of fertility behaviour is a first step towards devising population policy. This step is hard enough. The next step is even harder: finding a purpose behind such policy. The vast literature on political and moral philosophy, and in particular welfare economic theory and the economics of poverty, makes but perfunctory moves towards the foundations of population policy. For the overwhelming part it takes future numbers as given (see e.g. Graaff, 1962; Arrow, 1963; Sen, 1970: Rawls, 1972; UNDP, 1990; World Bank, 1990). But

---

[20] There are exceptions, of course, such as Pitt and Rosenzweig (1985) and Singh, Squire and Strauss (1986b). Behrman and Deolalikar (1988) is a useful survey of the literature on household allocations of health care and nutrition. The pioneering works on the analytical economics of the household are Becker (1960, 1981).

government policy can affect the size of future generations, and governments are continually urged by concerned world citizens to so affect them. Now to *say* that fertility rates are too high in most of the poorest of poor countries is easy enough; it is much harder, however, to establish arguments in support of the view.[21]

Three sets of arguments have recently been put forward against the view that the populations of poor countries are growing too rapidly. One appeals to simulation studies (Simon, 1977, 1981), another to historical evidence (Boserup, 1976, 1981), and the third uses analytical arguments from commonly accepted philosophical premises (Parfit, 1982, 1984, 1990).[22] None is ultimately persuasive. The problem with large-scale simulation studies is that they are often sensitive to the details of what are being assumed. This is the case with studies in this field. Whether growth in living standards follows from increased population size depends critically on the speed of response to the stimulus provided by the widening of markets. Moreover, the widening of markets itself involves resource inputs, something these simulations don't take into account.

At the same time, the historical evidence is so mixed that no such view as that which Boserup puts forward can persuasively be applied to poor countries in the modern world (see Birdsall, 1988). In any event, it is reasonable to ask today how long we should have to wait until rising numbers in the Indian sub-continent and sub-Saharan Africa finally unleash the technological and motivational forces that go to raise the standard of living.

It is analytical reasoning which over the long haul is the most enduring, and in Chapter 13 I shall argue that the well-known paradoxes of normative population theory recently proposed by Parfit (1982, 1984, 1990) and his followers are based on an implicit premiss, of treating possible people in exactly the same way as existing or future people. The premiss is that a decline in the level of well-being of an existing poor person by a given amount is ethically no more and no less significant than the prevention of the conception of a person whose well-being level would have equalled the amount of this decline. I shall argue that this is dotty, even if amiably so. We will see that in rejecting it we are able to avoid

---

[21] This is the one serious weakness in an otherwise admirable document on population problems in poor countries, World Bank (1984): it doesn't deal adequately with the question why we should regard current population growth rates to be overly high. When it does briefly face it (pp. 54–6), the document views matters solely from the perspective of existing people, and it asserts that they are locked in a Prisoners' Dilemma game over fertility matters. But this is to short-circuit some of the most telling considerations. There is much more to the problem than the Prisoners' Dilemma.

[22] I should add that Parfit (1982, 1984) doesn't himself express the belief that poor countries aren't for the most part growing too fast in numbers. He presents the implications of commonplace philosophical reasoning as paradoxes.

each of the several paradoxes that have been much discussed in normative population theory (see also Dasgupta, 1988c, 1989c, 1991b). Neither experience nor reasoning allows us to escape the view that population growth rates in many of the poorest of countries today is much too high.

These concerns, while seemingly disparate, hang together. It is simply no good merely repeating the catechism that destitution is a consequence of allocational failure (or 'entitlement failure', a term much in use today), to suggest improvements in the manner in which the produce finds itself finally allocated, and then to leave the matter at that. The poorest countries are also the ones whose resource bases appear to be dwindling at a fast pace, whose (per capita) incomes and food consumption have been falling, whose populations have been growing at furious rates, and which contain a substantial fraction of the world's undernourished (see Chapters 4, 5, 9–12, and 14–15). These can't be unrelated matters. But their links are not easy to discern. Destitution is a complex phenomenon, and it would be fatuous even to suggest that we are near to a good understanding of the variety of possible interrlationships resulting in it. For the moment, we will have to rely on a combination of formal and a good bit of informal theorizing, and we will have to appeal to crude and coarse data and some heroic inferences in order to arrive at a tentative picture of the matter. It may of course turn out to be a wrong picture. But the attempt is worth the risk.

1.6 *Theory and Policy*

These less-then-brief remarks were designed to provide an indication of the structure of the chapters that follow, and the reasoning underlying their themes and their order. Nevertheless, it will be as well to identify a central motivation governing this work. It is this.

Modern political economy has made enormous progress in incorporating into itself the continually shifting technology of commodity production. As a result, we have today a sophisticated apparatus for thinking about resource allocation in a world in which commodities and services can be transformed into further commodities and services by means of technological knowledge. The same progress has not been made on the consumption side. From our perspective here, the chief weakness of modern consumer theory is that it is oblivious of minimal physiological truths. It takes no account, for example, of the fact that there is a *fixed energy cost*, measured by what one may call *maintenance requirements* (see Chapter 14), which each person must cover before she can do anything else over the medium and long run. To be sure, it has been noted before that consumer theory is vulnerable to this charge.[23] But little has been done to rectify it.

---

[23] See the diagnosis of the analytical problem in Bliss and Stern (1978a). See also Dasgupta (1991c).

Admittedly, it is also possible that in many circumstances (for example if the economy under review is rich in assets) modern resource allocation theory is not at risk from this fixed cost. In Chapter 16 I shall confirm this. But it needs to be proved: it can't merely be assumed.

The matter is more awkward for development economics. It is to me curious that a large, and often impressive, literature should have been erected on the concept of absolute poverty, should then have been related to the phenomenon of undernourishment, and yet should not have felt the need to provide an analytical construct which makes essential the use of the physiological phenomenon of undernourishment. Thus, the concept of malnutrition has made repeated appearances in recent development economics (e.g. Underwood, 1983; Biswas and Pinstrup-Andersen, 1985; Reutlinger and Pellekaan, 1986; Berg, 1987; Bell and Reich, 1988; George, 1988; Dreze and Sen, 1990; UNDP, 1990; World Bank, 1990; Alamgir and Arora, 1991), but it has found little or no operational room in it. By this I mean that the underlying models on the basis of which these authors derive policies to alleviate undernourishment do not have under-nourishment as a phenomenon in them. This, as we noted earlier, has prevented policy-makers and academic economists from asking in clear contexts whether there is a necessary trade-off between growth in the standard of living, as caught, say, in estimates of national income per head, and the reduction in poverty among contemporaries. Put another way, it has prevented them from asking the related analytical question of whether 'trickle down' is the most appropriate route to take for the elimination of poverty. That there need not be a trade-off between growth and redistribution if redistributive policies are judiciously chosen is a point that has, of course, on occasion been made, most notably by Amiya Dasgupta (1975, 1976), Adelman (1979), and Streeten et al. (1981). (See also Chenery et al., 1974; Hicks, 1979.) But they were not provided with formal constructions built on adequate physiological foundations in which to undertake such inquiries. So they were unable to discuss the issue in any quantitative manner through the use of such a construct. For this reason, their claims are ultimately not convincing. If quantitative models glide over the pheno-menon of undernourishment, as for example current computable general equilibrium models do, they are by implication incapable of asking if growth in productivity is possible through redistributive policies. The claim that it is remains an act of faith, backed only by unquantified intuition. Until we are provided with quantitative models we will have to be content with recommendations such as the one offered by Reutlinger and Pellekaan (1986: 6) in their influential monograph: 'long run economic growth is often slowed by widespread chronic food insecurity. People who lack energy are ill-equipped to take advantage of opportunities for increasing their productivity and output. That is why policymakers in some countries may want to consider interventions that speed up food security for the groups worst affected without waiting for the general effect of long-run growth.'

It is in all probability because such claims do not as yet have either an analytical or a numerical grounding that economists are also led to advocate policies based upon an opposite causal mechanism, such as, for example, the one in the otherwise excellent report of the World Bank (1986a: 7): 'The best policies for alleviating malnutrition and poverty are those which increase growth and the competitiveness of the economy, for a growing and competitive economy facilitates a more even distribution of human capital and other assets and ensures higher incomes for the poor. Progress in the battle against malnutrition and poverty can be sustained if, and only if, there is satisfactory economic growth.'

There does not appear to me to be a conflict in values in the quotations here. It reads much more as though there is disagreement about the most effective means for eliminating destitution. One purpose of this book is to show why we need to have formal constructs accommodating these notions, and to provide the simplest examples of models capable of doing so. The models that will be offered here are simplified and they cannot be used to provide numerical assessment of alternative possibilities in economies we know.[24] But it is the sense of these models that will have to be reflected in numerical models of poor countries if notions of absolute poverty and undernourishment are to find operational significance. Until this is done, undernourishment in particular and destitution in general will provide the occasion for philosophizing in development economics, for undertaking cross-section studies of nations, for estimating how many there are who are so deprived, and for making assertions to the effect that those who are hungry are hungry because they are unable to obtain enough to eat. It won't provide the impetus for much else.

---

[24] However, in Ch. *16 I shall conduct a stylized calculation of such estimates.

2

Political Morality and the State

2.1 *The Government as an Agency*

We will be thinking of the production and distributional arrangements of commodities and services and, more generally, the protection and promotion of the rights of persons in a society as the outcome of a co-operative venture for mutual advantage. The approach adopted here will be to conduct this as a thought-experiment for testing and supporting commonly held beliefs about just distributions of benefits and burdens. Such a thought-experiment is useful because it allows us to capture something otherwise elusive, namely, the ideas of *impartiality* and *fairness*, notions that lie at the heart of any reasoned conception of justice.

I shall not try to present an account of modern theories of justice. (For this see, for example, Hamlin, 1986; Kymlicka, 1990.) In fact I shall work backwards, by first elaborating (this chapter) on a number of considerations relevant for *any* theory of justice, and then exploring (Chapter 3) the central implications of a hypothetical social contract. This will enable us to study the notion of impersonality in the public domain of life. Admittedly, we will be thinking of a society of persons in a manner that is a far cry from the nation-states that characterize much of the poorer regions of the world. The agency view of government doesn't fit a great deal of the world as we know it (see Chapter 5). Nevertheless, it is imperative to so idealize the role of the State, and thus government. Anything else leads us to view governments and their duties in ways that are prescriptively unjustifiable.

The government is thus an agency of the polity, and it is empowered with just the right kind of authority to enable it to perform as an effective agent. This view of government is broad enough to accommodate a number of rights-based theories, such as those of Hayek (1960), T. H. Marshall (1964), Bauer (1971, 1981, 1984), Rawls (1972), Nozick (1974), Buchanan (1975), Dworkin (1978), Fried (1978), Scanlon (1978), and Sen (1985); a variety of utilitarian theories, for example the preference-fulfilling and choice-theoretic utilitarianisms of Bergson (1938), Samuelson (1947), Arrow (1951), Harsanyi (1955, 1982), Meade (1955, 1976), Graaff (1962), Mirrlees (1967, 1971, 1982), Kolm (1969), Koopmans (1972a, b), Posner (1974, 1979), Hare (1981), Parfit (1984), Gauthier (1986), and

R. Hardin (1988); and also such pluralist conceptions as the one developed in J. Griffin (1986).[1]

This is not a new conception. It dates back at least to Aristotle. In his *Politics*, Aristotle saw the State as the perfect community, in fact a partnership, 'having the full limit of self-sufficiency, which came into existence for the sake of living, but which exists for the sake of living well'.[2] Thus, the State is a product of reason. Its political authority is concerned primarily with the resolution of conflicts which inevitably arise when individuals and groups pursue their own interests, or more generally their own conception of the good. In modern formulations this relates to the sharing of those benefits and burdens that arise from societal and communal living. We will be much concerned with this function of the State.

There is a related task before the State, which is at the centre of discussion whenever economists study social organizations. It is in co-ordinating the activities of individuals and groups in an interrelated world. By 'co-ordination' I mean something different from resolution of conflicts. I mean that there is a need for some kind of balance among various activities, for example production and consumption activities, so that shortages do not occur in some commodities and surpluses in others. Either would signal some form of waste, and thus a loss in terms of the goodness of a state of affairs. In order to achieve co-ordination, there is a need for some form of regulation (for example, enforcements of the laws of contract, and so forth), and this regulative function, in Aristotle's view, also falls properly on the government.[3]

For the modern organization theorist there is much of interest in Aristotle's views, and in those attributed to him by his medieval followers, such as Marsilius of Padua (see Marsilius, 1956). For example, the State is seen as comprising various functional parts. They function in different ways so as to provide collectively for human needs. Each part of the State is defined according to its caring for a different human function; farmers for their nutrition function, the mechanic artisan for the 'sensitive' function, and so forth. At a broader level of classification, Aristotle saw the State as comprising six parts, with their associated offices: agricultural, artisan, military, financial, priestly, and judicial or deliberative.

One should distinguish those elements of classical and medieval conceptions which are culturally specific from those that characterize their central

---

[1] With a bit of work, I believe it is possible to show that this conception is broad enough to accommodate even communitarian viewpoints. For a contrasting opinion, albeit confined to Rawls's contractualism, see Sandel (1982).

[2] Compare Bernard Williams's opening remark in Williams (1985): 'It is not a trivial question, Socrates said: what we are talking about is how one should live'.

[3] The substantive theory of such regulative function of government in Aristotle's work is, understandably, quite different from the one we would derive from modern resource allocation theory. See Ch. 6–7.

thrust. As an instance, we may note that the priest, the warrior, and the judge are, in Marsilius' view, strictly part of the State and are called the 'honourable' class (*honorabilitatem*). The remaining three are offices only in the 'broad sense of the term, because they are offices necessary to the state'. Persons belonging to them are referred to, collectively, as the 'common mass' (*vulgaris*) (Marsilius, 1956, Discourse I, ch. 5: 15). In Marsilius' account, the honourable class is seen as providing what we would today recognize as *public goods* (religious truths, warfare, and the law; see Chapter 6). The common mass are assumed to provide *private goods* (food, clothing, and implements; see Chapter 6). I do not know if the higher status bestowed upon the providers of public goods is on account of their being in charge of providing public goods, or whether it is because such commodities as defence, religious truths, and the law are regarded in some sense as being higher-order goods.[4] We should also note that in his *Politics* Aristotle talks of hunger, and of the State's duties concerning its prevention.

A not-dissimilar conception of the State is to be found in ancient and classical India. The classic on statecraft is the *Arthasastra* of Kautilya. The treatise does not address the question: 'What is justice?' Rather, it attempts to devise an efficient machinery for upholding a given conception of justice. Now once you address this problem, it is inevitable that you will not only discover problems of co-ordination and conflict, but you will also recognize the benefits of co-operation, the instrumental need for authority, and that it is altogether reasonable for people to dispense with unworthy rulers.[5] So, of course, the *Arthasastra* has long discourses on these, and it tries to solve these problems. The philosophical underpinnings of Kautilya's treatise are different from the Greek tradition, based as it is on the idea of *Dharma* (simultaneously, the cosmic order, the nature of things, moral righteousness, right rules of conduct), and the attendant duties it implies for people.[6] This tradition, which saw a fourfold division of functions in society along the lines of religion and education, warfare and politics, production and trade, and menial service, acknowledges the advantages of decentralization and specialization in activities. That by classical times Hinduism had ossified into a bizarre complex of rituals and horrifying inequities should not deflect us from recognizing this.

These considerations of the instrumental role of government are thus familiar matters, and rehearsing them here may appear to be a statement of the obvious. But much current debate in development economics *is* on

---

[4] See Dasgupta (1989a, 1990a) for further discussion. This chapter is based on them.

[5] The original Sanskritic meaning of the word *raja* is simultaneously 'one who rules' and 'one whose duty is to please'.

[6] W. N. Brown (1970) shows how this stress on duty and correct action has been a constant feature of Hindu thinking over 4500 years of development.

the proper role of governments in poor countries, on the constraints that ought to circumscribe their zones of control, and on their ability to be effective in many of the areas of action they frequently enter, and which in principle they ought to enter.[7] Morever, these issues transcend poor countries and development economics. They appear urgent whenever we reflect upon the idea of a civil society, and the rights, duties, and responsibilities of the various agents and agencies within it. Right and wrong carry with them no cultural or technological conditionality. That a tradition might not even acknowledge, let alone condemn, the violation of certain individual or group or gender rights does not make the violation right, and it is an error to think that it may.[8] To be sure, the state of an economy (for example, its level of economic development) will have an implication for the extent to which various public policies should be in effect and can be effective. But that is a different matter. To be sure also, there are countries for which the label of a civil society would be a travesty, where the fundamental conceptions of society and social interactions among their members are so much at variance that there is no meeting point. To use Professor Rawls's apt expression, these societies are not 'well-ordered'. However, even for them, there are on occasion narrow windows of concerned government action, and for this we require a language. Ethical theories of the State are designed to provide one.

The role of government is circumscribed for another reason. Much information relevant for the choice of public policy is only imperfectly known by it. To put it more sharply, a great deal of information is only privately known. This is a deep fact, not an incidental one, and the gap between what is privately observable and known and what is publicly verifiable is at the heart of the problem of incentives. Collective action, whether or not undertaken through the State, is constrained that much more, in that it cannot be founded upon unverifiable pieces of information, unless it is compatible with individual and group incentives. (Imagine, for example, a government trying to implement an income tax schedule when it has no means of assessing individual and corporate incomes.) All this is a way of saying that governments should not pursue courses of action that

---

[7] Among writings which reflect contrasting views, see Myrdal (1968), Adelman and Morris (1967, 1973), Bauer (1971, 1981, 1984), Adelman (1975a, b, 1979), Amiya Dasgupta (1975, 1976), ILO (1976), Streeten (1981, 1984), Streeten et al. (1981), Little (1982), Lal (1983), World Bank (1986a, 1990, 1991), Dreze and Sen (1990) and UNDP (1990).

[8] The view that ethical truths are culturally specific, what one might call ethical relativism, was held by early anthropologists. It says, roughly speaking, that among other things what is 'right' is to be thought of as that which is right for a given society, that this latter is to be understood in functional terms, and that therefore external criticism and condemnation is misplaced and wrong. This view has had some revival in recent years along communitarian lines (see e.g. Apffel Marglin and Marglin 1990). For a critique of ethical relativism, see Williams (1972) and Putnam (1989). I discussed this briefly in Ch. 1, and will return to it in the more applied parts of the book.

are incompatible with private incentives; a rather banal observation, perhaps, but one that is rarely put to use in theoretical political philosophy, and is often ignored by governments in practice.[9]

That different people know different things, and that not all people can observe the same things, have further consequences. This invites us to consider the *instrumental* worth of a wide variety of rights; for example, legal rights to certain kinds of property and to protected spheres of individual or agency discretion.[10] I do not deny that there could be patterns of rights that are basic, that is, that have intrinsic worth; what Dworkin (1978: 93) calls *background rights*: quite the contrary, and we will take this up in Section 2.3. I am only making the somewhat banal point that there are patterns of rights in society which ought to be located for their instrumental value only. Their protection and promotion advance basic rights or co-operative goals (see Chapters 6–10).

In this book I shall be advancing arguments for government involvement in a number of activities, and for its non-involvement in many others. The central problem in political philosophy is to locate the right mix of government, market, community, and household activities, given that the community and the household are not agencies in the sense that government is, nor are they institutions in the sense that markets are. There are two separate issues following from this: what are the duties of government, and what are good institutional arrangements for meeting these duties? The former can be discussed a good deal in the abstract; the latter cannot. The latter rests heavily on society's existing state, whereas the former does not. The latter requires us to judge the appropriate range and depth of government involvement in production and distribution, and it isn't possible to comment on how extensive a government's actual reach should be if we don't know something of the wealth of the country and its distribution, the reliability of its administrative capability, the motivation of the political authorities, and the performance of its markets and of existing patterns of communal security provided through the family, the village, the temple or mosque or church, or whatever. For example, it has been observed by social anthropologists that a growing problem faced by women in poor countries today is a continued deterioration in kinship support systems, a deterioration that has accompanied economic and cultural changes. (See E. Mueller, 1983. We will go into this in Chapters 9–11.) What we should conclude from this is not that in earlier times such

---

[9] The most notable exception among political philosophers is Professor Hayek (e.g. Hayek, 1945, 1960, 1976). Within current political philosophy R. Hardin (1988) has pursued this line of inquiry most systematically. See also Dasgupta (1980, 1982a, 1986a, 1989a). I shall address problems created by asymmetric information in Chs. 3, 7–9, and 17.

[10] See Dasgupta (1980, 1982a). See also Scanlon (1978), who emphasizes the instrumental role of rights from a different perspective.

support systems worked wonders,[11] but rather that, unless some alternative mechanism is provided, women will be increasingly vulnerable to destitution. Among other things, a State is characterized by its shared institutions and arrangements for the distribution of benefits and burdens. A normative theory of the State should be in a position to enable members of society to justify these arrangements to one another.[12] This cannot be done by merely looking solemn and uttering pious sentiments about the dignity of man, his autonomy, and the ability of persons to appear in public without shame. The most promising avenue available at the moment for finding such a justification lies in social contract theories. Among the aims is to find economic arrangements which no one can reasonably reject as a basis for informed, unforced general agreement. In Chapter 3 I shall present the reasoning behind contractual notions. To be sure, there are a number of philosophical systems other than contractual ones which address the same set of issues as those in this book, and which can in principle be used to arrive at similar conclusions regarding public policy. We will find though that there is much to commend thinking through these matters with the help of the device of a hypothetical social contract. For our purposes here, recourse to such a construct will be a tactical move, nothing more.[13]

2.2 *Acts and their Consequences*

There is a tradition in moral and political philosophy which distinguishes two broad types of considerations for reaching ethical judgments: *consequentialist* and *deontological*. The key to deontological reasoning lies in a recognition of the priority of the right over the good. The hallmark of

[11] The oft-repeated claim that in 19th-C. sub-Saharan Africa they did has been shown to be false by Iliffe (1984, 1987).

[12] See Scanlon (1982) for an expression of this. For further discussion, see J. Waldron (1984) and Gauthier (1986).

[13] O'Neill (1986) is an exploration of our obligations towards the alleviation of hunger in distant lands. This is in contrast to the focus here, which is on the duties of the State towards its own citizens, and the obligations citizens have to one another. O'Neill rejects both rights-based and beneficence theories, on the grounds that they are not helpful for her purposes, and pursues instead an obligation-based theory derived from Kant. Unfortunately, the implications she is able to draw from her own analysis are singularly weak, to wit that agencies like the World Bank and the International Monetary Fund should not be deceitful in their dealings with poor countries, and that they should not coerce them into pursuing policies not in their interest. I find it difficult to think that we need an elaborate ethical structure if this is all we conclude. The World Bank, for example, was created explicitly to help countries reconstruct and develop. Duties of international organizations are written into their charters, and they are forbidden to deceive and coerce. That they both may have practised deceit and coercion is not the point here, and no high-powered ethical theory is needed to be invoked to condemn them if they have.

consequentialism is just the reverse: it acknowledges the priority of the good over the right.[14]

Consequentialist theories judge actions, and policies that govern actions, in terms of their consequences. (For example, in utilitarian theories they are judged by their utility consequences.) They are often called *goal-based theories*. Among those states of affairs that are attainable, they identify those that are most desirable (for example, states of affairs in which the sum of individual utilities is largest), and they prescribe that all persons and agencies in society ought deliberately to seek and realize one of them.[15]

There are many versions of consequentialism, as, indeed, there are of utilitarian theories. They differ by way of the goals they advocate. Of these, classical utilitarianism, as expounded in Sidgwick (1907), evaluates actions in terms of their impact on the sum of human happiness. It remains the most well-known version. Then there are pluralist consequentialist theories. These pursue multiple goals all at once. For example, there are consequentialist theories which value both aggregate welfare and an equal distribution of welfare. (See Barry, 1965, for an account of this.) Such a theory may, but need not, specify weights reflecting the relative importance of goals when they are in conflict. If weights are not specified by the theory, not all consequences can be ranked by it. The moral theory in such an instance is able to offer only an incomplete ranking of states of affairs. This does not mean that ethical choice is not possible: it means that the theory offers only maximal sets of actions from which the chooser can select.[16] It does not identify optimal actions, or optimal policies. But no matter how much they differ from one another, consequentialist theories are thought to be related in one crucial respect: they judge actions and policies in terms of an aggregate evaluation of their consequences.

Not so with deontological theories, or so the philosophical tradition asserts. These theories judge actions and policies by their rightness or wrongness, not solely by their consequences. And how is rightness or wrongness judged? Well, it is judged in different ways by different deontological theories. Thus, for example, in absolutist rights-based theories such as that of Nozick (1974), it is wrong even to contemplate, let alone to undertake, an action that infringes a person's moral rights. Rights in

---

[14] Ross (1930) is the acknowledged modern classic on the distinction between the right and the good. Rawls (1972), as always, has an illuminating discussion of the contrasts, as do Dworkin (1978), and Fried (1978). Pluralist theories, such as that in J. Griffin (1986), do not search for a priority rule over these.

[15] This is in case there is more than one best state of affairs. If the optimum is unique, there is no further choice left.

[16] A *maximal set* in this context is a set of actions with the property that none of them can be bettered by any feasible action and where none of the actions in the set is better or worse than any of the others in the set.

absolutist theories identify protected spheres of individual discretion and treatment, which the claims of the general good cannot override. Thus, lying is wrong because in lying one is using a person as a means to one's own ends, and this is to violate her integrity. Thus also, it is wrong for a government to torture a prisoner, even if this is the only means of obtaining information for protecting the safety of its people; or to punish an innocent party, even if this implies an increase in overall welfare. Seen from such deontological perspectives, each one of us as a rational moral agent is protected by a cloak of rights, which even the general good is unable to override.

I have tried to fashion these all-too-brief remarks in such a way as to provide an explanation of why the philosophical literature over the years has seen it natural to begin by distinguishing consequentialist theories from deontological ones in terms of whether judgements on actions are made solely on the basis of their consequences, and then to glide into a seemingly different distinction when developing rights-based theories, a distinction based on their relative concerns for the claims of the individual *vis-à-vis* the aggregate mass of individuals, or, in other contexts, between the individual and the society of individuals. 'The distinction between rights-based and goal-based theories', writes J. Waldron (1984: 13) in an otherwise excellent essay on theories of rights, '[lies in the idea] that a requirement is rights-based if it is generated by a concern for some individual interest, goal-based if it is generated by concern for something taken to be an interest of society as a whole'. Rights-based theories, according to this reckoning, shudder at the thought of aggregation exercises, because it is held that in any such exercise the interests of the individual can all too readily get swamped by claims made on behalf of a multitude of others. 'A goal', writes Dworkin (1978: 91), 'is a non-individuated political aim'. Or to put it bluntly, goal-based theories are collectivist. Worse, they are algorithmic (O'Neill, 1986). Try as they might, consequentialists for the most part have not shaken their theories loose from this charge levelled against them recurrently by deontologists.

What are we to make of this? There is, of course, a problem with the distinction right at the outset, and this has been noted in recent years. (See the collection of essays in Scheffler, 1988.) It may seem easy to keep actions distinct from their consequences, but it isn't so easy. One reason is that they are both parts of a more general, more fundamental notion, that of a state of affairs, or a *social state* (see Arrow, 1963). In identifying a state of affairs, an evaluator is required to provide as complete a description of the world as it is possible to offer given the evaluator's information and powers of discrimination. It includes past actions, present actions, intended actions, Mother Nature's choice of actions, and the past, present, and future consequences of this stream of actions. It thus includes past, current, and future experiential states, the production and distribution of goods and services, and economic and social interchanges. In short, each social state is a complete history of the world, extending from the known past to the indefinite future—as complete, that is, as current powers of discrimination will allow.

All ethical theories evaluate social states. Theories differ in their identification of what is ethically significant in a social state. The distinction between acts and consequences in this broader framework of evaluation is formally so tenuous that it is difficult to sustain on its basis so central a classification as is provided by the labels 'deontological' and 'consequentialist'. If actions matter intrinsically, they can be made part of a description of consequences, and then the distinction collapses. What the concept of a social state does for us is to show that some deontological theories, such as that of Rawls (1972), can be regarded as consequentialist if we were to allow consequences to be defined in this wider manner. Thus, if an action is wrong because it violates someone's moral rights, it must be the case that one of the consequences of the action is a violation of these rights. A number of rights-based theories can be reinterpreted in terms of the weight placed on this harm. In these theories states of affairs bearing this feature will thereby appear low in the overall ranking of social states.[17]

Consequentialist theories of justice are often contrasted with one distinguished strand of deontological theories: those founded upon ideas of *procedural fairness* (see e.g. Hayek, 1960; Rawls, 1972; Nozick, 1974). The contrast, it is commonly asserted, lies in the fact that the criteria by which fairness of a procedure is judged are independent of any prior assessment of the possible outcomes in applying the procedure. Thus, 'pure procedural justice obtains when there is no independent criterion for the right result: instead there is a correct or fair procedure such that the outcome is likewise correct or fair, whatever it is, provided that the procedure has been properly followed' (Rawls, 1972: 86).

Problems lie with the prior notion of fairness. Examples are therefore often taken from gambling. For instance, if there are two people in a lifeboat and food enough for only one, a fair procedure would be to allocate the food on the basis of the toss of an unbiased coin. The rogue word here is 'unbiased'. While it means equal chance of either outcome, its ethical force obtains from the idea of empirical probability, that if such a coin were tossed over and over again each outcome would occur approximately 50 per cent of the time. Never mind that the procedure itself relies on a single toss. Were we to know nothing about empirical

---

[17] This, as I understand it, is the direction of analysis advocated in Dworkin (1978), Fried (1978), Mackie (1978), Sen (1982), and J. Griffin (1986). Sen has introduced the vocabulary of 'goal-rights' to highlight the commonality of the two frameworks of moral reasoning.

probabilities, we wouldn't even begin to have an intuitive sense of what an unbiased coin is. The fairness of the procedure, therefore, rests squarely on our previous evaluation of probable consequences. In Chapter 3 we will go further into this when distinguishing rules from discretion. We will see there that ideas of procedural fairness rest ultimately on consequentialist reasoning.

The more general claim, that deontological reasoning is averse to aggregative considerations, is probably more of a semantic matter. As noted earlier, the issue is not about aggregation *per se*, but about the extent to which people's claims may be permitted to be traded off against one another. In the following section I will argue that aggregation is an inevitable exercise in arriving at any public judgement.

There is, however, a type of consideration pulling us in two directions which can be used fruitfully for classifying ethical theories into consequentialist and deontological ones.[18] The consideration I have in mind is over the hold the *past* has over our evaluation of current and future actions and their consequences. It is a significant feature of ethical theories which are taken to be consequentialist that the past plays a role only through what is feasible today; it is allowed to play no role in our evaluation of those aspects of feasible states of affairs that lie in the future. For example, if current preferences have been moulded by experience, the past certainly plays a role in utilitarian evaluations of states of affairs, but only through the effect of the past on *future* experiential states. It is still the present and the future that ultimately count. Consequentialist theories in general, and utilitarian theories in particular, regard bygones as true bygones. If breaking a promise is judged wrong in a consequentialist theory, it is by virtue of its impact on what is to come. Under what is usually called deontological reasoning, it would be wrong even if it were to have *no* impact on the future. Bygones here are not bygones. We cannot of course affect the past. But the past affects our evaluation of what are today available options. We can't shake loose from it. This seems to be at the heart of much deontological reasoning, and it has found its deepest expression in recent years in Nozick (1974), where the idea of historical entitlements is made to play a decisive role in the delineation of individual rights. In Chapter 13 I will use a particular style of deontological reasoning to develop a prescriptive theory of fertility and the intergenerational transmission of knowledge, values, and general resources.

In a most suggestive passage on the tensions inevitably arising between individual aspirations and the claims of communal living, Arrow (1974: 28–9) recalls one of the early books of the *Iliad*, where Agamemnon is seen

---

[18] I have been influenced in this greatly by Paul Seabright. Our planned article for developing these ideas in a formal manner has, alas, still to be finalized.

raising the question whether the Greeks ought not to abandon their siege of Troy. They had been there for nine years and had got nowhere. Perhaps it was after all rather pointless. It is Odysseus who makes them realize however that such consequentialist reasoning is irrelevant. There was a commitment made a decade earlier, and this is all-important. They must stay and fight and cannot break the agreement. The Greeks remain, and all that is to follow from this decision follows. And Arrow remarks, 'It is this thinking which I think gives rise to the greatest tragedies of history, this sense of commitment to a past purpose which reinforces the original agreement precisely at a time when experience has shown that it must be reversed.' True enough, and from a consequentialist point of view, which is what Arrow adopts in this passage, the Greek sense of commitment would seem pointless and disastrous. But for better or worse, the claims of the past often have a deep hold on our sensibility. It is, of course, Arrow's intention to draw this out, to display the tension that often exists between the claims of living and the desirability of avoiding tragic consequences.[19] However, until relatively recently not much has been made of this distinction in the philosophical literature. As we have seen all too briefly, ethical theories for the most part have been classified in terms of the extent to which they entertain *trade-offs* between one person's interests and those of another. This is a different issue, an issue in aggregation. It is discussed next.

2.3   *Utility and Rights: Public Judgements and Aggregative Evaluations of Well-Being*

In talking of aggregate utility in utilitarian moral theories, we mean just that, nothing more. Summation of individual welfares, which different versions of utilitarianism urge upon us, is only one type of aggregation.[20] Judging states of affairs solely on the basis of the lowest welfare level attained in a society is another.[21] And there are many others besides, each embodying a different ethical viewpoint (see Roberts, 1980a, b; Blackorby,

---

[19] In a famous essay Bernard Williams explored this connection with a related motivation, that of linking moral realization to the contingencies of luck. (See Williams, 1976; see also Nussbaum, 1986, for a major development of this line of thinking.) It was central to Williams's thesis to introduce the idea that one may *regret* one's past choices, something that finds no room in the von Neumann–Morgenstern theory of choice under uncertainty (see Ch. 8). The idea has been put to fine use in modern decision theory by Loomes and Sugden (1982, 1986, 1987).

[20] I am continuing to use the terms 'utility' and 'welfare' interchangeably.

[21] Rawls's theory of justice was initially so interpreted in the economics literature. See Alexander (1974). Rawls, however, does not subscribe to this interpretation. See Rawls (1974).

Donaldson and Weymark, 1984). The argument that aggregative considerations cannot guarantee the protection of individual welfare interests (because, say, the claims of a large number can always swamp the claims of a few) isn't correct. It depends upon the type of aggregation being advocated. Admittedly, classical utilitarianism is vulnerable to such a charge, but not those theories that admit no trade-offs when the utility level of a person assumes low enough values. One way such utility security levels can be guaranteed is to build in constraints in the evaluative exercise, for example by insisting that the utility level of no individual falls below a stipulated level.[22] Such an ethical theory is a far cry from classical utilitarianism. It is none the less utilitarian: it judges actions and evaluates outcomes solely on the basis of their utility consequences, that is, the utility components of states of affairs. In some utilitarian theories (as in the hedonistic theory often associated with Bentham; but see Broome, 1991) utility is seen as a mental state, reflecting satisfaction, pleasure, or desire fulfilment; in others, as in social choice theory, it is seen as a numerical representation of a person's preference ordering over social states; and in yet others, as in much of welfare economics, it is seen as a numerical representation of the ordering over social states on the basis of which a person actually chooses. Ethical theories grounded on this third, and currently the most common, notion of welfare I shall call *choice-theoretic utilitarianism*. (For further discussion of this three-way distinction, see Chapters 3, 6, and 11).

Rights, on the other hand, are usually seen as providing a basis for protecting and promoting a certain class of human interests, such as agency, independence, choice, and self-determination. An individual has a right when there is a reason for awarding him some liberty, opportunity, or commodity even though mere considerations of welfare or utility would not warrant the award. Rights do not go against interest. They reinforce some interests against the claims of other, less urgent or vital, interests. Rights offer a way of distinguishing states of affairs with the same utility consequences. Rights-based theories are therefore non-utilitarian, but not all non-utilitarian theories are rights-based. For example, distributive principles founded upon the idea of desert, or *karma* (literally, 'deed'), can be quite different from those based on rights. Ethical theories that ignore experiential states are rationally repugnant and are therefore in error. It would be absurd, for example, if an ethical theory were to value only the formation of the capacity to form life plans and were indifferent to its realization and the experiential states that go with its realization. So the issue is not whether welfare is an appropriate ingredient in an ethical

---

[22] In all this I am assuming that welfare is a fully measurable numerical index and that one can make full interpersonal comparisons of welfare. See Scanlon (1992) for a recent discussion of the moral basis of making such comparisons.

theory, but whether it ought to be the sole ingredient. Put another way, rights-based theories not only scrutinize the utility consequences of public actions, they also evaluate certain features of states of affairs which give rise to the utility consequences. They distinguish different types of interest (see e.g. Rawls, 1972; Buchanan, 1975; Dworkin, 1978; Fried, 1978; Peffer, 1978; Scanlon, 1978; Sen, 1982).

But rights need to be justified. Even what are regarded as 'fundamental' rights have it as their basis that they are necessary for human flourishing. In this book we will call the degree to which a person is flourishing his flow of *well-being*. For analytical convenience we will on occasion think of it as a numerical measure of flourishing. But the concept is elusive, and at the end we will arrive at only a very limited understanding of it, and that too circuitously.[23] Neither happiness (as the word is currently used), nor pleasure, nor satisfaction, nor utility amounts to well-being. This is why rights-based and utilitarian theories often make different moves when explicating the nature of a just society. We will see later that in any justification of rights both the commonality of the human condition and the distinctiveness of every two human beings make their impact. Substantive theories of justice need to be sensitive to both.

In Chapter 3 we will try and formalize these thoughts, and we will arrive at a pluralist conception founded on modern decision theory. Empirical work on quality-of-life indices have been motivated by similar thoughts (see Chapters 4–5). But the literature displays a weakness, reflected in a somewhat narrowness of purpose. Writers have for the most part concentrated on a limited number of human interests; so limited that such quality-of-life indices as are currently on offer are misleading.[24]

Rights are often regarded inviolable, or absolute: 'Individuals have rights, and there are things no person or group may do to them [without violating their rights]' (Nozick, 1974: ix). This means they impose rigid constraints on what people may or may not do. Thus, states of affairs in which Nozickian rights are violated to the slightest extent are rejected in Nozick's scheme of things. Only those that are left after this pruning exercise are subject to social choice (Nozick, 1974: 166). But this is an aggregation exercise. The presence of 'deontological' constraints tells us how the aggregation is to be conducted; it does not offer an alternative to aggregation. The exercise is influenced in other theories by the suggested hierarchy of rights, as in Rawls (1972), where they are lexicographically

---

[23] In this I have learnt much from Williams (1985) and J. Griffin (1986).

[24] See Pant *et al.* (1962), Drewnowsky and Scott (1966), Adelman and Morris (1967, 1973), Nordhaus and Tobin (1972), Usher (1973), ILO (1976), Hicks and Streeten (1979), Streeten *et al.* (1981), and M. D. Morris (1979) for pioneering work in this field. See also Kakwani (1981), Sen (1981a, 1985), Silber (1983), Stewart (1985), Kaneko and Nidaira (1988), and UNDP (1990), for both analytical and empirical studies of living standards.

ordered. This poses a mathematical problem, in that a lexicographic ordering cannot be represented by a numerical function (Debreu, 1959). But this is of no significance for social choice. A Rawlsian citizen can still arrive at public judgements.

The brilliance of Professor Nozick's and Professor Rawls's writings has given the impression to many that rights by definition are inviolable, that rights-based theories do not entertain trade-offs among individual interests, and that they differ from utilitarian theories most vitally in that the latter are rapacious in their willingness to do so. But this would be wrong.[25] Rights are not all or nothing. For example, there are always degrees to which interests are frustrated and thus the corresponding rights, if there be corresponding rights, are not met. Even for rights there may be trade-offs, and, since inviolability means a zero rate of trade-off, we will not depart from the practical spirit of inviolability (if rights are inviolable) if we do allow trade-offs between rights, and between rights and other goods such as welfare—provided of course that the trade-off rate is very very small in appropriate regions of the space of states of affairs. From such a perspective, what distinguishes utilitarianism from rights-based theories is not that the latter avoid aggregation; nor, as seen from this perspective, do they differ in that the latter are incapable of admitting trade-offs where the former are most eager to admit them. Where they differ is somewhere else. They differ in terms of the kinds of objects that are aggregated.

A common objection to non-utilitarian theories is that they are paternalistic. (Indeed, utilitarianism is often identified in economics texts with consumer sovereignty.[26]) The argument stems from the twin observations that each rational person is the best judge of what is good for him, and that individual autonomy ought to be respected. Now, this conclusion does not itself depend upon individual preferences. It rests instead as the objective moral basis for giving rational preferences a fundamental role as the ground of ethically relevant valuation. But this means that when we

---

[25] 'Collective goals may, but need not, be absolute. The community may pursue different goals at the same time, and it may compromise one goal for the sake of another . . . Rights may also be absolute: a political theory which holds a right to freedom of speech as absolute will recognize no reason for not securing the liberty it requires for every individual; no reason, that is, short of impossibility. Rights may also be less than absolute; one principle might have to yield to another . . . We may define the weight of a right, assuming it is not absolute, as its power to withstand such competition. It follows from the definition of a right that it cannot be outweighted by all social goals' (Dworkin, 1978: 92). See also Gewirth (1981), who asks if there are *any* absolute rights.

[26] Strictly speaking, 'consumers' sovereignty' is associated with what we are calling here choice-theoretic utilitarianism. Such aggregates as those that are based on individual choice-theoretic utility functions are called Bergson–Samuelson *social welfare functions*. See Bergson (1938), Samuelson (1947), Arrow (1963), and Graaff (1962) for an account of such ethical theories, and Meade (1955), Atkinson and Stiglitz (1980), Boadway and Bruce (1984), Barr (1987), and Starrett (1988) for applications to economic problems.

talk of individual autonomy we are concerned, among other things, with the rights and liberties needed for persons to develop their goals and interests in an autonomous fashion, and to shape their lives in accordance with their reflective goals. Ironically, among these are rights that protect people from paternalistic interference. (Scanlon, 1978, develops this line of argument.) We are talking of political morality here. Not everything a person desires can legitimately form the basis of a claim on others. Going beyond choice-theoretic utilitarianism does not mean that others are presumed to know better what is good for us. It means only that others aren't obliged to take into account *all* of our desires when consenting to a public policy. This shows why choice-theoretic utilitarianism will not do, and why going beyond it isn't to invoke paternalism. We are pursuing a contractual view of the State. The object of a social contract is to further the prospects of human flourishing. This is why within contract theories each individual's well-being is ethically significant. It reflects a morally legitimate interest. It forms the basis of a claim on others in a contractually based State because a person could reasonably reject a political argument that gave no weight to his well-being. The ingredients forming the basis of collective action are, therefore, the rights and liberties of persons to pursue their own conception of the good.

These considerations also lead us to abandon the dichotomy based upon whether ethical theories are want-regarding or ideal-regarding. (Barry, 1965, pursues this distinction.) If wants were to be equated to desires, and thus to a certain kind of utility, the class of ideal-regarding theories would be far too large to be of use, including, as it then would, all non-utilitarian theories. It would include rights-based theories, duty-based theories, perfectionist theories, and theories that extol the virtues of nationalism. If, on the other hand, wants were to include interests, then want-regarding theories would in turn form too coarse a category: they would contain both utilitarian and rights-based theories. And, as we have seen, much the most telling distinctions lie among them.

We are inquiring into the legitimate role of the State, and thus with the claims we can make on others as members of a social union. Therefore, we are particularly interested in a certain set of human interests, those that give rise to claims on goods. It pushes us back, quite naturally, through the concept of well-being, to the concept of *commodity needs*.

2.4   *Commodity Needs*

A great many commodities do not possess intrinsic value. Their value derives from the uses to which they are put and is measured in terms of their contribution to the human good.[27] Social institutions (for example the family, kinship, the temple or mosque, village or commune, the State) are the medium in which this conversion occurs. These ideas have been the central dogma of economics and of recent political philosophy, and they realize their sharpest focus in those aspects of human functionings that are a precondition for the pursuit of different conceptions of the good. The idea of *basic needs*, as it appears in development economics (see ILO, 1976; Streeten *et al.*, 1981, for influential statements, and Pant *et al.*, 1962, for a pioneering early work), relates to positive-rights goods (see Section 2.5). Rawls's much discussed concept of *primary goods* is also related to this viewpoint: 'Primary goods . . . turn out to be those things which are generally necessary for carrying out . . . plans successfully whatever the particular nature of the plan and its final ends' (Rawls, 1972: 411; see also Rawls, 1982a, b, 1988). Rawls's primary goods include political and civil liberties, and an index of income and wealth, the latter being a prerequisite for the enjoyment of a class of positive freedoms we will discuss below. Later I shall try to decompose this index so as to identify the component commodities that go to make it up.

Such commodities as are required for satisfying basic needs have on occasion been called *merit goods* (Musgrave, 1959), and *natural-rights goods* (Weitzman, 1977). So far as I can tell, the term 'basic needs' was introduced into the modern literature in Benn and Peters (1959). In a related vein, Fried's (1978) and Dworkin's (1981) conceptions of *resources* are also needs-based goods. However, these authors were using the idea to identify a decent standard of living. The sense in which I am thinking of the notion here is starker. In classical political economy, this sense found an illustration in Marx's account of the transformation of food and fuel into labour power (Marx, 1970).[28]

One advantage of appealing to the concept of needs is that we are able to see commodity consumption as an input, political and civil liberties as the background environment, and welfare and individual functionings as an output vector, of what is in effect a complex 'production process'. Thus, Fried's (1978), Sen's (1982, 1985), and J. Griffin's (1986) focus on human functionings (the achievements of an individual) is on one aspect of the output side of the production process (see also Williams, 1985: chapter 3). Utility or welfare constitutes another aspect of the output side of

[27] I am thinking here of inanimate commodities. The valuation of animal protein poses deeper problems. (See e.g. Nozick, 1974, and Singer, 1986, for a discussion of how we ought to think on the problem.) I should also add that in the text I am thinking only of what one might call 'economic' commodities here. Goods like freedom possess so deep and fundamental an 'instrumental' worth (their absence diminishes us as persons) that their worth is often taken to be intrinsic.

[28] J. Griffin (1986), Braybrooke (1987) and Wiggins (1987) contain the most comprehensive modern discussion of needs that I am familiar with.

things. I sketched this viewpoint in Chapter 1. At one extreme are nutrition, shelter, bedding and clothing, potable water, medical care, and general environmental resources. They are inputs (indeed, complementary inputs) required for sheer survival. The production process here is physiological.[29] One class of what are often called *social indicators* are crude measures of commodity availability. They comprise the fraction of a population consuming less than an adequate diet, or owning no blanket to cover them at nights, or possessing no more than one piece of clothing; the extent of a population with access to drinking water; the number of hospital beds, doctors and nurses and lawyers per 100 000 individuals; the number of schoolteachers per 1000 children; the percentage of births attended by health staff; primary school enrolment rates for girls and boys; and a number of other things besides. Real income estimates are an attempt to summarize an individual's command over goods and services. Some of these indicators, as we can see from the list, are particularly crude because they do not tell us how easily accessible these goods are to *all* members of society. They do not on their own tell us of the distribution of their availability. Nevertheless, they try to capture the input side of the production process. And if they are buttressed by the distribution of their availability they reveal a good deal more.

Then there are indices that attempt to capture the *political* and *civil liberties* enjoyed by people in society. These consist of the extent to which people are able to play an active and critical role in the choice of the background political, legal, and economic structure (e.g. the freedom to determine who governs and what the laws are and will be), the degree to which people are able to express their opinions without fear of reprisals, and the extent to which they are protected from arbitrary arrests, from physical harm by others, from seizure of legitimately acquired property, and so on. They form the background environment within which people can engage in what we have been regarding as a production process, converting commodities and services, in conjunction with effort, ability, and ingenuity, into living.

On the output side is another class of social indicators, what we may call achievements. They include adult literacy rates, infant and child survival rates, life expectancy at birth, and the inverse of morbidity rates. They also include indices measuring the lack of group discrimination and internal conflict. The idea is to see them not only as a reflection of aggregate welfare realized in the economy, although they plainly affect welfare and so should be evaluated because of that; the idea is to see them also as they are, as measures of the extent to which certain real, vital

---

[29] In pure production models in economics a commodity is called 'basic' if it is a necessary input for the production of pretty much anything else. See Sraffa (1960).

interests of persons are being served and promoted, and to evaluate economies on such bases (see Chapters 4, 5, 10–11). In adopting the view I have just outlined, we are therefore making a break with the distinction between consumption and production which characterizes much economic analysis.

Commodity needs are not all or nothing. The ability of a person to perform tasks, whether mental or physical, can vary widely. Obviously, there are degrees of functioning. On some days we feel better and function better than on others. For those of us who are fortunate, this variation has little to do with nutritional fluctuations. For many who are not so fortunate, it can have a lot to do with it. As we will see in Chapters 14 and 15, nutritionists have shown in a quantitative manner that there are degrees of morbidity and malnourishment. In such work undernourishment is not identified with hunger. An undernourished person is usually also a hungry person, but undernourishment is not measured in terms of the experiential state of hunger. It is usually measured clinically or anthropometrically, and on occasion by the impaired ability of the person to perform simple tasks like walking, moving things, concentrating, caring about things.

Commodity needs are person-specific. For example, nutrition requirements vary from person to person. Individuals differ genetically, in their phenotypes, and in their history. To an extent, they can also alter their needs by behavioural adjustment, for example by cutting down on bodily movement. There is also the possibility of some adaptation at the physiological level.[30] Moreover, even basic needs are not nearly constant over one's life. An obvious example is the changing needs of a person from birth to death, through the growth phase, pregnancy, lactation, and so forth. Then there are special needs, such as those of handicapped persons. Furthermore, there are certain needs, for example those just mentioned, which are relatively easy to observe; but there are others, for instance certain psychological ones, such as the need to participate in political life, that are less easy. They are feelings and sensations, often communicable to others, but not readily verifiable publicly. This is of importance in the design of political and economic institutions (see Chapters 6–9 and 17).

The claims of needs suggest a sense of urgency. They hint, but only hint, at a preemptory argument. Basic needs display these features in a sharp form. We can postpone listening to a piece of music or going to a party, but we can't postpone the consumption of water when thirsty, or food when hungry, or medical attention when ill. Such needs have lexicographic

---

[30] See however Ch. 15, where we will see that the evidence of costless adaptation among poor people in poor countries is tenuous.

priority over other needs in our own evaluation of goods and services (Scanlon, 1975; Braybrooke, 1987; Wiggins, 1987). The meeting of these needs is a prerequisite for the continuation of one's life. Their fulfilment makes living *possible*. For life to acquire worth, for it to be *enjoyable*, other sorts of goods are required. Thus, calories make life possible; it is a good meal that makes life enjoyable. This suggests that, roughly speaking, there are two tiers of goods and services. The first tier, the one that makes living possible, comprises basic needs. The second tier consists of goods that are instrumental in making life satisfying. Political morality does not dictate that all activities must cease until each and every person's basic needs have been met. There are other claims on resources. As always, there is a multiplicity of claims, and thus objectives.[31] Nor does an appeal to the language of needs displace well-being as the central concern of political morality. Needs are patently an instrumental notion ('a need for what?'), and the concept's reach, as well as its limitations, lie there. In a society that takes liberty seriously, the production of living by means of commodity inputs is undertaken by people capable of assuming their agency role, and not by other agencies acting on their behalf. The political and economic structure of a society influences the distribution of benefits and burdens within it. Needs provide a most valuable marker for guiding public policy. The observation that needs vary, that there are different types of needs, that there are wants which are not needs, is not much more than a banality. We could make the same observation about well-being, or for that matter about preference fulfilment and functionings. But it would be grotesque if these concepts were for that reason banished from the political lexicon. What would political morality then be about?[32]

2.5   Freedom and Rights: Positive and Negative

In his classic essay on liberty, Isaiah Berlin distentangled two concepts of liberty which, although they had become fused in some of the literature, had historically developed in divergent directions until, or so he argued, they had come into direct conflict with each other. In contrast with the idea that a person can be said to be free to the degree to which no person or body of persons interferes within the area in which he could otherwise act (in other words, *negative freedom*), Berlin identified *positive freedom* with the ability 'to be somebody, not nobody; a doer—deciding, not being

---

[31] However, there are political philosophies, such as that of John Rawls, which do arrive at the primacy of such needs over all else.
[32] The language of needs finds less favour today than it used to. See e.g. Fried (1978), Goodin (1988), and Stern (1989), who advocate dispensing with the notion. The remarks in the text are designed as a counter to their position. For a modern restatement of the primacy of needs in political morality, see J. Griffin (1986) and Braybrooke (1987).

decided for, self-directed . . . conceiving goals and policies of [one's] own and realizing them', and the ability 'to be conscious of [oneself] as a thinking, willing, active being, bearing responsibility for [one's] choices and able to explain them by reference to [one's] own ideas and purposes' (Berlin, 1969: 131).[33]

At the coarsest level of discourse, the two concepts amount to the same thing. Being liberties, each measures the extent to which an individual has power and control over his own life, to shape it in line with his own conception of the good. At a finer level, they are different. Prototypical examples of negative and positive freedom are civil and political liberties, respectively. However, in developing the notion of positive freedom as it has evolved historically, Berlin focused on something else. He talked of the Marxian idea of 'false consciousness', the thesis that *real* freedom is exercised only when one's 'rational' self (some call it one's 'true' self) does the deliberation, and not one's 'empirical' self. One of Berlin's contentions was that this is dangerous stuff in the hands of fanatics, that the distinction between the rational and empirical self has often been perverted by political leaders and used for justifying policies of oppression.

One could not doubt it. On the other hand, we do not need to invoke the distinction to argue that people often act against their own interest in a systematic way. It is not for people in political authority to tell us what is in our real interest, but it is a desirable property of the institutions which guide resource allocation that people are able to reach a position where they can judge their own interests in a relatively unhampered way. To be literate and numerate is to enjoy a larger information base than one otherwise could. To have employment opportunities outside the home helps us to exercise our autonomy and to realize our interests better than we would be able to do were we not to have such options.

This brings us to a class of positive freedoms Berlin did not discuss in his essay, whose exercise requires goods and services in a pervasive way. The source of a foreclosure on such liberties is destitution. To illustrate this, consider a person who is chronically malnourished, and thereby prone to morbidity. We will study in subsequent chapters how this person may lack the motivation and physical capacity necessary to be employable in a freely functioning labour market (including self-employment). If he owns little in the way of physical assets, employment is his sole means of avoiding destitution. However, he is weak and physically not capable of doing much. So the range of activities from which he can choose is narrow, and it may be that the only movements he is capable of are those necessary for

---

[33] Positive and negative freedom are but two senses in which the word 'freedom' has been used. Berlin (1969: 121) informs us that there are more than two hundred senses in which the word has been used by historians of ideas. The mind boggles at the mere thought.

begging. He is in a trap from which he cannot escape. (See Chapter 16 for a formal analysis of such possibilities.) Nevertheless, he may be living in a society where citizens enjoy both civil and political liberties. The source of his being unfree is bad health, occasioned by a lack of basic needs—not a deprivation of political and civil liberties.

We are talking of the extent to which a person has power and control to shape his own life. At a basic level, we are talking about the actual extent of one's set of choices.[34] Admittedly, not all choices are of equal urgency or value to the person whose freedom is the object of inquiry. Different kinds of freedom of choice will have different worths when evaluated by the person in question. There is no one type of freedom that is real freedom. A person dying of starvation may well be negatively free; but the foreclosure on his freedom to do anything is terminal. At the opposite end, quality-of-life indices based exclusively on certain types of positive liberties, as in Sen (1981a) and UNDP (1990), will not do, either. It is an inadequate index of well-being which neglects primary negative liberties.

Among modern theories of justice embracing both positive and negative liberties, the most prominent is that of Rawls (1972). Among other things, Rawls studies the just distribution of those *commodities* that are essential to the exercise of freedom. He calls them (social) *primary goods*. His first principle of justice ('Each person is to have an equal right to the most extensive total system of equal basic liberties compatible with a similar system of liberty for all') covers both political and civil liberties; and his second principle ('Social and economic inequalities are to be arranged so that they are (a) to the greatest benefit of the least advantaged, consistent with the just savings principle, and (b) attached to offices and positions open to all under conditions of fair equality of opportunity': Rawls, 1972: 302) addresses what we may call *socio-economic freedom*. We should note though that among Rawlsian primary goods are some, such as an index of income and wealth, which have only instrumental value. By way of contrast, the others, such as self-respect and basic liberties, would seem to have intrinsic worth. I will argue subsequently that in the socio-economic sphere it is neither income nor wealth but, rather, a class of basic needs whose distribution will be the object of hypothetical social contracts in poor countries. Choice among alternative institutions for the production and distribution of basic needs is a different matter. They will typically involve a mixture of allocation in cash (e.g. income transfers, wages, and rents) and distribution in kind (e.g. primary health care). We will establish this later in the book.

---

[34] For recent discussions of the meaning of freedom, see Buchanan (1975), Joseph and Sumption (1979), Palczynski and Gray (1984), Dworkin (1986), Raz (1986), Kornai (1988), Lindbeck (1988), Sen (1988b), and J. Christian (1991).

There is more than one interpretation on offer of Rawls's theory of justice as fairness and of the substantive theory Rawls builds on the idea. In a long and important essay, Dworkin (1978: chapter 6) offers an interpretation different from Rawls's own. He suggests that the theory is based on the assumption of a natural right of all men and women to equality of concern and respect in the design of political institutions, a right they possess simply as human beings, with the capacity to make plans and give justice. He argues that Rawlsian principles are chosen behind the Rawlsian 'veil of ignorance' so as to protect this inviolable and most fundamental of rights.

The concept of positive freedom, with its emphasis on our ability to undertake motivated activities and to exercise our realized capacities (our innate or trained abilities), and on the recognition that the exercise of our natural powers is a leading human good, has strong historical antecedents, in as far-flung intellectual traditions as those of ancient and classical India. In the *Bhagavad Gita* of the *Mahabharata*, Lord Krishna reveals to the warrior-hero, Partha, the nature of the *virtuous* life; he does not dwell on the happy, or contented, life. The valuation of a person's life that Partha is urged to accept is one that is conducted on the actions he chooses, not on the consequences of his actions. To be sure, right action there is tied to one's status at birth, not to one's aspirations and talents, and this does not do. (There were social exceptions, the hero Karna being one, but as it happens he too was of noble birth.) The focus is rather on the link between the twin concepts of *Dharma* (right action) and *Karma* (deed). This is central to the *Gita*.[35]

The antecedents are more direct in Aristotle, most especially his *Nicomachean Ethics*.[36] Much attention is paid by Aristotle to the connection between enjoyment (alternatively, well-being) and the exercise of our capacities. Rawls (1972: 414), in an extended discussion, calls this connection the Aristotelian Principle (see also Williams, 1985: chapter 3). There is no suggestion though that enjoyment, as conceived of in this principle, is the same as happiness or utility as we use the terms today. It has, rather, to do with human flourishing, conducting a worthwhile life (see Vlastos, 1962; see also Scheffler, 1976). In this context, happiness has often been called the sweet exaltation of work well done. The point of interest is in

---

[35] It is a significant fact in the *Mahabharata* that Partha proves to be deficient in character. He is unable to absorb Lord Krishna's teachings. He fights nobly and well, he is the hero. But he doesn't think like a hero, and so he doesn't grow as a person as the epic unfolds. Self-realization eludes him. He loses the celestial bow he has obtained from his father, Indra, the King of the Gods, and he succumbs before finding his way to the abode of the gods on Mount Kailash. It has been said that one must think like a hero to behave like a merely decent human being. Partha lacked the gift of such thought.

[36] I have learnt much from ch. 5 of Jonathan Lear's excellent recent book on Aristotle, where he discusses the *Nicomachean Ethics*. See Lear (1988).

a person engaging in and bringing to fruition those activities which, upon rational deliberation, go towards making his total life well-lived.

The concept of a well-lived life is fraught with difficulties, but its basic features are not controversial. As regards personal growth, most people would place emphasis on their being able to realize a certain type of character, one they themselves can admire, something that is a source of self-respect—for example, having a disposition towards honesty and charitability, being able to stand up for one's principles, having the patience to probe and to discover where one's innate gifts lie (and to then develop them), being capable of displaying and receiving affection. In the related social sphere, most people would place emphasis on a successful family life, warm friendships, a meaningful job, fruitful vocational activities, an occasional trip to see other places and cultures, and at the end of it a reflective and useful old age. The centrality in all this of social organization and its implied role as a basis for resource allocation is clear enough: social life is an expression of a person's sense of social unity, and commodities and an absence of coercion are means by which persons can pursue their own conceptions of the good. We can curb our desires and needs and thus commodity requirements. We can as well escape into an inner world of self-sufficiency to accommodate an absence of both types of liberty. Several, what one might call mystical, systems in fact instruct us to do just that. But if the exercise of our natural powers is a leading human good, there is no getting away from commodity requirements and the need for negative liberty.

There is a connection between the modern concept of basic needs and the Aristotelian Principle. The principle affirms that enjoyment is by no means the result of returning to a normal or healthy life or of making up our deficiencies; for many kinds of enjoyment arise only when we exercise our faculties. What the Aristotelian system does is to show how such basic commodity needs are in themselves a part of what creates a claim-right to them.

There are several contemporary versions of this line of reasoning. For example, in his influential essay Vlastos (1962) explored the argument that rights have priority over utility or desert because their fulfilment provides the necessary background environment for persons to be capable of deliberating and acting *upon* considerations such as utility. When basic needs are not met our moral powers remain only potential; they are not attained. The satisfaction of these needs, as we noted earlier, is what makes life possible; it doesn't in itself make life enjoyable. Such goods have a different status from those that further our projects and purposes. In the absence of a set of background entitlements to basic needs, there would be nothing to guarantee the integrity of citizens as intelligent, free agents, capable in principle of deliberating over personal, political, civil, and socio-economic matters in a reasoned way. Dead people and chronically undernourished people are, understandably, not capable of rising to such heights. We can see then why a contractual theory of the State would require public institutions to be particularly concerned with basic-needs and civil and political liberties, among which are what we earlier called the first tier of goods, those that make living possible. The State cannot consistently keep its hands off such levers as may be necessary to pull in order to preserve the integrity of precisely those persons whose reasoned agreement *validates* the State. It is this argument that provides a link between freedom, commodity needs, and claim-rights.[37]

This link has more recently been explored in a powerful essay by Fried (1978), who distinguishes two types of rights, roughly along the lines of Berlin's two concepts of freedom. We are to think of positive rights as a claim *to* something, a share of material goods (such as Rawlsian or Dworkinian resources) or some particular commodity, such as education when young and medical attention when in need. It is to the satisfaction of such needs that we have positive rights, and Fried derives this from the primary morality of respecting the integrity of persons as free, rational, but incorporated beings. A negative right, on the other hand, is a right that something *not* be done to one, that some particular imposition be withheld. It is a right not to be wronged intentionally in some specified way. This too is derived from the primary morality alluded to above.

Now, it is a most interesting feature that positive rights are asserted to *scarce* goods, and so scarcity implies a limit to their claim. Negative rights, the right not to be interfered with in forbidden ways, on the other hand appear not to have such natural limitations. ('If I am let alone, the commodity I obtain does not appear of its nature to be a scarce or limited one. How can we run out of people not harming each other, not lying to each other, leaving each other alone?' Fried, 1978: 110.) This is not to say that protection against unauthorized violence does not involve material resources. But then the claim to protection from, say, the government

---

[37] Much contemporary ethics assumes at the start of the inquiry that these needs have been met: 'As for what typically goes on psychologists' lists of what constitutes "positive mental health"—things such as being healthy and confident, having self-esteem, being adaptable, caring—we might specify our subject by supposing that such traits are already present. The question then becomes: How should someone live who has reached the ample launching pad these traits provide?' (Nozick, 1990: 22). I shall not pursue here the important links tying rights to responsibilities, a matter that has been much neglected in the recent literature on political philosophy. (An exception are the Communitarians: see e.g. Selznick, 1987; Moravcsik, 1988). These lie at the heart of the notion of citizenship. See T. H. Marshall (1964) and Sec. 5.1 below. See also Rawls (1985) for a contractualist's perception of these matters, and how the notion of social unity may be integrated with that of an individual's self-fulfilment.

against such violence is a positive right, not a negative one.[38] This asymmetry in resource costs may explain the powerful hold negative rights have on our moral sensibilities. It is always feasible to honour negative rights (there are no direct resource costs, remember), but it may not be feasible to honour positive ones: the economy may simply not have sufficient resources to enable all to enjoy adequate nutrition, for example. It is then possible to entertain the idea that negative rights are inviolable, in a way that positive rights are not. (For how can a right be inviolable if it is not always possible to protect it?)

The asymmetry also offers a clue to why we typically find the thought compelling that all persons have *equal* negative rights, even while we eschew the idea of full equality in the distribution of goods to which we have positive rights. Negative rights don't have to be created, they have only to be protected. In contrast, positive rights are produced goods, and in deliberating their distribution we have to care about differences in individual talents *to* produce, we have to worry about incentives, and so we have to address the related matter of just deserts. Professor Rawls's two principles of justice are a notable illustration of this asymmetry.

That a given right is not inviolable does not make it any the less a right. While we may not possess an inviolable right to adequate diet and health care, we may nevertheless possess an absolute right to a fair share of whatever resources the economy possesses. And in certain contractual views of the State it is possible to argue that the government has an obligation to pursue policies that bring about situations where basic needs are obtainable by all.

2.6 *Impersonality and the Public Sphere*

I am being tentative here for good reason. We do not yet possess a fully developed contractual theory of the State. We can't tell what precisely the hypothetical contract would carry with it at different levels of economic development. By this I mean, among other things, that we don't have a method for obtaining the relative weights the contract would attach to different basic liberties. Even the most comprehensive modern contractual theory, that of Rawls (1972), isn't context-free, nor does Professor Rawls take it to be free of context (see especially Rawls, 1982a, b, 1985). The indefinite article in the title of his book can't be there by accident. The priority rule over political and civil liberties in *A Theory of Justice* is conditional on society enjoying a sufficiently rich resource and capital base. The social contract may well look different if matters were otherwise. We

---

[38] The agency on whom one is making the claim to protection is by hypothesis not the one committing the offence.

may view the state of economic development as a parameter of the social contract. It is possible that political and civil rights would not be awarded priority over socio-economic rights in a hypothetical social contract written by citizens of a poor society.

It would be a mistake to conclude from this that political and civil liberties would not, or do not, matter to the poor. This view is a piece of insolence that only those who don't suffer from their lack seem to entertain. If nothing else, the Indian election results of 1977 should have put at rest the thought that these basic liberties are a matter of indifference to the poor. They matter very much. Nevertheless, the relative weights on various categories of rights in a social contract may well depend on the state of economic development. A general theory of social contracts would specify how the weighting system would depend on this. We do not as yet have such a theory.

At an operational level this may not matter much. If faced with a choice between rights, one certainly needs a weighting system. It is debatable though whether, as a matter of fact, poor countries have to face this sort of choice. In Chapter 5 we will conduct a statistical investigation among fifty-one of the world's poorest countries to see if recent experience is any guide to this question.

There is another dimension in which we lack a general theory of social contracts. It has to do with the information that parties to the hypothetical contract are assumed to possess in the circumstances in which the contract is thought to be 'written'. Contract theories can differ over these issues. For example, Rawls's theory, in contrast to Gauthier's, doesn't invoke bargaining, because Rawls sees the contract to be agreed upon in a situation where all parties to the contract have the same point of view. The veil of ignorance in Rawls's 'original position' is sufficiently thick to warrant this treatment. This is also the case with Professor Harsanyi's 'utilitarian' theory, where impartiality, or *impersonality*, as he calls it, is modelled as individual choice under complete ignorance of whose situation one will occupy in any given state of affairs. (See Harsanyi, 1955, 1976, 1982. I should emphasize though that Harsanyi is a self-avowed non-contractarian: see Harsanyi, 1987.) Complete ignorance is in turn formalized as equi-probability, and the 'utilitarianism' Harsanyi proceeds then to derive follows from the axioms of rational choice under uncertainty.

Harsanyi's model, while only a sketch, is transparent. But it hasn't always been interpreted with the generosity it deserves. This is in part due to Harsanyi's own practice of calling his theory utilitarian, even although it is far removed from the classical version (e.g. the utilitarianism of Bentham and Sidgwick), or its modern variants (e.g. Hare, 1981). Furthermore, as the thought-experiment Harsanyi asks us to conduct isn't contaminated by our day-to-day wishes, desires, stresses, and strains, it isn't choice-theoretic utilitarianism either. A common criticism of classical utilitarianism, that it ignores the agency point of view, cannot be levelled against Harsanyi's theory: Harsanyi leaves open the motivations of agents. His moral agent has every opportunity and every reason to examine her own ends and the possible rational ends of all others when evaluating states of affairs. Harsanyi's theory, like Rawls's, inquires into our duties and obligations in the *public* sphere of life. That it is difficult for us to keep this sphere separate from the private sphere of our lives is all too apparent. But this does not imply that they are the same; it implies only that the demands of justice often conflict with those obligations arising from personal loyalites and commitments. As a theory of justice, Harsanyi too can ask moral agents to assume the 'perspective of eternity' urged upon us in the closing passages in Rawls (1972). Harsanyi's theory looks utilitarian only because aggregate well-being is argued in it to be the arithmetic average of individual well-beings. The objects being averaged bear no necessary relationship to hedonistic welfare or its modern variants.

Harsanyi's theory of justice, like Rawls's, is 'decision-theoretic'. It lies at one extreme. If the parties were permitted to know something of their own personal features (as in Gauthier, 1986), matters would be different, and we would require an explicit account of the bargain. Social contract theories differ on this matter.

Finally, there is the question whether the hypothetical social contract is binding upon oneself and upon future generations, or whether recontracting is possible, so that the original contract is constrained to take this into account. Theories of justice can differ over these issues as well (see Dasgupta, 1974a, b; Bernheim and Ray, 1987a; Binmore, 1989).

These reflections bring us back full circle to the point with which we began this chapter, that contractual reasoning will be used here as a thought-experiment for capturing something elusive, namely, the notions of fairness and impartiality which form the bedrock of any reasoned conception of justice. To say we do not yet possess a general theory of social contracts is to say we do not yet have a firm grasp of the idea of impersonality as it should govern our sense of justice. Putting it another way, we do not yet know if and how the *domain* on which impartiality ought to be practised changes with socio-economic, civic, and political development. That any reasoned notion of impersonality in these three spheres of life would have us throw some form of veil of ignorance over the circumstances governing the corresponding social contract is common to all modern contractual theories of justice. How thick the veil needs to be for arriving at the principles of justice remains contentious.

It is in these senses that we do not as yet possess a general theory of social contracts, one that would offer us a taxonomy of substantive theories of justice. But we possess some guidelines based on a veil which isn't overly transparent, and on their basis a few general observations can be made. In the next chapter we will collate them.

3

The Objects of Social Contracts

3.1 *Rules versus Discretion*

Social contracts, whether or not they are explicit, have to be simple to be effective. Contractual obligations should not be conditioned too much on events; they shouldn't be overly sensitive to contingencies. One reason for this is that the mind has a limited capacity for processing and evaluating information, and for acting upon information. So, it won't do for a contract to have too many qualifications, to allow for too many exceptions to the rule. Rules, rather than discretion, need to be the guiding principle in conceptualizing social contracts.

Admittedly, the distinction between rules and discretion disappears if rules are stated in a sufficiently refined manner. But then, rules would not be rules were they subject to too many qualifications. It is this coarseness, this seeming lack of sensitivity to special circumstances, that gives rules their chill and detachment. Rules are hard, discretion is soft. It is hard to *like* rules. But they are necessary. We have to live with them. Obedience to rules makes discretion possible.[1]

There is another reason why rules must not have too many qualifications. It is that a great many contingencies can be observed only privately; they are not confirmable publicly. But obligations that are conditional only on privately observable events are not enforceable unless the obligations are in the interest of persons to carry out even if they know they can get away with not carrying them out.[2] For these reasons, social contracts need to be simple if they are to be conducive to human flourishing.

A social contract must be acceptable over time. Earlier generations cannot bind later ones (see Chapter 13). But it must be durable if it is to be a contract. It must not, for example, be broken if some special, unforeseen, localized circumstance were to arise for a short period which

---

[1] Compare this with the distinction drawn by Harrod (1936) between *rule* and *act* utilitarianism, for a formalization of which see Harsanyi (1977a). For a distinction similar to the one we are making in the text, see Rawls (1955; 1972, ch. II, s. 14; 1987), and R. Hardin (1988). The classic precursor is Hume (1960).

[2] As a half-serious illustration, the reader should ask if it is feasible to engage in bets on people's states of mind. The idea of 'trust', when seen as a commodity, rests on these notions. See Dasgupta (1988d).

makes it beneficial for parties to break the contract for that period. Thus, if it transpired that for some previously unforeseen reason slavery (or, alternatively, bonded labour) would be an effective social institution for a short while (it would make all parties better off, including the slaves and bonded labourers), it would not be allowed. Nor would any public authority be allowed the discretion to punish an innocent party even if the authority were convinced that by so doing some general harm would be avoided. Were the social contract to allow for such exceptions, the number of qualifications could multiply indefinitely. This would then place a great strain on the contract, as people would spend much time and effort checking whether the contract were being violated, and getting upset if they thought it was. Mutual suspicion would rule the social climate. Civil wars and riots and the destruction they bring in their wake are a manifestation of this sense of injustice. In such circumstances there is little time or opportunity left for living. In saying all this, I am deliberately focusing on instrumental justifications. The rule that an innocent person should under no circumstances be punished would not be based solely on this: it would supplement the purer deontological consideration the contracting parties may wish to respect.

Of course, curtailment of freedoms would be deemed necessary in collective emergencies, for example when there is aggression by a foreign power. Such curtailments would fall equally on all citizens. But these occasions would be expected to be rare, and governments would be instructed to pursue foreign policies that would *make* them rare. So we will ignore these exceptions in the discussion that follows.

These considerations show why social contract theories have laid so much emphasis on freedoms. Liberties are not only intrinsically valuable, they have instrumental worth as well. It is possible that some of those goods that on the surface appear intrinsically worthwhile have only an instrumental value when probed at a deeper level. The character of a well-lived life varies from person to person, for if nothing else talents differ, aspirations differ, and people differ in their capacity for love and affection. What isn't obvious is the set of background circumstances in the political, civil, and socio-economic spheres that is most conducive to the realization of well-lived lives. The details will depend upon the circumstances of the society and its history. But certain features are incontrovertible: freedom, both in its positive and negative guises, is an essential requirement for the pursuit of well-lived lives. Thus, whatever else persons may want, they will rationally want such freedoms. These are basic needs. They are what we classified in the previous chapter as the 'first tier' of goods. They make living possible. Moral agency cannot act without them, and is devoid of content in their absence. The protection and promotion of freedoms are public goods. We may conclude that basic liberties comprise the domain of social contracts.

A desire for flexibility of choice will be strong among parties to the social contract.[3] They will be conscious that when the future becomes the present, vast quantities of what has been learnt about individual needs, skills, talents, wants, aspirations, affections, opportunities, and ideas will be private information. These facts bestow a supreme instrumental value to basic liberties. There will be no exceptions made, no qualifications added. Indeed, the Constitution will be so written as to prohibit trade in certain negative freedoms. Thus, for example, one would not be permitted to sell oneself into slavery. (Recall Mill's stricture (Mill, 1975) that people are not at liberty to sell their liberty.) Curtailment of basic liberties will be seen as a diminution of the humanity of a person. This diminution is an everyday affair in poor countries. We will see in Chapter 5 that the average citizen of these countries suffers either from a lack of food and health care, or from a lack of civil and political liberties. We will also see that in most poor countries she suffers from a lack of both.

What about happiness? It may be intrinsically good, but under a social contract it will not be of direct concern to the State. If nothing else, the State does not possess the information rational individuals possess about their capacities to lead happy lives. It is a deep fact that rational individuals know, and would be expected to know, a good deal more about their own purposes than the State. Now this does not mean that people do not miscalculate, or that bad luck does not befall them, frustrating their projects and purposes. Risk cannot be avoided. But it is their own mistakes that will prevail if it is they who choose, and it is this that is asserted when the claim is made that people must be allowed to be free to make their own mistakes. The idea here is that rational persons are the best judges of their own risks. There is also the parallel thought that people should be responsible for their lives, otherwise moral agency would be impaired. People would not be exercising their agency role were they not the ones who were doing the choosing. The State's role in a social contract is to provide the background environment within which persons are in a position to pursue their ends rationally. (J. Griffin, 1986, calls this the fulfilment of 'informed desires'.) This is why social contract theories recommend *decentralization* of power and control. The State's role being limited to implementing a just distribution of resources and of equal political and civil liberties in these theories is a reflection of this desire for decentralization.

---

[3] Koopmans (1964) and Kreps (1979) offer axiomatic approaches to the question of flexibility of choice. Neither grounds the idea directly on choice under uncertainty. The literature on *option values* does. (See Arrow and Fisher, 1974; C. Henry, 1974, for an application to environmental resources; and Black and Scholes, 1973; Merton, 1973, Cox, Ross and Rubinstein, 1979, for applications to financial markets.)

3.2 *Outcome- versus Resource-Based Evaluative Principles*

These considerations not only have a bearing upon the general design of economic organizations, they also hint at what are appropriate zones of responsibilities of various collectives: individuals, families, kinship groups, village communities, religious orders, local and voluntary organizations, and the State. Over which levers of control should the government exercise choice? What ought to be the protected spheres of individual and familial discretions? And so on. We noted earlier that constituent indices of well-being, such as utility and liberties, reflect the output side of a production process in which commodities are inputs and an absence of coercion is a necessary background environment. (Among other determinants there is, for example, the individual genotype. But this is a parameter, the person's characteristic. See below.) Indices such as the availability of basic-needs goods, or general resources, reflect the input side of this same process. Each reflects features of states of affairs. Where they differ is over something else: they differ in connection with the allocation of zones of responsibility in the just society.

The claims of rights require among other things that the State should be the protector of negative freedom. (The way government responsibility is established varies from theory to theory. Rawls's account invites persons to attain a reflective equilibrium in which, among other things, government responsibilities in a just society are deduced. Nozick's account proceeds along a hypothetical, evolutionary process in which the State emerges almost from a primeval social jungle.) The State provides the inputs necessary for the exercise of freedom; it does not force people to do so. I am free to cease typing this chapter and to go out of the house if I choose to. But I am not compelled to exercise this choice. If I were, I would not be free. For this same reason, it is a feature of contractualism that the State's obligation is limited to ensuring that citizens have access to adequate amounts of basic-needs, for such commodities are necessary if people are to enjoy the freedom to achieve their own ends.[4] A reasonable social contract would not allow the State to go farther. If it were to, it would encroach unduly upon negative freedom. From this we may conclude that the State is not to be entrusted with the duty of ensuring that people actually make use of basic-needs goods in an efficient manner. Citizens may be prohibited from trading these rights away (see Chapters 7 and 17); but they cannot be *made* to use them if they choose not to. For example, one can imagine a community in which all have access to

---

[4] As always, 'adequate' is an inadequate word. I am using it here for brevity. I should also add that whether the government facilitates the performance of markets, or publicly provides some of the basic needs, or enforces income and wealth transfers so as to enable all to have access to adequate amounts of them, is a different matter. See Chs. 6–7.

adequate medical facilities, but where a great many people, owing to deeply held religious convictions, choose not to make use of them. In terms of individual capacities to function (e.g. life expectancy at birth and morbidity rates), the community will score badly. The government cannot be faulted here.

To take a somewhat different example, nutritional historians have noted that during this century the periods when the population in England enjoyed some of their lowest mortality rates coincided with the two World Wars (see e.g. S. Davidson *et al.*, 1975; Winter, 1988). There are several reasons why this has been so, one of them being that the majority of people had no choice but to have a spartan, healthy diet during these periods. Obesity was not an option for them. However, I doubt if this points to the desirability of food-ration cards in today's England.

These examples suggest that in judging government performance citizens' achievements are the wrong things to look at. We should instead be looking at the extent to which they enjoy the freedom to achieve their ends, no matter what their ends turn out to be. The problem is that the extent of such freedoms depends upon the degree to which citizens make use of income and basic needs. So the thing to do is to look at the availability of those commodities that are necessary for the exercise of basic freedoms. Commodity availability is then a surrogate of what we are really after.

A social contract would stipulate that one role of government should be to obtain and provide information on the use and worth of commodities that are basic needs, and that people should have access to the means by which they are able to make use of this information (see Chapters 4 and 6). (Of particular importance will be freedom from disinformation.) However, the contract would not allow the government to force people to use it. There are exceptions, among which is the insistence that primary and secondary schoolchildren participate in free mid-day school meals to counter, say, biases in food allocation within households. But these are based on the argument that the interests of the very young need to be protected.

These considerations tell us to assess governments by the access citizens have to goods that satisfy basic needs. (Pfeffer, 1978, calls these rights against the State 'social contract rights'.) Primary (economic) goods, such as a suitable index of income and wealth, or specific resources (such as food and clothing, potable water, health care, shelter, legal aid, education facilities, and general information) as a focus of distributive justice are an articulation of this view; welfare, achievements, capabilities, and well-being are not.

Principles of justice based on the distribution of resources (such as Rawls's second principle of justice: see Rawls, 1972: 302) are frequently criticized on the grounds that, as formulated, they don't recognize differences in people's needs (see Arrow, 1974; Sen, 1985; Okin, 1989). Children and adults, for example, have different nutritional needs, as do pregnant and lactating women and the elderly (see Chapter 14). So a reference person has to be devised, against whom all people are compared and scaled. This is called an 'adult-equivalent scale'. Its construction is a much discussed exercise in applied economic statistics (see Deaton and Muelbauer, 1986, and Chapter 14). Admittedly, the construction of equivalent scales requires interpersonal comparisons, which are hard to make. But that is no harder than trying to compare people's achievements, or the freedoms people enjoy to achieve their own ends. We will put these thoughts to work when formalizing the notion of social well-being. (In a significant essay, Okin, 1989, has extended contractual theories of justice to include gender as a characteristic that is unknown in the original position. See Chapters 11–12. See also Okin, 1992.)

When evaluating government performance, there is another reason why we should study the distribution of resources, as opposed to outcomes. Achievements are often observable publicly; the innate ability of individuals and the efforts they make to realize them by the use of resources are often not. There are, of course, a great many needs that are publicly verifiable, such as those of physically handicapped persons, and average needs associated with such publicly identifiable circumstances as pregnancy, young and old age, illness, and so forth. Even here, however, there are always interpersonal variations. There are also a number of needs that only experts can ascertain, such as medical requirements. But there are many needs that aren't easy to ascertain in public, and this creates problems if we were to attempt to tailor resource allocation to persons according to their specific needs.[5]

One would not deny that human flourishing is what is ultimately of value; nor that there are needs that can be inferred only by studying a person's achievements (for example, inferring a child's nutrition requirements by observing his growth performance). This is only to affirm that a lack of information, among other things, may force us to evaluate the performance of governments by the distribution of resources and the political and civil liberties that people enjoy.[6] The (implicit) contract between a patient and his doctor is over the care and attention (i.e. the resource input) the doctor is to give to the patient's medical needs, not over his eventual state of health; for whether the patient gets well will depend upon the doctor's efforts, the care and attention he devotes to the case, and a wide variety of chance factors. If both personal effort and the

[5] That one would wish to use statistical information, say of the distribution of needs in an identifiable population, goes without saying. See Ch. 17.

[6] In an illuminating work, Seabright (1988) has made use of this argument to study more broadly the role of the State.

realization of chance factors could be publicly observable, it would be possible to draw up a contract specifying a payment contingent upon the patient's eventual state of health. As it is, it can't be done, and the parties are faced with a classic problem in moral hazard (see Chapter 9). Thus also for government performance.

3.3 *Political Competition and Civil Liberties*

All this bears on the way government performance should be assessed; none of it suggests a constitution offering the best chance for citizens to enjoy good government. Here the instrumental worth of political competition assumes importance. Competition in the political sphere not only enables citizens to shop for the ability among contenders to govern, it also enables them to shop for ideas on governance. Pluralism in the political domain is akin to 'contestable markets' in the economic sphere (see Chapter 6). Competition is desirable even in an unchanging environment. It discourages inefficiency. Potential competition is necessary to keep incumbents from slacking. However, when there are irrecoverable costs of entry, potential competition is not sufficient to discipline incumbents. The reason is this: knowing in advance that the incumbent will match their zeal and efficiency were there to be a true threat of entry, potential entrants will not enter. Armed with this knowledge, the incumbent will find it possible to slack (see J. Farrell, 1986; Dasgupta and Stiglitz, 1988a). Carried to the political sphere, this provides the rationale for the public subsidy of political parties not in power. It makes political markets contestable.

The analogy with competition among producing firms can be extended. You want your house decorated on a regular basis. For this you invite bids from rival decorators, and you engage the one who appears to offer the best contract. But you want to have the option of dismissing your decorator should he prove unsatisfactory. Otherwise you may find yourself in a monstrous situation: your decorator will have no further incentive to work efficiently.[7] Thus too with governments as an agency of citizens. We are, therefore, supposing that the background institutions include something like a Constitution and a Bill of Rights, which guarantee citizens their political and civil liberties.

Under changing circumstances and the birth and growth of new ideas, the argument for political competition is even stronger. It isn't merely personal dictatorships that are a harbinger of disaster over the long run.

---

[7] Unless the contract has been designed in a highly conditional way. But such complicated contracts as those that keep decorators from slacking have no counterpart in the political sphere. You can take your errant decorator to court should he violate the contract. But you cannot take your government to court if the judiciary is in the pocket of the executive and legislative branches. You would in all probability find yourself behind bars were you to try it.

Even party systems, unless disciplined by political competition, are prone to ossification. Admittedly, even single-party systems can field competition, as members vie with one another for control of party apparatuses. But for a political party to be definable, there must be something fixed in its agenda, at least over the short to medium run. It wouldn't be a party otherwise. For this reason single-party systems are incapable of fielding the spectrum of ideas that political democracies can. Moreover, the judiciary is unable to act independently of the legislative and executive branches of government under a single-party system. Over time this proves corrosive, stifling, and ultimately oppressive. Political competition enables citizens over the long run to change their portfolio of risks, much as they can in financial markets.

Unless they can be held accountable by independent bodies at every level, however, even democratically elected governments are not immune to the commands of powerful groups. But authoritarian regimes in general, and dictatorships in particular, are a different species altogether. Except during emergencies they are inefficient, because among other things they are bad at encouraging the production, dissemination, and use of information. Moreover, even seemingly benign authoritarian regimes turn nasty when economic circumstances run into awkward corners, or when citizens (often minorities) seek changes in their social and political situation, or begin demanding patterns of goods not currently obtainable in the economy, or, more generally, demand changes in the resource allocation mechanism currently in operation.

Admittedly, authoritarian regimes *can* leave citizens alone to pursue their lives. Authoritarian governments have also been known to provide a good environment for economic activity. But a commonly held belief that benevolent authoritarianism is a sure-fire route to sustained economic betterment is a belief in an incongruent object: sustained benevolent authoritarianism. Pointing to economies that have achieved significant economic progress under authoritarian regimes is no guide to political action. Citizens cannot will wise authoritarianism into existence, nor can they remove an authoritarian regime readily if the political leadership proves to be unsound. A central problem with authoritarianism is its lack of incentives for error-correction, a point that has repeatedly been made by advocates of liberal democracies.

From this it does not, of course, follow that political democracy guarantees economic progress, or that it propels growth. It does neither. What political pluralism does, when it is alllied to a commitment on the part of citizens that good government must protect and promote civil and political liberties, is to offer an environment where citizens have a chance to thrive. Of course, if civil order and general civic responsibility have broken down, there is no prescription to be had either one way or the other. In Chaper 5 we will see that the bulk of the world's poorest countries suffer either from dictatorial regimes or from single-party systems. Political pluralism and competiton for ideas are a scarce commodity in what are commonly referred to as developing countries. In the mid-1980s, citizens of 27 of the 45 nations in the continent of Africa were forced to live under militarily controlled governments (Sivard, 1985).

So too are civil liberties scarce in poor countries. Citizens in a large majority of such countries enjoy relatively few rights against the State. For instance, except for Botswana, the Gambia, and Mauritius, citizens in all countries in Africa routinely suffer from State repression in the form of torture, disappearances, and political killings (Sivard, 1985). The rule of just law is an alien figure there. Periodic riots and civil wars are endemic. Poor countries today are not only poor, they are for the most part not well-ordered societies. In a great majority of cases they are governed at best cynically, at worst brutally.

3.4 *Motivation and Choice*

For simplicity of exposition, I shall assume that each individual has a complete ranking over social states on the basis of which she actually chooses. Of course, no individual ever gets to choose a social state. Each person chooses only certain components of the social state, which gets selected through the mechanism guiding collective choice. (See below for a general formulation.) We will call any numerical function representing the ranking of social states on the basis of which an individual actually chooses, her *utility function*.[8] Modern-day applied welfare economic theory builds on the idea that public policy should serve an aggregate of individual utilities (earlier we called this *choice-theoretic utilitarianism*), even while it alludes to human welfare as the basis upon which policy is advocated in the theory. There is an implied suggestion that individuals choose on the basis of the conception they possess of their own good. But the literature doesn't inquire if the presumption is justified.

In poor countries at least, it is not uncommon for well-being and welfare not to be the basis on which individual choice is actually made. Mothers in impoverished circumstances routinely sacrifice their own interests for the sake of their families. There is little or no complaint, others' interests

---

[8] Let R (a binary relation, a ranking) define a complete ordering of social states. Social states are labelled x, y, z and so on. xRy is to be interpreted as 'x is at least as high in the ranking as y'. We say that a real-valued function $G(\cdot)$ defined on the set of social states represents R if, for all x, y, we have xRy if and only if $G(x) \geq G(y)$. From this we may note that if 'x is higher in the ranking than y', then and then only $G(x) > G(y)$. See any microeconomics graduate text, e.g. Varian (1984), for an account of this. The vital contributions to the development of modern decision theory and decision-theoretic ethics were Debreu (1954, 1958), Savage (1954), Harsanyi (1955, 1976, 1977a, 1982), Gorman (1968), and Koopmans (1972a, b).

having been internalized via her perception that the family's welfare is her own well-being. (See e.g. B. M. Popkin, 1983; E. King and Evenson, 1983. See also Chapters 10–11.) This identification is nurtured from an early age, and it isn't confined to mothers: older daughters of the household assume it as well. In the rural district of Birbhum in West Bengal, India, where my mother currently lives, I have known young women from poor families working thirteen- to fourteen-hour days, cooking, cleaning, and shopping, while their male siblings don't do anything in particular. Sons are a prize possession there (see Chapter 11). It doesn't quite do to insist that women are forced to behave thus. In one sense, *of course* they are, but this would be to miss the point. Nor would it do to suggest that they dislike fulfilling these obligations, for this is a sort of situation where a person's sense of duty may direct her to comply, and to comply in a way that is welfare-enhancing for her, because she is resigned to it. But they are a far cry from activities that would promote her own well-being. That a mother or daughter gladly offers or allows herself to be used does not obliterate the fact that she *is* used. The rupture between utility and advantage is complete here, as is the breach between desire-fulfilment and well-being.[9]

A striking, documented example of the internalization of social norms is offered by the extent to which women actively participate in the practice of female circumcision in parts of Africa. In a recent study, Lightfoot-Klein (1989) remarks that the practice is enforced by persons who have themselves been subjected to the torture. The picture one draws from her account is not that women are driven to practise this solely because they fear retribution if they don't, or that girls from their kinship will suffer indignities if they aren't circumcised (although these realities certainly do influence behaviour), but that they practise it also because they think it is right.

For certain kinds of analysis, it is useful to distinguish and to keep separate a person's values from her tastes. Values in such analyses are often seen as setting self-imposed constraints upon behaviour, with tastes guiding choice among those options from which a person permits herself to choose. This distinction can play no useful role in our analysis, because we are acknowledging that there is a difference between a person's utility and her well-being. In our analysis a person's utility function amalgamates her tastes, and the norms and values, both social and personal, that guide her. Nothing will be gained from our trying to unscramble from a person's utility function the various types of motivation that are the ultimate springs of action.

---

[9] That there are strong cultural bases in personal assessments of one's own well-being has been much discussed in the literature; see e.g. Birdsall and McGreevey (1983), Buvinic (1983), Low (1984), and Sen (1985, app. B).

3.5 *Social Systems: A Formulation*

We will label agents by the index k. We assume that there are M persons in all, numbered from 1 to M. M is therefore part of the data. A large number of these M persons will typically be future people. For the moment we are assuming that future population size is not subject to choice. (In Chapters 12–13 we will study fertility decisions.) We will first elaborate upon the idea of a social system.[10] This will enable us to offer a formal account of the domain of social contracts. It will prove expositionally helpful to amalgamate the government and its agencies, and regard them as a single additional actor. We will label this additional agency 0. Over time governments will come and go. But nothing will be gained here by giving new labels to future governments.

We are interested in the objects of individual choice. So we begin with the notion of an *elementary strategy*, or *elementary plan*, by which we will mean a conditional action. An elementary strategy is typically of the form: 'I will do this if that happens', or 'we will do that if he does this', and so on. Elementary plans form building blocks, in that what choosers usually choose are not elementary strategies, but a compound of elementary strategies, which we will call a *strategy*, or *plan*, for short. One example would be a person's plan of action for the day as he sets out for work; another, albeit the grandest of examples, would be his entire life plan. A plan consists of a number of conditional future actions.

We need to distinguish between the set of strategies from which a person can in principle choose and the set from which he can in fact choose. Were a destitute not a destitute, he would have had available for choice any number of plans he does not have available for choice. The advantage of keeping in mind the set of plans from which a person could in principle choose is that it enables us to have an idea of the many options that have been foreclosed by the existing distribution of benefits and burdens in a society. The object of agreement in a social contract is the set of rules governing this distribution. When we talk of freedom of choice, we mean among other things the range of plans from which a person can choose. Of course, a person's freedom of action would to an extent be protected even if someone else were to choose on his behalf, provided this choice is made on the basis of his interest. We will presently come to make this distinction (see also Dasgupta, 1980, 1982a), but for now we focus on the case where the person himself gets to make the choice.

My sole intention here is to provide a formulation of a social system. It will save notation to eschew time from the account, since nothing of

---

[10] The framework we develop here is an adaptation of Debreu (1952). See Dasgupta and Heal (1979, ch. 2) for an exposition similar to the one that follows.

substance will be lost in our making this move. When we come to analyse concrete situations in later chapters, time will be introduced explicitly.

Given this restriction, it makes no sense to talk of *conditional* actions; the appropriate elementary notion is, rather, that of an *action*. In the formal construction of this chapter the objects of choice will, therefore, be actions. Nevertheless, whenever I attempt to motivate the construction with general discussion, I will revert to using the term 'plan' in place of 'action'. Denote by a_k an action undertaken by k. The vector of actions $(a_0, a_1, \ldots, a_M)$ undertaken by all parties will be denoted by **a**.

An individual is characterized not only by his genotype, but also by his developmental history. The former is an unalterable attribute (at least as of now!), the latter is a function of the resources he has had at his command and service. I shall amalgamate both sets of k's attributes into one scalar object and call this his *state*, which is denoted by H_k, where $k = 1, \ldots, M$. Since H_k is dependent upon the extent to which k's basic commodity needs are met, we may express it by the functional relationship $H_k(r_k)$, where r_k is some suitable index of basic-needs goods at k's disposal.

The range of purposes and plans a person can reflect upon and choose from is itself dependent on his state. If he is badly undernourished and ill, most activities are out of his reach, and his freedom of achievement is severely restricted. In all probability he is even incapable of deliberating among those within his reach. His agency role is impaired in all senses. We may, therefore, say that the sets of plans from which a person can actually choose is dependent on his state. We may also say that his rational desires are definable only when he has attained a reasonable state. The reason is that when his moral powers are impaired it makes no sense to talk of his rational desires. One expects that his choices would be conditioned on reflex, not arrived at through deliberation. His instinct for survival would dominate his choice; for example foraging for food, engaging in few bodily movements so as to conserve energy, and so forth.

This isn't to say that one can't identify a person's *interests*, which in the case of a starving man will lie in the meeting of his nutritional needs. These interests are objective and incontrovertible. They will often have to be acted upon by others, because he may not be in a state to express either his desires or his needs, and he may not be able to act upon them even if he were able to make the choice. When in the closing passages of *The Grapes of Wrath* Rose of Sharon in an act of beatific compassion suckles the starving stranger, her thought isn't that his preferences should count. Rose's quite spontaneous action is directed at the stranger's needs. She sees no philosophical dilemma here.

The argument that a malnourished person ought to be fed is based not on the thought that his preferences ought to count, but that his interests count; that his choices would have reflected such interests had he been in a position to deliberate and choose. This is how we will interpret his utility function in that region of the function's domain where his state is impaired.

The range of plans (or actions, in an atemporal world) from which a person can in principle choose is vast. It includes plans the person would be able to pursue were all of society's resources (including other people's time and attention) to be placed at his disposal. Were he allowed to select a plan that makes use of such extensive entitlements, the options open to others would be severely limited. Social contracts address this vital issue: the delineation of permissible sets of plans.

Let us denote by X_k the set of actions from which the kth party can in principle choose, and by A_k the set of actions from which k can actually choose. Thus, $A_k \subseteq X_k$. A typical element of X_k is a_k. A_k will be called k's *permissible set*. (We could also call it k's *feasible set*.) We have noted on a number of occasions that, for individuals, A_k is dependent on k's state, H_k. A person's state is in turn dependent on the basic-needs goods he makes use of. So I express this recursive dependence as $A_k(H_k(r_k))$. For the government, a less elaborate notation is required. The notion of the government's state may as well be bypassed here, and so we can say that its permissible set is dependent upon the resources at its disposal. This we write as $A_0(r_0)$.

But there are further complications, arising from the fact that time has been eschewed from the formulation. Had it not been, we would have observed that the range of actions available to a party at a date depends upon the actions all relevant parties have undertaken until that date. Furthermore, we would have noted that a person's state at any date is in part dependent upon the actions others have undertaken until then (through, for example, the prices that have prevailed). In straitjacketing an intertemporal world into an atemporal formulation, we are in danger of overlooking this sort of interdependence among people. To avoid this pitfall we will take liberties with our notation. Thus, let $\mathbf{a}_{-k}$ denote the vector of actions chosen by all parties other than k.[11] We will now make an agent's permissible set of actions depend upon other agents' actions as well. We denote this overall dependence for individuals by the notation $A_k(\mathbf{a}_{-k}, H_k)$, and for the government by $A_0(\mathbf{a}_{-0}, r_0)$. Thus, $A_k(\mathbf{a}_{-k}, H_k(r_k))$ is a subset of X_k for $k = 1, \ldots, M$; and $A_0(\mathbf{a}_{-0}, r_0)$ is a subset of X_0.[12]

---

[11] In symbols, $\mathbf{a}_{-k} = (a_0, a_1, \ldots, a_{k-1}, a_{k+1}, \ldots, a_M)$. We will sometimes write $\mathbf{a} = (a_k, \mathbf{a}_{-k})$ for $k = 0, \ldots, M$.

[12] For simplicity, we are ignoring the functional relationship between H_k and $\mathbf{a}_{-k}$. The dependence of A_k on $\mathbf{a}_{-k}$ is artificial. We would not have required this contrivance in an intertemporal model. There, a person's plan is a compound strategy, a set of conditional actions. In an intertemporal construction each individual faces a decision tree. The generalized game (Debreu, 1952) to be considered (see below) should ideally be expressed in extensive form, and not in the normal form in which it will be cast below. See Fudenberg and Tirole (1991) for definitions.

This is still not the end of the matter. All social systems are subject to a wide variety of constraints on the availability and distribution of resources. Such constraints will figure prominently in this book. For the moment I shall simplify and assume that there is a single such constraint, given by the equation

$$F(r_0, r_1, \ldots, r_M) = L. \tag{3.1}$$

We will on occasion write $\mathbf{r}$ for the vector $(r_0, r_1, \ldots, r_M)$.

It is best to keep the formulation somewhat loose at this point. It allows for flexibility of interpretation. I want to think of L as being in some sense the total volume of resources to be devoted to the protection and promotion of both positive and negative liberties. It includes the allocation of basic-needs goods. If, as will be assumed below, the veil of ignorance is thick, the parties won't know their specific and special needs. So it is the *rule* governing the allocation of positive-rights goods (and not the actual allocation) which will be agreed upon behind the veil.

Actions lead to *consequences*. A typical consequence is expressed as C, and the functional dependence of consequences on plans as $C(\mathbf{a})$. For the moment we are ignoring environmental uncertainty and are regarding $A_k(a_{-k}, H_k(r_k))$ and $C(\mathbf{a})$ as deterministic functions. In Chapters 8–9 we will extend the formulation to accommodate uncertainty.

A person's utility is a function of the actions chosen by all. This is so even though what may matter to a person is the consequence and not directly the actions that lead to the consequence. We write person k's utility as $U_k(\mathbf{a}; H_k(r_k))$. k's utility may depend also on the extent of his choice, and not merely on what is chosen. In this case U_k will depend also on $A_k(\cdot)$, and possibly on the permissible sets of other agents. We will ignore this possible dependence for the moment in order to keep the exposition simple. In any case, this kind of dependence, that utility depends on the extent of one's choice, requires explanation, and we will provide one in Section 3.7.

No one is fully autonomous. Each of us is a member of many associations: our family, kinship, the local community and religious congregation, our network of friendships, the group we work with, and so forth. Some of these associations are ones we have inherited, others are to a greater or lesser extent those we have entered voluntarily. Decisions within an association are usually arrived at through agreement and co-ordination. It will be far too complex to introduce these institutions here as decision units. So I will regard individuals as the decision units. They choose their plans independently of one another, in a sense to be made precise below. We will study institutions, such as the family and the local community, in Chapters 8–12.

There remains the government, whose duties provided the theme of the previous chapter. We denote by $W(\mathbf{a})$ a numerical representation of the ordering on the basis of which the government is contracted to assess plans, including its own plan. $W(\mathbf{a})$ denotes: it doesn't explain, in that we have yet to formalize the government's motivation. We will do this in Section 3.9.

3.6 *Contractual and Optimization Theories*

In this and the previous chapter I have tried to bring together two disparate conceptual frameworks: contractual theories of justice, and theories that see justice as involving the maximization of some overall social objective. The contributions of Harsanyi (1955) and Rawls (1972) have been vital in demonstrating that the two strands come together in a formal sense if the (hypothetical) social contract is agreed upon at a stage when the veil of ignorance is opaque. Behind an opaque veil all parties have the same point of view. Reaching agreement does not involve bargaining. Therefore, in what follows I shall assume the veil to be opaque. For us it will be a tactical move. I am viewing social contracts here as a thought-experiment, to give shape to notions of fairness and impersonality. Contractual reasoning helps to set a standard by which we may evaluate not only the basic structure of society, but also public policy. More generally, it helps us to identify the domain on which social evaluation ought to be conducted.

We should imagine the contract as being agreed upon in the first stage of a multi-stage game. The veil is operative at this stage. The State is created at this stage as well. In the second stage the State is assumed to design and install those background institutions it is obliged to provide under the general terms of the contract. We could imagine the long-drawn-out third stage of the game to be the one in which citizens pursue their activities within the rubric established by these institutions. The government is now an active participant.

Now it cannot be emphasized strongly enough that this three-stage description of the game we are envisaging here has only simplicity to commend it. In practice, the third stage is divided into an indefinite number of steps.

What we need to do now is to work backwards in time. So we begin by studying the third stage (Section 3.7). This will enable us to have an idea of what rational contractees will agree upon in the *first* stage (Section 3.8). By a 'rational' person here I mean one who not only can reason through the most effective means towards her given ends, but one whose ends are rational too. The rationality of ends is something we considered all too briefly in the previous chapter, and we will return to in Chapter 13 (again briefly) when we view the household as a reproductive unit. Admittedly, persons behind an opaque veil would not know their rational ends, since they would know little to nothing of their personal circumstances. This is why their attitudes to risk must be rational as well (see Chapter 8). Contractees will recognize that in the day-to-day world the stresses and strains of living will contaminate their sense of the good. The social contract they will seek is designed in part to act as a cushion against this. We will look into it now.

3.7 Ex Post *Equilibria and* Ex Ante *Contracts*

At the third stage of the hypothetical game the veil has been lifted, and individuals know more of their plans and purposes. Let $\hat{r}_k$ be the index of resources available to k under the terms of the social contract agreed upon in the first stage. When the third stage 'commences', individual k's permissible set is, therefore, of the form $A_k(\mathbf{a}_{-k}, H_k(\hat{r}_k))$, and the government's set is $A_0(\mathbf{a}_{-0}, \hat{r}_0)$. The question now is: how should agents choose their actions? This poses an immediate problem, in that a person's utility is a function not only of what he does, but also of what others do, and a person's future capabilities depend not only on his own state, but also on what others choose to do. We can conclude that a rational agent has to form an expectation of what others will choose in order that he can make his own choice. This leads to the idea of *self-fulfilling*, or *equilibrium*, expectations. They are the natural focal point of any inquiry into expectations and, so, of any inquiry into the choice of actions. (See also Chapters 6–8, 11–12, and especially Chapter *12.)

The intuitive idea is to identify a set of feasible plans, one plan for each party, with the property that no party would choose to deviate from his plan in this set were he to expect all other parties to choose their respective plans in this set. Such a state of affairs is realizable only when agents' beliefs are self-confirming. To state it formally, we say that a vector of actions, $\mathbf{a}^* = (a_0^*, a_1^*, \ldots, a_k^*, \ldots, a_M^*)$, is an *equilibrium* if, for all k ($k = 1, \ldots, M$), we have $U_k(\mathbf{a}^*; H_k(\hat{r}_k)) \geq U_k(a_k, \mathbf{a}_{-k}^*; H_k(\hat{r}_k))$ for all $a_k \in A_k(\mathbf{a}_{-k}^*, H_k(\hat{r}_k))$; and if, for the government, $W(\mathbf{a}^*) \geq W(a_0, \mathbf{a}_{-0}^*)$ for all $a_0 \in A_0(\mathbf{a}_{-0}^*, \hat{r}_0)$. A vector of actions, one per party, satisfying this property is often called a *Nash equilibrium*, in honour of the person who first formalized the notion in a general context (see Nash, 1951). It is a state of affairs the social system could be expected to attain over the long haul were the background environment and the motivations of agents to remain approximately constant, that is, were the social system a *stationary* one (see Chapters 8 and *12).

Nash equilibrium strategies (a social system may well support more than one Nash equilibrium) are the natural objects of study in political philosophy. Such plans are self-enforcing: if all others were to choose their equilibrium strategies, there would be no reason for a person not to choose his equilibrium strategy.[13] The same cannot be said of plans that don't support a Nash equilibrium. To see this, consider a set of plans that is not a Nash equilibrium. We ask if the state of affairs resulting from this set of choices could prevail in a stationary environment. If the answer is 'yes', its justification would be based on the thought that a significant number of parties continually entertain wrong expectations of others' behaviour. We should then ask why those who have made mistakes in the past don't learn. (Recall that the background environment has been assumed stationary.) Admittedly, to ask it is not to answer it, and we won't know without formalizing the question whether plausible patterns of learning are capable of allowing parties over time to arrive at correct expectations. In Chapter *12 we will look at this question in a rudimentary way. But even without going into formal learning models, it seems clear that Nash equilibrium behaviour is the right set of objects to study. As an analytical attack on the problem of explaining and predicting behaviour in a social context, anything else would be flabby. We would be able easily to explain any pattern of behaviour, however bizarre. All we would have to do is to say that expectations were such as to have made this behaviour reasonable.

Not all social systems can support Nash equilibrium behaviour. It is not difficult to construct social systems where there are no Nash equilibria, that is, where there are no strategies satisfying the 'self-enforcing' property. So it is a natural next step to locate characteristics of social systems where Nash equilibrium strategies can be guaranteed to exist. This problem has been much explored in the game-theoretic literature, and we now have a codification of such systems (Nash, 1951; Debreu, 1952; Shafer and Sonnenschein, 1976; Topkis, 1979; Dasgupta and Maskin, 1986a, b; L. K. Simon, 1987; Milgrom and Roberts, 1990a, b; Simon and Zame, 1990; Caplin and Nalebuff, 1991).

All this is about stationary environments. Under changing circumstances matters are different. Nash equilibrium behaviour isn't then a compelling object of study. This explains why analyses of periods of rapid change are frequently so difficult. Simple learning rules can be postulated, but there isn't any firm experimental basis for any of them. This has implications for social contract theories. Social contracts specify permissible sets of plans (including the permissible set for the government). But this means, among other things, that the contract specifies rules for the sharing of benefits and burdens, in particular the material resources as circumscribed by condition

---

[13] Aumann (1987a) has argued that the central organizing idea of social interactions should instead be that of a *correlated equilibrium*, a generalization of Nash's concept. (A Nash equilibrium is a correlated equilibrium.) We will not analyse the circumstances in which this extended solution concept is the right one; to do so would take us into technical details. See also Aumann (1990) for examples that are problematic for the viewpoint we are adopting here. But our purpose is to study a schemata, nothing more. So I shall ignore problem cases.

(3.1). I have so far argued that, if men and women have to (hypothetically) come together and agree on a social contract, they will need to know in a broad sense the resource allocation they could expect to see prevail under alternative contracts. Otherwise they would not be in a position to assess the relative desirability of different types of contracts. But if next to nothing can be inferred by any of them about the behaviour of others, they will not be able to entertain firm expectations. This would place a severe strain on their ability to reach a decision.

One way out is to opt for a basic structure of society which doesn't involve too much interdependence among specifically related people (e.g. neighbours, kin, and so forth). If my life prospects are not heavily dependent on your (my kin's) behaviour, I don't need to base my decisions too much on what I expect you will do. I can then be somewhat independent of you. I won't have to rely on you in order to get on with my life. This affords me a special kind of protection. But to enjoy such independence I will need guarantees from the State, or at least from some public agency created especially for this purpose. Formally, this is to make the permissible sets, $A_k(\cdot)$, for each person as independent as possible of other persons' choices.

In a world where citizens are guaranteed reasonable social security, individuals do not have to depend upon neighbours and kin for support in times of need, for example, in old age, during periods of illness, or after harvest failures. Their plans don't have to be based on expectations of whether communal systems of security will continue to exist. We will note in subsequent chapters that one of the greatest tragedies in contemporary poor societies has been the breakdown of traditional patterns of support systems, unreplaced by any others. People's behavioural strategies have changed. This has come about by shifting, growing, and ageing populations, the widening of market opportunities, technological change, and exposures to new ways of living. The latter could be expected to alter people's utility functions, making kinship and group solidarity more fragile. When social security is strong, people are able to act somewhat more independently of one another without endangering one another's lives. The influence runs the other way as well. The erosion of intra-family support in Western Europe presumably has something to do with citizens enjoying extensive State protection against destitution.

This said, citizens would want their permissible sets to be as extensive as justice permits. (I will suggest why in the next section.) So we are back all the way to the State's obligation in a just society, a matter we explored earlier in less formal terms. In order that permissible sets are extensive, citizens have to be protected against force, fraud and theft, and so forth. Moreover, as people desire a measure of economic security in order to further their own ends, they will want their prospects in a changing world to be somewhat uncoupled from what others choose to do. The way they can ensure this is to have guarantees to basic-needs goods codified in the social contract.

We now have an explanation for the obsession that social contract theories have displayed towards freedom's various nuances. Basic liberties are guarantors of the ability of people not only to act, but to act independently of one another. To be sure, at the level of personal relationships, mutual dependence (both in the form of utility functions and permissible sets of strategies) is what makes life acquire meaning. As individuals, we *want* to enter into relationships that will bind us. Admittedly, also, governments could be required positively to help build and rebuild communal support systems. But we are not talking of any of these. We are talking instead of the basic structure of society. Here individual autonomy is a prized commodity.

3.8   *Measures of Freedom*

The government is an agency. Background institutions and government policies are directed at maximizing some aggregate of individual well-beings. This aggregate has been written as $W(\mathbf{a})$. We will call this a *social well-being function*. It is a numerical representation of that ordering over vectors of plans which is to guide the public realm of society. It reflects the outcome of an assumed bargain. The social contract hypothetically entered into is designed to maximize this function.

It has been suggested that, in seeking a complete social ordering over states of affairs, we seek too much, that public judgements can yield only an incomplete (or partial) ordering.[14] This is no doubt so in practice, although at the level of theoretical ethics it is hard to see what to do with this observation once it has been made. For analytical discourse it makes little sense not to think of a complete ordering of social states. It makes for expositional ease, and it keeps us away from inessential features of the exercise.

Since general well-being is an aggregate of individual well-beings, we need to formalize the latter first. Earlier we noted that a person's prospects for flourishing are dependent upon the nature and extent of the freedoms she enjoys. So we need a measure of her freedom. Since her permissible set of strategies is $A_k(\cdot)$, it is a numerical index of this we seek. We denote it by $Q_k(A_k(\cdot))$. Let us see how we may go about constructing such an index.[15]

---

[14] See the editorial Introduction in Sen and Williams (1982).
[15] The simplest measure of freedom is the number of elements in $A_k(\cdot)$. Suppes (1987) gives this as an example. An axiomatic basis for it is given in Pattanaik and Xu (1990), exposing the fact that the measure has only simplicity to commend it.

It is a deep and common intuition that freedom has intrinsic worth. But intuition is not always a reliable guide. What appears 'intrinsic' may have a deep instrumental root. As a research strategy, it makes sense to investigate whether freedom has instrumental worth. So we build on this idea.

Keeping our options open is desirable because we do not know in advance what we will rationally desire. A person may change in ways she can't now predict. Furthermore, she may rationally *wish* to change in ways she can't now predict.[16] To simplify the exposition, I shall restrict myself to a pure decision problem, that is, one where the actions of others, and the individual's entitlements to positive- and negative-rights goods, are taken by her to be given. She treats these objects as parameters, against which she does her best when choosing her own action. Let $V_k(\mathbf{a}; H_k)$ be a cardinal representation of person k's rational desires. We will take it to reflect her *good*. Of course, k does not know in advance what her good will be in the future. Certainly, in the circumstances in which the social contract is agreed upon, she will be expected to know little about it. So we denote by θ the parameter that reflects the functional form of the good. Thus, if $\mathbf{a}$ is the vector of chosen actions, and if θ is realized, then k's good is $V_k(\mathbf{a}; H_k; \theta)$.[17] Behind the veil of ignorance, let $\pi_k(\theta)$ be the probability that k's circumstances will be θ. (Each person may be thought of as a draw from the sample space of θs.) Now, in the three-stage game being envisaged here, the nature of admissible sets is established *before* individual θs are realized, and actions are chosen *after* they are realized.[18] Individual k chooses her action in accordance with her good. Her permissible set of actions is $A_k(\mathbf{a}_{-k}, H_k)$. Let $\bar{a}_k$ be an action from this set which maximizes $V_k(a_k, \mathbf{a}_{-k}; H_k; \theta)$. Since this choice depends on θ and $\mathbf{a}_{-k}$, and we wish to emphasize this, let us write it as $\bar{a}_k(\mathbf{a}_{-k}, \theta)$.[19] Therefore, $V_k(\bar{a}_k(\mathbf{a}_{-k}, \theta), \mathbf{a}_{-k}; H_k; \theta)$ would be her maximum good were θ to be realized. Consider the expression $\Sigma_\theta \pi_k(\theta) V_k(\bar{a}_k(\mathbf{a}_{-k}, \theta), \mathbf{a}_{-k}; H_k; \theta)$. It is the expected value of the maximum good k can realize if $A_k(\mathbf{a}_{-k}, H_k)$ is her permissible set of options. It can be thought of as the *option value* of her permissible set of choices, and is an index of the freedom she enjoys.[20] As a measure of the instrumental worth to k of her admissible set of choices, it has the right sort of properties. For example, the larger is the range of what may

---

[16] These form the basis for a concern with the distribution of primary goods in Rawls's account of a just society.

[17] Now H_k is a function of the basic-needs goods at k's disposal. Moreover, behind the veil k would be uncertain about H_k as well. To avoid any further notational complexity, I shall ignore these terms. Nothing will be lost in our doing so.

[18] This is a metaphor. With the passage of time a person learns more and more about herself. The formulation here is a pristine one, ignoring as it does such complications.

[19] It depends on H_k as well, but I am ignoring this for simplicity.

[20] I am grateful to Professor Kenneth Arrow for suggesting this index to me.

constitute a person's good, the wider should her permissible set be if it is to score well by this index. It is also evident that personal states (H_k in our notation), which are productive no matter what is k's good, contribute positively to this index. This means in turn that, in so far as H_k is affected by public policy, the social contract will lay stress on those policies that promote personal states. These properties give us a lead on what we should seek in practical measurements of freedom. A single numerical index is to be avoided: it will miss a great deal. Now health, education, income, and political and civil liberties are valuable no matter what the future holds. Therefore, we should focus on them. We will do so in Chapters 4–5.

3.9 *Social Well-Being Functions*

A person's well-being is an aggregate of its constituents: utility (because it is the most reliable approximate of her rational desires), and an index of the worth to her of the freedoms she enjoys. Its assessment needs to be made over her entire life. The accounting begins from the period when she has the right to be regarded as a person.[21] In practice this is a difficult task; it is easier to obtain information for a slice of time. Thus, income is easier to estimate than wealth, even thought it is wealth that is often of greater interest. These are familiar matters, that well-being at a moment of time is merely a constituent of a person's lifetime well-being, and that it is the latter that matters. We alluded to this in Chapter 2.

The thought-experiment concerning a social contract has now served its purpose. It has enabled us to identify freedoms as an essential feature of a just society. To the extent that freedoms are wide-ranging and enduring, a person's actual choices are likely to be a good reflector of her perception of her good. We therefore write individual k's well-being as

$$W_k(\mathbf{a}; H_k) = W_k(U_k(\mathbf{a}; H_k), Q_k(A_k(\mathbf{a}_{-k}, H_k))). \tag{3.2}$$

Since U_k and Q_k are constituents of her well-being, each contributes positively. It follows that $W_k(\cdot)$ is an increasing function of each.

That there are circumstances in which the well-being of all increases when suitable restrictions are imposed on each person's freedom is well known in game theory and political philosophy. The new social environment in such situations contains Nash equilibria where all are better off. (The Hobbsian social contract is a classic illustration.) This kind of possibility does not contradict the assumption we have just made. What game theory tells us is that strategic behaviour can make extensions of

---

[21] Constructing a person's lifetime well-being index poses yet another class of problems. It is simplest to think of it as an integral of the flow of well-being. This is how the classical utilitarians, such as Mill and Sidgwick, saw the matter and how, following Ramsey (1928), almost all of the literature on intertemporal planning sees it. See Chakravarty (1969) and Dasgupta and Heal (1979) for an account of the technical literature on this.

choice undesirable from everyone's point of view. Were this to be a possibility, it would be met in the design of the social contract. It would not be reflected in the individual well-being function. There is however another argument, often put forward, that increasing a person's set of choices reduces her well-being because of computation costs, anxiety over whether the right choice has been made, and so forth. We will ignore this here.

Social well-being in this M-person society is an aggregate of individual well-beings. Collective evaluation is based on them. We may therefore write aggregate well-being as

$$W(\mathbf{a}) = W(W_1(\mathbf{a}; H_1), \ldots, W_k(\mathbf{a}; H_k), \ldots, W_M(\mathbf{a}; H_M)). \quad (3.3)$$

This is a *social well-being function*. We will on occasion also refer to (3.3) as a *social evaluation function*, and often simply as *general well-being*.

Certain distinguished ethical theories can be derived as special cases from this conception. For example, modern welfare economic theory views the domain of $W(\cdot)$ as the space of individual utilities. As we observed earlier, a person's choices need not be based upon her conception of her own well-being, or of her own welfare. That a person's actual choices ought to be respected is almost self-evident. This means that social evaluation ought not to be insensitive to utility; it doesn't mean that utility is all that social evaluation ought to be sensitive to. This is a weakness of the conception.

Social choice theory is founded on a different basis from welfare economic theory. It takes individuals' preference orderings over options as primitives, and calls a numerical representation of an individual's preference ordering her *welfare function*. The social evaluation function is founded on individual welfare functions. It is called a *social welfare function*. Hammond (1976), Arrow (1977), d'Aspremont and Gevers (1977), Deschamps and Gevers (1978), Maskin (1978), Roberts (1980a, b), and Blackorby, Donaldson and Weymark (1984) provide axiomatic foundations of social welfare functions. The axiom of social choice which ensures that the social welfare function is defined solely on individual welfares is called the 'strong-neutrality axiom'. Sen (1982, 1985) calls this 'welfarism'. When individuals' preference orderings are consonant with well-being, the strong neutrality axiom does not have much work to do, and welfarism corresponds approximately to the pluralist viewpoint we have adopted here.

Libertarian theories are another special class of cases. They differ in terms of the liberties they espouse (see e.g. Rawls, 1972; Nozick, 1974; Buchanan, 1975; Friedman and Friedman, 1980; Sen, 1985, 1988b). We studied this in the previous chapter. This class of theories takes $W(\cdot)$ to be defined on indices of personal freedoms. But in order for it to give substance to the thought that not all freedoms have the same worth to a person, the idea of a person's good needs to be invoked. Our pluralist conception does that.

We will assume that $W(\cdot)$ is a smooth function, thereby allowing it to accommodate trade-offs between its various components. Nothing is sacrificed by this restriction, and much is gained. The trade-off rates will be negligible in certain parts of the space on which individual well-being is defined. This is an approximation to the idea that certain rights are inviolable. We noted this in the previous chapter.

It is not easy to think of reasons why aggregate well-being should not be an increasing function of individual well-being levels. Certainly, it is possible to construct social well-being functions so equality-conscious on the space of individual well-beings that they are not increasing in individual well-being. But this requires justification, and I have never seen one provided. We therefore take $W(\cdot)$ to be an increasing function of each of the component W_ks. Now each of the component of $W_k(\cdot)$ in formula (3.2) affirms person k's well-being. We therefore conclude that social well-being is in turn an increasing function of each of its $2M$ ingredients: utility, and the worth of the liberties enjoyed by each of the M persons in society as measured by the index $Q_k(\cdot)$.

3.10   Efficiency, Equality, and the Problem of Implementation

Thus far we have considered the constituents of general well-being. We have yet to address the problem of *implementation*, by which I mean bringing about the most desirable state of affairs out of all feasible states of affairs.

Implementability is a delicate concept. Not all feasible collections of individual plans are implementable. What is implementable depends not only on resource endowments and technological and ecological possibilities, but also on the distribution of knowledge. For example, individuals are most likely to know more than the State about their own talents, endowments, wants and desires. Certain allocations of goods and services, even while technologically feasible, will not be implementable: the State will not be able to so influence choices as to bring them about. These allocations will not be Nash equilibria. I alluded to this earlier, and in Chapters 6–9 and 17 we will study questions of implementability in greater detail. Here we note that the problem of incentives lies behind difficulties in implementation.

Let $\mathbf{a} = (a_0, a_1, \ldots, a_k, \ldots, a_M)$ be a feasible vector of actions. We will say that $\mathbf{a}$ is *well-being-inefficient* if there is a feasible set of plans, $\mathbf{a}^* = (a_0^*, a_1^*, \ldots, a_k^*, \ldots, a_M^*)$, such that, for all individuals, $k = 1,2, \ldots, M$, $W_k(\mathbf{a}^*, H_k) \geq W_k(\mathbf{a}, H_k)$; and if for at least one individual, say person m, $W_m(\mathbf{a}^*, H_m) > W_m(\mathbf{a}, H_m)$. We then say that a feasible set of plans is *well-being-efficient* if it is not well-being-inefficient. In words, a feasible set of plans, â say, is well-being-efficient if there is no alternative set of feasible plans along which each person achieves at least as high a level of well-being as along â, and along which at least one person achieves a higher level of well-being.

It transpires that the simplest social environment to study is also informationally the most stringent. In it the State knows everything each and every individual knows: all private information is in the State domain.[22] It is customary in economics to call a best implementable allocation of goods and services (there may be more than one best allocation) under these circumstances a *full optimum*. Sometimes it is called a *first-best*. We will use these terms interchangeably. In Chapter 7 we will apply these ideas to the fundamental resource allocation problem.

Since aggregate well-being is an increasing function of individual well-beings, a full optimum is obviously *well-being-efficient* (otherwise there is a contradiction). However, unless we impose further ethical structure on the social evaluation function, the mathematical projection of a full optimum will not necessarily be an efficient point in the M-dimensional subspace of utilities. (*Utility efficiency* can be defined analogous to well-being efficiency, by replacing $W_k(\cdot)$ by $U_k(\cdot)$ in the definition of well-being efficiency.) Nor will the mathematical projection of a full optimum necessarily be an efficient point in the M-dimensional subspace of liberties. Utility efficiency is often called *Pareto efficiency*. We conclude that a full optimum is generally not Pareto-efficient.[23]

The idea of *equality* is embedded in the social evaluation function. The domain of our concern being individual well-beings, it is the distribution of individual well-beings we will study here. We have adopted a pluralist conception. So we are able to obtain as special cases the wide variety of domains over which the notion of equality has been discussed in the literature—for example income, utility, welfare, opportunity, basic freedoms, and, more loosely, those objects that are implied by an equal respect and concern for all persons (see Williams, 1962; Kolm, 1969, 1977; Rawls, 1972; Sen, 1973; Amiya Dasgupta, 1975, 1976; Dworkin, 1978; T. Nagel, 1978; and Section 5.5 below).

At a full optimum there is a 'right' amount of equality. The tension much discussed in political philosophy between efficiency and equality is absent (there are no incentive problems at a full optimum), nor are there any other institutional constraints preventing otherwise feasible states of affairs from being realizable (see Chapter 7). However, in the world as we know

---

[22] Privacy matters to people and rightly so. This will be reflected in their well-being functions. So when I say the government 'knows' all that is relevant for it to be able to function effectively, I take privacy constraints into account.

[23] Sen (1970) noted this and drew attention to the general incompatibility of the requirement of Pareto efficiency with the inviolability of certain patterns of negative rights. My own formulation of social well-being functions has allowed me to present this result somewhat differently from the way it is usually presented in the literature.

it not all private information is in the domain of the government. The government has to operate with incomplete information. It has therefore a limited set of policy tools at its disposal. For example, it may be able to set a tax-subsidy policy founded on income, or on expenditure (the government may be able to observe both), but it may not be able to impose taxes on innate skills, or on the extent to which a person takes risks (the government may be unable to observe either). The natural question to ask then is this: why doesn't the State require citizens to divulge their private information so as to implement a full optimum?

There are two related answers. First, as we have already noted, there are problems of incentives, leading to issues studied in the theory of partial compliance in political philosophy. If it is in their interest to do so, individuals may claim that their own needs are greater than those of others, and seek a larger share of resources than they actually have a right to (see Chapters 8–9 and 17). To some (e.g. G. Cohen, 1991, in his criticism of Rawls) this argument smacks of expediency. They say citizens committed to a common conception of justice would not be expected to lie. But it isn't a matter of expediency, and this leads to the second answer, which has to do with privacy and the claims of negative freedom. It is an intolerable situation where citizens have constantly to divulge information about themselves, and to be then told what to do with their lives (where to work, what to work at, and so forth), all in the interest of some general good, or in the interest of the economically worst off members of society, or whatever. This is the stuff of totalitarianism. Hypothetical social contracts would have safeguards around such possibilities (Rawls, 1985, 1987). The protection of negative freedom would ensure checks against such forms of intrusion into people's lives. Citizens will desire this protection, otherwise justice will demand that all citizens constantly try to maximize something like expression (3.3). Were they to do so they would confound the very purpose of creating a just society: there would be no time left for living. There would also be enormous problems of co-ordination (a matter we studied earlier), making it a hopelessly inefficient society. So when we speak of 'incentives' in a just society, we mean that much information of relevance is privately held.[24] Autonomous people are not expected to divulge them, nor are they made to feel guilty when they don't constantly try to do good to others. Citizens have general obligations towards each other—paying their taxes, not intentionally harming others, and so forth. They are not obliged to bear the world's problems on their shoulders at all times.

---

[24] Optimal public policy in an environment where the government has incomplete information has been much discussed in the economics literature, and it parallels similar concerns in political philosophy. See Mirrlees (1971, 1985), Hammond (1979), Dasgupta (1980, 1982a), Dasgupta and Hammond (1982), Laffont and Maskin (1982), and Roberts (1984).

4

Well-Being: From Theory to Measurement

4.1 *Constituents and Determinants of Well-Being*

It is not an easy matter to use the analytical structure we have developed so far for empirical work. The constituents of personal well-being are quantitatively elusive. But leaving aside for the moment the practical problems of measurement, we should recall (see Chapters 2–3) that there are two ways of assessing social well-being and its changes. One is to measure the *constituents* of well-being (utility and freedoms, as in equation (3.2)), and the other is to value the commodity *determinants* of well-being (goods and services which are inputs in the production of well-being). The former procedure measures 'output' (e.g. indices of health), and the latter evaluates and aggregates 'inputs' (e.g. real national income). If undertaken with sufficient precision and care, either on its own will do (see Chapter*7). In practice, though, neither captures all there is in the idea of social well-being, and so it helps to make use of the two avenues simultaneously. This is what we will do in Chapters 5 and 11. In Chapter 5 we will study data bearing on social well-being in (what were in 1970) 51 of the poorest countries; and in Chapter 11 we will proceed along a finer route and look at the distribution of well-being along regional and gender lines by studying some crude data for India. But first, we must develop the rationale behind the choice of the indices we will be looking at.

What we are after, first of all, is a measure of personal well-being (W_k in equation (3.2)) which must not be too difficult to estimate.[1] The question of aggregation (equation 3.3)) comes after we obtain indices of personal well-being.

It is particularly hard to get a quantitative feel for the experiential state associated with the sense of well-being. The nub is that states of mind are involved. We observed in Chapter 1 that other minds are not as inscrutable to one as they are commonly made out to be; one's own experiences provide the right source of information. At a wider level, placing ourselves

---

[1] The cost of gathering information has to be taken into account when devising what are essentially surrogates for the ideal well-being index. See below in the text.

sympathetically in various possible situations is a way of obtaining the sort of information we seek. As examples, we could study indices of a country's divorce or suicide rate, and they have been suggested. But they are seriously deficient. Divorce rates in a society may be low not because marriages are happy, but because the cost of divorce is, for women, prohibitively high. Similarly, the rate of suicide picks out features of the lower tail of the distribution of states of mind, and we would wish to know something about the entire distribution.[2] In any event, whether we should include indices of the state of mind when evaluating a person's well-being depends on the point of the exercise. We noted in the previous chapter that a contractarian theory of the State would not allow the State to be concerned with whether citizens were happy: it would see the business of the State as being restricted to the availability of basic liberties. In what follows, we will confine ourselves to indices of such liberties. So our measure of well-being will be a partial one, although not excessively so.

Leaving aside for the moment the extent of civil and political liberties a person enjoys, there would seem to be at least three broad kinds of indices one can use in constructing a measure of a person's well-being: his current and prospective real income (inclusive of certain non-marketed goods and services), his current and future states of health, and his educational attainments. Now, these are different categories of goods. Health and education would seem to be an embodiment of positive freedoms, whereas income contributes to the enjoyment of these freedoms.[3] So then why do we wish to mix them up here?

The reason is that a person's real income measures the extent to which consumption goods like food and clothing, shelter, legal aid, and general amenities are obtainable by him *in the market*. But primary health care and education don't fall into this category. We will see in Chapters 6–8 that private markets do not provide an ideal resource allocation mechanism for their supply. Markets for these goods need to be allied to an explicit support by the State, in a way that assures citizens of their supply. Now government involvement in the provision of primary health care and education varies enormously across poor countries. For this reason it is possible for people on average to enjoy a higher disposable income in one country, and yet to suffer from worse health-care and education facilities than in another. Stating matters in the reverse way, it is possible for people in one country on average to be better educated and to enjoy better health

---

[2] Scitovsky (1976) offers an illuminating discussion of problems associated with the measurement of joy and joylessness. For earlier empirical work on these matters, see J. L. Simon (1974) and Easterlin (1975).

[3] Income affects a person's welfare as well, and it affects his utility in a direct way. So do health and education. But here I am regarding income, health, and education indices as constitutive of freedoms, nothing more.

than in another even while their access to other material goods is more restricted (see Table 5.1 below). Real income, health, and education indices capture in their various ways a number of constituents of a person's well-being.

The move towards extending the basis for estimating the standard of living has been impending for a long time. In 1954 a United Nations Expert Group recommended that, in addition to real per capita national income measures, use should be made of quantitative measures in the fields of health, education, employment, and housing for assessing the standard of living (see United Nations, 1954). The idea here was to leave the estimation of real national income pretty much the way it then was (see below), and to supplement this index by a further set of indices, reflecting various constituents and determinants of aggregate well-being.[4] This tactic (of compiling a heterodox collection of measures) has come to dominate international comparisons of well-being. For example, the annual *World Development Report* of the World Bank adopts this route.

To date, M. D. Morris (1979) and UNDP (1990) have been the most explicit attempts at an international comparison of well-being. The index in Morris's work was a weighted sum of life expectancy at birth, the infant survival rate, and the adult literacy rate. For reasons discussed in Chapters 2 and 3, there isn't much to commend in this measure. But the motivation behind the investigation is transparent. Morris was aiming to obtain a physical index of the standard of living.

Coming as it does some eleven years after Morris's work, it is difficult to view the UNDP's human development index (HDI) as a real improvement. HDI is the sum of certain normalized indices of per capita national income, life expectancy at birth, and the adult literacy rate. The normalization amounts to this. Suppose, for example, life expectancy at birth in a country is currently 55 years. Instead of entering it directly into its HDI, the procedure is to calculate the difference between 55 years and the minimum global life expectancy at birth (say, 45 years) and then divide it by the difference between the global maximum today (say, 80 years) and the minimum. The required index for life expectancy at birth in this country is then $(55 - 45)/(80 - 45) = 2/7$. Similar normalizations are obtained for the other two ingredients of HDI. There isn't much normative significance in this index. Nor is any account provided of HDI's normative significance. When UNDP (1991) attempts to give one, it ends up merely describing HDI. In fact, the index is not much good: it has too many unappealing properties. For example, were the adult literacy rate in the

---

[4] See United Nations (1954: 79–91). See also Bauer (1954: ch. 2; 1957) for a critique of current measures of real national income and their failure to record improvements in certain dimensions of utility, such as life expectancy at birth, and the large range of activities in what is euphemistically called the 'informal sector'.

country with the lowest rate in a sample to increase, the HDI of all other countries would decline. HDI is also excessively partial: it is oblivious of political and civil liberties. The second UNDP report (UNDP, 1991) on these matters pursues the very recent empirical literature on basic freedoms (see Dasgupta, 1990a; Chapter 5), and it tables one set of published indices on political and civil liberties. But nothing is done with the data.

In Chapter 5 I shall reintroduce civil and political liberties into the discussion, construct my own measure of social well-being, and conduct an empirical investigation of the quality of life in poor countries. In the remainder of this chapter we will elaborate upon a set of indices of positive freedoms which supplement both political and civil liberties.

4.2 Income

A person's real income is a measure of the command she has over marketed goods and services, for example food and clothing, shelter, transportation, and general amenities.[5] It is a coarse index of this command, because real income alone doesn't tell us what goods are on offer, nor does it tell us how much each good on offer the person can and does procure. But with constant relative prices, an increase in real income reflects a widening in her command over marketed goods and services. It follows that, if the ranking on the basis of which a person chooses also remains approximately constant, increases in real income indicate improvements in her utility level. If utility and welfare point approximately in the same direction, a rise in real income reflects an increase in welfare. For these reasons, movements in real income have been much used in empirical work: as a measure of changes in both welfare and the extent of choice over commodity bundles.

Poverty and low income are often taken to be synonymous. The most common practice in measuring the extent of poverty in a community or society is to select a cut-off level of income below which a person or household is deemed to be poor (the *poverty level*) and to estimate the percentage of the population whose income is below it. This is the *headcount index*. Thus, let y^* be the poverty level, let S denote the set of persons who are poor, and let M be the number of the poor (the cardinality of S). If N is the size of the whole population, the headcount index (HI) is

$$HI = M/N.$$

There are obvious weaknesses with the measure (see Watts, 1968; Sen, 1981b), but its strengths are also transparent. An alternative much in use is the *poverty gap*. The idea here is to sum over each poor person the gap

---

[5] I am thinking of persons as the unit of analysis, even though income usually accrues to households. We will discuss allocations within households in Ch. 11.

between the poverty level and her income, and then express the sum as a percentage of the total income (Y) of the population. Thus, if y_k is the income of the kth poor person, the poverty gap (PG) is

$$PG = \Sigma_{k \varepsilon S}(y^* - y_k)/Y.$$

There are obvious weaknesses with this too. But it has the attractive feature of telling us something important about the magnitude of poverty in a society. The poverty gap is the minimum amount of additional income, expressed as a percentage of society's aggregate income, which, if it is obtained by the poor, can eliminate poverty.

Table 4.1 presents estimates of the magnitude of poverty that prevailed in the world in the mid-1980s. Now, official exchange rates do not reflect relative purchasing powers within nations. Therefore, corrections have to be made to them if the incomes of different countries are to be comparable with one another. The idea is to use shadow exchange rates (see Chapters 7–*7). Summers and Heston (1988) address this problem and present the national income of 120 countries in purchasing power parity (PPP) dollars. (These are sometimes called international dollars. See also Chapter 5). The data in Table 4.1 are based on this measure of income. Two alternative poverty levels are considered: PPP $275 per year (extremely poor), and PPP $370 per year (poor). Even the larger figure buys a person

Table 4.1 Magnitudes of poverty, 1985

Region	Extremely poor[a]			Poor[a]		
	Number (m)	HI (%)	PG (%)	Number (m)	HI (%)	PG (%)
Sub-Saharan Africa	120	30	4	180	47	11
East Asia	120	9	0.4	280	20	1
China	(80)	8	1	(210)	20	3
South Asia	300	29	3	520	51	10
India	(250)	33	4	(420)	55	12
Middle East and North Africa	40	21	1	60	31	2
Latin America and the Caribbean	50	12	1	70	19	1
All developing countries	630	18	1	1110	33	3

HI: headcount index (%)
PG: poverty gap (%)

[a] The poverty line in 1985 PPP dollars is $275 per capita a year for the extremely poor, and $370 per capita a year for the poor.

Source: World Bank (1990, table 2.1).

very little (see Summers and Heston, 1988, World Bank, 1990). Despite the stringency of the criteria, the magnitude of poverty is large: about 1100 million people (or one person in every five in the world) are estimated to be poor, and of them something like 630 million are extremely poor. As we might have expected, the headcount index is highest in South Asia (the Indian sub-continent) and sub-Saharan Africa: about half their population is poor, and a third extremely poor.

The poverty gap is revealing. Resources required for eliminating poverty amount to approximately 10 per cent of their national income in sub-Saharan Africa and the Indian sub-continent. The amount needed to eliminate extreme poverty is less of course; it is something like 4 per cent of these countries' national incomes. Assuming a growth rate of income per head of 1 per cent per year, poverty in these parts could in principle be eradicated in 10 years, and extreme poverty in 4 years. (In saying this, I am supposing that the entire increase in income per head accrues to the targeted group.) Both Pakistan and India have routinely exceeded the growth rate of 1 per cent in income per head. But so far, neither country appears to have recorded a decline in her headcount index. Income hasn't trickled down to the poorest in these societies.

These are suggestive numbers, and we will find that they are in reasonable consonance with headcount indices of the world's under-nourished (see Chapter 15). But there are problems with income estimates. In poor countries household income is a difficult thing to measure because, among other things, a number of activities, products, and services remain unrecorded. Not only are many rural transactions not conducted in cash, a portion of rural household consumption is obtained from what are called 'common property resources'. (See Chapters 6 and 10. See also Nordhaus and Tobin, 1972; Fee, 1976; Dasgupta and Heal, 1979; Beneria, 1981; ILO, 1982; Dasgupta, 1982b; Jodha, 1986; Falconer and Arnold, 1989; Repetto et al., 1989; Agarwal and Narain, 1990; Dasgupta and Mäler, 1991.) Moreover, the volume of illegal transactions can be large (see de Soto, 1989). All this implies that estimates of household income are typically wrong, and possibly biased downwards. Income estimates need to be supplemented by other types of information bearing on the consumption of goods and services. The question is: what? In a pair of interesting recent explorations of poverty in a sample of village households in West Bengal, India, Bhattacharya et al. (1991) and Chatterjee (1991) have advocated the use of household data on clothing, bedding, furniture, and kitchen utensils, arguing that their paucity reveals more about the extent of household poverty than do income or nutrition estimates. The thought here is that a household containing undernourished members is almost certainly poor, but an absence of malnourished members does not mean that the household is not poor. Now the idea that even in empirical work we ought to work directly on the space of commodities is attractive. But these are early days yet for the use of disaggregate commodity data. In any event, there is a rationale for the use of income as a measure of access to commodities: income aggregates over commodities. Even though the aggregation is in practice deficient, income estimates are informative when used in conjunction with other data. This is the approach I adopt in this book.

From personal real income, it is conceptually but a short step to aggregate real income. And it is *real national income* and its distribution that are appealed to most often in judging movements in the aggregate well-being of a society. The practical limitations of this measure have been obvious ever since the concept was defined, but it is only recently that much has been made of them.[6] One reason critics are uneasy with national income estimates is that the concept has been used for at least two purposes: as a measure of aggregate well-being, and as a measure of economic activity in national accounting. What is a reasonable way of going about devising the latter isn't necessarily the best way of measuring the former. We are concerned with the former purpose here, and it is possible to show that, for any social well-being function, there is a corresponding formulation of real national income, which if used would reflect what is claimed of it (see Chapters *7 and *10). Towards this, it should be noted that a great many of the prices that would be used for computing an ideal national income index are shadow (or accounting) prices, not market prices. Moreover, a number of ingredients of the 'ideal' index remain unrecorded in practice. They consist of, for example, the shadow value of environmental resources, the social worth of commodities that go to enhance life expectancy at birth, a reduction in morbidity rates, and so forth. Conventional estimates of real national income present a misleading picture of aggregate well-being. The pioneering works of Nordhaus and Tobin (1972) and Usher (1973) began with this observation, and were an exploration of ways of improving upon conventional estimates. The authors' intentions were clear. Today they are a nearly forgotten pair of exercises (see also Usher, 1963).

4.3   Health, 1: Anthropometric Measures

A person's state of health can be assessed clinically (e.g. by looking for signs of oedema among infants to see if they are suffering from kwashiorkor);

---

[6] For varying reasons, among the most subtle being the one advanced and explored by Anand and Harris (1990). Using Sri Lankan budget survey data, they show that income variability over time results in systematic biases (e.g. the suggestion that in poor countries the bottom 80% of the population, ranked by income per head, dissave) and that a far more dependable ingredient of well-being is food expenditure per head. See Sect. 15.1 below.

anthropometrically (e.g. measuring height, weight, arm circumference, and skinfold thickness); by conducting biochemical tests (e.g. measuring the concentration of nutrients in a person's blood or urine); through questionnaires (e.g. asking the person to recall the frequency with which he has been struck down with illness in the recent past); and by observing behaviour (e.g. noting a person's appetite, the extent of bodily movement, and, more generally, his activity level). Each involves an expenditure of resources, and while they are partially substitutable as avenues of inquiry, their costs differ.[7] And they yield information at the individual level. Therein lies their attraction.

In a justly influential article, Waterlow *et al.* (1977) showed that a child's height (i.e. height-for-age) and weight-for-height are good indicators of his state of health, and thereby his *nutritional status*. Height is a person's summary statistic of past nutritional experience and morbidity. Weight-for-height, on the other hand, is a summary statistic of his current nutritional status. (See the multi-volume work of Falkner and Tanner, 1986; especially volume 3.) To take an example, low birth weight (under 2.5 kg) is a significant contributor to infant mortality. Relative to those whose weight at birth equalled or exceeded 2.5 kg, the risk of death among neonates with low birth weight is about 4; among post-neonates the corresponding figure is about 2 (Waterlow, 1992a: 332).

It transpires that both height-for-age and weight-for-height are effective indicators of morbidity and mortality.[8] In a classic longitudinal study in Matlab Thana, Bangladesh, on children who at the start of the study were in the age range 15–26 months, Chen, Chowdhury and Huffman (1980) demonstrated clear threshold effects in both height-for-age and weight-for-height. The risk of death was found not to differ much among those whose deficits in these anthropometric measures were mild to moderate. But there was a sharp increase for those whose deficits reached certain figures. These figures may therefore be used as indicators of severe stunting and wasting (see below).[9]

That weight-for-height influences morbidity and mortality risks for all age groups, at least at significantly low levels, is non-controversial (see Chapter 14). Indeed, among children it is a better predictor in the short run of morbidity and mortality than height-for-age. Recently it has been

[7] Biochemical tests are often the costliest of all. Surveys through questionnaires are usually cheap, but, as we noted earlier, respondents' replies are often culturally determined and, therefore, unreliable.

[8] See Chen, Chowdhury and Huffman (1979, 1980), Bairagi (1981), Martorell and Ho (1984), Martorell (1985), and Haas and Habicht (1990). In an earlier study in Bangladesh, Sommer and Loewenstein (1975) used arm-circumference-for-height as the predictor. See also Briend *et al.*, (1989), who have argued that absolute arm circumference is the best predictor of death.

[9] The threshold for height-for-age was a bit under 90% of the US standard, and for weight-for-height it was a bit over 70% of the standard.

suggested by Waaler (1984) that even among adult males height is a predictor of morbidity and mortality risks. (Waaler's data-base is several Norwegian villages, drawn from both this and the last century.) Fogel (1987, 1988) cites this to build an account of the decisive influence of nutritional improvements in increasing life expectancy at birth in eighteenth- and nineteenth-century Europe. That improvements occurred during this period is not to be doubted (Floud and Wachter, 1982; Fogel *et al.*, 1983; McKeown, 1983; Floud, 1987). But on the link between adult height, and morbidity and mortality risks, these are early days still. Waaler used Norwegian data pertaining to a time when tuberculosis (TB) was still a leading cause of death, and exposure to it virtually universal. High levels of TB are associated with stunting and wasting in a minority of more resistant children. These children, and the infected adults who happen to survive, are at higher risks of death. Uncoupling nutrition and infection from historical records is not going to prove easy. Much work needs to be done, on a wider range of evidence, to check if there is a systematic relationship of the kind suggested by the Waaler data.

Relative to populations of healthy persons in the United States and Western Europe, those with a deficit in weight-for-height are called *wasted* in the biomedical literature, and those with a deficit in height-for-age called *stunted*. (As a measure of nutritional status, weight-for-age has obvious shortcomings.) By 'deficit' here we mean more than 2 standard deviations less than the norms adopted in the United States. (For an account and use of these standards, see WHO, 1985. See also Chapter 14). The use of these norms, most especially those regarding stunting, has been criticized, and it has been argued that US–European standards of growth are inappropriate for use in poor countries. At an extreme is the suggestion by Seckler (1982, 1984) that on average a population can be short, and can yet be healthy.

There is no evidence to date that growth potentials at *childhood* differ substantially across the main ethnic groups (see Eveleth and Tanner, 1976; Satyanarayana, Naidu and Rao, 1980; WHO, 1985; Martorell, 1985; Martorell and Habicht, 1986).[10] Epidemiological studies show instead that it is nutrition and freedom from infections that are the major determinants of early growth. (We will go into this in Chapter 14.) Within ethnic groups in poor countries, differences in children's body size across socio-economic classes are usually large. At the same time, differences in body size between European, African, Latin American, and Indian children from the upper income groups are small. Martorell and Habicht (1986) provide a striking illustration of this: the mean height of a sample of 7-year-old

---

[10] An exception would appear to be Far Eastern people (Tanner *et al.*, 1982; Martorell and Habicht, 1986). Even for them, the differences are small, being about 3–4 cm between Japanese and US children aged 7.

children from Indian families of high socio-economic status was found to be about 121 cm. This is within 1 cm of the height of the 50th percentile of 7-year-olds according to the standard tables issued by the United States National Center for Health Statistics. However, the mean height of a sample of 7-year-old children from Indian families of low socio-economic status was 108 cm, fully 13 cm shorter than their privileged counterparts.

Where ethnic differences in growth are pronounced is during adolescence (F. E. Johnston et al., 1976; D. H. Rao and Sastry, 1977; Spurr et al, 1983a, 1984; Martorell, Mendoza and Castillo, 1989). The final height of a person is determined by both genetic and environmental factors. But the low average stature of persons in poor countries is for the most part to be attributed to poor nutrition and the heavy incidence of infectious diseases. Thus, the secular increase in mean Japanese height is an illustration of the impact of better health care and nutrition, the sharp increase having taken place during the period 1957–77 (Tanner et al., 1982). A different source of positive evidence is provided by food supplementation experiments among poor children in poor countries (Mora et al., 1981; Martorell and Habicht, 1986; Waterlow, 1988).

In an extensive study on Colombian children, Spurr et al. (1983a, b, 1984), Spurr, Reina and Barac-Nieto (1983), and Barac-Nieto, Spurr and Reina (1984) found that, compared with nutritionally normal children, undernourished boys in each of five age groups at 2-year intervals from 6 to 16 years have lower height and experience slower growth. Nutritional status in these studies was measured in terms of weight-for-age (the Gomez scale) and weight-for-height. Children whose weight-for-age and weight-for-height were both less than 95 per cent of Colombian standards were regarded undernourished. In addition to stunting and delayed spurts in growth, undernourished children attained sexual maturity later, and had lower values for maximal aerobic power (see Chapter 14) and skinfolds. Their capacity for work was less.

There is evidence that nutrition and morbidity in early childhood leave a large imprint on a person. The classic study on the importance of growth in the early years on final height is Satyanarayana, Naidu and Rao (1980). Heights of a group of 17-year-old boys in rural Hyderabad were measured and were compared with their heights when they had been 5 years of age. The sample was divided into four sub-groups, based on their level of stunting at age 5. (As it happens, all sub-groups had been stunted at that age.) The striking observation was that all sub-groups had gained approximately the same amount in height during the twelve-year interval, and the average increase (62 cm), was only 5 cm less than the increase that children on average experience in the United States over this same interval.

A recent longitudinal study in Guatemala analysed by Professor Martorell and his colleagues (see Martorell *et al.*, 1991) has controlled for differences in nutrition in early childhood. The experiment has revealed that the absolute difference in the average heights of two poor populations, one of which was the control group and the other of which was provided with food supplements, remained approximately constant from about age 3. Moreover, the intellectual performance of the control group in later years was significantly worse. Growth failure in early childhood in the data predicts functional impairment in adults (e.g. stature, strength, intelligence, numeracy, literacy, lean body mass (see Chapter 14), and in women, obstetric risks). The physiological mechanisms determining these outcomes aren't understood, but the behavioural ones are less opaque. For example, it is becoming clear that undernourished children save on energy by engaging in fewer bodily movements. They interact less with others and the world. So their cognitive and motor development is impeded. (See Chapters 14–15 for further discussion.) But the experiment conducted by Martorell and his colleagues does not determine if a population that has been nutritionally deprived for the first three years can catch up in later years should its diet improve. What the finding does display is that, unless conditions improve for a deprived group, whatever is the absolute gap in final heights due to nutritional differences among two populations, this gap is reached by age 3. It is in this sense that early history has an anthropometric stranglehold over our lives.[11]

The issue, therefore, isn't so much whether you can be a stunted but healthy adult male. (There isn't much evidence that I have seen which suggests you can't.) It is whether the fact that you are a stunted adult implies on average that you experienced periodic nutrition, sanitation, and health-care deprivation in some form during childhood (see e.g. Thomas and Strauss, 1992). Proponents of the 'small but healthy' thesis haven't taken note of this. Nor have they acknowledged that for stunted *women* health risks continue into adulthood: small women face obstetric risks.[12]

We should note as well that a determinant of prenatal and infant mortality rates is the mother's size and health. For example, birth weight is influenced by the mother's condition (Martorell *et al.*, 1981). It was

[11] I am most grateful to Reynaldo Martorell for explaining to me these, as yet unpublished, research findings of his group, and for allowing me to cite them here. In earlier work (Martorell, Rivera and Kaplowitz, 1990) he and his colleagues reported on a somewhat weaker finding, that stunting occurs by the age of 5 (see also Martorell, 1985). There is evidence that adolescents can catch up if they are given food supplementation, but the process is slow. Consequently, the additional energy and protein required per day is small. See Eveleth (1985) and Waterlow (1985, 1992a). We will study this further in Chs. 14–15.

[12] That stunted adults have markedly low lean body masses is well known. That lean body mass is closely related to both work capacity and endurance is also increasingly being appreciated, and we will study this in Ch. 14. For a reasoned critique of the 'small but healthy' thesis, see Beaton (1989) and Martorell (1990).

Table 4.2   Indicators of undernourishment in poor countries, mid-1980s

	Africa	Asia	Latin America[a]
Under-5 malnutrition			
Low weight-for-age[b] number			
(millions)	22	115	9
%	26	54	18
Low weight-for-height[b]			
number (millions)	4	33	2
%	7	16	4
Low birth weight[c] (%)	14	19	10
Anaemia in women (%)	40	58	17

[a] Excluding Argentina and Uruguay.
[b] More than 2 standard deviations below median value for reference growth patterns adopted by WHO.
[c] Below 2.5 kg.
Source: FAO (1987, table 3.3).

thought for some time that the placenta is to a large extent impervious to the mother's health status. This is in fact not so (Lechtig *et al.*, 1978; Falkner and Tanner, 1986). It is one way in which the effect of food and health-care deprivation in early childhood is passed on to the next generation, and thus on to the next, and so on.

Table 4.2 summarizes data on the nutritional status of children under 5 years of age, of infants, and of women in the three regions containing almost all the world's poor: Asia, Africa, and Latin America. The data are consonant with the incidence of poverty reported in Table 4.1. The bulk of the children who are wasted are in Asia. Over half of Asia's children under 5 suffer from overly low weight-for-age, and a third suffer from low weight-for-height. We may infer from this that, while wasting is a serious problem there, stunting is even more of a problem. Nearly one in five newborns in Asia have low birthweight (less than 2.5 kg), and nearly 60 per cent of women suffer from nutritional anaemia. Both women and children fare somewhat better in sub-Saharan Africa, and in Latin America they are the least badly off. Among Asian countries the figures vary widely. For example, about 30 per cent of newborns have low birthweight in the Indian sub-continent; in China the corresponding figure is 6 per cent, which is about the same as that in Japan and the Western industrial democracies (see World Bank, 1990). We will repeatedly observe large differences in various aspects of well-being across poor countries.

Anthropometric data are among the most revealing statistics concerning health. Weight-for-age is widely used among children, although its limitations are rather obvious. As noted earlier, arm circumference is a reliable index of nutritional status. In the Matlab Thana study referred to earlier, a third of all the deaths of children in the age range 6–36 months were found to be due to severe malnutrition, as measured by mid–upper-arm circumference (see Briend, Wojtyniak and Ronald, 1987; Fauveau *et al.*, 1990; see also Chapter 14). Mortality statistics tell us directly about something else, something even more urgent: the risk of death. The two most common indices in use are life expectancy at birth and mortality rates among infants and children. There is a reason for this. We will look into it now.

4.4 *Health, 2: Mortality Indices*

Life expectancy at birth is the number of years a random newborn baby can expect to live, on the assumption that current age-specific mortality rates will persist. It is the mathematical expectation of a person's longevity as seen from the vantage point of her date of birth if age-specific mortality rates aren't expected to alter.[13] It is a major constituent of utility. Indeed, it is difficult to think of a more important one, given that the desire for survival itself has had survival value over the long haul of time. To be sure, it is possible to think of situations where a shortish life is the more well-lived one and a long life one of wretchedness. From this it is but a short step to asking what is the optimal length of life, recognizing that resources are required to enable a person to lead a satisfactory life. The sharpest way (not the most realistic way, but the sharpest way) of posing the question is in the context of a person having an endowment of a durable, depletable resource, such as hard tack. If this is all she possesses, and all that she *can* possess, what is her ideal longevity? The answer is: neither a very long life (the quality of life at each instant would then be low), nor a very short one (there wouldn't be enough of a life *to* enjoy), but rather, somewhere in between.[14] However, across poor countries, at an aggregate level, we do not have to ask this question. We will see in Chapter 5 that national income per head is positively and significantly correlated with life expectancy at birth. They seem to go together. (But we will also see that a number of countries, such as Mauritius, Sri Lanka, and China, are outliers.) Differences in life expectancy at birth between rich and poor nations is large. In sub-Saharan Africa life expectancy at birth today is

[13] Thus, suppose M_t is the mortality rate of t-year-old persons in the population. (This is assumed unchanging with time.) Then, the probability that a random newborn will die at age t is $(1-M_0)(1-M_1) \ldots (1-M_{t-1})M_t$. Call this P_t. Life expectancy at birth is then $P_1 + 2P_2 + 3P_3 + \ldots$

[14] Koopmans (1973, 1974) analyses this problem in a formal way. As one would expect, given other things, the greater a person discounts future well-being, the shorter is her ideal longevity.

approximately 50 years, whereas in Western industrial democracies it is about 76 years.[15]

Life expectancy at birth tells us something quite different from anthropometric indices of the kind studied in the previous section. We noted there that newborns and children under 5 are less wasted in sub-Saharan Africa than they are in Asia. Within Asia the worst figures are, as always, in the Indian sub-continent. But life expectancy at birth in the Indian sub-continent is higher than in sub-Saharan Africa: it is 54 years as compared with 50 years. This tells us something about the limitation of the index, which is the expectation of longevity at *birth*. Ideally, we would be interested in longevity at different stages of life. This is another way of asking after age-specific mortality rates. Such data reflect the extent of threats a class or gender faces at various stages of life. Today, across countries the variation in life expectancy at age 5 years is much less than its variation at birth. For example, a 5-year-old girl in a Western industrial democracy should expect to live another 74 years, whereas her counterpart in sub-Saharan Africa could expect to live an additional 60 years or thereabouts. This is what we would expect. The impact of food, sanitation, and health-care deprivation is felt dramatically during early childhood. In hostile environments large groups of people get weeded out in the early years of their lives. We will see later (Chapter 11) that some of the weeding gets done at the household level by the parents practising differential child care.

All this pertains to overall populations. Across genders life expectancy at birth differs in almost all countries. (A current exception is India.) Differences have changed over time though changing technological possibilities and altered life-styles. For example, in the first half of the nineteenth century in England, female life expectancy at birth exceeded that of males, but female mortality rates in the age range 10–39 years were greater than those of males; today, female mortality rates in Western Europe and the United States are less than those of males at all age levels.[16]

At the prenatal and infant stages males are at a disadvantage relative to females. In the first place, they are vulnerable to congenital disorders

---

[15] The sense in which life expectancy is an index of liberties is complex. Women in Western industrial nations today live on average some 6 years longer than men. It would be hard to maintain though that women, even in these countries, do not suffer from disadvantages in the exercise of particular freedoms, such as entry into certain occupations under terms that are equal to men. It is possible that differences in life expectancy at birth between the genders will decline as women enter more fully occupations currently dominated by men.

[16] But across classes the matter is different. For example, in some sample studies in the USA, age-specific mortality rates of black females have been found to exceed the corresponding age-specific mortality rates of white males. For an illuminating general discussion of gender-based mortality differences, see I. Waldron (1985) and Johansson (1991b).

associated with their X-linked recessive gene. But this appears not to explain more than 10 per cent of the observed excess mortality of males at infancy in Western industrial countries. That the recorded ratio of females to males at birth is less than unity throughout the world has a great deal to do with the fact that more males are conceived than females. (Infanticide of females at birth and abortion of female foetuses provide the other major explanation.) The population ratio of females to males is less than 1 for the age range 0–4 years in most countries in the world, including industrial market economies and what used to be the Western socialist block (see World Bank, 1988, Table 33). In the United States and Western Europe, of every 1,000 births, about 515 are male. The ratio of females to males at birth is therefore about 0.94. However, the female–male ratio for the age group 0–4 years in these countries is about 0.96. The difference of 0.02 reflects the greater vulnerability of males at infancy.

Infant mortality rate is the number of live births out of every 1000 that die during the first year. We can then define the *infant survival rate* as 1000 minus the infant mortality rate. Plainly, this is not unrelated to life expectancy at birth, but it focuses on something quite different: nutrition and hygiene at the earliest stage of life. It is also related closely to the health of the mother and to the duration of lactation. We will see below that among poor families in poor countries it is related to mothers' education attainments as well.

As noted earlier, unless conditions improve for a person, there is a sense in which her first three years are crucial; they tend to leave a marked imprint on her future capacities. But a person is subject to different mixes of risks as she passes through infancy to early childhood. For many purposes, even the first year is too thick an interval to work with; the risks an infant is vulnerable to in the first month are different from those she faces in subsequent months. A good portion of infant deaths in the first month (the neonatal period) is composed not only of those suffering from congenital defects, but also of those who were born prematurely or experienced foetal growth retardation. Therefore, for certain purposes it makes sense to distinguish neonatal mortality rates from post-neonatal mortality rates. Now, such data are not easy to come by in many countries (but see Mata, 1985). As a pithy summary of the earliest set of risks to which a person is vulnerable, the infant mortality rate has much to commend it.

It has been normal practice to consider infant mortality rates separately from *child death rates*; the latter being the number of deaths of children per 1,000 in the age group 1–4 years of age in a given year. The primary reason for not aggregating the under–5 cohort is that the source of sustenance changes when an infant is weaned. An infant and a child are exposed to different sets of nutritional circumstances. They are thus vulnerable to different sources of infection. Weaning and complementary foods are a prime factor in this. On the one hand, malnourished mothers cannot provide sufficient fats in their milk, and in extreme cases the quantity of milk they are able to provide is low (Graves, 1976; Whitehead *et al.*, 1976; Jelliffe and Jelliffe, 1978; Prentice, 1980; Chavez and Martinez, 1984). On the other hand, weaning foods are a major source of the diarrhoeas, and these illnesses impede growth (see Jelliffe and Jelliffe, 1978; Mata, 1978a, b; Waterlow, Ashworth and Griffiths, 1980; Chapter 14). It is at age 1 year, or a little over 1 year, that infants are weaned completely. For this reason the incidence of diarrhoea is greatest among 6–18-month-old infants. (See, for example, the sample study from Guatemala in Martorell *et al.*, 1975.[17]) Despite this, UNICEF (1987) has advocated the use of a consolidated index, the *under-5 mortality rate*, this being the annual number of deaths of children under 5 years of age per 1000 live births. As a measure of the vulnerability of a person to the loss of all liberties in her early years, there is much to commend it. On the other hand, since the index aggregates over two rather significant stages of life, it is forced to suppress information concerning the differing nature of threats to one's life in the early years. This is a serious weakness.

4.5   *Health, 3: Morbidity*

Age-specific survival rates reflect a dramatic aspect of health. By reporting the incidence of death, mortality tables address life and death questions in the most direct way possible. And there are no three ways about it: either a person is alive or he is dead. Moreover, it is an easy matter to confirm whether a person is alive or dead. There are no cultural overtones to the matter.[18] This is what makes survival rates an attractive indicator of the average state of health of a population. It is also the source of its weakness:

---

[17] Difference in mortality rates between rich and poor nations is greatest in the second year after birth. It is a statistical fact that the ratio of the infant mortality rate to the child death rate is an increasing function of national income per head. For example, in 1984 the value of this ratio in Ethiopia was 172:39, or approximately 4.4, whereas the corresponding value for the Republic of South Korea was 28:2, or 14. (In Western industrial countries infant mortality rates are between 6 and 10 per 1000, whereas child death rates are well below 1 per 1000: see World Bank, 1988.) The explanation is that, with improvements in diet, sanitation, and health care, the child death rate can drop to negligible levels; but since there are so many other causes of infant deaths, it is unlikely that infant mortality rates can be brought down below 3 or 4 per 1000. Because of this, Mönckeberg (1983) has suggested that the nutritional status of children under 5 years of age should be measured by the ratio of the infant mortality rate to the child death rate. As always, there are dangers with such summary measures. A country could look good by neglecting its infants.

[18] With the coming of sophisticated life-support systems, this is obviously not true any more. But these developments are not yet of relevance for poor countries, where even public health measures are for the most part in an embryonic state.

the measure is far too coarse. A person can be alive, but weak and hungry and ill. Anthropometric indices distinguish various states of health, but we should now confront the possible argument that they don't reflect the experiential state associated with health.

A person's state of health can take a continuum of values. Later, in Chapter 14, I will illustrate this by considering the phenomenon of undernourishment, and the degrees of malnourishment an individual can be a prey to. But this will be to concentrate on the lower end of the state of health of a given population. A more refined indicator of community health is the extent of *morbidity* prevalent in it. The question therefore is whether morbidity data are a reliable guide to the 'actual' incidence of illnesses. To put it more operationally, we can ask if changes in morbidity rates in a society reflect changes in the actual incidence of illnesses.

The answer seems to be: not really, because 'illness' is not a purely physiological matter.[19] Thus, for the most part such data have to be collected from hospital records, or from questionnaires. ('Have you been ill, or have you felt ill, over the past three days?' or 'How often have you had to miss work over the past month on account of illness?') One can then see where the problem lies. Even while actual health improves, morbidity rates based on such data can increase. This is because, with growing wealth and increased education, people's standards become more demanding; their sights are aimed higher. We would expect this to be particularly so among women in poor countries, whose expectations are currently so low that they often may not acknowledge the physical and mental stress from which they routinely suffer. Illnesses that were not detected in earlier times (because they were unknown, or because people consulted doctors less frequently, or whatever) are acknowledged; the idea of 'stress' becomes accepted in the common culture; the possibility of doing something about stress and ill-health expands; and so forth. Granted that as wages rise the income one forgoes on account of illness increases, and this makes work that much more valuable, making people less prone to report sickness. (This is a 'substitution effect'.) On the other hand, with increased wages personal income itself rises, and this can lead to a shift towards greater health concerns, and to an increased demand for sick-leave (the 'income effect').

Morbidity has a direct effect on welfare (the pain and suffering), and it is this that we tend to notice most. It has also the indirect effect of reducing output, but this is less noticeable to the observer. Studies in Côte d'Ivoire, Ghana, and Mauritania suggest that potential income losses due to illness there are of the order of 15 per cent of gross national product. (This is to be

---

[19] I have learnt a great deal about these matters from the fine recent study by Johansson (1991a). For a wide-ranging collection of essays on public health, see Caldwell *et al.* (1990).

compared to the figure of about 1.5 percent for the United States. See World Bank, 1991a.) Of course, actual losses in output may be less, in that when there are underemployed people, they often replace their sick relatives in the fields. Typically, also, the sick person will try to make up by working longer hours later. But these substitutions themselves involve costs. When infants are ill, adolescent daughters often have to care for them. But this means that they miss school, and that affects future productivity.

The question therefore isn't whether morbidity is a source of pain and suffering and low output: it is. The question is whether increased morbidity is necessarily a sign of deterioration in health: and it isn't. Indeed, an increase in the availability of hospitals and doctors can in itself raise the morbidity rate. This would seem to have happened in Japan, where during the years when average height grew the fastest (1957–77) and life expectancy at birth increased substantially, there were periods when the recorded morbidity rate increased dramatically (see Research Committee, Japan, 1974).[20]

This is not to say that mortality rates and 'objective' morbidity rates must necessarily move together. It is easy to think of health-care practices that prolong life even while actual morbidity increases. A greater concern and care over one's health translates into a rise in recorded morbidity. However, this very concern and care protects one from an early death; and prolongation of life beyond a point is itself a cause of increased morbidity. Old age brings in its wake a number of ailments. Time-series from a number of countries show that it is normal for figures of morbidity and mortality to be negatively related (Riley, 1987). As communicable and parasitic diseases are eliminated with improved sanitation facilities, personal hygiene, and public health care, non-communicable diseases assume their place. In the United States about 12 per cent of gross national product, or something like US$2500 per person, is spent annually on health. This is in excess of the per capita national income of several countries labelled 'upper middle income' (see World Bank, 1988). And yet, in the late 1970s citizens in China and Sri Lanka, two countries that were (and are) very clearly 'poor', enjoyed a life expectancy at birth only about 6 or 7 years less than in the United States (see Table 5.1). A key reason behind this achievement has been the availability of sanitation facilities and public health care for most members in society. In addition to funds being made

---

[20] A striking, interregional illustration is provided by the state of Kerala in India, where life expectancy at birth (for both males and females) is about 70 years, in contrast with the current all-India average of 57 years. Income per head in Kerala is below the Indian per capita income, but male and female literacy rates are much higher than the Indian averages (see Ch. 11) and the provision of health care is a good deal better. It so happens that, among the states in India, Kerala registers the greatest rate of morbidity.

available, their delivery systems were reliable. Basic health care (including immunization, the provision of fluids for diarrhoeal illnesses, facilities for pregnant and lactating women, and medical attendance at childbirth) can be labour-intensive. Relative to what it can achieve, it does not require enormous capital expenditure. In the early 1970s, for example, expenditure on health by central government in Sri Lanka was about US$6 per head in 1975 prices. This was less than 2 per cent of income per head. (This should be compared with the expenditure on defence, which was about US$4 per head: see World Bank, 1983.)

So too has China's performance in the sphere of health been remarkable. It is all too easy to caricature the Chinese 'barefoot' doctors, as does Bhagwati (1988a: 548), and to assert that their professional competence occasionally exceeded that of the average grandmother only marginally. This may well have been true; but countries in the Indian sub-continent also have their share of grandmothers. Nevertheless, life expectancy at birth in the Indian sub-continent in the late 1970s was about 14 years lower than in China (see Table 5.1 below). There isn't that much of a mystery here: the contrast in public health measures between the two regions has been substantial. Differences in environmental sanitation and hygiene are also a part of the explanation. Among poor countries the contrast is even more striking when we compare the Chinese figure with that for Bolivia, a country with per capita income comparable to that of China (see Table 5.1), but where life expectancy at birth was 17 years lower in the late 1970s.

It is possible that facilities for health care have suffered a little in China since the economic and organizational reforms of the late 1970s. Judith Banister's reconstruction of mortality statistics for China suggests that both life expectancy at birth and the infant survival rate have dipped somewhat (or, at the very least, that improvements in these indices have slowed considerably) since then (Banister, 1984, 1987). But this is a controversial matter, and it can be argued (see Hull, 1990; Tomich, Kilby and Johnston, 1991) that the data are likely to be biased because parents in China today have an incentive to provide false information concerning births and deaths.

It bears emphasis that, unless the delivery systems of social services are reliable, it all comes to nought. If large fractions of the funds made available are looted along the way, nothing will come of such services. The experiences of Sri Lanka, Zimbabwe, and China show also that it is much easier to reduce mortality rates substantially than to remove hunger and malnutrition. Cross-country evidence suggests that doubling the spending on health per capita (from less than $2) in a group of countries with an average infant mortality rate of 137 per 1000 could reduce the rate by some 30 per cent (World Bank, 1991a).

Despite the difficulties in estimating morbidity, some guidelines are available. If we were to look at cross-country data on income per head and the number of deaths from each of a variety of causes in different countries, we would arrive at an indication of the income elasticity of the share of the contribution of each cause of death to the total number of deaths. The income elasticity of deaths arising from infectious and parasitic diseases is high at low income levels, and low at high income levels; and so on. Thus, the mix of the causes of death in a population changes with rising income, and it changes sufficiently to warrant its being called an *epidemiological transition*. Table 4.3 presents a breakdown of deaths in poor and advanced industrial countries by the causes of deaths. The striking contrast is that 45 per cent of deaths in poor countries are caused by infectious and parasitic diseases, while only 17 per cent are caused by circulatory and degenerative diseases (otherwise known as chronic illnesses). In industrialized countries, by contrast, the corresponding figures are 5 per cent and 54 per cent respectively.[21]

The number of healthy years gained by averting different types of illnesses varies considerably. For example, averting one case of sickle-cell anaemia saves about 25 healthy life-years on average, whereas averting a case of tuberculosis saves about 8 years (World Bank, 1991a). But costs vary, and this has to be taken into account in social cost–benefit analyses of health programmes. Experience suggests that the growth and impact of

Table 4.3   Epidemiological transition in less developed and industrialized countries

Cause of death	LDC (%)	DC (%)
Infectious and parasitic	45	5
Diarrhoeal	(13)	—
TB	(8)	—
Acute respiratory illness	(17)	(3)
Perinatal	8	1
Cancers	7	21
Circulatory (and degenerative)	17	54
Injury	6	7
Other causes	17	12

Key
LDC: less developed countries
DC: industrialized countries

Source: Jamison and Mosley (1990).

[21] For a quantitative historical account of the epidemiological transition in this century, see Preston, Keyfitz and Schoen (1972), Preston and Nelson (1974), and Preston (1980).

a number of life-threatening pathogens can be controlled at relatively little cost, something even poor countries for the most part would seem to be able to afford. It does not require elaborate social security, it does not demand maintenance programmes or employment guarantees, it most certainly does not require high income levels. It is in great part a little matter of medical application. These considerations form the intellectual basis of the claim that in poor countries attention needs to be given to public health—immunization against measles and whooping cough, for example, and environmental sanitation and potable water as a protection against diarrhoeas.

Allied to what is traditionally called public health are a number of pervasive sources of morbidity in poor countries, such as iron deficiency among pregnant and lactating women, and children, that are not beyond the reach even of poor countries. Field studies at the Narangwal Rural Health Research Centre in India show that perinatal mortality among the rural poor in that region can be reduced most effectively by diet supplementations or fortifications for mothers (for example iron and folic acid), to prevent, among other things, intrauterine malnutrition and premature delivery. Infection control had about half as much effect on perinatal mortality, mainly because of the reduction in neonatal tetanus by immunization of mothers and improved delivery practices of traditional birth attendants. On the other hand, infant mortality was reduced most in these studies by infection control, and less by improved nutrition. Mortality in children between the ages of 1 and 3 was reduced by both (see C.E. Taylor, 1983; and Chapter 14; see also Mata, 1985; Mosley, 1985). The evidence is compelling that most poor countries can afford to improve their general health care substantially. (See e.g. L.C. Chen, 1983; H. M. Levin, 1986; Jamison and Mosley, 1990; and for a collection of technical essays on the subject, Vallin and Lopez, 1985.)[22] But governments of few poor countries have taken notice of its imperatives.

Having said this, we should not ignore the danger of unbalanced attention in the reverse direction. It is being increasingly recognized that public health measures, such as immunization and oral rehydration, are cheap relative to measures that ensure that people have enough to eat. In recent years public bodies have had an incentive to concentrate their funds and attention on keeping infants and young children alive, at the expense of making those who are alive more productive. Admittedly, this is a horrifying sort of choice to make, even at the margin, but governments and international agencies have to make it all the time. The temptation on their part to shift entirely to public health measures directed at the very young has been considerable: they have quick and easily demonstrable

[22] The epidemiological problem of AIDS is a different matter.

yields. Moreover, deaths of infants and little children invoke a particularly strong emotional response. The 'food problem' has slowly yielded to the 'public health problem' on the agenda of international discourse. This has had far-reaching implications, in that school-age children and adults have been relatively neglected. Children in the age group 5–15 years in poor countries form about 25 per cent of the population. They represent the workforce of the next generation. Admittedly, they face the lowest risk of death among any age group; but their ability to concentrate and to attend to classroom work is significantly compromised by malnutrition (e.g. protein–calorie undernutrition, iron and iodine deficiency) and infection (e.g. intestinal parasites). This affects their ability to learn or master tasks. Quantitatively, the loss in future productivity would appear to be immense (see Pollitt, 1990; Leslie and Jamison, 1990; Section 14.2 below; and, in a different, more despairing, vein, M. King, 1990).

For rich nations the matter is different, and there is much to learn from them. In a series of illuminating writings on the state of health in the United States, Fuchs (1983, 1986, 1990) has argued that, beyond a fairly early point in the provision of food, hygiene, and basic health care, it is personal life-style that has the most telling impact on health (e.g. the incidence of heart diseases), and that it is 'normal' expectation of what a health service should provide which strongly affects overall expenditure. A comparison of, say, Western Europe or Canada with the United States reflects this. Health expenditure per person in Canada is about 70 per cent of the figure in the United States, and in Western Europe it lies between 35 per cent and 50 per cent of the US figure. But all the evidence suggests that people in Western Europe and Canada on average enjoy a standard of health at least as good as do people in the United States.

At least three explanations for this statistic suggest themselves. First, the average person in the United States demands more frequent medical attention, in the form of annual check-ups and so forth. Secondly, more attention is given there to 'luxury goods' in the health sector, for example the prolongation of life of the critically ill, or the very aged, and these are usually very capital-intensive. Thirdly, physicians charge a lot more in the United States (see Fuchs and Hahn, 1990). Inequality in the access to medical care in the United States is a reflection of this. Broad-based primary medical care would seem not to be an expensive commodity. By the same token, aggregate expenditure on health is not a good index either of the state of health or of the general availability of the health service.

There are thus numerous dimensions to the idea of morbidity, many of which are biologically based, but a number of which are quite blatantly cultural. Increases in morbidity among women in a poor country may reflect a growing autonomy of women and a better health service; it may have little to do with the purely clinical side of the matter. For the moment, therefore, it is difficult to see how data on morbidity can fruitfully be used in poor countries for judging the state of physical or mental health. For this reason, in Chapter 5 we will not study data on morbidity.

4.6 *Education: Numeracy and Literacy*

The output of education (knowledge, skills, and so forth) is a durable capital asset. A society's formal education system (comprising schools, colleges, training centres, and so forth) offers in principle a means by which people are able to acquire this asset. Other sources of education are the family, friends, and the community at large. We will be thinking here of the instrumental value of education in general, and of numeracy and literacy in particular.[23] Thus, we will ignore the direct consumption value of education, in the sense that the process of acquiring it and making use of it is usually a direct source of satisfaction to people. We will also neglect the thought that certain patterns of education have intrinsic value; intrinsic in the Aristotelian sense. This tactic will allow us to obtain a *lower* bound on the value of education. If for certain levels of education (e.g. primary education) this lower bound is found to be of high value relative to the economic return on other forms of capital assets, it can only mean that the society in question has been underinvesting in such levels of education.

In seeking an instrumental value of education, we will limit ourselves to measuring improvements in labour productivity brought about by education. We take it that increased knowledge and improved skills are a means by which this productivity gain is realized. There is now a wide body of evidence in support of this belief (see e.g. Chenery, Robinson and Syrquin, 1986; Morris and Adelman, 1987).

Although durable, the output of education depreciates over time if unused, and it grows if it is continuously used. (That is to say, there is learning: by doing, by using, by thinking, and by learning itself; see Chapter 6.) Thus, a person who learns to read and write but leaves school at the age of 10 and makes no further use of these skills will lose them over the years. She will be functionally illiterate. This is one reason why figures for adult literacy rates in poor countries are very suspect. They are often inferred from the percentage of adults who were enrolled in school for so many years. Also, they are often obtained from surveys, and in many countries the surveyor only gets to interview the adult males of the household. This leads to biases. Again, there is evidence of threshold levels in education. Schooling amounting to less than two years or so

---

[23] Data on numeracy are almost impossible to come by, and so, much of the discussion here will be centred on literacy.

would appear to be of no productive use. Beyond that, each additional year of education has productive value. We will look at estimates of this value.

In saying all this, I am thinking of education in a very specific way, as the acquisition of knowledge of other places, people, opportunities, and of the natural world, and of reading and writing and numerical skills and so forth. More generally, I am thinking of the acquiring of a certain attitude towards others and the world, one that imparts a distinct form of self-confidence, and encourages a judicious mix of conscious and trained reflection and experimentation to improve ways of doing things, and of understanding things.

The literature on human capital initially concentrated on the benefits of higher education (Becker, 1967, 1983; Chiswick, 1974). Here, we will be looking at the effects of the earliest stages of formal learning. That primary education has a considerable effect on industrial labour productivity has been much documented. Recently, Chaudhuri (1979) used data from the state of Punjab in India to show that primary education is important even for the cultivation of traditional varieties of wheat. He found that agricultural labourers who had been through primary education made more effective use of labour, and made better choices of production inputs. Chaudhuri also showed that the impact of secondary education increased significantly during 1961–72, suggesting that returns from secondary education increase with the coming of new technology of the kind embodied in the Green Revolution.[24]

There are now a number of cross-country estimates of social rates of returns on various levels of education. Table 4.4 (taken from Psacharapoulos, 1985) provides estimates for three regions: sub-Saharan Africa, Asia, and Latin America (and the Caribbean). The aggregation involved is heroic, but the figures are pithy, and they tell us something. In each region, among different levels of education it is the primary level that has the highest productive value (a rate of return of about 26 per cent), with secondary education having much less (about 15 per cent or a bit more) and higher education the least (about 13 per cent). One cannot escape the

[24] See also Singh (1990), who has shown that the earliest adopters of new hybrid varieties characterizing the Green Revolution were the most educated farmers (wealth was of secondary importance), and that the speed of adoption followed the classic logistic curve pioneered in the empirical work of Griliches (1957). The effect of education on farm productivity in other poor countries has been studied most thoroughly by Lockheed, Jamison and Lau (1980) and Jamison and Lau (1982). The latter, for example, have estimated that an additional year of schooling for the representative farmer in Malaysia would raise farm output by about 5 per cent, and that an additional year of schooling for the representative female would raise female wages by nearly 20 per cent.

Table 4.4   Social rates of return on education, 1980s (% per year)

Region	Primary	Secondary	Higher
Sub-Saharan Africa	26	17	13
Asia	27	15	13
Latin America and the Caribbean	26	18	16

Source: Psacharopoulos (1985).

thought that poor countries have consistently underinvested in primary education relative to education's higher reaches.[25]

These estimates are of the effect on output of changes in educational attainment. They don't entertain the possibility that education as a pooled stock may result in changes in output. I have in earlier chapters emphasized that negative freedoms, such as political and civil liberties, offer a background environment under whose protection people are able to pursue their lives. We explored the thesis that, at least up to a point, the wider are such commonly enjoyed background liberties, the greater are the possibilities open to people to achieve their aims. In Chapter 5 we will put this idea to the test. It appears that, like political and civil liberties, education as a stock is instrumental in generating economic growth, in that, *ceteris paribus*, economies with a larger stock of educated people tend to enjoy faster growth. The data suggest that each additional year of education as a stock is associated with a permanent increase in productivity growth by some 0.3 per cent per year (World Bank, 1991a). This is a substantial amount. Moreover, this figure augments the benefits from education captured in estimates of social rates of return. We will study the production and use of knowledge more closely in Chapter 6.

In recent years an additional effect of education has been investigated, and has been found to be powerful: the beneficial effects of parents' education, particularly mothers' education, on the well-being of their children. For the most part, the studies have explored the effect of up to 6 or 7 years of schooling, no more. Where they have differed is over the measurement of well-being. Some have looked at the 'input' side: for example household consumption of nutrients (Behrman and Wolfe, 1984a, b) and the use of contraceptives (Cochrane, 1979, 1983; Satahr and Chigambaram, 1984). Others have looked at the 'output' side, for example

---

[25] This is borne out in every country estimate I know of. See T. King (1980), Lockheed, Jamison and Lau (1980), Noor (1981), Jamison and Lau (1982), Psacharopoulos (1985), Psacharopoulos and Woodhall (1985), and World Bank (1989b, 1991a). Among the cognitive outcomes of education, it is numeracy (as compared with literacy) that would seem to affect productivity in agriculture more, especially wheat production. For a survey of the literature on the economics of education in the development process, see T. P. Schultz (1988a).

children's health in general, infant and child survival rates (Caldwell, 1979, 1986; Cochrane *et al.*, 1980; Cochrane, Leslie and O'Hara, 1982; Wolfe and Behrman, 1982, 1987; Hobcraft, McDonald and Rutstein, 1984; Mosley, 1985; Mensch, Lentzner and Preston, 1986; Victoria *et al.*, 1986; E. King, 1987; Cochrane and Farid, 1989; Strauss, 1990; Thomas, Strauss and Henriques, 1991), and children's height (Christian *et al.*, 1988; Strauss, 1990; Thomas, Strauss and Henriques, 1990, 1991).[26] Thus, maternal education has been found to have an influence on birth-spacing. Moreover, the survival chances of a newborn depends considerably on the length of the preceding birth interval; the longer the interval, the greater the survival chance. (In Cameroon, for example, the risk of death for children aged 1 year declines from about 55 to 35 and to 18 per 1000 according to whether the reference child was born less than 2 years, 2–3 years, or 4 or more years after the immediately preceding confinement; see Cochrane and Farid, 1989.) So the chain connecting parental educational attainment to the well-being of their children can have more than one link. At a more general level, these studies confirm that education helps mothers to process information more effectively, and enables them to use the various social and community services that may be on offer more intensively. Among other things, education appears to impart a degree of self-confidence enabling one to avail oneself of whatever new facilities may be on offer. This is invaluable for rural populations living through changing circumstances.[27]

Allied to this is the pervasive and significant effect of female education, especially secondary education, on women's reproductive behaviour (Cochrane, 1983). Although the links here are complex, female education as a general rule appears to lead to a reduction in fertility rates. We will study this in Chapters 11 and 12.

In poor countries, there is then a strong complementarity between social and community services, and literacy and numeracy taken together. Among the most important examples of the former are agricultural extension services, trade facilities with the rest of the world, provisions for health care, and advice on health care. Remove them, and rates of return on primary education are likely to be much lower. This is, of course, congenial to intuition. Literacy and numeracy are unlikely to be of much productive value if they have nothing to act upon. To cite an example,

[26] However, not all the studies I have cited here are methodologically immune to criticism. Indeed, in a few studies endogenous variables are treated as though they are exogenous. Strauss (1990) has a good discussion of such failings.

[27] Here is an indication of orders of magnitude. The infant mortality rate in households in Thailand where the mother had had no education (respect. has had primary and secondary education) was found to be 122 per 1000 (respect. 39 and 19 per 1000). See Jamison and Mosley (1990).

Chowdhury (1988) has used data from Bangladesh to argue that maternal education in his sample has little effect on child mortality rates because health services in rural Bangladesh are negligible. By the same token, literacy is of little use if you remain unemployed and are unable to make use of your literacy.

We may also look at matters the other way. The social value of community services and infrastructure (roads, marketing facilities, and so forth) is not likely to be high if reliable use is not made of them. They are unlikely to be reliably used if the population is illiterate.

So far as I am aware, estimates of social rates of return in the field of education and community services have all been of a partial nature: holding the level of one of the two categories constant and estimating the return on investment in the other. It is also possible that persons who were encouraged by their families to pursue primary and secondary education were the more productive ones anyway. There may then be a bias in the results. All this helps explain why some of the estimated rates are on the unusually high side.[28] It also goes some way towards explaining why there is little evidence of a rush on the part of poor people to acquire primary education, despite the high *ex post* aggregate rates of return. In those regions where the studies we have referred to have been conducted, the availability of complementary services has been a recent occurrence. It is possible that poor families had little idea of the economic benefits of education.

Calculations of rates of return on primary education are based on highly aggregated data, and cannot reveal another, possibly more important, reason for recalcitrance on the part of poor families in acquiring education. In a fine early empirical study, Bhagwati (1973) noted the large private costs that poor families have to bear when they send their children to school. By private costs I mean the opportunity costs of having their children attend school. Thus, by the age of six children in poor families in the Indian sub-continent tend cattle, goats, and younger siblings, fetch water, and collect firewood. Poverty forces parents to send children out to work at an early age. Child labour (of both girls and boys) in the market-place, including bonded labour, is a commonplace (see Cain and Mozumder, 1980). Such children are an early source of income, of much value to impoverished parents. Therefore, even when primary education is sub-sidized, schooling is costly for poor households, as the poor have limited access to credit (see Chapter 9), and so the benefits flowing from these

---

[28] *Ex post* cost benefit studies of investment in community services are rarer than those of investment in education. In a study of the effect on farm productivity of a programme of training and visit systems of agricultural extension in north-west India, G. Feder, Lau and Slade (1987) found a rate of return of over 15 per cent on investment in the programme.

subsidies are captured disproportionately by families that are well-off.[29] In the case of rural India, to the extent that wealth is correlated with caste hierarchy, education subsidies can be predicted to be captured mostly by the higher castes. And they are. In patrilineal societies, the benefits to poor parents from sending their daughters to school are less than the benefits from sending their sons. An educated girl may also be perceived as less pliable than an uneducated one. When this is the case, her parents will be at a disadvantage in the marriage market. We should expect a gender bias in education attainment, and there is such a bias (see Chapters 11–12).

These considerations imply that the private rate of return on primary education is higher for rich households than for poor households. Moreover, the return on a daughter's education is less than on a son's education. Furthermore, the large private cost of primary education for poor families facing credit constraints makes private returns lower than the figures that have typically been estimated in empirical studies, because current estimates often ignore such costs. In any event, data that aggregate over different income, caste and gender groups cannot expose these truths. Disaggregate data can, and they have exposed both caste and gender biases in primary education (Bhagwati, 1973; Sopher, 1980a, b). In Chapter 11 we will study evidence on sex differentials in health and education among poor children in the Indian sub-continent.

Across households within a country, therefore, poverty and illiteracy usually go hand in hand. Each reinforces the other. But across countries, the matter is different, since countries differ in their social ethos and their political design. In Chapter 5 we will see that among poor countries there was no systematic relationship between real national income per head and improvements in adult literacy during the decade of the 1970s. We will also see that there is a positive correlation between countries with a bad record on political and civil rights and those with a good record on improvements in literacy. I have no compelling explanation for this statistical fact, but that will not prevent me from speculating on the matter. What is incontrovertible is that it is possible for a poor country to break away quickly from the grip of illiteracy. It requires concerted effort from several parties: the household, local organizations and the village community, religious organizations, and the government. It involves government engagement in the form of free primary and secondary education,

---

[29] In many poor regions school terms coincide with periods when the need for agricultural labour is high, e.g. planting and harvesting. This provides another disincentive for parents to send their children to school.

free mid-day school meals, and so forth. All these are required to bring private returns on education closer to social returns.[30]

The supply side of education is not a complex matter to analyse. It is the demand side that is problematic. In certain circumstances, it has involved mass politicization; the examples of Tanzania, Cuba, and Vietnam testify to that. In others, such as in the south-western coastal areas of India, the role of the Christian church was substantial (Sopher, 1980a). In yet others, where there was already a strong, cultural commitment to general education (the influence of Buddhism and Confucianism has been much commented upon), as was the case in Sri Lanka, Korea, Thailand, and Taiwan, and in nineteenth-century Japan, this was not needed. Public demand was already there, despite the fact that the private opportunity cost of children's education was high for poor families.

---

[30] In Ch. 6 we will see that another source of the wedge between social rates of return on primary education and private rates of return is a range of educational externalities.

The Realization of Well-Being

5.1 *Citizenship: Civil, Political, and Socio-Economic*

The normative conception of the State explored earlier is far removed from the kinds of States we observe in most poor countries. In Chapters 2–3 I sketched the agency view of government in contractual theories of the State. Here, I will pull the various strands in that discussion into one overarching idea, that of *citizenship*, with its three constituent spheres: the civil, the political, and the socio-economic.[1]

Recall that the civil element of citizenship consists of the rights essential for basic liberties. It consists of the right to justice. Civil society is the sphere of autonomous institutions, protected by the rule of law, in which men and women may conduct their business freely and independently of the State.

Recall also that by the political element we mean the right of a person to participate in the exercise of political power, as a member of a body invested with political authority, or as an elector of the members of such a body. And, finally, recall that by the socio-economic element we mean a range that encompasses the right to a certain share of resources, the right to share to the full in the social heritage, and to live the life of a civilized being commensurate with the standards prevailing in the society in question. In earlier chapters I elaborated upon these various aspects of citizenship. The courts of justice; parliaments, and councils of local government; and the educational system and the social services are, respectively, the protectors and promoters of these three sets of rights. (See T. H. Marshall, 1964: 71–2. Marshall's classic statement on the nature of social democracies is further advanced in Marshall, 1981.)

Unhappily, in a great many poor countries civil society is woefully weak and fragmented. In some, even while they are formally so conceived, the concept of a nation-state is alien, with tribal, or clan, or religious, or ethnic loyalties prohibiting the emergence of the kind of dispassionate

---

[1] See T. H. Marshall (1964: 71–2). For convenience of exposition, I shall be thinking here of citizenship in the way it is viewed today, namely, citizenship of a nation-state. This is not to say that non-nationals do not have rights, nor that their rights aren't systematically violated in many parts of the world.

interpersonal concern and respect necessary for a well-ordered society. It would seem that to be a good citizen one has to be compartmentalized. We have to be able and willing to strike a balance between our own claims and the claims made upon us by our family and by the wide spectrum of associations of which we are members, ranging from those claims that can legitimately be made on us by our colleagues at the work-place, to those resulting from our membership of the polity. This is a very hard thing to do. On some occasions we rise to the moment, on most others we fall, sometimes hopelessly. But we can't avoid this multiplicity of obligations, and in subsequent chapters we will see that modern resource allocation theory encourages us to assume our multiple obligations not all at once, at all moments in our lives, but separately, as we step into our different positions. This protects our sanity. It also provides a way for us to discover what our own interests are. To be totally self-absorbed is bad. To be asked constantly to seek to do good to others is to be asked far too much; for the bulk of us it would involve a loss of our identities.

The roles (and by 'roles' I mean motivation and norms of behaviour) I am encouraged to assume as a son, husband, father, and friend are different from those I am asked to assume when performing as a teacher, researcher, shopper, voter, and member of the professional societies I belong to. I don't suppose it is immediately obvious how very radical in spirit this prescription is, this injunction that we somehow 'decentralize' ourselves each day of our lives into a number of selves. (See Rawls, 1955, for the development of a similar argument.) It is light-years away from the superficially more attractive prescription that we assume our complete selves at all times.

To not so decentralize ourselves can involve immense costs, as our loyalties and passions in one sphere of our lives interfere with our decisions in other spheres. No doubt there are psychic costs in compartmentalizing ourselves, but modern resource allocation theory tells us that this pattern of decentralization ultimately saves on resources. It thus widens the prospects of our being able to accomplish our projects and purposes.[2] Recognition of this multiplicity of obligations is a prerequisite for the implementation of a social contract which, as we noted in Chapter 3, is characterized more by rules than by discretion. In a just society, inequalities in income and wealth and attainments would not countenance a violation of equal citizenship, with the attendant right it confers on each person to be treated with the same respect and concern as all others.

These reflections, which have brought us back full circle to the abstract

---

[2] See Arrow (1974), who begins his monograph with the sage Rabbi Hillel's remarkably phrased questions: 'If I am not for myself, then who is for me? And if I am not for others, then who am I? And if not now, when?'

idea of a social contract, offer us a way to make a transition to the world as we know it. Here the idea of a social contract reduces to a weaker concept. The key notion is the *legitimacy* of political systems, which is the capacity of systems to sustain and promote the general informed belief that the existing institutional structure is the most appropriate one to have under the circumstances. (Lipset, 1960, has a fine discussion of this.) Such a general belief can only draw its support from a common set of values pertaining to the definition of the political community and the structure of authority within it. It is a necessary, though by no means sufficient, feature of a just society. Mutual sympathy and consideration among citizens and a sense of general trust among them are a prerequisite, as is periodic reaffirmation through political debate and uncoerced civic participation.

All this is absent from most poor countries. Both the idea of equal citizenship and the duties of citizenship are, for the most part, alien.[3] All too often, the weakness and fragmentation of civil society is taken advantage of by groups who gain control of the bureaucratic and military apparatus and pervert the purpose of government by repressing, and often obliterating, persons outside the groups. Examples abound, among the worst in recent years being Myanmar and Iraq, Ethiopia, Somalia, and the Sudan, Guatemala and El Salvador. In less hostile social environments (and they too exist in poor countries) votes are purchased, officials are bribed, agency loyalties are maintained, the courts are manipulated, the press are harrassed, and lobbyists succeed in getting their way.

There is a wide variety of groups exercising both power and control in poor countries. There are run-of-the-mill military dictatorships and land-owning aristocracies in parts of the Middle East and Latin America, élite tribes in sub-Saharan Africa, and industrial and landowning interests in the Indian sub-continent. There is also a variety of violations of the right to equal citizenship in poor countries. They range from the murderous, where life and property are continually at risk (see e.g. D. Collier, 1979; Morrison, Mitchell and Paden, 1989), to the 'benign', where the disadvantaged in the civic sphere have sharply restricted access to occupations, housing, and common-property resources.[4]

These are familiar matters today because they are visible, and are often written about. Less visible is an astonishing variety of modes through which resources, often public resources, are usurped by groups wielding power. They range from outright theft of official foreign aid (Bauer, 1981; Hancock, 1989), to State provisions of tax advantages, subsidized credit facilities, and infrastructure for landowning aristocracies (E. Feder, 1977,

---

[3] It is violated in other countries too, but we are not considering other countries here.
[4] See e.g. Beteille (1983) on the plight of low castes and untouchables in India, where disadvantages persist even although the law does not discriminate.

1979; Durham, 1979; Repetto, 1988; Binswanger, 1989), to producer-price controls of agricultural output for the benefit of urban populations (Bauer and Yamey, 1968, Bates, 1981, 1983; Bauer, 1987), to the widespread imposition of production and trade restrictions (Bhagwati and Desai, 1970; Krueger, 1974, 1990; Bhagwati, 1982; de Soto, 1989; Findley, 1989). Controls on producer prices and on trade and production create rents, which are often captured by those who foster such controls and restrictions. They can have woeful distributional consequences (see Chapters 6–10) and when extensive they border on a violation of civil liberties. They also erode the production and resource base of an economy.[5]

The chain linking the unjustifiable privileges of one class of persons to the erosion of the liberties of others is complex. In Chapter 10 we will, as an example, note the systematic urban bias that governments have demonstrated in most poor countries. This has gone to impoverish the rural poor even further. It has been possible for governments to do this because the rural poor are generally dispersed and unorganized. Unlike organized urban workers, the rural poor can't strike: they have nothing to strike *at*.

Case-histories of the political economy of nations offer a way of gaining an understanding of the nature of governments and societies, and of the extent of destitution in poor countries. A complementary route is the study of aggregate, internationally comparable data, to get a feel for the quality of life in various countries. In Chapters 3–4 I argued that figures for national income per head, life expectancy at birth, the infant (or child) survival rate, and the adult literacy rate are key indicators of general well-being. We will now combine internationally comparable figures for political and civil liberties with our four socio-economic measures to arrive at a comparison of the quality of life in the world's poorest countries.

Such exercises as those we will be undertaking here can only be regarded as exploratory. Cross-country data on such variables as national income, the literacy rate, and life expectancy at birth are well known to be defective. For several sets of countries the data are not quite comparable: not only were they not collected in the same year, but the methods deployed for collecting them were not the same (see the explanations accompanying the world tables in World Bank, 1991a, 1992). Some of the data, I am reliably informed, reflect not much more than interpolations on data collected in neighbouring countries. However, short of not addressing a number of questions that need to be addressed, there isn't very much I

---

[5] There are desirable forms of government restrictions on production and trade. We will study a few in Chs. 6–7. The recent economic history of South Korea illustrates how effective judicious control can be in fostering economic well-being (see Datta-Choudhury, 1978; Kim and Roemer, 1979; Bahl, Kim and Park, 1986; Kim and Yun, 1988; Amsden, 1989; Wade, 1990; World Bank, 1991a). In the text I am alluding to the effects of blatant forms of rent-seeking activities and resource usurpation.

can do about it. One has simply to be brazen about such matters and recognize the data for what they are. Nevertheless, the unevenness in the quality of data is something we should bear in mind throughout this book. My purpose in appealing to cross-country statistics is illustrative. Moreover, several of the analytical steps I shall take while conducting the exercises can be questioned. But they will not be *ad hoc*. I shall provide justifications, even though alternative steps will readily suggest themselves to the reader. I emphasize the exploratory nature of this inquiry only because there is a great deal that remains to be done in this field.

5.2   Inter-Country Comparison of the Quality of Life[6]

We will consider countries which, in 1970, enjoyed a per capita real national income less than $1500 at 1980 international dollars.[7] The idea is to look at a snapshot of the quality of life in each country. The year in question is 1979–80. Data on all six of the constituents of well-being to be studied here are available for only 48 countries out of the more than 55 that should be on our list.[8] Table 5.1 summarizes the data. Countries are listed alphabetically. Column (1) provides estimates of national income per head for the year 1980. Columns (2), (3), and (4) present life expectancy at birth, infant mortality rates, and adult literacy rates, respectively, for that year.[9]

Of the six columns of figures in the table, it is the last pair that will be of novelty to social scientists and political philosophers. They represent indices of political and civil liberties in our sample of countries for the year 1979. They are taken from the valuable compendium of Taylor and Jodice

---

[6] This section is taken from Dasgupta and Weale (1992).

[7] We are using data on purchasing power parity income rather than conventional income. This is open to the objection that it overstates income in those countries that choose to devote large amounts of resources to social services (see Isenman, 1987). Indeed, it may explain some of the results shown in Table 5.2. Nevertheless, the purchasing power parity income measure is the best indicator of income currently available.

[8] Data on per capita national income have been taken from Summers and Heston (1988), those on life expectancy at birth and infant mortality rates from World Bank (1989a), and the ones on literacy rates from World Bank (1983). The decision to use a 1970 figure of $1500 at 1980 international prices as the cut-off point is, of course, a bit arbitrary, but only a bit. In the following section we will study the performance of poor nations during the decade of the 1970s.

[9] Since life expectancy at birth is heavily influenced by the infant survival rate (see Table 5.3), one can argue that we are counting health twice—in other words, that we are giving health twice the weight we are giving to each of the other ingredients of aggregate well-being. It is easy to redo all our computations by deleting data on either of the health indices.

It would have been preferable to replace life expectancy at birth by life expectancy at age 1, to make the measure independent of the infant survival rate. An alternative would have been to use the child death rate in place of the infant mortality rate. Limitations of data have prevented me from doing any of this.

(1983). Political rights in Taylor and Jodice (1983) are taken to be the right of citizens to play a part in determining who governs their country, and what the laws are and will be. Countries are coded with scores ranging from 1 (highest degree of liberty) to 7 (lowest degree of liberty). Values for this index are given in the fifth column of the Table.

Civil rights are different. They are rights the individual has *vis-à-vis* the State. Of particular importance are freedom of the press and other media concerned with the dissemination of information, and the independence of the judiciary. The index measures the extent to which people, because they are protected by an independent judiciary, are openly able to express their opinions without fear of reprisals. Countries are coded with scores ranging from 1 (highest degree of liberty) to 7 (lowest degree of liberty). As indices of political and civil rights may not be familiar to readers, I provide their key in the Appendix to this chapter, where I also comment briefly on related work by others.

Even a glance at these columns tells us that for the most part political and civil liberties are scarce goods in poor countries. Citizens of thirty-three countries in our sample of forty-eight suffer from systems that score 5 or more for political rights, and those of no fewer than forty countries, from systems that score 5 or more for civil rights. As the Appendix makes clear, these scores reflect severe deprivation of these basic liberties. There are exceptions, of course, most notably Botswana, the Gambia, India, Mauritius, and Sri Lanka. But for the most part the columns make for dismal reading; and when they are combined with columns reflecting the socio-economic sphere of life the resulting picture is chilling. There is nothing to commend the state of affairs in a large number of the countries in our sample.

Our international comparison of the quality of life will be based on these six indices. Now, the quality of the data being what it is for many of the countries, it is unwise to rely on their cardinal magnitudes. We will, therefore, base our comparison on ordinal measures. This way, systematic biases in claims about achievement across countries will not affect the international comparison. But first, we need an ordinal aggregator.

Of the many we could devise, the one best known and most studied is the Borda Rule. This rule provides a method of rank-order scoring, the procedure being to award each alternative (here, country) a point equal to its rank in each criterion of ranking (here, the criteria being per capita income, life expectancy at birth, infant survival rate, adult literacy rate, and indices of political and civil rights), adding each alternative's scores to obtain its aggregate score, and then ranking alternatives on the basis of their aggregate scores. To illustrate, suppose a country has the ranks i, j, k, l, m, and n, respectively, for six criteria. Then its Borda score is $i + j + k + l + m + n$. The rule invariably yields a complete ordering of

Table 5.1 Living standards in 48 of the world's poorest countries, 1980

	Y (1)	E (2)	M (3)	L (4)	R_1 (5)	R_2 (6)
Bangladesh	540.0	48.0	140.0	26.0	4.0	4.0
Benin	534.0	47.0	124.0	28.0	7.0	7.0
Bolivia	1529.0	50.0	130.0	63.0	3.0	5.0
Botswana	1477.0	55.0	78.0	35.0	3.0	2.0
Burundi	333.0	46.0	126.0	25.0	6.0	7.0
CAR	487.0	47.0	143.0	33.0	7.0	7.0
Chad	353.0	42.0	147.0	15.0	6.0	6.0
China	1619.0	67.0	41.0	69.0	6.0	6.0
Ecuador	2607.0	63.0	75.0	81.0	3.0	5.0
Egypt	995.0	58.0	108.0	44.0	5.0	5.0
Ethiopia	325.0	44.0	155.0	15.0	7.0	7.0
Gambia	556.0	40.0	159.0	15.0	2.0	2.0
Haiti	696.0	52.0	132.0	23.0	6.0	7.0
Honduras	1075.0	60.0	87.0	60.0	3.0	6.0
India	614.0	54.0	107.0	36.0	3.0	2.0
Indonesia	1063.0	53.0	105.0	62.0	5.0	5.0
Jordan	1885.0	62.0	58.0	70.0	6.0	6.0
Kenya	662.0	55.0	83.0	47.0	5.0	5.0
Korea	2369.0	67.0	32.0	93.0	5.0	5.0
Lesotho	694.0	52.0	116.0	52.0	4.0	5.0
Liberia	680.0	52.0	100.0	25.0	4.0	6.0
Madagascar	589.0	51.0	146.0	50.0	5.0	5.0
Malawi	417.0	44.0	169.0	25.0	6.0	6.0
Mali	356.0	44.0	184.0	10.0	7.0	7.0
Mauritania	576.0	43.0	142.0	17.0	6.0	6.0
Mauritius	1484.0	65.4	45.2	85.0	2.0	4.0
Morocco	1199.0	57.0	102.0	28.0	4.0	3.0
Nepal	490.0	45.1	142.2	19.0	6.0	5.0
Niger	441.0	42.0	150.0	10.0	6.0	7.0
Nigeria	824.0	48.0	118.0	34.0	3.0	5.0
Pakistan	989.0	49.0	124.0	24.0	5.0	6.0
Paraguay	1979.0	66.0	47.0	84.0	5.0	5.0
Philippines	1551.0	61.0	52.0	75.0	5.0	5.0
Rwanda	379.0	45.0	127.0	50.0	5.0	6.0
Senegal	744.0	45.0	147.0	10.0	3.0	4.0
Sierra Leone	512.0	38.0	172.0	15.0	5.0	6.0
Somalia	415.0	44.0	145.0	60.0	7.0	7.0
Sri Lanka	1199.0	68.0	34.0	85.0	3.0	2.0
Sudan	652.0	46.0	123.0	32.0	5.0	5.0
Swaziland	1079.0	51.7	133.4	65.0	6.0	5.0
Tanzania	353.0	50.0	119.0	79.0	6.0	6.0
Thailand	1694.0	62.0	51.0	86.0	4.0	6.0
Tunisia	1845.0	60.4	91.8	62.0	6.0	5.0

Table 5.1   Continued

	Y (1)	E (2)	M (3)	L (4)	R_1 (5)	R_2 (6)
Uganda	257.0	46.0	113.0	52.0	7.0	7.0
Yemen	957.0	42.9	163.7	21.0	7.0	7.0
Zaïre	224.0	49.0	111.0	55.0	6.0	7.0
Zambia	716.0	50.1	90.4	44.0	5.0	5.0
Zimbabwe	930.0	55.0	82.4	69.0	5.0	5.0

Key:

Y: per capita income (1980 purchasing power parity)

E: life expectancy at birth (years)

M: infant mortality rate (per 1000)

L: adult literacy rate (%)

R_1: index of political rights, 1979

R_2: index of civil rights, 1979

Sources: Taylor and Jodice (1983); Summers and Heston (1988); World Bank (1983, 1989a).

alternatives. It can be viewed as a social well-being function, since the criteria can be thought of as 'voters'. Of Arrow's classic axioms on social choice, the Borda Rule violates the one concerning the independence of irrelevant alternatives (Arrow, 1963). The strengths and limitations of the Borda Rule have been investigated by Goodman and Markowitz (1952), J. H. Smith (1973), and Fine and Fine (1974). There is now a good intuitive understanding of it. So we will use it for our cross-country study.

The first column in Table 5.2 prescents the ranking of countries on the basis of the Borda index. Countries are listed in this order. The remaining six columns present the six constituents of well-being we are studying here. Rankings go up from the worst (score of 1) to the best (score of 48).

It is a useful exercise first of all to look at the best- and worst-off sets of countries. From column (1), we note that in *ascending* order the ten lowest-ranked countries in 1980 were: Mali, Ethiopia, Niger, Chad, Yemen, Malawi, Sierra Leone, Burundi, Somalia, and the Central African Republic. How does this list compare with the ranking of nations based exclusively on per capita national income? To scc this, we note from column (2) that, in ascending order, the ten poorest countries in our sample in 1980 were: Zaïre, Uganda, Ethiopia, Burundi, Chad, and Tanzania (tied at 5), Mali, Rwanda, Somalia, and Malawi. The lists aren't the same, but they are similar. All except one (Yemen) are in sub-Sahara, and the lists contain six countries in common.

Turning next to the ten highest-ranked countries, we note first that they are in *descending* order: Mauritius, Sri Lanka, Ecuador, South Korea,

Table 5.2   Rankings of living standards data of 48 of the world's poorest countries, 1980

	Borda Rank (1)	Y (2)	E (3)	M (4)	L (5)	R_1 (6)	R_2 (7)
Mali	1	7	7	1	1	1	1
Ethiopia	2	3	7	6	4	1	1
Niger	3	11	3	7	1	8	1
Chad	4	5	3	8	4	8	12
Yemen	5	30	5	4	10	1	1
Malawi	6	10	7	3	13	8	12
Sierra Leone	7	14	1	2	4	21	12
Burundi	8	4	14	20	13	8	1
Somalia	9	9	7	11	32	1	1
CAR	10	12	17	12	20	1	1
Mauritania	11	18	6	14	8	8	12
Benin	12	15	17	21	17	1	1
Uganda	13	2	14	27	29	1	1
Nepal	14	13	13	13	9	8	24
Haiti	15	25	28	17	11	8	1
Zaïre	15	1	21	28	31	8	1
Rwanda	17	8	11	19	27	21	12
Tanzania	18	5	23	24	42	8	12
Pakistan	19	31	21	21	12	21	12
Gambia	20	17	2	5	4	47	45
Sudan	21	21	14	23	19	21	24
Madagascar	22	19	26	10	27	21	24
Senegal	23	27	11	8	1	39	41
Bangladesh	23	16	19	15	16	34	41
Liberia	25	23	28	33	13	34	12
Swaziland	26	35	27	16	37	8	24
Zambia	27	26	25	35	24	21	24
Nigeria	28	28	19	25	21	39	24
Kenya	29	22	33	37	26	21	24
Lesotho	30	24	28	26	29	34	24
Egypt	31	32	37	29	24	21	24
Indonesia	32	33	31	31	34	21	24
Bolivia	33	40	23	18	36	39	24
Tunisia	34	44	39	34	34	8	24
Zimbabwe	34	29	33	38	38	21	24
Jordan	36	45	41	41	40	8	12
India	37	20	32	30	23	39	45
Honduras	38	34	38	36	32	39	12
China	39	42	46	46	38	8	12
Morocco	40	36	36	32	17	34	44
Philippines	41	41	40	42	41	21	24

Table 5.2   Continued

	Borda Rank (1)	Y (2)	E (3)	M (4)	L (5)	R_1 (6)	R_2 (7)
Botswana	42	38	33	39	22	39	45
Thailand	43	43	41	43	47	34	12
Paraguay	44	46	45	44	44	21	24
South Korea	45	47	46	48	48	21	24
Ecuador	46	48	43	40	43	39	24
Sri Lanka	47	36	48	47	45	39	45
Mauritius	48	39	44	45	45	47	41

Key:
Borda Rank: ranking using Borda Rule
Y: per capita income (1980 purchasing power parity)
E: life expectancy at birth (years)
M: infant mortality rate (per 1000)
L: adult literacy rate (%)
R_1: index of political rights
R_2: index of civil rights

Paraguay, Thailand, Botswana, the Philippines, Morocco, and China. The presence of Sri Lanka close to the top of our list of poor countries shouldn't be a surprise. The remarkable achievements of Sri Lanka (at least until recently) have been much studied and commented upon.[10] However, Mauritius rarely gets written about in development commentaries. Her presence at the top of our ranking was a revelation to me.

The closeness between China and India in our overall ranking deserves scrutiny. For a long while China and India have provided commentators with a classic tension: achievements in the socio-economic sphere of life, against those in political and civil liberties.[11] As Table 5.1 shows, China beats India hands down in each of the four socio-economic indices, while India wins over China in the spheres of political and civil rights. In a two-way Borda ranking between them, China scores 10 and India, 8. So China beats India. But it isn't a two-way comparison we are interested in: we are ranking forty-eight countries. In this setting, the *ordinal distance* between

[10] See Isenman (1980). See also Sen (1981a). I should add that the controversy over the question whether these achievements have been realized only over the past 30 years or so (see Bhalla, 1986; Pyatt, 1987; Isenman, 1987; Samarasinghe, 1988), or whether, as would seem to be the case, the quality of life in Sri Lanka was by the year 1960 already high relative to other poor countries (Bhalla and Glewwe, 1986), has no bearing on our discussion in the text. Here we are ranking countries on the basis of the quality of life at the close of the decade of the 1970s.

[11] For wide-ranging accounts of China's and India's achievements and failings, see Riskin (1987) and *Daedalus* (Special Issue on India, 1989), respectively.

China and India, as judged by the Borda Rule, depends on how many countries squeeze themselves in between them for each of the six constituent indices we are studying here. (The rule violates Arrow's axiom of the independence of irrelevant alternatives.) So the relative ranking of China and India could have gone either way, depending on how other countries were doing at the end of the 1970s. It transpires that the two-way ranking of China and India is preserved in the overall ranking of poor nations. (China is 10th from the top and India is 12th from the top.) But, given that they are close, it would have gone the other way had sub-Saharan countries been only a shade better in political and civil liberties.[12] In any event, it appears that the position of China relative to India is sensitive to the choice of the index of general well-being. This is useful information, and is consistent with our uninformed intuition.

How does the list of the top ten countries in terms of the Borda index compare with the list consisting of the ten least poor countries? It isn't dissimilar. The ten richest countries in our list are, in descending order: Ecuador, South Korea, Paraguay, Jordan, Tunisia, Thailand, China, the Philippines, Bolivia, and Mauritius. There are seven countries in common.[13] We conclude tentatively that among the poorest nations rankings in terms of general well-being are not too different from those based on income per head.

But this is a qualitative claim. It will be useful to get a quantitative feel for the relationship between our Borda ranking and rankings based on each of the six constituents of general well-being. Statistically, how close is the Borda ranking to the other six? In order to examine this, we look at *rank correlations*. Admittedly, our rankings are disturbed by inaccuracies in data. It is unlikely, though, that these would tend to do anything except depress the rank correlations below those that would be found were we to work with accurate data. The table of rank correlations may therefore be regarded as indicating underlying statistical relationships.

Table 5.3 provides the (Spearman) correlation coefficient for each pair of rankings from the seven rankings of nations. The correlation coefficient between the Borda ranking and the others are: 0.84 with national income

---

[12] The tying rule we have followed has something to do with it as well. What I have done is this. Suppose two countries tie for the second place (of badness). I have ranked both as number 2 and have given the rank 4 to the next country. Other procedures can be followed, and they will yield somewhat different overall rankings. I have stuck to the rule I began with before I knew what the answers were.

[13] The presence of China in the list of the 10 most affluent in our sample of forty-eight countries came as a surprise to me, used as I am to perusing the annual *World Development Report* of the World Bank, which hasn't as yet moved over to using international prices when making inter-country comparisons of real income. The Summers–Heston ranking of poor countries is quite different from those that rely on official exchange rates to reflect purchasing power.

Table 5.3 Correlation matrix of constituent rankings of well-being

	Borda	Y	E	M	L	R_1
Y	0.8407					
E	0.9133	0.7895				
M	0.8797	0.6943	0.9180			
L	0.7597	0.5942	0.8018	0.7934		
R_1	0.6842	0.4916	0.4105	0.4065	0.2420	
R_2	0.6881	0.5135	0.4347	0.3841	0.2654	0.7871

Note: All correlations are statistically significant at a 5% level.

per head; 0.91 with life expectancy at birth; 0.88 with the infant mortality rate; 0.76 with the adult literacy rate; 0.68 with political rights; and 0.69 with civil rights. I wasn't expecting this. I had no reason for thinking that health-related indices would be the closest to our measure of well-being. If we had to choose a single, ordinal measure of general well-being, life expectancy at birth would seem to be the best. At the same time, national income per head is not far behind indices of health in its closeness to the Borda index. Recent suggestions that national income per head is a vastly misleading index is not borne out by our exercise. We can do better than merely rely on national income, and this is what we have done. But we wouldn't have been wildly off the mark as regards an ordinal comparison of countries had we relied exclusively on national income per head. There must be a moral to this.

It is customary to regress national income per head against other socio-economic indicators, to see how closely they are related (see e.g. Kaneko and Nidaira, 1988). The second column of Table 5.3 presents Spearman rank correlation coefficients between national income per head and each of the other five constituents of well-being, together with the significance level of the correlation (i.e. the probability of the given correlation being generated by unrelated data). The highest correlation (0.79) is with life expectancy at birth. Again, I was not expecting this. I also had no prior notion that correlation with adult literacy (0.59) would be considerably less.[14]

Richer countries seem to enjoy greater political and civil rights. But the correlation is not overly high: the correlation is 0.49 with political rights and 0.51 with civil rights. Neither national income per head, nor political and civil liberties can be thought of as being exogenously given. Any such

[14] But that is only because I had not consulted historians. In 19th-c. Europe there was no systematic relationship between national income per head and literacy. Thus, England was Europe's wealthiest country, but only half its people could read and write by 1850; Sweden was relatively poor and agrarian in 1850, but had achieved universal literacy; Spain was poor and illiterate; Holland was comparatively well-off and literate; and so forth.

link between them as we observe in international data should be seen only as a link, nothing more; no causal relationship can be presumed from the data. Correlation coefficients of 0.49 and 0.51 mean that the claim that the circumstances that make for poverty are also those that make it necessary for governments to deny their citizens political and civil liberties is simply false. There are countries in the sample that are very poor and enjoy relatively high civil and political liberties.

We will note presently that the adult literacy rate is a rogue index: it stands somewhat apart from the other indices of socio-economic rights. The correlation coefficient between literacy and political and civil rights are 0.24 and 0.27 respectively. These are relatively low figures, far and away the lowest in Table 5.3.

5.3   *Political and Civil Liberties versus Economic Progress: Is There a Trade-Off?*[15]

In developing the arguments of Chapter 2, we built upon the idea that political and civil liberties provide the background environment within which people pursue their own conceptions of the good. For this they require, in addition, scarce resources. We elaborated upon this in Chapters 2–3 when developing a contractual theory of the State, and so far in this chapter I have tried to provide an operational content to this. Here I want to ask a question that makes the content more transparent: On a cross-country basis among the poorest of economies, is there a conflict between political and civil liberties and economic progress? The argument, which I have often heard expressed in conversation, that poor nations cannot *afford* the luxury of political and civil rights needs some form of testing. Now, a central conclusion of Chapters 2 and 3 was that these rights aren't luxuries at all. We argued that they possess an instrumental value as well: they delineate the environment in which men and women shape their lives. One might suppose that these freedoms protect and promote socio-economic rights. We should then ask whether, as a contingent matter, there is a trade-off between them when a country is poor, so that there is a question of choice, so that, if citizens desire fast growth in income or rapid improvements in health and education, they have to suffer from significant constraints on their political and civil liberties.

Towards this we will look at data for the decade of the 1970s. Table 5.4 summarizes these data. Since we are involved with a greater range of questions here, we will study a large pool of countries. I will vary the sample size as and when we need to. The criterion is the same as before. We are interested in those countries which, in 1970, enjoyed a per capita

---

[15] This section is taken from Dasgupta (1990a) and Dasgupta and Weale (1992).

national income less than $1500 at 1980 international prices. There are fifty-one such countries in Summers and Heston (1988).

The first column of Table 5.4 presents the average of the 1970 and 1980 figures for real national income per head. We study this average, rather than income per head at some given year during the decade, because growth rates varied across countries during the period. One common measure of economic performance is the percentage change in real income per head. This is provided in column (2). It will be noticed that an astonishing fifteen of the fifty-one countries experienced a *decline* in real income per head during the 1970s.

Column (3) gives life expectancy at birth in 1970. We need a measure of the change in this index over the decade. This is a delicate matter. Equal increments are possibly of less and less ethical worth as life expectancy rises to 65 or 70 years and more. But we are measuring performance here. So it would seem that it becomes more and more commendable if, with increasing life expectancy, the index were to rise at the margin. The idea here is that it becomes more and more difficult to increase life expectancy as life expectancy itself rises. A simple index capturing this feature is the ratio of the increase in life expectancy to the shortfall of the base-year life expectancy from some target, say 80 years.[16] Column (4) of the table gives this index of improvement over the period 1970–80 for 51 countries. All but two countries, Rwanda and Uganda, recorded an improvement.

Column (5) provides infant mortality rates in 1970. Construction of an index of improvement in these poses a similar problem. The ethical issues here, no doubt, are different from those concerning increases in life expectancy at birth. But we are trying to record performance in this field. A figure of 10 per 1000 for the infant mortality rate is about as low as it is reasonable for poor countries to aspire to for a long time to come. So we take the index of improvement to be the ratio of the decline in the infant mortality rate over the period in question (1970–80) to the base-year infant mortality rate minus 10. All countries in our sample have shown an improvement in infant survival rates. Column (6) presents values for this index of improvement.

The construction of an index of improvements in literacy rates doesn't pose problems of the kind we faced in connection with life expectancy at birth and infant survival rates. It isn't immediately clear why it should be a lot less or a lot more difficult to increase the literacy rate when people are more literate; except, that is, near 0 and 100%. This suggests that we should simply measure increases in adult literacy rates if we want to know what net improvements there have been in this field. Unfortunately, I have

---

[16] Thus, an increase in life expectancy at birth from 35 to 40 years is less difficult to achieve than an increase from 60 to 65 years (see Sen, 1981a). The mathematical representation of the index is given in the key to Table 5.4.

Table 5.4   Improvements in living standards in 51 of the world's poorest countries, 1970–1980

	Y (1)	ΔY (2)	E (3)	ΔE (4)	M (5)	ΔM (6)	L (7)	ΔL (8)	R_1 (9)	R_2 (10)
Bangladesh	499.0	17.9	45.0	8.6	140.0	0.0	22.0	4.0	4.9	4.2
Benin	552.5	−6.5	40.0	17.5	155.0	21.4	5.0	23.0	7.0	6.3
Bolivia	1383.0	23.6	46.0	11.8	153.0	16.1	39.0	24.0	5.6	4.1
Botswana	1179.0	67.7	50.0	16.7	101.0	25.3	41.0	—	2.1	3.1
Burundi	324.0	5.7	45.0	2.9	137.0	8.7	14.0	11.0	7.0	6.4
Cameroon	789.0	24.5	49.0	12.9	126.0	17.2	19.0	—	6.1	4.4
CAR	499.0	−4.7	42.0	13.2	153.0	7.0	7.0	26.0	7.0	7.0
Chad	409.5	−24.2	38.0	9.5	171.0	14.9	6.0	9.0	6.4	6.4
China	1315.5	60.0	59.0	38.1	69.0	47.5	43.0	26.0	6.7	6.7
Congo	986.5	−1.1	51.0	13.8	98.0	17.0	16.0	—	5.9	6.1
Ecuador	2005.0	85.8	58.0	22.7	100.0	27.8	68.0	13.0	6.4	3.7
Egypt	833.0	48.3	51.0	24.1	158.0	33.8	26.0	18.0	5.6	4.7
Ethiopia	333.0	−4.7	43.0	2.7	158.0	2.0	4.0	11.0	6.3	6.1
Gambia	561.0	−1.8	36.0	9.1	185.0	14.9	—	—	2.0	2.0
Ghana	494.5	−25.9	49.0	9.7	110.0	10.0	27.0	—	6.6	5.1
Haiti	623.0	26.5	48.0	12.5	162.0	19.7	15.0	8.0	6.4	6.0
Honduras	1001.0	16.0	53.0	25.9	115.0	26.7	45.0	15.0	6.1	3.0
India	595.0	6.6	48.0	18.8	139.0	24.8	28.0	8.0	2.1	3.3
Indonesia	811.0	90.2	47.0	18.2	121.0	14.4	39.0	23.0	5.0	5.0
Jordan	1653.0	32.7	55.0	28.0	90.0	40.0	32.0	38.0	6.0	6.0
Kenya	607.0	19.9	50.0	16.7	102.0	20.7	20.0	27.0	5.0	4.6
South Korea	1779.0	99.2	60.0	35.0	51.0	46.3	71.0	22.0	4.9	5.6
Lesotho	527.0	92.8	49.0	9.7	134.0	14.5	—	—	5.3	3.9
Liberia	694.0	−4.0	47.0	15.2	124.0	21.1	9.0	16.0	6.0	4.3
Madagascar	631.0	−12.5	45.0	17.1	183.0	21.4	—	—	5.1	4.4
Malawi	359.0	38.5	40.0	10.0	193.0	13.1	—	—	6.9	6.0
Mali	336.5	12.3	40.0	10.0	204.0	10.3	2.0	8.0	7.0	6.6
Mauritania	573.0	1.1	39.0	9.8	166.0	15.4	5.0	12.0	5.9	6.0
Mauritius	1254.5	44.8	62.4	17.0	61.4	31.5	—	—	2.7	2.3
Morocco	1037.5	36.9	52.0	17.9	128.0	22.0	14.0	14.0	4.6	4.4
Nepal	498.0	−3.2	41.6	9.1	157.4	10.3	9.0	10.0	6.0	5.0
Niger	421.0	10.0	38.0	9.5	170.0	12.5	1.0	9.0	6.7	6.0
Nigeria	727.0	30.8	44.0	11.1	158.0	27.0	15.0	19.0	5.7	4.0
Pakistan	893.0	24.1	46.0	8.8	142.0	13.6	15.0	9.0	4.3	4.9
Paraguay	1584.0	66.4	65.0	6.7	59.0	24.5	75.0	9.0	4.9	5.4
Philippines	1322.5	41.8	57.0	17.4	66.0	25.0	72.0	3.0	4.9	5.1
Rwanda	323.5	41.4	48.0	−9.4	135.0	6.4	16.0	34.0	6.9	5.3
Senegal	752.0	−2.1	43.0	5.4	164.0	11.0	6.0	4.0	5.6	4.4
Sierra Leone	485.5	11.5	34.0	8.7	197.0	13.4	7.0	8.0	5.6	5.0
Somalia	394.5	11.0	40.0	10.0	158.0	8.8	2.0	58.0	7.0	6.4
Sri Lanka	1108.5	17.8	64.0	25.0	52.0	42.9	75.0	10.0	2.0	3.0
Sudan	667.5	−4.5	42.0	10.5	149.0	18.7	13.0	19.0	5.9	5.7

Table 5.4   Continued

	Y (1)	ΔY (2)	E (3)	ΔE (4)	M (5)	ΔM (6)	L (7)	ΔL (8)	R₁ (9)	R₂ (10)
Swaziland	911.0	45.2	46.1	16.5	145.2	8.7	—	—	5.7	3.9
Tanzania	318.0	24.7	45.0	14.3	132.0	10.7	10.0	69.0	6.0	6.0
Thailand	1378.5	59.4	58.0	18.2	73.0	34.9	68.0	18.0	5.4	4.1
Tunisia	1460.5	71.5	53.9	24.9	127.2	30.2	16.0	46.0	6.0	5.0
Uganda	304.5	−27.0	47.0	−3.0	117.0	3.7	25.0	27.0	7.0	7.0
Yemen	742.0	81.6	38.6	10.4	187.8	13.6	3.0	18.0	7.0	7.0
Zaïre	291.0	−37.4	45.0	11.4	131.0	16.5	31.0	24.0	7.0	6.1
Zambia	752.5	−9.3	46.5	10.7	106.0	16.3	29.0	15.0	5.0	4.9
Zimbabwe	870.0	14.8	50.5	15.3	96.2	16.0	39.0	30.0	5.9	5.0

Key

Y: per capita gross national income; average of 1970 and 1980 values at 1980 international prices

ΔY: % change in Y over the decade 1970–80

E: life expectancy at birth in 1970

ΔE: life expectancy improvement index =

$$\frac{(\text{life expectancy at birth in 1980} - \text{life expectancy in 1970}) \times 100}{(80 - \text{life expectancy at birth in 1970})}$$

M: infant mortality rate in 1970

$-\Delta M$:   infant mortality improvement index =

$$\frac{(\text{infant mortality rate in 1970} - \text{infant mortality rate in 1980}) \times 100}{(\text{infant mortality rate} - 10)}$$

L: adult literacy rate in 1960

ΔL: adult literacy rate improvement index =
      (adult literacy rate in 1980 − adult literacy rate in 1960)

R_1:   political rights index, averaged over 1973–9 (decreasing with increasing liberty)

R_2:   civil rights index, averaged over 1973–9 (decreasing with increasing liberty)

Sources: World Bank (1983, 1989a); Taylor and Jodice (1983, tables 2.1 and 2.2).

not been able to locate adult literacy rate figures for a number of countries for the year 1970. I therefore present the figures for 1960 from World Bank (1983) in column (7). The net increase in literacy rates over the period 1960–80 is then provided in column (8). It will be noticed that all countries recorded an improvement.[17]

Columns (9) and (10) present indices of political and civil rights in our overall sample of 51 countries, averaged over the period 1973–9 (see Taylor and Jodice, 1983, tables 2.1 and 2.2). I commented earlier upon

[17] The coverage here is smaller. Figures for adult literacy rate are not available for a number of countries.

Table 5.5   Correlation matrix of indicators of improvements in living standards

	Y	ΔY	ΔE	ΔM	ΔL	R_1
ΔY	0.5883*					
ΔE	0.6578*	0.4113*				
ΔM	0.7546*	0.4129*	0.7917*			
ΔL	−0.0308	0.0660	0.2710*	0.0631		
R_1	0.5187*	0.2956*	0.2383*	0.4058*	−0.3769*	
R_2	0.4493*	0.2776*	0.2788*	0.3730*	−0.2806*	0.7290*

* Correlation is significant at a 5% level. The correlations are based on 51 observations, except for those for the changes in adult literacy, ΔL, which are based on 42 observations.

the extent to which poor people living in poor countries are deprived of such rights. Further comment is superfluous.

We begin with an analysis of rank orders. Table 5.5 consists of the 21 (Spearman) rank correlation coefficients associated with the seven columns of figures we are studying: namely, real national income per head and its percentage growth; improvements in life expectancy at birth, infant survival rates and adult literacy rates; and the extent of political and civil rights enjoyed by citizens. The correlation matrix tells us that the alleged choice between political and civil liberties and economic progress is a phoney kind of choice; that statistically speaking, societies aren't faced with this dilemma. But the matrix tells us more, and the morals that emerge appear to be these:

1. Political and civil rights are positively and significantly correlated with real national income per head and its growth, with improvements in infant survival rates, and with increases in life expectancy at birth. (The level of significance is 6.6 per cent for growth in real income per head. Each of the other figures is at a level of significance less than 5 per cent).
2. Real national income per head and its growth are positively and significantly correlated, and they in turn are positively and significantly correlated with improvements in life expectancy at birth and infant survival rates.
3. Improvements in life expectancy at birth and infant survival rates are, not surprisingly, highly correlated.
4. Political and civil rights are not the same. But they are strongly correlated.
5. Increases in the adult literacy rate are not related systematically at all to per capita incomes, or to their growth, or to infant survival rates. They are positively and significantly correlated to improvements in life expectancy at birth. But they are negatively and significantly correlated with political and civil liberties.

These observations suggest that literacy stands somewhat apart from other 'goods'. It doesn't appear to be driven with the three other socio-economic goods in our list. Furthermore, regimes that have bad records in political and civil rights are associated with good performances in this field. I have no explanation for this, which is compelling to me, but it is difficult to resist speculating on the matter. One possibility is that literacy has been used by a number of States in our sample to promote the acceptance of established order. This would seem plausible in rural communities, where the classroom provides a relatively cheap means of assembling the young and propagating the wisdom and courage of the political leadership. Education in this case would be a vehicle for ensuring conformity, not critical thinking. Nevertheless, there are beneficial by-products of education, and it is this aspect that I have emphasized in previous chapters. We observed earlier that not only do literacy and numeracy have beneficial effects on labour productivity on the farm, but female education has a strong influence on the well-being of children.

Of course, correlation observed in our data doesn't imply causation (each of the indices would in any case be 'endogenous' in any general political theory), and we should bear in mind that indices of political and civil liberties can change dramatically in a nation, following a *coup d'état*, a rebellion, an election, or whatever; and as we have used a six-year average index (the period 1973–9) for them in Table 5.4, we must be careful in interpreting the statistical results.[18] But I can't imagine that these difficulties provide reasons for ignoring civil and political liberties in estimations of the quality of life, even at this crude level of investigation. Subject to these obvious cautions, what the evidence seems to be telling us is that, statistically speaking, of the fifty-one poor countries on observation, those whose citizens enjoyed greater political and civil liberties also experienced larger improvements in life expectancy at birth, real income per head, and infant survival rates. This seems to me to be eminently worth knowing.

5.4 Wars and Strife

The indices of political and civil liberties we have used here are summary measures. They don't expose in any detail the kinds of deprivation a typical citizen suffers from. Constraints on one's freedom are often imposed by the State. Often enough, they are imposed by members of an opposing political, ethnic, or religious group. In times of strife, though, it may well be members of a person's own group who deprive him of his liberties.

---

[18] As a matter of fact, though, changes in political and civil liberties indices over the period 1973–9 were slight for most countries in the sample.

Violence is often inflicted by those involved directly in starting riots and waging wars for the purposes of righting wrongs.

Statistics of deaths and destitution don't offer us much guidance on the numbers of those who have been victims of civil disorders. We would expect infants and young children, women, and old people to be among them, but we would expect large numbers of young adult males to be among them too, those who found the activity of producing crops and raising families more purposeful than listening to local demagogues. And as soldiers themselves are among the most productive workers in an economy, wars take a heavy toll on this economic base.

Communal violence is a frequent occurrence in poor countries, a root cause of which frequently is opportunism on the part of civic and political leaders. In 1947 the Indian sub-continent was carved into three geographical (but two political) regions because the political leaders of the prime religious groups sought it. The partition of India was accompanied by communal violence in Bengal and the Punjab at a scale unprecedented in the sub-continent. In recent years communal violence has increased significantly in Kashmir and the Indo-Gangetic plain, and there are signs of political instability in several parts of India. As in other cases, it is possible to detect the progress of cumulative forces here: political advantages being sought through the incitation of communal strife, this in turn leading to greater State coercion to suppress such strife, this inevitably leading to greater strife, and so on.

In Sri Lanka, violence has marred its earlier (and as we saw quite spectacular) progress in general well-being. Elsewhere, in sub-Saharan Africa, threats to governments by disaffected communal or ethnic groups have resulted in large-scale violence on a number of occasions, for example in Zaïre, Nigeria, Sudan, Ethiopia, and Uganda. Violence has also characterized attempts at reunification across existing political boundaries by the Ewe (in Ghana and Togo), the Kongo (in Congo, Zaïre, and Angola), and the Somali (in Ethiopia, Somalia, and Kenya).[19]

Casualties of violence of the greatest urgency are, of course, those involving human lives, and it is the immediate human toll that is recorded most often. Since 1970 there have been sixty-three civil wars in what the World Bank refers to as developing countries (see World Bank, 1991a), directly claiming something like eight million lives. But the indirect toll is sizeable too, for another casualty of violence is the productive base. Wars and communal violence not only destroy private capital assets such as homes, looms, cattle, implements, seeds, and crops: they paralyse the infrastructure, particularly roads, cables, the water supply, health services,

---

[19] See Bates (1983) and Morrison, Mitchell and Paden (1989) for a wide-ranging quantitative study of the political economy of sub-Saharan Africa.

and, more generally, markets. For example, between a third to a half of the fall in food production in the territory of Eritrea in Ethiopia is attributable to the civil war there.

The chain of events resulting from the destruction of capital can take unusual turns. In a most revealing study, de Waal (1989) has shown that 100 000 of the deaths that occurred during the Dafur famine (in the Sudan) of 1984–5 were due not to starvation, but to a lack of potable water and sanitation. The greatest incidence of additional deaths occurred among children, the victims of diarrhoeas, measles, and malaria. The Dafur famine was a disease-ridden famine among those who were on the move in search of food and water. To be sure, these victims would have starved had they not fallen prey to diseases; the record shows only that diseases struck them first.

Government violence against citizens is also a commonplace occurrence in most poor countries. We noted this when commenting on indices of political and civil liberties, and we will confirm this when we interpret them in the Appendix to this chapter. Political instability is often allied to such violence. Over 50 of the approximately 115 so-called developing countries are run by militarily controlled governments. From 1958 to the end of 1981, there were more than fifty successful *coups* in twenty-five sub-Saharan countries, and more than fifty major attempts that proved unsuccessful.

Background environments which tend to encourage such instabilities are many and varied. They have been analysed with the help of cross-country data (Lipset, 1960; Janowitz, 1964; Russett, 1964; Adelman and Morris, 1967; Bienen, 1968; Gurr, 1968, 1970; J. Nagel, 1974; Siegelman and Simpson, 1977; Morrison, Mitchell and Paden, 1989). Inequalities in the distribution of land and sectional incomes have been found to be a contributing factor. Cultural pluralism (in particular, linguistic heterogeneity) is another source of tension, most especially in situations where one cultural group monopolizes economic or political power. The sub-Saharan experience suggests in addition that linguistic heterogeneity, when allied to a high concentration of wage-earners in the government sector, is associated with political instability. One plausible explanation for this is that the public sector is a source of political patronage. It promotes inequality. High rates of social mobilization (education, urbanization, exposure to information) allied to economic stagnation are another source of political instability. Moreover, greater political instability is associated with a higher growth of the military apparatus, most especially in countries that are linguistically heterogeneous. It appears though that greater political legitimacy of the State apparatus reduces the likelihood that linguistic heterogeneity will result in political instability. This indicates that cultural heterogeneity on its own isn't a problem, an encouraging conclusion in what is mostly a depressing literature (see Morrison, Mitchell and Paden, 1989, chapter 5).

The coercive powers of the State are enhanced by the accumulation of machinery for warfare. Excluding India and China, among those that are classified by the World Bank as 'low-income countries' (per capita gross national product less than US$480 in 1988), expenditure on the military as a fraction of government spending in 1988 was about 10.5 per cent. This should be contrasted with the corresponding figures for health and education, which were 2.8 and 9.0 per cent respectively (see World Bank, 1990, table 11). The Indian sub-continent, as always, is a telling case. In the late 1980s, government expenditure as a proportion of gross national product was 18 per cent in India and 22 per cent in Pakistan. As Table 5.6 shows, expenditure on the military as a fraction of government spending in 1988 was about 21.5 per cent in India, and 29.5 per cent in Pakistan. This is to be contrasted with the sums allocated to health and education, the contrast being particularly stark when we consider the lack of achievement in these countries in life expectancy at birth, infant survival, and literacy. India and Pakistan have fought three wars, and each country's military accumulation has been dominated by a display of paranoia about the other. Neither country can at all afford their armaments expenditures (Table 5.1), and yet there are no signs of a breakthrough in this long-drawn stalemate. There are no regional trade agreements in the offing, no collaborative ventures, and no serious cultural exchanges; nothing remotely like what has developed over the years among members of the European Community. That in earlier times each was supported by a rival super-power is on occasion offered as an excuse on its behalf. (The metaphor here is that of children at the mercy of drug-pushers.) But it is no excuse. Each is a sovereign nation. If their political and civic leaders had displayed the required courage and vision, the governments of India and Pakistan would have entered into negotiations long ago, and kept the super-powers at bay.

In recent years the most dramatic example of destructive behaviour has been the eight-year Iraq–Iran war. One estimate of the total cost in military expenditure and lost output during the first five years of the war

Table 5.6   Pattern of government expenditure in India and Pakistan, 1988

	% of government expenditure		
	Military	Health	Education
India	21.5	1.8	2.9
Pakistan	29.5	0.9	2.6

Source: World Bank (1990, table 11).

Table 5.7   Living standard indicators of some middle-income countries

	Y	E	M	L
Costa Rica	2650	75	18	94
Iraq	2813	64	68	88
Chile	3486	72	20	94
Iran	3922	63	64	55

Key
Y: 1985 real per capita national income in 1980 international prices.
E: Life expectancy at birth in 1988.
M: Infant mortality rate (per 1000) in 1988.
L: Literacy rate (per cent) in 1988.

Sources: for *Y*, Summers and Heston (1988); for *E, M,* and *L*, World Bank (1990).

amounted to a staggering US$415 billion (see World Bank, 1991a). To no end. Their borders as of now are pretty much what they were when the war began. There was no requirement of reasoned accountability to the citizens of the aggressor by its leadership. Granted, neither Iran nor Iraq is a poor country; on the other hand, no country can afford this waste. Costa Rica sits in the middle of a troubled region as well, but spends nothing on the military: she *has* no army. And she has not merely survived, she has thrived. As Table 5.7 shows, there is a wide variation in achievements even among middle-income countries.

5.5   Inequalities

A putative weakness in our quantitative assessment of the quality of life in this chapter is that these are international comparisons. Each country in the sample we have studied has been a unit of observation. I have said nothing directly about the distribution of well-being within a country, even though the quality of life ranges widely even within a locality, let alone a country.[20] In the previous chapter (Tables 4.1 and 4.2) we looked at intercontinental data to obtain an idea of the extent and incidence of absolute poverty and ill-being in the world. Those data reflected the starkest end of well-being inequality in the world. As such, they were insensitive to the various nuances in the idea of inequality. In any event, they revealed little about inequalities within countries.

The most common measure of living standard is real income. Thus, in quantitative empirical work economic development itself has often been

[20] To give an example, the infant mortality rate in India, as noted in Table 5.1, was about 94 per 1000 live births in the early 1980s; but among low-caste people in the shanty towns of Bombay and Delhi, it could be as high as 300 per 1000 live births.

identified with growth in real income per head, and the idea of inequality has been associated with one or other measure of income inequality.[21] These measures have varied in sophistication: from those that look at only one portion of distributions (e.g. percentage share of household income going to the poorest 20 or 40 per cent of households, or percentage share of income accruing to the richest 5 per cent of households, as in Kuznets, 1955; Adelman and Morris, 1973; Ahluwalia, 1976a, b; Lecaillon *et al.*, 1984; Yotopoulos, 1988), through summary measures (e.g. the Gini coefficient, as in Atkinson, 1970, 1975; Lydall, 1979; Yotopoulos, 1988) to the very refined (e.g. measures that feed the entire income distribution into a social evaluation function, as in Kolm, 1969; Atkinson, 1970).[22] In this chapter we have not studied income inequality within nations; rather, we have made an international comparison of general well-being. Nevertheless, our data allow us to infer something about inequalities within countries.

Per capita income says nothing about the distribution of income. But infant mortality rates, life expectancy at birth, and the literacy rate say a good bit about inequalities in resource allocation within countries. We observed in the previous chapter that, provided the public delivery system is not overly tainted, public health measures relative to armaments and luxury durables are not expensive. Even among poor countries, low figures for infant survival rates and life expectancy at birth are indicative of serious inequalities in the access to resources. Inequality in well-being is a recurrent theme of this book. It will appear in a number of guises in the chapters that follow.

---

[21] Of a vast literature, see e.g. Kuznets (1955, 1966), Dandekar and Rath (1971), Pen (1971), Fishlow (1972), Paukert (1973), Atkinson (1975), Cline (1975), Jain (1975), Ahluwalia (1976a, b), Kakwani (1980, 1981), Glewwe (1986), S. Robinson (1976), Frank and Webb (1977), Sahota (1978), Adelman (1980), Fields (1980), Bigsten (1983), Lindert and Williamson (1985), Yotopoulos (1985, 1988), and Papanek and Kyn (1986). A much-discussed theme in the interface of income inequality and economic growth has been the suggestion by Kuznets that there is an inverted U-shaped relationship between income inequality and the stage of economic development (as measured by income per head), in that income inequality increases in the early stages of development, and then falls when income per head is large. However, the definitive work of Anand and Kanbur (1989a, b) shows that there is nothing, after all, in this empirical claim. For a survey of the literature on income distribution and development, see Adelman and Robinson (1989).

[22] The pure theory of income inequality measures was developed in a highly original, remarkably complete, but as yet rarely cited article by Kolm (1969). The work was presented in 1966 at a Round Table conference of the International Economic Association on Public Economics. The article made such a break with the then existing research agenda in welfare economic theory that it remained unnoted. Kolm's results were later rediscovered independently in two steps by Atkinson (1970), and by Dasgupta, Sen and Starrett (1973) and Rothschild and Stiglitz (1973).

Table 5.8   Nutrition and health in Chile and Cuba, 1980

	Chile	Cuba
Programme		
National Health Service		
Number of hospital beds	34 000	35 000
Health centres	1 422	1 232
In-hospital deliveries		
(% of total deliveries)	(92)	(96)
Free distribution of milk and weaning foodstuff (0–6 years		
of age) (% of total population)	93	96
Homes for pregnant mothers from rural areas (number of		
homes)	42	63
Centres for recovery of severely malnourished infants		
(number of beds)	1 320	1 010
Health statistics		
Infant mortality rate (per 1000)	31	26
Life expectancy at birth (years)	67	66

Source: Mönckeberg (1983, tables I and II).

5.6   The Point of Cross-Country Studies

The results reported in Section 5.4 are statistical. They should be seen and interpreted as such. It is simply no good arguing against the force of such findings by pointing to the small number of countries where citizens have had their political and civil liberties severely restricted, and where economic progress has been spectacular, and then pointing in almost conditioned reflex to India as a case in contrast. There is no policy prescription flowing from such examples as Singapore and Hong Kong.[23] Nor is there a case for suggesting that one form of dictatorship necessarily displays greater social conscience than another. Table 5.8, taken from Mönckeberg (1983), shows how similar (and impressive) public health statistics were in Cuba and Chile in the early 1980s. These are countries with approximately the same population size (about 11 million at the time). Their national incomes in the early 1980s were not far apart either. But the nature of their dictatorships were quite dissimilar.[24]

This is only to show that there are exceptions to our findings, which are, after all, statistical. From our perspective here, not much follows from

[23] See e.g. Stern (1991: 429), who muses: '. . . it would be hard to be confident from comparative history that democracy is good for growth. Has it been democracy that has propelled Hong Kong and Singapore?' In the text I am implying that this is the wrong question to ask.

[24] Underwood (1983) contains a number of additional essays evaluating nutritional intervention programmes in Chile.

these exceptions. It is absurd to tell citizens to establish for themselves a one-party system of government, or to locate for themselves a reliable and efficient dictator. 'Good authoritarianism' cannot be willed by citizens, and bad authoritarian regimes are hard to dislodge. To be sure, had our main finding in Section 5.4 (as stated in moral 1 above) gone the other way, there would have been something urgent to discuss and to think through. As it is, the data give us no reason to question the instrumental virtues of civil and political liberties.

The limitations of statistical analysis more generally are often noted by social scientists, and there are many who find them mechanical, bloodless, and lacking in the kind of insight that only micro-historical studies can offer. There is something in this, but it is also good to recognize their strength. Statistical analyses such as ours should be seen only as a complementary route to the case-studies of nations and regions. Their strength lies in the fact that we avoid getting enmeshed in historical details, which can mesmerize us into thinking that whatever happens to be the case has had a certain inevitability about it. The claim that 'historical forces' have led poor societies to their present plight is one which, however true, is not only a conversation-stopper, but also a plank that has often been used by social scientists for condoning the most predatory of political regimes and oppressive of social practices. To take the claim too literally is to overlook the existence of choice, and thus responsibility. And that is to deny persons the respect that is owed to them.

Appendix: Political and Civil Rights Indices

In this appendix I will explain briefly the indices of political and civil rights used in this chapter. It is perhaps unnecessary to emphasize that any such index will have a subjective element, but it is necessary to remind ourselves that there is a subjective element in the estimation of any index, even the familiar index of national income, in the construction of which it is necessary to dispense with information, to arrange what is not dispensed with, and so forth. The fact that we have got used to dealing with economic and social statistics and are unfamiliar with political and civil ones should not make us blind to this. However, the indices themselves (as opposed to their estimates) are no less objective than national income. For example, freedom from police detention without charge, or the freedom to practise any religion, or the freedom to publish books and to read them, or the right to seek information and to teach ideas, or freedom from political press censorship, or freedom of movement within one's own country, or freedom from police searches of homes without warrants, or the right of women to equality (with men) of movement and physical protection and of access to occupations, or freedom of radio and television broadcasts from State control, or freedom from torture or coercion by the State—all are fairly concrete ideas, most especially perhaps for people who have suffered from a severe denial of any of them.

There is a reaction, which I have recently had from colleagues in response to the material of this chapter, that political and civil rights indices are culture-specific, that they merely reflect the well-known liberal obsession with the individual. It is not easy to know how best to respond to this. Perhaps the most direct response is that a concern with mortality tables or sex ratios (which we all seem to find revealing statistics) reflects no less a concern with the individual. In any event, the following are uncompromising facts: it is individuals who suffer from malnourishment, who fall ill, who grieve, who bear children, who are prevented from entertaining any ambition, who are tortured, and who die. It is fatuous to make a plea for one sort of concern and not for the others. Political and civil rights are political and civil rights, nothing else. That there are other rights merely tells us that we have studied an incomplete set of rights in this chapter. They don't cease to be important rights because of that.

Taylor and Jodice (1983: 60–1) provide an account of their scoring system for political rights. Those countries that score 1 enjoy political systems in which the great majority of persons or families have both the right and the opportunity to participate in the electoral process. Political parties in these countries may be formed freely for the purpose of making the right to compete for public office fairly general. Countries scoring 2 are those enjoying political systems with an open access, which, however, do not always work, owing to extreme poverty, a feudal social structure, violence, or other limitations on potential participants and results. However, as with countries coded 1, a leader or party can be voted out of office. A score of 3 is associated with political systems in which people may elect their leaders or representatives, but in which *coups d'état*, large-scale interference with election results, and frequent non-democratic procedures are at work. A score of 4 is associated with systems in which full democratic elections are blocked constitutionally or have little significance in determining power distributions; of 5, with systems in which elections are either closely controlled or limited, or in which the results have little significance. Countries scoring 6 have political systems without elections or with elections involving only a single list of candidates, in which voting is largely a matter of demonstrating support for the system, but where nevertheless there is some distribution of power. Finally, a score of 7 is associated with systems that are tyrannies, without legitimacy either in tradition or in international party doctrine.

Taylor and Jodice (1983: 64–5) also provide an account of their scoring system for civil rights. Those countries that score 1 enjoy political systems in which the rule of law is unshaken. Freedom of expression is both possible and evident in a variety of news media. Countries scoring 2 are those with political systems that aspire to the above level of civil rights, but are unable to achieve it because of violence, ignorance, or unavailability of the media, or because they have restrictive laws that seem to be greater than are needed for maintaining order. A score of 3 is associated with political systems that have trappings of civil liberty, and whose governments may be successfully opposed in the courts, although the courts may be threatened or have unresolved political deadlocks, and may have to rely often upon martial law, imprisonment, or sedition, and the suppression of publications. A score of 4 is awarded to political systems in which there are broad areas of freedom, but also broad areas of illegality. States recently emerging from a revolutionary situation or in transition from traditional society may easily fall into this category. Countries scoring 5 are those with political systems in which civil rights are often denied, but in which there is no doctrine on which the denial is based. The media are often weak, controlled by the government, and censored. Countries scoring 6 are those in which no civil rights are thought to take priority over the rights of the State, although criticism is allowed to be stated in limited ways. Finally, countries scoring 7 are those that suffer from political systems of which the outside world never hears criticism, except when it is condemned by the State. Citizens have no rights in relation to the State.

The Taylor–Jodice rankings of countries are based on scores for human rights published regularly by Freedom House, recent publications from which are Gastil (1984, 1986). The scores themselves are awarded to countries on the basis of a wide range of information, and the indices R_1 and R_2 in our text are composites of a number of indicators of political and civil rights, respectively. The estimates have been criticized for being impressionistic (see in particular, McCamant, 1981; Scoble and Wiseberg, 1981). However, it does not do to infer from this that these estimates should be rejected. The reason is that other people have also, independently, estimated political and civil rights, and the rankings of nations based on them are highly correlated with the rankings reported here.

For example, Humana (1983, 1986) has undertaken parallel work, in which forty specific freedoms were rated for each country in his sample and were used to assess political and civil rights. In contrast to the seven-point scale in the Taylor–Jodice compilation, Humana presents a four-point scale. It transpires that there is a very high correlation between Humana's scores on political and civil rights and the scores presented here. Banks (1989) reports correlation coefficients between the two scores on civil rights and the two scores on political rights to be 0.895 and 0.900, respectively. In any event, criticisms of Freedom House rankings have in the main been over their implied assessment of political and civil liberties in rich nations, not in poor ones. For the moment, then, we may as well use the rankings reported in Taylor and Jodice (1983) for aggregate quantitative work in this field when applied to poor countries.

There are a number of other exercises that can be conducted with quantitative indices on negative and positive rights and liberties. Banks (1989) presents a wide-ranging statistical analysis of cross-country human rights indices, identifying clusters of nations on the space of these rights, and also demonstrating that in the current data a few identifiable human-rights indicators capture most of the information we need to have on these matters. This literature reinforces the view that civil and political liberties can be given a quantitative footing and that their indices can, therefore, be placed on par with the socio-economic indicators of citizenship. Our aim in this chapter has been to do just that.

PART II

Allocation of Resources among Households:
The Standard Theory

6

Resource Allocation Mechanisms

6.1 *Resources and Property Rights*

In Chapters 2–5 I placed the allocation of resources in a context wider than is usual in the social sciences. I did this so as to enable the notion of human flourishing to occupy the centre-stage in our inquiry. The approach allowed us also to use a broad contractual argument to establish that it is the singular responsibility of the State to protect and promote general well-being. The State should be charged with implementing those distributions of benefits and burdens that go most towards furthering it. This duty needs to be undertaken by the State through a range of background institutions empowered to enforce just distributions of rights and resources. A concern with resource allocation is only part of a wider interest we all have in the distribution of liberties.

In this and the following chapters our concern will be narrower. I will take the background and the political and civil liberties in a society as given, and will concentrate on the allocation of resources. In doing so I will develop in this and the following six chapters what we may today call the *standard theory of resource allocation* and its extensions. Our findings in Chapters 2–5 will have warned us that such a research strategy has its risks, in that it is not possible to isolate the allocation of resources from the allocation of negative rights. Nevertheless, it is essential to work on a narrow footing if we are to arrive at an understanding of the phenomenon of destitution. The ideal procedure then would be to alternate between the wider viewpoint and the narrower outlook and search for a conceptual mechanism that converges.[1] Unhappily, I shall be unable to provide a formal account of any such mechanism. Our piecemeal approach, when backed by empirical findings on the distribution of negative rights and resources, should nevertheless give us a broad idea of a reasonable balance over conflicting values and competing claims. Along the way I will identify the kinds of policies the State in poor countries ought to be pursuing, and in the final chapter I will gather these together.

I take it then that there is a given structure of property rights in society.

---

[1] In a related context, Rawls (1972) calls the stationary point of any such process a *reflective equilibrium*.

We will subsequently note (Chapter 10) that in pastoral and dry agrarian societies much productive capital, particularly natural resources, is communally held, and we will see a rationale for this. However, even in these societies there are private property rights over a wide variety of productive assets. These include milch and draught animals, agricultural tools (such as ploughs, hoes, and spades), seeds, agricultural land and crops, household utensils, spinning wheels, implements for manufacturing 'cottage industry' products, and, in many situations, living accommodation.

The idea behind a private right over an asset is that an individual (or household) has exclusive title to it and its uses. This is an extreme notion, of course, and in all societies there are constraints on the use to which even private property resources may be put. Thus, you may own your house, but you may need permission to extend it. In some rural communities you may own the land you have cleared, but you can't sell it or bequeath it to whomever you wish without obtaining permission from the clan or village head. Then in some communities there are elaborate rules over the sharing of rights to resources offering multiple uses, such as land whose use is rotated over cultivation and grazing, or on which there are trees providing fuelwood and fruit. The piece of land may also have a water source. The person (or family line) who owns the land and cultivates it may have to acknowledge others' rights to some of the joint services it provides. For example, in some communities the agricultural crop is private property, but the post-harvest stubble is not (Feder and Noronha, 1987). Similarly, the agricultural land may be private property, but the produce of the trees may not be.

Inevitably, a great many rights over resources are incompletely specified. There may be many rights in need of overhaul if general well-being is to be promoted, and we will return to this issue later. But for now we take the underlying set of property rights to be given. By a *resource allocation mechanism* I will mean a rule that translates any combination of household utility functions and social well-being function, technological and ecological transformation possibilities, initial endowment of goods and services, the dispersion of information, and the environmental events that transpire into a final allocation of goods and services. In Chapter 3 I developed an account of this when explaining the notion of an equilibrium of a social system. In this and the following chapters we will study more concrete societies. I suggested earlier that for our purposes it makes sense to limit ourselves initially to two extreme types of agencies: households and the State. We will consider intermediate layers, such as village communities, in later chapters.

It is simplest to think of single-membered (or, what is analytically equivalent), autocratic households. We are not restricted to them, though. By a *household utility function* in the definition of a resource allocation mechanism, I mean a numerical representation of the ordering on the basis of which a household's actual decisions are made. Whether household decisions are made by a patriarch or a matriarch, or whether it is an outcome of bargaining among members of the household or is based on household welfare, is immaterial to our present discussion. But it is not immaterial to the interpretation of the results we will report in Chapter 7. Nor will it be immaterial to later discussions of allocations within the household. We will study these questions in Chapters 11–12.

The reason I am including the social well-being function in the domain of resource allocation mechanisms is that it allows us to include the government as an active party. This way the notion has a large reach, and it captures a wide range of societal forms. We should also note that for any structure of property rights there are many possible resource allocation mechanisms. By the same token, a resource allocation mechanism sustains different patterns of final allocations for different assignments of property rights.

6.2 *Markets and Market Mechanisms*

A key ingredient of resource allocation mechanisms is the market. By a market, I mean an institution that makes available to interested parties the opportunity to negotiate courses of actions. Thus, by a malfunctioning market I will mean a market where such negotiations are not possible, that is, where the market is missing (because, say, property rights are vague, or the costs of establishing the market are high, or whatever), or where negotiations can at best be carried out partially (because, say, the parties don't know one another well, and they conclude their negotiation without being able to exploit all possible gains from trade: see J. Farrell, 1987), or where they are overly one-sided. (The latter allows us to capture the distributional aspects of rights and resource allocations in bargains and transactions.) Nothing will be lost in our adopting what may seem an absurdly wide definition of markets. And there are advantages. Our wide definition will encourage us to interpret a number of activities within what are traditionally called 'non-market' institutions (such as the household and extended family), and a variety of social norms in rural communities (such as 'reciprocity'), as transactions in goods and services. We will find this a useful viewpoint.

Of all resource allocation mechanisms, the *market mechanism* is the one most commonly discussed. Even though it is rarely defined in formal terms, its broad outlines are familiar. The idea is that the State plays a very restricted role in the socio-economic sphere of life. Regarding other spheres, however, matters are unspecified. We are usually not told of the extent to which citizens enjoy political and civil liberties in a society where resources are allocated by the market mechanism. So we will ignore the extent of such liberties for the moment. By a market mechanism I will mean a resource allocation mechanism in which the State restricts its activities in the socio-economic sphere to facilitating the operation of private markets. This it does by developing and enforcing commercial laws (e.g. the law of contracts), protecting private property rights (e.g. guaranteeing the safety of legitimately acquired merchandise), and so forth. Professor Nozick's Minimal State sustains a market mechanism (Nozick, 1974). But market mechanisms are not limited to the Minimal State; a society where political democracy is absent can also support a market mechanism.

A special distinguished example of this is the *competitive market mechanism*. The version whose analysis is to all intents and purposes now complete is the one where all commodities have markets, and where all parties are price-takers in these markets. (For expositions of varying levels of technicality, see Koopmans, 1957; Debreu, 1959; Arrow and Hahn, 1971; Hildenbrand, 1974; Bliss, 1975; Hildenbrand and Kirman, 1976). In the following chapter we will review some of its formal properties, and place it within a wider social context.[2]

Defence, and in many instances total advocacy, of market mechanisms, with their attendant sets of private property rights, has ranged from supremely instrumental grounds (for example, that under certain conditions they sustain allocations of resources that are Pareto-efficient: see Chapter 7) to those that see their exclusive and unfettered play as a requirement of any society taking individual rights seriously (Nozick, 1974). Neither viewpoint is justified. This was a central implication of Chapter 2. In Chapter 1 we noted that the theory of competitive market mechanism assumes certain minimal positive rights to be protected by the State. This it does for the most part by assuming that each household enjoys initial rights over sufficient amounts of commodities. Of particular interest is potential labour power, which almost every person may be said to possess, even were he to possess nothing else. In Chapter 16 we will see that in poor countries self-ownership of potential labour power isn't enough for a market mechanism (and not merely the competitive market mechanism) to promote basic liberties. The problem is that the labour power realized by an otherwise assetless person under a market mechanism

---

[2] The game-theoretic concept of a core is another example of a market mechanism. There is an intimate connection between the core and the competitive market mechanism in an economy where individuals are self-regarding. In a large society they sustain, roughly speaking, the same set of resource allocations. Nozick (1974), Hildenbrand and Kirman (1976), and Aumann (1987b) have excellent, non-technical discussions of this. However, the bargaining process leading to a core allocation of resources is not explicitly modelled in the theory. Gale (1986a, b) has shown how competitive equilibrium allocations of resources can emerge from an explicit bargaining situation.

is not necessarily marketable if the distribution of property rights is overly unequal to begin with. But this means that some reallocation of property rights may prove necessary if market mechanisms are to get going and realize the instrumental virtues often claimed for them. That in poor countries the bulk of those who are most vulnerable to acute and chronic deprivation are from the assetless has been much documented (Cline, 1975; K. Griffin, 1976, 1978; Griffin and Khan, 1977; ILO, 1977; Berry and Cline, 1979; Chen, Chowdhury and Huffman, 1979; Fields, 1980; Sen, 1981b; Kutcher and Scandizzo, 1981; FAO, 1987; Ghai and Radhwan, 1983; Herring, 1983; Sinha, 1984; Lipton, 1985; Ravallion, 1987a; Bardhan and Srinivasan, 1988; World Bank, 1990). This evidence provides indirect confirmation of the theory I will develop in Chapter 16. I conclude for now that, when seen purely in instrumental terms, market mechanisms do not suffice. Under the terms of a social contract, the State is obliged to do more than merely sustain a market mechanism.

On the other hand, we miss a good deal when we view markets purely in instrumental terms. Markets are themselves an expression of an entire class of liberties, namely freedom of association, freedom of movement, freedom to develop one's own talents, freedom to exchange legitimately acquired goods and services, and so forth. Thus, while the State is obliged to go beyond market mechanisms, it is also bound by the terms of the social contract not to suppress them systematically. The State has to tread a delicate line, facilitating the formation of markets, and at the same time complementing markets in a number of ways (see below).

Neither political freedom nor extensive civil liberties are implied by market mechanisms (see, e.g. Lindblom, 1977). Nevertheless, there are grounds for thinking that the extent of government accountability, the reach of civil liberties, and the functioning of market mechanisms are connected. In a study conducted on the Peruvian economy, de Soto (1989) has estimated that, as a consequence of bureaucratic controls on the establishment of new businesses, up to 50 per cent of Peru's active population and about 60 per cent of its working hours are devoted to illegal activities—all of which accounts for something like 40 per cent of the country's gross national product. Needless to say, none of this gets acknowledged in Peru's national income statistics. With justification, de Soto calls this sort of resource allocation mechanism 'crony capitalism', where an unaccountable (though democratically elected) government imposes economic controls of complexity and detail reaching Byzantine proportions. The situation in Peru would appear to be stable. Because entrepreneurs in the illegal sector have no legal title to their businesses, or access to credit and insurance facilities from the legal sector, they individually have no incentive to exert political pressure to bring about a change in the government's controls. Democratically elected governments, unless they can be held accountable by independent bodies at every level, are not immune to activities aimed at syphoning hidden 'rents' in an economy. Nor are they immune to pressures for creating rents, which are then syphoned by interested parties. Authoritarian regimes in general, and dictatorships in particular, are of course capable of operating at a much higher scale of corruption than unaccountable democracies. We looked at some examples of this in the previous chapter.

6.3   *Culture and Market Transactions*

There are goods whose characteristics depend upon their not being marketable, 'love', 'loyalty', 'autonomy', and 'bodily integrity' being prime examples. A number of institutions, such as the family, kinship, and village communities, in part form networks where such goods are created and exchanged. These institutions fall somewhere between the individual and the State.[3] We will omit such goods from our analysis in this and the following chapters. I shall also take civil and political liberties as established, and not subject to bargains. We will be interested only in the allocation of those commodities that have direct instrumental value— commodities like food, clothing, shelter, legal service, characteristics of work, transport, resources for health care, information, means of entertainment, and many other things besides. We will call them *economic goods.*

This said, we should not overlook that the household, kinship, and the temple or mosque or church are also much involved in the production and distribution of economic goods. No doubt the anthropologist's notion of 'gift exchange' is different from the idea of 'market exchange'; but what is being 'transacted' in a gift exchange is not merely a smile, a bonding, and a promise of good faith: economic goods are involved as well. So we will view the phenomena of 'gift exchange' and 'patron–client interchange' as involving transactions in economic goods. This strategy may not take us all the way to an understanding of such phenomena, but it will take us a good way. In any event, to not so regard such phenomena would be to put blinkers on; it would be to disregard a large common core in the human experience, among which are the need for survival and, often, the search for improvements in the conditions of life. This explains why I have adopted a wide definition of markets here.

We will not be studying every type of activity individuals are engaged in, only a restricted set. For example, we will not explore the idea that cultures can be codified in terms of the way symbols are manipulated. Nor

---

[3] They are a central concern in anthropology. Among non-anthropological writings, see Arrow (1972) and Rawls (1972) for wide-ranging discussions of these goods.

will I take the position that culture is wholly instrumental to the realization of biological necessities. In any event, the approach we will pursue here does not amount to ecological functionalism.[4] Instead, it will offer a large role to historical accidents in giving shape to the detailed way resources are allocated in a society (Chapters 8, 12 and *12). But we wish to understand how established resource alllocation mechanisms are sustained. This involves analysis, not history.

The account of transactions to be developed in this and the next chapter will be of impersonal (or anonymous) market transactions. Transactions will be assumed possible at prices that are independent of transactors' names. (Prices in many situations will be only implicit.) This is a far cry from the personalized nature of many transactions in agrarian and pastoral societies of poor countries, and we will look into this in Chapters 8–10. Of course, all societies rely on a mix of market transactions and non-market interchanges; and within the broad class of market transactions there is throughout the world a mix of personalized and impersonal transactions. But the composition of these mixes varies across societies. Even the poorest of traditional societies are known, and have been known, to sustain market transactions (see e.g. Malinowski, 1921, 1960; Sahlins, 1968; Colson, 1979), and it is pure romanticism to think otherwise. Where poor countries appear distinctive is in the ratio of the value of personalized to impersonal market transactions, which would seem to be much higher there than in modern industrial democracies. It is then tempting to define differences in these mixes in terms of differences in culture.

No reductionist research programme could countenance the use of 'culture' as an explanatory variable. Instead, it would try to explain cultural differences in terms of differences in finer primitives, such as individual motivation, ecological circumstances, transaction costs, pure historical accidents, and so forth.[5] The problem is that individual motivation is in turn under the influence of cultural values and norms. There is a two-way influence here. So pure reductionism won't do. Now dynamic processes with such mutual feedback in an environment containing a multitude of actors are a commonplace in the social sciences. Cultural anthropologists are, however, often suspicious of the coherence of such models. Writing about two contrasting paradigms of anthropological theories, Sahlins (1976, p. 55) says:

The alternatives in [the] venerable conflict between utilitarianism and a cultural account may be broadly phrased as follows: whether the cultural order is to be

---

[4] See Sahlins (1976, ch. 2) for a criticism of ecological functionalism in the form it appears in Malinowski (1921, 1960).

[5] In the natural sciences reductionism is often identified with the hypothesis of linearity, the assumption that the whole equals the sum of the various parts of the system being studied. See e.g. Davies (1988). This is not how I am using the term in the text.

conceived as the codification of man's actual purposeful and pragmatic action; or whether, conversely, human action . . . is to be understood as mediated by cultural design, which gives order at once to practical experience, customary practice, and the relationship between the two. The difference is not trivial, nor will it be resolved by the happy academic conclusion that the answer lies . . . on both sides (i.e. dialectically).

I have not fully grasped Professor Sahlins's account of why the difference can't be resolved dialectially, but I have the sense that he fears it is incoherent. This it is not.

Any process that ties individual motivations to social values and norms, and back again, would be expected to be *path-dependent*. The term is almost self-explanatory. The broad idea is that the consequences to an actor of her actions depend on how often people have undertaken similar actions in the past. This can imply that a social system's long-run tendencies depend upon where it is today. In path-dependent processes the past is present in the future. History (indeed, pure accidents) assumes a strong role in any such programme of research (Schelling, 1978; David, 1985, 1988, 1991, 1992a; Anderson, Arrow and Pines, 1988; Arthur, 1989; Milgrom, Quian and Roberts, 1991; we will study this further in Chapter *12). The approach is very different from crude functionalism.

One such programme has explored the thesis that the mix of institutions supporting production and exchange in a society is dependent upon relative transaction costs (Coase, 1960; Demsetz, 1966, 1967, 1972; J. R. Hicks, 1968; Furubotn and Pejovich, 1972, 1974; Williamson, 1985; North, 1986, 1988a, b, 1989; Ensminger, 1990; Feder and Feeny, 1991; Migot-Adholla, 1991). Impersonal markets are seen to develop only when transactions are supported by the law of contract and are backed by the rule of law. This ensures that product quality (not only chemical and physical properties, but also date of delivery) is not much at risk despite the anonymity of sellers. Otherwise, many vital markets remain unestablished, and when they do get established they are sustained by extra-government enforcement agencies such as, for example, the Mafia in Sicily (Gambetta, 1988, 1992). Similarly, the availability of infrastructure, such as roads, ports, and cables, reduces transaction costs. Larger markets being reachable, a greater division of labour is then possible.[6] Large markets also facilitate the diffusion of ideas. Increased division of labour and a greater absorption of new ideas together propel growth in productivity (see below). This in turn leads to increases in the standard of living.

It is a mistake to think that the model of the competitive market economy (Chapter 7) is devoid of institutional content. (For the suggestion

---

[6] For a formalization of the idea that the division of labour depends upon the extent of the market, see Dasgupta and Stiglitz (1980a), Dasgupta (1986b), and Locay (1990).

that it is, see North, 1989). The model assumes a range of background institutions for supporting transactions, for example the enforcement of contracts. It assumes that the costs of establishing markets, often fixed costs, are low in comparison with other costs, and that the State has the means and ability to protect property rights and to enforce the terms of contracts that are voluntarily entered into.

The growth of impersonal market transactions in poor countries is necessary for long-run improvements in the standard of living. Both history and economic analysis tell us this. In subsequent chapters we will look at other institutions, such as kinship and the village community, as mediators of production and exchange in economic goods. These markets are by the nature of things *thin*. (I am borrowing the terminology from Arrow, 1971a). They involve few transactors; often they involve only bilateral exchanges of goods. Transactions in these institutions are personalized (Chapters 8–9). Thinness is a weakness, not only because of the reasons we have identified (they don't encourage much division of labour, and they are not propitious for the diffusion of knowledge across distant regions), but also because power relations are overly personalized. Consequently, they are highly asymmetrical (see Rudra, 1984; and Chapter 9 below). Personal service, for example, is particularly subject to abuse in poor countries.

6.4 *Externalities: Public Goods and Common Property Resources*

The definition of markets I have chosen to work with here is unusually wide. This has an advantage, in that we are not limited to searching only for impersonal transactions when studying economic relationships. On the other hand, it poses the danger of swallowing within its net pretty much any type of transaction. Thus, my definition allows us to entertain the thought that, if it is possible for all parties to get together and bargain, the market mechanism will sustain a Pareto-efficient outcome; for if it were not to (or so it might be argued), the grand coalition of all parties would block it.

This is not a good argument. The statement is loose (the bargaining process isn't specified) and, unless qualified, it is simply false. One reason we appealed to contractual theories of the State was to sharpen the statement. (As we have seen in earlier chapters, there were other reasons too.) Contractual theories formalize the hypothetical coming together of the grand coalition of all parties. We have already postulated an elaborate set of background institutions. We may as well then be flexible in our interpretation of transactions and allow ourselves the thought that market mechanisms cannot necessarily be relied upon to attain efficient allocations of resources. One of the duties of the State is to aid markets in achieving this, just as its other duties are to provide services that markets aren't at all equipped to provide, such as a just distribution of benefits and burdens. Thus, even within the category of economic goods there is a range of vital commodities whose provision ought not to be left to market mechanisms. Our task in this section is to identify them.

Goods and services such as security from external threats, laws of property and contracts, the means for the enforcement of contracts, and the protection of persons or groups against force, fraud, theft, and violence are essential to basic liberties. Among many other things we identified in Chapters 2–3, they enable interested parties to engage in market transactions. Any political philosophy that acknowledges the right of citizens to equality in basic negative liberties will insist that the State be empowered with the task of providing these essential services, and be accountable for them. This is the way to ensure that their distribution does not depend upon citizens' abilities to pay.

It is significant that these commodities are jointly consumable: consumption by one party does not, as a reasonable approximation, reduce the amount available for consumption by others. Another example of jointly consumable goods is knowledge (or, more technically, information: see below). Some of these goods possess the additional property that no one can feasibly be excluded from consuming them once they have been produced. Commodities satisfying both these properties are called *public goods*. All citizens get to consume the same amount of a public good. (That a public good is jointly consumable does not, however, mean that it is equally useful to all.) National security and a community's non-material cultural heritage are prime examples. It is not possible to enforce private property rights on public goods, even when they can be defined. This means that in practice not all interested parties, acting individually, are capable of negotiating the production and protection of such goods. Markets on their own do not constitute the right resource allocation mechanism for the supply and maintenance of public goods. In Chapter *6 I will present a formal account of this observation.[7]

Immunization against contagious diseases, sewage systems, and sanitation in general are examples of approximate, albeit spatially localized, public goods. They are not quite public goods, but they nevertheless involve strong *externalities*. The benefit to me, for example, in getting myself immunized against measles falls short of the overall benefits this act confers, since others in my locality are as a result that much more protected

---

[7] In England the movement to enact laws that make monuments and buildings of historical importance on private land the nation's property began only in the 19th c. But the prevailing conception of private property was so all-embracing and unyielding that Parliament did not, until this century, pass a law that would transfer monuments of historical importance into what we will call the public realm. See Sax (1990).

against the disease. So my personal interest in getting myself immunized falls short of the general interest. Private action here has an external effect. If left solely to individual choice, the extent of immunization in a society will typically fall short of the socially desirable amount. This provides a now well-known argument for State involvement (Pigou, 1920; Arrow, 1971a; Meade, 1973; and Chapter *6).

In a weaker form, literacy and numeracy also have elements of this feature. When a person becomes literate and numerate she increases her own productivity. At the same time, she increases the productivity of those others who are literate and numerate; it makes it that much easier for them to communicate with her. In this respect (and only in this respect) literacy and numeracy are rather like telephones and fax machines: they display *network externalities*. Conformity to social norms and cultural values also generates network externalities. The value here lies in making it easier for each party to predict others' behaviour. It also makes it less necessary for people to monitor each others' actions and to verify that others have done what they said they would. It reduces both uncertainty and transaction costs.

Knowledge is not a public good. While it is jointly usable, exclusion is up to a point feasible; it is possible legally to prevent people from making use of what they know. Patents and copyrights protect private rights to knowledge. An alternative method of excluding others from making use of what one knows is secrecy. This can be an effective way of 'cashing in' on the fruits of one's newly acquired knowledge, at least for a while. Information about new commodities and new techniques of production (e.g. high-yielding varieties of wheat and rice), about ecological matters, about external markets, and so on are vital commodities in poor countries. They are essential for the undertaking of innovation, production, trade, and for the adoption of superior technologies. While they are not exactly public goods, they resemble public goods more than they do goods like tea, sugar, rice, and fish. So we will treat them as though they are public goods, and we will pay special attention to them in what follows.[8]

A number of commodities we are calling public goods are really public 'bads', environmental pollution being a prime example. They share with public goods their 'publicness', but are quite dissimilar as regards their desirability.

There is another class of economic goods, different from public goods, that is of importance for poor people in poor countries. They happen

---

[8] For analyses of alternative resource allocation mechanisms for the production, dissemination, and use of knowledge, see M. Polanyi (1943–4), Nelson (1959), Arrow (1962a), and Dasgupta and David (1987, 1991). The latter two papers explore both historically and analytically the institutions of science and technology as producers of knowledge. For a mathematical account of a number of ideas developed there, see Dasgupta (1988a, b).

usually to be renewable natural resources; forests, coastal waters, threshing grounds, grazing lands, village ponds and tanks, rivulets and aquifiers are prime examples. As with public goods, private property rights to these commodities are often difficult to define. Even when they are definable, they are difficult to enforce. So they are *common property resources*. However, unlike public goods, consumption of these commodities is competitive: it is possible for one party to increase its consumption at the expense of others' consumption. In Chapter 10 we will see that, even though it is possible to assign private property rights to them in some cases (e.g. local forest lands), it is usually undesirable to do so.

From the economic point of view, the central common characteristic of public goods and many common property resources is the difficulty they pose for the enforcement of private rights to them. Some four decades of work in the theory of externalities has built on this fact to elucidate reasons why the provision of public goods and the use of common property resources ought not to be left to purely individualistic allocation mechanisms; why allocative decision at the collective level is required. I shall present a formal account of the problem of the commons in Chapter *6.[9]

The appropriate level of this collectivity will depend upon the geographical extent of the 'publicness' or 'commonality' of the good in question. I will argue later (Chapter 10) that, while the State ought to ensure that local decisions aren't usurped by the powerful, decisions on the control of local common property resources, such as village ponds, grazing, and forest lands and rivulets, and of local public goods, such as local public order, should be left to the village community. But in impoverished regions funding for the production of local common property resources, such as bore holes and irrigation canals, needs to come from the State.

Two types of collective policies for public goods suggest themselves. The first is free collective provision, possibly State provision, the cost of production being recovered through taxes (Samuelson, 1954; Stiglitz and Dasgupta, 1971; Atkinson and Stern, 1974). The second is to leave the provision to the private sector, but have the State subsidize its production. (The subsidy would in fact be a tax in the case of a public bad.) This is a Pigovian subsidy (Pigou, 1920). At the level of analysis we are pursuing here, it does not matter which of these two routes a community chooses to follow. In practice it does matter, and it has to do with the conditions of production, which can vary greatly across public goods. The production of knowledge, for example, involves different considerations from the supply of national security.

---

[9] The literature on public goods is far larger than the one on common property resources. The modern classics on public goods are Samuelson (1954), Musgrave (1959), and Arrow (1971a). Starett (1988) and Stiglitz (1988a, 1989) are recent, more formal accounts. To the best of my knowledge, Gordon (1954) is the first clear statement of possible allocation failure when a commodity is a common property resource.

The analysis of common property resources is a bit different, and two collective policies suggest themselves: charges for their use, and quantitative controls on their use. A third would be to privatize the resource if it is feasible to do so. This last is often advocated in the literature on public economics. But it doesn't mean that the prescription is right. In Chapter 10 we will look at these alternative policies and judge their relative merits.

6.5 *Infrastructure and Fixed Costs*

There is another category of goods, such as roads, electricity, cables, ports, irrigation canals, and potable water supplies, whose availability is a precondition for the growth of anonymous markets, and for the production and distribution of raw materials and outputs (Rogers and Shoemaker, 1971; L. A. Brown and Lentneck, 1973). They form an economy's *infrastructure*. Wilbanks (1980), for example, has used evidence from India to show that accessibility of roads is a significant factor in the rate of adoption of new ideas even at the intra-district level. Now it is a contingent fact that the production of infrastructure involves large fixed costs relative to the size of the population involved in their use. (Commodities that we have labelled public goods also often satisfy this property.) In rural communities of poor countries they are often large relative to average income, which is another way of saying the same thing. Commodities whose production involves large fixed costs are called *natural monopolies*.

Potable water and fuel prompt greater urgency than the rest: they are basic needs. But over the medium and long run, general infrastructure is also a critical set of commodities. Poor countries usually suffer from a lack of infrastructure. For example, World Bank (1989b: 25–9) traces the low return on investment in sub-Saharan Africa in substantial measure to the paucity of infrastructure. At an extreme is the remarkable fact, even by the appalling standards of the worst of poor countries, that the Sudan, with a population of about twenty-five million and an area of about 2.5 million sq. km. (which is about as large as the United States east of the Mississippi River), even now has only about 3000 miles of roads, 2500 miles of which are gravel or unpaved tracks. It is not difficult to imagine the role this paucity has played in the incidence of famines there. (On this see Bonner, 1988).

It can be argued, both analytically and by an appeal to evidence, that the production and use of infrastructure is hampered if decisions are left exclusively to the private sector (Scherer, 1980; Stiglitz and Mathewson, 1986; Tirole, 1988; Panzar, 1989). The reason is that, because of large fixed costs, the average cost of production is less than the marginal cost when the level of output is optimal. This means that setting price equal to marginal cost of production entails losses, something a private producer would wish to avoid. This forms the classical reason for government involvement in the production of infrastructure.[10] However, the theory of contestable markets, developed in Baumol, Panzar and Willig (1982), has identified circumstances in which a natural monopoly could well be left to the private sector, the role of government in this theory being relegated to ensuring that the monopolist faces potential competition. If the market is contestable, the natural monopolist sets price equal to average cost of production, a policy a nationalized natural monopoly would follow were it instructed to balance its books. But it can be shown that the necessary circumstances for contestability are especially stringent, in that they require the structure of production to involve no *sunk costs*; that is, costs which are irrecoverable (see J. Farrell, 1986; Dasgupta and Stiglitz, 1988a). When an important component of industry costs is irrecoverable (advertisement and research and development are prime examples), private natural monopoly is not an efficient institution. This on its own doesn't imply that the industry should be nationalized. Nationalization creates its own problems, and one must reckon with losses caused by government mismanagement. (For an assessment of the empirical evidence on this, see Cubbin, 1988; Vogelsang, 1990).

Some forms of government regulation (for example pricing and geographical reach), allied to an encouragement of potential competition, are required if production of a natural monopoly is left to the private sector. Regulation of private natural monopoly is the norm in the United States. An alternative is nationalization. The rule that the State enterprise would ideally follow would be for it to determine the optimal level of output, set price equal to the marginal cost of production, and ensure that its losses are covered by a lump-sum subsidy from the State. (The Electricité de France is a state-owned public utility following something like this rule.) It is unlikely to work in poor countries, where governments are strapped for revenue. In any case, optimal lump-sum taxes are not feasible even in advanced industrial economies (Chapter 7). So the correct thing to do is to set price equal to marginal cost of production plus a tax. The magnitude of the unit user tax depends on the necessary revenue to be collected, the pattern of consumption by income classes, and so forth. For very poor regions the infrastructure has to be supplied free of charge, the expenditure being financed by general taxation. But these are matters of institutional detail over which it is hard to theorize.

Credit markets are notoriously imperfect in poor countries; they are especially thin (see Chapter 9). Moreover, because they would suffer badly

---

[10] See Guesnerie (1975), D. Brown and Heal (1979, 1983), Beato and Mas-Colell (1985), Dierker (1986), and D. Brown, Heller and Starr (1990). For an overview of the analytical foundations of decentralized planning in the face of increasing returns to scale in production, see D. Brown (1990).

from the problem of 'moral hazard' (Chapter 9), rental markets for durable commodities, such as bullocks, tractors, and bicycles, are for the most part non-existent. Together, they imply that such goods are indivisible. Unless some other institution were to be established to stand in place of credit and rental markets, households would have to save from current income for the purchase of indivisible investments. This would be hopelessly inefficient: savings would have to lie idle while households separately accumulated funds for their purchases. Rural communities in poor countries have for long devised rotating savings and credit associations (Roscas) as a means of overcoming this inefficiency.[11] One version has members committed to depositing a fixed sum of money in each period of life of the Rosca to a common 'pot'; in every period lots are drawn and the pot is allocated randomly to one of the members. (The period and the amount contributed by each member in each period is chosen on the basis of the number of contributors and the cost of the durable good.) Once a member has won the pot, his name is withdrawn from all future draws. But he keeps on contributing, and the Rosca continues until all members have received the pot once.

And there are other versions of Rosca. None of the existing versions supports an optimal allocation rule (on this see Besley, Coate and Loury, 1992), but they all take the form of a collective savings association. This is an example of the way collective associations at the local level can help mitigate a resource allocation problem occasioned by the indivisibility of certain durable commodities.

6.6 *Private and Public Realms, and Private and Collective Goods*

There is, finally, a class of commodities to which people have positive rights, such as nutrition, shelter, clothing, primary and secondary education, basic health care, and legal services. Under the terms of the social contract, an individual's access to them at an acceptable level should not depend upon an ability to pay.[12] Within this class of commodities, education, health care, and legal services share the feature that, unlike nutrition, clothing, and to a lesser extent shelter, they are not easily transferable among individuals. This means that it is possible for these goods to be allocated in *kind*; no illicit trade in one's entitlements could vitiate the original intent of the social contract.

---

[11] See Geertz (1962), and for a fine analytical treatment of the institution in its various existing forms, see Besley, Coate and Loury (1992).

[12] We studied the reasoning behind this in Chs. 2–5. In the previous section we noted that the argument for State involvement in public health care and primary and secondary education in fact goes beyond this, since immunization, literacy, and numeracy involve externalities.

A social contract provides citizens with an opportunity to pre-commit themselves to an access to these goods. Pre-commitment is a rational strategy under the circumstances of such contracts, because citizens recognize that poverty typically prevents people from obtaining education for their children, and from protecting themselves against the exigencies of life. It does not do to argue that even poor parents have the option of borrowing from the market to buy education and health insurance for their children. Credit markets are particularly imperfect in poor countries. Poor people don't possess much by way of collateral. Furthermore, as it is embodied in a person, education (i.e. human capital) does not function well as a collateral. One can't easily borrow against it. We noted this in Chapter 4.

These considerations suggest that a social contract would establish terms for the direct provision of primary and secondary education and health care; it would not recommend income transfers, enabling people to purchase them. Contractees will recognize that, were income to be transferred for their purchase, individuals might end up not purchasing them. This is where pre-commitment plays its hand. It is not that social contracts would not countenance general income transfers to enable people to have access to other things (see Chapter 7), nor that the private provision of education and health care would be forbidden. It is rather that the contract would envisage guaranteed access to these goods to be honoured in kind, not in cash. This it can do because provision of the guarantees in kind could be expected to stick. It is difficult to sell one's rights to immunization, for example; or one's place in school: the State can observe the fraud.

While nutrition and clothing are also basic needs, they are easy to market. Moreover, preferences differ considerably over their characteristics (people have divergent tastes), and this matters. Distribution in kind is generally a wrong allocation mechanism for these rights. Income guarantees or commodity subsidies are more reasonable ways of meeting them. There are exceptions, of course, most notably when children's well-being is involved. Here, commodity-specific income allowances for poor households (e.g. food stamps), free school meals, and subsidized school uniforms may be the right ingredient of the chosen allocation mechanism (see Chapter 7).

We can now usefully divide commodities into two categories. The first consists of those goods and services whose production and allocation should fall within the domain of private markets, that is, transactions among households and private firms. We may call the social environment within which such decisions are made the *private realm*. Decisions governing the production, maintenance, and allocation of commodities in the second category fall under what we will call the *public realm*. We will refer to the former as *private goods*, the latter as *collective goods*.

By the public realm I don't mean the realm of the State only; I mean institutions at 'lower' levels as well, including religious organizations, village communities, charities, non-governmental agencies, and so forth. Collective goods include public goods (e.g. laws of contract, a community's non-material cultural heritage, the institution of government), non-rivalrous goods (e.g. knowledge, and cultural artefacts), merit goods (e.g. school-books), natural monopolies (e.g. general infrastructure), goods involving significant externalities (e.g. common property resources, public health), and so forth. In the private realm are the large numbers of goods and services whose consumption should be tied sensitively to individual pre-ferences and requirements, and whose determination requires private information about such matters. Income guarantees are a means of ensuring that citizens have an access to those basic needs (e.g. food and clothing) falling within the private realm.

This is a rough and ready division, of course. So rough that, in practice, a number of commodities will co-exist in the two realms. For example, that health measures should fall within the public realm does not imply that it should be banned from the private realm: quite the contrary. Moreover, the division should not be fixed once and for all, even within a country. With changing circumstances, goods that earlier properly belonged to the public realm may preferably be transferred to the private realm. Furthermore, State guarantees of collective goods does not imply that the government ought to be engaged in its production. It may be advised to issue contracts to private firms to produce them. And so on.

These are details of implementation, but they are often misunderstood. Consider as an example Bernard Williams's assertion that, for a needs-based good such as medical care, any allocation other than one based on needs is socially 'irrational' (Williams, 1962). Nozick (1974: 233–5) argues against this by showing that there is no reason why medical doctors ought not to seek high salaries and offer their services to those who can most afford it. Now, the two are talking about different things: one is insisting that those who are in need of the service ought to be able to receive it, the other is arguing that the supplier of the service should be paid adequately for it. State guarantees for medical care are a way of reconciling the two claims. This entails consumption subsidies. It does not pose a deep intellectual problem.

6.7   *Knowledge, Organization, and Economic Growth*

The organization of production and exchange is influenced in part by the extent to which those who are engaged in it are educated, and is in part complementary to it. It is also influenced by information about new materials and products, and about new ways of doing things. This sort of information is often obtained from elsewhere. But it has to be absorbed and processed. Moreover, if it is to be put to use effectively it has to be adapted to suit local tastes, ecology, and resource endowments. Education is of enormous value here, as are external contacts. Product and process innovations don't occur in a vacuum, even when innovations consist of the transfer of foreign technology. Formulae for new products and processes can't simply be taken off the shelf and rented. Above all, people must have the incentives to undertake this complex set of activities. Progressive technological change involves a delicate mix of private initiatives and public support.[13] Later (in Chapters 7–10) we will see that not only is the organization of production influenced by who knows what and can observe what and does what best, but also, the institutional arrangements defining exchange and production are constrained by them. If wage-based and household production systems require explanation in an agrarian context, so do fixed-rental and sharecropping arrangements demand investigation.[14]

Earlier I remarked that knowledge is a non-rivalrous good. It is also durable. (The wheel does not need to be invented twice). But the transmission of knowledge isn't uniformly easy. In addition to the absorptive capacity of the recipient, it depends on the language in which knowledge is transmitted. By *information* we usually mean knowledge reduced and converted into messages that are easily communicable. *Codification of knowledge* is a step in the process of this reduction and conversion, and it renders the transmission, verification, storage, and reproduction of knowledge less costly. Much scientific and technological activity is directed at the codification of knowledge, through the development of uniform notation, specialized language, and so forth. The transfer of codified knowledge is often occasioned through publications. Literacy and numeracy are essential for deciphering it.

In contrast, *tacit knowledge* refers to the common perceptions we all are often generally aware of without being focused on them.[15] Tacit knowledge as a stock of capital forms the context within which focused perception is possible. Both science and technology draw crucially upon

---

[13] In the context of the spread of hybrid corn in the USA, Griliches (1957, 1958) has shown that the rate of return on agricultural research and development can be substantially higher than the average rate of return on investment (see also Evenson and Kislev, 1973). Evenson and Kislev (1975) provide a breakdown of expenditures on agricultural research and extension in a wide range of countries. The work that drew attention to the importance of technological change in agriculture for growth in the standard of living in poor countries is T. W. Schultz (1964).

[14] For accounts of tenurial arrangements in rural South Asia, see the vital contributions of Rudra (1982) and Singh (1988a, b, 1990).

[15] The distinction between codified and tacit knowledge is due to M. Polanyi (1962, 1966). It has been put to use in resource allocation theory in Dasgupta and David (1991), upon which much of this section is based.

skills and techniques that are acquired experientially, and are transferred by demonstration, instruction, and the provision of expert advice (e.g. agricultural extension services, maternal and paediatric care, and so forth).

Poor countries typically would not be expected to invest heavily in the production of basic knowledge (the kind of knowledge that is used as an input in the production of further knowledge). Understandably, the bulk of the world's basic research and development activity is undertaken in advanced industrial nations. Since basic knowledge travels well across international borders (much of it is codified), it is right and proper for poor countries to rely on this, and to invest in scientific and technological expertise so as to unravel and absorb it, and then disseminate it. Adaptation of foreign technology is a different matter, though, and much of the skills involved are packaged in a tacit form, even though what is ostensibly being paid for by the importing country is codified knowledge. There is then a need for local scientific and technological expertise to fashion such a transfer. Moreover, patent licensing agreements need to be written in a form that provides foreign firms with the incentive to transfer their tacit knowledge as well. Otherwise, what is paid for isn't of much use. Were this to continue, imports of foreign technology would merely decline in the long run.[16]

An economy's output depends not only on the material inputs put to use, but also on the knowledge and organizational basis of production. It is possible to decompose changes in a country's gross output into movements of the various determinants of production. This enables one to estimate the relative contributions of changes in material factor inputs on the one hand, and alterations in the knowledge and organization base on the other. The exercise has a heroic air about it, but it is illuminating: it is a necessary ingredient in policy debates. For this reason much work has been done on it since the pioneering studies of Abramovitz (1956) and Solow (1957). (See e.g. Denison, 1962; Crafts, 1985; Chenery, Robinson and Syrquin, 1986; Maddison, 1989; Boskin and Lau, 1990a, b.) It will be useful to study it.

Let L_t denote aggregate labour use and K_t an index of the flow of services from stocks of material capital in an economy at date t. We will amalgamate land and natural resources and write an aggregate of the flow of services from them as T_t. Denoting by Y_t the gross national product (GNP) at t, we may write the relation between GNP, factor inputs, and the state of knowledge and organization as:

$$Y_t = A_t F(K_t, L_t, T_t). \tag{6.1}$$

For purposes of illustration, it is helpful to consider the case where $F(\cdot)$

---

[16] Arora (1990) has investigated how transfer agreements in practice ensure that the tacit knowledge too is passed on to the importing country.

displays constant returns to scale in K_t, L_t, and T_t (that is, $F(\cdot)$ is linear-homogeneous in the three variables). So we will do so. What remains is A_t. We will regard it as a compound index of the state of knowledge and the organization of production. It has been found to be the main source of growth in living standards.

Equation (6.1) is a sharp specification, so it has been much used. It assumes, among other things, that technological change is neutral across the material factors of production. There are good reasons for thinking, at least in rich countries, that it isn't neutral, that it is biased, and that for the most part it augments the value of material capital because it is tied up with its improvements (see Boskin and Lau, 1990a, b).[17] To the best of my knowledge, the question of bias in technological progress hasn't been systematically explored for poor countries. So we will work with the formulation in (6.1).

It is simplest to consider competitive markets for the material factors of production. We therefore assume that there are private property rights to material capital, labour, and land, and that their markets are approximately competitive. At an equilibrium (see Chapter 7), factor payments equal their marginal products.[18] Thus, write by s_t the rental rate on capital (i.e. the price of capital services), by w_t the wage rate paid by employers, and by r_t the rental paid on land, all at time t. We then have from (6.1):

$$Y_t = s_t K_t + w_t L_t + r_t T_t, \tag{6.2}$$

where $s_t = A_t F_K$, $w_t = A_t F_L$, and $r_t = A_t F_T$. Understandably, the relative shares of material capital, labour and land and resources in GNP ($s_t K_t/Y_t$, $w_t L_t/Y_t$, and $r_t T_t/Y_t$, respectively) differ between poor countries and industrial market economies. Table 6.1 provides orders of magnitude. In poor countries shares of material capital and labour in GNP are each of the order of 40 per cent, and the share of land and natural resources combined amounts to 20 per cent. (The corresponding figures in industrial market economies are 20, 75 and 5 per cent, respectively.) The relative importance of the environmental resource base of production in poor

Table 6.1 GNP shares, poor countries v industrial countries, 1980s

	Share of GNP (%)		
	Capital	Labour	Land and resources
Poor countries	40	40	20
Industrial market economies	20	75	5

[17] Were technological progress purely capital-augmenting, we would write GNP as $Y_t = F(A_t K_t, L_t, T_t)$, and not as in (6.1).

countries is something we should have expected. We will have much to say on this in Chapter 10. We now consider movement through time.

Differentiating both sides of equation (6.1) yields

$$(\mathrm{d}Y_t/\mathrm{d}_t)/Y_t = [(\mathrm{d}A_t/\mathrm{d}t)/A_t] + F_\kappa[(\mathrm{d}K_t/\mathrm{d}t)/K_t]$$
$$+ F_t[(\mathrm{d}L_t/\mathrm{d}t)/L_t)] + F_r[(\mathrm{d}T_t/\mathrm{d}t)/T_t]. \qquad (6.3)$$

This is an accounting identity, and it has decomposed the percentage rate of change of GNP into four constituents, consisting of the four terms on the right-hand side of equation (6.3). In earlier days it was common to refer to the first of these as the rate of technological change. Since the determinants of technological change were thought not to be well understood, it was also called the *residual*, a catch-all term for all the determinants of growth that economists couldn't account for. Today, it is referred to more accurately as the rate of *total factor productivity growth*, to capture the idea that it reflects not only growth in knowledge, but also changes in the organization of production. The remaining three terms represent the contributions of changes in the use of material capital, labour, and land and natural resources, respectively. Since wages reflect the productivity of labour, private returns to human capital are embodied in wage rates. Educational externalities are a different matter, and they are reflected in total factor productivity, A_t.

Growth in total factor productivity (it can be negative, as we will see shortly) is not a happenstance. Both the public and private realms influence it. A key influence is the act of production. There is now much accumulated evidence that production is a source of knowledge to the producer of how to do things better. This is often called learning-by-doing (see Chapter 7). In addition, public policy shapes total factor productivity. In the absence of infrastructure, neither capital equipment nor labour effort amounts to much. Being in the public realm, infrastructure has to be paid for by taxation, and from foreign aid, domestic borrowing, and international loans.

Thus far theory. What have been the orders of magnitude of the model's relevant variables in recent years? Table 6.2 presents estimates of the annual percentage rates of growth of output, of the factors of production, and of total factor productivity in four regions containing the bulk of the world's poor people. The estimates are over two periods: 1960–73 and 1974–87. For the purposes of comparison, the corresponding figures for West Germany are presented for the period 1960–73. It is implicit in the table that changes in the use of land and natural resources have been negligible. They are not mentioned.

What is most striking is that in (sub-Saharan) Africa and Latin America

---

[18] I am tacitly assuming for simplicity of exposition that $F(\cdot)$ is differentiable. One may then talk of marginal products.

total factor productivity *declined* over the latter period 1974–87, and in South Asia it declined during the earlier period 1960–73. The organization of production and the extent to which production capacity is in use affect output. They thereby affect changes in output. Growth in total factor productivity changed dramatically over the two periods in both South Asia (primarily the Indian sub-continent) and Latin America. In South Asia it switched from an annual average decline of 0.1 per cent to an annual average increase of 1.4 per cent, whereas in Latin America it switched from an annual average increase of 1.3 per cent to an annual average decline of 1 per cent. The performance of sub-Saharan Africa in this, as in other matters, has been consistently bad: a move from 0.7 to −0.8 per cent. In contrast, the performance of East Asia has been spectacular. A consistently high rate of growth of GNP has been reflected in a balanced increase in the determinants of GNP.

Table 6.2   Growth rates of productive factors

Region	G_Y		G_K		G_L		G_A	
	(i)	(ii)	(i)	(ii)	(i)	(ii)	(i)	(ii)
Africa	4.0	2.6	6.3	6.3	2.1	2.3	0.7	−0.8
East Asia	7.15	6.5	9.8	10.7	2.8	2.6	2.6	1.4
Latin America	5.1	2.3	7.4	5.6	2.5	2.8	1.3	−1.0
South Asia	3.8	5.0	8.0	7.2	1.2	2.3	−0.1	1.4
(West Germany)	(5.4)		(7.0)		(−0.7)		(3.0)	

Key
G_Y: % annual growth in GNP.
G_K: % annual growth in material capital stock.
G_L: % annual growth in labour force.
G_A: % annual growth in total factor productivity.
(i) : Figs. for the period 1960–73.
(ii) : Figs. for the period 1974–87.
Sourcs: World Bank (1991a), Chenery, Robinson and Syrquin (1986).

What have been the contributions of the various constituents of output to its growth? Equation (6.3) is the basis on which estimates are made. Table 6.3 provides estimates for the same regions over the period 1960–87. Notice that, in contrast to poor countries, in West Germany total factor productivity growth has been much more important than growth in the factors of production.[19] It is often argued that this should come as no

---

[19] The period over which the West German estimates have been made is a bit different: 1957–85. See Boskin and Lau (1990b), whose key new finding is that $F(\cdot)$ has displayed decreasing returns to scale and that technological progress in West Germany (as well as Japan, UK, France, and USA) has been capital-augmenting. For this reason the figures for West Germany are not quite comparable with those for the other regions.

surprise. Rich countries work with a larger capital base than do poor countries, so it is only natural that in rich countries growth in total factor productivity should play a relatively important role in the growth of final output. It is argued that in contrast, growth in total factor productivity should be expected to be relatively unimportant in poor countries. Table 6.3 would seem to confirm this. But countries have been aggregated in the table, and this has suppressed an important truth. Even poor countries are capable of making significant advances in total factor productivity if investment in infrastructure is strong, and if producers are able both to put into effect organizational changes and to exploit the potentials of learning-by-doing. In South Korea, Singapore, Taiwan, and Hong Kong (countries that in 1960 were poor) total factor productivity contributed a greater share to growth in their GDPs during 1960–87 than the 28 per cent recorded in Table 6.3 for East Asian growth. (On this see Lucas, 1991). Even these aggregate figures reflect a good deal of differences among poor countries. The dismal share of total factor productivity growth in sub-Saharan Africa and Latin America is striking. These regions have languished badly.

Table 6.3   Share of GNP growth, 1960–1987 (%)

Region	Capital	Labour	Total factors of production
Africa	73	27	−1
East Asia	57	16	28
Latin America	69	30	1
South Asia	67	19	14
(West Germany)	(22)	(−9)	(87)

Sources: Boskin and Lau (1990a, b), and World Bank (1991a).

Both education and an ability to exploit the gains from foreign trade and competition have played significant, complementary roles in the remarkable performance of a number of East Asian countries (Japan, South Korea, Taiwan, Hong Kong, and Singapore being the dominant performers). State participation in creating private incentives for engaging in technological innovations and displaying an openness to trade are likely to prove synergistic. We have also noted why these in turn are likely to improve the domestic organization of production and exchange and learning-by-doing. This is where educational externalities would be thought to be potent (see Romer, 1986; Lucas, 1988). Education can be effective only when it has the scope to be effective. (The Philippines and South Korea were similar in respect to education attainments in 1960, but their economic performances have been quite different since.) We would conjecture nevertheless that education as a stock of human capital has a positive effect on growth in total factor productivity.[20] Recent estimates are consistent with this line of thought, although their meaning isn't as yet fully clear (see World Bank, 1991a). Cross-country data suggest that in 1960 an additional year of mean education in a country would have resulted in a permanent increase of 0.3 per cent in the annual growth rate of its GNP. In 1960 the average citizen in sub-Saharan Africa had acquired only 1 year of education; GNP growth rate since then has averaged at about 3.3 per cent per year. In contrast, the average citizen in East Asia had enjoyed 4.4 years of education in 1960; since then the growth rate of GNP there has averaged at about 6.8 per cent annually. If the estimates are to be interpreted literally, this difference in education stock between sub-Saharan Africa and East Asia in 1960 would explain almost a third of the difference in their GNP growth rates since then. These are crude estimates of counterfactuals and they should not be interpreted literally. But they serve to indicate a possible additional effect of education.

---

[20] Formally, the thought here is that $(dA_t/dt)/A_t = \delta(E_t)$, where $\delta(\cdot)$ is a non-decreasing function of the stock of human capital, E. Thus, if the *level* of this stock were to remain constant, *growth* in total factor productivity would remain constant; the higher this level, the higher the corresponding growth rate.

Public Goods and Common-Property Resources[1]

*6.1 *The Theory of Public Goods*

Public goods have been much discussed in both economics and political philosophy. Here it will be useful to present the arguments in a somewhat different way from the standard treatment of the subject (e.g. Stiglitz, 1988a). What I shall do is to define public goods through the language of externalities and then deduce the conclusions of the standard theory of resource allocation.

There are M households, labelled $j, k = 1, \ldots , M$. They are interested in two commodities, one private (e.g. income) and one public. Each household has an initial endowment of 1 unit of the private good, and none of the public good. They all have access to a technology (e.g. trade with the rest of the world) by means of which, for every p units of the private good, a unit of the public good may be obtained. Let x_k be the quantity of the private good consumed by household k, and g_k be the quantity of the public good produced by k. It follows that k gets to consume Σg_j units of the public good.

For simplicity of exposition, households are taken to be identical. k's utility function is assumed to be of the form $U(x_k, \Sigma g_j)$, where $U(\cdot)$ is a strictly concave function, and increasing in each of its two arguments. In a decentralized market economy, k's problem is:

Choose x_k and g_k so as to maximize $U(x_k, \Sigma g_j)$, subject to the constraint

$$x_k + pg_k \leq 1. \qquad (\ast 6.1)$$

Notice that k's choice depends on the choice of g_j by household j, for all $j \neq k$. So we seek to locate a Nash equilibrium of this game. Since households are identical, we look for a symmetric equilbrium (i.e. one where all households choose the same commodity bundles).

It will prove useful to parameterize our problem by supposing that utility is logarithmic. So we now assume that

$$U(x_k, \Sigma g_j) = \log x_k + \log(\Sigma g_j).$$

---

[1] This chapter is taken from Dasgupta and Heal (1979: Ch. 3).

To compute the symmetric Nash equilibrium we proceed as follows. Suppose household j (all $j \neq k$) produces g^* units of the public good. Then k's utility from consuming x_k units of the private good and producing g_k units of the public good is

$$\log x_k + \log[(M - 1)g^* + g_k]. \qquad (\star 6.2)$$

Maximizing ($\star$6.2) subject to the budget constraint in problem ($\star$6.1) yields as the first-order conditions:

$$1/x_k = \mu \qquad (\star 6.3)$$

and

$$1/[(M - 1)g^* + g_k] = \mu p, \qquad (\star 6.4)$$

where μ is the Lagrange multiplier associated with k's budget constraint.

At the symmetric Nash equilibrium, the solution of g_k from equations ($\star$6.3) and ($\star$6.4) must equal g^*. Let the pair (x^*, g^*) denote household k's choice at this equilibrium. We may now solve the equations explicitly to conclude that

$$x^* = M/(M + 1), \quad \text{and} \quad g^* = [(M + 1)p]^{-1} \qquad (\star 6.5)$$

It will be noticed that if M is large each household transforms only a tiny amount of its initial endowment into the public good. That there is an *undersupply* of the good in equilibrium may be confirmed by asking what this community of M households would collectively do if it acted in concert. So we search for the symmetric Pareto-efficient allocation.

We assume that households know they are identical. This means each household knows the others' endowments and utility functions. This is a very strong assumption, and we will weaken it in later chapters when developing the notion of incentives. But we make the assumption here so as to develop concepts.

Households collectively pool their initial endowments and co-ordinate their choices. Let x be the consumption of the private good by the representative household and g the quantity of the public good produced by it. Then for (x,g) to sustain the symmetric Pareto-efficient allocation, x and g must be the solution of

Choose x and g so as to maximize $\log x + \log(Mg)$, subject to the constraint

$$x + pg \leq 1. \qquad (\star 6.6)$$

Let $(\hat{x}, \hat{g})$ be the solution of problem ($\star$6.6). It is a routine matter to check that

$$\hat{x} = 1/2, \quad \text{and} \quad \hat{g} = 1/2p. \qquad (\star 6.7)$$

Compare the solutions in ($\star$6.5) and ($\star$6.7). So long as $M \geq 2$, there is an undersupply of the public good at the symmetric Nash equilibrium. This is an instance of market failure brought about for reasons we identified in Chapter 6.

We now look for resource allocation mechanisms which may sustain the allocation given by (*6.7). Two suggest themselves.

1. *Pigovian subsidies*. As a collective body, the community offers each household a subsidy of τ units of the private good for each unit of the public good the household produces. (In a larger context, what we are calling the community would be the State.) The cost each household now incurs in producing the public good is $(p - \tau)$ per unit. This makes the public good more attractive to produce. At the same time, the collective imposes a household tax (i.e. a poll tax) so as to finance the subsidy. Let T be the poll tax. Household k's problem now is to

Choose x_k and g_k so as to maximize $\log x_k + \log(\Sigma g_j + g_k)$, subject to the budget constraint

$$x_k + (p - \tau)g_k \leq 1 - T. \qquad (*6.8)$$

It is now a routine matter to confirm (see Dasgupta and Heal, 1979, chapter 3) that, if the State sets $T = (M - 1)/2M$ and the public-good subsidy at $\tau = (M - 1)p/M$, the symmetric Nash equilibrium in the economic environment given by problem (*6.8) will be the allocation in (*6.7). We should note that this tax-subsidy scheme balances the State's budget.

2. *Public supply*. The idea here is that the State supplies $M/2p$ units of the public good free of charge (see equation (*6.7)), and imposes a household poll tax (amounting to $\frac{1}{2}$ unit of the private good per household) to finance it. Households are at liberty to produce the public good. But now they will not wish to do so. (Why?)

*6.2   The Problem of the Commons

Consider a piece of grazing land, of size S, which is common property among M herdsmen (labelled $j, k = 1, \ldots, M$). If X is the number of cows grazed on the land, the output of milk, Y, is given by the production function $Y = G(X,S)$, where $G(\cdot)$ is strictly increasing, constant-returns-to-scale, and concave in X and S. There are no fences; so cattle mingle freely on the commons. The model is atemporal. Since the commons is fixed in size, we may as well suppress S and write $G(X,S) = F(X)$, where $F(0) = 0$, $F'(X) > 0$, and $F''(X) < 0$. We take it that $F(X)$ is bounded above. All this means that $F(X)/X > F'(X)$; that is, average product per cow is greater than the marginal product of the cow on the grazing land, and average product is a declining function of the size of the herd grazing on the land (see Fig. *6.1). Let x_k be the number of cows grazed by herdsman k. Then $X = \Sigma x_k$. Denote by y_k herdsman k's output of milk. Since cattle mingle, we take it that $y_k = x_k F(X)/X$. Let the price of a cow be q. Without loss of generality, we set the price of milk at unity.

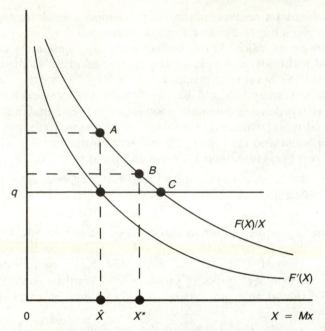

Fig. *6.1   Average and marginal productivity curves of the commons. A is the point of efficient use of the commons. B is the symmetric Nash equilibrium outcome with M herdsmen, $M \geqslant 2$. C is the limiting case of B when $M = \infty$.

It follows that k's profit, π_k, is

$$\pi_k = x_k F(\Sigma x_j)/\Sigma x_j - q x_k. \qquad (*6.9)$$

Herdsmen are profit-maximizing, and we take it to begin with that they behave non-cooperatively. The outcome we are interested in is then the symmetric Nash equilibrium of the economic environment; that is, one where all the hersdmen graze the same number of cows. To have a non-trivial problem, we take it that $F'(0) > q$. Assume now that herdsman k thinks that each of the other herdsmen will introduce x^*. In this case equation (*6.9) reduces to

$$\pi_k = x_k F[(M - 1)x^* + x_k]/[(M - 1)x^* + x_k] - q x_k. \qquad (*6.10)$$

We take it next that k's profit-maximizing choice of x_k is positive. (This will be justified in equation (*6.12).) Then it follows that x_k must satisfy the first-order condition

$$\{(M - 1)x^* F[(M -)x^* + x_k]\}/[(M - 1)x_k + x]^2$$
$$+ x_k F'[(M -1)x^* + x_k]/[(M - 1)x^* + x_k] = q. \qquad (*6.11)$$

At a symmetric equilibrium we must have $x_k = x^*$, and so the equilibrium number of cows on the commons is the solution to

$$F(X)/X - \{[F(X)/X] - F'(X)\}/M = q. \qquad (*6.12)$$

This is the fundamental result in the problem of the commons. Denote its solution by X^*. It is an easy matter to compute that in equilibrium each herdsman's profit, π^*, is

$$\pi^* = [F(X^*) - X^*F'(X^*)]/M^2. \qquad (\star6.13)$$

We will now study how the size of the equilibrium herd changes with M. It is an easy matter to check that X^* increases with M. If $M = 1$, equation ($\star$6.12) reduces to

$$F'(X) = q. \qquad (\star6.14)$$

and if $M = \infty$, it reduces to

$$F(X)/X = q. \qquad (\star6.15)$$

Thus, total surplus (or industry profit) from the grazing land is largest when $M = 1$; it is zero when $M = \infty$. Equation ($\star$6.14) yields the efficient size of the total herd on the land, and there *is* no problem of the commons. This is obvious, since property rights are well defined when there is only one herdsman. The problem of the commons occurs whenever $M \geq 2$; the equilibrium sustains more than the right number of cows. The problem arises because the grazing land is free to all. The only grazing cost incurred by hersdmen is the cost of purchasing cattle (and tending them). With $M \geq 2$ there is an externality which each herdsman inflicts on all other herdsmen, in that, when a herdsman introduces an additional cow into the land, he reduces the average product of cows. (Cattle are assumed to intermingle and compete for grass.) Granted, when M is large each herdsman can reduce average profits ever so slightly. But the number of herdsmen being harmed is large, and the overall effect is non-negligible (equation $\star$6.11). Indeed, the larger is the number of herdsmen, the more acute is the problem of the commons. Equation ($\star$6.15) represents the problem in its most acute form. See Fig. $\star$6.1.

Assume $M \geq 2$. the herdsmen recognize that they face a problem, somewhat akin to the Prisoners' Dilemma. Unless they take collective action, each will be making lower profits than he could. What they wish to do is to ensure that each grazes $1/M$ of the efficient size of herd. Let $\hat{X}$ be the efficient size (i.e. the solution of equation ($\star$6.14)). We will take it that the number of cows each herdsman introduces into the grazing land can be publicly monitored. Three arrangements for implementing the efficient solution suggest themselves:

1. *Quantity control (or quotas)*. The herdsmen agree that each will be allowed up to $\hat{X}/M$ cows. They impose a fine for any violation sufficiently stiff to deter anyone from doing so.

2. *Taxes*. The idea here is to introduce a tax per cow grazed on the commons. If τ is the tax, the net price of a cow is $q + \tau$, and so the

symmetric Nash equilibrium size of herd is given not by equation (*6.12), but by

$$F(X)/X - \{[F(X)/X] - F'(X)\}/M = q + \tau. \qquad (*6.16)$$

The idea now is to choose τ so that equation (*6.16) reduces to equation (*6.14). It is a simple matter to confirm that this is achieved by setting

$$\tau = \hat{\tau} \equiv (M - 1)\{[F(\hat{X})/\hat{X}] - F'(\hat{X})\}/M. \qquad (*6.17)$$

Equation (*6.17) can be thought of as an optimal 'pollution' tax, or charge. Here it is a tax per cow for the use of the grazing land.

The total tax revenue is $\hat{\tau}\hat{X}$. We are assuming this is distributed equally among the herdsmen. This way they maximize their profits. On the other hand, suppose that the tax is imposed by some other agency (e.g. the State, a land baron) and expropriated. In this case, the herdsmen enjoy less profits than they would have had no tax been imposed. (See Dasgupta and Heal, 1979: chapter 3 for a proof.) The efficient size of herd is no doubt $\hat{X}$. But the distributional implication of expropriated taxes needs to be borne in mind whenever policy is discussed on such matters as the commons.

3. *Privatization.* Imagine that fences can be built relatively cheaply. The M herdsmen could then divide the grazing land into M equal bits and award private property rights to them. Consider now herdsman k. Given that he has exclusive rights to his plot (of size S/M), his output of milk is:

$$y_k = G(x_k, S/M) = G(Mx_k, S)/M = F(Mx_k)/M. \qquad (*6.18)$$

We may now write k's profits as $\pi_k = F(Mx_k)/M - qx_k$. This means k will choose the size of his herd to satisfy

$$F'(Mx_k) = q,$$

which is equation (*6.14). After privatization, each herdsman will introduce $\hat{X}/M$ cows into his own plot of grazing land.

We have studied three institutional arrangements for mitigating the problem of the commons. Which one is most effective depends on the activity causing the problem and on the extent to which activities can be monitored; international fisheries are different from local grazing lands, and the atmosphere isn't the same sort of sink for pollutants as are village tanks. The distributional implications of altered property rights need also to be borne in mind. Privatization of the commons may be appropriate in some examples, while quantity controls on the use of the commons may be appropriate in others. An external agency may be needed to enforce agreements in one case, and the local community may suffice for another. The matter is complex, and we will go into it in Chapter 10.

Decentralization and Central Guidance

7.1 *Competitive Mechanisms in the Private Realm*

Social scientists and political philosophers frequently allude to the virtues of competitive markets. It is time to formalize the underlying ideas of these markets. We will continue to assume that the production and allocation of collective goods occur in the public realm. For the moment we will take it that the State imposes *lump-sum taxes* for the purposes of financing its expenditures. By lump-sum taxes I mean taxes that, at the margin of choice, leave agents' chosen plans unaffected.[1] I include transfers across households and firms, so the idea covers lump-sum subsidies as well. Up to Section 7.4 we will take the State's decisions regarding lump-sum taxes (and subsidies) and the supply of collective goods in the public realm as given. What remains is the large class of private goods in what we earlier called the private realm. The *competitive market mechanism* is an idealization of what ought to guide resource allocation there. We now turn to this.

In order to obtain the most parsimonious picture, we will restrict our attention to households and firms. Households are decision units, and although firms are owned by households they too take decisions. Managers of firms may be required to act in the interest of shareholders. Nevertheless, it is 'management' that decides.

It is appropriate to consider first the competitive market mechanism in its strongest guise. This is also the form that is best understood. There it is assumed that all transactions in the private realm are mediated by prices quoted today. This means that each and every commodity and service (now and in the future) has a market today, and thus a price today. Moreover, individual parties, whether households or firms, are taken to be sufficiently small relative to the markets as to be unable to affect prices by their choice of plans. In short, we assume that all parties are price-takers. (This last explains the use of the qualifier 'competitive' in a competitive market mechanism.) The markets we are studying here are not thin.

These assumptions taken together are plausible only when transaction costs are small and households are *self-regarding*. By this I mean that a

---

[1] To give an example, a poll tax is a lump-sum tax. It is not based on anything over which an agent has choice.

household's utility is dependent solely on its own net consumption of goods and services, including leisure. This is usually taken to imply greed. It is sometimes seen to mean that the 'economic man' is not much better than a potential swindler, the kind of person one wouldn't want to know. But this isn't so. The idea of a compartmentalized citizen is relevant here (see Section 5.1). The standard theory of resource allocation sees a household's total expenditure as being constrained by its net wealth; the theory is silent on what keeps the household from violating the constraint. This leaves open our reading of the motivations of the household. We could imagine, for example, that the constraint on expenditure is self-imposed. It is perfectly consistent for an individual to be concerned with his own self and at the same time to abide by norms of behaviour pertaining to production and exchange, even when the risks of being caught violating them are negligible. Being self-regarding in the private realm is not the same as being immoral, nor is it the same as being amoral. When a person is in search of the best buy in a market, it isn't necessarily his intention to chisel anyone. Nor is the notion of a fair price alien to the self-regarding household. A London restaurant recently broke with the tradition of charging for items on its menu. Instead, it invited its patrons to pay whatever they wished for the meal they had, *after* they had had it. Patrons were under no obligation to pay anything. The majority of customers apparently chose to pay the 'market price' for their meal, including many who weren't expecting to patronize the restaurant again. I have economist friends who find this behaviour at odds with the standard theory of resource allocation. It isn't. There is nothing paradoxical in self-regarding agents behaving justly when they can afford to so behave. Matters of social justice pertain to the public realm. The boundary between the public and private realms may be fuzzy, but it exists. Coming to terms with this is a key to good citizenship.

Thus far we have concentrated on households in the standard theory. The theory sees firms as being engaged in the transformation of goods and services into further goods and services. This transformation can be effected domestically, in which case it is called domestic production of goods and services. It can also be effected internationally, by trade with the rest of the world. In the latter case exports should be thought of as inputs and imports as outputs, with the international terms of trade acting as foreign transformation possibilities.

The assumption that households are self-regarding in the private realm rules out a number of interactions among households which are labelled 'externalities' in the economics literature. Indeed, we saw earlier that it is because activities such as immunization carry with them strong externalities that their allocation should properly be in the public realm (Chapters 4 and 6). I shall also take it that there are no production externalities among firms and among households and firms. This too is a reasonable move to make, because a central point in creating the *public* realm was to accommodate all those goods and services for which private markets are likely to malfunction. We are assuming here that all commodities and services in the private realm have competitive markets. (Recall that the private realm sustains the allocation of private goods.) This implies there are no significant externalities in the private realm, because externalities are a manifestation of missing markets. A clean separation between the public and private realms provides the most pristine setting for the standard theory of resource allocation.

Economists, even development economists, tend to ignore the role of traders in resource allocation mechanisms. (An exception is the classic by Bauer, 1954.) One reason for their absence from the literature may well be that their role is not transparent. Farmers produce crops, industrial firms produce industrial goods, restaurateurs serve food, and builders build; what do traders do? Well, they save buyers and sellers the cost of search and transport. Since these are less tangible goods, they are easy to overlook. Traders are important everywhere, and it is easy to take them for granted. But they shouldn't be taken for granted, especially in poor countries, where transport costs are high relative to incomes. Because of large transport costs, existing markets are often thin there, and specialization in production is more limited than in rich societies (see Section 9.2). So it is as well to remind ourselves that traders matter very much. They need to find room in any theoretical construct. Traders are firms in our account here. They 'transform' goods produced by producing parties into goods purchased by purchasers.

Firms are small relative to the markets in which they operate. This means, among other things, that there are no large fixed costs in production. (Recall that natural monopolies have been placed in the public realm.) Formally, we suppose that each firm's set of production possibilities is *convex*.[2] We take it that firms are profit-maximizing. This is a reasonable assumption in the environment we are alluding to here. Since all commodities in the private realm have their prices quoted, profits can be defined unambiguously. (By a firm's profits, I mean the present discounted value of the sum of its profit flow.) This means that shareholders will agree on what are profit-maximizing production plans. By assumption, there are many households and many shareholders per firm. So it is in their interest to instruct firms to maximize their profits, and they do so; the theory envisages that management can be monitored closely. It follows that a firm

---

[2] A set is convex if the straight line joining any two points in it lies in the set. In Chapters 16 and *16 we will be better placed to understand the far-reaching role convexity plays in the standard theory of resource allocation. Koopmans (1957) and Debreu (1959) are the classic expositions on this.

engaged in the production of a single commodity produces at a point where the price of its output equals its marginal cost of production. Households in turn use their non-labour and labour endowments to purchase commodities in the market. Each household is subject to a linear budget constraint, which is that its expenditure on goods and services must not exceed its wealth less the lump-sum tax imposed on it by the government. This defines the household's *budget set*. It is the set of feasible consumption bundles for the household. The budget set corresponds to what in our formulation of a social system (Chapter 3) we called an individual's permissible set. What was called a plan in that formulation should in the present context be thought of as a consumption bundle. We may therefore borrow the intellectual machinery we developed earlier. A household's utility function is to be thought of as a numerical representation of the ordering over options on the basis of which it actually chooses. To state matters in shorthand, the household maximizes its utility subject to its budget constraint. We will assume that each household's budget set is convex irrespective of the market prices and its wealth. In Chapters 16 and *16 we will find that the economics of destitution requires that we drop this last assumption.

A *competitive equilibrium* (in the private realm) is a set of prices, one for each and every distinguishable commodity and service, such that total demand made for each commodity and service by all households and firms is no greater than its total supply. (If, as is almost always the case, the price of a commodity is positive, then its demand equals it supply.) It is today called an *Arrow–Debreu equilibrium*, in honour of the two economists who presented the definitive modern version of it (see Arrow and Debreu, 1954; Debreu, 1959; Arrow, 1964). It formalizes the stationary outcome of a wide variety of possible transaction processes.

A competitive equilibrium, as we have formulated it here, has a single price for each commodity (the Law of Single Price). Net of transport costs and the like, sellers receive what buyers pay: there are no commodity taxes or subsidies. Government revenue required to support the public realm is collected through lump-sum taxes. The mechanism provides a sense in which prices can co-ordinate the activities of autonomous parties in an interrelated economy, and can co-ordinate them in an informationally parsimonious way. At an equilibrium, each household needs only to know its own endowments (goods and services it has an initial right to, including what is on offer in the public realm in the form of public goods and so forth), its own 'mind', and market prices. Each firm in turn needs only to know market prices and its own production possibilities. Co-ordination is achieved with a minimum of public information. The only publicly known objects in the private realm are prices.[3] Of course, we are leaving

---

[3] That the price mechanism in a competitive setting provides a parsimonious setting for households and firms in their need for public information has been much discussed in the economics literature. Sonnenschein (1974) addresses this issue in a formal manner.

unanalysed the government's role for the moment. Its activities are being taken as given. So we don't ask what the government knows and how it arrives at its decisions.

7.2 *Existence of Competitive Equilibrium*

Why study equilibrium allocations? One reason (there are others) is this: In defining and characterizing an equilibrium, we do not have to describe the underlying economic process whose stationary state corresponds to the equilibrium in question. There are usually a great many possible dynamic processes which have this same equilibrium as a stationary outcome. A significant advantage of working with an equilibrium concept, rather than with an explicit dynamic process, is that it allows us to study a large class of possible economies. It does mean though that we have to investigate whether the concept is coherent. This means that we need to identify properties which, were an economy to possess them, would ensure that it is capable of sustaining an equilibrium allocation of goods and services. Economists refer to this problem as one of 'existence of equilibrium'. In Chapter 3 we discussed this in the more general context of a Nash equilibrium of a social system.

We can put the matter differently. For an equilibrium concept to be fruitful, it needs to be coherent in a wide enough class of economies. Codification of this helps us judge which activities ought not to be left to the private realm, and which ones ought to be left to it. It also helps explain why. Of course, we have already made use of this reasoning; for example in our earlier suggestion (see Chapter 6) that a natural monopoly ought not to be left entirely to the private realm; or in the argument we deployed in Chapters 3 and 6, that the protection of basic positive and negative liberties should be a matter for the public realm. For all these reasons, much intellectual energy has been directed at identifying general characteristics of economies which guarantee the existence of competitive equilibrium. This hasn't been self-indulgence on the part of mathematical economists: it has been a necessary research enterprise. Here I merely note that, details apart, the assumptions we have made about households and firms in the previous section imply that the economy we are studying sustains competitive equilibrium allocations.

In Chapters 16 and *16 we will define a competitive equilibrium in formal terms and prove an 'existence theorem' for it diagrammatically as a by-product of our inquiry into the phenomenon of destitution. We should note, however, that both in intention and in delivery the standard theory assumes away the phenomenon. Indeed, the theory in its textbook guise assumes that each household is capable of surviving in good health even were it to be autarkic. This means it can survive by consuming its initial endowment of goods and services and engaging in household production. Plainly, if it can do that, it can survive by trading as well, and survive better. Exchange in the theory allows households to improve their lot; it is not necessary for survival.

I am referring to the conception of the competitive market mechanism as it appears in economics texts and treatises (see Koopmans, 1957; Debreu, 1959). There are specially structured models where labour skills are the only initial endowments of many households. But one can't live merely on leisure. So households sell their labour so as to enable them to purchase commodities. These special models exemplify that trade is necessary for survival (and not merely for an improvement in the quality of life), and that in equilibrium people are able to exchange their labour services for consumption goods, and survive.[4] An implicit assumption in these examples is that the economy in the aggregate is rich enough in assets. As it is a key assumption, it renders the model less than appropriate for poor countries. In Chapter 16 we will see all this, and we will extend the notion of an equilibrium to encompass situations where markets don't clear. Inevitably, we will pay special attention to the labour market. We will study circumstances where the labour market is rationed, so that many are driven to a state of destitution.[5] For the moment we continue to assume that markets don't malfunction. In particular, I shall suppose that the economy is sufficiently rich in assets, and that the public realm is just.

7.3   Competitive Markets and Efficiency

We have now seen how prices can co-ordinate the consumption and production activities of households and firms in the private realm. But the competitive price mechanism provides more service to a society than mere co-ordination. What is widely known as the First Fundamental Theorem of Welfare Economics says that a competitive equilibrium allocation is also Pareto-efficient.[6]

As we noted in Section 3.10, Pareto efficiency is efficiency in the space of utilities. The theory I have outlined does not specify whether in the private realm households choose on the basis of what they value, or whether what they value is based on what they think will give them satisfaction. We are not told whether the household's ordering of consumption bundles (its 'utility ordering') is arrived at through a process of bargaining among its members, or whether it reflects households' well-being. (On this see Chapter 11.) The motivation underlying households is

---

[4] McKensie (1981) has addressed this issue in a general context.
[5] The argument will be based on Dasgupta and Ray (1986, 1987). Hammond (1991) is a generalization of these studies.
[6] For proofs, see e.g. Varian (1984).

left unstated. This is what gives the theory flexibility of interpretation, and allows for a rich set of contexts in which it may be put to work.

The First Fundamental Theorem of Welfare Economics provides both the sharpest and the bluntest justification of the price mechanism. It is the sharpest, because it makes precise an analytical feature of the mechanism. There is nothing mystical about the claim, nor does the justification rely on historical evidence. It is at the same time the bluntest, because Pareto efficiency yields a mere partial ordering: not all states of affairs are comparable by this criterion. Pareto efficiency is silent on the distribution of pretty much anything—of utility or welfare or well-being, of freedoms or interest or advantage (see Section 3.10). What determines the extent of choice for a household is its initial endowment of goods and services (including its innate skills and other characteristics); the goods and services, lump-sum taxes, and subsidies determined in the public realm; and the terms on which the household can convert skills and commodities into further commodities and skills via household production and market exchange. A household with limited endowments, living in a society where the public realm offers little, will not have much power to ensure that its interests and advantages are sufficiently realized in the state of affairs that emerges under the price mechanism. It will also have precious little, in the way of control, to shape its life on the basis of its own choice from a sufficiently rich set of projects and plans. In short, the First Fundamental Theorem is non-committal about the distribution of power and control and, at a step nearer, non-committal about the distribution of utility among society's members.[7] It is the Second Fundamental Theorem of Welfare Economics that addresses distributional issues. We turn to this.

7.4 *The Implementation of Just Allocations in the Private Realm*

We will continue to ignore environmental uncertainty. In order to present the theorem in the form it is almost always discussed, we will take it that the social contract empowers the State to judge outcomes in the *private* realm on the basis of choice-theoretic utilitarianism (see Chapter 3, Section 3.4). In Chapters 2 and 3 (Section 3.9) I provided reasons why overall the social contract will go beyond choice-theoretic utilitarianism and include wider notions of freedom when evaluating a person's well-being.[8] But we

---

[7] This is so for any market mechanism, and not merely the competitive price mechanism, since equilibrium allocation of market mechanisms is dependent upon the initial allocation of rights.

[8] There are many who identify justice with choice-theoretic utilitarianism; see e.g. Friedman (1962); Bauer (1971, 1981, 1984), and Friedman and Friedman (1980), whose 'libertarianism' is founded upon choice-theoretic efficiency. See also Atkinson and Stiglitz (1980), Boadway and Bruce (1984), Barr (1987), and Dreze and Stern (1987), all of whom assume that State policy even in the public realm is fashioned upon choice-theoretic utilitarianism.

are studying a limited sphere here: the private realm. Within it, citizens would be expected to regard choice-theoretic utilitarianism as a reasonable guide to the evaluation of resource allocations. (See the form of the individual well-being function in equation (3.2).) It is a good approximation because the protection of negative liberties and the supply of rights-based goods have been assured in the public realm by our background assumptions (see Section 7.5).

A key requirement of the Second Fundamental Theorem of Welfare Economics is that the State have full information about household needs, endowments, utility functions, and firm's production technologies, including international trade possibilities. A second requirement is that the economy in the aggregate be rich enough to enable all households in principle to function. The theorem offers an account of a resource allocation mechanism capable of implementing just distributions of benefits and burdens.

We are to imagine that the State helps organize decisions in the public realm and sets the background circumstances that enable the private realm to operate under the competitive price mechanism. We continue to assume that households are self-regarding in the private realm. The Second Fundamental Theorem of Welfare Economics states that, provided household utility orderings and firms' production possibilities satisfy the assumptions that were made in Section 7.1, *any* Pareto-efficient allocation can be supported by a competitive equilibrium in the private realm, provided the government in advance implements suitable household-specific lump-sum wealth transfers, and ensures that the required provisions to be made in the public realm are realized.[9] This means that, if it is a good approximation for society to subscribe to choice-theoretic utilitarianism in the private realm, then the full optimum (or first–best allocation; see Section 3.10) can be attained by a judicious combination of public choice and the competitive price mechanism. In Section 7.5 we will study the problem of implementation of the first-best allocation in the public realm. (A formal account is provided in Chapter *7.) Loosely speaking, the theorem tells us that public judgements concerning the distribution of utilities (and therefore the distribution of goods and services) ought to be implemented by household-specific lump-sum taxes and subsidies. It also tells us that the efficient co-ordination of economic activities ought to be divided suitably between the competitive price mechanism in the private realm and State involvement in the supply of collective goods in the public realm.[10] In

---

[9] See Koopmans (1957), Debreu (1959), Meade (1964, 1976), Arrow (1971a), and Arrow and Hahn (1971) for expositions of this theorem at varying levels of technicality. We will study a variant of this in Chapter *16.

[10] The way I have put it isn't quite accurate, in that, if there are multiple competitive equilibria associated with a given distribution of endowments and collective goods, the government will require a policy on how to bring the 'right' equilibrium about. The theory of indicative planning can be made to address this question. See Meade (1970).

the circumstances envisaged by the theorem, there is something of a separation of 'efficiency' from 'distributional' considerations. This separation has long been at the centre of discussion on welfare and public economics: the distribution of purchasing power in the private realm is not met by the imposition of income or commodity taxes and subsidies; for lump-sum taxes and subsidies emerge as superior public tools. The Second Fundamental Theorem of Welfare Economics offers a form of social organization in which households exercise both power and control over their own lives. If either is vastly restricted, it is because the economy as a whole is poor, not because opportunities and achievements are concentrated among a few households.

It is easy to overlook how radical are the theorem's implications. The question it addresses and answers isn't based on marginal, reformist motives. Lump-sum redistribution of assets in rural societies would, for example, involve agrarian reform, politically perhaps the most explosive of economic measures.[11] The theorem also envisages a smoothly working price system. There aren't any sectoral price rigidities, or rent-seeking activities in the political sphere. There are also no distortionary commodity taxes or subsidies. So domestic prices of tradable goods equal their international prices. The measures that governments are expected to take in implementing the theorem go very much beyond marginal reforms. The State is called upon to introduce radical, structural changes.

7.5 Pluralism and Exchange Restrictions in the Public Realm

Thus far the operations of the private realm. To be sure, the distinction between the public and private realms has been kept deliberately vague. Extreme precision can mislead. Nevertheless, we are able to deduce a number of guidelines concerning ideal resource allocation mechanisms, which are summarized below.

The Second Fundamental Theorem of Welfare Economics provides an account of the conditions in which the price mechanism should be allowed to play a dominant role in the private realm. Market prices ought to rule there because, under the circumstances envisaged by the theorem, they reflect social scarcities of private goods. We now consider implementation of the full optimum in the public realm. For reasons we have already studied, it would be injudicious of a society to rely exclusively on market prices there. But the idea of social scarcities remains a key ingredient in allocation decisions. Now social scarcities of goods and services in the

---

[11] For a wide-ranging discussion of the difficulties of agrarian reform, see Montgomery (1984). As with any pattern of redistribution, there are moral tensions here. Land expropriation without suitable compensation violates negative rights. There is simply no getting away from this. See Ch. 17 for further discussion.

public realm can often be estimated in such ways as to allow decisions there to be reached and implemented in a decentralized manner, much in the way that the Second Fundamental Theorem of Welfare Economics envisages market prices to function in the private realm (see e.g. Dasgupta, Marglin and Sen, 1972; Little and Mirrlees, 1974; Ahmad and Stern, 1989, 1991; Chapters *6 and *10.) They involve the use of *shadow prices*, or *accounting prices* (Section 7.7 and Chapter *7.) To give a qualitative example, public health care would typically be expected to be on offer at a price far below its cost of supply. But the government would be expected to ensure that its provision is cost-effective. The use of shadow prices can be very fruitful here, and they are often quite simple to estimate. For instance, a large number of inputs for the service (e.g. medicines and equipment) would be purchased from the private sector at market prices, or from abroad. Often enough, they would reflect their accounting prices.

These considerations can now be used to explore the sort of resource allocation mechanism which ought ideally to encompass the public and private realms. In doing this we will proceed by steps, and with the help of examples. It will prove instructive to begin by extending the Second Fundamental Theorem of Welfare Economics to cover a good part (the 'convex' part) of the operations of the public realm as well. In Chapter *6 we developed an idea of what guidelines the theorem will offer. Our examples will show that, under the circumstances envisaged by the theorem, the promotion of general well-being requires governments to impose, in conjunction with household-specific lump-sum transfers, household-specific commodity taxes and subsidies for needs-based goods.

To see this, consider the social evaluation function in Chapter 3, equation (3.3). It is not in general Paretian: the first–best allocation of resources is not efficient on the space of utilities. (Remember that unlike Section 7.4, where I focused on allocations in the private realm, I am considering both the private and public realms in this section.) If a government were attempting to implement the full optimum, it would in general need to impose some trade restrictions domestically. Why? Because we are trying to implement an allocation that is not Pareto-efficient. Considerations arising from well-being typically clash with the right that persons may be thought to have to *all* voluntary transactions.[12] What forms ought these exchange restrictions ideally take? If we were to extend the Second Fundamental Theorem of Welfare Economics to the social well-being function (3.3), governments would be required to impose (optimal) household-specific commodity taxes and subsidies, in addition to the

---

[12] Nozick (1974) emphasizes that rights may imply exchange restrictions. But he considers only negative rights. In the text we are thinking of material, or economic, goods, in particular basic needs.

(optimal) lump-sum wealth transfers. And commodity taxes and subsidies imply exchange restrictions.

To illustrate this, imagine that household 1 has a special need for commodity y, and needs find expression in social evaluation through, say, its effect on an index of health. Let us assume also that the unit cost of producing y is \$1.50. (This would be its import price if the commodity had to be obtained from abroad.) Then the extended version of the Second Fundamental Theorem of Welfare Economics when applied to this economy would have \$1.50 as its price for all households not having a special need for it. For household 1, though, it would recommend a subsidy, the subsidy reflecting the social evaluation of household 1's special need for the good.[13] Imagine that the optimum subsidy is \$0.50 per unit of y. Then this household gets to purchase y at \$1.00. There will clearly be some temptation for household 1 to establish a black market, purchasing y from the official market at \$1.00 and selling it to other households at a price anywhere between \$1.00 and \$1.50. The State will have to prevent this kind of transaction. Fortunately, for a number of goods and services in the public realm black markets aren't too much of a problem: health and education services aren't easy to resell by purchasers. This makes it possible to charge differential prices for them. (In the literature on public economics, the idea that certain commodities ought not to be exchangeable is called *specific egalitarianism*. See Tobin, 1970; Stiglitz, 1988a.)

There are a number of empirical correlates of household- (or person-) specific commodity taxes and subsidies. In the United Kingdom, medical prescriptions are free for people 16 years of age or under, for people 65 years of age or over, for expectant women and nursing mothers, for people with continual medical needs, for full-time students under the age of 21, and for households receiving the Family Income Supplement. Of these, it is only the last category that receives the prescription subsidy on grounds of its inability to pay. It is a non-distortionary subsidy when applied to each of the other categories of recipients.[14]

The problem with household-specific commodity taxes and subsidies is, as always, enforcement. The incentives for black markets would be high in any society that was to try implementing too many such schemes. But recall the rationale for these taxes and subsidies: the non-congruence of utility and well-being. On the space of goods and services, this non-congruence manifests itself in poor countries mainly through the social valuation of those commodities that are basic needs. But basic needs are a limited category of goods. For all intents and purposes, then,

---

[13] The government would finance the subsidy from (optimal) lump-sum taxes.

[14] I am not suggesting that people deliberately earn less in order to qualify for free medical prescriptions; merely that in principle they can.

the extended version of the Second Fundamental Theorem of Welfare Economics envisages household-specific commodity subsidies to be employed only upon a select set of commodities and services. There is no reason for thinking that this bit of economic analysis is impractical. Difficulties with the Second Fundamental Theorem of Welfare Economics lie elsewhere.

7.6   *Producer versus Consumer Taxation*

Lump-sum taxes and subsidies are always feasible, but it is impossible to design them optimally. This is because much information pertinent to their optimal design is private, and so governments are unable to base optimal taxes and subsidies on them. This is what makes the Second Fundamental Theorem of Welfare Economics operationally of no use. It has didactic use, though. It directs us to what is intellectually the right point of departure for deliberating public policy.

The State may have statistical information of needs, endowments, and utilities, but it invariably has limited knowledge at the individual or household level. However, the State needs to raise revenue for redistributing purchasing power and for ensuring the supply of appropriate amounts of the goods and services in the public realm. If it is to do things well, it has to use whatever information it has, and to base the taxes and subsidies on this limited knowledge. The full optimum being unattainable, the best a society can hope for are what are called *second-best* allocations (see Meade, 1955). Second-best taxes and subsidies are 'distortionary', because they are based on the production, purchases, and sales of commodities, and on household and corporate incomes. In contrast to a full optimum, second-best allocations are not well-being efficient. (For a formal demonstration see Chapter *7.) Income taxes, family supplements, general commodity taxes, and subsidies are familiar controls. They may not be optimally chosen in the world as we know it, but this merely offers us grounds for discussing their best design, or the direction of desirable reforms; it isn't an argument for rejecting them.[15]

---

[15] The pioneering contributions in the study of public policy under incomplete information on the part of the State are Diamond and Mirrlees (1971) and Mirrlees (1971). Diamond (1975), Hammond (1979), Mirrlees (1976, 1985) and Roberts (1984) are major syntheses. There is now a large literature extending these works on second-best taxation. One strand has put the theory to use in studying public finance in poor countries; see Ahmad and Stern (1984, 1991), Heady and Mitra (1986, 1987a, b, 1990) Sah and Stiglitz (1987), Besley and Kanbur (1988), Sah and Srinivasan (1988), Dahl and Mitra (1989), and Burgess and Stern (1991). For a fine empirical assessment of the pricing of two vital collective goods in poor countries, namely education and health, see Jimenez (1987, 1990). It is often argued that land provides a non-distortionary source of taxation, since it is thought to be inelastic in supply. (If all taxes on agricultural outputs and inputs are reduced in the same proportion, the effect is identical to a proportional tax on land.) However, as the quality of land is affected by investment in it, the thought that land is in inelastic supply is a non-starter.

A vector of net outputs of goods and services in an economy is *production-efficient* if there is no feasible net output vector which displays greater net output of at least one commodity and no less net output of any other commodity. It is obvious that there is a significant difference between well-being efficiency and production efficiency. So, even though information and administrative constraints preclude well-being efficiency from being a desirable goal, it doesn't necessarily make production efficiency undesirable. Indeed, assuming that it has a sufficiently wide range of fiscal tools at its disposal, the State ought to provide incentives to ensure production efficiency, even though it would wish to violate well-being efficiency. The problem is, the width of the required range of fiscal tools is very large indeed, and it cannot be expected to prevail in economies we know.[16] Thus, as a social objective, even production efficiency has to be abandoned, particularly so in poor countries, where the State is heavily constrained in its choice of policy tools. The right question then to ask is this: Given the social environment, what is the best set of distortions to have if the economy has to have them?[17] By distortions here I mean departures from economy-wide production efficiency. Taxation of producer goods in these circumstances is necessary for raising revenues as well as for redistributing purchasing power, and there is now a large literature on the structure of optimum second-best taxation under diverse circumstances.[18] In the presence of such taxes, the rates at which purchasing firms transform goods and services into further goods and services differ from the rates at which supplying firms do so. Even though each individual firm may be doing the best it can (in particular, it may be producing efficiently), there is none the less a slack in economy-wide production. When this is so, the gap between social well-being at the first-best and at the realizable second-best is large. But that is life.

The sorts of production distortions prevalent in poor countries aren't usually founded on such considerations as those we have reached so far in this book. Agricultural production as a frequent rule is subject to punitive taxation, often in the form of an implied tax on marketed surplus. (A recent study of eighteen developing countries has concluded that on average the rate of agricultural taxation there was about 30 per cent during the period 1960–85. See Krueger, Schiff and Valdes, 1988. See also World Bank, 1986a, 1991a.) This turns the terms of trade against agriculture, via government procurement schemes, collectivization of agriculture, and

---

[16] See Diamond and Mirrlees (1971) and Dasgupta and Stiglitz (1972). These articles provide a codification of circumstances where economy-wide production efficiency is a desirable objective.

[17] See e.g. Stiglitz and Dasgupta (1971) and Dasgupta and Stiglitz (1974).

[18] Good summaries can be found in Bhagwati and Srinivasan (1983), and Auerbach and Feldstein (1985, 1987).

over-valued exchange rates. Domestic producers of food crops as a result face prices lower than their international values. Now, the desire that food should be cheap calls for consumer subsidies (on both imported and domestically produced food; see Chapter 17); it does not recommend depressed producer prices, nor does it point to the collectivization of agriculture. These latter routes are a harbinger of disaster. They stifle incentives to produce. In addition, collectivization, ushering as it does uniform production strategies, induces greater correlation among the risks borne by production units (see Chapters 8–9). The collapse of food production in sub-Saharan Africa (Tanzania is merely the most publicized example) in recent years has had much to do with government policies against agriculture. The Chinese agricultural crash, where grain output fell by nearly 100 per cent in one year (1959–60), is an instance of policy failure of a catastrophic kind.

International-trade taxes (sometimes called border taxes) on producer goods are a commonplace for manufactured products in poor countries. Most often this involves taxation of imports. (Import quotas and outright bans will be regarded here as an extreme, non-linear form of taxation.) Imports and exports of producer goods are production activities. So border taxes on them lead to a particular kind of production inefficiency.[19] Import tariffs on producer goods have a particularly detrimental effect. In the manufacturing sector foreign producers are often the sole competitors of domestic producers. Levying import duties on them allows domestic manufacturers to enjoy an easy life.

The traditional argument for import duties on manufactures was based on the idea that for agrarian economies they are an 'infant industry'. The argument ran thus: domestic producers would not initially be expected to be as efficient as established foreign manufacturers. Now engineering and management studies show that the very act of production causes domestic producers to learn more about *how* to produce. More importantly, economic studies confirm this.[20] Over time, however, through the accumulation of experience, domestic manufacturers should be expected to become at least as efficient as their international competitors. There are

[19] The remarks here pertain to commodities whose prices at the border of the country in question are independent of the country's volume of imports or exports of them. For commodities whose international price can be affected by the country, the matter is different. But other than a few countries and a few raw materials and minerals, such considerations can be ignored.

[20] See, Asher (1956) and Alchian (1963) on airframe production, Zimmerman (1982) on nuclear power technologies, and Lieberman (1984) on production and investment in chemical process industries. (Learning was found to be small in this last study.) Hollander (1965) has investigated the phenomenon of learning in the technology of research and development.

The idea of learning-by-doing is very old. I have discovered that even the expression itself is not new: 'Anything that we have to learn to do we learn from the actual doing of it: people become builders by building and instrumentalists by playing instruments' (Aristotle, 1976 edn.: 63). Professor Kenneth Arrow has told me that he got the term 'learning-by-doing' from the writings of John Dewy, an Aristotelian.

thus dynamic economies of scale in production in infant industries. The catch is that, unless they are enabled to produce, domestic industries can't learn and become efficient; and they can't learn and become efficient if they aren't permitted to be inefficient for a while. For this they need initial protection against foreign competition.

The argument is correct. The infant industry argument recommends an export (more generally, production) subsidy (see Baldwin, 1969; Negishi, 1972; Dasgupta and Stiglitz, 1988b). The problem is that for it to work the government must commit itself to definite time horizons over which it would offer protection to domestic manufacturers (the relevant learning periods). In practice, governments don't commit themselves to a time duration; instead, protection is granted over a long period, literally decades. If domestic manufacturers know they can influence this, they can slack. As they are smart, they do indeed slack. This should come as no surprise. Poor countries are replete with both public and private enterprises that are elephantine.[21] There have been exceptions, for example East Asian countries, which have pursued this policy most subtly and judiciously. Yotopoulos (1990), in an analysis of the Japanese experience, calls this 'state-led capitalism'.

The early modern literature on learning-by-doing (Arrow, 1962b; Kaldor and Mirrlees, 1962; Wan and Clemhout, 1970) was based on economy-wide aggregate models. Its main weakness was that it saw learning to be a public good: learning by a firm was assumed to spill over instantaneously and costlessly to all other firms. This is an extreme assumption. It is also a delicate assumption, in that if it were to be dropped one would be forced to study an oligopolistic industry (see Dasgupta and Stiglitz, 1988b). The presence of oligopoly in domestic and foreign countries is itself a reason why a government may wish to pursue a discretionary policy towards domestic firms against oligopolistic outsiders. Oligopoly sustains super-normal profits (or rents), and the thought is that judicious industrial policy on the part of the domestic government can syphon rents away from foreign firms into the home economy (see e.g. Helpman and Krugman, 1989; Levy and Nolan, 1991). One problem with the argument is that foreign governments could retaliate, vitiating the intention of the domestic government. In any event, what quantitative evidence there is suggests that the gains from unilateral protectionism are unlikely to offer much to the home country (see Bhagwati, 1988b).

These arguments imply that the productivity of investment is adversely

---

[21] See World Bank, (1986a, 1990, 1991a). In Eastern Europe the phenomenon has been studied most comprehensively by Kornai (1988). For an identification of the kinds of distortions induced by government soft-budgets, see Qian (1990). See also Barro (1991), who, in a cross-country study of over 100 countries, has shown that during the period 1960–85 growth in national income per head was negatively related to the extent of market distortions.

Table 7.1   Trade protection and the productivity of investment

Trade protection	Rate of return on investment (%)	
	Public sector	Private sector
High	13.6	9.2
Moderate	15.4	8.7
Low	19.3	18.9

Source: World Bank (1991a, table 4.2).

affected by excessive protection of domestic production. With one minor and informative exception, this is consistent with Table 7.1, which provides estimates of *ex post* rates of return on both public and private investments of some 1650 projects supported by the World Bank and the International Finance Corporation. The exception pertains to relative rates of return of private-sector projects between countries with high and moderate overall restrictions on trade. The difference is slight and goes the other way: the rate of return is higher in economies with high rates of protection than in economies with moderate protection. It could be a statistical artefact. It could also be that the private sector genuinely benefits from a move from moderate to high protection, in that it passes on the resultant higher costs of inputs to consumers in the form of yet higher prices.

Taxes and subsidies on consumer goods is a different matter. If the consumption of luxury goods is to be discouraged, the thing to do is to impose a stiff consumption tax on it. There is no a priori reason for discouraging its production: it may, for example, be an exportable commodity. Likewise, if the commodity is a basic need, consumption should be subsidized: producers should not be forced to sell at a low price. Producer and consumer taxation involves quite different sets of consideration.

Rations and exchange restrictions are extreme special cases of taxes and subsidies; and the idea that certain commodities ought not to be exchangeable (earlier we called this 'specific egalitarianism') is an old one. In the previous section I presented an argument for exchange restrictions in the allocation of certain basic needs. The criterion adopted for social evaluation was a pluralist one, and we assumed that the government possessed the all-encompassing range of information required of it by the Second Fundamental Theorem of Welfare Economics. I will now argue that, when the government does not possess information about matters of relevance (e.g. individual 'preferences'), exchange restrictions can be a recommendation of even choice-theoretic utilitarianism.

This may appear counter-intuitive at first blush, for it could be thought that, if the government were to effect the allocation of basic needs by distributing cash (i.e. purchasing power), people would be able to engage in mutually beneficial trades to obtain the commodity allocations they 'want'. The problem is that people could claim transfers intended for others. Thus, imagine that the government can't tell which citizens have a special need for a certain commodity. If its distribution were to be effected by cash transfers, all citizens would have to be awarded the same transfer. Those not having the need would then spend their cash entitlement on other commodities. This could well be a waste. Distribution in kind can be so tailored that the problem is overcome (those who don't have the special need will have no incentive to claim it), provided of course that the emergence of 'black-markets' can be prevented (see Blackorby and Donaldson, 1988; Chapter 17). By their very nature, it is difficult to re-sell health care and education in the market, and so they are prime candidates for the practice of specific egalitarianism. Admittedly, exchange restrictions mean that the resulting allocation is Pareto-inefficient. But this is to be expected whenever the government chooses policies under incomplete information.

The theory of taxation is both subtle and complex. For example, even if it were desirable, a subsidy on basic food items for all consumers would not typically be feasible in poor countries, because the ability of governments to tax is severely restricted there. (See Pinstrup-Andersen, 1988a, b, 1989, for country experiences.) This means that only a few basic food items can be subsidized. Which ones should be chosen? Subsidy on even a single food item may prove to be overly expensive if it were to be offered to all consumers. (For example, in poor countries consumer expenditure on cereals is some 15 per cent of gross domestic product (GDP). Therefore, a 20 per cent subsidy on cereals amounts to 3 per cent of GDP, a substantial figure.) This implies that the subsidy should be offered only to certain groups of consumers. Since the needy are the target (Chapter 2), how are they to be identified, given that observable income is imperfectly correlated with need? Should the government then seek to offer a subsidy to individuals (or households) possessing certain observable characteristics (e.g. children in the age range 6–36 months, pregnant and lactating women, widows, and households with a female head) that are correlated with need (this is called 'tagging'), or should it so design the subsidy that consumers 'self-select' in some way (e.g. subsidizing coarse grains which the rich don't care to consume)?

In a related context, should the government establish a cash-for-work programme to eliminate destitution? If so, how should it be designed if it is to attract only the needy? These questions are at the heart of the economics of incentives, and they arise because governments possess incomplete information about matters of relevance to their activities. We will go further into these questions in Chapter 17.

7.7 *National Income in a Pluralist Society*

All this has a direct bearing on how national income ought to be computed if it is to serve as an index for measuring changes in general well-being. In Chapter 5 (Section 5.2) we attempted to compare the quality of life in different countries by looking directly at some of the constituents of well-being: life expectancy at birth, infant survival rate, adult literacy rate, and the extent of political and civil rights enjoyed by their citizens. We studied these in conjunction with figures for national income per head. Now, as we saw earlier (Chapters 3 and 4), per capita income is a measure of affluence. It provides an estimate of the extent of choice among marketed goods. The question arises whether it is not in principle possible to construct an overarching measure of real national income which could be made to reflect aggregate well-being itself; or, to put it another way, whether it is not possible to measure changes in aggregate well-being by changes in a suitable index of the *determinants* of well-being. The answer is 'yes', provided certain technical conditions are satisfied. The prices that need to be used for this purpose are not 'market prices', but household-specific shadow prices (or accounting prices). It pays to study this.

For our purposes here we may define the shadow price of a commodity as the increase in the maximum feasible level of aggregate well-being were the economy in question to be awarded a unit more of this commodity free of charge (see e.g. Intriligator, 1971). A commodity's shadow price therefore measures the maximum this society would be willing to pay in terms of general well-being for one more unit of it. It measures the social scarcity value of the good. Plainly, this depends on both social objectives and feasibility constraints, including in particular information constraints. Optimum commodity taxes and subsidies can be defined as the differences between the market and shadow prices of goods and services. In Chapters 10 and *10 we will see how figures for (net) national product need to be revised in the light of resource depletion and environmental degradation. In Chapter *7 we will prove a general theorem, applicable to an optimizing, pluralist economy facing any number of constraints—transactional, informational or whatever.[22] What we will prove is this: provided certain mathematical conditions are satisfied, associated with any social evaluation function (equation (3.3)) and any set of technological, institutional, and informational constraints, there exists a set of household-specific shadow prices for commodities and services which ought to be used in the evaluation of real national income. At constant relative (shadow) prices, changes in real national income reflect changes in aggregate well-being.

---

[22] The reach of this theorem is therefore far beyond that of the Second Fundamental Theorem of Welfare Economics. For example, it allows for informational asymmetries.

Moreover, changes in the income of a group (e.g. expectant or lactating mothers) reflect changes in the well-being of that group. Furthermore, changes in the income generated in each sector reflect changes in its contribution to aggregate well-being. And so on. Thus, were we to be confident that shadow prices have been estimated accurately, there would be no special need for augmenting real national income with figures for 'socio-economic indicators', such as those in Table 5.1.[23] Real national income would be an adequate summary index of the quality of life.

As it inevitably happens, we don't possess such shadow prices. This means that we can't aim at a single summary measure. We have to construct a multiplicity of indices of the constituents of well-being. This, allied to conventional national income figures, formed the basis of our empirical evaluation of countries in Chapter 5.

---

[23] We would still want to have them to know what they are. What I am saying in the text is that we would not need to have a heterodox collection of indicators for judging the quality of life.

7

Real National Income as a Measure of General Well-Being

Earlier, I remarked that if we wish to estimate changes in social well-being, there are two routes available. The first is a direct one. The idea is to measure changes in the *constituents* of well-being, such as health, longevity, basic liberties, literacy, and also real income, as indicators of the extent of commodity choice. In so doing, we measure changes in well-being itself. This is the route we followed in Chapter 5 (Section 5.2) when making an international comparison of well-being.

The other route is roundabout. It is to measure changes in the value of the *determinants* of well-being. Since commodities are inputs in the production of well-being, we measure changes in the accounting (or shadow) values of goods and services. In short, the idea is to measure changes in real national income. The heart of the matter is to estimate shadow prices. This is the difficult part.[1] If real national income as an index of social well-being has come to acquire a bad name, it isn't because the measure is unsound; it is because all too often the prices used to estimate it are vastly inappropriate. Because of this, we didn't rely entirely on national income figures when making international comparisons of the quality of life in Section 5.2. However, the general principle remains: provided the social evaluation function, production possibilities, and institutional and informational constraints satisfy certain mathematical properties (see problem ★7.4 below), then, for any social evaluation function, feasibility constraints, and initial endowments of commodities and skills, there is a corresponding set of shadow prices which can be used for the evaluation of real national income.

In what follows, I demonstrate this. Recall the formulation of aggregate well-being in Chapter 3 (Section 3.9). For convenience, we reproduce equations (3.1) and (3.2) in a simplified form as

$$W_k(\mathbf{a}; H_k) = W_k[U_k(\mathbf{a}; H_k), Q_k(H_k)] \qquad (\text{★}7.1)$$

---

[1] Methods of estimation of shadow prices were developed in Little and Mirrlees (1969, 1974), Dasgupta, Marglin and Sen (1972), and Helmers (1979). See also Dasgupta (1982b), Heady and Mitra (1987a), and Squire (1989).

and

$$W(\mathbf{a}) = W[W_1(\mathbf{a}; H_1), \ldots, W_k(\mathbf{a}; H_k), \ldots, W_M(\mathbf{a}; H_M)]. \quad (\star 7.2)$$

(Here, $W_k(\cdot)$ is person k's level of well-being; $U_k(\cdot)$ and $Q_k(\cdot)$ are, respectively, k's utility and a scalar index of the ability to function; $W(\cdot)$ is the social well-being function; and M is the number of people.)

This is an abstract framework, and we need to put some structure into it. So we consider a resource allocation problem. Without a loss of generality, let us consider a two-person, two-commodity economy involving no production. (Extensions are trivial.) Both commodities, x and y, contribute positively to each person's utility, but only commodity y influences the ability of people to function. To give an example, y could be a basic need, and x a good that is not basic. Let x_k and y_k ($k = 1, 2$) denote k's consumption of the two goods and let X and Y be the economy-wide endowments of x and y. The six-vector (X, Y, x_k, y_k: $k = 1, 2$) is an allocation of resources. We can think of it as a social state, or state of affairs.

Let us suppose that a change in aggregate well-being is brought about by an alteration in resource allocation. To measure this change by the first method, we would seek to estimate changes in the values of the constituent functions, $U_k(\cdot)$ and $Q_k(\cdot)$, and use the differential of equation ($\star 7.2$). This differential we write as

$$\Delta W = \Sigma(\partial W/\partial W_k)[(\partial W_k/\partial U_k)\Delta U_k + (\partial W_k/\partial Q_k)\Delta Q_k]. \quad (\star 7.3)$$

(Δ denotes a small change.) As noted in Section 5.2, the route we followed in making an international comparison of average well-being was in this spirit. I say 'in spirit' because we had only ordinal information for political and civil rights, and so our social evaluation function (the Borda Rule) relied only on ordinal data.

The evaluation of real national income is trickier. We consider making this evaluation for an optimizing economy.[2] In all other respects, our treatment will be general, and we certainly don't wish to restrict our discussion to a fully optimal economy, which is where the Second Fundamental Theorem of Welfare Economics holds. We want to allow for informational and transaction constraints. So, the canonical formulation of the economy's planning problem is:

Choose x_k, y_k ($k = 1, 2$) so as to maximize
$$W[W_1(x_1, y_1), W_2(x_2, y_2)],$$

---

[2] An alternative would be to study an economy at an arbitrary resource allocation (say, an equilibrium allocation) and obtain criteria for evaluating shifts to neighbouring social states; see Dasgupta, Marglin and Sen (1972) and Dasgupta (1982b, ch. 5). Formal treatments can be found in Meade (1955, 1976), Boadway (1975), Starrett (1988), and E. Ahmad and Stern (1989, 1991).

where

$$W_k(x_k, y_k) = W_k[U_k(x_k, y_k), Q_k(y_k] \text{ (for } k = 1, 2); x_1 + x_2 \le X,$$
$$y_1 + y_2 \le Y, x_1, x_2 \ge 0, \text{ and } I(x_1, x_2, y_1, y_2) \ge 0. \tag{*7.4}$$

In this problem, the first set of constraints is technological (total commodity consumptions must not exceed their available supplies), and the final constraint, $I(\cdot) \ge 0$, is taken to reflect informational and institutional constraints.[3]

We will now express and interpret the first-order conditions of (*7.4). Assuming that we can use the Kuhn–Tucker theorem, we may conclude that there exist (positive) shadow prices for x and y, say λ and η, and a nonnegative shadow price for the final constraint. $I(\cdot) \ge O$, say ρ, such that[4]

$$(\partial W/\partial W_k)[(\partial W_k/\partial U_k)(\partial U_k/\partial x_k)] + \rho \partial I/\partial x_k = \lambda \tag{*7.5}$$
$$(\partial W/\partial W_k)[\partial W_k/\partial U_k)(\partial U_k/\partial y_k) + (\partial W_k/\partial Q_k)Q_k'(y_k)]$$
$$+ \rho \partial I/\partial y_k = \eta \quad \text{for } k = 1, 2. \tag{*7.6}$$

I shall presently show that, with well-being as numeraire, real national income in this economy is

$$\Sigma(\lambda - \rho \partial I/\partial x_k)x_k + \Sigma(\eta - \rho \partial I/y_k)y_k. \tag{*7.7}$$

The shadow price of x_k is $(\lambda - \rho \partial I/\partial x_k)$, and that of y_k is $(\eta - \rho \partial I/\partial y_k)$. We may conclude that the shadow price of x is in general household-specific. It is not household-specific if

$$\rho \partial I/\partial x_1 = \rho \partial I/\partial x_2 \tag{*7.8}$$

Similarly, the shadow price of y isn't household-specific if

$$\rho \partial I/\partial y_1 = \rho \partial I/\partial y_2. \tag{*7.9}$$

But equations (*7.8) and (*7.9) hold true only in special circumstances. They hold true, for example, at the full optimum, where the Second Fundamental Theorem of Welfare Economics obtains; at the full optimum, the constraint $I(\cdot) \ge 0$ is non-binding, and so $\rho = 0$. They also hold in what is widely referred to as a Diamond–Mirrlees (second-best) optimum, relevant for a society in which the only constraint other than technological ones is the inability of the government to impose optimal lump-sum transfers (see Diamond and Mirrlees, 1971; Mirrlees, 1969, 1971; Dasgupta and Stiglitz, 1972; Hammond, 1979). However, in general, equations (*7.8) and (*7.9) will not be expected to be valid. For this reason, the appropriate shadow prices to use in the estimation of real national income are in general household-specific.

---

[3] Generally speaking, there will be a multitude of such constraints. But we would gain nothing by writing a whole host of them. One suffices.

[4] I am assuming that at the optimum each person gets to consume positive quantities of both goods.

When developing the idea of household-specific taxes and subsidies in Section 7.5, we saw that there is often a reason for having different people (or households) face different market prices for needs-based goods. (For these to be feasible, transactions need to be observable by the State). This is an additional complication, and it requires formal demonstration. So now recall that, by hypothesis, the utility function $U_k(x_k, y_k)$ is a numerical representation of the ordering over commodity bundles on the basis of which household k chooses. Let us assume that the optimal allocation is achieved in a decentralized manner. If P_k is the ratio of the price of y relative to x which household k faces at the optimum, we have

$$(\partial U_k/\partial y_k)/(\partial U_k/\partial x_k) = P_k, \qquad k = 1, 2. \qquad (\star 7.10)$$

It will be noticed from ($\star$7.5) and ($\star$7.6) that, unless the society in question subscribes to choice–theoretic utilitarianism, P_k in equation ($\star$7.10) depends on k (i.e. is household-specific) even at a full optimum (that is, even when $\rho = 0$). We conclude that the price consumers should face for a needs-based commodity ought to vary according to needs. This is so even when conditions ($\star$7.8)–($\star$7.10) are satisfied, and shadow prices aren't household-specific.

With these preliminary observations completed, we can proceed to prove that expression ($\star$7.7) represents real national income.

We look first at changes in aggregate well-being. Let α be a parameter of $W(\cdot)$. We can let the interpretation of α vary. It would denote time if we were interested in changes in aggregate well-being of a community over time; alternatively, it would be geographical location if we were to make interregional comparisons. Now,

$$dW/d\alpha = \Sigma(\partial W/\partial W_k)[\partial W_k/\partial U_k)(dU_k/d\alpha) + (\partial W_k/\partial Q_k)(dQ_k/d\alpha)].$$
$$(\star 7.11)$$

But

$$dU_k/d\alpha = (\partial U_k/\partial x_k)(dx_k/d\alpha) + (\partial U_k/\partial y_k)(dy_k/d\alpha) \qquad (\star 7.12)$$

and

$$dQ_k/d\alpha = Q'_k(y_k)dy_k/d\alpha, \qquad \text{for } k = 1, 2. \qquad (\star 7.13)$$

We may now use equations ($\star$7.12)–($\star$7.13) and ($\star$7.5)–($\star$7.6) in equation ($\star$7.11) to obtain

$$dW/d\alpha = \Sigma(\lambda - \rho\partial I/\partial x_k)(dx_k/d\alpha) + \Sigma(\eta - \rho\partial I/\partial y_k)(dy_k/d\alpha) \qquad (\star 7.14)$$

Now write $q^x_k = \lambda - \rho\partial I/\partial x_k$, and $q^y_k = \eta - \rho\partial I/\partial y_k$, for household-specific shadow prices of x and y in units of aggregate well-being.[5] Real national income in this optimizing economy is

$$Y = \Sigma q^x_k x_k + \Sigma q^y_k y_k. \qquad (\star 7.15)$$

---

[5] From equations ($\star$7.5) and ($\star$7.6), we know that $q^x_k, q^y_k > 0$ for $k = 1, 2$.

At constant shadow prices, we would conclude from equations (*7.14) and (*7.15) that

$$dW/d\alpha = dY/d\alpha.$$

This proves the claim.

8

Uncertainty, Insurance, and Social Norms

8.1 *Environmental Uncertainty*

We have so far studied resource allocation mechanisms shorn of environmental uncertainty. Goods and services have been identified not only by their physical characteristics (such as colour, taste, or nutrition content), but also by their location and the date at which they are made available. The locational specification of goods and services enables us to discuss trade across villages, districts, regions, and nations; and the temporal specification offers us the way to analyse trade across time, be it among a group of people (for example, commercial borrowing and lending, patron–client transactions in agrarian cultures, and the institution of gift exchange supported by norms of reciprocity), or with oneself over time (the problem of saving and accumulation). Both Fundamental Theorems of Welfare Economics envisage an array of forward markets (or markets that are equivalent to forward markets). Future commodities are traded in such markets.

Uncertainty is the reason why commodities need also to be specified in terms of the environmental events in which they become available. Irrigation water in a dry year is a different commodity from irrigation water in a wet year, because its use-value is different. Therefore, we extend the notion of a commodity to include in its characterization the contingency in which it appears on the scene. This extended notion of an economic good is called a *contingent commodity*, and prices of such goods are called *contingent-commodity prices* (which are in effect insurance premia). This extension allows us to view insurance as a commodity, and it gives us a route to a formal analysis of markets for insurance. But first we need to make precise the idea of an environmental contingency.

We have on occasion referred to Mother Nature's choice of action. This is a self-consciously colloquial way of speaking about environmental uncertainty. A tight way of discussing it is to begin by considering a state of nature, which in statistical decision theory is seen as 'a description of the world so complete that, if true and known, the consequence of every action would be known' (Arrow, 1971b: 45). Arrow is here confining his attention to the case of a single decision-maker. If there are two or more persons involved, the definition would need to be changed trivially to the form, 'the consequence of the set of actions of all parties involved would be known'.[1] An *event* can now be defined as a collection of states of nature. Thus, 'drought next year in sub-Sahara' is an event, being the union of all possible natural histories of the world consistent with drought next year in sub-Sahara.[2] From this it follows that no one can possibly know what the true state of nature is, since it will never be revealed. (Unless, that is, there is a known termination date for the world; in which case the true state of nature will be revealed at the last date.) What we observe instead are events. The descriptions of realized events become more and more detailed as more and more is observed and recorded with the passage of time. Thus, for any observer the partition of the states of nature is coarsest at the initial date, becoming finer and finer with every observation she makes.[3] At any date, the partition a person's powers of observation and discrimination confine her to is called her *information partition*, or, alternatively, her *information structure*. A key assumption underlying the two Fundamental Theorems of Welfare Economics when they are extended to incorporate environmental uncertainty is that at any date all individuals have the same information structure.

An example will help. Let us assume that the world lasts for three periods (indexed $t = 0,1,2$). Assume too that the only environmental uncertainty pertains to the weather in each period, which may be either wet, W, or dry, D. At $t = 0$ (the initial period) there is uncertainty about weather at dates 1 and 2. There are then four states of nature: WW, WD, DW, and DD; where WD means 'wet at date 1 followed by dry at date 2', and so forth. At date 0 no one knows what the true state of nature is. Assume next that at date 1 all individuals can costlessly observe the weather in that period. This is an event, and it will be either W or D. If it is W, they will all know that the true state of nature belongs to the set {WW, WD}. In the language we are developing now, this set {WW, WD}

---

[1] A state of affairs, or social state (see Ch. 2), is a thicker concept than a state of nature. A social state includes in its description the state of nature. It includes a good deal more, such as people's actions.

[2] Formally, the set of all events is given the structure of a sigma field. The primitive notion is that of a state of nature. States of nature are in fact elementary events. They are at the same time elements *of* events.

[3] We take it that all individuals have perfect recall: they remember what they have observed in the past. A collection of sets whose union is the set S is said to be a *partition* of S if no two sets in the collection have a common element in them. A partition, say P_1, of a set S is said to be *finer* than a partition, say P_2, of this same set S if P_1 contains a greater number of sets and if each member of P_1 is a subset of some member of P_2. In this case we also say that P_2 is *coarser* than P_1. All this is illustrated in Fig. 8.1. An excellent elementary exposition of statistical decision theory is Raiffa (1968). See also Dasgupta and Heal (1979: chs. 13 and 14).

is the event W at date 1. If, on the other hand, the weather is dry, they will all know that the true state of nature belongs to the event D at date 1, which we write as {DD, DW}. At date 2 all individuals will be able costlessly to observe the weather once again. By this second observation they will all have learnt the true state of nature.

Figure 8.1 portrays the *information tree* generated by this example. At date 0 the information partition is the coarsest: it is the entire set {WW, WD, DW, DD}. At date 1 the partition is finer; there are now two possible events, {WW, WD} and {DW, DD}; and only one of them can occur. At date 2 the partition is finer still; it consists of the four events {WW}, {WD}, {DW} and {DD}. There is a single node at date 0, two at date 1, and four at date 2. An event is a node in this information tree. The Fundamental Theorems of Welfare Economics assume that this information tree is common to all individuals in the economy. In short, individuals are

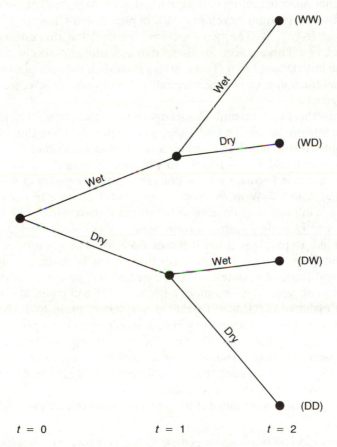

Fig. 8.1   Information tree in a 3-period world

identical in their powers of observation and discrimination. The theorems assume all individuals to be travelling along the same information tree.

It will prove useful to formalize this. Thus, suppose, without any loss of generality, that there is a single commodity, let us call it *income*, which is the object of desire at each node along the information tree we have just studied. Let $N(t)$ be the number of nodes at t. (In the present example, $N(1) = 2$, and $N(2) = 4$.) Furthermore, let $n(t)$ be the index of nodes at t, with $n(t) = 1, \ldots, N(t)$. We now denote by $X^k_{tn(t)}$ the amount of income available to household k at node $n(t)$. Notice that income here is not a single commodity. Looked at from the vantage point of the initial date $(t = 0)$, its use-value depends upon the date and upon the contingency. Income is a *dated-contingent commodity*. Since there are six nodes following the initial date, there are six dated-contingent goods in the model. The Fundamental Theorems of Welfare Economics envisage that household k's utility function at the initial date is defined over these six dated-contingent goods. In the notation developed in Chapter 3 and Chapter ⋆7, we can write it as $U_k(X^k_{tn(t)})$. The two theorems assume that this household will face a set of relative prices for these dated-contingent goods, to be paid for at the initial date, $t = 0$. These prices should be thought of as insurance premiums for a unit of income claimable if and only if the corresponding node is reached.

Why do the Fundamental Theorems require the strong assumption of common information structure? The reason is this. Imagine that household k is unable to distinguish the two events (or nodes), W and D, at date 1, but that household $k + 1$ is able to distinguish them.[4] To be concrete, imagine that it is known by both households that $k + 1$ will have stocks of grain at date 1 if W were to occur, but not if D were to occur. Let us assume k is in need of grain at date 1. Granted, there is no grain to be had in the event D (unless k stores grain against this contingency); however, k would like to purchase grain if the event is W. The question is whether k can purchase from $k + 1$ grain contingent on W at date 1 at a price quoted and charged at date 0. The answer is 'no', and the reason is this: k knows in advance that, no matter what, $k + 1$ will claim at date 1 that the true event is D. He will therefore not supply grain to k. As neither event at date 1 is publicly observable, k won't be able to prove $k + 1$ to be lying were the true event D. This means that Arrow–Debreu markets for this particular dated-contingent grain will not exist. In the language of modern organization theory, such contingent commodity markets are not compatible with individual incentives.

People can of course enter into contracts with others even when they

---

[4] If weather appears an implausible example for the point I am trying to make, we could interpret D as ill-health and W as good-health for household $k + 1$.

don't share the same information structure. However, such contracts as would be compatible with individual incentives when household information structures are different will look different from those embodied in the price-taking competitive hypothesis assumed in the standard theory. Later, we will study resource allocation mechanisms that are compatible with household incentives when the information that households possess does not coincide. Until then we will continue to assume that households have identical information structures.

8.2   Choice under Uncertainty and Risk Aversion

People typically differ in their beliefs about the likelihood of events. This divergence of opinion provides one reason why households engage in trades that are contingent on specific events. Insurance markets are the setting for such trade. Prices in the theory of resource allocation under uncertainty are prices for contingent goods and services. Contracts in resource allocation mechanisms under uncertainty are contingent contracts. We anticipated these matters earlier. To give an example, a price for irrigation water next year if there is a drought is a price to be paid now for delivery of irrigation water next year *if and only if* there is a drought next year. It will be recalled that in the Arrow–Debreu theory there is a complete set of markets at the initial date. This means that there is a market for each and every distinguishable commodity.[5] All decisions concerning exchange, production, and consumption must therefore be made at the initial date. Most of these decisions concern contingent actions; so actions are specified in terms of date–event pairs.

Household utility functions and indices of liberties are defined on the space of dated-contingent commodities. Both a household's behaviour and its revealed attitude towards risk are reflected in its utility function. There is no presumption in the standard theory that household choices maximize anything as special as their expected utility. This is important to note; it makes the account of household behaviour quite generally usable. By a careful specification of the domain of utility functions, it is possible for the theory to accommodate the many seeming oddities in individual choice which have been uncovered in recent experimental work.[6]

[5] As we observed earlier, this hypothesis requires all parties to have the same information structure. Otherwise there will be missing markets.

[6] By oddities I mean oddities when viewed from the perspective of the expected-utility theory of choice under uncertainty (otherwise known as the von Neumann-Morgenstern theory: see below). It should be noted that the argument that a sufficient set of securities markets, allied to spot markets for commodities in each possible contingency, can substitute for a complete set of contingent-commodity markets does require that households maximize expected utility. Arrow (1964) is the pioneering article on this.

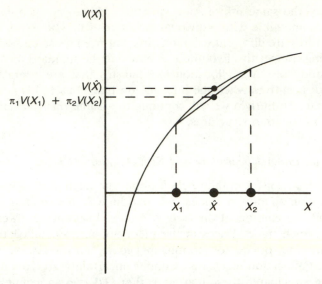

Fig. 8.2   von Neumann–Morgenstern utility function: $\hat{X} = \pi_1 X_1 + \pi_2 X_2$

It is useful to distinguish general models of choice under uncertainty from special ones. In the latter, household utility functions over contingent commodities are given strong additional structures. The best-known special construction is the 'expected utility' model of von Neumann and Morgenstern (see von Neumann and Morgenstern, 1944; Marschak, 1950; Savage, 1954; Luce and Raiffa, 1957; Arrow, 1971b). We turn to this in the context of our example.[7]

Consider household k, whose utility function satisfies the expected-utility hypothesis. Imagine that it is a self-regarding household. Then its utility function would be reducible to the form

$$U_k = \Sigma \pi_s V_s^k(X_{st}^k) \equiv E[V_s^k(\cdot)], \qquad (8.1)$$

where X_{st}^k denotes income enjoyed by household k at date t ($t = 1,2$) in state of nature s ($s = 1,2,3,4$), π_s denotes the probability of s occurring, and E is the expectation operator. (The underlying probabilities could be subjective.) In the language of the theory, $V_s^k(\cdot)$ is k's state-dependent utility function, and by its choice k maximizes the expected value of this, which is U_k.[8]

---

[7] Yaari (1987) has developed a model that is dual to this.

[8] I need hardly add that this phrasing of matters ought not to be taken literally: U_k is the numerical representation of the ordering over alternatives on the basis of which household k actually chooses. I should add though that, since the household is unable to distinguish between states of nature 1 and 2 and between 3 and 4 at date 1, it will have to respect the constraints $X_{11} = X_{21}$ and $X_{31} = X_{41}$.

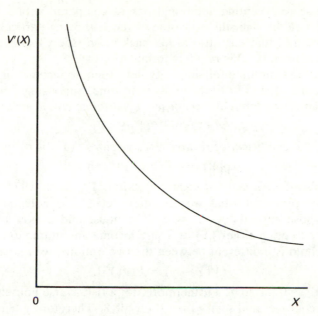

Fig. 8.3   Marginal utility function

For expositional ease, I shall simplify further and assume household k's utility function to be independent of the state of nature. Then we may write expression (8.1) as

$$U_k = \Sigma \pi_s V^k(X^k_{st}). \qquad (8.2)$$

To say that k is risk-averse at all points is to say that $V^k(\cdot)$ is a strictly concave function of its argument. This is shown in Fig. 8.2, which considers two states of nature and a single date. Income is desired, so V^k is an increasing function of income. Given a choice between a sure income, $\hat{X}$, and an uncertain income, $\{X_1, X_2\}$ with mean $\hat{X}$, the household will choose the sure income: expected utility is higher. This is shown in the figure.

The idea can be generalized. Consider an income (or consumption) lottery $\{\bar{X}^k_{st}\}$. Superimpose on this a risky income $\{\tilde{Y}^k_{st}\}$, which is probabilistically independent of $\{\bar{X}^k_{st}\}$, and whose expected value is nil. Call this $\{\tilde{Z}^k_{st}\}$.[9] A risk-averse household, k, always prefers $\{\bar{X}^k_{st}\}$ to $\{\tilde{Z}^k_{st}\}$ (Rothschild and Stiglitz, 1970). Other things being the same, a risk-averse individual, or household, prefers a smooth consumption stream to a fluctuating one. We will make much use of this when studying household saving behaviour.

The extent to which a household is averse to risk depends on how wealthy it is. It seems plausible that a poor household would be that much

---

[9] That is, $Z^k_{st} = X^k_{st} + Y^k_{st}$.

more averse to accepting additional risk as compared with a (relatively speaking) wealthy one, the downside of the risk being particularly harsh for a household that has little to fall back upon (see Chapter 9; but see below, Section 8.3). This requires formulation.

Abstracting from time for simplicity, let Y denote income, or wealth (it does not matter), and $V(Y)$ the utility of income. Supposing V to be thrice differentiable, we define the *coefficient of absolute risk aversion*, $\gamma(Y)$, as

$$\gamma(Y) = -V''(Y)/V'(Y). \tag{8.3}$$

Similarly, the *coefficient of relative risk aversion*, $\rho(Y)$, is defined as

$$\rho(Y) = -YV''(Y)/V'(Y). \tag{8.4}$$

($\rho(Y)$ is also the *elasticity of marginal utility*). To see in which way these coefficients represent what we are after, let $\{\tilde{Y}\}$ denote an uncertain income whose expected value is $\hat{Y}$. The household is now offered the option of accepting either $\{\tilde{Y}\}$ or a sure income amounting to $(\hat{Y} - y)$. If the household is indifferent between the two options, we must have

$$V(\hat{Y} - y) = E[V(\tilde{Y})]. \tag{8.5}$$

Now $V'(Y) > 0$ for all Y. Furthermore, for a risk-averse household, $V(Y)$ is strictly concave, and so $V''(Y) < 0$ for all Y. Therefore $y > 0$, which is as it should be, since y is the premium the household attaches to the risk associated with $\{\tilde{Y}\}$.

Now suppose $\{\tilde{Y}\}$ is a small risk. Then y must be small. Applying Taylor's expansion round $\hat{Y}$ up to the first order in y to both sides of (8.5), we can express it as

$$-yV'(\hat{Y}) \approx V''(\hat{Y})\sigma^2/2,$$

where σ^2 is the variance of $\{\tilde{Y}\}$. This we can rewrite as

$$y \approx -\sigma^2[V''(\hat{Y})/V'(\hat{Y})]/2. \tag{8.6}$$

Using (8.3) in (8.6), we have

$$y \approx \gamma(\hat{Y})\sigma^2/2, \tag{8.7}$$

or, on using (8.4), we may write it equivalently as

$$y/\hat{Y} \approx \rho(\hat{Y})[\sigma/\hat{Y}]^2/2. \tag{8.8}$$

Equations (8.7) and (8.8) give us the sense in which $\gamma(Y)$ and $\rho(Y)$ are measures of risk aversion. For a given variance, σ^2, the risk premium is proportional to γ, and for a given coefficient of variation, $(\sigma/\hat{Y})$, the risk premium, as a fraction of mean income, is proportional to ρ (see Pratt, 1964; Arrow, 1965). There are grounds for inferring from studies of household behaviour that $\gamma(Y)$ is a decreasing function of Y (see Arrow, 1965; Binswanger and Rosenzweig, 1989; Chapter 9). From (8.3) we know this to require the condition $V'''(Y) > 0$ for all Y. This is another way of saying that $V'(Y)$ is a strictly convex function of Y (see Fig. 8.3). Now, it is an easy matter to confirm that $V'(Y)$ is strictly convex if $V(Y)$ is iso-elastic (i.e. $\rho'(Y) = 0$). Iso-elastic utility functions provide a good labora-tory for exploring consumption behaviour over time (Mirrlees, 1967), under risk (Mirrlees, 1965; Levhari and Srinivasan, 1969; Hahn, 1970), and in connection with fertility choice (Dasgupta, 1969; Chapter *13) and the depletion of exhaustible resources (Solow, 1974; Dasgupta and Heal, 1979). We will discuss the effect of increasing risks in future income on current consumption in Section *9.2.

It will prove useful to have a sense of orders of magnitude. Suppose that $\rho = 3$ and $(\sigma/\hat{Y}) = 0.3$. From (8.8), it follows that $y/\hat{Y} = 13.5$ per cent. In other words, a household would be willing to settle for 13.5 per cent less income on average if this were the price it had to pay for eliminating income risk entirely. This isn't a negligible amount, and, as ρ has been assumed to equal 3, it reflects only moderate risk aversion. We will find these ideas useful subsequently when we study household behaviour under risk.

The purpose of imposing such structure as the expected-utility formula-tion is to obtain testable implications. Further structure; such as for example declining absolute risk aversion with increasing wealth, yields even sharper results. Because of its simplicity, and because as a model of *rational* choice under uncertainty there is much to commend the expected-utility theory (see below), this special construct has been greatly explored. The problem is that a large array of experimental investigations in recent years has shown that individuals violate the 'expected-utility hypothesis' systematically.[10]

The claim that a rational individual *ought* to obey the von Neumann–Morgenstern axioms of choice is a contentious one. But it has one impressive grounding. It can be shown that a person violating any of the axioms is a potential 'money pump': a sequence of monetary bets can be so tailored for him that he will inevitably lose an arbitrarily large sum in the long run (see Raiffa, 1968; Yaari, 1985; Machina, 1990). The argument then is that, were he made aware of this fact, he would recognize the error of his ways, and would proceed to choose in accordance with the von Neumann-Morgenstern axioms. There is consequently a tension between how people actually choose, and how they would choose if they thought through such problems as the one we have just identified. In any case, it

---

[10] Machina (1987), in a most illuminating essay, provides a classification of the various patterns in which the von Neumann-Morgenstern theory has been observed to be violated by subjects under experimental conditions. (The classification is based on what are known as 'common consequence' and 'common ratio' effects, the phenomenon of preference reversal, and the framing effect.) Kahneman, Slovic and Tversky (1982), Hogarth and Reder (1986), D. E. Bell, Raiffa and Tversky (1988), and Gardenfors and Sahlin (1988) are collections of essays that report these violations.

isn't clear if choice under experimental conditions of what are usually small sums of money provides adequate information about choice involving matters such as planting crops, taking out insurance, storing food-grain, and so forth. Moreover, the bulk of the experimental work on attitudes to risk has been conducted on people who are not poor. We can't conclude from this body of work that in regions of low income the von Neumann-Morgenstern axioms are off the mark for risks involving substantial sums.

In fact, we may tentatively so conclude from an exceptional investigation by Binswanger (1981). This study, based on a sample of poor farmers in India, offered options involving sums of money which were not small relative to their wealths. It was discovered that farmers' attitudes to risk violated the expected-utility hypothesis. The question arises whether models of individual choice under uncertainty can be made sufficiently broad to accommodate many of the systematic patterns of choice so far exposed in the experimental literature, including Binswanger's, and yet be sufficiently structured to yield further, testable implications.

In a remarkable series of essays, Machina (1982, 1987, 1989, 1990) has not only shown that this is possible: he has also shown how to extend the vocabulary associated with the expected-utility theory (such as the idea behind risk aversion) to more general circumstances.[11] For example, it is possible to show (see Quizon, Binswanger and Machina, 1984) that a number of simple formulations that depart from the expected-utility hypothesis are consistent with Binswanger's original findings.[12] The expected-utility hypothesis can be expected to be with us because of its simplicity, its heuristic value, and because there is a sense in which the axioms underlying it are those that a rational strategist would subscribe to. We will also see subsequently that it has enormous explanatory power for the kind of data economists are normally limited to. (The data would not be able to tell the expected-utility theory apart from any number of more general theories.) Because we now know there are simple extensions which enable us to accommodate those observed behaviours the theory can't handle, we can have greater confidence in appealing to the expected-utility theory for heuristic purposes. But as a universal model of individual choice under uncertainty, it has now to be abandoned. Machina's work has shown that, fortunately, this is not a cause for alarm.

[11] For certain violations of the von Neumann-Morgenstern axioms, such as those uncovered in the so-called 'Allais paradoxes' (covering as they do what are called the common consequence and common ratio effects), the thing to do is to seek representations of preferences which, unlike expression (8.1) are not linear in probabilities. For other types of violation, such as 'preference reversal' and the 'framing effect', the thing to do is to expand the space on which the orderings are defined. This last move is not a contrivance. If the way in which options are framed has an effect on how a person ranks them, then patently, his ranking is sensitive to such additional characteristics of options as the way in which they are expressed.

[12] The extension consists of utility functions, $U_k(\cdot)$, that are non-linear in probabilities.

On the production side, matters are simpler for theories of resource allocation under uncertainty. Technological and ecological transformation possibilities need to be defined among contingent commodities. Thus, a peasant can be assumed to know agricultural transformation possibilities. What he does not know in advance is how much harvest he will enjoy with a given allocation of inputs. Therein lies the uncertainty. Since there is a complete set of contingent-commodity markets in the Arrow–Debreu theory, producing firms in it do not face any uncertainty in their profits. All the uncertainty is borne by households. Both the Equilibrium Existence Theorem and the First Fundamental Theorem of Welfare Economics therefore extend themselves trivially, with the provision that households' utility functions pertain to the initial date. For example, the First Fundamental Theorem states that a competitive equilibrium sustains an *ex ante* Pareto-efficient allocation of risk-bearing.

Extension of the Second Fundamental Theorem is for this reason a bit delicate in its reach, in that the social well-being function has now to be regarded in an *ex ante* fashion. It is defined on individual well-beings which are themselves evaluated *ex ante*. Put another way, the theorem assumes well-being to be assessed at the initial date, over all possible contingencies and over all possible dates. As it stands, it is silent on whether social choice can be expected to be consistent as events follow upon events, or whether it is known in advance that social choice will be revised. Further structure is required to ensure that it is consistent. (On this see Starr, 1973; Jacques Dreze, 1974; Machina, 1989).

8.3   *Avoiding Disasters*

In fact, we shouldn't expect households to be averse to risk at very low levels of income. One imagines that every household faces something like a threshold level. Were its income to fall below it, the household would be in a state of crisis. Further deprivation wouldn't matter much; it wouldn't be felt. When household income is extremely low, members face starvation, and then marginal additions to income are of little or no value. The household is in the throes of a disaster, and only a discrete addition to income can lift it out of the mire.[13] Of course, we have no reason at all for thinking that individuals, let alone households, in such circumstances choose in conformity to the expected-utility theory, or even close to conformity. Nevertheless, the theory can aid us in predicting and explaining choice under uncertainty in stressful circumstances.

---

[13] Needless to say, even for a given household there is no actual line that defines the threshold. It is more like a band which, when crossed, dramatically reduces its survival chances. See Chs. 14–*16 for further discussion.

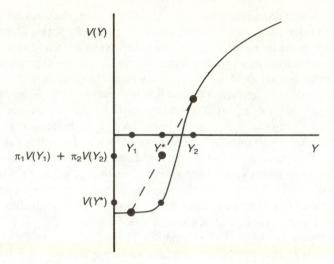

Fig. 8.4   von Neumann–Morgenstern utility function at very low income: $Y^* = \pi_1 Y_1 + \pi_2 Y_2$

Fig. 8.4 describes a utility function, $V(Y)$, which is more or less flat at very low levels of income, and which rises sharply near the threshold income, Y^*. $V(Y)$ assumes a concave, increasing form a bit beyond Y^*, so the expected-utility theory predicts risk-averse behaviour there. But $V(Y)$ is convex in the neighbourhood of Y^*; and so, for very poor households the theory predicts risk-taking behaviour over income lotteries which offer them the chance of avoiding disaster. In short, very poor households choose gambles of a certain kind. This is shown in Fig. 8.4 via a simple example. There are two states of nature, $s = 1, 2$. As between a sure income Y^* and an uncertain income (Y_1, Y_2) with mean Y^*, the household would choose the uncertain income. Expected utility is lower at Y^*.

There is an alternative way of formulating the idea that at very low levels of income households choose to gamble. It is to assume that, when choosing among risky income streams, households first choose safety, and from among those that are safe they choose in accordance with expected utility, or possibly expected income. This is called the *safety-first* model of choice under uncertainty. To illustrate, imagine that the household sets a safety level of 5 per cent. This means it rejects any income lottery offering more than a 5 per cent chance of yielding an income either less than or equal to Y^*. We could then imagine that, from among those that remain after this pruning exercise, the household chooses the option with, say, the highest expected value. This displays a lexicographic ordering over income lotteries. (Therein lies its weakness; the underlying ordering is discontinuous.)

Formally, let Ξ be the set of available income lotteries, and let $\{\tilde{Y}\}$ be a typical lottery. The safety-first model can be expressed as:[14]

Choose $\{\tilde{Y}\}$ from Ξ so as to maximize $E(\{\tilde{Y}\})$
subject to the constraint that $\text{prob}[\{\tilde{Y}\} \le Y^*] \le 0.05.$ \qquad (8.3)

We would like to confirm that the criterion can lead to the household favouring risky income streams. To do this, let us assume that there are two states of nature, $s = 1, 2$, and two income lotteries, $\{\tilde{Y}\} = (Y_1, Y_2)$ and $\{\tilde{X}\} = (X_1, X_2)$ to choose from. Imagine that the probability of $s = 1$ occurring is 4 per cent. Suppose $\{\tilde{X}\}$ is a sure income equal to Y^*, and that $Y_1 = Y^* - \delta$ and $Y_2 = Y^* + \varepsilon$, where δ and ε are positive numbers. Select their values so that $E(\{\tilde{Y}\}) = Y^*$. In this case $\{\tilde{Y}\}$ is unambiguously more risky than $\{\tilde{X}\}$, and has the same mean value. Nevertheless, under criterion (8.3), it is $\{\tilde{Y}\}$ that will be chosen.

The safety-first model has been much analysed in decision theory.[15] In an instructive study Kunreuther and Wright (1979) have used it to explain the cultivation of cash crops (a risky activity) as opposed to food crops (the safer activity) among samples of the smallest landholders in Bangladesh, Nigeria, and late nineteenth-century southern United States. The model has also been used to explain high fertility rates in poor countries. The idea here is that parents set targets for the size of their families with an eye to a sufficiently high probability that they will have someone to support them in old age (see Cain, 1983, and Chapter 12). As a model of choice under uncertainty, the safety-first principle has a rough-and-ready air about it. This is one of its attractions. As a method for capturing the way people living in extreme poverty try to fend off disaster, there is much to commend it. That some of this behaviour can be culled from the expected-utility hypothesis near threshold income levels means only that it is a matter of research convenience which of the two models we use to analyse some of the critical problems facing the poorest of the poor.

8.4   *Trading in Risks: Pooling and Spreading*

Household attitudes to risk are embodied in their utility functions. In the competitive price mechanism, these attitudes get reflected in the prices of contingent commodities, the latter being in effect insurance premia. When risks are 'objective', as for rainfall, prices are related to the relative probabilities of various contingencies. In agrarian and pastoral societies of poor countries we do not typically observe competitive contingent-commodity prices. In Chapter 6 we identified a number of reasons why we

---

[14] $E[\{\tilde{Y}\}]$ denotes the expected value of $\{\tilde{Y}\}$.
[15] For reviews, see Jock Anderson (1979) and Boussard (1979). See also Majumdar and Radner (1991).

would not expect to see competitive markets in poor countries. With the exception of casual labour markets, such formal markets as exist in rural areas there are usually thin, and we would not expect competitive prices to emerge. In the rural credit market in Pakistan, the price of loans has been observed to equal their average cost, not their marginal cost (see Aleem, 1990). One reason markets are thin is that transport costs in rural areas of poor countries are large relative to incomes. An additional reason, which is a consequence of this, is that buyers and sellers across villages do not possess the same information about product or factor quality. Village enclaves are the result. Labour and credit markets are geographically segmented.

The thinness of markets can on occasion mean that the terms of trade are only implicit, as in the practice of gift exchange. As there are often no enforcement possibilities via a third party, such as the courts, many contracts have to be personalized. The absence of contingent prices doesn't mean that risk markets don't exist in poor societies. Nor does it mean that resource allocation mechanisms in these societies aren't sensitive to the exigencies of life. Nor indeed does it mean that people with little by way of assets are not averse to risk. Quite the contrary: trading in insurance is of paramount importance to any household that knows that it can be obliterated under a single bad contingency were it to operate in an autarkic manner.[16] We would then expect insurance against hunger and destitution to be among the most important organizational problems facing poor communities. This need for trading in risks in a world where there are few formal risk markets leads to the highly integrated network of interpersonal and inter-household obligations (including marriage patterns) that anthropologists and economists have often observed in agrarian and pastoral communities in poor countries.[17]

When risks are household-specific (these are otherwise known as individual risks), such as illnesses unconnected with infections, or fire damage

---

[16] There is no contradiction between this and the analysis of the previous section, where risk-taking behaviour was explained. Given the shape of the utility function in Fig. 8.3, we would expect poor households to avoid risk and to welcome it at the same time. The mix of the two depends upon the composition of income lotteries on offer. See Friedman and Savage (1948) for a similar analysis for middle-income households.

[17] See e.g. Provinse (1955), Turnbull (1972), Wynne (1980), Hayami and Kikuchi (1981), Rudra (1982, 1984), Binswanger (1986), Binswanger and Rosenzweig (1986a, b), Rosenzweig (1988a, b), de Garine and Harrison (1988), Rosenzweig and Stark (1989), Townsend (1989), and Lim (1991). See also Piddocke (1965) for an account of the Potlatch system prevailing among North American tribes; Wiessner (1982) for an account of the *hxaro* system of hunger insurance among the !Kung San hunter-gatherers; Cashdan (1985) for an account of the corresponding system among the Nata River Bushmen; Caldwell, Reddy and Caldwell (1986) for a study of hunger insurance among non-resident in-laws in the state of Karnataka in India (see also Ch. 11); and Platteau and Abraham (1987) for an account of hunger insurance through credit exchanges in a fishing community in the state of Kerala in India. Cashdan (1989) is a useful collection of essays on communal-security arrangements in traditional societies.

to one's home, mutual insurance is a way of reducing them. This is often called *risk-pooling*. Insurance companies pool risks by this device, having a large number of insurees whose risks are approximately independent of one another. Health and accident insurance are examples. Insurance companies like to call this 'risk-spreading' rather than 'risk-pooling', the difference in the terminology reflecting largely the agency point of view. Households can be viewed as pooling their risks through the insurance company, while the insurance company can simultaneously be viewed as spreading its risks by offering insurance to a multitude of independent households. By 'household-specific risks' we mean risks that are approximately independent across households. (They are also often called 'idiosyncratic risks'.) Within households there is also risk-pooling, in that many risks are specific to persons, illness or accidents being prime examples. Here then is an advantage of the extended-family system (Cain, 1981, pursues this line of thought). Other things being the same, the larger is the population size, the greater is the extent to which independent risks can be reduced by pooling. In the limit, the coefficient of variation facing each household can be reduced to nil. This follows from the Law of Large Numbers.[18]

In small village communities, the Law of Large Numbers would not be expected to apply. Nevertheless, mutual insurance can reduce household risks. We would also expect to see norms of behaviour consistent with the exchange of contingent goods and services. We have earlier noted that, for insurance contracts to work well, contracting parties need to be in a position to verify jointly that stipulated events have occurred as and when they occur. Unless the relationship is expected to be enduring and the parties farsighted, they must also be in a position to confirm that all concerned parties have undertaken the actions they have agreed to undertake in specified circumstances.[19] It helps if a third party can also verify claims. This makes enforcement of contracts easier. But as we will see later, for people expecting to encounter one another repeatedly, it isn't always essential. This makes resource allocation mechanisms in what are often called traditional societies look quite different from those in societies sustained by the law of contracts and private property.

At the household level, risk-spreading is a way of reducing uncertainty.

---

[18] See Malinvaud (1972b, 1973) for properties of Arrow–Debreu contingent-commodity prices in situations where the Law of Large Numbers applies. They are proportional to the probabilities of various contingencies. See also Dasgupta and Heal (1979: ch. 13).

[19] Radner (1981, 1985, 1986) has shown that useful insurance arrangements can be arrived at between farsighted parties even if effort on the part of clients (agents) can't be monitored by patrons (principals). Radner's argument is that, if the environmental uncertainty is independently distributed over time, a patron can use the accumulated record of outcomes to infer with confidence if the client has been cheating.

It is a form of self-insurance. Agricultural households can often diversify their activities (or locations of activities), engage in intercropping patterns of cultivation, and so forth, with the hope that bad fortune in one activity will be compensated by good fortune in another (see Walker and Ryan, 1990). For the spreading of risks to be possible, it is necessary that risks are not positively correlated to any great extent. For this reason poor agrarian households not only produce crops, they often also produce artefacts for the market, such as rugs, trinkets, baskets, ropes, and general art and craftwork. This supplements income. Also, such sources of income are not overly correlated with agricultural output. These supplementary activities provide a form of hunger insurance, by reducing the fluctuation of total household income.

Another form of risk-spreading for the individual household in some societies is land allocation. In parts of the Himalayas and the Andes, each household cultivates a diversified portfolio of land, the diversification being in terms of slope, soil characteristics, and altitude (see Mayer, 1985; Platteau, 1991). The idea behind this, again, is to smooth the inevitable fluctuations of household income.

It is instructive to note the difference between risk-pooling and risk-spreading in this example. Were each household to cultivate contiguous pieces of land, there would be no risk-spreading on the part of any household. There would then be a need for risk-pooling *among* households. For reasons of moral hazard in agricultural (see Chapter 9), pooling is a less effective mode of reducing individual risk when spreading is an available option. By diversifying the portfolio of cultivable land, each household reduces its need for pooling its risk with others. This gain may exceed the loss that each household incurs from diversification, the loss being the greater cost involved in managing non-contiguous pieces of land. Therein lies the rationale for locational diversification of household plots.

8.5   *Correlated Risks in Agriculture*

Neither risk-spreading nor risk-pooling is a possibility when environmental uncertainties are positively correlated to any great extent, and when outside credit facilities are unavailable. As we observed earlier, credit facilities within a community would be expected to be heavily constrained because of positive correlations in risks. (For empirical confirmation, see Binswanger and Rosenzweig, 1986b; Hazell, Pomareda and Valdes, 1986.) I will hardly offer you a loan if I think you will be unable to repay me precisely when others are unlikely to be able to repay me, when thereby my need for income would be greatest. This is a central problem for agrarian communities. Weather can impose highly correlated risks among farmers.

One way out, even in such circumstances, is to hold stocks of grain.

Inventories offer a method of smoothing consumption over time, some-thing a risk-averse household would prefer over fluctuations in consump-tion (see Chapters 9 and *9). The holding of inventories is common household practice in rural communities. It offers insurance against hunger even when in any given season household risks are correlated. But we are studying poor households here. Their inventories are typically small and are inadequately protected against damp and pests.[20] An important area of State action in this situation is the pooling of agricultural risks across different regions. A region suffering from drought can then be protected against famine and destitution if the government is able and willing to transport food from its own granaries and from purchases made from surplus areas;[21] similarly for the correlated risks of floods, and the consequent losses that they inflict on life and property.

Another way out is to use the body as a store of 'food' (i.e. energy). We will see in Chapters 14 and 15 that, in those parts of rural sub-Saharan Africa where there is only one agricultural season, people's body weights move with the annual cycle: farmers gain weight after harvest, and lose weight during the hungry season, when agricultural tasks are particularly heavy. We will study the problem of saving and the attempt on the part of households to smooth their consumption over time in greater detail in Chapter 9. Here we should note that using the body as a store of energy does not help to smooth consumption; it merely enables a person to meet energy requirements over the annual cycle.

From the perspective of households, uncertainties in both agricultural yields and the prices of inputs and outputs are much like correlated environmental risks within the village (or district). Thus, for example, were all households to engage in the production of pretty much the same crop, they would face large, positively correlated risks. (This is the kind of risk mono-crop communities are vulnerable to.) It would then prove difficult to establish mutual insurance among households within a village.

These are qualitative statements. To present matters in a form that enables the analyst to determine the extent to which households in a village can insure themselves against risks in income, let $\tilde{I}_{ht}$ be household h's income at time t. For simplicity of exposition, let us assume that we can decompose it into three parts: X_h, a time-invariant, household-specific income; $\tilde{Y}_{ht}$, a time-varying, household-specific (or idiosyncratic) shock with zero mean; and $\tilde{Z}_t$, a time-varying village-specific shock with zero

---

[20] In sub-Saharan Africa, anything between 10% and 25% of grain is lost in on-farm storages. See Pariser (1982).

[21] That the Chinese government did not perform this function during its Great Leap Forward had much to do with the famine that resulted in more than 20 m. deaths there. See Dreze and Sen (1990).

mean which is faced by all households. (This last is the positively correlated component of household incomes.) Thus,

$$\tilde{I}_{ht} = X_h + \tilde{Y}_{ht} + \tilde{Z}_t. \qquad (8.9)$$

As noted above, efficient risk-sharing among households within the village can protect them only against the idiosyncratic component of their incomes, not against the component that is correlated positively. We have also observed that households diversify their activities with a view to reducing the riskiness of $\tilde{I}_{ht}$, both by reducing the extent to which their incomes are correlated among one another (enabling them to try to pool their risks) and by lowering the uncertainty in their idiosyncratic shocks (so as not to have to try to pool). That they are able considerably to achieve the former has been observed by Udry (1990) in a set of panel data for Northern Nigeria, and by Morduch (1991) for south India. These authors have estimated that the share of idiosyncratic risk in the variance of total household income in the data is over 75 per cent. Of course, the two methods available to a household for reducing income fluctuation may conflict with each other: the attempt on the part of households to diversify their activities so as to spread their risks may lead to an increase in their correlated risk. When this is so, it is the lack of insurance possibilities that results in a high covariance in household incomes, and not that a high covariance in household incomes blocks the possibility of risk-pooling (see Alderman and Paxson, 1992).

Covariances among household incomes within ecological zones are a reason why government ought to be involved in the supply of insurance. Maintaining stocks in public granaries are one way governments can insure households against drought, smoothing food supply over time and events. It is not necessarily the cheapest way (depending on the circumstances, additional food imports in times of crisis could be cheaper), but the Indian experience since the 1970s suggests that it can be very effective (see Reutlinger and Pellekaan, 1986; Drèze and Sen, 1990).

Insurance, whether through pooling or spreading, is especially potent when it proves possible to pursue activities whose risks are correlated negatively. For pooling to be effective, large numbers are not essential in this case. Consider an extreme example. Assume that there are only two possible events, e_1 and e_2. There is an activity, say a_1, which yields income of 100 units in e_1 and nothing in e_2. There is another activity, say a_2, which yields income of 100 in e_2, and nothing in case of e_1. The correlation coefficient of the two risks is -1. In this situation it makes perfectly good sense for me to pursue a_1 and for you to pursue a_2 and for us to agree to a guaranteed income of 50 units each in either event. This arrangement offers each of us complete insurance.

Such simple extreme cases don't usually exist; but there are on occasion situations that offer parties the opportunity of obtaining insurance through the choice of negatively correlated risks. Consider the choice of investment projects. Other things being the same, a project that is negatively correlated with national income is preferable to one that is positively correlated with it. In the literature on social cost–benefit analysis, it has been argued that in agrarian societies irrigation projects possess an insurance value that fertilizer projects do not: irrigation projects have high use-value precisely when its yield is most needed (i.e. when rainfall is low and thus national income is low), where fertilizers have high use-value only when there is ample water, which there would be only when rainfall was high, and therefore when national income was high.[22]

There are thus different layers of insurance against hunger and destitution in any society. (For an empirical study, see Walker and Ryan, 1990.) As regards the pooling of risks, the household itself offers an insurance arrangement to its members. Across households in traditional village communities there are, as I have noted in all too sketchy a manner, any number of systems of mutual insurance arrangements. These are often, though not always, codified through social norms of behaviour (see below). The various institutional layers are not, of course, distinctive. For example, the government has an obligation to ensure that individuals have protection against destitution. This may cut across insurance schemes at the household, village, and district levels. There are insurance mechanisms at the level of the individual and the household in all societies. They are often hopelessly inequitable, in that income gains from insurance arrangements are disproportionately shared among parties. They are also often inefficient. We will look into this in Chapter 9.

None of this implies that the government should impose draconian measures by forcibly obliterating existing institutions and replacing them by new ones. There is much we should have learnt by now from the recent history of revolutionary intentions. Under a hypothetical social contract, the State's role in these layers would be to supplement existing institutions, by offering additional opportunities (for example credit facilities, an agricultural extension service, public health care, a family-planning service), and by advertising these new options vociferously. If better opportunities were made available to rural people, they could be expected to exploit them and to further them. More than forty years of research on rural practices and peasants' responses to new opportunities should at last

---

[22] See Dasgupta, Marglin and Sen (1972). (See also Dasgupta and Heal, 1979: 378–88, for a formalization.) For the sake of expositional ease, I am restricting myself to covariances only when talking of insurance. In general, higher moments of probability distributions will also matter. However, if the risks are small we can restrict ourselves to the first two moments, no matter what the distribution (see e.g. Dasgupta and Heal, 1979; Newbery and Stiglitz, 1981). Alternatively, and this is the real justification here, it could be that the distributions are defined in terms of two moments, e.g. the normal distribution.

have laid to rest the thought that such folk may not know where their real interests lie.

8.6 *Reciprocity as a Social Norm in Stationary Environments*

The near-stationarity of both kinship lines and the circumstances facing people in traditional societies together imply that mutual insurance arrangements don't always look like mutual insurance arrangements.[23] There can be layers of behavioural norms and rules whose compliance sustains a variety of insurance agreements. You come and help in my field when I fall ill, fully expecting that you in turn will be helped by me should you fall ill. Should it happen that you are ill longer than I was when you helped me, I would not cut short my help to keep it commensurate with the help you gave me. This is because, for all I know, the next time I may be ill for an even longer spell and will need even more help from you. And so on. There is nothing mysterious in such acts of reciprocity; certainly, there is no reason to invoke the idea that there is greater innate generosity and fellow-feeling among poor people in poor communities than exists among members of modern urban societies.[24] Substantial inequities have been unearthed in resource allocation mechanisms in poor societies, for example, between landlords and tenants, and in patron–client labour and insurance relationships in rural Asia. They are all too visible even to the privileged in these societies.

Within rural communities there is thus an integrated system of mutual insurance against illness, production failure, and general bad luck. We have not as yet studied how these implicit contracts are enforced. We have to investigate what sustains (non-contractual) systems of reciprocity, what encourages people to meet their obligations even when there is no law to enforce them (that is, law in the modern judicial sense).

At least three answers suggest themselves. Each has force, to a greater or lesser extent depending on the context in which the exchange occurs. (Of course, none of the answers may work in a particular context, in which case people will find themselves in a hole they cannot easily get out of, and what could have been mutually beneficial exchanges will not take place.) The first is that rural communities are themselves village-level States, with an established structure of power and authority, vested in

---

[23] I am thinking of societies where the land–person ratio hasn't changed rapidly. The assumption that society is nearly stationary is not a good one when the society experiences rapid population growth within a fixed cultivable land mass.

[24] The idea that traditional societies were closer to being 'moral economies' than market economies was explored by J. C. Scott (1976). See also Giddens (1986). Platteau (1991) contains a rich discussion of why this is a questionable viewpoint. For analytical discourses on social norms and conventions, see D. Lewis (1969). Ullmann–Margalit (1977), Boyd and Richerson (1985), Richerson and Boyd (1987), and Elster (1989).

some cases in tribal elders (as within nomadic tribes in sub-Saharan Africa), and in other cases in dominant landowners (such as the zamindars of eastern India), feudal lords (as in the state of Rajasthan in India), chieftains, and priests. On occasions there are even attempts at making rural communities mini-republics. Village Panchayats in India try to assume such a form. The idea there is to elect offices, the officials being entrusted with the power to settle disputes, enforce the agreed-upon uses of communally owned resources, communicate with higher levels of State authority, and so forth. Wade's account (see Wade, 1987, 1988) of the collective management of common-property resources in South India describes such a mechanism of enforcement in detail.

The question why such a structure of authority as may exist is accepted by people is a higher-order one, akin to the question why people accept the authority of government. General acceptance itself is a Nash equilibrium: when all others accept the structure of authority, each has an incentive to accept it. Contrariwise, when a sufficiently large number don't accept it, individual incentives to accept it weaken, and the system unravels rapidly. General acceptance of the structure of authority is held together by its own bootstraps, so to speak. (See Chapter *12 for an illustration in a different context.)[25]

The second answer is that the practice of reciprocity is *internalized* by each of us over time through communal living, role modelling, education, and through experiencing rewards and punishments. This process begins at the earliest stages of our lives. We internalize social norms, such as that of paying our dues, keeping agreements, returning a favour; and higher-order norms, as for example frowning on people who break social norms, and so forth. To use the language we have developed earlier, the claim here is that a person's utility function is itself a reflection of an ordering over actions in part driven by social norms. By internalizing a norm, a person makes the springs of his actions contain the norm. He therefore feels shame or guilt in violating a norm, and this prevents him from doing so, or at the very least it puts a brake on his violating it unless other considerations are found by him to be overriding. In short, his upbringing ensures that he has a disposition to obey the norm. When he does violate it, neither guilt nor shame is typically absent, but the act will have been rationalized by him.

Now it is evident that people differ in the extent to which they internalize social norms. They also differ in the extent to which they are willing to trade off the dictates of norms against personal desires, other

---

[25] The political process is often usurped by the economically powerful in rural communities. A central problem facing applied political theory is of devising ways of making participatory democracy work in village communities. See Chopra, Kadekodi and Murty (1989) and Seabright (1990) for case studies of this.

commitments, competing loyalties, and so on. In Chapter 3 I touched upon this when discussing the direction of the socialization process for poor women in poor countries. That we internalize social norms goes partly to explain why utility is not congruent with well-being interests.

Social norms are injunctions on behavioural strategies. They say 'do this if that', or 'do that if he does this', and so forth. To attain the status of social norms, such injunctions must be accepted by members of society generally. We are talking of norms of behaviour here; we are not talking of cultural beliefs, which are a sharper set of objects.[26] Where people repeatedly encounter one another in similar situations, norms could be established and sustained even without people internalizing them. Thus, social norms could be self-sustaining even were the socialization process ineffectual. This is the third kind of answer to the question we are addressing here.

How does this argument work? A simple set of contexts in which it works is where farsighted people know both one another and the environment, where they expect to interact repeatedly under the same circumstances, and where all this is common knowledge.[27] For expositional purposes, it helps to simplify further and to consider circumstances where actions are observable, and where there is perfect recall on each person's part of how others have behaved in the past.[28] One idea is to require social norms to be supplemented by an entire sequence of meta- (i.e. higher-order) norms, all of which can be succinctly stated in the form of a basic norm, requiring each party to co-operate with any other if and only if that other party is *deserving*. We now assume that the norm requires all parties to start the process of repeated interactions by co-operating. By recursion, it is then possible for any party at any date to determine who is deserving and who is not. If someone is found to be non-deserving in any period, the norm enjoins each of the other parties to impose a sanction on him for

---

[26] See Greif (1991), who argues that cultural beliefs concern commonly held beliefs by each member of a cultural group about what others in the group will do *off* an equilibrium path, that is, along a path where one or more members violate the norm. In this interpretation a cultural belief can never be falsified along an equilibrium path. We will explore this issue in the following section.

[27] See Kreps and Wilson (1982), Milgrom and Roberts (1982), Kreps *et al.* (1982), and Benoit and Krishna (1985) for demonstrations that co-operative behaviour is possible even when people know that the interactions will be for a (large) finite number of periods. For a non-technical discussion of the force of the assumption of common knowledge, see Binmore and Dasgupta (1986) and Aumann (1987a). We entered this briefly in Ch. 3 (s. 3.4). See also Milgrom, North and Weingast (1990) for an application of this mode of reasoning to the development of merchant codes in medieval Europe which led to the revival of trade.

[28] Each of these qualifications can be relaxed. See Radner (1981, 1985, 1986) and Fudenberg, Levine and Maskin (1986) for weakening the first qualification, and Sabourian (1988) for relaxing the second. In the text we will eliminate the qualification that the same set of people are expected to interact indefinitely. We will present an example where social norms can be self-enforcing in a situation where no two parties interact more than once.

that period. (This amounts to non-cooperation with him for that period.) In long, the social norm requires that sanctions be imposed upon those in violation of an agreement; upon those who fail to impose sanctions upon those in violation of the agreement; upon those who fail to impose sanctions upon those who fail to impose sanctions upon those in violation of the agreement; and so on, indefinitely. (This is the sequence of meta-norms mentioned earlier; see Akerlof, 1976, 1980; Axelrod, 1986.) Provided agents are sufficiently farsighted to give sufficient weight to their future gains from co-operation, this basic norm, which tells each person to co-operate with (and only with) deserving persons, can lift communities out of a number of potentially troublesome social situations, including the repeated Prisoners' Dilemma. The reason each person conforms to the basic norm when a sufficient number of others conform is pure and simple self-interest. If a person does not conform, he will suffer from sanctions for the duration of his non-conformism.

This sort of argument, which has been established in a general setting only recently (see Aumann and Shapley, 1976; Rubinstein, 1979; Aumann, 1981; Fudenberg and Maskin, 1986; Abreu, 1988), has been put to effective use in explaining the emergence of a number of institutions which facilitated the growth of trade in medieval Europe. Greif (1989), for example, has shown how the Maghribi traders during the eleventh century in Fustat and across the Mediterranean acted as a collective to impose sanctions on agents who violated their commercial codes. Greif, Milgrom and Weingast (1990) have subsequently offered an account of the rise of merchant guilds in late medieval Europe. These guilds afforded protection to members against unjustified seizure of their property by city-states. Guilds decided if and when a trade embargo was warranted against the city.[29]

Such analyses as I am referring to here have been cast within contexts where the same group of people expect to interact repeatedly and indefinitely. This strong requirement is unnecessary. In a wide-ranging and illuminating essay on social norms, Elster (1989: 113) suggests otherwise: 'Intergenerational reciprocity is . . . found between parents and children. Assuming that parents cannot disinherit their children, the latter have no

---

[29] See also Milgrom, North and Weingast (1990), for an analysis of the role of merchant courts in the Champagne fairs. These courts facilitated members in imposing sanctions on transgressors of agreements. Professor Paul David has remarked to me that a somewhat reverse set of actions occurred as well in medieval Europe, where transgressions by a party were sometimes met by the rest of society imposing sanctions on the entire kinship of the party, or on the guild to which the transgressor belonged. The norm provided collectives with a natural incentive to monitor their own members' behaviour. For a different instance of this, the context being the use of common-property resources, see Howe (1986). We will study the mutual advantages of peer monitoring in Chapter 17, when we come to study credit co-operatives.

incentive to take care of their parents in old age. . . . Yet, most societies have a norm that you should help your parents; in return for what they did for you when you were at a similarly helpless stage.' Elster uses this thought (allied to other thoughts) to argue that this third type of answer we are considering here is of no use; that internalization of norms is the central means by which norms are in fact sustained.

Now this cannot be right when we try to account for the way trade sanctions were used against unreliable city states and potentially dishonest merchants. These institutions did not internalize norms; they followed their mandates, among which were that they pursue such behavioural strategies as I have outlined here. One may argue, however, that behavioural strategies of guilds aren't what one calls 'social norms', which, after all, refer to those that are *generally* accepted. It may then seem that the third kind of answer we are exploring here, while suitable for explaining the development of institutions, isn't equipped to explain behaviour at the personal level. But this would be to miss the point of the exercise. The sort of answer we are seeking here, when applied to personalized exchanges, should be seen as a supplement to the one which says that social norms exist by virtue of our having the disposition to obey them. It isn't inevitably a *competing* answer; it enables us to address a prior question: What explains the norms enshrined in our educational process, those that are instilled into us from the beginning of our lives, by our kith and kin, and by our friends, acquaintances, and teachers? That we internalize norms is not in doubt. (When we refrain from littering the streets it isn't entirely because we are afraid of being caught. We often think it is simply the wrong thing to do.) But to explain the existence of norms by saying that the educational process creates such a disposition in us is facile. It doesn't come to grips with why the educational process in a given community is what it is, why our social dispositions take the shape they do. We should ask if underneath it all there isn't a more basic consideration, something that is hidden from view by the process of socialization, and by the language we use to explain our acts. We should ask if it isn't possible that the *grounds* of our disposition to follow social norms has something to do with individual interest. The third type of answer we are exploring here has the virtue that it enables us to explain social norms in terms of localized interests, and ecological and technological constraints. It has the considerable merit of being parsimonious. It may, of course, be wrong. But as a programme of research it is worth pursuing. To be sure, if the claim in the above quotation from Elster (1989) is analytically correct, this third route we are exploring here will be a minor starter. As it happens, it is not correct.

8.7   *Overlapping Generations and the Transmission of Resources*

Consider a stylized model of a society of dynastic families, in which each generation lives for precisely three periods: childhood, adulthood, and old age.[30] If a person is to survive a period, she needs to consume at the beginning of the period at least $\hat{X}$ units of a perfectly perishable commodity. Furthermore, each person in her adulthood produces at no cost $3\bar{X}$ units of the good, where $\bar{X} > \hat{X}$. To give the example some bite, we assume that no one is capable of producing anything in her childhood and old age. At the beginning of adulthood each person gives birth to a child, and, so as to avoid unnecessary complications, we will also assume that each generation in a dynasty has one member. We may thus treat a generation synonymously with a person. If someone were to receive less than $\hat{X}$ she would die in that period. Were a child ever to die, the dynasty would end.

Let $(X_{1t}, X_{2t}, X_{3t},)$ be the lifetime consumption profile of generation (or person) t, where $t \geq 0$. I assume that the lifetime utility of this person is of the form $V(X_{1t}) + V(X_{2t}) + V(X_{3t})$, where $V(\cdot)$ is an increasing function of its argument. This means in particular that each individual's utility function depends solely upon her own lifetime consumption. People do not suffer from any sense of filial or parental responsibility. They have not internalized social norms and the obligations embedded in norms; nor have they any natural feelings of concern for their children or parents. The example we are studying here has been designed to make the point I want to make in the sharpest and simplest way. Thus, it eschews one of our most enduring sensibilities: the strong concern we have for our offspring and our parents.[31] I could easily introduce all such features without changing the example's substance, but it would blunt the purpose of the exercise, so it is best not to do so. To provide urgency to consumption when it is precariously low, I take it for concreteness that $V(X)$ tends to minus infinity when X tends to $\hat{X}$ from above. This is an extreme version of the notion that everyone desires very much to consume in excess of the survival level of consumption.

Children, when young, can't do anything for their parents. Nor can parents, when old, do anything for their children or grandchildren. Children and old people are helpless in this example. Food storage is impossible. Therefore, if old-age support is not arranged, the elderly starve; and if someone were not to look after her child when young, the child would starve; and this in turn would mean starvation in the next period for this someone. The problem is to devise a social norm that is *self-enforcing*, and which ensures that children take care of their parents when old and parents take care of their children when young.

---

[30] The model is a simple adaptation of the classic by Samuelson (1958). Samuelson's motivation was different from the one here, in that he wanted to provide an explanation for the existence of money as a social contrivance.

[31] That we may have been evolutionarily wired to have a concern for our offspring in a way we may not for our parents when we are adults and they are old, has been much discussed by evolutionary biologists.

Let us suppose that the consumption profile $(\bar{X},\bar{X},\bar{X})$ over the three periods of each person's life is the one this 'society' is trying to sustain. $(\bar{X},\bar{X},\bar{X})$ could be realized only if each adult were to give her child and her mother one-third each of what she produces. The problem before society is to devise the necessary incentives. This is how it can do so.

Consider the following norm: support your child in the required manner (i.e. give her at least a third of what you produce) during her childhood no matter what; support your aged parent in the required manner (i.e. give her at least a third of what you produce) if she is deserving, but give her $\hat{X}$ if she is undeserving. At the very beginning, when the norm is being established from scratch, the first set of working people are required to give at least a third of their output to their aged parents and at least a third to their children. By recursion, we can then determine at any future date whether a parent is deserving. We now confirm that the required inter-generational transfer can be supported by the norm. We need to establish that it is in every generation's self-interest to obey the norm on the assumption that all other generations do so.

Suppose I am in my adulthood and my parent is deserving. (This can mean one of two things: either she gave at least a third of her output to me when I was a child and at least a third to my deserving grandparent, or she gave at least a third of her output to me when I was a child and gave $\hat{X}$ to my *un*deserving grandparent.) Then it is in my interest to give precisely a third of my output to my child and precisely a third to my parent, because otherwise *my* child will give me only $\hat{X}$ in *my* old age (I won't be deserving!), and that is far too horrible a state of affairs for me.[32] Alternatively, suppose my parent is undeserving. (This can mean one of four things: (i) she gave less than a third of her output to me when I was young and she gave at least a third to my deserving grandparent; (ii) she gave at least a third to me when I was young but gave less than a third to my deserving grandparent; (iii) she gave less than a third to me when I was young and less than a third to my deserving grandparent; or (iv) she gave more than $\hat{X}$ to my undeserving grandparent.) In this event it is in my self-interest to give precisely a third to my child and $\hat{X}$ to my parent. Otherwise I shall not be deserving, and will receive only $\hat{X}$ from my child.

Social sanctions in this example are fierce. We don't see anything as draconian as this in the world as we know it. (Of course, in equilibrium we would not observe them because sanctions would not be needed!) But then, our natural concern for our parents and children is also substantial, and this was eschewed in the example. The greater is the extent to which such concern is present, the less is the need for norms to be established.

[32] Greif (1991) calls this belief about what the child will do off the equilibrium path a 'cultural belief'.

Likewise, the more primary norms are internalized, the more blunted is the role of higher-order norms. This is intuitively congenial.

The idea that *society* solves an allocation problem by recourse to a social norm is a metaphor here. We have shown that $(\bar{X},\bar{X},\bar{X})$ can be supported as a Nash equilibrium.[33] We are not supposing that the even pattern of consumption follows from a collective decision, in the sense of being an injunction from Government House. The underlying idea is that the (non-cooperative) equilibrium is arrived at through a societal evolutionary process. The social norm we have just studied sustains the evenly distributed allocation $(\bar{X},\bar{X},\bar{X})$. We may ask how this has come about, why some other allocation has not got 'chosen'. The question has bite, because any allocation over one's lifetime adding up to $3\bar{X}$ and involving greater consumption than $\hat{X}$ in each of the three periods of one's life can be sustained by a suitably worded social norm. (We need merely to repeat the argument we have constructed by replacing $(\bar{X},\bar{X},\bar{X})$ by the allocation in question.)[34] Thus, game theory is unable to eliminate a very large set of allocations. The theory is successful in explaining which allocations can be sustained and which cannot; it can't explain why or how the allocation being sustained has come to be chosen. For this we need something more.

There is a distinction between a generalized social norm (for example, the norm of reciprocity) and a specific norm (for example, that reciprocity involves making a gift commensurate with the gift you had received). Generalized social norms are universally applicable. We observe all societies to practise reciprocity, in one sphere or other, to a greater or lesser extent. The problem is that, when stated in a generalized form, a social norm doesn't convey much information; it does not tell us which allocation the norm actually sustains, or how it got established in the first place. To account for the latter, we need to study a society's history, and

---

[33] In fact, the argument I have deployed has established that it is a *subgame-perfect* Nash equilibrium: in each period the strategies of all present and future people are a Nash equilibrium of the subgame emanating from that period. The notion of subgame perfection is the game-theoretic counterpart of dynamic programming. See Fudenberg and Tirole (1991) for a formal account of this.

[34] In game theory a precise statement of this in the context of repeated games (i.e. where the players are infinitely lived and play the same single-period game over and over again) is called the Folk Theorem. The literature on this is vast. The vital early papers on this are J. Friedman (1971), Aumann and Shapley (1976), Rubinstein (1979), Fudenberg and Maskin (1986), and Abreu (1988). Game theorists among readers will have noted that all the allocations I have identified as being subgame-perfect Nash equilibria are 'renegotiation-proof'. (There is no one with whom an errant woman can renegotiate with: she has nothing to offer her grown-up daughter.) On the usefulness of the idea of renegotiation-proof equilibrium as a refinement of subgame-perfection in repeated games, see J. Farrell and Maskin (1989), Evans and Maskin (1989), and Abreu and Pearce (1989). What we have just studied in the text is an overlapping-generations game: it is not a repeated game. Renegotiation-proofness has no bite in our example.

pure accidents may play a major role in this selection process.[35] Social norms on their own cannot be relied upon to sustain Pareto-efficient resource allocations, nor can they be relied upon to sustain just allocations. Generalized norms are there to sustain allocations; on their own they cannot do the picking of allocations.

Norms can be exploitative, or just plain silly. (Anthropologists often call the latter 'dysfunctional'.) Moreover, the speed with which external circumstances change is often faster than the rate at which social norms can adjust. If internalization of norms has been successfully conducted, people will feel commited to upholding not so much the norm as the allocation supported by the norm. We may then observe anachronistic practices in a society, whose rationale may lie in the past, far from sight, and which nevertheless remain alive and have a stranglehold over the lives of people. Here lies a central weakness with the internalization of social norms. They are difficult to give up when their purpose ceases to exist, or when it is commonly recognized that they are sustaining unjust or inefficient allocations, or when the underlying belief system is altering. Thus, in rural communities of the foothills of the Himalayas in the state of Uttar Pradesh in India, women give birth to their children in cowsheds and remain there for one to two weeks. They aren't permitted to return to their homes any earlier because they are regarded as impure. The (Indian) Centre for Science and Environment (CSE, 1990) reports that village folk in these parts believe cowdung and urine to be good disinfectants. They also believe that the mother and child are protected by the cows from evil spirits. Infant and maternal mortality rates are significantly higher on account of this practice, cowsheds being notoriously unhygienic. The custom appears to be another manifestation of the widespread idea that physiological displays of female reproductive capabilities are *polluting* (see Douglas, 1984). The rationale for the custom is not that it offers a brief respite to the mother from domestic chores.[36] Within three to five days of giving birth, mothers are expected to collect firewood and fodder and to leave it in the cowshed for others to collect. (For her to deliver the firewood to her home would be to defile her home.) Modern-day women in these parts, especially those with some education, are breaking with the practice. But it is a slow process. Meanwhile, both mothers and their infants are exposed to avoidable infections.

Cases of this sort are pervasive, and it is tempting to condone them on grounds that not to do so would be to show disrespect to the value systems of other cultures. But this would be tantamount to making the sharp

---

[35] For a more formal discussion of the evolution of cultural norms, see Boyd and Richerson (1985) and Greif (1991).

[36] This was the rationale I attributed to the practice when I first read of it.

fact–value distinction we had cause to reject earlier (Chapter 1). Writing about an earlier cultural practice, Putnam (1989: 20) says:

the feature of the Aztec way of life that troubles us (the massive human sacrifice) and the belief about the world that conflicts with science were interdependent. If we can say that the Aztec belief about the Gods was false, why can we not say that the practice to which it led was wrong (although, to be sure, understandable given the false factual belief)? If we are not allowed to call the practice wrong, why are we allowed to call the belief false?

Social norms and cultural practices are a minefield for the enactment of public policy.

PART III

The Household and its Setting: Extensions of the Standard Theory

9

Land, Labour, Savings, and Credit

9.1 *The Peasant Household*

Peasant households are involved in both production and consumption. The prototypical household owns a small plot of land, purchases agricultural inputs and consumer goods from the market, sometimes leases in more land, grows subsistence crops, engages in cottage industry, tends domestic animals, relies on common-property resources for a number of essential services, cooks food, rears children, sometimes hires out labour, and on occasion hires labour in to work on the land.

It will prove useful to formalize the deliberations involved in this sort of choice. This will be done in a sequence of steps in this and the next three chapters and their starred counterparts. We will also study the setting in which households in rural communities have to operate. Towards this we will develop some theory and look at evidence from the Indian sub-continent and sub-Saharan Africa which go towards validating the theory. Later (Chapter 16), the theory of household interactions will be extended by including physiology in the account. At that point it will be useful to return to a number of stylized facts we will be collating here.

It is as well to be somewhat loose with the idea of a household. This will afford us flexibility when we study prevailing resource allocation mechanisms. As a rough guide, we may think of the *household* as a group of people who jointly cultivate at least one plot of land, and who share a common store of food (Meillassoux, 1981). We begin by thinking of the household as a decision-making unit. (In Chapters 11–*11 we will peer inside the household.) For simplicity of exposition, we will also ignore domestic activities, such as cooking, collecting firewood, fetching water, rearing children, and so forth. (These activities will be studied in Chapters 10–*12.) I shall for the most part be thinking of communities where there are private property rights to agricultural land.[1] We will imagine that the household owns a plot on which food crops can be grown. These are often subsistence crops. Inevitably, cultivation involves fixed costs (learning about conditions of factor markets, new

[1] This is not a good assumption in sub-Saharan Africa, where fallow agricultural land is often communally owned (by the kinship). See Sect. 9.6, and Ch. 12.

varieties of seeds, methods of pest control, and so forth). If such costs bite, a small landholder will lease out his plot and work simply as a labourer. (Landless households are, of course, a special case of this class.) If fixed costs are sufficiently small and economies of scale are absent, even a landless household may become a tenant farmer, either on a rental basis or as a sharecropper (see below). Here we will be thinking of households that cultivate. The household can sell farm output at a quoted price. Farming requires material inputs (e.g. seed, irrigation water, fertilizers) and labour. The household purchases material inputs from the market (or from government) at a given price.

As an opening, it is useful to think of the case where the total available quantity of household labour power is independent of the household's consumption of food. So we take this stock to be a given quantity. (This is blatantly unrealistic, and we will drop the assumption in Section 9.7 and in Chapters 14–17.) It is also useful to begin by supposing that the agricultural labour market is competitive. At the prevailing wage rate the household can hire labour if it requires it or, alternatively, it can offer labour should it have labour to spare. (We will drop this assumption in Chapter 16.) As it is simplest to think that household and hired labour are perfect substitutes in agricultural production, we will do so. (But see Section 9.2.) Household utility is taken to be defined over the consumption of food crops, consumer goods which the household can obtain only from the market (e.g. clothings and untensils), and the leisure it enjoys.

In the next section we will study the organizational structure of this household more closely. Chapter *9 (Section *9.1) contains a formal account of it. Here we will look at the various responses the household would make to changes in the price of its farm output and of the material inputs of agricultural production (e.g. seeds, fertilizers, pesticides, water, draught-animal power). This will prove useful when we come to discuss agricultural policy in poor countries.

The landowning peasant household has four possible sources of income: selling its produce, hiring out labour and capital assets, leasing out some of its land, and common-property resources. Combined with its savings from the previous season, these yield the household its funds. Consider a household that sells some of the agricultural crop it produces. As it is a net producer of the crop, an increase in the price of that crop can only be beneficial to it, the magnitude of the benefit depending upon the share of agricultural profits in the household's full income. This share varies widely; for example, it has been found to be 50 per cent in a sample from Malaysia and 20 per cent in a sample from Thailand, (Singh, Squire and Strauss, 1986a). For a landless household it is, of course, zero.

Would a landowning household consume more, or would it consume less, of a food crop were its price to increase? The first column of figures

Table 9.1 Elasticities with respect to food crop prices

	Crop	E_f	E_m	E_π	E_L
Malaysia	Rice	0.38	1.94	0.66	−0.57
Nigeria	Sorghum	0.19	0.57	0.20	−0.06
Sierra Leone	Rice	−0.66	0.14	0.71	−0.09
Thailand	—	−0.37	0.51	8.10	−0.62

Key
E_f: elasticity of household consumption of food crops.
E_m: elasticity of purchased consumer goods.
E_π: elasticity of farm profit.
E_L: elasticity of household labour supply.

Source: Singh, Squire and Strauss (1986a, table 2).

(E_f) in Table 9.1 presents estimates of own-price elasticities of demand for agricultural produce (a subsistence crop) in four of the countries for which such estimates have been made in recent years. The typical household in each of the samples owned land. It will be noticed that in two (Malaysia and Nigeria) the elasticity is positive, indicating that the positive response in consumption arising from increased profits swamps the negative response arising from the fact that the household is also a consumer of the product. The elasticity is negative in the two remaining countries (Sierra Leone and Thailand). The absolute values of the elasticities are all low.

The second column of figures (E_m) in the table provides estimates of the elasticity of the purchased consumer good with respect to the price of the subsistence crop. The elasticity is positive in all four countries, implying that an increase in income leads households to consume more of the commodity. The value is really low in Sierra Leone. A possible explanation is that, as average income is low and transport costs are large there, market-mediated transactions in non-farm goods among rural folk are relatively sparse.

The third column of figures $(E\pi)$ gives estimates of the elasticity of farm profits with respect to the price of the subsistence crop. They are positive everywhere, with a remarkably high value in Thailand. And the fourth column (E_L) gives estimates of the elasticity of labour supply with respect to the price of the food crop. This is negative in each of the countries, implying that leisure is a normal good and that farm profits play a strong role in household decisions.

An increase in the price of material inputs in farm production harms the landowning household. This much is obvious. In Table 9.2 the peasant household's responses to an increase in its price in terms of farm production, subsistence consumption, agricultural profits, and demand for

Table 9.2   Elasticities with respect to fertilizer prices

	$\bar{E}_f$	$\bar{E}_m$	$\bar{E}_\pi$	$\bar{E}_L$
Malaysia	−0.03	−0.18	−0.15	0.05
Thailand	−0.03	−0.03	−0.41	0.05

Key
$\bar{E}_f$: elasticity of household consumption of farm output.
$\bar{E}_m$: elasticity of purchased consumer good.
$\bar{E}_\pi$: elasticity of farm profit.
$\bar{E}_L$: elasticity of labour household supply.

Source: Singh, Squire and Strauss (1986a, table 4).

material inputs in production are given for samples from Malaysia and Thailand. The material input in question is fertilizer.[2] The first three pairs of elasticities are negative (the first two pairs being very low in absolute value), while the fourth pair is positive, indicating that an increase in the price of fertilizer would lead households to produce less of the food crop, consume less of it, earn lower profits, and supply more labour as a substitute for fertilizers.

All this is in conformity with intuition, but the effect of reductions in the prices of both the subsistence crop and the material input in agricultural production, taken together, is ambiguous. This is problematic, because governments in poor countries frequently tax agriculture (through export taxes, and marketing boards) so as to earn revenue, and simultaneously subsidize material inputs in crop production (e.g. fertilizers, tractors) to restore farmers' incentives.[3] In Chapter 7 (Section 7.6) we observed that this kind of distortion is hard to justify. This policy would typically look bad even were we to examine only its short-run effect on the peasant household's real income. Computations based on Malaysian data suggest that a 10 per cent reduction in the price of food crops would reduce household real income by 7 per cent, while a 10 per cent reduction in the price of fertilizers would increase real income by less than 1 per cent, (Singh, Squire and Strauss, 1986a; see also D. Mazumdar, 1989). Food crops loom larger than material inputs of agricultural production in the peasant household's budget.

9.2   *Credit Constraints and the Organization of Production*

Family labour does not require as much supervision as hired labour. This is partly because family members can be expected to share an emotional

---

[2] Sierra Leone and Nigeria are missing from this table because fertilizer is rarely used there.
[3] Overvalued exchange rates discourage agricultural production as well. We will go into this more fully in Ch. 10.

bond, and so to a great extent can trust one another not to shirk. It is partly also because family members have a stake in the household fortune; that is, each is a *residual claimant* (Alchian and Demsetz, 1972). The need for supervision of hired workers stems from the fact that otherwise an employer would be unable to detect shirking. For a big landlord there may not be enough household members to do the supervision, in which case he will need to employ supervisors. But then, who will supervise the supervisors to ensure that *they* don't shirk? Well, no one needs to if the supervisors are also made residual claimants. It has, for example, been argued that one reason (there are others; see Chapters 16 and *16) landlords employ permanent workers (often called farm servants) at considerable cost is that they serve as supervisors of the many casual workers hired during the busy agricultural season. When farm servants are remunerated at a sufficiently higher rate than casual workers, they have an incentive to supervise without shirking. The reason is that if they were ever to be discovered shirking, their reputation would be tarnished; they would lose their wage differential and be forced into casual employment.[4]

One has an incentive to shirk when work is unpleasant or strenuous. Not only does a person's work *effort* involve the expenditure of resources (e.g. time), his *ability* (i.e. his productive capability) too is often difficult to fathom, especially when he is a stranger. Mechanization of production eases the burden of monitoring both effort and ability, because machines can set the pace of work, and the pace is known from their specifications. In rural communities of poor countries matters are different, for agricultural production is for the most part unmechanized. This means that the reach of the two Fundamental Theorems of Welfare Economics discussed in Chapter 7 is extremely limited there. The law of contracts, in the sense that it is in operation in Western democracies, has little relevance. For this and other reasons (Chapters 6–8), markets are thin. This being so, people need to have personal information about others' doings and beings in order to enter into contracts with them. But a great deal of such information is not known publicly, and it is known that much future information will not be publicly known. The cost of acquiring information about people and their circumstances in even neighbouring villages, let alone distant ones, can be huge. This provides one explanation for the fact that privacy is a scarce commodity within rural communities. Village folk in poor countries appear to know more about one another than would be regarded seemly in modern cultures.[5] Behaviour that

---

[4] See Eswaran and Kotwal (1985a). The pioneering work by Shapiro and Stiglitz (1984) deployed this idea towards a related end.

[5] Townsend (1989), Udry (1990), and Lim (1991) have indirectly confirmed this by studying credit markets within villages and kinship groups in India and Nigeria, respectively. See below.

encroaches upon privacy has an instrumental role to play: it enlarges the scope of transactions in risks by the pooling of information. Local gossip as a means of acquiring information is prominent there (see e.g. Hayami and Kikuchi, 1981; Gambetta, 1988b). But it is not possible to eliminate all differences in information. So the types of contracts we observe in markets are conditioned by what can or cannot be observed jointly, or publicly. These features reinforce the argument we have so far offered on why village communities in poor countries are often self-contained enclaves of production and exchange relationships.

By reporting on a number of studies on rural India, we will presently look at evidence on how self-contained these enclaves can be. One would imagine, though, that even within village communities much information is only privately known. (Lack of privacy reduces asymmetries in information, it does not eliminate it.) These private pieces of information include: (i) an individual's personal characteristics (e.g. his preferences and personal endowments, including his productive capability); that is, what kind of a person he *is*; (ii) the actions he takes (e.g. how hard he works at a given task); that is, what he *does*; and (iii) knowledge about the world; for example certain aspects of specialized technological or ecological possibilities. Following the insurance literature, the term *adverse selection* is often used to characterize resource allocation problems raised by the first and third categories of private information (*hidden knowledge*), and the term *moral hazard* is often used to characterize problems raised by the second category of private information (*hidden action*).[6]

As they lead to similar analytical problems, the distinction has little bite. When one individual reports to another (or takes a jointly observable action) on the basis of information known only to him (this is the hidden information), the strategy he uses (that is, the function that maps what he knows to what he does) is not observable by the other person, and so resembles a hidden action. The potent distinction therefore lies not between hidden action and hidden knowledge, but elsewhere. The distinction that should be drawn is between cases where an agreement (or contract) is made *before* the parties' private pieces of information are known to them, and cases where an agreement (or contract) is made *after* the parties' private pieces of information are known to them. We will refer to the former class of cases as those resulting in moral hazard, and the latter as those leading to adverse selection.[7]

---

[6] See Grossman and Hart (1983), Arrow (1985), Myerson (1985), Binmore and Dasgupta (1986), and Stiglitz (1988b), who make this distinction explicitly.

[7] I am grateful to Paul Milgrom for pointing this out to me. I have gained much from reading his unpublished manuscript on this point (Milgrom, 1987) and from Hart and Holmstrom (1987), which contains a fine presentation of what was known (*c.* mid-1980s) about the analytical problems in agency relationships under moral hazard.

Consider agricultural labour contracts between employers and employees. An Arrow–Debreu wage is a payment for a unit of a particular quality of work. So the Arrow–Debreu model assumes the quality of hired labourers' work to be jointly observable by the relevant parties. In traditional agriculture, resources have to be spent in order to assess labour quality, or to ensure that hired workers have the incentive to provide good-quality service. This goes to shape the organization of agricultural production in its various guises. The Arrow–Debreu model is unable to account for them.

Seasonality also plays a role in the determination of agricultural institutions. A good part of the costs of agricultural production (weeding, planting, fertilizing, irrigating, and so forth) are incurred months before harvest. Moreover, running an agricultural operation involves fixed costs: the scale must be of a minimal size before it is worth organizing production. If the fixed cost is sufficiently small (as typically would be the case in traditional agriculture) the minimal size is small enough to warrant our ignoring it. So often we will do so. But its existence should be borne in mind.

In the Arrow–Debreu model households can borrow against future profits to finance current expenditure. Each household faces a single budget constraint. (Hahn, 1973, calls exchange economies with this feature *inessential sequence economies*.) This is true nowhere in the world as we know it, and it is most especially untrue in poor countries, where the credit market is notoriously stringent against small landholders (see Sections 9.4–9.5). This sets greater limits on the ability of poor households to obtain working capital. Given their inability to transfer funds from the future to the present, poor households face more than one budget constraint. In an exceptional pair of articles, these considerations have been put together by Eswaran and Kotwal (1985b, 1986) to explain the diverse modes of agricultural production observed in poor countries. In Section *9.1 we will look at the formal structure of the household's decision problem. Here I shall sketch its resolution by appealing to the Eswaran–Kotwal analysis. My treatment will be informal and intuitive.[8] We will find that the character of a household depends upon its circumstances (e.g. size of its landholding). This is at variance with the household in the Arrow–Debreu model (as expounded, for example, in Koopmans, 1957; Rosenzweig, 1980; Singh, Squire and Strauss, 1986a, b), where it is to a large extent independent of its endowments.

Empirical studies have shown that to a good approximation peasant agricultural production involves constant returns to scale in the variable

---

[8] See also Binswanger and Rosenzweig (1986a) for a fine theoretical analysis of agrarian production relations in poor countries. I have drawn on their work quite freely in this chapter.

factors; land, labour, and material inputs, with diminishing returns to each factor (see Cline, 1970; Lau and Yotopoulos, 1971; Bardhan, 1973a). We will therefore assume this. We will assume also that there is a competitive market for wage labour, and a rental market for land. It will be seen that this too has the backing of a good deal of evidence. Now, supervising hired workers requires time; the greater the size of the employed labour force, the longer the time required for supervision. Imagine that households with larger landholdings have greater savings at their disposal for use as working capital. Landless and near-landless households typically have next to nothing in the way of savings. They are particularly constrained in their ability to buy intermediate goods (e.g. seeds, fertilizers, pesticides). Unless these inputs are made available by the lessee, the poorest households are at best able to lease in tiny plots of land. So they work small plots. Since the marginal product of household labour on the plot it cultivates is low, the household finds it in its interest to hire out a fraction of its labour time. Such a household is a *labourer–cultivator*. If the plot it owns is not negligible in size (but not significantly large either), all available household labour is needed for farming the land that is tilled. So it does not at all enter the labour market. Nor does it employ labour. To do so would require monitoring employees' work effort (in addition to having to pay them the going wage), and this would prove too costly. Such a household is a *self-cultivator*. It is the prototypical peasant household.

Larger landowners have greater access to working capital. They find it profitable to lease in quantities of land sufficiently large to make it necessary to employ agricultural workers. These households allocate their time between cultivation, supervision of hired labourers, and leisure. Really large landowners find it most expedient to devote all their non-leisure time to supervising hired help. They don't work the land. They are *capitalists*.[9]

These considerations suggest that the amount of hired labour increases with farm size, as does supervision cost. This means that the cost of a unit of labour increases with farm size. Since the rental on land is the same for all, it has the effect of making the ratio of land to labour an increasing function of farm size. This in turn means that, when there are sharp diminishing returns to the use of intermediate inputs, output per acre decreases with the size of the farms. The model therefore predicts an 'inverse' relationship between farm size and the productivity of land. This has been much documented in the empirical literature.[10] We will return to

---

[9] The classification adopted by D. Mazumdar (1989), in terms of owner-operators, tenants, and agricultural labourers, cuts across the one we are adopting here, but is accountable by the model being sketched here.

[10] The pioneering work is Bauer (1946). Subsequent studies which have found an inverse relationship include D. Mazumdar (1965), Cline (1970), Dorner (1972), Bharadwaj (1974), C. H. H. Rao (1977), Berry and Cline (1979), Kutcher and Scandizzo (1981), Carter (1984), G. Feder (1985), and Singh (1988a).

it in the final chapter when we come to discuss the efficacy of agrarian reform.

9.3 *Moral Hazard, Wage Labour, and Tenancy*

The discussion so far has assumed that labourers who are not household members are paid a wage. Now wage contracts are viable only if labour can be monitored at relatively little cost. When it is possible to observe the tasks a worker accomplishes, he can be paid on a *piece-rate* basis. If his effort can be observed, payment can be made on a *time-rate* basis. Both objects can be observed costlessly in the Arrow–Debreu model. So it is a matter of indifference which system of payment is agreed upon (see Chapter 16). In reality there is a difference. For example, Foster and Rosenzweig (1992a), in an ingenious study of longitudinal data from the Philippines on agricultural workers' body masses, calorie intakes, and wages, have shown that both share-tenancy (see below) and a wage system where payment is based on a time rate are subject to moral hazard. This they do by estimating that under self-cultivation and a piece rate system of payment workers lose more weight over a work period. It enables the authors to infer that under the latter two modes of agricultural organization workers supply more labour effort.

Wage labour is different from tenancy, something the Arrow–Debreu model wasn't designed to recognize. Agricultural mechanization has often been associated with a move from tenancy to a wage system. Within wage employment, casual labour is more prominent than permanent labour in many parts of the world (e.g. India). In a sample of villages in West Bengal, for example, over 80 per cent of the hired labour force was found to be casual labour (see Bardhan and Rudra, 1981; Rudra, 1982; Bardhan, 1984a). I will provide explanations for these observations in this section and in Chapter 16.

Tenancy is an important agricultural institution in a number of poor countries (e.g. Egypt and Pakistan). Contrary to what is sometimes thought, tenants are not necessarily small farmers. In the sample covered by the well-known ICRISAT panel, between 42 and 69 per cent of total area leased in was by large farms, and the bulk of the land leased out was from small- to medium-size landholdings.[11] Increased possibilities of

---

[11] ICRISAT is the acronym for the International Crops Research Institute for the Semi-Arid Tropics, in Hyderabad. Its panel data initially covered 240 households in six villages in the semi-arid regions of two states (Andhra Pradesh and Maharashtra), over an extended period commencing in the early 1970s. It is a pioneering investigation. Accounts of its findings on credit, tenancy, and labour relations in this data-set are in Binswanger *et al.* (1984), Jodha (1984), Ryan and Ghodake (1984), Shaban (1987), and an excellent synthesis by Walker and Ryan (1990). The most extensive accounts of land and labour relations in the broader context of South Asia with which I am familiar are Singh (1988a, b, c, 1990) and Mazumdar (1989), all of which include analyses of the ICRISAT data.

mechanization (making large landholdings more profitable than small ones), and the existence of a government Employment Guarantee Scheme in the state of Maharashtra (see Chapter 17) provide part of the explanation for this phenomenon. A more encompassing explanation follows from the theoretical analysis I shall now develop.

Two particular forms of tenancy have been found to predominate: *fixed-rental contracts* and *sharecropping*. The former is straightforward enough: the tenant is expected to pay a fixed rent to the landlord for the land he leases. The latter institution is more complex. In its simplest guise, sharecropping involves an agreement between the landlord and the tenant over the ratio in which agricultural produce is to be divided between them. As the tenant does not retain the whole fruit of his marginal level of effort (his marginal product), sharecropping does not offer him adequate incentives to work, at least not when contrasted with land-rental or self-cultivation systems. (For empirical confirmation, see Shaban, 1987; Foster and Rosenzweig, 1992a.) So its practice requires explanation. We will look into this by building on the ideas introduced in the previous section.

Sharecropping as an institution is no longer as prevalent as it used to be. Today less than 10 per cent of the cultivated land and less than 10 per cent of agricultural labourers in India operate under this system. But that is because tenancy-farming itself is in decline there, for reasons we will discover below.[12] However, sharecropping is common within tenancy-farming: in India during the early 1970s it accounted for a little over 50 per cent of land under tenancy contracts that were in the size group less than 2.5 acres (see Singh, 1988b, Table 3). Between 77 and 99 per cent of transactions in land covered by the ICRISAT data on central India involved sharecropping.

Traditional agriculture requires labour to be applied flexibly. There is uncertainty in labour requirements, arising from capricious weather, idiosyncratic field conditions, variability in the populations of pests, and so forth. Earlier, we observed that monitoring work effort is a central problem in agricultural production. It is also on occasion a problem for an employer to verify the number of tasks a worker accomplishes. Supervision of labour is crucial, and it involves time and resources. As yield is always uncertain, it isn't possible for an employer to infer unerringly from observing yield how his workers have performed on an individual basis. In any case, cereals are harvested months after the planting season; even if an employer is able to judge individual labour effort after measuring yield, it may be too late to do anything.[13] These observations highlight the fact that labour effort is often an unmarketable commodity. The employer faces moral hazard in agricultural production. But the worker is a residual

---

[12] For an account of the prevalence of this institution, see Bardhan and Rudra (1980), Rudra (1982), and Singh (1988c).

[13] Were the parties to discount future income at a high rate, the threat of punishment would prove to be no threat.

claimant under tenancy. Since household labour is easier to supervise than hired labour, tenancy involves a contract to hire not merely the labour of the tenant, but also the supervised labour of the tenant's family. Therein lies the subtlety of the institution. It dilutes the landlord's moral hazard.

There are other important asymmetries in the distribution of information about knowledge, effort, and ability. Knowledge both of market conditions and of new inputs and techniques of production is more likely to be held by large landholders than by landless and near-landless people (see Feder, Just, and Silberman, 1985). The former have better contacts and greater political power. As a class, they also have better access to education (Chapter 4). What one may call 'managerial skill' resides more among landowners than among landless workers. But the use of such skills by their possessors cannot be enforced by those who don't possess it. So it isn't a marketable commodity. Large landowners typically also have greater access to credit and working capital. The exercise of such credit and capital cannot be enforced by those who don't have access to funds. This too is a non-marketable ability. These features of agricultural production provide yet another source of moral hazard. But, unlike the case of labour effort, the hazard here is faced by peasants.[14]

Let us return to the decision problem facing a landowner. He has three options. One would be to practise capitalist farming. In this case he would have to offer hired labour a fixed-wage contract, supervise the work, and provide the necessary managerial service. A second option would be for the landowner to lease out his land at a fixed rental. In this case the tenant would be responsible for both management and the supervision of labour: the landowner would sit back, relax, and enjoy rents. The third option would be for the landlord and tenant to agree on a share contract. The landlord would be expected to provide managerial service, and the tenant would be in charge of supervising labour.

Consider first a wage contract. The landowner is a residual claimant; the worker is not. The landlord therefore has the incentive to provide managerial service, while the labourer has little interest in organizing the finer details of agricultural work. This means that the landlord has to organize and supervise labour, something he is less capable of doing than the labourer. It is a source of inefficiency. The wage system is particularly inefficient when the organization and supervision of labour is of prime importance, when the landowner does not have enough time (or ability) to accomplish this, and when specialized knowledge of the market for inputs and products is of no prime importance. Traditional agriculture could be expected to possess these features. Tenant farming is a more efficient institution in these circumstances. We will confirm this below.

---

[14] I am grateful to Mukesh Eswaran and Ashok Kotwal for these insights. They have developed the required analysis in Eswaran and Kotwal (1985b). This section is based on it.

Consider now tenancy under a fixed rental contract. Here, the tenant is a residual claimant, the landlord is not. The tenant has the incentive to provide quality labour-service, while the landlord has little incentive to provide good management. So the tenant finds it necessary to provide managerial service as well, even though he is not very good at it. This is a source of inefficiency. The fixed rental system is particularly inefficient in those environments where agricultural work is routinized (so supervision is not that vital), where information about market conditions is of importance in generating farm profits, and where the tenant does not possess this knowledge to any great extent. Agriculture under rapidly changing circumstances would have these features. The wage-based system is the more efficient institution under these conditions.

Consider finally share-tenancy. The system makes both parties residual claimants. This encourages the tenant to supply supervised labour and the landlord, managerial services. Sharecropping allows each party to specialize in what he is good at. It thereby blunts the two-way moral hazard problem in agriculture. The system's weakness lies in the fact that neither party has full incentives to work at his respective tasks, because each receives only a fraction of his marginal product. This means not only that labour effort could be expected to be less under sharecropping than under a system where farmers own their own land, but also that tenants are less eager to invest in the land they till. A fraction of the return on any such investment goes to the landowner, and this dulls tenants' incentives. (But see below for variations in contractual arrangements under share-tenancy.) In those circumstances where labour supervision and managerial services are both important, and where each party is significantly better in its specialized skill than the other, share-tenancy is a reasonably efficient institution. Mechanization of agriculture would render it relatively inefficient. This explains why share-cropping is not prevalent in advanced industrial countries.[15]

Share contracts are remarkably similar across regions. They appear to specify a fixed share (i.e. a share that is independent of the size of the output). Even more remarkably, the share seems to hover close to 50 per cent (see Binswanger and Rosenzweig, 1984a; Stiglitz, 1988b). I do not know of any persuasive argument for explaining these two features of share-tenancy (but see Allen, 1985). The thought that a 50–50 split is *fair* is misleading: the allocation of agricultural production does not resemble the division of a cake of fixed size. Moreover, the circumstances of

---

[15] A precursor to this account of sharecropping, based on the theory of contracts between 'informed' agents (labourers) and 'uninformed' principals (landowners), was explored in a pioneering paper by Stiglitz (1974) (see also Newbery and Stiglitz, 1979; Stiglitz, 1987b, 1988b). As a theory it is less satisfactory, because it does not offer a convincing account of the differences between wage and rental systems of agricultural production. More generally, it does not exploit the two-way moral hazard present in production.

production differ widely across regions, and the theory of agency informs us that efficient contracts would stipulate shares that are dependent on the volume of output (see Mirrlees, 1971, 1985; Grossman and Hart, 1983; Rogerson, 1984). The matter remains a theoretical puzzle.

Having said this, one should note that there are variations in share contracts even within small geographical areas. For example, the sharing rule has been known to vary as regards the rights the parties have to the by-products of crops, which in some cases go entirely to the landlord and in others to the tenant. Then again, the share going to the tenant is in many situations increased when he undertakes investment in the land, for example, digging irrigation ditches and terracing (see Singh, 1988b). This possibility improves the institution's performance. Often, there are also elaborate cost-sharing arrangements, for example, those that stipulate that the tenant is to provide animal- and man-power, seeds, and agricultural implements, and the landowner is to provide fertilizers and the costs of irrigation. The rationale behind cost-sharing is easy to locate. The tenant farmer is more likely to know localized production possibilities. A contract that stipulates not what mix of inputs is to be used in production, but rather how costs are to be shared, leaves allocative decisions to the tenant. This is desirable because the tenant knows better. Cost-sharing allows for flexibility in the choice of production technique.[16]

Sharing rules differ across villages. More broadly, they differ across ecological zones. Furthermore, the same village may have casual labour paid on the basis of a daily time-rate, a daily piece-rate, and a daily harvest-share.[17] No theoretical model can have the capability of explaining all that has been observed in as complicated a human interchange as that embodied in agricultural labour contracts. For example, the detailed evidence Rudra (1982) produced in his remarkable work on labour contracts in the state of West Bengal is a theorist's nightmare. But only if he is weak-kneed: the evidence isn't a nightmare if we acknowledge that the purpose of building analytical constructs is to provide major signposts, not to explain every wrinkle of 'fact'. In any case, the institutional arrangements underlying agricultural work in poor countries are so complex and so specific to regions that no single model can entirely get off the ground. We can but nibble at an understanding, and that too only from various ends. To do this it is best to suspend disbelief and capture a few

[16] See Braverman and Stiglitz (1986). The argument in the text regarding the advantages of cost-sharing rules is identical to the one that says that in a wide range of circumstances the use of prices is superior to the use of quantity controls in production when regulators know less about production possibilities than production managers. See Weitzman (1974). See also Dasgupta (1982b).

[17] On all this see Bardhan and Rudra (1980, 1981), Rudra (1982), Binswanger et al. (1984), Binswanger and Rosenzweig (1982), Jodha (1984), Singh (1988b, c), and Walker and Ryan (1990).

compelling features of the conditions of living among the rural poor in poor countries, and see what together they tell us. We should not, of course, take any of the constructions literally, but we should take them seriously.

9.4 *Village Enclaves as Production Units*

In the previous chapter we observed that labour and credit markets in rural communities of poor countries are often thin. A pervasive reason is *mobility cost*, which is large relative to general income levels. Costs of mobility include those associated with transportation, but they involve many other things besides. Markets being thin, the outside world presents considerable uncertainties to the individual. Life in the village may be harsh, but there is an element of security provided by the family and the community. This is sustained by norms of behaviour by which people abide. You can't simply pack up and leave for better prospects in a neighbouring village. For one thing, you may not be welcome; for another, your departure would be seen as an unsocial act, and this could inflict costs on your kin through a reduction in the support system your village community provides for them. To be sure, large-scale migration does take place on occasion, for example when far-reaching technological changes in a region give rise to labour scarcity there. But the prospect elsewhere has to be substantially good before long term migration is judged worth while. For all these reasons, migration within spatially proximate villages is not so common.

If this sounds like a circular reasoning (markets are thin because mobility is costly and mobility is costly because markets are thin), it is meant to be. In the previous chapter (Section 8.7) we encountered a social environment possessing *multiple equilibria*. The example we studied had an infinity of equilibria. In Chapter 12 and *12 we will see that societies where norms of behaviour have been internalized are likely to possess multiple equilibria. This means in particular that equilibrium allocation is not determined uniquely by technology and individual motivations. Models of social systems possessing multiple equilibria are to be commended for having this feature, they are not to be decried. Analysis of the kind with which we are engaged in this book enables us to identify self-enforcing beliefs and behaviour. It makes it possible for us to locate those resource allocations that can be sustained, and by implication those that cannot. Now, when a social system possesses multiple equilibria, analysis on its own can't tell us which of the equilibrium resource allocations will prevail. To be able to do this, we would need to study its history. So multiplicity of equilibria provides a role for history. Admittedly, it also means that two societies which to begin with possess similar characteristics may eventually sustain quite different resource allocations. This is the source of the seeming circularity in reasoning. But it isn't a flaw, it is a virtue.

The sparseness of inter-village transactions accentuates the difficulties people in one location face in obtaining information about another locality, both about labour quality and about the risks associated with loans. For example, it has been observed widely in Indian villages that the agricultural labour market is closed, in that the hiring of labour across neighbouring villages is rare. Each village is an enclave (see Rudra 1982, 1984; Binswanger and Rosenzweig, 1984b; Bardhan and Rudra, 1986; Walker and Ryan, 1990). One reason employers may not wish to hire workers from a different village is that they are unknown commodities. Hiring them would involve large risks; 'foreign' workers may be unreliable, or simply incompetent. But the following expressions of rural needs in West Bengal reported in Rudra (1984: 255), identify mobility costs and uncertainty as the reasons for geographical segmentation of labour and credit markets, and the persistence of uniform patron–client relationships within villages:

Landowner (patron): I may require a labourer to come and help me in the middle of the night, for example, if it has rained and the living quarters and the paddy godown have got flooded. There are no rates for such work to be done at such an hour. Such a service cannot be purchased.

Peasant worker (client): I am a poor man and I do not even have enough to eat every day. I may require urgently some money for a funeral in the family. To whom shall I go?

Spot markets for such needs are an awkward thing. Contractual terms in spot markets would be volatile. They would add to the uncertainty each party faces. Patron-client relationships involve less uncertainty, because they amount to long-term contracts. So we may expect landlords and peasants within a village to enter into them. In India these 'long-term' contracts are often of a few months' duration: the peasant worker borrows when in need with the promise of being available for work for so many days during the next busy season, when the requirements of the landowner are greatest. The forces of competition make the terms of such contracts roughly uniform within villages. But, mobility costs being large, contracts can differ across villages (Rudra, 1984). Because their histories are different, even neighbouring villages would be expected to settle on different equilibria.

The wage for casual labour has been found to possess a similar characteristic: it is uniform within villages, but it varies across villages considerably (Bardhan and Rudra, 1981, 1986; Rudra, 1982, 1984; Walker and Ryan, 1990). Table 9.3 displays a remarkably wide range even within a cluster of villages (in Illambazar, West Bengal). Forces of competition can explain the former, but mobility costs are a necessary ingredient in any analysis aiming to explain the latter. In Chapter 16 I shall offer an explanation based on spatial differences in the availability of local common-property resources. An alternative is to construct models possessing multiple equilibria.

Table 9.3   Wage rates in Illambazar cluster, West Bengal

Daily wage rates	Number of villages
Cash only	
Rs4.00	4
Rs5.00	10
Rs6.00	6
Rs8.00	1
Cash and kind	
Rs2.00 + 1.5 kg rice	5
Rs3.00 + 1.5 kg rice	22
Rs3.50 + 1.5 kg rice	1
Rs4.00 + 1.5 kg rice	2
Rs6.00 + 1 meal	1

Source: Rudra (1984, table 2).

One way of doing this for the casual labour market (see Mukherjee and Ray, 1992) is to suppose that, provided the private cost of unemployment during part of the year is not too high, a worker finds it an affront to work for a landowner in the peak season if he feels that, relative to other landowners, the one in question offered too low a wage to workers in the previous slack season.[18] In the busy agricultural season, time is of the essence. So the cost of refusal to a landowner isn't negligible. We would now expect the economy to sustain multiple equilibria because wages in the slack season are held up by their own bootstraps: if all other landowners offer a relatively high (low) slack-season wage, it is in the interest of the typical landowner to offer a relatively high (low) wage; the argument being that, if the wage he offers is substantially lower than those offered by others, he is sure to be refused by workers in the next busy season.

In earlier days, long-term contracts between patrons and clients were really long-term. Among the most intensively studied patron–client relationships was the Hindu *jajmani* caste system, predominant in south India (see Wiser, 1936; Gough, 1960/1; Epstein, 1967; Bowes, 1978). The trade here was labour service and crop output for land. Labour service and crop output were offered by the low-caste (more accurately, the untouchable) client, in exchange for the 'lease' of land owned by the high-caste *jajman*. The arrangement was entered into by two or more families and was founded on hereditary ties. It was for all practical purposes non-negotiable; the arrangement was governed by custom. The client owned insufficient land to make ends meet in bad years; so he had to 'lease' land

---

[18] This is where the externality associated with an internalized 'norm' comes in. It involves what are known as *strategic complementarities*. See Ch. *12.

from the *jajman*. In bad years output was so shared as to meet the 'subsistence' requirements of the client tiller. This was in effect what set the client's income, even for good years. The client's income was pretty much fixed at this level. What was not fixed by the arrangement was the client's labour effort. Here his obligations were often extensive. The patron could call upon additional time and effort from the client in good years (when labour requirements were expected to be heavy), could have the client's spouse do some of the patron's domestic chores, demand that the client be generally there to serve the master, and so forth. The system survived for long because formal savings and credit institutions were not available to the low-caste tiller. The *jajmani* system offered him insurance against bad years. However, the terms of trade on offer were stiff enough to prevent him from accumulating wealth in good years sufficient to cover deficits from his personal landholdings in bad years. In short, the client was unable to provide self-insurance. So he had to comply with the customary arrangement, and, in effect, remain perpetually in debt. The client's family gained as well by this arrangement. (Even when it was socially acceptable, opting out was usually the worse option: see Ray, 1984, for a formal demonstration.) But it was a cruel arrangement in a cruel agrarian setup.

The *jajmani* system has all but disappeared today. The commercialization of agriculture (with the attendant importance of agricultural investment) has meant that landowners find it in their interest to be in charge of their own lands. Moreover, a tenant has the right (in law at least) to continue tilling the land if he has cultivated it for so many years. In the state of West Bengal this has in recent years been enforced under what has been called Operation Barga. All this makes long-term tenant farming, such as that under the *jajmani* system, unprofitable to the landowner: he loses flexibility.

Earlier in this section we noted that the labour market is often linked to the market for credit. Labour effort serves as a collateral for the landless. Modern institutions, such as those that provide formal savings and credit facilities, break this link. The success of the Grameen Bank in Bangladesh (see Chapter 17) is a reminder of how what are essentially small loans can transform the lifetime opportunities of the very poor.[19] My conclusions in Chapter 6 on the guidance the State should offer in the production of goods that are a natural monopoly are relevant here. In poor countries even credit and savings facilities assume the status of natural monopolies. The extent of the market is small when most people are very poor. They may have little or no security to offer against loans. Because the cost of monitoring loans across distances is high, the private

---

[19] It contrasts sharply with the failure of the Brazilian regulation on private banks to disperse specified volumes of credit to small farmers. See J. Anderson (1990).

market for loans is geographically segmented. So credit is often localized within village communities and kinship groups (see Rudra, 1984; Walker and Ryan, 1990; Udry, 1990). Now, the risks rural people face in any given locale are correlated positively. If my crops fail, so presumably do my neighbour's. Therefore, village money-lenders need money most especially when potential borrowers are in need of it. They are unable to diversify their loans sufficiently, and so are averse to the risks associated with their activity. This means in turn that risk markets are restricted even within locales. The State has an advantage here. That it has a role to play in the establishment of credit services to the poor in poor countries is evident. (For a contrasting opinion, see Besley, 1992.) It is in a position to spread the fixed cost of establishing insurance markets. It is also in a position to pool geographically dispersed risks.[20]

Thus far analysis. It will prove illuminating to study something about the workings of agrarian institutions. In the next section I shall sketch what is known about such matters in India. Section 9.6 will address sub-Saharan Africa. They offer contrasting pictures.

9.5   Land, Labour, and Credit Markets: Observations on Rural India

Let us begin with the market for casual agricultural labour. In India, where labour markets have been much studied, this market meets as frequently as daily, and it is usually wage-based. The wage is agreed upon in advance of the day, in return for an effort level over a stipulated number of hours. Hired labourers are almost invariably supervised by someone in the employer's household, who in fact works alongside them (see Binswanger and Rosenzweig, 1984a, 1986a; Singh, 1988a, b, c; Walker and Ryan, 1990). As we have seen, resource allocation theory predicts this practice.

An alternative is a daily piece-rate system, the worker's remuneration being dependent on the number of tasks he completes by the end of the day. (See Chapter 16 for further discussion.) There is no need for supervision under this arrangement, so the system operates in cases where accomplishments are relatively easy to monitor, such as picking tea, cutting sugarcane, and transporting loads.

Participation rate in the daily market is defined as the number of person-days of wage work sought plus the number of person-days of wage work done as a proportion of the total number of person-days where participation could have occurred. (Work on one's own farm is excluded from this

---

[20] As the success of the Grameen Bank has shown, non-government organizations can be even more effective in this field. We will study desirable forms of credit contracts in Ch. 17.

computation, as is work as a tenant farmer.[21]) It is an index of labour supply in the daily labour market. It can be significant and, just as the theory I sketched in Section 9.2 predicted, it is highest among households owning little or no land. The ICRISAT panel data records it as high as 87 per cent. Within the village the market for casual agricultural labour is, at least in the Indian sub-continent, very competitive. There is little evidence of monopsonistic behaviour on the part of landlords (see Bardhan and Rudra, 1981, 1986; Binswanger and Rosenzweig, 1984b; Singh, 1988b, c; Walker and Ryan, 1990). It is also impersonal, an agricultural labourer working for as many as twenty employers during a year. Of these employers, there may be one from whom the labourer had borrowed earlier (Section 9.4); he will have a commitment to work for that man for so many days in the busy season. On other days he is free to obtain work from other landlords.

Agricultural daily wages are usually sex-specific, female hourly wages in the ICRISAT data being on average 60 per cent of male hourly wages. So are tasks sex-specific. For example, men do the ploughing, while women do the transplanting, threshing, and winnowing. Women often comprise a disproportionate portion of the casual workforce; anything between 60 and 90 per cent of the casual labour hired are women. In later chapters we will try to find at least partial explanations for these facts.

Land is a most valued possession, even more than cattle. Most transactions in land in the Indian sub-continent are in tenancy, not in outright sales and purchases. In the early 1970s only about 1.5 per cent of agricultural households in India sold land in any year. A large proportion of sales by small holders are distress-sales, the owners facing food crises, deaths in the family, or stresses of similar magnitude. (See below.) In contrast, the market for bullocks is relatively buoyant, and in the early 1970s some 10 per cent of agricultural households in India sold livestock annually, a large proportion of sales being bullocks. Bullocks are typically bought and sold in regional markets, not village ones. This provides a way of smoothing consumption against village-specific risks (see Chapter 8; Lim, 1991). Livestock are a capital asset. Bullocks, for example, can also serve as a collateral on loans. They are therefore a prized commodity, and prestige is attached to their ownership (see D. Mazumdar, 1989).

There are two reinforcing reasons we would expect the market for land to be dormant. In the absence of financial capital markets, land, cattle, and children offer poor households the primary means of holding their savings. In India in the early 1970s, land accounted for about sixty-five per

[21] The total number of person-days where participation could have occurred excludes the person-days of family members who are disabled, who are regularly at school, who are children, and who are employed in regular or professional jobs.

cent of all rural household assets (see Singh, 1988b, c). (Children were not counted as capital assets.) For small landholders land is something of an indivisible asset. Moreover, poor households are particularly constrained in their ability to borrow. So buying and selling assets are about the only viable way of smoothing consumption over fluctuations in income.[22] However, owning little wealth, the coefficient of absolute risk aversion of a poor household is typically large (see Section 8.2). The household would be willing to sell land only if the prospects from doing so were very promising. It would not wish to reduce its asset for the mere possibility of increased future consumption; the downside of the risk would loom large in its consideration. Poor households, therefore, part with land only when faced with an economic crisis, when the present moment dominates all thought. (Cain, 1981, uses this argument to explain why in rural Bangladesh, where farmers face exceptional risks, land sales are more frequent than in ICRISAT villages.) For this same reason, landless people part with their livestock only when they face a crisis. In extreme situations even children are sold. I shall provide a formal expression of the precautionary motive for saving in Chapter *9.[23]

What we have adduced about men's behaviour holds equally true about women, of course. Women's most valued physical asset is usually their jewellery. It is pretty much the last thing they will part with, and for the same reason. Now, when we talk of household decisions concerning land or cattle sales, we typically mean male decisions (see Chapters 11 and 12). Except in some parts of south India, land and cattle in the Indian sub-continent are overwhelmingly owned by men. Even widows of landowning men find it difficult to claim the land as theirs.

A second reason land sales are rare in India is this: land is not homogeneous, and so under traditional technology part of the knowledge a peasant acquires about farming practices is farm-specific.[24] So the value of a piece of land to an adult who has cultivated it since childhood is greater than to an adult who hasn't. This means that land has the features of a differentiated commodity. *Ceteris paribus*, each farmer has his own most preferred plot of land, the one he has cultivated since boyhood. There is a sense in which peasants are locked into their plots of land. Such localized

---

[22] That the sale and purchase of bullocks serve this function for poor farmers in semi-arid rural India has been shown by Rosenzweig and Wolpin (1989) to be consistent with the ICRISAT data. In an unpublished paper, Binswanger and Rosenzweig (1989) have directly tested for the hypothesis that farmers in the ICRISAT sample choose their asset portfolios in such a way as to reflect aversion to risk. Their results were positive.

[23] In a recent overview of the savings problem in poor countries, Deaton (1990) has confirmed this intuition through simulation studies. See also Zeldes (1989b) for the argument that, even were they able to, poor and finitely lived households would not borrow for fear that a run of bad luck would wipe them out.

[24] The learning-by-doing involved in traditional farming is to some extent geographically localized. Modern farming technology irons out spatial differences. Rosenzweig and Wolpin (1985) have developed this argument.

learning-by-doing in agriculture also makes family labour cheaper than hired labour, and it makes the elderly particularly valuable as repositories of knowledge specific to the farm. This provides part of the reason why households in the Indian sub-continent have several generations living together. Adult farmers have an incentive to keep the elderly with them.[25]

Tenancy periods are short, as short as a season in irrigated regions. Elsewhere they are annual, but rarely greater than 2 to 3 years. Tenancy laws in India confer ownership rights on the actual tiller of leased-in land after a specified period. Jodha (1984) reports that in the ICRISAT data between 66 and 96 per cent of land transactions involved leases that were for one year or less in duration (see also Walker and Ryan, 1990). Between 14 and 46 per cent of operational land changed hands in the sample recorded in the ICRISAT data. In all but one village, between 89 and 97 per cent of transactions were in tenancy. Absentee-landlords are not uncommon, and they lease out their land at a fixed rental. This is what theory predicts, since in practice an absentee-landlord is unable to observe much of what is going on in his land. However, tenant farming is now becoming a rarity in the country as a whole.

The leasing of land and transactions in credit are on occasion intertwined. This may be compared with the link between the labour and credit markets we studied earlier. It is another instance of what in the development literature are often called *interlinked rural markets*.[26] The credit market is notoriously fragmented in poor countries. The informal credit system assumes a dominant role. In India, as late as 1971 the share of credit in agriculture obtained from formal institutions was only about thirty per cent.[27] A large volume of loans is obtained from friends and relatives, and from village and town money-lenders. We have anticipated reasons for this. Town money-lenders typically demand a collateral (sometimes twice the amount borrowed), whereas village money-lenders often do not. Both adverse selection and moral hazard regarding 'creditworthiness' play a role in this. (The would-be borrower typically knows more relevant facts about his own circumstances than the town money-lender; and the village money-lender typically knows more about the borrower than does the town money-lender.) For relatively wealthy households this may not matter much; their assets are the security on loans. Indeed, when some other

[25] In the early 1970s over 60% of all farm households contained at least two generations of adults. The argument that the elderly in pre-literate societies enjoyed special status because they were the repositories of knowledge has been developed by Goody (1986).

[26] See e.g. Braverman and Srinivasan (1981, 1984), Braverman and Stiglitz (1982), Rudra (1982), Mitra (1983), Binswanger and Rosenzweig (1984a, 1986a), Braverman and Gausch (1984), K. Basu (1987, 1990), C. Bell (1988), Bardhan (1989), Bell and Srinivasan (1989), and Hoff, Braverman and Stiglitz (1992).

[27] But by the early 1980s it had increased to 60%. To cite other examples, the share in Chamber, Pakistan, was 25% in 1980–1 (see Aleem, 1990); and in Zaria, Nigeria, it was a mere 8% in 1987–8 (see Udry, 1990).

transaction is linked to a loan (e.g. the leasing of land), it can be interpreted as a collateral. For landless households, the promise of labour service during the next peak agricultural season is a form of collateral. As a rule, however, the absence of collateral prevents landless households from investing in alternative types of capital assets, such as a small retail trade, or a cottage-based manufacturing unit (see below, and Chapter *9).[28]

Which creditor one goes to depends to an extent on the purpose behind the loan. A villager may need a loan for buying agricultural equipment, for food in bad times, for seeds and fertilizers, for wedding and funeral expenses, for replacing a draught animal, and so forth. Institutions offering investment credit, such as a nationalized bank, are not approachable for consumption loans, or for loans to meet social or familial obligations. They also operate with less information about borrowers than do local money-lenders. Moreover, since their interest rates are usually fixed by government policy, they typically have to ration their loans among potential borrowers. This gives rise to a complicated segmentation of the credit market. There is more than one reason for differences in interest rates across types of creditors.[29]

A large landowner may offer a loan to a small landowner in exchange for the lease of his land on a share-tenancy basis. In their study of ICRISAT villages, Binswanger et al. (1984) note that assetless people on occasion contract themselves out as farm servants for 3 months to a year, the primary motive being to obtain credit from the employer. However, casual labourers aren't able to obtain credit from employers by promising labour in peak seasons. (This is in contrast with the findings of Bardhan and Rudra, 1978, in West Bengal.) Where there are old debts to be paid back, the reverse can happen, and the small landowner (the debtor) may lease out his land to the creditor on a sharecropping basis *and* work on the tenant's farm as a labourer.

Often enough, the tenant is landless (or at best a small landholder) and owns a draught animal. For reasons of moral hazard, the rental market for draught animals on their own is pretty much non-existent. (How can the owner ensure the animal isn't mistreated?) He therefore offers himself and his draught animal in the market as a combined agricultural input, or he leases land from a large landholder on a share-tenancy basis (see Bliss and Stern, 1982).

[28] For more detailed accounts of these matters, see Jodha (1981), Binswanger et al. (1985), Feder, Just and Silberman (1985), Bhende (1986), Binswanger (1986), Binswanger and Rosenzweig (1986a, b; 1989), Gersovitz (1988), Dreze and Mukherjee (1989), Eswaran and Kotwal (1989), Deaton (1990), Walker and Ryan (1990), and Morduch (1990).

[29] In India in the early 1980s, the average nominal interest rate on rural credit in the formal sector was 10% per year; in the informal sector it was 22%. See C. Bell (1990), and Hoff and Stiglitz (1990).

9.6 Agrarian Relations in Sub-Saharan Africa

The semi-arid regions of sub-Saharan Africa offer both similar and contrasting pictures. There is a short growing season, the technology of production is primitive (there is little irrigation), population density is low, transport costs are particularly high, and soil productivity is both low and variable.[30] Land is still relatively abundant. These features have over the centuries led to the emergence of *shifting cultivation* as the dominant mode of farming. Household plots are small, for reasons we will see below. During cultivation the soil is usually covered by a mixture of crops which utilize soil nutrients from different depths and provide a varied canopy to shelter the soil surface (see Chapter 10). At the end of the cropping cycle, the natural system of resting the land restores the nutrients removed by crops; it also drives out opportunistic pests and diseases. So long as the fallow period is long enough, the system is sustainable. Consequently, fertilizers are of no importance (Section 9.2). Gathering and hunting from common property supplement agricultural income (Falconer and Arnold, 1989; Falconer, 1990; Chapter 10).

Taken together, the low productivity and variability of soil provide an explanation of the fact that fallow land is communally owned within kinship groups. Farming consists of cultivation by those clearing and occupying the land. The proportion of rural households that are landless is thus low; about 10 per cent. This form of property rights, even though inefficient in most ways, affords insurance to the household against misfortune specific to it. Strong bonds enable kinship to be a major source of credit. In Chapters 10–12 we will study the implications of communal ownership of land for gender relations and fertility behaviour. Here we note three immediate consequences: (i) land cannot be used as a collateral on loans; (ii) it has no market; and (iii) tenancy is virtually non-existent.

Land being abundant, the direct opportunity cost of labour is its average agricultural productivity, which to a good approximation may be assumed to be independent of population size. Now hired labour requires supervision. So the productivity of hired labour (net of supervision costs) will be lower than self-cultivation. Moreover, labour has to be paid before harvest, and, as elsewhere, credit is hard to come by. Taken together, this explains why the market for agricultural wage labour is only nascent. For the greater part farms are self-cultivated. Since shifting cultivation is practised, the soil can be tilled with hoes (making for small household plots). Farming by women is thereby viable. In an ingenious analysis,

---

[30] As with any such description of a large land mass, there are exceptions and variations. For instance, colonization led to private ownership among European settlers. I am abstracting from this. The material in this section has been drawn from P. Hill (1972), P. Collier (1983), Binswanger and McIntire (1987), Binswanger, McIntire and Udry (1989), D. Mazumdar (1989), World Bank (1989b), Feder and Feeny (1991), and Migot-Adholla *et al.*, (1991).

Pingali, Bigot and Binswanger (1987) have demonstrated a rationale behind farming with hand tools, by showing that the unit cost of production is lower with hoe cultivation than under farming with the plough.[31] So women frequently do the farming while their husbands work in towns and plantations as wage-labourers (see Chapter 11). This has an added advantage: male employment in the organized sector provides a form of collateral on loans.

Agricultural risks among neighbouring households are highly correlated. So markets for insurance and credit are restricted. In Chapters 11 and 12 we will see how patterns of conduct within kinship groups are a partial substitute for them. But they are an imperfect substitute. So further alternatives have to be found. The accumulation of capital provides an option for partially circumventing the problem.

As fallow land is communally held and shifting cultivation is practised, there is little incentive on the part of households to invest in it. Therefore, what is elsewhere a substantial form of private capital has a small role to play in the accumulation process. Common granaries are not useful for pooling agricultural risks (they are highly correlated), and are plagued by moral hazard. (The incentive to take more than one's due is not negligible.) So households store their own grain. Storage is at risk from pests. Vital though they are, granaries are an unreliable asset. What remains is livestock.

As in the Indian sub-continent, cattle are seen as durable capital. Households invest in them. *Transhumance* (i.e. the seasonal migration of cattle by herdsmen to suitable grazing grounds in different ecological zones) ensures that the values of crops and cattle are not quite as correlated as they would otherwise be. So livestock also provides households with a means of diversifying the portfolio of risks. As it happens, transhumance is a necessity. In the semi-arid regions both pasture and water vary over time and location. Stationary cattle would be extremely vulnerable. If cattle are to be watered and fed, they have to be on the move, from one water source to another. Peasant households are tied to the soil, at least during the planting and weeding season. Being sedentary, their knowledge of climatic and ecological conditions over large distances is understandably limited. So they can't be involved in the management of migratory livestock. Unlike in the Indian sub-continent, herding is therefore a specialized activity. Herdsmen, acting as 'tenants', manage peasants' livestock.

---

[31] The use of ploughs requires land to be de-stumped. This involves much greater energy costs. It is in the form of a fixed cost, and is worth bearing only if the land is permanently cultivated. There were probably other, parallel reasons for the prevalence of hoe-farming, the fragility of the soil in semi-arid Africa, and the prevalence of the tse-tse fly in large parts being only two.

Binswanger, McIntire and Udry (1989) note that this creates a moral hazard problem. (How are peasants to know if their cattle have been mistreated, or simply killed for their meat?) They trace the fact that the farmer–herder relationship extends over many years to this: it reduces moral hazard (Chapter 8). Furthermore, payment to herders includes milk and a share of the cattle's offspring. This further reduces the hazard.

9.7   *Consumption as Investment*

The standard theory of resource allocation takes the household as its unit of analysis. I have on occasion suggested why this is a weakness. We have also seen its strengths. The distinction between individual and household savings provides another illustration of its strength. It will pay to look into this.

Individual savings are a problematic concept in poor countries, where the many anonymous markets we take for granted elsewhere malfunction, or do not function at all. *Saving* is conventionally taken to mean consumption forgone today for the purposes of greater consumption in the future. Presently we will see that this can be misleading, and that it is more appropriate to regard saving as an activity that is undertaken today for the purpose of increasing productivity (of, say, labour), and thereby consumption, in the future. It is often a delicate matter to judge when a transaction amounts to saving and when it does not. This is so even when the notion of saving we deploy is the conventional one. Thus, consider again our stylized model of intergenerational food allocation in the previous chapter (Section 8.7). Food was taken to be non-durable, and households were assumed not to have access to capital markets. As a resource allocation mechanism, the household needed stringent norms of behaviour. (Of course, the need for norms is negligible when emotional ties are sufficiently strong.) The norm we studied had adults giving a fraction of their produce to the young and a fraction to the deserving old (but none to the undeserving old), and consuming the rest. This norm was shown to sustain pretty much any allocation over a lifetime, but it seemed natural to study the constant consumption stream. As the commodity was taken to be non-durable, the question of investment in the aggregate did not arise. (The model had no capital stock to augment or deplete.) However, adults in the economy saved: their consumption fell short of their income. Consumption transfers to the young and to the deserving old were forgone consumption; they guaranteed adults consumption in their old age. By the same token, not giving anything to an undeserving old person would also have constituted an act of investment. Cast in a 'non-market' environment, the model was, in disguise, one of *life-cycle saving* on the part of individuals.[32] The young in the model 'borrowed', the old dissaved, and the household as a whole neither saved nor dissaved. In short, household consumption equalled household income at each date. This is what made aggregate saving equal aggregate investment in the economy: each was nil. The economy we considered there was stationary. In such an environment it makes sense to treat the household as an economic unit for the purposes of constructing national accounts. It saves on accounting costs.

That intergenerational consumption transfers within families should, at least in part, be seen as a substitute for imperfect capital and annuity markets in industrial market economies has been suggested by Kotlikoff and Spivak (1981). They have argued that such transfers can be interpreted as a method for smoothing consumption over time when annuity markets are imperfect and the date of death is uncertain. Their simulations suggested that something like seventy per cent of the self-insurance that would have been achieved were annuity markets perfect could be attained through intergenerational transfers even within small families (see also Kotlikoff and Summers, 1981; Kotlikoff, 1988; Bernheim, 1991). Bernheim, Schleifer and Summers (1985) and Cremer and Pestieau (1991) have carried the argument further. They have proposed that we view bequests as a payment for care and support in old age. Parents commit themselves to the total figure for bequests and determine the sharing rule among offspring, but leave open the option of disinheriting errant children. This way parents can play one child off against another, and are able to obtain all the utility surplus to be had in the intergenerational exchange.

The pattern of exchange is in some ways reversed in poor countries (see Chapter 12). Meillassoux (1981), in a well-known work, argued that heads of households (the old) in sub-Saharan Africa provide consumption insurance for the young in exchange for labour services. This the old manage to do by maintaining ownership of cattle, and control over household foodstocks. If this insurance benefit were to be ignored, the aggregate transfer of resources would be from the young to the old, a matter that has figured prominently in Caldwell (1977a, b, 1981, 1982). The allocation mechanism is sustained by norms of behaviour. The example studied in Chapter 8 (Section 8.7) provides a way of explaining how such behaviour is sustained.

The effect of changes in household income and investment opportunities on its savings behaviour, and the link between savings and fertility

---

[32] Models of life-cycle savings in the presence of perfect capital markets have been explored in Modigliani and Brumberg (1953), Meade (1966), and M. Farrell (1970), among many others.

Table 9.4 Sources of aggregate savings (%)[a]

	Household	Enterprise	Government
India	65	20	15
United States	35	58	7
China	46	34	20
	(15)	(34)	(51)

[a] Data for mid-to-late 1980s. Figures for China in parentheses are from 1978.

Source: Lim and Wood (1985, table 9.1); Qian (1988, table 2).

decisions in poor countries, are both complex and ill-understood.[33] One reason we know little is that national statistics on savings don't often incorporate household investments in cattle; and they almost never incorporate the maintenance and improvement of land (e.g. terracing, reforesting, digging storage tanks and irrigation ditches). For rural households with little access to the capital market, land, and agricultural equipment, children, seeds, and cattle are vital capital assets. They provide ways of congealing household savings. The non-congruency of saving as recorded in national income statistics, and saving as perceived by poor households, is then self-evident.

As Table 9.4 shows, households are the primary saving institution in poor countries. This is in contrast to industrial market economies, where private enterprises are the dominant savers. The presence of constraints on a household's ability to obtain credit removes the clean separation between consumption and production which is the hallmark of the household in the Arrow–Debreu model of resource allocation (see Koopmans, 1957; Singh, Squire and Strauss, 1986a; Section *9.1). While worth making, however, this is somewhat of a technical point, and not much conceptually hangs on it. Fundamental issues are involved in a feature of the standard theory lying elsewhere. The theory treats current consumption as forgone investment. Even though this is a good basis for classifying economic activities in rich economies, it isn't so good for poor households in poor economies. At low levels of nutrition and health care, increases in current consumption improve future labour productivity: if nothing else, morbidity is reduced. For example, Pitt and Rosenzweig (1985) observed from Indonesian data that an increase in the consumption of fish, fruit, or vegetables by 10 per cent reduces the chance of illness there by 9, 3 and 6 per cent respectively. The general effects of nutrition and health care on productivity were described in Chapters 1 and 4, and in Chapters 14 and 15 we will study these matters in sharper detail. Here we should note that

---

[33] We will study these questions in Chs. 11–13.

at the margin consumption of basic needs amounts to investment. One may go further and argue that consumption and investment at the margin are, over time, synergistic with each other up to a point; they are not competitive (see also A. Marshall, 1920; Leibenstein, 1957a, b; Myrdal, 1968; Gersovitz, 1983; Chapters 14–17).

The presumption about industrial market economies is that a vast majority of the population are well fed and well cared for in health. Marginal changes in consumption expenditure have no effect on nutrition and health care, so future productivity of labour is unaffected. In this context it makes sense to treat consumption and investment as competing activities. National income accounting practices reflect this thought. Admittedly, in saying this I am ignoring obesity, which is a problem in industrial countries. Nutrition affects future productivity there as well, but it works in the opposite direction, making the competition between consumption and investment more severe than accounting conventions allow.

In the past, a neglect of such links as we are identifying here has deflected the intellectual and administrative energies of many poor countries into unproductive channels. Consider, for example, the oft-quoted passage from perhaps the most influential article to have been written to date on economic development in poor countries:

The central problem in the theory of economic development is to understand the process by which a community which was previously saving and investing 4 or 5 per cent of its national income or less, converts itself into an economy where voluntary saving is running at about 12 to 15 per cent of national income or more. This is the central problem because the central fact of economic development is rapid capital accumulation (including knowledge and skills with capital). (W. A. Lewis, 1954: 155)

It is perhaps unfair to fix on this one passage when there are so many illuminating ones elsewhere in the article. But the central point of the essay—the importance of accumulation of physical capital and of rapid industrialization—did catch the mood of the period and greatly influenced the way models of the development process were fashioned, at least until recently.[34] The problem is that it is a pretty wrong-headed diagnosis of the dilemma poor countries in general faced at the time Lewis wrote on the matter, and it continues to be so now; and for two reasons.

First, the saving rates used as illustrations in the passage are those taken

---

[34] I am here thinking of the large, influential literature on dual economies and dualistic growth (see e.g. Marglin, 1976). Roughly speaking, this literature envisages a stagnant and passive agricultural sector, from which labour is drawn into the dynamic, usually urban, industrial sector along the process of capital accumulation there. Timmer (1988) provides a short, but powerful, critique of this vision.

from official statistics, and we have seen the sense in which they are based on a conceptually flawed dichotomy between saving and consumption. Second, and more importantly, the passage doesn't quite acknowledge that it isn't merely saving that matters, it is also the productivity of investment. If the latter is really low, even a 20 per cent rate of saving (let alone 12–15 per cent) will not do much for growth in national income. By official estimates, poor countries in recent years have routinely managed to invest at a rate 20 per cent or more of their gross domestic product. During the 1980s the rate of investment in even low-income sub-Saharan countries (excluding Nigeria) averaged somewhere around 18 per cent of their aggregate output. However, the rate of growth of output averaged only 1.4 per cent per year.[35] This translates itself into a rate of return on investment of about 8 per cent per year (0.014/0.180), a dismally low figure (see also Table 7.1). Among the poorest countries, there has in fact been a negative correlation between savings rates and rates of growth of national income per head (Stern, 1989). Admittedly, the passage quoted above contains within parentheses an elaboration of what constitutes capital accumulation. It nevertheless contains an incomplete set of markers to guide us.

These reflections on the sense in which dualistic models of development are misleading are connected, of course. Investment in infrastructure, shelter, primary health care, education, and nutrition guarantees enhance labour productivity. This is a recurring refrain in this book. In Chapters 6–8 we studied the organization of production as a determinant of productivity. We will do that again in this and the following chapter. Here we are adding to it the thought that patterns of investment matter. Increases in the consumption of basic needs are a form of investment with high returns in poor countries. Of course, good social cost–benefit analysis of alternative activities has always been able to pick up such features as we are identifying here. The standard model of resource allocation requires only slight extension to accommodate them.

9.8 Lack of Credit among the Assetless

Earlier, I observed that, because the phenomena of adverse selection and moral hazard would be expected to increase sharply with geographical distance, markets for insurance and credit in poor countries are fragmented into tiny enclaves, such as villages and kinship groups (see e.g. Rudra, 1984; Townsend, 1989; Udry, 1990).

The costs of screening are not negligible even within locales. For

---

[35] See World Bank (1989b, tables 2 and 4). The inclusion of Nigeria would not change the figure for the investment rate, but it would yield an even worse figure for growth in aggregate output, namely −0.4% per year. It doesn't bear asking how an oil-rich country could have so mismanaged its affairs.

example, Aleem (1990) has estimated that in the early 1980s non-institutional lenders around the town of Chambar (Pakistan) on average spent one day and $2 in transportation for screening each loan applicant, even though many of the lenders had been operating in the area for several years. This amounted to about 6.5 per cent of the value of the average loan. Large covariances among household incomes within geographical enclaves provide an additional reason why neither insurance nor credit offers a way for poor, risk-averse households to smooth their consumption across contingencies and time. A large covariance ensures on average that the supply of credit reduces precisely at those moments when demand increases. These are moments of collective crises, when people are trying to obtain distress-loans. If at such moments the credit market in any locale is to clear, its price would have to rise sufficiently to equate supply with demand. This would mean either a rise in the interest rate or an increase in collateral requirements on loans, or it could mean both. Assetless households would be especially hurt—in the latter case because they have little to offer in the way of collateral, in the former because they are less inclined than rich households to bear additional risk. (Walker and Ryan, 1990, provide an excellent account of this.) Taken together, these features imply that in times of especial stress the price of credit becomes too high, and the assetless are shut out of the market. This is not only tragic, it is ironic, for poor people need credit more than rich people do. The rich can save more easily for the purposes of smoothing their consumption.

Thus far the analysis has been simple, addressing as it does the need for loans for the purposes of riding through a crisis. We expect markets for credit (as also for insurance) to be ruthless towards the poorest of the poor. In fact there is a pervasive problem with loan markets. It is that the interest rate on credit not only serves the function of a price, but also serves as a mechanism for screening loan applicants, and for providing them with the incentives for repaying the loans.[36] Because the interest rate plays several roles, credit markets can't even be guaranteed to clear. Credit in many circumstances is rationed, in that, among loan applicants who appear to be identical, some receive credit while others do not; moreover, those who don't would not receive credit even if they were to offer to pay a higher rate of interest.

Let us see how this may happen. (Section *9.4 contains a formal analysis.) Loan applicants typically differ as regards the investment projects they would like to undertake. So let us assume for simplicity that all potential investment projects have the same mean return, but differ in

---

[36] The key paper on this is Stiglitz and Weiss (1981). See also Stiglitz and Weiss (1983, 1986, 1987), in which they develop the basic argument in rich detail. In Chapters 16 and *16 I shall develop a theory of rationing of the labour market which is based on a different mechanism. For excellent syntheses of models of rationing, see Stiglitz (1987b) and Weiss (1990).

their riskiness. Imagine also that each borrower has at his command precisely one project, and that all borrowers are risk-neutral. In terms of their ability to repay loans, therefore, each potential borrower is a different risk. But this risk may be assumed to be private knowledge (this is the source of the adverse selection problem facing lenders); and so all potential borrowers (i.e. investment projects) look the same to lenders. We can now see how the interest rate can act as a screening device. The expected return to a lender depends on the probability of repayment (or, to put it another way, the probability of default). For example, those who are willing to pay a high interest rate will on average be the worse risks: they are willing *because* they know that the probability of having to repay is low. If a lender were to increase his interest rate in these circumstances, the pool of borrowers would get worse, because those whose projects are less risky would withdraw from the market. Thus, the presence of 'bad' projects would drive out the 'good' ones. If this effect were sufficiently powerful, the expected return to a lender would be a declining function of the interest rate he charged. In many circumstances it would result in credit rationing, because lenders would prefer to restrict the amount people are permitted to borrow, rather than raise the interest rate they charge on the loans. Moral hazard and adverse selection can provide lenders with a reason for imposing a ceiling on the interest rate on loans.

In the credit market we are envisaging here, the interest rate would be determined by the average quality of the pool of potential loan applicants. This is the source of an externality: even though each potential borrower is affected by the quality of all other potential loan applicants, no applicant takes into account the effect he has on others. In the case under consideration, every high-risk borrower inflicts a damage on all low-risk borrowers by the fact that there is a marginal increase in the interest rate the latter group faces as a consequence. The externality is *pecuniary* (the term was invented by Scitovsky, 1954, for classifying externalities), and the market equilibrium allocation of credit is Pareto-inefficient. It can be shown that, in the market we are considering here, there is in the aggregate too little credit on offer, relative to what there would have been had lenders been able to distinguish the various projects in terms of their riskiness. A public subsidy on interest rates could in principle sustain a Pareto-efficient allocation of loans. The efficient level of subsidy could be computed by the government even if it were to suffer from adverse selection to the same extent as the private creditors.

That markets characterized by moral hazard and adverse selection sustain Pareto-inefficient allocations is a general result: such markets suffer from pecuniary externalities. Allied to it is a deeper result, which is that these markets are (almost) never Pareto-efficient even in a relevant, constrained sense. Even if the government is subject to the same informational constraints as private agencies, it can (almost always) devise Pareto-improving policies; that is, policies that would be 'utility-improving' for at least one party without being 'utility-reducing' for any party. (The key paper here is Greenwald and Stiglitz, 1986). In the above example, the government could so subsidize credit as to result in a Pareto-improving credit allocation, even though it may not be able to distinguish potential borrowers in terms of the quality of their projects. We will study public policy and the problem of incentives in Chapter 17.[37]

Credit-rationing is analytically a different phenomenon from the poor being shut out of the credit market because the price of borrowing is too high. For the poor, however, analytical distinctions are of no direct moment. What is of importance to them is that, generally speaking, the terms on which they are able to obtain credit are stiff relative to the returns they expect on alternative investment opportunities open to them. It matters to them also that the avenue of credit is not really open to them for smoothing their consumption across contingencies and time.

9.9 *Consumption Smoothing*

Except under a special set of circumstances (identified in the Arrow–Debreu model, Chapter 7), it isn't possible for households to separate their decisions on investment from their decisions on consumption. A household's investment decisions in the Arrow–Debreu model depend only on market interest rates and the production technology it has at its disposal: they are independent of preferences. The avenue of borrowing allows risk-averse households to smooth their consumption across time and contingencies. In short, the possibility of smoothing consumption through borrowing allows households to engage in high-risk activities with large expected returns. All this breaks down when the household is constrained in its ability to borrow.

The poor are often in debt, sometimes perpetually so. We have seen why borrowing terms for the poor are harsh, to an extent that they are usually loath to borrow. They do so from money-lenders only in conditions of real distress. Therefore, saving on their part in such an economic environment mediates between low current consumption and uncertain

[37] The pecuniary externalities associated with adverse selection do not inevitably result in an under-supply of credit: it could lead to an over-supply. In our example in the text, projects were assumed to differ only by their riskiness, not by their expected yield. There are circumstances in which the presence of borrowers with good projects enables borrowers with bad projects to 'free-ride' and secure loans they would have not been able to obtain had lenders been able to distinguish bad projects from good ones. In the example in the text, the situation is the reverse (bad projects drive out good ones) and so there is underinvestment. See de Meza and Webb (1987) for a general analysis.

future agricultural income. The household aims to smooth its consumption in the face of uncertain income. The motive for saving (e.g. carrying inventories) is a precautionary one; it isn't the life-cycle savings motive we considered in the previous chapter. We will formalize this intuition in Section *9.2.

Suppose that at some arbitrary date the household's level of assets is precariously low (owing, say, to a run of bad harvests allied to a degradation of common-property resources, during which the household has been forced to dissave). If it were possible to do so, the household would wish to borrow so as to keep consumption from falling yet further. But it is unable to borrow. (Rich households don't face this problem.) So the household is forced to dip into its assets and dissave some more (e.g. sell draught animals, pull children out of school and put them to work; see Jacoby and Skoufias, 1992). In less bad times the household has prepared for such eventualities. Thus, savings and agricultural investments are used as a means of smoothing consumption. The household invests in safe, low-yielding crops instead of risky, high-yielding crops. This strategy enables it to smooth the flow of income. Consumption credit for the poor household enables it to smooth consumption without having to engage in precautionary savings, enabling it to accept risks it otherwise would not be able to accept. Eswaran and Kotwal (1989) have made this observation to argue that the unavailability of consumption credit forces poor households to invest in safe, low-yielding agricultural activity. We will study this argument formally in Section *9.3.

There are empirical correlates of this. Moscardi and de Janvry (1977) found in Pueblo, Mexico, that farmers with larger landholdings took greater risks in their selection of crops, as did farmers belonging to solidarity groups who pool their risks. The Eswaran-Kotwal argument provides a link between consumption loans and the choice of investment activity. We will see subsequently that it also describes a mechanism (there are others; see Chapter 16) by which disparities in well-being widen over time among poor households which are similar to begin with.

Consumption loans are not the same as insurance. You buy your insurance before you know your output of crops, whereas you try and obtain consumption credit only after you have experienced bad luck with your crops. With credit you can smooth consumption completely over time, but not over events. Provided you are charged actuarially fair premia, you can equalize consumption over both time and events by buying insurance. So insurance is better. But among villagers in poor countries crop insurance is non-existent, for reasons we have already studied.

These are loose statements, and can be made tight only by specifying a formal model. But the intuition is clear enough. Deaton's (1990) simulations based on a model of an agricultural household facing credit constraints shows consumption to be much smoother over time than income, and to be strongly autocorrelated; the household engages in precautionary savings to smooth consumption partially (see also Deaton, 1991). I will return to this observation in Chapter 15, when I come to argue that observing autocorrelation in nutrition intake does not imply nutritional adaptation: autocorrelation in consumption over the medium and long run is an implication of credit constraints among the poor.

Whether credit-rationing is pervasive in poor countries has become a contentious issue of late. The anecdotal evidence has appeared so over-whelming that until recently credit-rationing as a phenomenon was taken pretty much for granted. However, in a carefully designed work, Kochar (1991) has studied the Government of India Household Survey data on credit transactions, indebtedness, and household and farm investments, to conclude that in rural India there is little evidence of credit-rationing. But her findings are not at odds with the suggestion that the poor are often shut out of the market because the terms they face are unfavourable. If this is true (and there is a rather large battery of evidence suggesting that it is), the rural poor are unable to accomplish much consumption-smoothing. Recently, Morduch (1990) has studied an 8-year household panel data from ICRISAT, and has used a model of household production possibilities similar to the one I have deployed here (and in Section *9.2), to conclude that in a number of villages poor farmers diversify their crops more than rich farmers do, even at the expense of mean earnings. (See also Binswanger and Rosenzweig, 1989; Walker and Ryan, 1990; Alderman and Paxson, 1992.)

There is also anthropometric evidence of credit constraints in a number of countries, for example Kenya, the Gambia, Ethiopia, and Bangladesh. In rural communities of poor countries there is often a hungry season, when stocks are low and agricultural work is intensive. In the post-harvest season nutritional stress is reduced (households carry inventories of grain), and there is less work to be done in the fields. Adults and newborn children in poor households there often display seasonal fluctuations in weight.[38] This does not look much like consumption-smoothing to me.

9.10   Unemployment

Except possibly during periods of peak labour demand (harvest and sowing times), there is, in South Asia at least, strong evidence of labour

---

[38] See Chambers, Longhurst and Pacey (1981), Prentice et al. (1981), Prentice (1984), Payne (1985a, b), Chen, Chowdhury and Huffman (1980), Ferro-Luzzi, Pastore and Sette (1987), de Garine and Harrison (1988), Neumann et al. (1989), Whitehead (1989), Ferro-Luzzi et al. (1990), Norgan et al. (1992), and Ch. 14.

unemployment.[39] At this point it is as well to be loose in our use of the term 'unemployment'. The thing to avoid is a recount of debates on the matter, which took place among development economists during the decades of the 1950s and 1960s. The literature for the most part remains incomprehensible to me. Later, in Chapter 16, I will define and discuss both *disguised unemployment* (i.e. *surplus labour*) and *involuntary unemployment*, and I shall provide an explanation for their presence. Inevitably, the evidence is that unemployment is experienced among the landless and near-landless, and disproportionately by the women among them. The seasonally unemployed are also among the poorest in society: the poorest aren't too poor to be unemployed (see Visaria, 1980; Singh, 1988c).

The unemployment observed in poor countries isn't voluntary. It is as though there are agricultural 'insiders' and 'outsiders', with the outsiders inhabiting the casual labour market.[40] Over time, the less productive among the outsiders are weeded out during slack periods, and they become permanently unemployed (Rudra, 1982). In a number of regions there is unemployment even during peak seasons. For example, in a large cross-sectional sample of household survey data in West Bengal, Bardhan (1984b) estimated unemployment among male casual workers to be about 8–14 per cent in peak periods and about 23 per cent in slack periods, and for female casual workers to be about 20 per cent in peak periods and 42 per cent in slack periods. Unemployment was measured by Bardhan to be the number of days in the reference week respondents reported seeking work or being available for work as a proportion of the total number of days in the reference week they worked or reported seeking work or being available for work.[41]

The seasonally unemployed poor are usually not as well off as those who have long-term employment. But it is the extreme outsiders who are the most wretched of people. They are society's outcasts, unable to obtain even seasonal work. They are disfranchised, and they become destitutes. They are often the migrants and dispossessed in search of jobs, who in the course of time become the emaciated beggars to be seen in the streets of large towns and cities, leading what in a different context has been called 'lives of quiet desperation'. How this process operates, where, from an initial situation of near equality, people find themselves facing different life chances, is one of the most profound questions in the social sciences.

---

[39] See e.g. Krishna (1975), Gulati (1976), Visaria (1980), Rudra (1982), Bardhan (1984a), Ryan and Ghodake (1984), Singh (1988c, 1990), and Dreze and Mukherjee (1989).

[40] The terminology I am using here is due to Lindbeck and Snower (1988), but the mechanism I allude to which creates insiders and outsiders here is different from theirs. See Ch. 16.

[41] See Ryan and Ghodake (1984), and Ch. 16, for comparable figures in the semi-arid regions of central India.

Thus, workers may initially be similar in their characteristics, and they may not be indifferent between the types of contracts prevailing. If the resource allocation mechanism enforces involuntary unemployment, we would expect some form of rationing in the labour market, with those who are fortunate enough to become 'insiders' enjoying a higher living standard than those who remain seasonal 'outsiders'. We would also expect these seasonal outsiders to enjoy a higher living standard than the outcasts of society. With the passage of time, having experienced different nutrition and work histories, these different classes of people would, inexorably, no longer *be* the same, and would no longer *look* the same. Emaciated beggars have no marketable labour quality to offer. No rationing would then be required by the allocation mechanism to keep them disfranchised. From the perspectives of the market, they would be non-people. In Chapter 16 we will look into one class of mechanisms under which all this can happen.

Households and Credit Constraints

★9.1 Model of the Peasant Household

In this section I shall offer a formal account of the peasant household sketched in Sections 9.1–9.3. The formulation has been adapted from Eswaran and Kotwal (1986). Their aim was to study the force of credit constraints on household behaviour in a world where larger landowning households are able to obtain more credit. The authors used this to explain the joint presence of different types of organizations in agricultural production.

The household in the Arrow–Debreu model faces a single budget constraint, and so is a special case of the one we will be studying here. It can decentralize its production and consumption decisions on the basis of market prices. This latter fact was stressed in Koopmans (1957). It has been put to empirical work by Rosenzweig (1980) and Singh, Squire and Strauss (1986b), among others (see also Singh, Squire and Strauss, 1986a). In the Arrow–Debreu model it does not matter whether agriculture is under tenancy or whether landowners hire wage-labourers: there are no differences in efficiency in the two systems of production. Indeed, both are efficient (Chapter 7). So the model doesn't explain institutional differences, and was not designed to do so. In Chapter 9 we noted that the Arrow–Debreu premiss (that households don't face credit constraints) is false in poor countries. So we will not study the Arrow–Debreu household here.

We assume that the household's landholding is $\hat{T}$. (For a landless household, $\hat{T} = 0$.) Farm production and household consumption of the food-crop are denoted by Y_f and C_f, respectively. I take it for simplicity that, provided hired labour is supervised, it is a perfect substitute for household labour in agricultural production. Total available household time is taken to be L^*. Let L_h denote the amount of time devoted by the household to cultivation on the farm, and L_o the amount hired out in the labour market. Supervision of hired labour on the farm also requires time. I denote this by S. If L_e is the quantity of hired labour, supervision time amounts to $S = S(L_e)$, where $S(0) = 0$, and $S'(0)$, $S''(L_e) > 0$. The amount of leisure is denoted as C_s. It satisfies the equation

$$C_s + L_h + L_o + S(L_e) = L^*. \qquad (\star 9.1)$$

Let X denote material inputs in farm production, and let C_m be the household's consumption of an index of commodities purchased in the market (e.g. clothing, utensils). The amount of labour used in farm production is denoted by Z, and T represents the quantity of land the household farms. (If the household has rented out some of its land, then $T < \hat{T}$; if it has leased in some land, then $T > \hat{T}$.) We may now represent farm production possibilities by the function

$$Y_f = F(Z, X, T), \qquad (\star 9.2)$$

where $Z \equiv L_e + L_h$.[1] The household's utility function is taken to be $U(C_f, C_m, C_s)$, a strictly concave function. Since each of the final consumption goods is desired, $U(\cdot)$ is increasing in each of its arguments. For expositional ease, we will assume that each commodity is much desired when its consumption level is low. This will guarantee that all three consumption goods will be consumed, even if at very low rates.

The price of the purchased consumer good is normalized to be unity. We denote the market wage rate for unskilled labour by w, the price of food crops by p_f, that of material inputs in farm production by p_x, and the rental on land by p_T. The household is assumed to be a price-taker in these markets.

It is convenient to think of production occurring in two stages: (i) preparing the soil, seeding, irrigating, fertilizing, weeding, and so forth; followed by (ii) harvesting, marketing, and so on. Factor payments have to be made during the first stage. Constraints on the availability of working capital set limits on what the household can do at this stage, and therefore on what it can achieve at the second stage. For simplicity of exposition, I shall ignore the credit market altogether and assume that the household can gather together in the first stage a certain sum based on past savings. This sum, which I write as B, is taken to be an increasing function of the size of household's landholding; that is, $B = B(\hat{T})$, with $B'(\hat{T}) > 0$.[2] It follows that production costs must satisfy the condition,

$$B(\hat{T}) + P_T\hat{T} + wL_o \geq p_xX + wL_e + p_TT. \qquad (\star 9.3)$$

Write

$$\pi \equiv [B(\hat{T}) + p_T\hat{T} + wL_o - p_xX - wL_e - p_TT] \geq 0. \qquad (\star 9.4)$$

Once crops have been harvested, the household's budget constraint is[3]

---

[1] $F(\cdot)$ is assumed to be constant-returns-to-scale, concave, and an increasing function of each of its arguments. For expositional ease, I shall also assume that the marginal product of each of the three variable factors of production is large when the level of the corresponding factor use is very low. This will ensure that each factor is in use in production.

[2] We may imagine that B is *negative* when $\hat{T}$ is very small, to underline the fact that agricultural production incurs fixed costs.

[3] I am assuming implicitly that the interest rate is nil.

$$p_f C_f + C_m \leq p_f F(L_h + L_e, X, T) + \pi. \qquad (*9.5)$$

For simplicity of exposition, I shall assume that, relative to the fixed costs of cultivation, the household owns sufficient land to make it worth while to maintain a farm. Thus, we now need to record explicitly that

$$L_o \geq 0; \qquad (*9.6)$$

$$L_e \geq 0; \qquad (*9.7)$$

$$L_h \geq 0. \qquad (*9.8)$$

Therefore, the household's problem is

Choose C_f, C_m, C_s, X, L_o, L_e, L_h, T, so as to maximize $U(C_f, C_m, C_s)$, subject to constraints (*9.1), (*9.3), (*9.5)–(*9.8). $\qquad (*9.9)$

Inspection of problem (*9.9) tells us that it is a concave programme. So let μ_1, μ_2, μ_3, μ_4, μ_5, and μ_6 be the Lagrange multipliers associated with constraints (*9.1), (*9.3), (*9.5)–(*9.8) respectively. Denote the Lagrangean by L. It takes the form

$$
\begin{aligned}
L = U(C_f, C_m, C_s) &+ \mu_1[L^* - C_s - L_h - L_o - S(L_e)] + (\mu_2 + \mu_3)[B(\hat{T}) \\
&+ p_r \hat{T} + w L_o - p_x X - w L_e - p_r T] + \mu_3[p_f F(L_h + L_e, X, T) \\
&- p_f C_f - C_m] + \mu_4 L_o + \mu_5 L_e + \mu_6 L_h, \qquad (*9.10)
\end{aligned}
$$

where each of the six (non-negative) multipliers satisfies the complementary-slackness condition with the constraint it is associated with. The assumptions we have made imply that $\mu_1 > 0$ and $\mu_3 > 0$. Interest, therefore, lies in μ_2, μ_4, μ_5, and μ_6. We will see presently that the values they take are the defining characteristic of the organization of agricultural production.

Problem (*9.7) has eight first-order conditions. From the Lagrangian in (*9.10), we conclude that they are:

$$\partial U/\partial C_f = p_f \mu_3 \qquad (*9.11)$$

$$\partial U/\partial C_m = \mu_3 \qquad (*9.12)$$

$$\partial U/\partial C_s = \mu_1 \qquad (*9.13)$$

$$p_f \partial F/\partial X = (\mu_2 + \mu_3) p_x/\mu_3 \qquad (*9.14)$$

$$w = (\mu_1 - \mu_4)/(\mu_2 + \mu_3) \qquad (*9.15)$$

$$p_f \partial F/\partial Z = [(\mu_2 + \mu_3)w + \mu_1 S'(L_e) - \mu_5]/\mu_3 \qquad (*9.16)$$

$$p_f \partial F/\partial Z = (\mu_1 - \mu_6)/\mu_3 \qquad (*9.17)$$

$$p_f \partial F/\partial T = (\mu_2 + \mu_3) p_r/\mu_3. \qquad (*9.18)$$

It is an easy matter to confirm that, if at an optimum $L_e > 0$, then $L_o = 0$. An *Arrow–Debreu household* is characterized by the condition $\mu_2 = 0$. It faces a single budget constraint. A large landowning household in our model will satisfy this condition: it will not face a constraint on the ability to mobilize working capital. It will also pursue a capitalist form of agriculture, in that it is possible to show that, if $\hat{T}$ is large (and therefore $B(\hat{T})$ is large), the household will find it optimal to set $L_o = L_h = 0$, and $L_e > 0$.

If $\hat{T}$ is small but positive, we would typically find $L_e = 0$, and L_o, $L_h > 0$. This is a *labourer–cultivator household*. An exploration of special functional forms for $F(\cdot)$, $S(\cdot)$, and $U(\cdot)$ suggest that, if $\hat{T}$ is in some intermediate range of values, then $L_h > 0$, and $L_o = L_e = 0$. This is a *self-cultivator*, the peasant household in its pristine form.

★9.2   *Precautionary Motive for Saving*

Consider a rural household planning its present and future. The present is taken to be date 0. Denote the household's assets at date t (≥ 0) as A_t. (We are simplifying and aggregating its assets into one.) There are three things a household can do with its assets: it can consume part of them, it can invest in agricultural production, and it can lend what remains at the going rate of interest. The market interest rate is assumed to be r (> 0). The household can invest in two agricultural crops, and we denote their rates of return by α_t and β_t. They are taken to be independent random variables.[4] By assumption, α has a lower mean than β, but it is less risky. (We say that β is more risky than α if there is a random variable, say ϕ, which is independent of α and has zero mean, such that $\beta = \alpha + \phi$. See Rothschild and Stiglitz, 1970.) Furthermore, we assume that α, $\beta \geq -1$ for all possible realizations. Let C_t be household consumption and Y_t and Z_t the amounts it invests in the two agricultural crops.

The household has potential labour power. However, the labour market is capricious, and in really bad circumstances work may involve foraging from common-property resources. So we denote by X_t, a random variable, the household's exogenous income at t.[5] Time is discrete, so the household's asset level moves according to the equation

$$A_{t+1} = (A_t + X_t - C_t - Y_t - Z_t)(1+r) + (1+\alpha)Y_t + (1+\beta)Z_t$$
$$\text{for } t \geq 0. \tag{★9.19}$$

The household is assumed to be risk-averse. It begins with assets equal to A_o. This represents inheritance from the past. It is the household's initial condition. For agricultural production to be worth while at t, we must suppose that $E(\alpha)$, $E(\beta) > r$, where $E(\cdot)$ is the expectation operator. (This is because the household is risk-averse.) We next take the household's intertemporal utility function to be of the form

$$E[\Sigma_t(1+\delta)^{-t}V(C_t)], \tag{★9.20}$$

---

[4] For simplicity of notation, we will assume that α_t and β_t are both identically and independently distributed over time. So we may as well drop their time subscripts.

[5] This too is assumed to be identically and independently distributed over time. We are simplifying and regarding the source of this exogenous income to be unconnected with agricultural production.

where δ (≥ 0) is the household's pure rate of time-discount, and $V(\cdot)$ its per-period utility function.[6] As before, we assume that $V'(C) > 0$. As it is risk-averse, $V''(C) < 0$. Furthermore, we take it that $V'''(C) > 0$. This is necessary if the coefficient of absolute risk aversion is to decline with increasing wealth (see Chapter 8).

Finally, the household must respect the constraints

$$C_t, Y_t, Z_t \geq 0, \qquad \text{for } t \geq 0. \tag{*9.21}$$

We will now assume that $A_t \geq 0$ for all $t \geq 0$. This captures the idea that the household is unable to borrow. It is an extreme assumption, for, as we have noted in this and the previous chapter, the poorest are often in debt, sometimes perpetually so. The idea we are trying to catch here is that borrowing terms for the poor are harsh. The simplest way of capturing this is to suppose that they can't borrow at all.[7] This is what we now assume. Saving in such an environment mediates between low current consumption and an uncertain future agricultural income. The household aims to smooth its consumption in the face of uncertain income. The motive for saving is, therefore, a *precautionary* one, it isn't the life-cycle-savings motive considered in Section 8.7.[8] The household can decumulate its asset, but it can't allow it to become negative. From equation (*9.19), this means

$$A_t + X_t - C_t - Y_t - Z_t \geq 0, \qquad \text{for } t \geq 0. \tag{*9.22}$$

The household's problem is therefore to choose an intertemporal profile ($t \geq 0$) of consumption and agricultural investments (which I write as $\{C_t\}$, $\{Y_t\}$, and $\{Z_t\}$, respectively), so as to maximize (*9.20) subject to constraints (*9.19), (*9.21), and (*9.22).

To simplify, X_t will be assumed to be positive under all contingencies. Now, consumption in bad circumstances can be very low, but we will assume it will never be allowed by the household to be nil. This means we may ignore the first of the constraints embodied in (*9.21): it will never be binding. This can be justified by the further assumption, $V'(C) \to \infty$ as $C \to 0$. Since the household enjoys a flow of exogenous income, should it need to, it can afford to drive its assets to zero. Of course, consumption

---

[6] We will be informal here. So we will not invoke a bequest motive for the household, but instead will regard it as a dynasty, with no end to its planning horizon. The rate of discount, δ, should be thought of as being small.

[7] We could set a negative floor on the asset level. This would not alter the analysis. So we set the floor at zero.

[8] The pioneering works on this are Phelps (1962) and Mirrlees (1965). Important subsequent contributions include Leland (1968), Levhari and Srinivasan (1969), Hahn (1970), Rothschild and Stiglitz (1971), Mirrlees (1974b), Bewley (1977), Schechtman and Escudero (1977), Foldes (1979), Rosenzweig and Wolpin (1989), Zeldes (1989a, b), Deaton (1990, 1991), and Morduch (1990).

will be low in times of stress, when assets have been drawn down and, by misfortune, X_t is low. In these circumstances the latter two constraints in (*9.21) will bind: the household will be forced to refrain from investing in agricultural production.

Let ϕ_t and θ_t (≥ 0) be the Lagrange multipliers associated with the latter two constraints in (*9.21), respectively; and let μ_t (≥ 0) be the multiplier associated with the credit constraint (*9.22). Each multiplier should be interpreted as a shadow price, to be imposed on the household were it to break the corresponding constraint, so as to prevent it from doing so. Routine arguments in dynamic programming then imply that, for all $t \geq 0$,

$$V'(C_t) = E\{[(1 + r)/(1 + \delta)]V'(C_{t+1})\}+\mu_t \qquad (*9.23)$$
$$V'(C_t) = E\{[(1 + \alpha)/(1 + \delta)]V'(C_{t+1})\}+\phi_t \qquad (*9.24)$$
$$\text{and} \qquad V'(C_t) = E\{[(1 + \beta)/(1 + \delta)]V'(C_{t+1})\}+\theta_t. \qquad (*9.25)$$

These are the three Euler equations of the household optimization problem. They are direct generalizations (to the case of uncertain farm productivity) of Frank Ramsey's famous rule (see Ramsey, 1928), requiring the household's marginal rate of indifferent substitution between consumption at dates t and $t + 1$ to be equated to the productivity of investment.[9]

Consider a date, t, when $\mu_t = 0$. This means that the credit constraint (*9.22) is non-binding. We have assumed that $V'''(C) > 0$. It follows that an increase in the riskiness in consumption at $t + 1$ increases the right-hand side of (*9.23), and therefore the left-hand side of the equation; and this in turn means that C_t declines. Deaton (1990: 66) uses this observation to conclude that the condition $V'''(C) > 0$ guarantees a precautionary motive for saving. But since consumption at $t + 1$ is endogenous to the analysis, it would be wrong to infer any such thing. The conclusion is in any case incorrect.

To see this in a simple way, let us depart from the dynastic household and consider instead a two-period (dates 0 and 1) model of household consumption (see Leland, 1968; Rothschild and Stiglitz, 1971). Simplify further by assuming that the household faces a single investment opportunity, which offers a random gross yield of θ. If s is the household's saving rate, its expected present discounted value of the two-period flow of utility is

$$V[(1 - s)A_0] + E[V(s\theta A_0)]/(1 + \delta). \qquad (*9.26)$$

The value of s that maximizes (*9.26) satisfies the first-order condition

$$V'[(1 - s)A_o] = E[\theta V'(s\theta A_0)]/(1 + \delta). \qquad (*9.27)$$

From (*9.27) we may conclude that an increase in the riskiness in θ leads

---

[9] They are also generalizations to an intertemporal setting of the first-order conditions in the previous section.

to an increase in the rate of saving (i.e. reduces current consumption) if $\theta V'(s\theta A_0)$ is strictly convex in θ, and reduces the rate of saving (i.e. increases current consumption) if $\theta V'(s\theta A_0)$ is strictly concave in θ. A straightforward calculation shows that $\theta V'(s\theta A_0)$ is strictly convex in θ if $V'''(C) > -2V''(C)/C$ for all C, and is strictly concave in θ if $V'''(C) < -2V''(C)/C$ for all C.

Consider the class of iso-elastic utility functions. Denote the elasticity of marginal utility by ρ. (ρ is also the degree of relative risk aversion; see Chapter 8.) Clearly $V'''(C) > 0$. However, if $\rho > 1$ (respect. < 1), $V'''(C) > -2V''(C)/C$ (respect. $< -2V''(C)/C$) for all C. This means that the household displays a precautionary motive for saving if $\rho > 1$, and a precautionary motive for *consumption* if $\rho < 1$. We will look at the intuition behind this result. (The argument is taken from Hahn, 1970.)

What is relevant in a saving decision is the marginal gain, in any period, from consuming a little less in the preceding period. Now notice that if $\rho > 1$, $V(C)$ is bounded above but unbounded below, whereas if $\rho < 1$, $V(C)$ is unbounded above but bounded below. This means that when $\rho > 1$ there can be infinite disasters but only finite gains; on the other hand, when $\rho < 1$ there can be infinite gains but only finite disasters. Thus, when $\rho > 1$ the household wants to ensure its future consumption standard, whereas when $\rho < 1$ it wants to gamble on its future consumption.

The empirical evidence suggests that, if we are to restrict ourselves to iso-elastic utility functions, we should consider only those for which $\rho > 1$. This brings out the reason why we would expect households to display a precautionary motive for saving; that is, why an increase in uncertainty in the household's (exogenous) future income would cause it to reduce its consumption today, and thus increase its consumption growth (Phelps, 1962; Mirrlees, 1965, Leland, 1968; Levhari and Srinivasan, 1969; Hahn, 1970; Rothschild and Stiglitz, 1971). In what follows we will confine ourselves to the case $\rho > 1$.

Let us return to the dynastic household. It is not possible to solve equations (*9.23)–(*9.25) explicitly. What we are after are optimal C, Y, and Z as functions of the asset level, A, and the exogenous income, X. Simulations are a way of obtaining insights about the general characteristics of these functions. But we can glean something about them under extreme situations. Notice that, even though the household has been prohibited from borrowing, it can accumulate and decumulate its assets so as to smooth its consumption pattern over time. If assets aren't hopelessly low, and there is a sharp decline in income as a result of a bad harvest, consumption can be maintained by decumulating capital. In Chapter 9 we noted that for poor peasant households the sale of bullocks often serves this purpose (Rosenzweig and Wolpin, 1989). However, for a poor household only a short run of bad luck is required before its assets come perilously close to zero. Such households are then most reluctant to part with their assets. Obviously, when assets are very low and there is a sharp decline in income owing to yet more bad luck, consumption follows suit: smoothing consumption isn't possible for the very unlucky. The borrowing constraint binds whenever (*9.22) is an equality, so that $\mu_t > 0$ in (*9.23). But when assets are down to really low levels, the probability of hitting the constraint in the near future becomes positive, and extreme caution is practised by the risk-averse household. In short, the optimal consumption of a poor household tracks income more closely than does the consumption of a wealthy one.

From our earlier arguments we know that, because of the credit constraint, very poor households will not invest in agriculture at all (i.e., they will set $Y_t = Z_t = 0$, since both crops are risky), and will invest only in the safe asset, earning a return r. As we go up the asset ladder, we will find that not-so-poor households invest in both the safe asset and the safer crop, α, but not in the risky crop, β. Rich households do not worry about credit constraints, and invest only in the risky crop (see Eswaran and Kotwal, 1990). Morduch's findings of ICRISAT data (Morduch, 1990) are consistent with these observations.

*9.3   Credit, Insurance, and Agricultural Investment

The availability of credit enables households to smooth consumption across time without having to engage in precautionary saving. This releases resources for investment in relatively good times. It simultaneously enables risk-averse households to better absorb risks in investment (e.g. agricultural investment). Often, investments with a high expected yield are especially risky. In Chapter 9 we noted that this provides a synergistic link between the availability of consumption credit and agricultural investment. We illustrate these considerations formally by way of a two-period model deployed by Eswaran and Kotwal (1989).

There are two techniques of agricultural production whose input costs are the same. One is safe, and yields X units of output per unit of land in each of the two periods. The other technique has a safe yield in the second period (Y units of output per unit of land), but its first-period output is risky, in that it is $(Y - \sigma)$ with probability $\frac{1}{2}$ and $(Y + \sigma)$ with probability $\frac{1}{2}$. To make the problem interesting, we take it that $Y > X > Y - \sigma$.

A given household owns a unit of land. Its per-period utility of consumption (C) is $V(C)$, where $V(C)$ is an increasing and strictly concave function ($V'(C) > 0$ and $V''(C) < 0$). The utility discount rate is zero and the market rate of interest for consumption loans is also nil. We now assume that there is no insurance market for crop failure. Imagine that the household cultivates a fraction, p (> 0), of its land using the risky technique, and the remainder, $(1 - p)$, by using the safe technique. Assume to begin with that the household faces no borrowing constraints. It is a simple matter to confirm that, in order to smooth consumption across dates, the household will borrow $p\sigma/2$ units of consumption should output from the risky technique be a failure $(p(Y - \sigma))$, and lend $p\sigma/2$ units should output from the risky technique be a success $(p(Y + \sigma))$. Indeed, by doing this it will fully smooth its consumption over time, although not across the two events. (There is no insurance market.) We conclude that the household's intertemporal expected utility is

$$\{2V[pY + (1 - p)X - p\sigma/2] + 2V[pY + (1 - p) X + p\sigma/2]\}/2. \tag{*9.28}$$

The household chooses p so as to maximize (*9.28). Denote the maximizing value by p^*. For expositional ease, we assume that the parameters of the problem are such as will ensure $1 > p^* > 0$.

Now suppose that the household faces a borrowing constraint. For simplicity, we take it that it can borrow at a zero rate of interest up to a maximum, B, where $B < p\sigma/2$. It is a simple matter to confirm that the household will borrow up to the full amount B in case of failure with the risky technique. However, its choice of the fraction of land given over to the risky technique will itself be a function of B. We write this as $p^*(B)$. Routine calculations show that $dp^*(B)/dB > 0$. This establishes our claim.

*9.4 Why May Credit be Rationed?

In Chapter 9 (Section 9.4) we observed that the phenomena of moral hazard and adverse selection can lead to credit being rationed among potential borrowers. The argument there was informal. In this section, therefore, I provide a formal sketch of the ideas involved. (It is taken from Stiglitz and Weiss, 1981.)

Consider a peasant who would like to borrow an amount B this year so as to finance a project with uncertain income $R(\theta)$ to be realized next year, where θ is the index of relevant events next year. If r is the interest rate on the loan and C the collateral required, the peasant is able to pay back the loan in the event $C + R(\theta) \geq B(1 + r)$; otherwise he is bankrupt. His net income, $Y(R, r)$, from the project is therefore

$$Y(R, r) = \max \{R - B(1 + r), - C\}. \tag{*9.29}$$

Similarly, should credit be offered and accepted, net income of the creditor, $I(R, r)$, is

$$I(R, r) = \min \{R + C, B(1 + r)\}. \tag{*9.30}$$

In order to make the point in the sharpest possible way, we will assume that the peasant's von Neumann-Morgenstern utility function is linear in his income, Y. The peasant is therefore risk-neutral. For the moment we

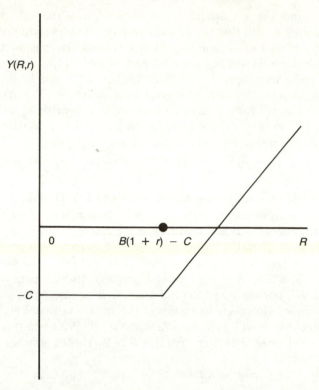

Fig. *9.1   Borrower's utility function

take the interest rate to be given. In Fig. (*9.1), equation (*9.29) has been used to plot the peasant's income as a function of the project's gross yield, R.[10] Notice that bankruptcy offers a floor on the peasant's income. This renders his utility function strictly convex in the neighbourhood of the bankruptcy point, $R = B(1 + r) - C$.[11]

Now imagine there are many peasants, indexed by n. Each peasant has his own potential investment project, represented by the gross yield R_n. All projects cost the same, namely B. Moreover, they all have the same expected yield. Where they differ is in their riskiness: the larger the value of n, the greater the riskiness of R_n. Let $\pi(\theta)$ be the probability that event θ will occur.

Should peasant n undertake his project, his expected income would be[12]

[10] I am assuming for simplicity that there is no utility loss attached to bankruptcy *per se*. Nothing would be gained were we to assume otherwise.

[11] This shows that risk aversion on the part of the peasant would not change the analysis substantially, although it would make it a bit more complicated.

[12] As before, $E(\cdot)$ is the expectation operator.

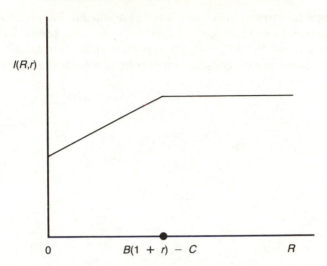

Fig. *9.2 Lender's utility function

$$E[Y(R_n(\theta), r)] = \Sigma_\theta \max \{R_n(\theta) - B(1 + r), - C\}\pi(\theta). \quad (*9.31)$$

Given the interest rate, r, let us assume there is a peasant, $n^*(r)$, whose expected income is nil. At this interest rate all peasants whose indices exceed $n^*(r)$ will wish to borrow, and all whose indices are less than $n^*(r)$ will wish not to borrow. It is also a simple matter to confirm that $n^*(r)$ is an increasing function of r. This means of course that raising the interest rate would increase the overall riskiness of the portfolio of investment projects that are undertaken; the safer bets would be weeded out. (By assumption, the mean would not change.)

Using equation (*9.30), the creditor's net income has been plotted as a function of R in Fig. (*9.2).[13] It is strictly concave in the neighbourhood of the yield $B(1 + r) - C$. Let $U(I)$ be the creditor's von Neumann-Morgenstern utility function. We assume that $U'(I) > 0$, and that $U''(I) \leq 0$. (The creditor is not risk-loving.) Figure (*9.2) then informs us that the creditor's expected utility from a loan decreases as the riskiness of the loan increases. We can now see that in raising the interest rate the creditor invites two effects, working in opposite directions with regard to his expected utility. The direct effect is positive: the expected income from any given loan (i.e. peasant) increases with r (equation (*9.30)). But there is an opposing effect, caused by adverse selection: it is that the pool of peasant borrowers changes slightly, making the overall portfolio more risky. At sufficiently high interest rates the latter effect could be expected

---

[13] For our purposes here it does not matter if there is a single creditor in the village or an entire class of them. So we will assume there is only one.

to dominate the former. When this is the case, further increases in the rate of interest would merely reduce the creditor's expected utility. Let $\hat{r}$ be the interest rate at which the creditor's expected utility is maximized. If the demand for loans at $\hat{r}$ exceeds the amount he is able to lend, he will ration credit.

10

Poverty and the Environmental Resource Base

10.1   *The Resource Basis of Rural Production*

People in poor countries are for the most part agrarian and pastoral folk. In 1988 rural people accounted for 65 per cent of the population of what the World Bank classifies as low-income countries.[1] As Table 10.1 shows, the proportion of total labour force in agriculture was a bit over this. The share of agriculture in gross domestic product in these countries was about 30 per cent. These figures should be contrasted with those from industrial market economies, which are 6 and 2 per cent respectively. Come what may, poor countries can be expected to remain largely rural economies for a long while to come.

Agricultural performance has been bad in all those countries that have remained poor. Since about 1965, with the notable exceptions of China (but see below) and India, it has been deplorable. Table 10.2 presents figures for growth rates in population and agricultural production over two periods (1965–80 and 1980–8) in China, India, and sub-Saharan Africa. They offer contrasting pictures.[2]

Table 10.1   Agriculture and rural labour

	Rural labour force (%)	Share of agriculture in GDP (%)
Low-income countries	68	30
Industrial market economies	6	2

Source: World Bank (1990).

[1] See World Bank (1990). There are 41 low-income countries in this list for which figures are provided in the report. (I am ignoring countries where the population size is less than 1 m.) Nearly all of them are contained in Table 5.1 above. I should add that, for obvious reasons, several Asian countries in Table 5.1 (e.g. South Korea and Thailand) are not to be found in the World Bank's current list of low-income countries. The rural population in what the World Bank classifies as high-income, OECD-member countries is about 23% of their total population.

[2] Sub-Saharan Africa consists of forty-five countries. (See World Bank, 1989b, for a demographic breakdown.) In mid-1987 the populations of China, India, and sub-Saharan Africa were 1.07 bn, 0.80 bn, and 0.45 bn, respectively.

Table 10.2   Population and agricultural growth in poor regions

	G_p		G_a		g_a	
	T_1	T_2	T_1	T_2	T_1	T_2
China	2.2	1.3	2.8	6.8	0.6	5.2
India	2.3	2.2	2.5	2.3	0.2	0.1
Sub-Saharan Africa	2.7	3.1	1.3	1.8	−1.4	−1.3

Key

G_p: annual % rate of growth of population
G_a: annual % rate of growth of agricultural production
g_a: G_a-G_p
T_1: period 1965–80
T_2: period 1980–88

Source: World Bank (1989b, 1990).

In 1965 grain output in China was only 8 per cent higher than its 1957 figure (see Wong, 1977, Table 3). The intervening years saw the rise and demise of the Great Leap Forward (see Banister, 1987; Riskin, 1987; Nolan, 1988; Perkins, 1988). It is in this light that we should interpret the relatively good performance of Chinese agriculture during 1965–80. The more pertinent period for China is the one following its agricultural reforms of the late 1970s, consisting of partial privatization, and the encouragement of market incentives. As Table 10.2 confirms, Chinese agricultural performance has been spectacular since then.

The Indian performance in agriculture, as in other economic spheres, has been middling: it has just kept ahead of population growth.[3] Unlike governments in much of sub-Saharan Africa, the Indian government hasn't acted *against* agriculture: rather, it has displayed an attitude of benign neglect over agriculture in some parts of the country, and given considerable support in others.

One early policy that helped producers in India has been much commented on, since it was originally intended to help the poor among the consumers. Government procurement policies on staple food (wheat, rice, and sugar during the 1960s and 1970s) in India were so fashioned that farmers in effect were able to employ discriminatory pricing.[4] They were obliged to sell a fraction of their produce to the government at a low, administered price, and were allowed to sell the rest in the open market.

---

[3] The noted agricultural economist and international civil servant, Dr S.R. Sen, likens India's economic performance to the progress of a bullock-cart; reliable, but excruciatingly slow.

[4] Government procurement policies are less extensive now, and so I am reporting on matters as they prevailed when they were extensive.

Government procurement was in turn put out for sale at fair-price stores, to consumers with ration cards. The motivation behind this was to provide poor households with inexpensive essential foods (see Dantwala, 1967; Mellor, 1968). But there were problems of implementation, and the outcome was different from what was ostensibly desired. First, government fair-price stores were in the main located in urban locations (which in the mid-1960s housed less than 20 per cent of the population); furthermore, as in other spheres of life, the poorest urban dwellers could not even afford to avail themselves of these opportunities. Second, the quality of products in fair-price stores was inferior. Third, one had to queue to obtain the rationed quantities. The latter two features meant that cheap staples were in the main not consumed by the urban rich, who obtained their requirements from the open market. Now, the higher is the income per head of a household, the more inelastic is the household's demand for staple foods. So the Indian food procurement policy enabled farmers to sell the remainder of their produce in the open market at a price sufficiently high to enable them to make a larger profit than they would have had the government not intervened. Broadly speaking, the policy redistributed purchasing power from wealthy urban consumers to those urban residents who were *relatively* poor, and the redistribution took place without dampening the incentives of food producers (see Hayami, Subbarao and Otsuka, 1982).

But there were other factors at work, and growth in agricultural productivity has varied across Indian ecological zones. Implicit government subsidies for the use of fertilizers (thereby countering an overvalued exchange rate), and the provision of irrigation water and extension services have made their impact most strongly in the northern plains (the states of Punjab and Haryana), where the successful new hybrid varieties of wheat have transformed living standards (see Singh, 1990). Hybrid varieties of rice haven't proved equally robust, so the rest of India has not enjoyed the agricultural transformation of the North. This goes some way towards explaining why, overall, agricultural production in India has been only moderately good over such a long stretch of time.[5]

All this is in contrast with sub-Saharan Africa, where per capita agricultural production has declined systematically over the past 25 years (see Table 10.2). It is not feasible for me to try to analyse how this has come about here. But some of the broad features of what would amount to an explanation are clear. (See also Section 5.4.) During 1970–84 food production per head in sub-Saharan Africa fell at an annual average rate

[5] Food grain production grew from 90 million tons in 1970 (just after the drought-affected years) to about 140 million tons in 1985. In the text I have emphasized the incentives for farmers to produce crops. The fact that government food procurement policies in India did little for the rural poor is of vital importance, but that is another matter.

of 1.3 per cent (see World Bank, 1989b). This can't be attributed to a move to cash crops, because the output of cash crops declined simultaneously. Nor is it simply that the terms of trade have gone against cash crops in the international market. This wouldn't explain why sub-Saharan Africa's shares of world exports for most of its major crops have fallen during this extended period. (Between 1970 and 1984, sub-Saharan Africa's world market share for three central agricultural exports, namely coffee, cotton, and cocoa, declined by 13, 29 and 33 per cent, respectively. See World Bank, 1989b, p. 19.) A major cause was the systematic bias against rural production in much of this region. As noted in Chapter 7, agricultural produce has often been subject to punitive taxation, through producer price controls, the intrusions of marketing boards, and overvalued exchange rates. Such interventions not only change the domestic terms of trade against agriculture, they depress domestic agricultural prices relative to their international prices. Farmers in a number of sub-Saharan countries received less than 50 per cent of the world market price for their crops from government procurement agencies. Moreover, there has been a systematic dearth of credit and rural infrastructure for small farms, for example of production inputs such as storage facilities and water. In a number of countries (Ethiopia, Mauritania, and Tanzania being prime examples) agricultural land has been transformed into collective farms, often with uncertain residential tenure for their members. This has dulled private incentives in agricultural investment.[6] It has simultaneously eroded the environmental resource base.

Agricultural taxation isn't uniform across commodity groups. In sub-Saharan Africa as a whole, governments have discriminated against export crops relative to cereals since the early 1970s. This has proved environmentally damaging in the drylands of sub-Saharan Africa (see below).[7] The impoverishment of the African rural community and a deterioration of its production base have taken place even while world food production has grown faster than either its population or its market demand (see Chapter 12).

Given the importance of agriculture in poor countries, a bias against it should be expected to make investment in general yield less. (The rise in industrial productivity in the West occurred *after* agricultural productivity

---

[6] For further dissection of such kinds of policy failure, see Bauer and Yamey (1968), Bauer (1971, 1984, 1987), Johnston and Kilby (1975), Lipton (1976), T. W. Shultz (1978), Bates (1981), Timmer, Falcon and Pearson (1983), Raikes (1986), Mellor and Ahmed (1988), World Bank (1986a, 1989b), FAO (1985, 1986), Mellor and Desai (1985), Norse (1985), Braun and Kennedy (1986), IIED/WRI (1987), Timmer (1988), and B. F. Johnston (1989).

[7] See World Bank (1986b: 68). I will not speculate why they have done so. See Repetto (1988) for a fine recent analysis of the kinds of agricultural policy reforms governments in poor countries ought now to be engaged in.

had grown over a period of decades, making available sufficient surplus to 'finance' industrialization. See Timmer, 1988; Maddison, 1989.) This is consistent with the findings in an *ex post* evaluation of about 1650 investment projects financed by the World Bank and the International Finance Corporation. The average rate of return on public-sector projects in economies where the bias against agriculture has been high was about 11.5 per cent; it was 18 per cent in those countries where the bias was moderate or low. Average rates of return on private-sector projects in these two classes of economies were 13 and 16 per cent, respectively (see World Bank, 1991a). We studied related evidence in Chapter 7 (Table 7.1).

There has been a parallel weakness in academic development economics on matters concerning the environmental resource basis of rural production. The dependence of poor countries on their natural resources, such as soil and its cover, water, forests, animals, and fisheries, should have been self-evident. Nevertheless, if there has been a single thread running through 40 years of investigation into the poverty of poor countries, it has been the neglect of this base. Environmental resources make but perfunctory appearances in government planning models, and they are cheerfully ignored in most of what goes by the name 'development economics'. These resources appear in the literature about as frequently as rain falls on the Thar.[8]

It should not have been so. Poor countries are for the most part *biomass-based subsistence economies*, in that their rural folk eke out a living from products obtained directly from plants and animals. For example, in their informative study of life in a micro-watershed of the Alaknanda River in the central Himalayas in India, CSE (1990) reports that, of the total number of hours worked by the villagers sampled, 30 per cent was devoted to cultivation, 20 per cent to fodder collection, and about 24 per cent was spread evenly between fuel collection, animal care, and grazing. (Some 20 per cent of time was spent on household chores, of which cooking took up the greatest part, and the remaining 6 per cent was involved in other activities, such as marketing. See also A. Agarwal, 1990.) Ignore the environmental base, and we will obtain a misleading picture of productive activity within rural communities of poor countries.

---

[8] Here are a few illustrations. Dreze and Stern (1987) and Stern (1989) are surveys of cost–benefit analysis and development economics, respectively. The former, a 90-pp. article, contains precisely one sentence on the subject of renewable and non-renewable natural resources (and it is to tell readers where to go if they wish to learn about such matters); and the latter, an 88-pp. article, also contains a single sentence (and this too tells readers where to go if they wish to learn about such matters). A third example is provided by the two-volume *Handbook of Development Economics* (Chenery and Srinivasan, 1988, 1989), which contains no discussion of environmental resources and their possible bearing on the development process. And a fourth example is provided by Dreze and Sen (1990) on hunger and public action. For the most part this is concerned with the distribution of national product. It does not say anything about the environmental production base of poor countries.

10.2 *What Are Environmental Resources?*

Environmental problems are almost always associated with resources that are regenerative (we could call them *renewable natural resources*), but which are in danger of exhaustion from excessive use.[9] The earth's atmosphere is a paradigm of such resources. In the normal course of events the atmosphere's composition regenerates itself. But the speed of regeneration depends upon, among other things, the current state of the atmosphere and the rate at which pollutants are deposited. It also depends upon the nature of the pollutants. (Smoke discharge is clearly different from the release of chemicals or radioactive material.) We need first of all a way of measuring such resources. In the example above, we have to think of an atmospheric quality index. The net rate of regeneration of the stock is the rate at which this quality index changes over time. Regeneration rates of atmospheric quality are immensely complex, ill-understood matters. There is a great deal of synergism associated with the interaction of different types of pollutants in the atmospheric sink. Despite these qualifications, the analytical point I am making, i.e. that even pollution problems involve the depletion of renewable natural resources, is both true and useful (see Ehrlich, Ehrlich and Holdren, 1977).

Animal, bird, plant, and fish populations are other typical examples of renewable natural resources. There are now a number of studies addressing the reproductive behaviour of different species under a variety of 'environmental' conditions, including the presence of parasitic and symbiotic neighbours. Land is also such a commodity, for the quality of arable and grazing land can be maintained only by careful use. Population pressures can result in an extended period of overuse. By overuse I mean not only an unsustainable shortening of fallow periods, but also deforestation and the cultivation and grazing of marginal lands. This causes the quality of land to deteriorate, until eventually it becomes a wasteland.

The symbiotic relationship between soil quality and vegetation cover is central to the innumerable problems facing sub-Saharan Africa, most especially the Sahel. (D. Anderson, 1987, contains an authoritative account of this.) The management of the drylands in general has to be sensitive to such relationships. It is, for example, useful to distinguish between on the one hand a reduction in soil nutrients and humus, and on the other the loss of soil due to wind and water run-off. The depletion of soil nutrients can be countered by fertilizers (which, however, can have

---

[9] Minerals and fossil fuels are unrenewable (they are a pristine example of exhaustible resources), but they raise a different set of issues. For an account of what resource allocation theory looks like when we include exhaustible resources in the production process, see Dasgupta and Heal (1979), Hartwick and Olewiler (1986), and Tietenberg (1988). For a non-technical account of the theory and the historical role that has been played by the substitution of new energy resources for old, see Dasgupta (1989b).

adverse effects elsewhere in the ecological system), but in the drylands a loss in topsoil can't be made good. (In river valleys the alluvial topsoil is augmented annually by silt brought by the rivers from mountain slopes. This is the obverse of water-runoff caused by a lack of vegetation cover.) Under natural conditions of vegetation cover it can take anything between 100 and 500 years for the formation of 1 cm of topsoil.[10]

Soil degradation can occur if the wrong crops are cultivated. Contrary to general belief, in sub-tropical conditions most export crops tend to be less damaging to soils than are cereals and root crops. (Groundnuts and cotton are exceptions.) Many export crops, such as coffee, cocoa, oil palm, and tea, grow on trees and bushes which enjoy a continuous root structure and provide continuous canopy cover. With grasses planted underneath, the rate of soil erosion associated with such crops is known to be substantially less than the rate of erosion associated with basic food crops (see Repetto, 1988, Table 2). But problems are compounded upon problems in poor countries. In many cultures the men control cash income while the women control food (see Chapter 11). Studies in Nigeria, Kenya, India, and Nepal suggest that, to the extent that women's incomes decline as the proportion of cash-cropping increases, the family's nutritional status (most especially the nutritional status of children) deteriorates (see e.g. Braun and Kennedy, 1986). The indirect effects of public policy assume a bewildering variety.

The link between irrigation and the process by which land becomes increasingly saline has also been much noted in the ecological literature (see Ehrlich, Ehrlich and Holdren, 1977). In the absence of adequate drainage, continued irrigation slowly but remorselessly destroys agricultural land through the salts left behind by evaporating water. The surface area of agricultural land removed from cultivation worldwide through salinization is thought by some to equal the amount added by irrigation (see United Nations, 1990). Desalinization of agricultural land is even today an enormously expensive operation.

The environment is affected by the extent to which the rural poor have access to credit, insurance, and capital markets. In the previous chapter we studied some of the limitations of the market for credit among the rural poor in poor countries. For the most part such folk do not have access to

---

[10] One notable, and controversial, estimate of worldwide productivity declines in livestock and agriculture in the drylands due to soil losses was offered in UNEP (1984). The figure was an annual loss of $26 bn. For a discussion of the UNEP estimate, see Gigengack *et al.* (1990). The estimate by Mabbut (1984), that approximately 40% of the productive drylands of the world are currently under threat from desertification, gives an idea of the magnitude of the problem. For accounts of the economics and ecology of drylands, see Wischmeier (1976), Pierce *et al.* (1987), Falloux and Mukendi (1989), Dixon, James and Sherman (1989, 1990).

the capital market either. Even when banks are located close by they are often viewed with suspicion. For this reason, domestic animals assume a singularly important role as a capital asset. But they are prone to die when rainfall is scarce. In sub-Saharan Africa farmers and nomads therefore carry extra cattle as an insurance against droughts. Herds are larger than they would be were capital and insurance markets open to the rural poor. This imposes an additional strain on grazing lands, most especially during periods of drought. That this link between capital markets (or rather, their absence) and the degradation of the environmental resource base is quantitatively significant (World Bank, 1992) should come as no surprise. The environment is itself a gigantic capital asset. The portfolio of assets a household holds depends on what is available to it. In fact, one can go beyond these rather obvious links and argue that in principle even the fertility rate is related to the extent of the local environmental resource base, such as fuelwood and water sources. In Chapter 12 we will see why we should expect this to be so.

Underground basins of water also have the characteristic of a renewable natural resource. The required analysis is a bit more problematic, though, in that we are interested in both its quality and its quantity. Under normal circumstances an aquifer undergoes a self-cleansing process as pollutants are deposited into it. (Here, the symbiotic role of microbes, as in the case of soil and the atmosphere, is important.) But the effectiveness of the process depends on the nature of pollutants and the rate at which they are discharged. Furthermore, many aquifers are recharged over the annual cycle. The recharge rate depends not only on annual precipitation and the extent of underground flows, but also on the rate of evaporation. This in turn is a function of the extent of soil cover. In the drylands, reduced soil cover lowers both soil moisture and the rate of recharge of underground basins, which in turn reduces the soil cover still more, which in turn implies a reduced rate of recharge, and so on.[11] With a lowered underground water table, the cost of water extraction rises.

In fact, aquifers display another characteristic. On occasion the issue isn't one of depositing pollutants into them. If, as a consequence of excessive extraction, the groundwater level is allowed to drop to too low a level, there can be saltwater intrusion in coastal aquifers, and this can result in the destruction of the basin.

Environmental resources, such as forests, the atmosphere, and the seas, often have multiple competing uses. This accentuates management problems. Thus, forests are a source of timber, bark, saps, and, more

---

[11] See e.g. Falkenmark (1986, 1989), Olsen (1987), Nelson (1988), Reij, Mulder and Begemann (1988), and Falkenmark and Chapman (1989). A good technical account of groundwater hydrology is Domenico (1972).

particularly, pharmaceuticals. Tropical forests also provide a habitat for a rich genetic pool. In addition, forests influence local and regional climate, preserve soil cover on site, and, in the case of watersheds, protect soil downstream from floods. Increased runoff of rainwater owing to deforestation helps strip soil away, depriving agriculture of nutrients and clogging water reservoirs and irrigation systems. The social value of a forest typically exceeds the value of its direct products, and on occasion exceeds it greatly (see Hamilton and King, 1983; D. Anderson, 1987).

These examples suggest that a number of issues in the economics of environmental resources are 'capital-theoretic': environmental resources are a part of our natural capital base.[12] But there are added complications. among which is that the impact on the rate of regeneration of environmental resources of a wide variety of investment decisions is not fully reversible, and in some cases is quite irreversible.[13]

If this were all, life would have been relatively simple. But it isn't all. Admitting environmental resources into economic modelling ushers in a number of additional, potent complications for development policy. These occur because for poor people in poor countries some environmental resources are often complementary to other goods and services, while other environmental resources supplement income, most especially in times of acute economic stress. So an erosion of the environmental resource base can make certain categories of people destitutes even while the economy on average grows (see Chapter 16). This explains the frequent intellectual tension between aggregate concerns (such as the greenhouse effect, or the appropriate mix of resources and manufactured capital in aggregate production) which sweep across regions, nations, and continents, and those (for example the decline in fuelwood or water availability) that are specific to the needs and concerns of poor people of as small a group as a village community. This tension should be borne in mind. Environmental problems present themselves in the form of different images to different people. At this stage of our understanding it would be a wrong research strategy to try to put them all together into one large basket.

I have so far presented an outline not only of the resource basis of production, but also of the various ecological linkages through which communities can experience resource degradation. The next step will be to present an illustrative pair of calculations about resource *needs*, and thus an account of what resource *stress* amounts to. In Section 10.4 we will

---

[12] This guides the exposition in C. W. Clark (1976) who, however, concentrates on fisheries. See Dasgupta (1982b) for a unified capital-theoretic treatment of environmental management problems.

[13] As always, one shouldn't be too literal. A very slow rate of regeneration produces a strong flavour of irreversibility.

study the place of these resources in national accounts and in cost–benefit analyses of investment projects, while continuing to ignore the detailed, institutional features that surround the use of local environmental resources. We will pick up the institutional trail in Section 10.5.

10.3   Needs, Stress, and Carrying Capacity: Land and Water

How much land does a man need?[14] Later, in Chapters 16 and *16, when we come to an analysis of public policy for countering destitution, we will find a use for an answer to this question. Here we will provide some orders of magnitude, and for simplicity we will ignore uncertainty in production.[15]

Rice cultivation in the drylands using conventional techniques requires something like 130 person-days of labour time per hectare each year, and it yields about 15 billion joules (GJ), or 1000 kg, of rice. If the average energy input in cultivation per working day is taken to be 3 million joules (MJ), total energy required for cultivation amounts to 390 MJ, or 0.39 GJ, per hectare over the year. Therefore, the net energy produced amounts to 14.61 GJ. Assuming that an individual's energy requirement is 2200 kcal per day, a family with five members would require 17 GJ of food energy per year.[16] This in turn means that the family would need approximately 1.2 h of land to remain in energy balance. Inversely, a family of five would be the *carrying capacity* of 1.2 h. Total work input on this amount of land is 0.39 × 1.2 GJ, or approximately 0.5 GJ. Therefore, the ratio of energy output to energy input in this form of cultivation is 34 : 1. This is quite high, and compares very favourably with the energy output–input ratios associated with the technologies available to hunter-gatherers, pastoralists, and food-garden systems in fertile tropical coastal areas.[17]

Crude but revealing calculations of this kind can also be done for water requirements. While 70 per cent of the earth's surface is covered by water, about 98 per cent of this is salt-water. Most of the earth's fresh water is stored as polar ice-caps and in underground reservoirs. (Only about 0.015

---

[14] I am putting the question in the way Tolstoy did.

[15] The computation is taken from Payne (1985a: 7). An original source of this kind of calculations is Leach (1975), who provided estimates of energy inputs and outputs per hectare for a variety of agricultural systems. See also Bayliss Smith (1981), and Higgins *et al.* (1982), for estimates of the carrying capacity of different types of land in poor countries.

[16] It will be recalled that 1 kcal is the amount of heat required to raise the temperature of 1 kg of water from 15° to 16°C. In 1948 this common heat unit in nutrition was redefined to equal 4.184 kJ.

[17] The carrying capacity of land can be increased enormously by suitable investment. In irrigated rice cultivation a hectare can support as many as 15 people, provided fertilizers, pest controls, and improved seeds are used. See Norse (1985) for sample calculations of this sort. It may be noted that China averages only about 0.09 ha of arable land per capita, while Indonesia, India, and the USA average 0.12, 0.20, and 0.55, respectively. See W. C. Clark (1989).

per cent is available in rivers, lakes, and streams.) It is distributed most unevenly across regions.

The three sources of water for any given territory are trans-frontier aquifers, rivers from upstream locations, and rainfall. The water that is available from precipitation comes in two forms: soil moisture, and the annual recharge of terrestrial water systems, namely aquifers, ponds, lakes, and rivers. Rain-fed agriculture consumes an amount of water roughly proportional to the produced biomass. (The water is returned to the atmosphere as plant evapotranspiration.) Water can be recycled, and so the water utilization rate can be in excess of the water supply. (Israel, Libya, and Malta have utilization rates well in excess of annual water supplies.) The problem is that in semi-arid and arid regions losses due to evaporation from natural vegetation and wet surfaces are substantial, and not much effort is made in the poor drylands to develop technologies for reducing them (e.g. improved designs of tanks and reservoirs). The mean annual precipitation divided by mean annual potential evapotranspiration is less than 0.03 in hyper-arid regions (annual rainfall less than 10 cm); between 0.03 and 0.20 in arid regions (annual rainfall between 10 and 30 cm); between 0.20 and 0.50 in semi-arid regions (annual rainfall between 20 and 50 cm); and between 0.50 and 0.75 in sub-humid regions (annual rainfall between 50 and 80 cm). According to most classifications, it is this set of regions that comprises the *drylands*. Within the drylands, rain-fed agriculture is suited only to sub-humid regions. Occupying about a third of the earth's land surface, the drylands are the home of some 850 million people (see Dixon, James and Sherman, 1989: 3).

Losses due to evaporation in the drylands are accelerated by disappearing biomass. For example, only about 10–20 per cent of rainfall finds use in the production of vegetation in the Sahelian rangelands (where the annual rainfall is in the range 10–60 cm); some 60 per cent is returned to the atmosphere as unproductive evaporation. Irrigation schemes in the drylands, bringing water from distant parts, are unlikely to be cost-effective. This is a solution more appropriate to temperate zones. It has been argued that in the drylands the proportion of rainfall that is productive can be increased to 50 per cent if vegetation is allowed to grow, and if suitable catchments are constructed (see Falkenmark, 1986; see also Barghouti and Lallement, 1988).

Something like 1250 cubic metres of water per person is required annually for the supply of habitats and for the production of subsistence crops in the drylands. This does not include the water required for municipal supplies, for industry, and for the production of cash crops. (Agriculture currently uses about 75 per cent of the world's use of fresh water, industry about 20 per cent, and domestic activities the remaining 5 per cent.) A community experiences *water stress* if, for every 1 million cubic metres of water available annually for use, there are 600–1000 persons having to share it. When more than 1000 persons are forced to share every 1 million cubic metres of water annually, the problem is one of severe shortage. Currently, well over 200 million people in Africa are suffering from water stress or worse (see Falkenmark, 1989). The tangled web of population growth, deforestation, water stress, and land degradation defines a good deal of the phenomenon of destitution in today's world.

10.4 *Environmental Shadow Prices, Project Evaluation, and Net National Product*

It is as well to remember that renewable natural resources are on occasion of direct use in consumption (as with fisheries), in production (as with plankton, which serves as food for fish species), and sometimes in both (as with drinking and irrigation water). Their stock, as we noted earlier, are measured in different ways: in mass units (e.g. biomass units for forests, cowdung, and crop residues), in quality indices (e.g. water and air quality indices), in volume units (e.g. acre-feet for aquifers), and so on. When we express concern about environmental matters, we in effect point to a decline in their stock. But a decline in their stock, on its own, is not a reason for concern. This is seen most clearly in the context of exhaustible resources, such as fossil fuels; to not reduce their stock is to not use them at all, and this is unlikely to be the right thing to do.

To be sure, we could in principle limit the extraction and use of renewable natural resources to their natural regeneration rate and thus prevent their stocks from declining. But this too may be the wrong thing to do, in that there is nothing sacrosanct about the stocks a community has inherited from the past. Chapters 2, 3, 6 and 7 are relevant here. Policies directed at the environmental resource base can only be derived from considerations of population change, intergenerational well-being, technological possibilities, environmental regeneration rates, and the existing resource base. They can't be pulled out of the air by mere reference to sustainable development.

In Chapter *7 we developed an approach to the estimation of real national income. We demonstrated that, provided certain technical restrictions are met, for any conception of aggregate well-being, and for any set of technological, transaction, information, and ecological constraints, there exists a set of shadow prices of goods and services which can be used in the estimation of real national product. The index in question has the following property: small projects that increase the index are at once those that increase aggregate well-being.[18] By real national product for an intertemporal economy, I of course mean real net national product (or NNP). The shadow value of the depreciation of fixed capital, and by this I mean both manufactured and natural capital, needs to be deducted if the index of national product is to play the role we are assigning to it here (see Chapter *10).[19]

It is because depreciation of environmental resources is not deducted from estimates of NNP that current assessments are biased. Stated another way, NNP estimates are biased because a biased set of prices is in use. Prices imputed to environmental resources *on site* are usually zero. This amounts to regarding the depreciation of natural capital as zero. But these resources are scarce goods, so we know their shadow prices are positive. Profits attributed to projects that degrade the environment are therefore higher than the social profits they generate. This means in turn that wrong sets of projects get chosen. This happens in both private and public sectors. The extent of the bias will obviously vary from project to project, and from country to country. But it can be substantial: in their work on the depreciation of natural resources in Costa Rica, Solórzano *et al.* (1991) have estimated that in 1989 the depreciation of three resources—forests, soil and fisheries—amounted to about 10 per cent of GDP and over a third of gross capital accumulation. We conclude that, in the absence of such corrections, resource-intensive projects look better than they actually are. Installed technologies are usually unfriendly towards the environment.

One can go further: the bias extends to the prior stage of research and

---

[18] It will be recalled (see Ch. *7) that the technical restrictions amount to the requirement that the Kuhn–Tucker theorem is usable, i.e. that both the set of feasible allocations and the social ordering reflected by the social well-being function are convex. The assumption of convexity is dubious for pollution problems, as was illustrated by Starrett (1972). Nevertheless, in a wide range of circumstances it is possible to separate out the 'non-convex' sector, estimate real national income (or product) for the 'convex' sector, and present an estimate of the desired index as a combination of the real product of the convex sector and estimates of stocks and their changes in the non-convex sectors. This is a simple inference from the work of Weitzman (1970) and Portes (1971).

[19] See the calculations in Repetto *et al.* (1989), Solórzano *et al.* (1991), and Devarajan and Weiner (1989). See also CSE (1982, 1985), IIED/WRI (1987), and World Bank (1989b). For a discussion of the appropriate framework for national income accounts, see Dasgupta and Heal (1979), Peskin (1981), Dasgupta (1982b), Ahmad, El Sarafy and Lutz (1989), A. Harrison (1989), Gilbert (1990), Dasgupta and Mäler (1991), Mäler (1991), and Sefton and Weale (1992). Suggestions that conventional measures of net national product (NNP) should be augmented by measures of *net nature product* (see Agarwal and Narain, 1989) are related to what we are discussing in the text. By 'net nature product' Agarwal and Narain mean a measure of net changes in the environmental resource base. The correct measure of NNP is, of course, the sum of conventional NNP and net nature product. It is this aggregate that I am elaborating upon in the text. For tactical reasons it may well be desirable to present valuations of changes in the environmental resource base separately from figures of net national product. But I am concerned in the text with analytical issues. For this reason we will concentrate on an overall measure of NNP.

development. When environmental resources are underpriced, there is little incentive on anyone's part to develop technologies that economize on their use. The extent of the distortion created by this underpricing will vary from country to country. As noted in Chapter 6, poor countries inevitably have to rely on the flow of new knowledge produced in advanced industrial economies. Nevertheless, poor countries need to have the capability for basic research. The structure of shadow prices there is likely to be different from that in advanced industrial countries, most especially for non-traded goods and services. Now we observed earlier that, even when it is publicly available, basic knowledge is not necessarily usable by scientists and technologists unless they themselves have a feel for basic research. Thus, ideas developed in foreign lands ought not merely to be transplanted to the local economy: they need to be adapted to suit local ecological conditions. This is where the use of shadow prices is of help. It creates the right set of incentives among both developers and users of technologies. Adaptation is itself a creative exercise. Unhappily, as matters stand, it is often bypassed. Foreign technologies are simply bought and installed with little by way of modification. There is great loss in this.

The prior question, how we should estimate shadow prices for environmental resources, is a complex one. But it isn't uniformly complex. For commodities like irrigation water, fisheries, and agricultural soil, there are now standard techniques of evaluation. These techniques rely on the fact that such resources are inputs in the production of tradable goods.[20] For commodities such as firewood and drinking and cooking water, the matter is more complex. But even they are inputs in production, namely, in household production. This implies that we need to have an estimate of household production functions. As an example, transportation costs (in particular calorie costs) for women and children would be less were the sources of fuelwood and water not far away and receding. The value of water or fuelwood resources for household production can then be estimated from these caloric needs.[21] In some situations (as on occasion with

---

[20] See e.g. G. Brown and McGuire (1967) for irrigation water; C. W. Clark (1976), Richard Cooper (1975), and Dasgupta (1982b) for fisheries; Magrath and Arens (1989) and Repetto et al. (1989) for soil fertility; Newcombe (1984) and D. Anderson (1987) for forestry; and Solórzano et al. (1991) for all three.

[21] Here is a simplified model for illustrating how one would go about it. Let a representative woman's (or child's) daily calorie consumption be c, and let x be the harvest of fuelwood (or water) per day. Let F denote the stock of fuelwood (or water) resources on site. Let $s(F)$ be the energy cost of bringing home a unit of fuelwood (or water). The point to note is that $s(F)$ is a decreasing function of F. Now household production of services is an increasing function of x. It follows that well-being is an increasing function of net calorie intake and x. Write this as $B(c-s(F)x,x)$. Assume for simplicity that a person chooses x so as to maximize this intake. This maximized value we write as $V(c,F)$; it is the *indirect* well-being function. Assume next that there are M such people using the resource stock, F. Then, for an additive social well-being function, the shadow price of the resource is simply

fuelwood) the resource is a substitute for a tradable input (for example, paraffin/kerosene); in others (as with cooking water) it is a complement (sometimes a weak complement) to tradable inputs (for example, food grain). Such facts allow one to estimate shadow prices of non-marketed goods in terms of the shadow prices of marketed goods (see Mäler, 1974, 1992; Schecter, Kim and Golan, 1989).

The approach I have outlined above (the 'production function approach') allows us to capture only the known use-value of a resource. As it happens, its shadow price may well exceed this. Why? The reason is that there are additional values embodied in a resource stock. One additional value, applicable to living resources, is their intrinsic worth *as* living resources. (We plainly can't think that the value of a blue whale is embodied entirely in its flesh and oil, or that the value of the 'game' in Kenyan safari parks is simply the present discounted value of tourists' willingness-to-pay!) It is almost impossible to get a quantitative handle on 'intrinsic worth' (sometimes called 'existence value'). So the right thing to do is to take note of it, keep an eye on it, and call attention to it whenever the stock is threatened. (For further discussion, see Chapter 13.)

There is another source of value of environmental resources, which is more amenable to quantification. It arises from a combination of two things common to such resources: uncertainty in their future use-values, and irreversibility in their use. (Genetic material in tropical forests provides a prime example.) The twin presence of uncertainty and irreversibility implies that, even if the social well-being function were neutral to risk, it would not do to estimate the shadow price of an environmental resource solely on the basis of the expected benefit from its future use. Irreversibility in its use implies that preservation of its stock has an additional value, the value of extending society's set of future options. Future options have an additional worth because with the passage of time more information is expected to be forthcoming about the resource's use-value. This additional worth is often called an *option value*. The shadow price of a resource is the sum of its use-value and its option value.[22] We studied this idea in Chapter 3 when exploring alternative measures of freedom.

$- M(dc/dF)_B = MV_F/V_c = - Ms'(F)x$. (Here V_F and V_c denote the partial derivatives of V, and $(dc/dF)_B$ denotes the marginal rate of substitution between c and F in the indirect well-being function.) In a more detailed model c will have to be endogenous, and the effect of Mx on future values of F will also have to be taken into account. See Ch. *10.

[22] The pioneering works are Arrow and Fisher (1974) and C. Henry (1974). See also Dasgupta (1982b), Fisher and Hanemann (1986), and Mäler (1989).

10.5 *Markets and their Failure: Unidirectional and Reciprocal Externalities*

All this has been from what one might call the 'programming' or 'operations research' side of things. It is an essential viewpoint, but it is limited. By way of its complement there is the institutional side, with all its attendant difficulties. We noted in Chapter 6 that interested parties would be unable to negotiate courses of actions were property rights to be either incompletely specified or insubstantially enforced. Environmental resources by their very physical characteristics present difficulties in this regard. Consequently, markets for environmental resources often don't exist, and they are prone to malfunction when they do exist. The theory of externalities addresses the problems arising from this fact, and it is to this that we now turn.[23]

Market failure is prominent in those hidden interactions that are *unidirectional*, for example deforestation in the uplands, which often inflicts damages on the lowlands in integrated watersheds.[24] It pays first to concentrate on the assignment of property rights before seeking remedies. The common law in many poor countries, if we are permitted to use this expression in a universal context, *de facto* recognizes polluters' rights, and not those of the pollutees. Translated into our present example, this means that the timber merchant who has obtained a concession in the upland forest is under no obligation to compensate farmers in the lowlands. If the farmers wish to reduce the risk of heightened floods, they will have to compensate the timber merchant for reducing the rate of deforestation. Stated this way, the matter does look morally bizarre, but that is how things are with polluters' rights. Had property rights been the other way round, i.e. one of pollutees' rights, the boots would have been on the other set of feet, and it would have been the timber merchant who would have had to pay compensation to the farmers for the right to inflict the damages that go with deforestation. However, when the cause of damages is hundreds of miles away, when the timber concession has been awarded to public land by government, and when the victims are thousands of impoverished farmers, the issue of a negotiated outcome doesn't really arise. Thus, judged even from the viewpoint of Pareto efficiency, a system

---

[23] See Pigou (1920), Meade (1973), Mäler (1974), Baumol and Oates (1975), and Dasgupta and Heal (1979).

[24] Watersheds are fairly self-contained ecological systems. The most critical sector of a watershed is forest cover. The forest not only offers direct yield to its population, it maintains ecological balance and water regime, dampens floods and droughts, retards wind and water erosion, and sedimentation. Watershed lowlands are typically used for the production of staple food, and are usually flat plains of alluvial and heavy soil. See Easter, Dixon, and Hufschmidt (1986) for an account of the economics of watersheds. The classification of externalities into two categories, unidirectional and reciprocal (see below in the text), follows Dasgupta (1982b).

of polluters' rights in such an example would be disastrous. The private cost of logging being lower than its social (or shadow cost), we would expect excessive deforestation.[25]

In some parts of the world, community leaders, non-government organizations, and a free press (where they exist) have been known to galvanize activity on behalf of the relatively powerless pollutees. In recent years this has happened on a number of occasions in different contexts. One of the most publicized has been the Chipko Movement in India, which involved the threatened disfranchisement of historical users of forest products. This was occasioned by the State's claiming its rights over what was stated to be 'public property' and then embarking on a logging operation. The connection between environmental protection and civil and political rights is a close one. Our discussions in Chapters 2 and 5 are pertinent here. As a general rule, political and civil liberties are instrumentally powerful in protecting the environmental resource base, at least when compared with the absence of such liberties in countries run by authoritarian regimes.

When the shadow prices of environmental resources are higher than their market prices, resource-based goods can be presumed to be underpriced in the market. Naturally, the less roundabout, or less distant, is the production of the final good from its resource base, the greater is this underpricing, in percentage terms. Put another way, the lower is the value added to the resource, the larger is the extent of this underpricing of the final product. We may then conclude that, when unidirectional externalities are present in countries that export primary products, there is an implicit subsidy on such products, possibly on a massive scale. (See Dasgupta, 1990b.) Moreover, the subsidy is paid not by the general public via taxation, but by some of the most disadvantaged members of society: the sharecropper, the small landholder or tenant farmer, the forest dweller, the fisherman, and so on. The subsidy is hidden from public scrutiny; that is why nobody talks of it. But it is there. It is real. We should be in a position to estimate such subsidies. As of now, we have no estimate.[26]

---

[25] The classic on the subject, Coase (1960), contained an argument proving the neutrality of the assignment of property rights on allocative efficiency. Coase's theorem requires stringent assumptions, including the little-noticed one that there are only two parties involved. With more than two parties, matters are different and Coase's theorem is a non-starter, because the very existence of a bargained outcome can depend upon the assignment of property rights. For example, Shapley and Shubik (1969) and Starrett (1973) have shown that an economy can fail to possess a core allocation if there are polluters' rights over *private bads*, such as household rubbish. In their examples, however, a core allocation would exist if property rights were to be awarded to pollutees.

[26] But see Dixon (1992) and Hodgson and Dixon (1992) for an attempt at such an estimation for the Bacuit Bay and the El Nido watershed on Palawan, in the Philippines. The cause of the damages (to tourism and fisheries) was due to logging in the uplands. Dixon's computations were incomplete, but such as they were, the analysis did point to the desirability of a ban on logging.

We will see in Section 10.7 that matters can be quite different for economic and ecological interactions that are *reciprocal*. Here, each party's actions affect all. Reciprocal externalities are the hallmark of common-property resources (Chapters 6–*6), such as grazing lands, forests, fisheries, the atmosphere, aquifers, village tanks, ponds, and lakes. Some of them, for example the atmosphere and aquifers, have to remain common property by virtue of their physical characteristics. Others, such as local forests, grazing lands, village ponds, and rivulets, are often common property because that is how they have been since time immemorial. Moreover, such resources in poor countries have been common property for so long because they are basic needs which are at the same time geographically contained. Rivers may be long, but they are narrow, and don't run through everyone's land. Upstream farmers would have untold advantages over downstream farmers were they in a position to turn off the 'tap'. Exclusive private territoriality over these resources would leave non-owners at the mercy of the owners at the 'bargaining table', most especially in societies where markets are thin. No such society could risk the institution of private-property rights over such resources.[27] However, and we noted this in Chapter *6, unless there is collective action at some level, a common property is over-exploited: the private cost of using the resource falls short of its shadow price. This was the point of Gordon's classic article (see Gordon, 1954; see also A. D. Scott, 1955; Milliman, 1956). It was popularized subsequently by G. Hardin (1968) who coined the phrase, *the tragedy of the commons*.

Economic analysis is thought by some to have implied that common-property resources can be managed only through centralized co-ordination and control, where by a 'centralized agency' I mean the government, or some agency external to the community of users. Referring to solutions to the problem of the commons in the theoretical literature, Wade (1987: 220), in a much-cited article, writes: 'The prevailing answer runs as follows: when people are in a situation where they could mutually benefit if all of them restrained their use of a common-pool resource, they will not do so unless an external agency enforces a suitable rule.' And he proceeds to describe enforcement mechanisms in his sample of villages which do not rely on external agencies. This is a bad reading of modern economic analysis. The theory of games has unravelled a number of institutional mechanisms (ranging from taxes to quantity controls) which can in principle support effective allocations of common-property resources. The theory makes clear, and has made clear for some time, that enforcement

---

[27] In many early societies rulers had control over such resources. But that wasn't the same as private property rights. Rulers were obliged to make them available to the ruled. Indeed, one of the assumed duties of rulers was to expand such resource bases.

of the controlled allocation can in a variety of circumstances be undertaken by the users themselves. In many cases such participatory arrangements of control may well be the most desirable option (see Dasgupta and Heal, 1979, chapter 3; Chapter *6).[28]

Common-property problems can rear their head through all sorts of unsuspected sources. The introduction of cotton as an export crop in Tanzania was successful in increasing farmers' incomes. But other than for the purchase of cattle there was little outlet for this income. The quantity of livestock increased significantly, placing communal grazing lands under stress —to the extent that herds declined through an increase in their mortality rate.

As always, monitoring, enforcement, information, and transaction costs play a critical role in the relative efficacy of the mechanisms that can be used for controlling common-property resources. It matters whether the common property is geographically contained (contrast a village pond with the open seas); it matters whether the users know one another and whether they are large in number (contrast a village grazing ground with a tuna fishery); and it matters whether individual use can easily be monitored, so as to prevent 'free-riding' (contrast the use of a village tube-well with littering the streets of a metropolis; or the grazing of cattle in the village commons with firewood collection from forests in mountainous terrain). We touched on related issues in Chapter 8 when developing the notion of social norms of behaviour, and I will have something more to say on methods of control in Section 10.7. The confirmation of theory by current evidence on the fate of different categories of common-property resources has been one of the pleasing features of modern economic analysis.

Public concerns about environmental degradation are often prompted by disasters, such as nuclear leakage or floods.[29] The environmental impact of large undertakings (e.g. dams and irrigation systems) also catch the public eye. This is not surprising. Large-scale effects caused by single happenings are easy to detect, and thereby invite debate. In contrast, the examples of environmental externalities offered for study here are not so easy to detect. They often involve large numbers of resource-users, each inflicting only a tiny damage to each of the others. It would seem that much of the environmental degradation in poor countries is due to this kind of subtle interaction, and not to large projects (see Repetto, 1988).

In Chapter *6 I presented a game-theoretic analysis of common-property resources with an arbitrarily given number of users. We observed that particular interest attaches to the case where the number of users is large

---

[28] Not everyone writing on the subject has misread the literature. For illuminating accounts of the way communities have often jointly controlled common-property resources, see Howe (1986), Feeny et al. (1990) and Ostrom (1990).

[29] Kreimer and Munasinghe (1991) is an excellent collection of studies on the management of natural disasters.

(in the extreme, infinite), where each user contributes a tiny amount to degradation (in the extreme, no damage at all), but where the total effect, by virtue of the large numbers involved, is substantial. Gordon (1954) studied this extreme case. It appears illogical to some. ('This is surely absurd. If each contribution is literally "imperceptible" how can all the contributions together add up to anything?' Barry (1978: 32)). But it isn't absurd, and it hasn't been absurd since the discovery of Lebesgue integrals some ninety years ago.

10.6   *Property Rights on Land*

Property rights on land have assumed a bewildering variety across regions; land rights in sub-Saharan Africa have traditionally been quite different from those in, say, South Asia. Chance events have undoubtedly played a role in the way patterns of land tenure developed in various parts of the world, but so have economic, demographic, and ecological circumstances. We observed earlier that rights to assets that offer multiple services are often complex. Thus, someone may have the right to cultivate a piece of land (in many contexts if he has inherited it from his father, in others if he is the one to have cleared it), while others may share the right to the products of the trees growing on this land, while still others may have a concurrent right to graze their animals on the stubble following each harvest, and so forth. On occasion, the person who has the right to cultivate a piece of land does not have the right to rent it, or to sell it, and on most occasions he does not have the right to divert water-flows through it. These last are often group rights (see e.g. Breslin and Chapin, 1984; Feder and Noronha, 1987). However, for clarity it pays to think of polar cases, which are *territorial* (or private property) systems, and *communal* property systems. Even these on occasion can be hard to distinguish in practice. For example, social groups could assert territorial rights over land and at the same time practise reciprocity over access. This would have much the same effect as controlled communal ownership of all the lands. Or it could be the other way round; ownership could be communal across groups, but residence could be confined to given territories. Right of access to resources by one group from the territories of another would have to be monitored to avoid free-riding. But this would look pretty much like private ownership with reciprocity over access (see Cashdan, 1983).

Two aspects of spatially spread resource bases are of vital importance: *density* and *predictability* (see Dyson-Hudson and Smith, 1978; E. A. Smith, 1987). By density I mean the average value of the resource, say per square mile; and by predictability I mean the inverse of the variance in the value of the resource per unit of time per square mile, with the allied assumptions that the probability distributions are not overly correlated across spatial groupings of land, and not overly correlated over time. Two extreme types of spatially spread resources are then of particular interest. The first is characterized by both high density and high pre-dictability (for example, river valleys), and the second by low density and low predictability (for example, semi-arid scrublands and grasslands). The standard theory of resource allocation informs us that communities would tend to institute private property rights over the former category and remain geographically stable. We noted in the previous chapter that the theory also tells us that communities would be dispersed and mobile were they dependent upon the second category of resources. The prevalence of nomadic herdsmen in the Sahel is an instance of this.[30] In any event, we would expect a greater incidence of common-property resources in regions where resources have low density and low predict-ability, and we will note in the next section that this is to some extent confirmed by recent field studies in villages in the drylands of the Indian sub-continent.

Observations appear to be consistent with these predictions (see Agarwal and Narain, 1989; Chopra Kadekodi and Murti, 1989; CSE 1990; for studies on India). P. Hill (1963), J. Cohen (1980), Netting (1985), Feder and Noronha (1987), Feder and Feeny (1991), and Migot-Adholla *et al.* (1991) have provided accounts of the evolution of land tenure systems in sub-Saharan Africa. These accounts also seem consistent with our reasoning. In Africa land rights were typically held by groups, not by individuals. It is this which is being transformed, a good deal by State fiat (which often claims ownership, as in Ethiopia, Mauritania, Zaïre, Zambia, Nigeria, and Tanzania), and some by individuals themselves, who break with traditional norms of ownership when land values rise.

Resource density increases with investment and technological improve-ments, for example terracing, the maintenance of windbreaks, woodlots, and farm trees and shrubs, or the introduction of high-yielding varieties of wheat. Predictability can be made to increase at the same time, for example by the creation of irrigation facilities. (Poor countries today account for about 75 per cent of the world's irrigated land area.) The opening of new markets for cash crops also raises resource density. Changing patterns of land tenure often observed in poor countries would seem to be explainable along the lines we have outlined (Ensminger, 1990). We will go more deeply into these issues in the next section.

---

[30] The payoff (or utility) to a community is the net return of resources per unit of time spent in harvesting the resource and in defending it. For a review of the evidence, see E. A. Smith (1987). Boserup's well-known thesis (see Boserup, 1965), that high population density is usually associated with private-property rights and the use of the plough, is somewhat different from the classification I am discussing in the text.

10.7   *Public Failure and the Erosion of Local Commons*[31]

There is a vast difference between global commons and local commons. The open seas are common-property resources, as are usually village ponds. As economic analysis makes clear, what are problems for the former are by no means necessarily problems for the latter. However, it is the global commons, and popular writings on them (for example, the influential article by G. Hardin, 1968), which have shaped popular images of *all* common-property resources. This has been unfortunate because, unlike global commons, the source of the problems associated with the management of local commons is often not the users, but other agencies. The images invoked by 'the tragedy of the commons' are mostly not the right ones when applied to local commons. The point is that local commons (such as village ponds and tanks, pastures and threshing grounds, watershed drainage and riverbeds, and sources of fuelwood, medicinal herbs, bamboo, palm products, resin, gum, and so forth) are not open for use to all in any society. In most cases they are open only to those having historical rights, through kinship ties, community membership, and so forth. Those having historical rights of use tend, not surprisingly, to be very protective of these resources. Local commons are easy enough to monitor, so their use is often regulated in great detail by the community, as noted earlier, either through the practice and enforcement of norms, or through deliberate allocation of use.

An empirical investigation of the latter mode of control has been conducted by Wade (1987, 1988). Forty-one south Indian villages were studied and it was found, for example, that downstream villages had an elaborate set of rules, enforced by fines, for regulating the use of water from irrigation canals. Most villages had similar arrangements for the use of grazing land. In an earlier work on the Kuna tribe in the Panama, Howe (1986) described the intricate set of social sanctions imposed upon those who violate norms designed to protect their source of fresh water. (See also Breslin and Chapin, 1984.) Even the iniquitous caste system of India has been found to provide an institutional means of checks and balances by which communal environmental resources have been protected (see Gadgil and Malhotra, 1983).

The extent of common-property resources as a proportion of total assets in a community varies greatly across ecological zones. In India they appear to be most prominent in arid regions, mountain regions, and unirrigated areas. They are least prominent in humid regions and river valleys (see Agarwal and Narain, 1989; Chopra, Kadekodi and Murty, 1989). In the previous section I provided an explanation for this in terms of relative

---

[31] This section is based on Dasgupta and Mäler (1991).

resource predictability and density. An almost immediate empirical corol-
lary of this is that income inequalities are less where common-property
resources are more prominent. However, aggregate income is a different
matter, and it is the arid and mountain regions and unirrigated areas that
are the poorest.[32] This needs to be borne in mind when policy is devised.

In an important and interesting article, Jodha (1986) used data from over
eighty villages in twenty-one dry districts from seven states in India to
estimate that among poor families the proportion of income based directly
on common-property resources is for the most part in the range 15–25 per
cent (see also Jodha, 1990; Das Gupta, 1987b). This is a non-trivial
proportion. Moreover, as sources of income, these resources are often
complementary to private-property resources, which are in the main
labour, milch and draught animals, cultivation land and crops, common
agricultural tools (e.g. ploughs, harrows, levellers, and hoes), fodder-
cutting and rope-making machines, and seeds. Common-property resources
also provide the rural poor with partial protection in times of unusual
economic stress. For landless people they may be the only non-human
asset at their disposal. A number of resources (such as fuelwood and water
for home use, berries and nuts, medicinal herbs, resin and gum) are the
responsibility of women and children.[33]

A similar picture emerges from Hecht, Anderson and May (1988), who
describe in rich detail the importance of the extraction of babassu (palm
oil) products among the landless in the Brazilian state of Maranhão. The
support that such extraction activity offers the poorest of the poor, most
especially the women among them, is striking. These extractive products
are an important source of cash income in the period between agricultural
crop harvests (see also Murphy and Murphy, 1985; and for a similar picture
in the West African forest-zone see Falconer, 1990).

It is not difficult to see why common-property resources matter greatly
to the poorest of the rural poor in a society, or therefore, to understand
the mechanisms through which such people may well get disfranchised
from the economy even while in the aggregate the society is enjoying
economic growth. As we observed in Chapter 8, if you are steeped in social
norms of behaviour and understand community contractual obligations,

---

[32] As might be expected, even within dry regions dependence on common-property
resources falls with rising wealth across households. The interrelationship between destitution
and the erosion of the rural environmental resource base is developed in an analytical
context in Ch. 16.

[33] The most complete account I have read of the centrality of local forest products in the
lives of the rural poor is Falconer and Arnold (1989). On kinship support systems in northern
India, which enable certain critical natural resources to be common property, see Das Gupta
(1987b). The importance of common property resources for women's well-being in historical
times has been stressed by Humphries (1990) in her work on 18th-c. rural England. The
parallels with modern-day poor societies are remarkable.

you do not calculate every five minutes how you should behave. You follow the norms. This saves on costs all round, not only for you as an 'actor', but also for you as 'policeman' and 'judge'. It is also the natural thing for you to do if you have internalized the norms. But this is sustainable only so long as the background environment remains pretty much constant. It will not be sustainable if the social environment changes suddenly. You may even be destroyed. It is this heightened vulnerability, often more real than perceived, which is the cause of some of the greatest tragedies in contemporary society. They descend upon people who are, in the best of circumstances, acutely vulnerable.

The sources triggering destitution by this general means vary. The erosion of common-property resource bases can come about in the wake of shifting populations (accompanying the growth process itself), rising populations and the consequent pressure on these resources, technological progress, unreflective public policies, predatory governments, and thieving aristocracies. There is now an accumulation of evidence on this range of causes, and in what follows I will present an outline of the findings in three sets of studies.

1. In his work on the drylands of India, Jodha (1986) noted a decline in the geographical area covering common-property resources ranging from 26 to 63 per cent over a twenty-year period. This was in part due to the privatization of land, a good deal of which in his sample had been awarded to the rural non-poor. He also noted a decline in the productivity of common-property resources on account of population growth among the using community. In an earlier work, Jodha (1980) identified an increase in subsistence requirements of the farming community and a rise in the profitability of land exploitation from cropping and grazing as a central reason for increased desertification in the state of Rajasthan in India. Jodha argued that, ironically, it was government land reform programmes in this area, unaccompanied by investment in improving the productive base, which had triggered the process.[34]

2. Ensminger's (1990) study of the privatization of common grazing lands among the Orma in north-eastern Kenya indicates that the transformation took place with the consent of the elders of the tribe. She attributes this willingness to changing transaction costs brought about by cheaper transportation and widening markets. The elders were, quite naturally, from the stronger families, and it does not go unnoted by Ensminger that privatization has accentuated inequalities. However, she provides no data to tell whether the process has increased the prevalence of destitution among the economically weak.

---

[34] For a formalization of the dynamics of such a process, see Dasgupta (1982b, Ch. 6).

3. In earlier, much-neglected work on the Amazon basin, E. Feder (1977, 1979) described how massive private investment in the expansion of beef-cattle production in fragile ecological conditions has been supported by domestic governments in the form of tax concessions and provision of infrastructure, and loans from international agencies, such as the World Bank. The degradation of vast tracts of valuable environmental resources was accompanied by the disfranchisement of large numbers of small farmers and agricultural labourers from the economy. At best it made destitutes of traditional forest dwellers; at worst it simply eliminated them (see also Barraclough, 1977; Dasgupta, 1982b: chapter 2; Hecht, 1985). The evidence suggests that during the decades of the 1960s and 1970s protein intake by the rural poor *declined* even while the production of beef increased dramatically. Much of the beef was destined for exports, for use by fast-food chains.[35]

These matters, which are an instance of the intricate link between economic, social, and financial institutions, have been taken up anew by Repetto (1988), Mahar (1988), and Binswanger (1989). The latter in particular has shown how in Brazil the exemption from taxation of virtually all agricultural income (allied to the fact that logging is regarded as proof of land occupancy) has provided strong incentives for the acquisition of forest lands by the higher-income groups and for deforesting them. The subsidy the government has provided to the private sector to undertake deforestation has been so large that it is arguable that a reduction in this activity is in Brazil's interests, and not merely in the interest of the rest of the world. This has implications for international negotiations. The current consensus appears to be that Brazil in the aggregate has much to lose from reducing its rate of deforestation. Were this true, there would be a case for the rest of the world to subsidize her if she is to restrain herself. But it isn't clear if the consensus is correct.

The sources of the transformation of common-property resources into private resources described in the three sets of studies mentioned above are different. Consequently, the ways in which they have had an impact on those with historical rights have been different. But each is understandable and believable. (Noronha, 1990, provides an illuminating discussion of a number of other case-studies.) Since the impact of such forms of privatization are confirmed by economic theory, the findings of these case studies are almost certainly not unrepresentative. They suggest that privatization of village commons and forest lands, while hallowed at the

---

[35] Durham (1979) provides a compelling analysis of the 1969 'Soccer War' between El Salvador and Honduras. The explanation he provides of the disfranchisement of the poor is based not on reduced land–man ratios, but on the expansion of commercial agriculture by the largest landholders in the region.

altar of efficiency, can have disastrous distributional consequences, dis-
franchising entire classes of people from economic citizenship.[36] They also
show that public ownership of such resources as forest lands is by no means
necessarily a good basis for a resource allocation mechanism. Decision-
makers are in these cases usually far removed from site (living as they do
in imperial capitals), they have little knowledge of the ecology of such
matters, their time-horizons are often short, and they are in many instances
overly influenced by interest-groups far removed from the resource in
question.

All this is not at all to suggest that rural development is to be avoided.
It is to say that resource allocation mechanisms which do not take
advantage of dispersed information, which are insensitive to hidden
(and often not-so-hidden) economic and ecological interactions (what
economists would call 'general equilibrium effects'), which do not take the
long view, and which do not give a sufficiently large weight to the
claims of the poorest within rural populations (particularly the women
and children in these populations) are going to prove environmentally
disastrous. It appears that during the process of economic development
there is a close link between environmental protection and the well-being
of the poor, most especially the most vulnerable among the poor.
Elaboration of this link has been one of the most compelling achievements
at the interface of anthropology, economics, and nutrition science.

10.8 *Work Allocation among Women and Children and the Desirable Locus of Environmental Decisions*

The links between environmental degradation and an accentuation of
deprivation and hardship can take forms that even today are not always
appreciated. The gathering of fuelwood and fodder, and the fetching of
water for domestic use in most rural communities, fall upon women and
children. When allied to household chores and their farming obligations,
the work-load of women in South Asia in terms of time is often one and
a half to two and a half times that of men.[37] This work-load has over the
years increased directly as a consequence of receding resources. Now it
should be remembered that we are speaking of a category of people of
whom more than 50 per cent suffer from iron deficiency, of whom only a
little less than 50 per cent suffer from wastage, and who in some parts of

---

[36] For alternative demonstrations of this theorem, see Cohen and Weitzman (1975) and
Dasgupta and Heal (1979, Ch. 3). The analysis in these works assumes that the property is
perfectly divisible. Often, in poor communities an asset is a common property because it is
indivisible (see Noronha, 1990). Privatization of any such property increases inequality.
[37] See e.g. Cecelski (1987), Fernandes and Menon (1987), S. K. Kumar and Hotchkiss
(1988), and CSE (1990). See also Ch. 11.

the world work 15 to 16 hours a day during the busy agricultural season. Thus, communities in the drylands of the Indian sub-continent and in sub-Saharan Africa today often live miles away from fuelwood and fodder sources and permanent water sources. As noted earlier, women and children spend up to 5 hours a day collecting water during the dry season in India and Africa. The consequence is that anything between 10 and 25 per cent of daily daytime energy expenditure is required for the purposes of collecting water. Later I will argue that this influences fertility decisions within the household. (See L. C. Chen, 1983, for a review of the link between improved water supply and health benefits among the rural poor.)

A similar problem is associated with fodder and fuelwood collection. In Africa, some 90 per cent of the population use fuelwood for cooking. In northern India some 75 per cent of firewood for domestic use comes from twigs and fallen branches. A substantial part of the remaining fraction comes from cowdung. From data now available from the drylands of India on time allocation on the part of women in fuelwood collection, the energy costs in this activity would seem to be also in the range 10–25 per cent. Estimates of the energy cost of collection are essential ingredients in the calculation of the shadow prices of fuelwood and water.

Information concerning the ecology of local commons is often dispersed, and is usually in the hands of the historical users who, as we observed earlier, are often the women of rural populations. There are exceptions, of course, but as a general rule this makes it desirable that local commons be protected as commons and that decisions regarding local commons be left in the hands of the users themselves. This is because the local commons will almost certainly remain the single source of vital complementary and insurance goods for poor people for a long time to come. To be sure, it is essential not only that governments provide infrastructure and credit and insurance facilities, but also that they make available to users new information concerning technology, ecology, and widening markets. However, there is little case for centralized control.[38] Quite the contrary: there is a case for facilitating the growth of local, community decision-making, in particular decision-making by women, since it is the women who are the actual users of these resources and thus know something about the ecology of the matter. More generally, there is a strong case for the State to ensure that local decision-making isn't usurped by the economically powerful among rural communities. This tension—the simultaneous need for increased decentralization of rural decision-making, and for government

[38] The need for reinforcing the capacity of rural communities to make decisions about matters pertinent to them is the subject of a special issue of *The Administrator* (Lal Bahadur Shastri National Academy of Administration, New Delhi), 35 (1990). On the role of local organizations in rural development, see Esman and Uphoff (1984), Wignaraja (1990), and Ghai and Vivian (1992).

involvement in ensuring that the seat of local decisions is not usurped by the powerful—poses the central dilemma in the political economy of rural poverty. The large, often fragmented, literature on local common-property resources is beginning to offer an unequivocal impression that during the process of economic development the protection and promotion of environmental resources would best be served if a constant public eye were kept on the conditions of the poorest of the poor in society. Environmental economics and the economics of destitution are tied to each other in an intricate web. We should not have expected it otherwise.

Net National Product in a Dynamic Economy

★10.1 *The Economics of Optimal Control*

In Section 10.2 I sketched a number of methods that are currently available for estimating shadow prices of environmental resources *in situ*. We shall now seek to put shadow prices to use in judging the relative desirability of alternative economic activities. Of particular interest to us is social cost–benefit analysis of investment projects. In Chapter ★7 it was noted that the measurement of real national income is intimately connected to this. In this chapter we will extend the earlier analysis by taking explicit account of time. We wish also to take environmental resources into consideration. The index we now seek is *net national product* (NNP) as a measure of general well-being.[1] I shall show that the question of how to measure it for the purposes of cost–benefit analysis isn't a matter of opinion: it has an un-ambiguous answer. We need a formal model to establish this. In this chapter I present what I hope is a canonical model of an economy for doing so.[2]

My aim here is to display the connection between shadow prices, rules for project evaluation, and national product accounting in a context that is simple but at the same time has sufficient structure to allow us to obtain a number of prescriptions that were alluded to in Chapter 10. In order to keep to what for our purposes in this chapter are essential matters, I will ignore the kinds of 'second-best' constraints (e.g. market disequilibria) which have been the centre of attention in the literature on project evaluation, as for example in Dasgupta, Marglin and Sen (1972) and Little and Mirrlees (1974). The principles we will develop here carry over to disequilibrium situations.[3] For expositional ease we will restrict ourselves

---

[1] There are other purposes to which the *idea* of national product has been put; e.g. as a measure of economic activity. They require different treatments. We are not concerned with them here.

[2] My analysis extends the ones in Samuelson (1961), Arrow and Kurz (1970), Weitzman (1976), Dasgupta and Heal (1979), Dasgupta (1982c), Solow (1986), and Hartwick (1990). This chapter is taken from Dasgupta and Mäler (1991). For a more comprehensive account, see Mäler (1991).

[3] In Chapter ★7 the final constraint in problem (★7.4) was a typical 'second-best constraint'. See also Blitzer, Dasgupta and Stiglitz (1981).

to a closed economy. (The analysis here has been extended to an open economy by Sefton and Weale, 1992.) I shall also take it that the social well-being function*al* is the (possibly discounted) *integral* of the flow of instantaneous social well-being. This strikes many as a strong assumption, and in some ways it is. But we know properties of linear functionals best, and so optimization theory has advanced most of the class of social well-being functions that are integrals over time and people. This is our real justification (see Koopmans, 1965, 1967, 1972a, b).

I begin by recalling the main features of intertemporal optimization exercises.[4] The theory of intertemporal planning tells us to choose current controls (for example, current consumptions and the mix of current investments) in such a way as to maximize the current-value Hamiltonian of the underlying planning problem. As is well known, the current-value Hamiltonian is the sum of the flow of current well-being and the shadow value of all the net investments currently being undertaken. (The planning exercise generates the entire set of intertemporal shadow prices.[5]) It will be seen below that the current-value Hamiltonian measures the social return on the value of all capital assets. In short, it is a measure of *wealth*. This provides us with the necessary connection between the current-value Hamiltonian and real net national product. NNP is merely a linearized version of the current-value Hamiltonian, the linearization amounting to a representation of the current flow of well-being by the shadow value of all the determinants of current well-being. In the simplest of cases, where current well-being depends solely on current consumption, NNP reduces to the *sum* of the shadow value of an economy's consumptions and the shadow value of the changes in its stocks of real capital assets.

The Hamiltonian calculus in fact implies something more. It implies that the present discounted sum of today's current-value Hamiltonian is equal to the maximum present discounted value of the flow of social well-being (equation *10.13). Thus the current-value Hamiltonian is the maximum sustainable flow of social well-being. It is a measure of *sustainable development*. This was not seen immediately as an implication of the mathematical theory of programming, although it should have been obvious from the work of Arrow and Kurz (1970) and Solow (1974). Each of these matters will be illustrated in our formal model.

*10.2   *NNP in a Deterministic Environment*

We consider an economy that has a multi-purpose, man-made, perfectly durable capital good, whose stock is denoted by K_1. If L_1 is the labour

---

[4] The best economics treatment of all this is still Arrow and Kurz (1970).

[5] The current-value Hamiltonian will in general also contain terms reflecting the social cost of breaking any additional (second-best) constraint that happens to characterize the optimization problem. As mentioned in the text, we ignore such additional constraints for expositional ease.

effort combined with this, the flow of output is taken to be $Y = F(K_1, L_1)$, where $F(\cdot)$ is an aggregate production function.[6] The economy enjoys in addition two sorts of environmental resource stocks: clean air, K_2, and forests, K_3. Clean air is valued directly, whereas forests have two derived values: they help keep the atmosphere (or air) 'clean', and they provide fuelwood, which too is valued directly (for warmth or for cooking). Finally, we take it that there is a flow of environmental amenities, Z, which directly affects aggregate well-being.

Forests enjoy a natural regeneration rate, but labour effort can increase it. Thus we denote by $H(L_2)$ the rate of regeneration of forests, where L_2 is labour input for this task and $H(\cdot)$ is, for low values of L_2 at least, an increasing function. Let X denote the rate of consumption of fuelwood. Collecting this involves labour effort. Let this be L_3. Presumably, the larger is the forest stock, the less is the effort required (in calorie requirements, say). I remarked on this in Chapter 10. We thus assume that $X = N(K_3, L_3)$, where $N(\cdot)$ is an increasing, concave function of its two arguments.

Output Y is a basic consumption good, and this consumption is also valued directly. However, we take it that the production of Y involves pollution as a by-product. This reduces the quality of the atmosphere both as a stock and as a flow of amenities. We assume however that it is possible to take defensive measures against both these ill-effects. First, society can invest in technologies (e.g. stack-gas scrubbers) for reducing the emission of pollutants, and we denote the stock of this defensive capital by K_4. If P denotes the emission of pollutants, we have $P = A(K_4, Y)$, where A is a convex function, decreasing in K_4 and increasing in Y. Second, society can mitigate damages to the flow of amenities by expending a portion of final output, at a rate R. We assume that the resulting flow of amenities has the functional form $Z = J(R, P)$, where J is increasing in R and decreasing in P.

There are thus four things that can be done with output Y: it can be consumed (we denote the rate of consumption by C); it can be reinvested to increase the stock of K_1; it can be invested in the accumulation of K_4; and it can be used, at rate R, to counter the damages to the flow of environmental amenities. Let Q denote the expenditure on the accumulation of K_4.

Now, the environment as a stock tries to regenerate itself at a rate that is an increasing function of the stock of forests, $G(K_3)$. The net rate of regeneration is the difference between this and the emission of pollutants

---

[6] In what follows I assume that all functions satisfy conditions that ensure that the planning problem defined below is a concave programme. I am not going to spell out each and every such assumption, because they will be familiar to the reader. For example, I assume that $F(\cdot)$ is concave.

from production of Y. We can therefore express the dynamics of the economy in terms of the following equations:

$$dK_1/dt = F(K_1, L_1) - C - Q - R \qquad (\star10.1)$$
$$dK_2/dt = G(K_3) - A[K_4, F(K_1,L_1)] \qquad (\star10.2)$$
$$dK_3/dt = H(L_2) - X \qquad (\star10.3)$$
$$dK_4/dt = Q \qquad (\star10.4)$$
$$X = N(K_3, L_3) \qquad (\star10.5)$$
$$Z = J\{R, A[K_4, F(K_1, L_1)]\} \qquad (\star10.6)$$

The current flow of aggregate well-being, W, is taken to be an increasing function of aggregate consumption, C, the output of fuelwood, X, the flow of environmental amenities, Z, and the quality of the atmospheric stock, K_2. However, it is a decreasing function of total labour effort, $L = L_1 + L_2 + L_3$. (As noted in the text, labour effort could be measured in caloric terms.) We thus have $W(C, X, Z, K_2, L_1 + L_2 + L_3)$.

Stocks of the four types of assets are given at the initial date; the instantaneous control variables are C, Q, R, X, Z, L_1, L_2, and L_3. The objective is to maximize the (discounted) sum of the flow of aggregate well-being over the indefinite future; that is,

$$\int_0^\infty W(C, X, Z, K_2, L_1 + L_2 + L_3)e^{-\delta t}dt, \text{ where } \delta > 0.$$

We take well-being to be the numeraire. Letting p, q, r, and s denote the (spot) shadow prices of the four capital goods, K_1, K_2, K_3, and K_4 respectively, and letting v be the imputed marginal value of the flow of environmental amenities, we can use equations $(\star10.1)$–$(\star10.6)$ to express the current-value Hamiltonian, V, of the optimization problem as

$$V = W[C,N(K_3,L_3),Z,K_2,L_1 + L_2 + L_3] + p[F(K_1,L_1) - C - Q - R]$$
$$+ q[G(K_3) - A(K_4,F[K_1,L_1])] + r[H(L_2) - N(K_3,L_3)] + sQ$$
$$+ v(J\{R,A[K_4,F(K_1,L_1)]\} - Z). \qquad (\star10.7)$$

Recall that the theory of optimum control instructs us to choose the control variables at each date so as to maximize $(\star10.7)$.[7] Writing by W_c the partial derivative of W with respect to C, and so forth, it is then immediate that along an optimal programme the control variables and the shadow prices must satisfy the conditions[8]

(i) $W_c = p$;　　(ii) $W_x N_2 + W_L = rN_2$;　　(iii) $W_z = v$;
(iv) $W_L = (qA_2 - vJ_2 - p)F_2$;　　(v) $W_L = -rdH(L_2)/dL_2$;
(vi) $p = vJ_1$;　　(vii) $p = s$. $\qquad (\star10.8)$

---

[7] Notice that we have used equation $(\star9.5)$ to eliminate X, and so we are left with 7 direct control variables.

[8] F_2 stands for the partial derivative of F with respect to its second argument, L_1; and, as mentioned earlier, $L = L_1 + L_2 + L_3$. I have used this same notation for the derivatives of $N(\cdot)$, $J(\cdot)$, and $A(\cdot)$.

Moreover, the accounting prices p, q, r, and s satisfy the auxiliary conditions

(1) $dp/dt = -\partial V/\partial K_1 + \delta p$;   (2) $dq/dt = -\partial V/\partial K_2 + \delta q$;

(3) $dr/dt = -\partial V/\partial K_3 + \delta r$;   (4) $ds/dt = -\partial V/\partial K_4 + \delta s$.   (*10.9)

Interpreting these conditions is today a routine matter. Conditions (*10.8) tell us what kinds of information we need for estimating shadow prices; (*10.9) are the intertemporal 'arbitrage conditions' the shadow prices must satisfy. We may now derive the correct expression for net national product (NNP) from equation (*10.7): it is the linear support of the Hamiltonian, the normal to the support being given by the vector of accounting prices.

It will pay us now to introduce time into the notation. Let us denote by $\mathbf{O}_t^*$ the vector of all the non-price arguments in the Hamiltonian function along the *optimal* programme at date t. Thus,

$$\mathbf{O}_t^* = (C_t^*, Z_t^*, Q_t^*, R_t^*, K_{1t}^*, K_{2t}^*, K_{3t}^*, K_{4t}^*, L_{1t}^*, L_{2t}^*, L_{3t}^*).$$

Write $I_{it} \equiv dK_{it}/dt$, for $i = 1, 2, 3, 4$. Consider now a small perturbation at t round $\mathbf{O}_t^*$. Denote the perturbed programme as an unstarred vector, and $d\mathbf{O}_t$ as the perturbation itself. It follows from taking the Taylor expansion around $\mathbf{O}^*$ that the current-value Hamiltonian along the perturbed programme is

$$V(\mathbf{O}_t) = V(\mathbf{O}_t^*) + W_c dC_t + W_x dX_t + W_z dZ_t + W_L(dL_{1t} + dL_{2t}$$
$$+ dL_{3t}) + pdI_{1t} + qdI_{2t} + rdI_{3t} + sdI_{4t},   (*10.10)$$

where $Z^* = J\{R^*, A[K_4^*, F(K_1^*, L_1^*)]\}$.

Equation (*10.10) tells us how to measure net national product. Let $\{\mathbf{O}_t\}$ denote an arbitrary intertemporal programme. NNP at date t, which we write as NNP_t, in the optimizing economy, measured in well-being numeraire, is the term representing the linear support term in expression (*10.10). So,[9]

$$NNP_t = W_c C_t + W_x X_t + W_z J\{R_t, A[K_4, F(K_{1t}, L_{1t})]\} + W_L(L_{1t} + L_{2t}$$
$$+ L_{3t}) + pdK_1/dt + qdK_2/dt + rdK_3/dt + sdK_4/dt.   (*10.11)$$

Notice that all resources and outputs are valued at the prices that sustain the optimal programme $\{\mathbf{O}_t^*\}$.[10] To stress the points I want to make here, I have chosen to work with a most aggregate model. Ideally, (income) distributional issues will find reflection in the social well-being functional. These considerations can easily be translated into the estimates of shadow prices (see Dasgupta, Marglin and Sen, 1972).

---

[9] We may divide the whole expression by W_c to express NNP in aggregate consumption numeraire. It should also be recalled that by assumption W_L is *negative*.

[10] One could alternatively think of a sequence of policy reforms, and to use shadow prices defined at the existing structure of production. Given that the planning programme has been taken to be concave, a sequence of such moves would take the economy ultimately to the optimum. For a simplified exposition of the connection between these two modes of analysis (reforms and optimization), see Dasgupta (1982b, ch. 5).

Why should expression (*10.11) be regarded as the correct measure of net national product? The clue lies in (*10.10). Suppose we are involved in the choice of projects. A marginal project is a perturbation on the current programme. Suppressing the index for time once again, the project is the ten-vector $(dC, dX, dR, dL_1, dL_2, dL_3, dI_1, dI_2, dI_3, dI_4)$, where $I_i = dK_i/dt$, $(i = 1,2,3,4)$; and dC, etc., are small changes in C; and so forth. If the project records an increase in NNP_t (the increase will be marginal of course), it will record an increase in the current-value Hamiltonian, evaluated at the prices supporting the optimal programme. Recall that optimal control theory asks us to maximize the current-value Hamiltonian. Moreover, we are assuming that the planning problem is concave. So, choosing projects that increase NNP (i.e. are socially profitable) increases the current-value Hamiltonian as well, and therefore such projects should be regarded as desirable. Along an optimal programme, the social profitability of the last project is nil; that is, its contribution to NNP is nil. This follows from the fact that the controls are chosen so as to maximize expression (*10.7). This is the justification. All this is well-known, and our purpose here is to obtain some additional insights. Expression (*10.11) tells us:

1. Were wages to equal the marginal ill-being of work effort, wages would not be part of NNP. In other words, the shadow wage bill ought to be deducted from gross output when we estimate NNP. (However, if labour is supplied inelastically, it is a matter of indifference whether the wage bill in this optimizing economy is deducted from NNP.) On the other hand, were we to recognize a part of the wage bill as a return on the accumulation of human capital, that part *would* be included in NNP.

2. Current defensive expenditure, R, against damages to the flow of environmental amenities should be included in the estimation of final demand. (See the third term in expression (*10.11).)

3. Investments in the stock of environmental defensive capital should be included in NNP. (See the final term of expression (*10.11).)

4. Expenditures that enhance the environment find expression in the value imputed to changes in the environmental resource stock. We may conclude that this change should not be included in estimates of NNP. (Notice the absence of sQ in expression (*10.11).)

5. The value of *changes* in the environmental resource base (K_2 and K_3) should be included in NNP. However, anticipated capital gains (or losses) are not part of NNP.

*10.3 *The Hamiltonian and Sustainable Well-Being*

The idea of *sustainable development* has been much discussed in recent years (see Brundtland *et al.*, 1987), for the most part in an intuitive way. We can give a formal expression to it. It transpires that the current-value Hamiltonian is intimately connected to the notion. Differentiate expression ($\star$10.7) and use conditions ($\star$10.9) to confirm that, along the optimal programme,

$$dV_t^*/dt = \delta(pdK_1/dt + qdK_2/dt + rdK_3/dt + sdK_4/dt)$$
$$= \delta(V_t^* - W_t^*), \tag{$\star$10.12}$$

where W_t^* is the flow of optimal social well-being.

This is a differential equation in V_t^* which integrates to

$$V_t^* = \delta\int_t^\infty W_\tau^* e^{-\delta(\tau-t)}d\tau,$$

and thus

$$V_t^*\int_t^\infty e^{-\delta(\tau-t)}d\tau = \int_t^\infty W_t^* e^{-\delta(\tau-t)}d\tau. \tag{$\star$10.13}$$

Equation ($\star$10.13) says that the present discounted value of a constant flow of today's current-value Hamiltonian measures the maximum present value of the flow of social well-being. Thus V_t^* is the maximum sustainable flow of social well-being.

Define $K \equiv pK_1 + qK_2 + rK_3 + sK_4$ as the aggregate capital stock in the economy. The first part of equation ($\star$10.12) can then be written as

$$V_t^* = \delta K_t. \tag{$\star$10.14}$$

In short, the current-value Hamiltonian measures the current return on the economy's aggregate capital stock, inclusive of the environmental resource base.

$\star$10.4 Future Uncertainty

We will now extend the analysis for the case where there is future uncertainty. An an example, we would imagine the discovery and installation of cleaner production technologies which make existing abatement technologies less valuable. For simplicity of exposition, we will assume that such discoveries are uninfluenced by policy, for example research and development policy.[11]

It is most informative to consider discrete events. We may imagine that at some random future date, T, an event will occur which is expected to affect the value of the then existing stocks of capital. We consider the problem from the vantage point of the present, which we denote by $t = 0$, where t, as always, denotes time. Let us assume that there is a (subjective) probability density function, π^t, over the date of its occurrence. (We are thus supposing for expositional ease that the event *will*

---

[11] R&D policy can easily be incorporated into our analysis. The following account builds on Dasgupta and Heal (1974), Dasgupta and Stiglitz (1981), and Dasgupta (1982c). These earlier contributions, however, did not address the measurement of NNP, our present concern.

occur at some future date.) From this we may define the cumulative function ϕ^t.

We take it that the social good is reflected by the expected value of the sum of the discounted flow of future aggregate well-being. Were the event in question to occur at date T, the economy in question would enter a new production and ecological regime. We continue to rely on the notation developed in the previous section. As is proper, we use dynamic programming, and proceed to work backwards. Thus, let K_i^T (with $i = 1, 2, 3, 4$) denote the stocks of the four assets at date T. Following an optimal economic policy subsequent to the occurrence of the event would yield an expected flow of aggregate well-being. This flow we discount back to T. This capitalized value of the flow of well-being will clearly be a function of K_i^T. Let us denote this by $B(K_1^T, K_2^T, K_3^T, K_4^T)$. It is now possible to show that until the event occurs (i.e. for $t < T$), the optimal policy is to pretend that the event will never occur, and to assume that the flow of aggregate well-being is given not by $W(\cdot)$, as in Section *10.1, but by $(1 - \phi^t)W(\cdot) + \pi^t B(\cdot)$ (see Dasgupta and Heal, 1974). Suppressing the superscript for time, we may then conclude from the analysis of the previous section that NNP at any date prior to the occurrence of the event is given by the expression

$$NNP = (1 - \phi)(W_cC + W_xX + W_zJ\{R, A[K_4, F(K_1, L_1)]\} + W_L(L_1 + L_2 + L_3) + pdK_1/dt + qdK_2/dt + rdK_3/dt + sdK_4/dt). \quad (*10.15)$$

Notice that, if the event isn't ever expected to occur, then $\pi^t = 0$ for all t, and consequently, $(1 - \phi^t) = 1$) for all t. In this case expression (*10.15) reduces to (*10.11). Notice that the shadow prices appearing in (*10.15) are Arrow–Debreu contingent-commodity prices. Notice too that, while we have used the same *notation* for the accounting prices in expressions (*10.11) and (*10.15), their values are quite different. This is because future possibilities in the two economies are different.

11

Food, Care, and Work: The Household as an Allocation Mechanism

11.1 *Gender Differentials among Adults*

I have on a number of occasions observed that for the most part the household is treated as a unit of analysis in what I have called the standard theory of resource allocation. This obviously makes sense for single-membered households. It doesn't necessarily make sense otherwise. Recall that we are interpreting a household's utility function to be a numerical representation of the ranking of options on the basis of which its choice is actually made. This makes for a consistent analysis, but it puts strain on the normative significance of household choice. Choice may reflect a ranking that systematically favours some members (for example males), and it may discriminate against others (for example higher-birth-order girls and elderly relatives). Household choice assumes strong normative significance only when the underlying ranking of options is based upon a defendable aggregate of each member's well-being. But this may not be common, at least not when the family is impoverished, and the stresses and strains of hunger, illness, and physical weakness make themselves felt.

The matter is a delicate one. For the State to interfere with household choice and to probe its inner workings systematically can have catastrophic consequences, if recent evidence in a number of poor countries is any guide. Nevertheless, there are indirect levers the State can pull which do not amount to direct interference with what happens inside the household, but which protect vulnerable members and enable them to reach a stronger strategic position. Fertility decisions and allocations of food, health care, and work are among the most important determinants of household well-being. We need to have some understanding of what happens within poor households. In this and the following chapter we will look into this, first by presenting some aggregate data, and then by reflecting upon the data.

Gender and age differences in the access to resources and over patterns of approved activities and roles are a commonplace in poor countries.[1] In

---

[1] I hasten to add, it isn't that discrimination doesn't occur elsewhere, but that I am not writing about elsewhere. I should also add that the kinds of discrimination addressed in this chapter

recent years the former has been much studied. Much less has been written in the social sciences on differences based on age (after correcting for differences in needs among the young and old). With increasing life expectancy and changing social mores, the plight of the assetless elderly will inevitably assume more and more quantitative importance in poor countries. A beginning is provided by Deaton and Paxson (1990), who present a comprehensive statistical picture of the state of the elderly in Thailand and Côte d'Ivoire. The overall picture, though horrifying, is sketchy, and so we concentrate on gender differences.[2]

Certain patterns of differences are pervasive, while others of a more specific kind are regional. Some are local. I have had occasion to remark on this in earlier chapters. Let us first look at a few of the more pervasive forms of differentiation. Their extent varies considerably across ecological zones and continents. But I shall use the broad brush here.

Girls in poor countries are on average allowed less education by their families. The ratio of male to female adult literacy rates among countries where the under-5 mortality rate exceeds the high figure of 175 per 1000 is (42/21) per cent, or 2 (see UNICEF, 1987). Women on average have far fewer employment opportunities in the market (see Chapter 9). Moreover, they earn less than men when they do find employment and, with monotonous regularity, they work longer hours (see e.g. Buvinic, Lycette and McGreevey 1983; M. A. Chen, 1989). They face a variety of social restrictions on their movements, and they are particularly constrained in the ability to acquire capital, loans, and information. This is especially so within certain religious and ethnic groups. Those who work outside the home, whether farming or sowing or knitting or selling wares or earning a wage, do so in addition to their work at home, which consists of cooking, cleaning, feeding the children, collecting fuelwood and fodder, grinding grain, fetching water, and so on. For example, in a study based on a sample of Nepalese villages, Kumar and Hotchkiss (1988) found that during the period April–September women work approximately twice as long each day compared with men (10 hours to men's 5 hours). However, for the rest of the year they have it easy, and they work only one and a half times as long. Women in rural Java have been found to work on average 11 hours a day, compared with men's 8 hours (see Nag, White and Peet, 1978). A study in Côte d'Ivoire found that rural women on average fetch

---

are for the most part practised in poor households, for reasons we will explore below. For a far-reaching analysis of gender inequalities in households of advanced industrial societies, and the need for theories of distributive justice to accommodate such inequalities, see Okin (1989).

[2] Good overviews are Piwoz and Viteri (1985), and two special issues of *Food and Nutrition Bulletin* (1988, 10(3); 1989, 11(4)) on 'Women and Nutrition', most especially, the articles by McGuire and Popkin (1988, 1989) and Bennett (1989). A pioneering collection of quantitative studies is Buvinic, Lycette and McGreevey (1983). See also A. Ahmad (1991).

some 600 kg of water to their kitchen every week, and spend some forty-five minutes a day doing so (see Lunven, 1983). In parts of East Africa, women often work a 14-hour day, producing 60–80 per cent of the food for the family.[3] To this we must add the bearing and rearing of children (Chapter 12), which increase nutrition requirements. It is then easy to see why poor women in poor countries often fall prey to the debilitating effects of undernourishment.

Total fertility rate is the number of live births a woman would expect to give were she to live through her child-bearing years and to bear children in accordance with the prevailing age-specific fertility rates. The measure pertains to the number of live births, not pregnancies. In Chapter 12 we will place international figures for the total fertility rate in perspective (see Table 12.1). Here, we need only note that in all poor countries it exceeds the *population replacement rate*, which is the total fertility rate that would maintain a constant population size in the long run. The population replacement rate in poor countries today is just over 2.1. The total fertility rate varies enormously within poor countries; towards the end of the 1980s it ranged from a high of just over 8 in Rwanda to approximately 2.3 in China and Sri Lanka.

Table 11.1 presents aggregate data concerning the status of women from seventy-nine so-called Third World countries (see also Saflios-Rothschild, 1985). The pattern is unmistakable. High total fertility rates, high rates of female illiteracy, low age-of-marriage for women, low share of paid employment for women, and high percentages of women working as unpaid family workers—all these hang together, and in what follows we will try to see why they would be expected to hang together. The seeming oddity is the last pair of columns of the first two rows. That an increase in women's age at marriage (from 18.6 to 20.3 years) should be associated with a reduction in women's illiteracy rate (from 76.9 to 65.7 per cent) is something one would expect when reflecting upon such matters. But it is associated also with an increase in the total fertility rate, from the range 6.1–7.0 to above 7.0.

Cochrane (1979) has noted this seemingly unexpected association between education and fertility at low levels of education (up to three or four years of school enrollment). The countries where the total fertility rate is in excess of seven are all in sub-Saharan Africa. (At a more disaggregated level, one would find such high levels of fertility also in North Africa and the Middle East.) We will study this link more closely in the next chapter.

---

[3] There is now an extensive literature on the role of women in the generation of household income in poor countries. See e.g. Boserup (1970), Fagley (1976), Meillassoux (1981), Beneria (1981, 1983), Buvinic, Lycette and McGreevey (1983), V. Mazumdar (1983), G. Sen and Sen (1985), Fernandes and Menon (1987), Dwyer and Bruce (1988), Hecht, Anderson and May (1988), Agarwal and Narain (1989), and McGuire and Popkin (1989).

Table 11.1   Aggregate data on the status of women from seventy-nine 'Third World' countries

N	TFR	PE	UE	I	MA
9	> 7.0	10.6	46.9	65.7	20.3
35	6.1–7.0	16.5	31.7	76.9	18.6
10	5.1–6.0	24.5	27.1	46.0	21.0
25	< 5.0	30.3	18.1	22.6	21.8

Key
N: number of countries
TFR: total fertility rate
PE: women's share of paid employment (%)
UE: % of women working as unpaid family workers
I: women's illiteracy rate (%)
MA: women's average age of marriage
Source: IIED/WRI (1987, table 2.3)

Here we need only observe that extended breast-feeding and postpartum female sexual abstinence form methods of birth control in sub-Saharan Africa. It has been suggested that these methods are likely to be less firmly practised with a rise in female education, and that, the levels of poverty and female discrimination practised in these parts being what they are, one wouldn't expect to see an emergence of the kinds of counterbalancing forces that would militate against high fertility rates. But, from an analysis of the World Fertility Survey, Cochrane and Farid (1989) have shown that the evidence that is currently available does not support the thesis; for example, in a sample of sub-Saharan countries, breast-feeding has not been found to decline much with education; a revealed preference for large family size would have seemed to dominate fertility choice.[4]

Men's allocation of time doesn't vary much over the working life-cycle. It is often fixed, independent of the number of other household members (see especially King and Evenson, 1983; Henn, 1984). For the most part their work is directed at income outside the home and hearth, in the form of wages, or agricultural production and earnings. On the whole, it is men who control households' cash incomes. This appears to be true both in the Indian sub-continent and in sub-Saharan Africa. In rural Africa nearly half the households are headed by women. They do the subsistence farming, but this doesn't mean they have much cash income. Men from poor households are involved in cultivating cash crops, and working in the

---

[4] I should emphasize that Table 11.1 presents highly aggregate data, and should be treated as such. At a more disaggregate level, the link between any two of the items in the table is much harder to identify empirically. See e.g. Hammer (1986).

cities.[5] In contrast, women's time allocation varies. Poor women in poor countries are always working women. That they often get recorded as unemployed is a pure fudge. Moreover, that they are outside the home for part of the day does not reduce their workload in the realm of home maintenance, child care, and food preparation. There are no substitution possibilities open to them. Their choice of occupation is dictated by an almost universally inflexible role they must assume, of being at once mother, wife, and housekeeper. So they must aim at jobs that allow flexible hours. Out of necessity, they seek jobs that require little or no education. All this implies low financial returns (see e.g. B. M. Popkin, 1983; King and Evenson, 1983; Da Vanzo and Lee, 1983; Hay and Stichter, 1984).

Women have little control over cash income, even when they earn it. The sphere over which they have control is food and health-care allocation. But the choices are hard. When there is little food and general resources to go around, most especially when the rains have just arrived, and food stocks are low, and agricultural tasks are intensive, draconian allocation rules are forced upon them—for example, giving priority to the adult male, favouring sons over daughters, favouring lower-birth-order daughters over higher-birth-order ones, neglecting elderly relatives, and so forth (see e.g. Feierman, 1985; Behrman, 1987, 1988a, b; Das Gupta, 1987a; A. M. Basu, 1989; Pitt, Rosenzweig and Hassan, 1990). Poor women in poor countries face a variant of Sophie's Choice every day.[6]

11.2   *Allocations among Girls and Boys*

Applied research in household allocations entails hard work. It is difficult enough to monitor work allocation among members of a household; observing food allocation is harder still. Direct observation is very costly (but see Chen, Huq and D'Souza, 1981), and answers to questionnaires are unreliable. Data on household expenditure provide a possible route to detecting biases in the allocation of nutrition. Evidence of relative food deprivation among household members is mixed in this body of research. The practice isn't uniform across regions. In a study of household expenditure for Côte d'Ivoire and Thailand, Deaton (1989) found little or

---

[5] Their lives are wretched as well, but it is gender comparisions we are concerned with here. See Faruqee and Gulhati (1983), Hay and Stichter (1984), and Kamarck (1988).

[6] The coarsening of maternal feeling among those who have to make household allocational decisions under conditions of chronic poverty was the central motif in Satyajit Ray's 1955 masterpiece, *Pather Panchali*. A leading image in the film is the discrimination the mother practises against her daughter and, even more tellingly, against the elderly widowed aunt of the family. It will be recalled that towards the end of the film the aunt is driven out by her, to die abandoned, a destitute.

no sign that girls are discriminated against in the allocation of children's goods. More tellingly, Caldwell and Caldwell (1992) have emphasized that in sub-Saharan Africa there is no evidence of gender differences in the child death rate. (See also Svedberg, 1990; Pinstrup-Andersen, 1991.) On the other hand, Behrman's work on (rural) Indian data (see Behrman, 1987, 1988a, b; Behrman and Deolalikar, 1988) shows that there is a bias against female children in the allocation of household nutrients, most especially against higher-birth-order girls. This bias is pronounced in the northern states of India, and it is sharpest during the lean season. When food is scarce in northern India, it is the less endowed, female, and low-caste children who are placed at greater nutritional risk. However, during the surplus season parents appear to allocate food among their children more along the lines of need.[7] Acute scarcity forces households to practise discrimination in a remorseless way. There is some evidence though, that discrimination, when mapped against household food availability, is ∩-shaped; so that when food is severely scarce less discrimination is practised than when it is only acutely scarce (see Haddad and Kanbur, 1989). We will come back to this point later in the book (Chapter 16).

Evidence that female children in rural Bangladesh receive less food than their male siblings was reported from direct observation in Chen, Huq and D'Souza (1981).[8] Often, children in poor households are made to eat from the same bowl; this puts the youngest and weakest children at special risk, as they scrabble for grains at the edge of the bowl while their elders divide up the meat which is placed in the middle. The medical profession in sub-Saharan Africa calls this the 'communal-feeding-victimization disease' (see Lacville, 1991). Recently, Subramanian and Deaton (1990) have found in household expenditure data from the Maharashtra state sample of the National Sample Survey of India that parents give up more of certain adult commodities (cigarettes and *paan*, to be precise) when the child is a boy than when it is a girl. To date, the evidence from the Indian sub-continent, at least, seems to be that the sphere in which discrimination against female children manifests itself most strongly is health care. Utilization of even free medical services is often lower for females (see Dandekar, 1975; Chen, Huq and D'Souza, 1981; Miller, 1981; Kynch and Sen, 1983, A. M. Basu, 1989; Harriss, 1990).

Most studies on gender discriminations have been more direct. They have looked at what in Chapter 2 we called 'output' indicators; anthropometric measures (e.g. Chen, Huq and D'Souza, 1981; Sen and Sengupta,

---

[7] See also Valdeverde *et al.* (1979) and Ferro-Luzzi, Norgan and Paci (1981) for evidence from Guatemala and Papua New Guinea, respectively. See also Payne (1985b).

[8] See also Das Gupta (1987a), who noted that mortality rates increase with the birth order of girl children in a sample of villages in north India.

1983), mortality indices (e.g. D'Souza and Chen, 1980; Chen, Huq and D'Souza, 1981; Miller, 1981; Das Gupta, 1987a), and literacy rates (Sopher, 1980a). In their pioneering, quantitative studies on the general theme of gender inequality, D'Souza and Chen (1980) and Chen, Huq and D'Souza (1981) analysed data from Matlab Thana in Bangladesh for the period 1974–7 (a time of acute scarcity) and found nearly 15 per cent of female children to be severely malnourished, in that they were less than 60 per cent of the Harvard weight-for-age standard; the corresponding figure for male children was 5 per cent. They also found that male children in the age range of 1–5 years enjoyed a 66 per cent higher rate of treatment from diarrhoeal diseases. As expected, this was associated with a significantly greater incidence of mortality among girls: in the age-group 1–5 years, the female mortality rate exceeded that of males by some 45 per cent. In view of all the other evidence, the inference to be made isn't that discrimination in health support disappears when times are economically less stressful, but that the biases take on a different complexion, and have less drastic consequences. We will wish to provide an explanation for these findings.

11.3   *Bridewealth and Dowry*

There are two issues here: gender differentials among children, and among adults. We presume they are related, in that we should expect the extent of the former to be influenced by the presence of the latter. The pioneering investigation into the influence of relative rates of return from household members on food and health-care allocation rules within poor families is Rosenzweig and Schultz (1982). They found that male–female differentials in child survival rates in India can be explained by relative returns on male and female labour.[9] Later, when we come to identify some common underlying motivations of household behaviour, we will try to put these observations to work. But it is as well to note here that by 'relative rates of return' Rosenzweig and Schultz mean relative private rates of return, or in other words returns to parents. Under a dowry system parents provide a benefit to their future selves-in-law[10] when they raise a daughter, and it isn't obvious from the evidence if this benefit is typically paid for. The system harbours a notable form of externality if it isn't paid for, and we should expect investment in the object of benefit to be low when it isn't.

[9] They found predicted female employment rates to be a significant and negative determinant of the differential. The policy implications of this are rather immediate. But it isn't clear if this negative relation is universal. See Leslie (1988). On the other hand, female employment rate isn't the only indicator of the economic value of a girl in the household; see below. So the matter is an open one.

[10] I can't tell if the term 'self-in-law' is self-explanatory. My father-in-law, James Meade, invented it for the purposes of referring to my father, Amiya Dasgupta. In Bengali there is a standard term to denote the relationship. In English there seems to be none.

Whether societies do in fact harbour this kind of externality is a complex matter, and I don't know the answer. One can argue that the son-in-law's family does offer a payment—to wit, food, clothing, shelter, and protection for the daughter after her marriage. However, the daughter offers a range of services in return, so there is payment from both sides. No 'externality' is involved if the dowry equals the difference between the present discounted values of the two flows of services.

One may reasonably ask how such powerful externalities as we are referring to in the text can possibly survive in a society. In Chapter *12 we will see that they can easily persist when externalities take the form of cultural norms. These externalities are particularly difficult to dislodge in those regions where girls are not socially entitled to parental assets, and where their outside employment opportunities are severely restricted. The only significant form of employment open to poor women in these environments is as child-bearers and housekeepers. Marriage is the institution offering a scope for both roles. Unless there is a severe shortage of girls in a community, we wouldn't expect the dowry system to disintegrate once it has taken root. In any case, the protection that marriage offers women is available should the parents have a daughter to give away in marriage. It would be absurd to think that parents try to have daughters *because* there are potential selves-in-law offering protection to them.

The Rosenzweig–Schultz finding is suggestive. Parents don't gain anything directly from their (married) daughters' employment prospects in the labour market: it is their selves-in-law's households that do. However, parents do benefit indirectly when the marriage dowry is negatively related to female employment opportunities. The Rosenzweig–Schultz study can be seen as providing indirect evidence that in the Indian sub-continent such a negative relationship exists. A direct test would clinch the matter. For the moment it is a prediction of resource allocation theory.

By way of contrast to the Indian sub-continent, bridewealth is the normal pattern of marriage transaction in sub-Saharan Africa. Here we will distinguish dowry from bridewealth in terms of the direction of marriage payment.[11] Relative to the Indian sub-continent, women in sub-Saharan Africa are far more involved in agricultural production. Our framework identifies this as an explanation for the differing nature of marriage transactions in the two continents (see also Boserup, 1970; Pryor, 1977). That polygyny is widespread in sub-Saharan Africa only goes to reinforce the explanation: competition among men bids up the price of women (and men's age at marriage); it doesn't run counter to it.

---

[11] But when probed, neither dowry nor bridewealth is a pure category. Both institutions are fiendishly complex (see Goody and Tambiah, 1973). The characterization I have presented in the text is only a caricature. For our purposes this will suffice.

In what follows we will look at some more quantitative evidence of gender differentials, and in the process of trying to explain the data we will further extend the standard theory of resource allocation outlined and developed in Chapters 6–10. As in other matters pertaining to poverty, the most intensively studied country has been India, and it continues to be so. It is also the country I know best. Consequently our figures are from there.[12]

11.4   *Regional Patterns of Household Allocations: The Case of India*

Male and female life expectancy at birth in India are today pretty much on a par: about 59 years. Until recently, life expectancy at birth for females was less than for males (by about 2 years in the early 1980s), a fact almost singular to the Indian sub-continent, and which still applies to Pakistan and Bangladesh. Female mortality rates are considerably higher than those of males during infancy and childhood. (I am, of course, reasoning backwards, since life expectancy figures are based on current mortality tables.) Until recently the ratio of male to female mortality rates in India lay between 0.70 and 0.85 at ages 1–9; it remained substantially less than 1 (never greater than 0.93) through the child-bearing years; and it exceeded 1 only at about age 48 (see Mitra, 1979; G. Kumar, 1989). (These figures are for the early 1970s.) The ratio is a bit in excess of 1 in the first year of life. But being in excess of 1 in the first year is a universal phenomenon, male infants being more vulnerable than female ones (see Chapter 4). Beyond 10 years of age, the ratio of male to female mortality rates is greater than 1 in almost all countries outside the Indian sub-continent.[13]

The overall *sex ratio* (i.e. the ratio of the number of females in a population to the number of males) is a revealing summary statistic. In a justly famous study, Visaria (1971) noted that in India the sex ratio has fallen almost consistently during this century. Starting from 1901, the sex ratio at the end of each decade has been: 0.972, 0.964, 0.955, 0.950, 0.945, 0.946, 0.941, 0.930. (The 1981 census showed a slight improvement: 0.933.) This does reflect discrimination, because, except for China and

[12] But I should add that the evidence from Bangladesh, Pakistan, and Nepal are accentuated versions of the picture that emerges from north India. See in particular D'Souza and Chen (1980), Chen, Huq and D'Souza (1981), Lopez (1984), Chatterjee and Lambert (1989), and McGuire and Popkin (1989).

[13] In most countries the ratio becomes greater than 1 at an earlier age. For example, it lies between 1.2 and 1.7 from age 5 onwards in Costa Rica, which is only a middle-income country (see United Nations, 1985). In Western industrial economies female mortality rates in the aggregate (though not necessarily across classes) are lower than male rates at every stage of life. Why, beyond childhood, female mortality rates are lower in most countries is something not fully understood as yet. Possible genetic reasons have often been explored (see the survey by I. Waldron, 1985). But Johansson (1991b) shows that in Western Europe excess (adult) male mortality has been only a post-industrial phenomenon.

Table 11.2 Gender inequalities in Indian states, early 1980s

	L		SR	MR		WI	Y
	M	F		M	F		
	(1)	(2)	(3)	(4)	(5)	(6)	(7)
South							
Kerala	75	66	1.03	12	13	0.34	1761
Tamil Nadu	58	35	0.98	37	38	0.41	1827
Andhra Pradesh	39	20	0.97	39	34	0.53	1955
Karnataka	49	28	0.96	27	27	0.50	1957
Maharashtra	59	35	0.93	22	22	0.44	3032
North							
Gujarat	54	32	0.94	36	43	0.52	2795
Rajasthan	36	11	0.91	50	61	0.36	1881
Uttar Pradesh	39	14	0.89	55	76	0.19	1567
Madhya Pradesh	40	16	0.94	49	56	0.60	1636
Punjab	47	34	0.89	32	38	0.06	3691
Haryana	48	22	0.88	30	38	0.10	3147
East							
Bihar	38	14	0.94	35*	35*	0.33	1174
West Bengal	51	30	0.91	26*	26*	0.17	2231
Orissa	47	21	0.98	42	43	0.25	1339
All India			0.93			0.33	

Key
L: literacy rate, 1981 (M: male, F: female).
SR: female–male sex ratio, 1981.
MR: under-5 mortality rate per 1000, 1971.
WI: female–male agricultural wage income ratio, 1974.
Y: income per head in rupees, 1983–4.
*   rural population only

Sources: Government of India (1986); Dyson and Moore (1983, table 1); G. Kumar (1989, table 3); Bardhan (1988, table 3); M. Das Gupta (1987a, table 8).

west Asia, the sex ratio exceeds 1 in all regions, including Africa.[14] These statistics are a mute testimony to the marked difference between the levels of well-being of men and women in India, and they extend beyond the sphere of health. Indian women are also on average less educated. The literacy rate today is about 58 per cent for males and 30 per cent for females.[15]

[14] In Africa as a whole the figure is about 1.02. In Christian Africa the figure is yet higher. As we will see below, the sex ratio within India varies greatly, reaching pretty much a bottom in the north-western state of Rajasthan, where in some districts it is as low as 0.75. See also El Badri (1969) for an account of the sex ratio in the wider context of South Asia.
[15] For a vivid account of female discrimination in India, with a focus on the rural-urban traffic, see Karkaria (1989).

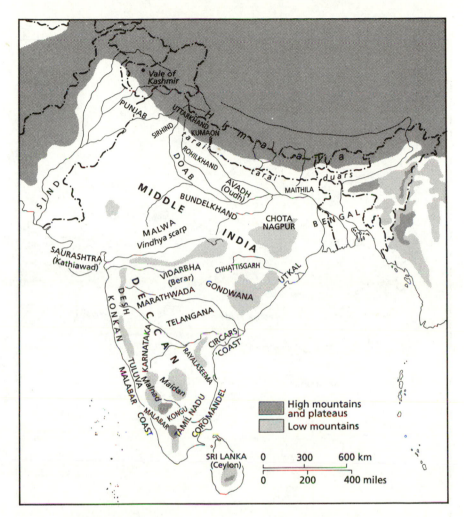

Map 1   Physical map of India

We will look at some disaggregate data from India to study regional variations in gender differences in well-being. As in Chapters 4 and 5, we will wish to study indices of health, education, and income. Now household income is impossible to unscramble between the sexes, and so we can't really talk about 'income' differences between the genders. I have been in several minds over what to use in its stead. One idea is to explore male–female inter-state differences in their access to cash income. To capture this I use the ratio of the annual wage income of a woman to that of a

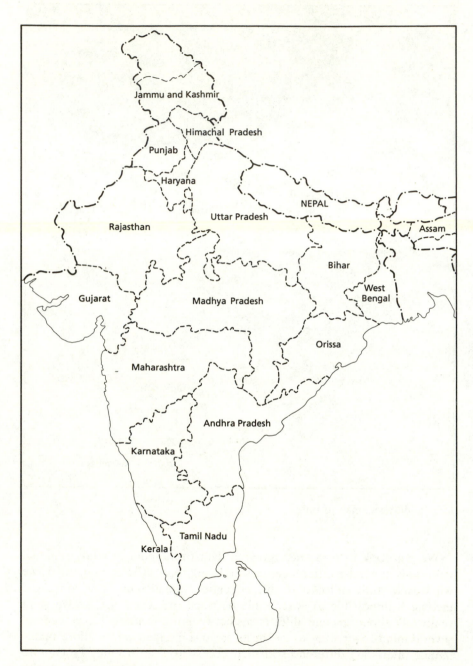

Map 2   Indian states

man.[16] One weakness with this (there are a number of other weaknesses) is that the data pertain only to households consisting of agricultural labourers. However, it is this class of households that predominates among the rural poor, so this isn't a serious matter. It transpires that women are at a disadvantage in this regard as well.

Table 11.2 presents evidence on male–female literacy rates, the sex ratio, male–female under-5 mortality rates, female–male wage income ratios, and income per head, in fourteen of the largest states of India in the early 1980s.[17] Women score less than men in every criterion used here, except for sheer numbers in the south-western state of Kerala, the only state in India where the sex ratio is above 1. The regional breakdown, into South, North, and East, follows the lead provided in the innovative work of Sopher (1980a), who demonstrated that a west–east boundary could be drawn along the line of the Vindhya scarp in the centre of India to demarcate northern and southern regions, between which gender differentials in literacy rates show a marked dissimilarity (see Maps 1 and 2). He suggested that the sex ratio displays a similar geographical pattern, something I will confirm below. It was observed by Sopher that the greatest disparity is between the north-west (i.e. the northern triangle comprising the Brahmanic land proper of antiquity) and the south, with the eastern states (Bengal and Assam) having features of both. He also suggested that for most purposes it is as well to treat the non-northern lands as one, distinguishing them as the south from the north across the Narmada River. We will on occasion do the same.

A glance at Table 11.2 shows the North/South/East breakdown to be appropriate even when we include other indicators of well-being. To demonstrate this, I have used Table 11.2 to construct state rankings on the basis of three indicators of gender differentials: the sex ratio (SR), male–female differentials in literacy rates (LD), and gender disparities in annual wage income (WI).[18] These rankings are provided in the second, third, and fifth columns of Table 11.3. The ranking in terms of the sex ratio (the larger the sex ratio, the better) is straightforward and can be read off

---

[16] The annual wage income per male (or female) is the product of the estimated number of days worked in wage employment and the estimated average daily wage earned by the number of wage-earners, divided by the number of males (females) belonging to the agricultural labour household. I am grateful to Pranab Bardhan for suggesting that I use this index as a proxy for what I am after. The data on this presented in Table 11.2 are taken from Bardhan (1988, Table 3). The original source is Government of India (1986).

[17] Of the large states, only Assam and Jammu-Kashmir are missing from the table. Figs. for the female–male wage income ratio are for 1974–5. The definition of under-5 mortality rate adopted in Table 11.2 is different from the one in use by UNICEF (see Ch. 4). Here, the female (male) under-5 mortality rate has been estimated per 1000 female (male) children under 5, and not per 1000 live births.

[18] Since gender-based under-5 mortality rates are closely related to the sex ratios, I have not used them as a basis for ranking the states.

Table 11.3   Rankings of Indian states in terms of gender inequalities[a]

	Y	SR	LD		WI	A	
	(1)	(2)	(3)	(4)	(5)	(6)	(7)
South							
Kerala	10	1	1	(0.13)	8	8	(16)
Tamil Nadu	9	2	3	(0.49)	6	1	(38)
Andhra Pradesh	7	4	7	(0.63)	2	2	(31)
Karnataka	6	5	6	(0.54)	4	5	(22)
Maharashtra	3	9	8	(0.65)	5	6	(21)
North							
Gujarat	4	6	4	(0.51)	3	8	(16)
Rajasthan	8	10	14	(1.78)	7	14	(6)
Uttar Pradesh	12	12	12	(0.92)	11	11	(10)
Madhya Pradesh	11	6	11	(0.85)	1	8	(16)
Punjab	1	12	2	(0.42)	14	13	(7)
Haryana	2	14	9	(0.74)	13	12	(8)
East							
Bihar	14	6	12	(0.92)	9	7	(18)
West Bengal	5	10	4	(0.51)	12	3	(30)
Orissa	13	2	10	(0.76)	10	4	(23)

[a] 1 denotes highest and 14 the lowest.

Key
Y: income per head
SR: sex ratio
LD: index of gender inequality in literacy: difference in male–female literacy rate divided by average literacy rate. (Figs. given within parentheses.)
WI: female–male agricultural wage income ratio
A: percentages of rural households who are asset-poor (i.e. households owning less than Rs1000 in mid-1971). (Figs. given within parentheses.) *Source*: Bardhan, 1988.

directly from Table 11.2. It displays the north–south-east divide almost perfectly: 4 of the top 5 performers are southern states, while 4 of the bottom 5 performers are in the north.

Comparing gender differences in literacy is more delicate, since it won't do to take the ratio of literacy rates. The index used in Table 11.3 is the difference between male and female literacy rates divided by the average literacy rate. (The figures are provided in parentheses in the fourth column.) Sopher's general thesis is supported by this, but not as sharply. All 5 southern states are among the top 8 performers, while 4 of the 6 northern states are among the bottom 6.[19]

[19] I am using the ratio of the range to the mean as our index of disparity. The one employed by Sopher (1980a) is different. Designating by L_m and L_f the proportions of males and

The distribution of the female–male wage income ratio also supports Sopher's thesis, but less decisively: 4 of the top 6 states are in the south, while 3 of the worst 5 states on this count are in the north.

The first column in Table 11.3 presents state rankings on the basis of income per head. It is clear that gender differentials can't really be explained by per capita income. For example, the two richest states in India, the northern states of Punjab and Haryana, have the two worst figures for the sex ratio, whereas the southern state of Kerala, whose income per head is less than the national average, is an outlier, and resembles Sri Lanka in many respects, including its high literacy rate. (We will come to discuss the last two columns of Table 11.3 presently.)

How do we account for these regional differences in the way men and women are treated from their earliest years? Two broad explanations suggest themselves, and they both identify senses in which a daughter's usefulness to a household falls short of a son's. (There is a third, which relates to cultural and religious values, and we will touch upon it at the end.) The first (see Bardhan, 1974, for the original exploration) notes that female agricultural labour is less used in the north-western wheat growing areas than in the eastern and southern rice growing regions. Current technological practices in the production of rice require a good deal of labour in post-harvest operations, much more so than for wheat. Many of these operations can currently be undertaken at home, which is what makes them suitable for women. Admittedly, even within these broad agricultural zones there are differences. Female labour participation is higher in the high-productivity irrigated paddy fields of some of the southern states than in the rain-fed lower-productivity paddy fields of the eastern states. Moreover, female participation rates are lower in the high-productivity, irrigated wheatfields of Haryana and the Punjab than in the low-productivity fields in the coarse-grained wheatfields of Maharashtra.[20] More recently, differences in labour participation rates have intensified in the north-west with the introduction of high-yielding varieties of wheat, as this has brought in its wake increased mechanization of farmwork, which has typically displaced female labour more than male labour.

There are counter-examples to the thesis in the way it has been stated; in particular, the use of female participation rates as a proxy for the valuation of women within the household. The point can be made that

females, respectively, who are literate, and by $P_m = L_m/(1 - L_m)$ and $p_f = L_f(1 - L_f)$, Sopher's 'disparity index' is $\log(p_m/p_f)$.

[20] See P. K. Bardhan (1974, 1984a, 1988), Rosenzweig and Schultz (1982), K. Bardhan (1985), G. Sen and Sen (1985), G. Sen (1987), M. A. Chen (1989), and G. Kumar (1989), for accounts of varying refinements along this line. I should add that, in contrast to the labour market participation rate defined in Sec. 9.4, by 'female participation rate' I mean here the proportion of all women who are usually in the labour force.

West Bengal has low female participation rates as compared with the drylands of Rajasthan (where women are also much involved as manual labourers in construction sites). As we have observed in Table 11.2, gender inequalities are far greater in Rajasthan. But no broad-stroke thesis as I am sketching here can fit all details. Furthermore, estimates of labour participation rates miss a great deal of what the concept aims to capture; as an index of the value of women as wage-earners, they can be misleading. In any event, what we have described is only one prong of what must surely be a multi-pronged reason for regional gender differences in well-being.

The second explanation traces differences between the north and south in the valuation of girls relative to boys within the household to differences in property rights in land, and to related differences in marriage trans-actions. In parts of the south (most especially in parts of Kerala), inheritance is along matrilineal lines. To be sure, there are a great number of sub-regional variations, and inheritance of land is most often patrilineal in the south as well. Nevertheless, historically there may well have been 'demonstration effects' at work through imitation, with the standard practice of one group displacing that of another following even an accidental disturbance. (See Morgan, 1963; David, 1987, and Chapter *12 for such mechanisms.) In contrast, the north is pretty uniformly patrilineal, and marriages are typically characterized by village and clan exogamy. Brides move away from their homes at marriage and become a part of the groom's family. Residence is thus patrilocal.[21] Endogamy is more common in the south, and male ties with their relatives by marriage are stronger.

In a wide-ranging essay on the spatial structure of marriage in India, Libbee (1980) showed that high endogamy rates are correlated with small marriage distances, and low endogamy rates with large marriage distances. He argued that women in the south are not as restricted in their movements and associations as women in the north: large proportions of marriages confined to women's natal villages are positively associated with the economic position of women in society. He speculated that, when a known member of an extended family network is taken as a bride, her treatment is different from that accorded a stranger coming into a totally new situation: it is typically better. He argued that as compared with the south there is neglect of daughters relative to sons in the north because in the north it is the sons who remain at home to support their parents in old age, while daughters leave home on marriage and cease to be members of the natal household.[22]

---

[21] There are a number of exceptions, of course, such as in the foothills of the Himalayas, where high search and transport costs make universal exogamy impractical. Village endogamy is practised even where affinal and consanguineal ties are taken to be mutually exclusive. See Berreman (1962).

[22] See also Dyson and Moore (1983), who pursue this line of reasoning. A preference for sons on account of the security they provide in old age has been explored by Cain (1978, 1982, 1984), Cain, Khanam and Nahar (1979), and Mason and Taj (1987). See Ch. 12.

Taken as a whole, this second explanation is blunted somewhat for assetless households. It is true that the daughter leaves home even from assetless north Indian households. On the other hand, the property system is irrelevant for assetless parents, since there *is* no property to bequeath. So one may ask whether states in which a large proportion of households are assetless are also the ones where gender differentials are low. The last column of Table 11.3 gives the percentage of rural households who have little or no assets (less than or equal to Rs1000 in mid-1971). The figures are given in parentheses. The penultimate column provides the ranking of states on this basis: the greater the proportion of asset-poor households, the higher the rank. It will be observed that this ranking also breaks down roughly into a north–south divide: four of the six states with the highest percentage of asset-poor rural households are in the south, and the four states with the lowest percentage of asset-poor rural households are in the north.

These are two broad explanations of the north–south divide. There is, finally, an explanation based on cultural practices. In this context the influence of Brahmanic culture in north India has been invoked to explain gender differentials in literacy. (See also Debysingh, 1980, for a study of the geographical dispersion of poultry-keeping and vegetarianism in India.) Cross-sectional data at the district level show male literacy to decline with increases in the proportion of Muslims in a population, and the disparity between the sexes to grow larger with increases in the proportion of Brahmans in a population (see Sopher, 1980a: 168). Quantitative evidence suggests that regional differences in women's place in the household and in society at large are an aspect of gender differences in Hindu society; they aren't so much a Muslim legacy.[23] Nor have the liberating influence of Christianity and international commerce on the southern, coastal regions of the sub-continent (most especially Kerala, Goa, and the southern tip of India) gone unnoted. Moreover, the cult of male honour, what is elsewhere called *machismo*, is prevalent in the north-west, most especially in the deserts of Rajasthan, and among the Sikhs of the Punjab. That there is a dark side to any such conception has been much noted in literature. (The writings of Gabriel García Márquez are especially illuminating.) The idea that men should be protectors (or trustees) of women may sound grand, but it doesn't do much for female autonomy in the best of circumstances; it can in the worst of circumstances be devastating.

[23] See Visaria (1971) and Sopher (1980b). See also Bhattacharji (1991) for an account of gender inequalities in ancient India. Among other things, she notes that the *Brahmanas* were explicit that a son is a blessing and a girl a curse. At a broader level, Boserup (1965, 1970, 1976, 1985) has adduced the use of the plough (as against the hoe in sub-Saharan Africa) in agriculture as a force that has helped accentuate gender differentials.

11.5 *Marriage and Inheritance in India*

None of this really explains why marriage patterns assume the forms they do in the Indian sub-continent, or why the related matter of inheritance should be so pronounced in the direction of patrilineality. One promising line of inquiry is to see at least some of the established practices as being directed by the need to reduce household risk. First, patrilocal residence and patrilineality together enable men to exploit the knowledge they have acquired since their early years as cultivators, of the idiosyncrasies of the land they cultivate. (Recall that a good deal of this knowledge is held only tacitly.)[24] Second, we may presume that, where information channels are otherwise restricted, kinship networks offer an alternative to credit agencies as a source of income in times of stress (Chapter 9). The thought here is that within a kinship (e.g. among selves-in-law) there are greater grounds for trust (e.g. because the patriarch's daughter resides with his self-in-law), and so moral hazard and adverse selection problems are typically less than they are outside it. Now, help from a kin is usually regarded as a transfer, not a loan. Nevertheless, inasmuch as reciprocity is the norm, such transfers are part of an implicit exchange over time and contingencies. So they do have the characteristics of credit. We explored this in Chapter 8.

Third, we would expect that in stationary agricultural environments spatial covariance in income is a general feature. By this I mean that the larger is the distance between any two villages, the smaller is the correlation coefficient between their incomes. These observations imply that village and clan (or, in the Hindu context, *gotra*) exogamy together offer a way of widening the sources of income in times of stress. So we should ask if village exogamy is pronounced in regions where economic fortunes among neighbouring households are particularly correlated, as they would be in the drylands. In the one study on this with which I am familiar (Rosenzweig and Stark, 1989), the evidence is consistent with this line of reasoning. Among households of six ICRISAT villages (see Chapter 9) whose longitudinal data were studied, rural households facing greater fluctuations in income tended to form marriage alliances in villages located at greater distances.

Quantitatively, transfers from relatives do not appear to be as important as credit from village money-lenders and loan institutions (see Caldwell, Reddy and Caldwell 1986; Rosenzweig, 1988a, b; Walker and Ryan, 1990). But the bulk of income transfers received by households are from relatives outside their villages, the most important source being the family of the patriarch's wife, more so than offspring living and earning in towns.

---

[24] Steward (1955) has used this argument for communities that hunt for non-migratory, but scattered game. Rosenzweig and Wolpin (1985) have also used this argument for explaining why there are so few land sales in India (see Ch. 9).

That rural–urban migration in India is small relative to inter-village migration was revealed in the 1981 Population Census of India. Net migration from rural to urban areas for reasons of employment amounted only to 1.6 per cent of the 1971 rural population. However, the census also revealed 30 per cent of India's population to be residing in places not of their birth; and, most strikingly, approximately 80 per cent of these 'migrants' were women, who attributed their move to marriage.[25]

The economic dependence of women on men in India reflects itself most sharply in the plight of widows from poor households who have no surviving sons. Patrilocal residence and patrilineal inheritance together act as a potent force. Muslims enjoy a different set of marriage and inheritance laws from the rest of the community. Despite the enactment of the Succession Bill of 1956, Hindu widows in India in practice often do not inherit their husband's property. If sons are young, widows are seen by the community as trustees of the estate. When they have no surviving sons, their deceased husbands' families can be relied upon to usurp the property. This plight is faced also within the Muslim populations, despite their inheritance laws which allow a daughter one-half the share received by a son: in practice women receive less, and in any case, when she does inherit it her husband can (and usually does) regard it as his own. In Bangladesh, where the *purdah* system (female exclusion) is practised vigorously, the economic dependence of women on men shows itself in sharp relief.

All this puts widows in a vulnerable position, forcing them routinely into destitution.[26] In the early 1980s there were over 25 million widows in India, amounting to some 8 per cent of the female population. Were we to ignore leviratic unions (which is more common in north India than in the south, and which is often forced upon widows), widow remarriage is rare among caste Hindus. Age-specific survival chances among widows are low relative to non-widows, and they are lower in the north and north-west of India than in the South. The north-south divide over gender matters thus manifests itself in the fate of widows in a seemingly peculiar manner: the ratio of widows to the female population in the north is lower than in the south.

The arguments I have offered about variations in India are arguments writ large. They emerge from the broad brush. There are any number of local variations and district oddities which simply don't mesh with all this.

---

[25] On this see Skeldon (1986). Das Gupta (1987b) has argued that it is because of the prevalence of intra-village support systems in north India that the magnitude of rural–urban migration has typically been low. But hers are studies of two villages and three shanty towns, at a point in time. There is no cross-sectional test to check if the argument should be rejected.

[26] The plight of widows in India has been much written about in the Indian press in recent years. See especially the fortnightly magazine, *India Today*. Of a growing academic literature, see Visaria and Visaria (1985), Sahayam (1988), and Dreze (1990).

But discrepancies at the village and even district level are not counter-examples. We have been looking at statistical relationships at the state level, what we may call central tendencies. Chance events in the past will have much to do with local variations in the cultural mores. Within any culture, resource allocation mechanisms are responsive to relative prices. In the long run they are even more responsive, as cultural values themselves are put at greater and greater strain with increasing changes in resource costs. We are currently witnessing changing mores throughout the world, as relative prices alter in conjunction with technological change, population growth, the widening of markets, and changes in the information base. The strains on traditional support systems is something we have commented upon earlier. They arise from the powerful forces of cultural externalities. Nevertheless, resource allocations within poor households are responsive to the relative costs of basic needs. As we have seen, they depend also on the values household members attach to one another's *usefulness*. Analytical accounts of such matters need to incorporate these features. Of course, none of this should come as a surprise. Poor people in poor countries have to work at the margin because they live at the margin. They can't afford to be flippant in their computations; there is no slack for them to enjoy. The study of gender differentials in the Indian sub-continent is still in its early stages. For the moment we are left with knowledge of such differentials in well-being, and a few observations about what might account for their differing presence across regions—not much more.

11.6 *Bargaining Theory as a Framework for Household Choice*

We have so far speculated on the forces affecting household decisions, those that bear on gender inequalities among adults, and in food and health-care allocations among children. But, as there is usually more than one parent in a household, we need to know how decisions are reached. Fortunately, I will lose nothing qualitatively in this and the following chapter by not specifying the household model in any sharp detail. I want to avoid doing the latter in any case. These are early days yet in our understanding of the exact springs of household behaviour, even in poor countries. So it is better to squeeze as much out of a partially unspecified model than to start with a precise model and work through its implications.[27] In any event, this is how I will proceed.

The current debate on how best to model the household isn't about the reasonableness of viewing it as an 'optimizing agent'. At a technical level all current constructs of the household are optimization models. Where

---

[27] Singh, Squire and Strauss (1986b) pursue this route to good effect.

they differ is this: one class of models sees some household agent consciously optimizing, for example by taking reasonable account of the claims of all household members (Gary Becker's 'altruistic dictator': see Becker, 1960, 1965, 1981; Sen, 1966; Mirrlees, 1972; Stiglitz, 1976; Nerlove, Razin and Sadka, 1987a, b; Becker and Barro, 1988; Cigno, 1991; Lee and Miller, 1991), while another interprets household choice in terms of an 'as if' optimization (as in the theory of bargaining invoked by Manser and Brown, 1980; McElroy and Horney, 1981; Sundstrom and David, 1988; Haddad and Kanbur, 1989; Cremer and Pestieau, 1991). Given this commonality, all the formal apparatus of optimization theory can be brought to bear on analyses of household decisions, for example on household demands and supplies of goods and services at various prices and income levels. However, the normative significance of such decisions depends on the basis upon which choices are actually arrived at. In what follows, we will develop an account of household choice by appealing to the elements of the theory of games and will see where they lead us. We will then compare the implications of this viewpoint with those of the perspective that sees household choice as being arrived at from welfare, or well-being, maximization. Our analysis will be exploratory. These are early days in our understanding of household behaviour. Nevertheless, we will see that our framework accommodates a number of observed features within poor households in poor countries.

We may to begin with think of the household as comprising two members who may have concern for each other, but whose motivations aren't necessarily the same. As we are studying household decisions, we can ignore children from our analysis. Parents will be taken to act on their behalf, to a greater or lesser extent, and for better or worse. As household resources are inevitably scarce, well-being interests can never be entirely congruent. However, it is the members' utilities with which we are concerned here; and the pair's utility functions over allocations of goods, services, and responsibilities could in principle be the same. When they are, the household can be regarded as a *team*, in the sense of Marschak and Radner (1972). What then remains to be analysed is the co-ordination of their tasks when the two know different things.

At the other extreme is a household composed of two people with totally opposed orderings over allocations. That they remain together should be a cause for concern, but we may be unable to do anything about it. If they are forced to stay together, the couple is involved in something akin to a zero-sum game. There is no scope for co-operation here.

Neither model is of any relevance. Interest lies rather in those situations where both parties perceive that they add something by acting together (there are gains in forming a household and co-operating), where the pair can break up should either party be placed under undue stress (there is an *exit option* for each party), and where the parties' utility functions aren't the same. This is not to say that an individual's ranking of household allocations may not reflect interpersonal comparisons of well-being, interest, or advantage. Mutual care and concern will not be absent, but we would expect identification to be partial. This is the most common type of situation analysed in the theory of games, and I will appeal to the two-person version of this theory, which is usually called *bargaining theory*.

By a *co-operative infrastructure* I will mean a set of institutions, or mechanisms (e.g. the village head, the feudal lord, the often-credible threat of social, personal, or self, sanctions), which ensures that agreements are binding (see Binmore and Dasgupta, 1987). A good deal of pre-play activity forms a part of what we mean by a co-operative infrastructure. It should not be thought that co-operative solutions have necessarily much to commend them (the distribution of well-being under co-operation could be awful); nor should it be thought that co-operative infrastructures are necessarily benign. Credible threats (e.g. periodic physical assault) by one party are a way of getting the other party to do his bidding, and such mechanisms are included in the notion of a cooperative infrastructure.[28] Bargaining theory—and, by implication, models of the household based on bargaining theory—assumes that there is a co-operative infrastructure in the background. At the opposite extreme of games backed by a co-operative infrastructure are non-cooperative games, where parties have no occasion even for pre-play communication. In Section 8.7 we studied an intergenerational resource allocation game which was capable of sustaining co-operative outcomes despite an absence of a co-operative infrastructure.

We will assume that household members bargain (or negotiate) over allocations of goods, services, tasks, and responsibilities. Both their real interests and their perceived interests lie in such allocations, as do their conceptions of desert or legitimacy—for example, those that are related to the perceived productive contributions of each party to family income. The idea of household members bargaining is to be seen here as something of a metaphor, in that negotiation procedures are unlikely to be explicit, unlike bargaining between managements and unions. This provides us with all the reasons why we should be hesitant in modelling the 'negotiation process', and we will see below (and in Chapter *11) how to avoid this. As before, we define a household member's utility function as a numerical representation of the ordering over allocations on the basis of which he or

---

[28] The term 'co-operative infrastructure' is therefore something of a misnomer here, but I wish to refrain from using any new term. To do so would be to give it the aura of a new theory, whereas what I shall be doing is to use a theory which has been much studied in the game-theoretic literature.

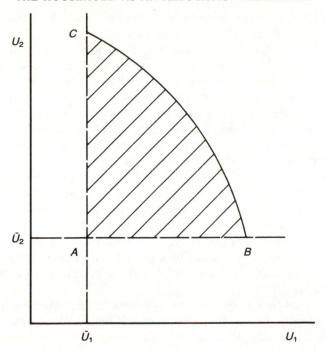

Fig. 11.1   Household negotiation set

she 'bargains'. It is then an obvious move to work on the space of utilities, even though the bargaining is over the allocation of resources and tasks.

Our interest to begin with lies in those situations where there are feasible allocations that are higher in both parties' rankings than the allocation implied by their exit options. It will simplify the exposition if we assume that utility functions of both parties are cardinal. So we do this, and we denote them by U_1 and U_2. These are to be interpreted as 'expected utilities' (see Section 8.2).[29] Furthermore, we let $(\bar{U}_1, \bar{U}_2)$ denote the utility pair for the couple when either party exercises the exit option.[30] In what follows, I will identify $(\bar{U}_1, \bar{U}_2)$ with what is known as the *status quo point* (or *threat point*) in bargaining theory. Given the context in which the theory is being used, I shall refer to $(\bar{U}_1, \bar{U}_2)$ as the *alienation point*.

---

[29] But see Rubinstein, Safra and Thomson (1992) for an extension of the Nash bargaining theory (see below) to circumstances where the parties do not maximize their expected utilities.

[30] If one party exercises his exit option, the other party has to as well. What we are calling the exit option is referred to as the *outside option* in strategic theories of bargaining. See Shaked and Sutton (1984) and Sutton (1986), who show that in certain classes of games the status-quo point differs from the pair of utilities that is attained when either party exercises the exit option.

Figure 11.1 describes the set of feasible utility pairs for a given pair of cardinalizations of the utility functions. (See Chapter *11 for details.) Our interest lies in the shaded area ABC with the origin at the point $A = (\bar{U}_1, \bar{U}_2)$. We will call this the *negotiation set*. As the figure shows, there are gains to be had from co-operation. If the negotiation set is common knowledge among the two parties (see Section 3.4), then in terms of their motivations it isn't collectively rational for them to agree on a point inside the set: further gains from co-operation would be possible by moving further north-east. Points on the boundary are different, however. Choice among these points involves a tussle between the two. The boundary consists of the Pareto-efficient points of the negotiation set. We assume that randomizations of strategies are allowed, so that the negotiation set is convex. This is a technical but vital requirement, and I make it because at this stage of development I can't do without it if we are to have an underlying theory of household decisions which we can debate, discuss, and test.[31] We denote the parties by k $(k = 1, 2)$. Simple though it is, the structure I have outlined allows us to address a number of issues much discussed in recent years.

Now it cannot be emphasized strongly enough that the negotiation set is influenced by tradition, by social norms of behaviour, by the extent of mutual affection and loyalty, and by work opportunities. In the Indian sub-continent, for example, single women are economically more vulnerable than men. We noted earlier that they usually have no access to credit, they usually don't inherit any land, and in all regions employment opportunities and wages are far less than those for men. Women are invariably responsible for their children, and, in addition, they are more subject to physical assault. For them the exit option is hardly an option. Moreover, since a person's utility function reflects the ordering on the basis of which he or she chooses, there is no presumption that points inside the negotiation set reflect greater well-being for either party than the alienation point. Armed with this formulation, we can immediately explain one observed phenomenon in the Indian sub-continent: men's desertion of their families during periods when households face acute food and employment scarcity.[32]

Under the circumstances of a famine, both outside opportunities and household production possibilities open to a poor household are extremely

---

[31] We will see subsequently (Ch. 15) that randomization of food and work allocations is often a desirable feature of household decision-making procedures. It is an essential ingredient of *fair* procedures. See Ch. 2.

[32] See Gangrade and Dhadda (1973), Alamgir (1980), and Greenough (1982). See also Vaughan (1987) for the same observation in the context of the 1949 famine in Malawi. And see B. Agarwal (1989) for further references. In Fig. 11.1 I have drawn the outer boundary of the shaded area (what is somewhat forbiddingly called the set of individually rational, Pareto-efficient utility pairs) to be downward-sloping throughout. We don't need to assume this, but it eases the exposition.

limited. This means that the afflicted household faces a shrunken negotiation set. It also typically means that the exit options decline in utility value. Suppose now that circumstances are so extreme that there is no feasible household allocation higher in the male's ranking than his (new) exit option. (We are to imagine his exit option as involving departure for the city in search of a job and abandoning his family, or throwing out his wife, or whatever.) This means that the negotiation set has shrunk to nothing. Now this may be so even when there are feasible household allocations that are higher in the female's ranking than her (new) exit option. In this situation the woman won't make the move and depart, but the man will. Of course, at the end of the day she too will be forced to face her exit option. But this is because she has been abandoned, or has been thrown out. It isn't because she has willed it.

It may be thought that I have used a huge intellectual apparatus to arrive at what could be seen as a trite explanation of a not-uncommon phenomenon during famines, that of men's desertion of their families. The explanation seems almost to amount to a description. But a tightly woven apparatus is needed if we are to make any progress in what is a profoundly complex matter, the understanding of household decisions. There are no short-cuts to be had in this, and it is treacherous to try one. Here is an example of how easy it is to get things wrong unless one is careful.

In an essay on social security and the family in rural India, B. Agarwal (1990: 344) writes: 'A crisis which leads to a total collapse of, or even a large decline in, the wife's fall-back position (as could happen, for instance, during a famine) while that of the husband sustains in relative terms, could weaken her bargaining power even to a point where non-co-operation is found more beneficial by the man than cooperation, creating a tendency towards the disintegration of families, and the abandonment of spouses.'

This is odd. You (a male) and your spouse form a household. Other things remaining the same, your spouse's exit option (i.e. fall-back position) weakens relative to what it was before. How can this be an inducement for you to leave the co-operative arrangement? Quite the contrary: the bargaining situation has improved for you. If you were involved in co-operation before, you would most certainly remain and try to reap some additional benefits from the household arrangement.

The point then is this. The man deserts his wife during a famine not because *her* fall-back position weakens. (It typically does, but that isn't the point.) He deserts her because *his* outside option in these circumstances emerges higher in his ranking than any feasible allocation within the household. It is the shrinking of the shaded area in Fig. 11.1, and not a reduction in the wife's exit option, that makes the man abandon his wife in times of economic crises.

11.7 *The Nash Programme: A Formalization*

But these are extreme circumstances. We need to put the construct to work in situations where the couple remains as a unit. What then can we say about 'negotiated' outcomes?

In a remarkable series of articles, the mathematician John Nash provided an answer to this for one class of circumstances. Perhaps more importantly, he also proposed a programme of research for attacking the problem under a wide class of settings (see Nash, 1950, 1951, 1953), and the Nash programme after a long slumber has recently become one of the most productive enterprises of social science research.

Nash's approach is stictly game-theoretic, and he was careful to say so. He was concerned with most effective plays by rational strategists having well-defined goals. These goals he left unspecified: they were data for the theory, not matters to be deliberated over. He used the term 'satisfaction' as a metaphor to describe individual 'utility', but the metaphor plays no role in the theory. It is utility in the sense I have repeatedly defined it here that he makes use of. His is *not* a normative theory (of justice, or overall goodness, or fairness, or whatever), and he never claimed it to be so. The purpose of the analysis is to see what points in the negotiation set are possible outcomes of negotiation.[33]

This suggests that the negotiation process needs to be modelled explicitly. Solutions to the bargaining problem (there may be more than one solution even if the negotiation process is specified) are then non-cooperative (Nash) equilibrium points of this larger negotiation game. In a negotiation game a strategy is a statement of how to conduct the negotiations under all possible eventualities, and how finally to choose a strategy (e.g. proposing a household allocation) on the course the negotiations took. Since the co-operative infrastructure is specified for the model, non-cooperative equilibria of the negotiation game are 'co-operative' outcomes of the bargaining problem. As an example, consider a situation where one party in the household has the capability of moving first with a pre-emptive, self-binding commitment (e.g. a convincing 'I shall desert you if you don't agree to this allocation'). In this case he will do so (unless his code prohibits him from using this kind of strategy) and his spouse will then be left with a 'take it or leave it' situation. Negotiation games are therefore to be thought of as strategic forms of bargaining games.

---

[33] See also Harsanyi (1977b), who perhaps more than any one else was for a long while involved in the development of the Nash programme; and see Binmore and Dasgupta (1986, 1987). I emphasize the motivation behind the programme only because it has been much misunderstood. (See Luce and Raiffa, 1957, for an early misreading.) For example, A. Sen (1987: 22), in an influential recent essay, says: 'Nash had seen his solution as a normative one . . .' And he shows why it won't do as a basis for justice. My point is not one of historical exegesis. It is that in misinterpreting Nash's articles one does violence to a serious research programme currently under way in co-operative game theory. See below in the text.

The problem is that, in having always to specify the negotiation game before thinking of solutions to bargaining problems, one is embarking on a formidable taxonomy. As it also happens, except in the simplest of negotiation games, computing non-cooperative equilibria is very hard. Furthermore, it is foolhardy to try to formalize as complex a negotiation process as is involved in a household.[34] A parallel research strategy is therefore to avoid modelling the negotiation process, and to consign the details of the process to intelligent speculation and informed guesswork. In practical terms this means choosing an appropriate solution concept, such as the core, or the Nash bargaining solution, or the Kalai–Smorodinsky solution (see below, and Chapter *11), and to see them as outcomes of non-cooperative negotiation games whose negotiation procedures haven't been formalized.[35]

This parallel route often consists of straightforward axiomatization. The idea is to propose properties that non-cooperative equilibrium outcomes of the underlying 'negotiation game' can be expected to satisfy, and then to check which points in the negotiation set satisfy them. Nash illustrated this overall approach both by proposing a set of axioms the solution of a particular class of bargaining problems could be expected to have (what is now called the *Nash bargaining solution*), and by formalizing a class of simple negotiation games whose non-cooperative equilibria approximate this solution (see Nash, 1953). We will be interested in the axiomatic approach here, and in Chapter *11 we will study Nash's axioms and their extensions. For the moment, we need only to have a description of the outcome that is implied by his axioms.

Consider that point on the negotiation set at which the expression $(U_1 - \bar{U}_1)(U_2 - \bar{U}_2)$ is maximized. Call it $(\hat{U}_1, \hat{U}_2)$. Taken together, the axioms that Nash (1950) proposed imply that $(\hat{U}_1, \hat{U}_2)$ is the unique solution to the underlying bargaining problem. This is the Nash bargaining solution (Fig. 11.2).

It will be noticed that an increase in $\bar{U}_k$ increases $\hat{U}_k$. This is congenial to intuition, and it is not at variance with broad observations. Suppose that the exit option of a member of the household were to improve, because of, say, the acquisition of human capital, or credit, or physical capital, or, perhaps, even a new job opportunity arising from, say, a cash-for-work programme (see Chapter 17). This is to increase her autonomy. It would

---

[34] I should add that there is no reason to think that Nash had the household in mind when defining the bargaining problem. His solution (see Ch. *11) on the face of it may have no bearing on household decisions.

[35] See Binmore and Dasgupta (1987) for a collection of essays exploring the Nash programme. Stahl (1972), Harsanyi (1977b), Rubinstein (1982), and Binmore (1987) are among the key modern contributions to this line of research.

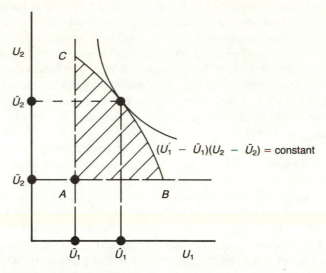

Fig. 11.2 Nash bargaining solution

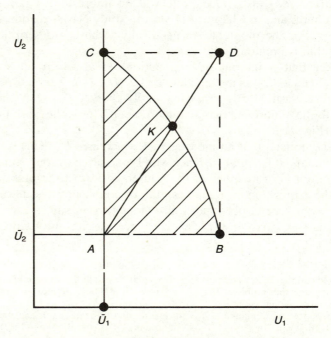

Fig. 11.3 Kalai–Smorodinsky bargaining solution

be odd if this were not to place her in a better bargaining position, enabling her to improve her lot.

Nash's axioms have been much discussed, and one of them ('the independence of irrelevant alternatives': see Chapter *11) has proved controversial (see e.g. Luce and Raiffa, 1957; Roth, 1979.[36]) So one looks for alternatives. An alternative which on the face of it seems more natural for solutions to household bargaining problems is the one proposed by Kalai and Smorodinsky (1975). In Chapter *11 we will study the axiom system that yields the *Kalai–Smorodinsky solution*. Here I will merely describe it.

We first construct the rectangle which has the alienation point at one corner, and the points on the negotiation set that award maximum utilities to the two individuals as two other corners (the rectangle *ABDC* in Fig. 11.3). The Kalai–Smorodinsky solution is the intersection of the south-west–north-east diagonal of this rectangle and the outer boundary of the negotiation set (the point *K* in Fig. 11.3).

The Kalai–Smorodinsky solution, like the Nash solution, is responsive to changes in the alienation point. If, to take an example, other things were to remain the same and the woman's utility level at the alienation point were to increase, the Kalai-Smorodinsky solution would award the woman more than she had received previously. Where the Kalai-Smorodinsky formulation looks more credible than Nash's is in the axioms themselves, which in the context of households seem intuitively more plausible. In Chapter *11, when we come to study the two sets of axioms, we will see that, despite this, it will prove very difficult to discriminate between the two solutions on the basis of empirical observations. But analytically they are quite different. They are driven by different considerations.

11.8 *Bargaining vs. Well-Being Maximization within the Household*

It is also possible to analyse household allocations by assuming that the household is governed by optimization on the part of one member (the 'dictator' in an autocratic household, or the 'first mover' with a take-it-or-leave-it opportunity in a negotiated household). This doesn't commit us to saying that the maximizer is maximizing household well-being. Of course, the maximizer may well have the habit of taking each member's well-being into account, but even in this case he may not award defendable weights to them. The relative weights upon which he bases his decisions

[36] One of the axioms, that the outcome of two-person negotiations must inevitably be Pareto-efficient, has been much less frequently questioned, but it is suspect. See Fernandez and Glazer (1991) for a negotiation game possessing multiple non-cooperative equilibria, some of which are Pareto-inefficient.

will typically depend upon how much voice the various members are capable of exercising, what their outside opportunities are, and what their contributions are perceived to be. They will also depend upon the extent of mutual care, concern, and affection, and many other things besides. Allocations in such hypothetical households would be qualitatively the same as in households where allocations are arrived at through more elaborate bargaining.

I have found it natural to think of household allocations as solutions of bargaining games, and not as allocations that maximize household well-being or utility. A great deal of empirical work on the household, however, assumes the latter. Why is this? The reason is pure convenience. We can arrive at solutions of complicated goal-maximizing problems in a way we can't of even relatively simple bargaining problems. Decision theory is much simpler than game theory. In any event, often it doesn't matter which modelling route we follow; the qualitative results are much the same, and the data are often too coarse to discriminate between.

Consider as an example the profoundly disturbing phenomenon of unequal food and health-care allocation in poverty-stricken households which we studied earlier in this chapter. One doesn't need bargaining theory to account for it. The phenomenon would occur in a household even if allocations were determined on the basis of aggregate well-being. In extreme situations, sharing equally (in adult equivalent scales) would place the entire household at risk of extinction, whereas unequal sharing might allow a few to survive and carry on. Even in less extreme circumstances, unequal sharing would be an appropriate policy, because different oocupations require different nutrition-intakes if a breakdown in health is to be avoided (see Pitt, Rosenzweig and Hassan, 1990). Unequal sharing is necessary in a poor household because of the fixed costs involved in the transformation of calorie-intake into work output.[37]

Seen in this light, the dilemma is akin to the well-known life-boat problem (see Chapter 2), where there are two on the life-boat with food adequate for only one. What should the parties do? Flipping a fair coin to decide who should live might seem the right procedure. The solution displays *ex ante* equality in treatment, but severe inequality *ex post*. What if one of the parties is hardier than the other, and neither's survival can be ensured by the ration? Maximizing expected aggregate welfare would have all of the ration going to the hardier person, whereas fairness would suggest flipping a coin. Both procedures prescribe *ex post* inequality.

This is a textbook example. In life, as we read about it and see it on

---

[37] See Chs. 1 and 14. See also Mirrlees (1975), Stiglitz (1976), and Dasgupta (1988e, 1991c). This fixed cost yields unequal shares as optimal only when the household is poor, not when it is well-endowed in food. See Ch. *16.

television, such tragic choices are routinely faced by relief workers in times of famines. Food aid is limited and not all can be helped. So relief workers implement draconian allocation rules, where only a few are chosen for survival and the rest are kept out of the feeding area.

These considerations suggest that maximization of expected aggregate welfare can involve inequality within poor households. In times of especial stress it can even imply *gender*-based inequality among children, since the long-term survival chances of the household as an entity are often better served by sons than daughters in rural communities of poor countries. What it doesn't imply is systematic gender-based inequality among *adults* in the sharing of resources across the wide range of poor societies. Nor is it consistent with the fact that the allocation of food and care among children in poor households depends upon the extent to which mothers have control over household income (Gross and Underwood, 1971; Kennedy, 1989). We have to reach out to a wider theory, based on something like the theory of bargaining, to account for these. At the moment we have only a rudimentary theory (see Chapter *11).

We should expect such patterns of inequality as we have been studying to transcend current expenditure. Wherever household demands for goods and services in the market reflect male concerns, the direction of technological change can be expected to follow suit. We would expect technological inventions in farm equipment and techniques of production to be forthcoming in regions where cultivation is a male activity (there would be a demand for them); we would not observe much in the way of process innovations in threshing, winnowing, grinding grain, and preparing food. Thus, cooking in South Asia is a central route to respiratory illnesses among women: women sit hunched over ovens fuelled by cowdung, or wood, or leaves. It is inconceivable that design improvements couldn't be realized at a slight cost. But entrepreneurs have no incentive to bring about such technological innovations. Household demand for them would be low.

The argument extends to collective activity in general, and State activity in particular. In poor communities men typically have the bulk of the political voice. We should expect public decisions over rural investment and environmental preservation also to be guided by male preferences rather than female needs. Over reforestation in the drylands, for example, we should expect women to favour planting for fuelwood and men for fruit trees, because it is the women and children who collect fuelwood, while men control cash income; and fruit can be sold in the market. Such evidence on this as I am aware of is only anecdotal. But as it is confirmed by theory, it must be generally true.

It seems to me that it is ultimately on such counts as these that the maximization of well-being as a model for explaining household behaviour must be rejected.[38] The nub of the matter isn't whether household behaviour can safely be viewed as emanating from an 'as if' maximization. For the moment there is no reason for thinking that it can't. The problem lies somewhere else, namely, in what interpretation we give to this maximization. Even though it is often difficult to design and effect it, the target of public policy should be persons, not households. Much follows from this.

However, no matter which route we follow in studying behaviour within households with more than one person, the right framework for analysing public policies here is no different than in a world where households are composed of single persons. Our general conclusions in Chapters 2, 3, 6, and *6 continue to hold. Social well-being is an aggregate of individual well-beings, even when decision units are multi-membered households. Governments need to be conscious of the household as a resource allocation mechanism. They need also to be aware that there are other mediating institutions, such as the village community, voluntary organizations, the temple, the mosque, the church, and so on, some of whose deliberative mechanisms can legitimately be shaped by the State. It is through an understanding of such interlocking resource allocation mechanisms that governments can arrive at appropriate kinds of public policy.

Can the nutritional status of girl children be improved were free midday meals to be provided in State schools? If so, by how much? In answering this there has to be some assessment of what this provision would imply by way of increased school attendence. There has also to be some estimate of the extent of declines in household food allocation for girls that would result from this—the 'crowding out effect'. Modern resource allocation theory remains central for the purposes of locating optimal public policy, even though the theory has typically not peered inside the household.

---

[38] McElroy (1990) explores the empirical implications of demand theory based on Nash bargaining theory, and compares and contrasts them with those of household welfare-maximizing models.

Axiomatic Bargaining Theory

In the previous chapter (Section 11.7) I sketched the idea underlying the Nash programme and argued that for the moment the axiomatic mode is likely to be the more fruitful route to an understanding of household allocations of food, health care, and work. I also described two well-known solutions to the bargaining problem. In this chapter I shall go more deeply into them, by providing proofs and extensions. In Section ★11.1 the Nash bargaining solution is analysed. In Section ★11.2 I take up the Kalai-Smorodinsky solution.

We are concerned here with two-person bargaining problems. (For axiomatic bargaining theory, which is what we are pursuing here, extension to more than two parties is trivial.) I assume, as is appropriate for a theory of bargaining, that the outcome of 'negotiation' doesn't depend upon any particular pair of cardinalizations of the utility functions. This is another way of saying that interpersonal comparisons of utilities are ruled out in arriving at a solution of the bargain. (We are discussing bargaining, not choice-theoretic justice.) Therefore, each axis of the negotiation set (see Section 11.6) can be stretched or squeezed independently of the other without affecting the allocation of goods and services, tasks, and responsibilities realized by the couple (so long, of course, as the stretching and squeezing amount only to positive linear transformations).

★11.1 *Nash Bargaining Solution*

Nash (1950) proposed four axioms for characterizing solutions to a class of bargaining problems.[1]

1. Allocations of goods and services are independent of utility calibrations.
2. Solutions lie on the outer boundary of the negotiation set (Pareto Efficiency).
3. If there is a pair of utility calibrations for which the negotiation set is symmetric about the 45° line going through the alienation point, then the solutions lie on this 45° line.

---

[1] There were several implicit assumptions of significance in his treatment. We will glide over these. See Binmore and Dasgupta (1987).

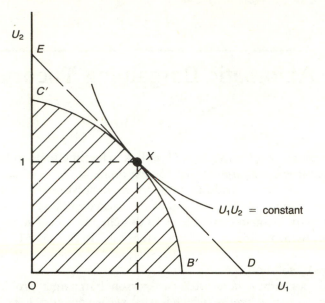

Fig. *11.1   Normalized Nash bargaining solution

4. Suppose that, *ceteris paribus*, the negotiation set were to shrink, but
   in such a way that solutions of the original bargaining problem are
   contained in the new negotiation set. Then the original solutions are
   also solutions of the new bargaining problem (Independence of
   Irrelevant Alternatives).

I will now show that axioms (1)–(4) together imply the Nash bargaining
solution. In doing so I refer to Fig. 11.3. I will show that the point on the
negotiation set at which the function $(U_1 - \bar{U}_1)(U_2 - \bar{U}_2)$ is maximized
is the unique solution of the bargaining problem if solutions are required
to satisfy assumptions 1–4.

Recall Fig. 11.1. We first use axiom 1 to translate the two utility
functions in such a way as to shift the alienation point to the origin, as in
Fig. *11.1. Consider now that point on the transformed negotiation set at
which the function $U_1 U_2$ is maximized. We now use axiom 1 again and
rescale the utility calibrations in such a way as to move this point to (1,1)
on the recalibrated utility space. In Fig. *11.1 I have labelled this point as
X. $OB'C'$ is the recalibrated negotiation set. We can work with it because,
by assumption 1, it is equivalent to the original negotiation set. At X the
slope of the isoquant of $U_1 U_2$ is -1. At X the slope of the outer boundary
($B'C'$) of the negotiation set is also -1.

Now draw the tangent line to $B'C'$ at X. I have labelled this line DE.
It 'separates' the negotiation set $OB'C'$ from the set of all points at which

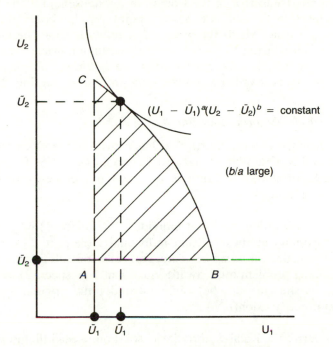

Fig. *11.2 Nash bargaining solution with unequal bargaining power

the function $U_1 U_2$ is at least as large as 1. We are able to draw this separating line DE only because the negotiation set is, by assumption, convex. Furthermore, we know that $OD = OE$.

Next consider a different bargaining problem, in which the negotiation set is the triangle ODE. Recall that $X = (1,1)$. On using axioms 2 and 3, we may then conclude that X is the unique solution to this new bargaining problem. Finally, return to the negotiation set $OB'C'$. This is contained in the triangle ODE. But X is a point in $OB'C'$. We may then use axiom 4 to conclude that X is the unique solution when the negotiation set is $OB'C'$. This concludes the proof. We now study some generalizations.

Axiom 3 embodies the idea that the two parties have equal bargaining power. As a characterization of relative bargaining powers in poor households in poor countries, this will clearly not do. So suppose we were to drop it. Consider then the utility pair that maximizes the function $(U_1 - \bar{U}_1)^a (U_2 - \bar{U}_2)^b$, where a and b are positive constants. Call this pair $(\tilde{U}_1, \tilde{U}_2)$. This is the natural generalization of Nash's bargaining solution when the parties have different bargaining powers. We are to think of the ratio b/a as capturing the unformalized notion of the 'bargaining strength' of the man relative to that of the woman in the household.[2] The larger is b/a, the closer is the solution to the point on the boundary of the negotiation set which yields the woman her utility level at the alienation point. This approximates the outcome of a negotiation where the man can make a convincing 'take it or leave it' offer as a first move. The man enjoys almost all the surplus arising from the joint enterprise (see Fig. *11.2).

*11.2   The Kalai–Smorodinsky Bargaining Solution

Of Nash's axioms, it is the fourth that has proved the most controversial (see Luce and Raiffa, 1957; Kalai and Smorodinsky, 1975; Roth, 1979). The Kalai–Smorodinsky solution is obtained by retaining axioms 1–3 above, and replacing 4 by:

> 5. If, for every utility level that individual 2 (respect. 1) may demand, the maximum utility level that individual 1 (respect. 2) can obtain either remains the same or increases, then the solution to the new bargaining problem must award individual 1 (respect. 2) at least as much as she (respect. he) obtained under the original agreement (monotonicity axiom).[3]

We now derive the Kalai–Smorodinsky solution. Recall that in Fig. 11.1 the negotiation set is ABC. Now suppose that solutions of the bargaining problem satisfy assumptions 1–3 and 5. Let us translate the utility functions in such a way as to shift the alienation point A to the origin. We can rescale the two utility functions independently in such a way that the maximum feasible utility for either party is 1 (see Fig. *11.3). These transformations are admissable under assumption 1, so we can work with the negotiation set OGH in Fig. *11.3, where $G = (1,0)$ and $H = (0,1)$.

We now construct the unit square $OGIH$ and draw the diagonal OI. Let its intersection with the outer boundary of the negotiation set be Y, where $Y = (d,d)$. Connect Y to G and H by the straight lines YG and YH, and construct the kite-shaped figure $OGYH$ in Fig. *11.3. This is symmetric around the line OY. Let us now consider a new bargaining problem,

---

[2] See Roth (1979). Rubinstein (1982) and Binmore (1987) have developed a negotiation game whose non-cooperative equilibrium point approximates the asymmetric Nash bargaining solution under certain conditions. In their model relative bargaining powers are reflected by the agents' relative time discount rates. Being more patient than one's rival gives one power over her. In Fig. *11.2 person 1 is the female.

[3] For non-technical discussions of this axiom, see Gauthier (1986) and Elster (1989). Recall that the axioms pertain to the space of utilities. It can easily be that the antecedent clause in axiom 5 has come about in a particular household because the woman's perception of what she is worth has changed. A. Sen (1987) calls condition 5 a 'perceived contribution response'.

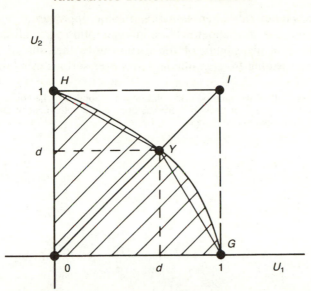

Fig. *11.3   Normalized Kalai–Smorodinsky solution

whose negotiation set is the kite-shaped figure *OGYH*. Using assumptions 2 and 3, we may conclude that *Y* is its unique solution.

Return to the bargaining game whose solution we are seeking. Its negotiation set is *OGH*. Denote a solution of this game by the utility pair (m,n). We should notice that, in moving from the kite-shaped negotiation set *OGYH* to the negotiation set *OGH*, the antecedent clause of assumption 5 is satisfied for both parties. (This is an implication of the assumption that the negotiation set *OGH* is convex. The kite-shaped region *OGYH* is contained in *OGH*.) We may then conclude from 5 that $m \geq d$ and $n \geq d$. But the outer boundary of the negotiation set *OGH* is downward-sloping throughout. It must then be that $m = n = d$. Therefore *Y* is the unique solution of the bargaining game whose negotiation set is *OGH*. This proves our claim in Section 11.7.

The two solutions we have studied are quite different. But at the level of empirical inquiry it may prove difficult to test for their relative appeal. Increased earning potentials for women will typically alter both the alienation point and the shape of the outer boundary of the negotiation set. Suppose we were to discover from cross-sectional data that women fare better inside the home when they face greater income opportunities outside the home (see e.g. Boserup, 1970; Acharya and Bennett, 1983). Are we to interpret this result in terms of the Nash solution and claim that it is an improvement in their position at the alienation point that is responsible for this? Or are we to interpret it in terms of the Kalai–Smorodinsky solution and claim that, when women's income opportunities outside the home improve, the antecendent clause in assumption 5 is realized? For the moment it is the plausibility of the assumptions that should guide our choice. Direct testing from available data poses serious problems.[4]

---

[4] A weakness of the Kalai–Smorodinsky solution when applied to the household is axiom 3, that of symmetry. I do not know if there has been any development of an *a*symmetric solution of the Kalai–Smorodinsky model.

12

Fertility and Resources: The Household as a Reproductive Unit[1]

12.1 *Income, Fertility, and Food: The Environmentalist's Argument*

Except for sub-Saharan Africa over the past 25 years or so, gross income per head has grown in nearly all poor regions since the end of the Second World War. Moreover, growth in world food production since 1960 has exceeded the world's population growth rate: by an annual 0.8 per cent during 1960–70, by an annual 0.5 per cent during 1970–80, and by an annual 0.4 per cent during 1980–7. (see World Bank, 1984, Table 5.6; FAO, 1989, Annex, Table 2). As we observed in Chapter 5, this has been associated with increases in the value of a number of indicators of well-being, such as the infant survival rate, life expectancy at birth, and literacy. All this has occurred in a regime of population growth rates substantially higher than in the past. Except for parts of east and south-east Asia, modern-day declines in mortality rates have not been matched by reductions in fertility. Moreover, a number of places that did experience a decline in total fertility rates for a while (for example Costa Rica, Thailand, Indonesia, and India), have stabilized at levels well above the *population replacement rate* (the fertility rate at which population would be expected to stabilize in the long run; a figure just over 2.1). Table 12.1 presents total fertility rates in several countries (and groups of countries). In the late 1980s, total fertility rate in the World Bank's list of low-income

Table 12.1 Total fertility rates in the late 1980s

India	4.2
China	2.3
Sub-Saharan Africa	6–8
Japan, and Western industrial democracies	1.5–1.9

Source: World Bank (1990).

[1] This chapter and Chapter *12 are based on Dasgupta (1991a, 1992).

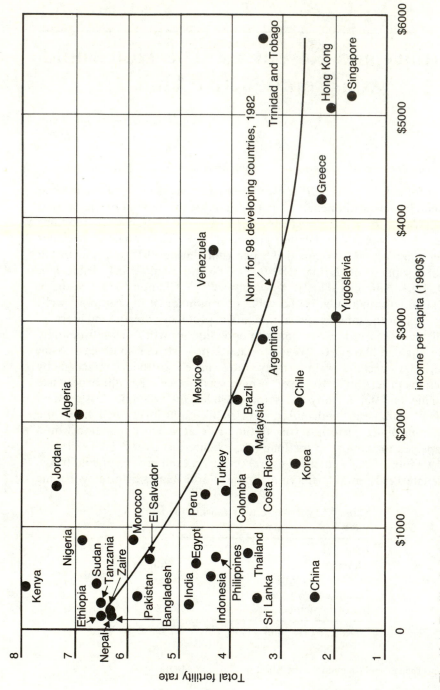

Fig. 12.1 Fertility in relation to income in developing countries, 1982
Source: Birdsall (1988)

countries (excluding China and India) was 5.6. The figures for China and India were 2.3 and 4.2, respectively.

Cross-sectional curve-fitting on data from ninety-eight so-called developing countries displays a declining relationship between the fertility rate and national income per head (see Fig. 12.1). China, Sri Lanka, Thailand, and South Korea are outliers, with fertility rates much lower at their levels of income than would be predicted by the statistical relationship. So are most nations of sub-Saharan Africa, but they all lie on the other side of the curve. Nevertheless, *ceteris paribus*, there would appear to be a link between income and fertility. A regional breakdown of even the Chinese experience displays the general pattern: fertility is lower in higher-income regions (see Birdsall and Jamison, 1983). With the notable exception of China and Sri Lanka, poor countries are a long way from the so-called *demographic transition*, that is, the transition to a regime of low fertility and low mortality rates.

Both time series and, as we have just observed, cross-sectional data are suggestive of a broad 'inverse' (more accurately, declining) relationship between fertility (and mortality) rates and national income per head. That mortality rates would decline with increasing income is something to be expected. Rising income usually carries with it more education, improved diet, and better health care and sanitation.[2] However, a decline in the fertility rate isn't self-evident. And to understand why fertility rates have fallen in many societies, and why at the same time the decline has been so sluggish in so many others (even while the mortality rate has been falling, as in modern sub-Saharan Africa), we need a theory. One of my purposes in this chapter is to develop such a theory.

What we have been talking about is commodity production, not the commodity basis of production. Now, statistics concerning past movements of income and agricultural production per head can lull us into neglecting the environmental-resource basis of human well-being. They can encourage the thought that human ingenuity can be guaranteed to solve the problems that resource stress poses for growing populations (see J. L. Simon, 1981; Simon and Kahn, 1984). They may even explain why environmental resources have been so comprehensively neglected in the economics of poor countries. But, as noted in Chapter 10, gross income

---

[2] Preston and Nelson (1974) and Preston (1980, 1986) are illuminating dissections of the evidence bearing on the causes of the decline in mortality rates during the 20th c. (see Preston, Keyfitz and Schoen, 1972, for world tables). To me their most striking finding from international data has been that reductions in respiratory diseases (e.g. influenza, pneumonia, and bronchitis) and infectious and parasitic diseases (e.g. tuberculosis, the diarrhoeas, whooping cough, malaria, cholera, diphtheria, measles, and typhoid) have contributed equally (about 25–30%) to this decline. (There are exceptions, of course, such as Sri Lanka.) In Chapter 4 (Table 4.3) we studied the contrast between rich and poor countries in terms of the epidemiological transition.

and its attendent benefits do not capture future consumption possibilities. So they don't quite bear on the confluence of concerns people have about population growth and the environmental-resource basis of human well-being, both of which are in large measure directed at the future.

While economists by and large have neglected these themes, demographers and ecologists have not. Much of this discussion has been conducted at an aggregate plane (see e.g. Ehrlich, Ehrlich and Holdren 1977; J. L. Simon, 1977; Kelley, 1988; L. R. Brown *et al.*, 1991), with a heavy emphasis on the macroeconomic consequences of population growth. In this literature, population growth isn't explained, it is taken as datum. Thus, in the literature on the environment it is a commonplace to read estimates of declining land–man ratios and of dwindling natural-resource bases associated with increases in the size of populations at both the global and regional levels. That rising numbers in the face of a finite environmental-resource base will have catastrophic effects has been argued eloquently by Ehrlich and Ehrlich (1990), among others. The assertion here is that beyond a point there are no substitution possibilities between environmental resources (e.g. genetic diversity, fresh water, breathable air, and so forth) and manufactured goods. I observed in Chapter 10 that policy-makers often aren't sensitive to ecological processes, which in any case are for the most part ill-understood.[3] Moreover, urban decision-makers can be relied upon to underestimate the dangers of environmental degradation. The social value of additional knowledge about ecological processes is therefore large, certainly larger than its private value, and possibly a good deal larger than is officially acknowledged. This calls for greater expenditure on the acquisition and dissemination of such knowledge. Moreover, as long as uncertainty about the value of environmental resources is large and environmental destruction is at least partially irreversible, there is a case for awarding special weight to keeping our future options open. In the present context, this means that we ought to pursue what one could call a 'conservationist' approach to environmental policy: we should preserve more than what standard cost–benefit analysis of the use of environmental resources will warrant (see Arrow and Fisher, 1974; C. Henry, 1974). This is at the intellectual heart of the ecological movement.

12.2   *The Population Problem*

Such estimates as are currently on offer about population and resources at the aggregate level are valuable. They alert us to problems. But on their

---

[3] It is remarkable how little even ecologists know about ecological matters of importance. I am grateful to Professor Paul Ehrlich for emphasizing this to me. See Ehrlich and Ehrlich (1991) for an account of the value of biological diversity.

own they aren't a guide to action. The reason is that neither the rate of population growth nor the intensity of environmental-resource use is given from outside. They are determined jointly by a complex combination of opportunities, human motivation, ecological possibilities, and chance factors. To identify and affect population policy, one needs to peer into the locus of decision-making over fertility matters. As human society is currently organized, this locus is in large measure the household.[4] I conclude that it is once again the household we must study. Formal accounts of fertility behaviour haven't often placed the household explicitly in the context of rural poverty, and it is poor rural populations that are growing the fastest. Nor has the household been analysed in the context of environmental-resource use, a matter examined only briefly in Chapter 10. We will see that the context matters.

In this chapter I shall put resource allocation theory to work on findings in applied demography so as to identify what we could today call 'the population problem' in the poorest regions of the world, namely, the Indian sub-continent and sub-Saharan Africa. Both theory and evidence indicate that current rates of population growth in these regions are overly high, and we will try to identify the directions in which public policy needs to be put into effect. In addition to the ecologist's concerns, which we have noted, the population problem in these parts displays itself starkly in the form of unacceptable risks of maternal death for poor, illiterate women, and of new lives doomed to extreme poverty. This identification has the air of banality about it, but it needs to be made. I have not found in the literature an exploration of household behaviour that yields anything like the population problem we will uncover here. For example, even in the influential and informative report on population and development by the World Bank (see World Bank, 1984), there are only three pages (pp. 54–6) devoted to the question why households may be producing *too many* children. Moreover, the answer it provided was rough and limiting: the report said that households can get locked into a Prisoners' Dilemma game over fertility decisions, and that they are typically ignorant of family planning measures.

In their search for the population problem, demographers have for the most part attempted to locate varieties of externalities in household reproductive activities (see e.g. Lee and Miller, 1991). The kinds of externalities they have mostly studied are those that yield the Prisoners' Dilemma. However, there are forms of reproductive externalities which do not lead to the Prisoners' Dilemma (see below and Chapter *12). They have been neglected, to such an extent that a central implication of

---

[4] However, we will see below that, for fertility analysis in sub-Saharan Africa and the Caribbean, the household isn't a very useful category.

such externalities (multiplicity of social equilibria) has gone unnoted. In any event, we will find that there is a lot more to the population problem than externalities, the Prisoners' Dilemma, and ignorance (or fear) of birth control techniques. Thus, consider as an example gender-differences in the costs of reproduction. Assume that each successful birth involves a year and a quarter of pregnancy and breast-feeding. (It can be longer if really extended breast-feeding is practised, as in sub-Saharan Africa.) On making the obvious corrections, we can then conclude that, in a society where female life expectancy at birth is 50 years, and where the total fertility rate is 7 (this is approximately the average figure in sub-Saharan Africa today), well over a third of a woman's expected adult life will be spent either carrying a child in her womb or breast-feeding it. And we haven't allowed for unsuccessful pregnancies.[5] In most poor countries maternal mortality is the largest single cause of death among women in their reproductive years, nutritional anaemia playing a central role in this. In parts of sub-Saharan Africa (e.g. parts of Ethiopia), 1 woman dies for every 50 births.[6] We may conclude that, at a total fertility rate of 7 and over, the chance that a typical woman entering her reproductive years will not make it through them is about 1 in 6. The reproductive cycle in such a woman's life involves her playing Russian roulette. This is one manifestation of the population problem. It is unacceptable.

I shall argue that *wrong* relative prices of household goods and services are as much a potential source of the population problem as are externalities. Among other things, we will find that for poor rural households environmental degradation (e.g. vanishing sources of water, receding sources of fodder and household fuel) can be both a cause and an effect of an increase in the net reproductive rate. To the best of my knowledge, this last has not been given any attention in the applied demographic literature.[7] But for a weak empirical substantiation in World Bank (1991b), I have not been able to locate any empirical work that tests the thesis. It isn't known how powerful the mutual feedback is in the rural communities we know of. Should it prove important, the policies that governments will be urged to pursue for bringing down fertility rates will be of a different nature from the ones usually espoused (see below). It would also go some way towards explaining the fact that fertility rates in sub-Saharan Africa have not responded to a decline in infant mortality rates. The theory deserves investigation, and it explains the title of this chapter.

---

[5] In Bangladesh about 60% of a woman's reproductive life is spent in pregnancy or lactation. The corresponding figure in Pakistan is 50%. See McGuire and Popkin (1989).

[6] By way of contrast, we should not that the maternal mortality rate in Scandinavia today is 1 per 20 000 (see World Bank, 1988).

[7] For example, Johnson and Lee (1987), Birdsall (1988), and T. P. Schultz (1988b) have nothing on it. Exceptions are Dasgupta and Mäler (1991) and Nerlove and Meyer (1991), which have explored the thesis analytically.

Having said this, it is as well to note that, to anyone who is not a demographer, economic demography is a most frustrating subject. It would seem that, for any theoretical prediction on, say, fertility matters, no matter how innocuous, there is some set of data from some part of the world over some period that is not consonant with it. The springs of human behaviour in an activity at once so personal and so social as procreation are so complex and interconnected that empirical confirmations of ideas are always shot through with difficulty.

Faced with this, there are two avenues that are open to me here. One would be to try and collate what we know about fertility matters from international and interregional data. The other is to brazen it out and appeal to some simple theoretical constructs, and to highlight a few of the forces that we may expect to have an important effect on the demographic structure of a community. World Bank (1984) and Cochrane and Farid (1989) provide excellent illustrations of the former route. In keeping with the spirit of the rest of this book, I shall follow the latter route here. To begin with, we will study directional changes in fertility behaviour arising from changes in the 'environmental' parameters households face (prices of goods and services, employment opportunities, distances to sources of water and fuelwood, and so forth). We will be concerned with the signs of these directional changes, not their strengths; for the latter can most certainly be expected to differ widely across communities and cultures. However, even the signs are often not unambiguous, and so they can be expected to differ across regions as well (see e.g. Easterlin, Pollak and Wachter, 1980; Nerlove, Razin and Sadka, 1987a, b).

A concern with the representative household's behaviour has engaged most of the attention in the demographic literature. We have noted repeatedly in this book that many of the items that a household treats as parameters are endogenous to the social system as a whole. Therefore, the next step involves the study of interactions among households, which enables us to analyse social equilibria. This step is still nascent in the literature on population and development ('The next step is to apply . . . microeconomic models [of household behaviour] to understand aggregate developments in a general equilibrium framework. But progress in this field has been slow.' T. P. Schultz, 1988b: 418.) Not surprisingly, we will not be able to move very far in this direction. But we will be able to reach several, possibly important, conclusions, even while we theorize in an informal manner.

12.3 *Population Externalities: Household versus Societal Reasoning*

That many parts of the globe are even now experiencing severe resource scarcity is widely recognized. This doesn't mean individual households are making irrational or abnormal choices. In an otherwise most illuminating essay Bauer (1981: 61, 64) goes farther. Arguing that it would be wrong of us to think that large families in poor countries necessarily pose a problem, he writes:

The comparatively high fertility and large families in many ldcs (less developed countries) should not be regarded as irrational, abnormal, incomprehensible or unexpected. They accord with the tradition of most cultures and with the precepts of religious and political leaders . . . Allegations or apprehensions of adverse or even disastrous results of population growth are unfounded. They rest on seriously defective analysis of the determinants of economic performance; they misconceive the conduct of the peoples of ldcs; and they employ criteria of welfare so inappropriate that they register as deterioration changes which are in fact improvements in the conditions of people.

Now, even when men and women at the household level rationally prefer large numbers of children to small numbers, it doesn't follow that there is no population problem, a problem they themselves might acknowledge were they asked about it. As in every other field of individual choice, we need here to ask as well if a collection of reasoned decisions at the individual level might be sub-optimal at the collective level. Putting it in a slightly different way, we need to ask if there can be a 'resource allocation' failure here.

There are two broad reasons for a possible dissonance between household and societal levels of decision-making in the field of procreation. The first is that the relative prices of various goods and services that households face may simply be 'wrong', for whatever reason. The second is provided by the ubiquitous phenomenon of externalities. In this section and in Chapter *12 we will study the latter; in Sections 12.5 and 12.6 we will identify the former.

Two sources of externalities suggest themselves. The first is simple enough: it has to do with the finiteness of space. Increased population size implies greater crowding, and one would not typically expect households, acting on their own, to 'internalize' crowding externalities. This isn't a precious argument. The human epidemiological environment becomes more and more precarious as communication and population densities rise. Packed centres of population provide a fertile ground for the spread of viruses, and there are always new strains of these in the making. That environmental resources are usually common property is also cited as a harbinger of externalities. The point here is that, because households have access to common-property resources, parents don't fully bear the cost of rearing children, and so they produce too many. Admittedly, as we noted in Chapter 10, local common-property resources in poor countries have in recent studies been found to be a good deal less of a source for free-riding than they have traditionally been taken to be; nevertheless, the static misallocation, however small, can cumulatively have a large effect on population, as we will see presently.

The second source of externality lies elsewhere, and is more subtle. It arises from imitative behaviour, and it often lies behind what is often called 'traditional practice'. Procreation is not only a private matter; it is also a social activity. By this I mean that household decisions about procreation are influenced by the cultural milieu (see e.g. Easterlin, Pollak and Wachter, 1980; Cotts Watkins, 1990). In many societies, there are practices encouraging high fertility rates which no household desires unilaterally to break. These practices may well have had a rationale in the past, when mortality rates were high, rural population densities were low, the threat of extermination from outside attack was high, and mobility was restricted. But practices can survive even when their original purpose has disappeared, something I commented upon in Chapter 8 when developing the idea of social norms. It can then be that, so long as all others follow the practice and aim at large family sizes, no household on its own will wish to deviate from the practice; however, if all other households were to restrict their fertility rates, each would desire to restrict its own fertility rate as well. Thus, there can be multiple social equilibria, each sustained by its own bootstraps, so to speak, and a society can get stuck in one which, while it may have had a collective rationale in the past, does not have one any more.

This does not mean that society will be stuck with it for ever. As always, people differ in the extent of their absorption of traditional practice, their readiness to digest new information, and to act upon new information. There are inevitably those who, for one reason or another, experiment, take risks and refrain from joining the crowd. They are the tradition-breakers, and they often lead the way. In the context of fertility, educated women are among the first to make the move towards smaller families (see, e.g. Farooq, Ekanem and Ojelade, 1987; A. Ahmad, 1991). Female education is therefore a potent force in creating tradition-breakers, as are employment opportunities for women. Special costs are inevitably borne during transitional periods, when established modes of operation are in the process of disintegration without being replaced immediately by new institutions to soften the costs. Demographic transition is possibly a prime example of this. When this is the situation, only a concerted effort (e.g. a massive literacy drive) can dislodge the economy from the rapacious hold of high fertility rates without at the same time inflicting misery on those who alter their mode of behaviour. In Chapter *12 we will study a formal account of it. (In applying such reciprocal externalities as we are studying here to urban residential choice, Schelling (1978) refers to constructs such as this as 'tipping models'.)

In their informative study of fertility behaviour in sub-Saharan Africa,

Cochrane and Farid (1989) remark that both the urban and rural, the educated and uneducated in sub-Saharan Arica have more, and want more, children than do their counterparts in other regions. Thus, even the younger women there expressed a desire for an average of 2.6 more children than women in the Middle East, 2.8 more than women in North Africa, and 3.6–3.7 more than women in Latin America and Asia. There are probably many concurrent explanations for this fact; I shall point to a few in what follows.

First, recall (Chapters 6 and 8) that the multiplicity of social equilibria offers a role for history. Thus, two societies may be indistinguishable in terms of underlying 'preferences' and technologies, and may nevertheless sustain different behaviour patterns, including professed desires concerning fertility rates. High fertility goals in sub-Saharan Africa do not necessarily imply that folk there are intrinsically different from people in other parts of the world facing environmental circumstances: they may be very similar and yet be operating in a different social equilibrium.

Admittedly, I am simplifying by implicitly assuming that social processes are costlessly reversible. This enables us to fix ideas and concentrate on those analytical matters that need to be grasped before all else. Typically, however, social processes are not costlessly reversible (in the extreme they are irreversible), in the sense that the structure of relative prices prevailing at any date depends upon the course of history.[8] We touched upon this in Chapter 6 when alluding to path-dependent processes, and in Section 12.6 we will make an informal study of a process involving fertility choice and degradation of the local environmental resource base which too is path-dependent. Thus, in speaking of multiple equilibria here, I am taking the long view. Kicking an economy from one equilibrium into another by means of some such policy as that which involves a 'big push', attractive though it may seem, is no easy matter. The government would need to possess information about states of affairs far away from the current equilibrium state (see Chapter *12).

It is of course, very hard to test for multiple equilibria, but the work of Paul David (e.g. David, 1985, 1988, 1991, 1992a, b) on technological adoption involving 'network externalities' suggests that it can be done. For the moment, we simply note that the reciprocal externality arising from imitative behaviour (with the attendant possibility that there is a multiplicity of social equilibria) cannot be ruled out as a part of an overall explanation of the puzzle that sub-Saharan Africa continues to offer demographers.

---

[8] See David (1975) for a classic deployment of this observation in his critique of Fogel (1964), who was attempting to demonstrate that the railroads were not of any special significance for the growth of the US economy during the 19th c.

There is an additional force operating in rural communities of poor countries which further encourages high fertility rates. It has to do with the relative prices of alternative sources of a number of vital household needs, which are nowhere in line with what they ought to be if human well-being is to increase there. From the household's perspective, the local environmental-resource base offers the relatively cheap sources of such needs. We will see that this can encourage high fertility rates and unsustainable resource use. But in order to develop the argument, we need to study the determinants of fertility. So we do this first.

12.4   Birth Control and Female Education

All societies practise some form of birth control. Fertility is below the maximum possible in all societies. Even in poor countries, fertility is not unresponsive to the relative resource costs that households face.[9] Extended breast-feeding and postpartum female sexual abstinence have been common practices in Africa. In a noted study on !Kung San foragers in the Kalahari region, R. B. Lee (1972) observed that among them the nomadic, bush-dwelling women had an inter-birth interval of nearly 4 years, while those settled at cattle-posts gave birth to children at much shorter intervals. From the perspective of the individual nomadic !Kung San woman, it is significant that the social custom is for mothers to nurse their children on demand, and to carry them during their day-long trips in search of wild food through the children's fourth year of life. Anything less than a four-year birth interval would therefore increase mothers' carrying loads enormously, impose a threat on their own capacity to survive, and reduce their children's prospects of survival. In contrast, cattle-post women are sedentary, and are able to wean their children earlier.[10]

Except under conditions of extreme nutritional stress, nutritional status does not appear to affect fecundity (see Bongaarts, 1980; Menken, Trussell and Watkins, 1981). During the 1974 famine in Bangladesh the rural population lost over 1.5 million additional children; the stock was replenished within a year (see Bongaarts and Cain, 1981). Of course, undernourishment can still have an effect on sexual reproduction, through its implications on the frequency of still-births, maternal and infant mortality, and a possible reduction in the frequency of sexual intercourse. The central questions in economic demography are then these: what determines fertility, and what grounds are there for our thinking that there is a

---

[9] See Coale and Trussell (1974) for an attempt at constructing a measure of the extent to which members of a society consciously control their fertility.

[10] See also Blurton Jones and Sibly (1978) and R. B. Lee (1980). Child-spacing in sub-Saharan Africa is the subject of empirical inquiry in Page and Lesthaeghe (1981).

population problem? In the following section (and in Chapter *12) we will look at the latter question. The remainder of the body of this chapter studies the two together.[11]

The first and most obvious determinant is the nature of the available technology of fertility control. (Bongaarts, 1984, and World Bank, 1984, contain good discussions.) Traditional methods have consisted of abortion, abstinence or rhythm, prolonged breast-feeding, and coitus interruptus. These options are often inhumane, and usually ineffectual, and unsafe. Contraceptives are superior on all three counts. Nevertheless, their use has been uneven within poor countries. In East Asia over 65 per cent of married women in the age range 15–49 years use contraceptives as against somewhat under 10 per cent in sub-Saharan Africa. In South Asia as a whole the figure in the early 1980s was about 25 per cent, but in Sri Lanka it was a high 55 per cent (see World Bank, 1984, Table 7.1). These large variations across regions not only reflect a divergence in the public provision of family planning and health-care services; they reflect variations in demand as well. Surveys indicate that women themselves perceive an unmet need for access to methods for reducing their fertility. However, the extent of this felt need varies across regions substantially (see World Bank, 1984; Chomitz and Birdsall, 1991; K. Hill, 1992). Successful family planning programmes have proved more difficult to institute than could have been thought possible at first. At one extreme (South-east Asia, Sri Lanka, and the state of Kerala in India), household demand and State commitment to family planning programmes and public health services have merged in a successful way. China in particular has pursued an active policy of limiting family size; total fertility rate was brought down, though not monotonically, to a remarkable 2.3 by 1978 from a high 5.9 in 1960.[12] In many places, however, there has been a paucity of demand for such programmes. In Thailand, for example, the population growth rate has fallen from an average of 3.1 per cent per year during the decade 1960–70 to 1.9 per cent during the decade 1980–90, but now shows signs of having stabilized there. At another extreme (most of sub-Saharan Africa), next to nothing has been done at the State level to supply such services. The population growth rate has increased in these decades from about 2.5 per

[11] For illuminating empirical analyses of the determinants of fertility, see Leibenstein (1974), Easterlin (1975, 1978), Birdsall (1977, 1988), Bongaarts (1978), Preston (1978), Cochrane (1979), Freedman (1979), Easterlin (1980), Cain (1981, 1982, 1984), Bongaarts and Potter (1983), Bulatao and Lee (1983), and Easterlin and Crimmins (1985).

[12] See World Bank (1984, 1988). However, rather draconian measures would appear to have been in use, and the cost has not been negligible. Hull (1990) has collated data reflecting the growing increase in the male–female sex ratio at birth in China. The 1987 One Percent Survey in China shows in addition dramatic patterns of high sex ratios for second and higher-order births. There are three possible explanations for this, all of which may be presumed to be operating: female infanticide, gender-specific abortions, and concealments of births. Tomich, Kilby and Johnston (1991) provide a fine discussion of the possibilities.

cent per year to something like 2.9 per cent per year. We will see below that the absence of conjugal bond (in particular the practice of polygyny) as a norm in sub-Saharan Africa has something to do with such high rates, although it has little to do with the fact that fertility rates haven't declined there.[13]

We should not be surprised that, in those regions where family planning programmes have had an impact, it has occurred mostly in the initial stages. Couples could be expected to adopt new methods of birth control to satisfy unmet needs; however, over time it is the net demand for children that would be expected to dominate household decisions. Here is a substantiation. Starting in 1977, 70 'treatment' villages were serviced by a programme of birth control in the famous experiment in Matlab Thana in Bangladesh, while 79 'control' villages were offered no such special service. The contraceptive prevalence in the treatment villages increased from 7 to 33 per cent within 18 months, and then more gradually to a level of 45 per cent by 1985. The prevalence also increased in the control villages, but only to 16 per cent in 1985. The difference in total fertility rates between the two groups reached a figure of 1.5 (see Phillips *et al.*, 1988; K. Hill, 1992).

In the intial stages, however, family-planning programmes do not work on their own: it matters greatly if women have a measure of education and autonomy. This has been a central conclusion of a large number of empirical studies. The links between female education, especially secondary education, and reproductive behaviour are varied (Cochrane, 1983, is an illuminating study). The acquisition of education delays the age of marriage, and this would be expected to reduce fertility. Moreover, at low levels of education and low levels of contraceptive prevalence, literacy and receptiveness to new ideas complement the efforts of family planning programmes. Family planning programmes have been known to result in longer birth-spacing, and thus in reduced infant mortality rates. Furthermore, education increases women's opportunities for work and so their opportunity cost of time. (The cost of child-rearing is higher for educated mothers.) And finally, educated mothers would be expected to value education for their children more highly, so would be more likely to make a conscious trade-off between the quality and number of their children (see below).

Set against these is an effect on fertility which runs the other way. Taboos against postpartum female sexual activity, where they exist, may well be weakened through education. In sub-Saharan Africa, where polygyny is widely practised, postpartum female sexual abstinence can last

---

[13] The current tragedy over the rapid spread of AIDS in sub-Saharan Africa is also in part a consequence of this. See Caldwell (1991), and a periodic feature article entitled 'A Continent's Agony', in the *New York Times* (especially 16–19 September, and 19 and 28 October 1990).

up to 3 years after birth. It is also not uncommon for women to practise total abstinence once they have become grandmothers. The evidence, as we noticed in the previous chapter, is curious: in Latin America and Asia, increased female enrolment in secondary education has had the effect of lowering fertility rates, while in parts of sub-Saharan Africa there is evidence that the effect has been the opposite.[14]

In poor, illiterate societies there is, then, a complementarity between family planning programmes, and literacy and numeracy taken together. At a more general level, social and community services and female autonomy are complementary factors. Neither on its own will be of much use. In the remainder of this chapter I shall take this for granted and try to identify the motivations for having children.

The 'cost' side of the ledger in bearing and rearing children is self-evident. Pregnancy involves forgone work-capacity for women, and it can involve a considerable additional risk of dying. After birth the offspring have to be fed, clothed, taught, and cared for. Each of these tasks involves time and material resources. Reproductive costs differ enormously between men and women. Conflicts of interest between the genders arising from this is a key ingredient of the population problem. We will also see that in some regions (e.g. sub-Saharan Africa) the cost of rearing children is shared among kith and kin. This can lead to reproductive free-riding, most especially by men. Understanding and modelling the cost side of reproduction doesn't pose any serious intellectual challenge.[15]

12.5 *Children as Consumer and Insurance Goods*

The 'benefit' side is more delicate. Two broad types of reproductive motivations have figured prominently in analyses of population growth in poor countries. The first stems from a regard for children as children. Not only are children desirable in themselves, they carry on the family line or lineage, and they are the clearest avenue open to what one may call *self-transendence* (see Chapter 13). We are genetically programmed to want and to value them. In short, children are *durable consumer goods*.[16] This

---

[14] How powerful this countervailing force has proved in sub-Saharan Africa is a controversial matter, and it is possible that the increased fertility response to increased education seen in some of the data reflect aggregation biases. But see Hess (1988) for a time-series analysis which attests to there being such an effect in parts of sub-Saharan Africa. However, see Barro (1991), who analyses data from over 100 countries to show that during 1960–85 countries with a higher human capital base (as evidenced by school enrolment figures) had lower fertility rates.

[15] This is not to say that estimating the cost of having children isn't formidable. See Lindert (1980, 1983) and Lee and Bulatao (1983) for useful discussions of this.

[16] Models with this general motivation have been explored in Becker (1960, 1981), Dasgupta (1969, 1974c), Mirrlees (1972), Becker and Lewis (1973), Willis (1973, 1987), Becker and Tomes (1976), Behrman, Pollak and Taubman (1982), Caldwell and Caldwell

provides the broadest type of motivation. It comprises a disparate set, ranging from the desire to have children because they are playful and enjoyable to the dictates of injunctions emanating from the cult of the ancestor, which sees religion as essentially the reproduction of the lineage. This latter motivation has been emphasized by Caldwell and Caldwell (1987, 1990) in explaining why sub-Saharan Africa has for the most part proved so resistant to fertility reduction. But it isn't a good argument. It explains why fertility rates there are high, but it doesn't explain why they haven't responded to declining mortality rates. The cult of the ancestor may prescribe reproduction of the lineage, but it does not stipulate an invariant fertility rate. Even in sub-Saharan Africa, total fertility rates have been less than the maximum possible rate.

The second kind of motivation stems from the *old-age security* children can provide in an economic environment where capital, or annuity, markets are next to non-existent. One way of formalizing this is to assume that parents are interested in some form of household welfare, subject, however, to the condition that the chance of there being an offspring to care for them in old age (i.e. providing sustenance, time, and attention) is no less than a certain amount. In many societies this translates itself to a requirement that the chance of there being a *son* alive when the parents are old is no less than a certain amount. As a numerical example, we may consider the simulation study by May and Heer (1968), who estimated that an average Indian couple in the 1960s needed to have 6.3 children in order to be 95 per cent sure of having a surviving son when the father reaches the age of 65. This is a high figure, about the same as the total fertility rate in India during the decade of the 1950s. This 'safety first' model of fertility decision has recently been much explored in a series of articles by Cain (1981, 1982, 1983, 1984). Here we should note that a preference for sons leads parents to discriminate against higher birth-order girl children, a not-infrequent practice in China and in the northern parts of the Indian sub-continent (see Chapter 11). In much of sub-Saharan Africa even today, rural women lose something like a third of their offspring by the end of their reproductive years. This provides a strong reason for pro-natalism.[17]

(1987, 1990), Nerlove, Razin and Sadka (1987a), Barro and Becker (1989), Cigno (1991), Lee and Miller (1991), and in a powerful philosophical essay by Heyd (1992). Note that in evolutionary biology phenotypic costs and benefits of reproduction are important only to the extent that they are correlated with reproductive measures. Offspring in this theory are valued in terms of the end of increasing fitness. This isn't the point of view in economic demography, where instead children are valued as durable consumer goods, or as producer and investment goods (see below).

[17] Leibenstein (1957b) is an early exploration of the old-age security hypothesis regarding fertility behaviour. See also Neher (1971), T. W. Schultz (1974), Willis (1980), Sundstrom and David (1988), and Cremer and Pestieau (1991). Nugent (1985) provides an assessment of the then existing literature on the subject.

Old-age security as a motivation for having children in poor countries is intuitively appealing. The question remains whether there is anything to it in the world as we know it. In a significant study, Nugent and Gillaspy (1983) used Mexican evidence to show that old-age pension and social security do act as a substitute for children. This doesn't mean that fertility rates must inevitably decline when fully functioning capital markets are introduced; they may well rise if parents display a mixed motivation for having children, viewing them both as investment and as durable consumer goods (see Nerlove, Razin and Sadka, 1987a, b).

Old-age security provides a potentially strong motive. In 1980 people aged 65 and over in South Asia formed about 4 per cent of the total population. The sex composition among the aged is far from even, being of the order of 80–85 men for every 100 women among the elderly. In South and South-east Asia female life expectancy at birth is 59 years, while that of males is about 54 years; at age 60, however, they are approximately 15 and 14 years, not much less than the life expectancy at age 60 in advanced industrial countries (see Trease and Logue, 1986). In the Indian sub-continent the proportion of the elderly who live with their children (for the most part, sons) is of the order of 80 per cent or more. (In the United States the corresponding figure is about 15 per cent.) Sons are an absolute necessity in these circumstances. A poor widow with no sons in northern parts of the India sub-continent is faced with a near-certain prospect of destitution.

12.6   *Environmental Degradation, and Children as Producer Goods*

In poor countries children are also useful as income-earning assets, that is, as *producer goods*. This provides households in these parts with a third kind of motivation for having children. It has important consequences. There are exceptions, of course (e.g. E. Mueller, 1976), but on the whole this motivation has not been explored much in the demographic literature.

In Chapter 10 we explored a number of implications of the fact that poor countries for the most part are biomass-based subsistence economies. We noted that poor rural folk in such countries eke out a living from products obtained directly from plants and animals. Production throughput is low. Households there do not have access to the sources of domestic energy available to households in advanced industrial countries. Nor do they have water on tap. (In the semi-arid and arid regions, water supply isn't even close at hand.) This means that the relative prices of alternative sources of energy and water faced by rural households in poor countries are quite different from those faced by households elsewhere. Indirect sources (e.g. tap water nearby) are often prohibitively expensive for the household. As we will see presently, this provides a link between high fertility, degradation of the environmental-resource base of a rural community, and an accentuation of hardship among its members.

From about the age of 6 years, children in poor households in poor countries mind their siblings and domestic animals, fetch water, and collect fuelwood, dung, and fodder. These are complementary to other household activities. They are necessary on a daily basis if the household is to survive. As many as 5 hours a day may be required for obtaining the bare essential amount of firewood, dung, and fodder. (One should contrast this with the direct time spent by households in acquiring water and fuel in advanced industrial economies, which is nil.)

All this may be expected to relate to the high fertility and low literacy rates in rural areas of most poor countries. Poverty, the thinness of markets, and an absence of basic amenities make it essential for households to engage in a number of complementary production activities: cultivation, cattle grazing, fetching water, collecting fodder and fuelwood, cooking food, and producing simple marketable products. Each is time-consuming. Labour productivity is low not only because capital is scarce, but also because environmental resources are scarce.[18] Children are then continually needed as workers by their parents, even when the parents are in their prime. A small household simply isn't viable. Each household needs many hands, and it could be that the overall usefulness of each additional hand increases with declining resource availability.[19] In their study of work allocation among rural households in the foothills of the Himalayas, CSE (1990) recorded that children in the age range 10–15 years work one-and-a-half times the number of hours adult males do, their tasks consisting of collecting fuelwood, dung, and fodder, grazing domestic animals, performing household chores, and marketing. Now, a high rate of fertility and population growth further damages the environmental resource base (to the extent that this consists of unprotected common property), which in turn in a wide range of circumstances provides further (private) incentives for large families, which in turn further damages the resource base, and so on, until some countervailing set of factors (whether public policy, or falling productivity of additional children) stops the spiralling process. But by the time this happens millions of lives have usually suffered.[20] Such an explosive process can be set off by any number of factors. Government or private usurpation of resources to which rural

[18] Cooking in a poor household is a vertically integrated activity: nothing is processed to begin with. It is time-intensive.

[19] This can happen especially if households discount the future at a high rate.

[20] For a mathematical treatment of this kind of spiralling process, see Nerlove and Meyer (1991). See also Dasgupta and Mäler (1991). In an important empirical document, World Bank (1991b) has subsequently provided partial confirmation of the thesis in the context of sub-Saharan Africa.

communities have had historical access is a potential source of the problem; so is the breakdown of collective agreements among users of common-property resources. Indeed, even a marginal decline in compliance can trigger the process of cumulative causation. The static efficiency loss associated with minor violations is, to be sure, small; but over time the effect can be large.

As workers, children add to household income. They are often costless to rear by the time they are adolescents. This line of argument has been emphasized by E. Mueller (1976) and Lindert (1980, 1983). Cain (1977) has studied data from the village Char Gopalpur in Bangladesh. He showed that male children become net producers at as early an age as 12 years, and work as many hours a day as an adult. Using a zero (calorie) rate of interest, he estimated that male children compensate for their own cumulative consumption by the age of 15. This may not be typical in Bangladesh. I cite it, nevertheless, to show the vast difference in the motivation for having children between households in rich countries and poor households in poor countries.

It appears then that the transfer of *material* resources over a life-cycle in poor households in poor countries is from offspring in the aggregate to their parents. The qualification is important. I have seen no study that includes in the calculation of resource transfers the value of time forgone in the rearing of children, or the risks borne by the mother during the process of reproduction. These amount to resource transfers from parents to their children. There is nevertheless a sense in which children are more valuable to parents as producers of income within poor households in poor countries than they are in rich communities. So I shall take it that the flow of resources there is from the offspring to their parents. However, it isn't mere poverty that leads to this directional flow. If people are mobile (and this was the case in early nineteenth-century England), poor parents are not able to effect this transfer readily. In such circumstances much of the motivation for having children is absent, and even a poor society may display a move towards the *demographic transition*, that is, the transition from high to low fertility.[21] But this isn't so in the Indian sub-continent and sub-Saharan Africa, and its absence makes for a strong parental motivation for having large families.

In the previous chapter we explored the suggestion that in many societies daughters are a net drain on resources, and we used it to explain the preference for sons in these cultures. It also helped explain why daughters in their childhood are expected to work relatively harder for their parents. All this is in sharp contrast with advanced industrial nations, where material resources are transferred on average from the adult to the young.

---

[21] I am grateful to Sheilagh Ogilvie for this point.

In a long sequence of writings, Professor Caldwell (see e.g. Caldwell, 1976, 1977a, b, 1981, 1982) has argued that whether a society has made the demographic transition is related to the direction of the intergenerational flow of resources. This is not dissonant with what we have been calling the standard theory of resource allocation (see also Willis, 1982).

The motivation for fertility that I have been emphasizing in this and the previous section springs from a general absence of certain basic needs goods in rural parts of poor countries: public health services, old-age security, water, and sources of fuel. Children are born in poverty, and they are raised in poverty. A large proportion suffer from undernourishment. They remain illiterate, and are often both stunted and wasted. Undernourishment retards their cognitive (and often motor) development (Chapter 14). Labour productivity is dismally low also because of a lack of infrastructure, such as roads. In this background it is hard to make sense of the oft-expressed suggestion (e.g. J. L. Simon, 1977, 1981) that there are increasing returns-to-scale in population size even in poor countries; that human beings are a valuable resource. They are *potentially* valuable as doers of things and originators of ideas, but for this they require inputs of the means for development. Moreover, historical evidence on the way pressure of population has led to changes in the organization of production, property rights, and ways of doing things, which is what Boserup (1965, 1981) studied in her far-reaching work, also does not seem to address the population problem as it exists in sub-Saharan Africa and the Indian sub-continent today. Admittedly, the central message in these writings is that the spectre of the Malthusian trap is not to be taken seriously. But we should be permitted to ask of these modern writers what policy flows from their visions. The Boserup–Simon thesis (if one may be permitted to amalgamate two sets of writings) implies that households confer an external benefit to the community when they reproduce. This means that fertility ought to be subsidized. I have not seen this implication advocated by its proponents.

12.7 *Some Special Features of Sub-Saharan Africa*

Even among poor regions, sub-Saharan Africa is special case on fertility matters, and it is worth asking why.[22] To be sure, as in matters of land tenure (Chapter 9), sub-Saharan Africa is not a homogeneous entity even when it pertains to fertility norms. There are regional differences in the social ethos within this large land-mass (see Cochrane, 1991). But for our purposes we will lose little by thinking in aggregate terms. There are

---

[22] Cochrane and Farid (1989) and Caldwell and Caldwell (1992) contain accounts of fertility trends in sub-Saharan Africa.

central tendencies in any broad cultural group, and a number of features within sub-Saharan Africa would seem to be pertinent when we seek to locate them. When we have identified a few, we will contrast them with those prevailing in the Indian sub-continent, another region experiencing a population problem.

Unlike the Indian sub-continent, the 'household' is not a very meaningful organizing unit for production, consumption, and fertility decisions in Africa (see e.g. Dow, 1971; Caldwell, 1975; Cain, 1984; Bleek, 1987; Caldwell and Caldwell, 1987, 1990; Kamarck, 1988; Goody, 1990). Often, there is no common budget for a man and wife. Polygamy is widely practised. In the late 1950s some 35 per cent of all married men in sub-Saharan Africa were polygamists (see Goody, 1976). In rural areas matters would not appear to have changed much (see Farooq, Ekanem and Ojelade, 1987). (By 'polygamy' we really mean 'polygyny' here: it is the men who have more than one spouse.) Women in sub-Saharan Africa, like women among non-caste Hindus in India, often have more than one relationship at any given time; but these are extra-marital relationships, not marriages.[23] Recall also that the dowry system is virtually non-existent in sub-Saharan Africa. For the most part it is the man's family that has to accumulate wealth to obtain a bride. This affords a reason why the median age difference between spouses in Africa is large; a fact of considerable importance, since it enables women to have spouses despite the prevalence of polygyny: women on average become widows at an early age, and widow remarriages are not only permissible, they are a commonplace.

The sexual division of labour in sub-Saharan Africa is powerful, but it assumes a different form from that in the Indian sub-continent. We noted in Chapter 9 that, even though women do not inherit land, the primary responsibility for raising subsistence crops for the household usually rests with women, who as a consequence have greater power and control over food distribution than their counterparts in the Indian sub-continent. Over 30 per cent of rural households are headed by women; the men are absent (see Jazairy, Alamgir and Pannucio, 1992). (This goes a little way towards explaining why the dowry system is absent.) Nevertheless, women's sexuality and labour power are firmly under control by the husband's lineage. Among other things, it is the extent of kinship control of women that differentiates societies in sub-Saharan Africa from those in the Indian sub-continent. All this makes for a considerable difference in the resource implications of having offspring. Children aren't raised by

---

[23] Among some non-caste Hindus in India extra-marital relationships offer a means of fertility control. Abortion of a foetus resulting from a marital union is frowned upon, whereas the abortion of a foetus resulting from an extra-marital relationship is pretty much mandatory. I am grateful to Paul Seabright for this observation concerning norms of behaviour in rural South India.

their parents in the way they are in the Indian sub-continent; rather, this responsibility is more diffuse within the kinship group, affording a form of insurance protection to be expected in semi-arid regions (see Chapters 9–10). In much of West Africa, about a third of the children have been found to live with their kin at any given time. Nephews and nieces have the same rights of accommodation and support as biological offspring. Sub-Saharan Africa has often been characterized by strong descent lineage and by weak conjugal bond. For the most part, as in much of the Indian sub-continent, descent is patrilineal and residence is patrilocal. (An important exception are the Akan people of Ghana.)

Cochrane and Farid (1989) remark that the high levels of fertility in sub-Saharan Africa are a consequence of early and universal marriage, allied to little reliance on contraception. Thus, average age at marriage for sub-Saharan women is 18.9, and the proportion of those 15–19 years of age who are married is 40 per cent. The comparable figures for Asia are 21.3 years and 26 per cent, respectively, and for Latin America, 21.5 years and 19.8 per cent, respectively. The overall usage of contraceptives is very low in sub-Saharan Africa: even among the most educated of people, the prevalence is only 20 per cent or so. But the proximate causes identified by Cochrane and Farid are themselves in need of explanation. The importance of women in farming has often been adduced to explain in part sub-Saharan Africa's marriage patterns, and we touched upon this in Chapter 9. In the previous section we identified an additional set of reasons why children would be particularly attractive to rural folk in the drylands. Earlier, we noted that social externalities may provide one more set of reasons. In the following section we will locate yet another factor, connected with the diffused nature of children's maintenance costs in sub-Saharan Africa, which would be expected to contribute to making fertility rates particularly high there.

12.8 Modelling Fertility Decisions

Household fertility and savings decisions are interrelated. Indeed, children as old-age security identifies the two. Nevertheless, it will prove useful to consider them separately. It makes for expositional ease.

Earlier, we identified three different motives behind procreation. Hybrid models of fertility decision contain all of them in varying strengths. They enable us to analyse the matter in a unified way. We need to consider the 'reduced form' of household utility as a function of, among other things, the number of children a couple have. Should the child mortality rate decline, the fertility rate would be expected to follow suit among households averse to facing risks in the number of children who survive. But even when mortality rates decline, it takes time for households to recognize this. Demographic transitions would be expected to display sharp declines in fertility rates only some time after steep declines in mortality rates.[24]

The effect on fertility of changes in income and the cost of rearing and bearing children is more complex. (The pioneering works are Becker, 1960; Becker and Lewis, 1973; Becker and Tomes, 1976.) Letting c denote current parental consumption, n the number of children, and z an index of the quality of each child, we may assume household utility, U, to be a function of these three variables: $U(c,n,z)$. It is appropriate to assume that U is an increasing function of both c and z.[25] We should view $U(\cdot)$ as a 'reduced form' of household utility, in that, in those circumstances where children are seen at least partially as investment goods, z would in part reflect future parental consumption.

The quality of a child depends on the amount of time and resources devoted to him; it depends as well on the time and effort devoted by the child in acquiring education and skills. In a hybrid model, z itself would be an aggregate of different characteristics. The problem is that parents are faced with a trade-off between c and z, and between n and z. Moreover, as we have seen, c is itself up to a point an increasing function

---

[24] I am assuming that the cost of rearing children remains approximately the same despite falling mortality rates. Thus, let n be the number of children produced, and $\pi(N,n,\alpha)$ the probability that N will survive, where $0 \leq N \leq n$ and where α is an underlying parameter of the distribution. Now no matter what is the motivation for having children, we can always represent the reduced form of *ex post* parental utility (net of the *ex post* cost of child-rearing) as $V(N)$. For vividness, we may suppose that $V(N)$ is increasing in N for low values of N and decreasing in N for high values of N. If the von Neumann–Morgenstern axioms are satisfied, *ex ante* parental utility is $U(n,\alpha) \equiv \Sigma\pi(N,n,\alpha)V(N)$. Parents choose n. Suppose, to take a sharp example, $\pi(\cdot)$ is the binomial distribution, with α representing the probability that any one child will survive. This means that $\pi(n,N,\alpha) = {}^nC_N\alpha^N(1 - \alpha)^{(n-N)}$. It can then be shown that, if $V(N)$ is concave in N, an increase in α leads to a decline in the utility-maximizing choice of n. The argument generalizes to the case where there are child-bearing costs, provided they are increasing and convex in n; and it generalizes to the case where reproductive decisions are sequential. See Sah (1991).

The critical assumption is the concavity of $V(N)$. Since $V(N)$ is a reduced form (what we may call *indirect utility*), we should ideally derive it from postulates on primitives, and not merely stipulate it. Preston (1978) contains valuable empirical evidence on the matter. It offers a varied picture. See in particular the essays by Ben-Porath and by Chowdhury, Khan and Chen. In the former study (based on Israeli data) child replacement is shown to be a significant phenomenon, and it occurs quickly. In the latter study (based on data from Bangladesh and Pakistan) the influence of child mortality on subsequent fertility was found to be of no great significance. But see Bongaarts and Cain (1981), who record substantial replacement through increased fertility following the Bangladesh famine of 1974; and Caldwell (1991) on sub-Saharan Africa.

[25] Children are taken to be identical, and are assumed to be identically treated. I do this simply in order to pose the problem in its pristine form. We will also ignore the externalities that social norms create.

of n in poor households: children are valuable as producer-goods. This accentuates the trade-off parents face between n and z.[26]

In Chapter 4 we observed that improvements in education appear to have a salutary effect on household circumstances. The effects of parents' education, particularly mothers' education, on fertility behaviour has also been much studied in recent years (see e.g. World Bank, 1984). Earlier, in Chapter 11 (Table 11.1) we observed a negative relationship between women's educational status and the total fertility rate. I have had much to say about the beneficial effects of education on the realization of well-being.

It is also useful to study the effect of an increase in parental income on fertility. (This leads us back to the aggregate data we studied in Section 12.1.) To begin with, we may trace the increase in parental income to a rise in their labour productivity—as a consequence, for example, of rural investment or, more generally, better employment opportunities for men and women in the labour market. Now a rise in women's labour productivity implies an increase in the opportunity cost of rearing children. At the same time, with increasing parental income, children are needed less as producer goods, and possibly less also as investment goods, since one would imagine that rising income brings in its wake greater access to the capital market. (For an empirical exploration of this last link, see Rosenzweig and Evenson, 1977.)

Improvements in labour productivity are often associated with urbanization. This accentuates the directional changes we have already identified. Urbanization tends to break households down into 'nuclear' units. This raises the cost that parents have to bear in rearing their children. (The contribution of grandparents, aunts, and other kin is in this situation greatly reduced.) Growing urbanization in a growing economy also offers children better employment prospects, which improve their bargaining strength relative to their parents. This in turn lowers the gross return on children as investment goods, since children become less dependable as a source of income to their parents in their old age. (Sundstrum and David, 1988, deploy this argument in the context of ante-bellum United States.) Moreover, State legislation on elementary schooling (for example, making it compulsory) and increased private returns to education (arising from general industrialization) make children relatively less useful as producer goods. Compounding all these considerations, we can glimpse those forces at work which relate fertility to household income. The broad 'inverse'

---

[26] Increased life expectancy increases the return on children's education, and so human capital formation could be expected to assume a larger share of total investment. The Indian data conform to this expectation. See Ram and Schultz (1979), who in addition estimated that during the 1970s human capital accumulation in India was of the order of 55% of physical capital accumulation.

relationship between income and fertility does not require of us to postulate that children are 'inferior goods', in the sense made familiar in consumer-demand theory. Increased parental income, especially maternal income, raises the cost of children; children become more expensive relative to other goods. The causal chain is therefore more complex and somewhat reinforcing, and the 'inverse' relationship between household income and the desired family size holds for a wide class of household utility functions.[27]

Both the costs and benefits of having children are experienced in different proportions by the parents. The cost of bearing and nursing a child is inevitably borne by the mother, but the cost of rearing children is culturally conditioned. In some cultures, as in much of sub-Saharan Africa, these costs are diffused across the kinship. (That women are vigorously engaged in agriculture presumably has something to do with this.) When this is so, there is an allocation failure, in that neither parent bears the full cost of the couple's decision to have a child. In societies characterized by weak conjugal bond (as in much of sub-Saharan Africa and the Caribbean) male parents often bear little of the cost of rearing children. Here, then, we would expect to see another source of asymmetry in parental motivations over reproductive decisions. Men's desire for children would on balance be expected to exceed that of women by far, and this would bring in its wake all the attendant implications we observe in the data. Patriarchy, a weak conjugal bond, and a strong kinship support system of children taken together are a broad characteristic of sub-Saharan Africa. It provides a powerful stimulus to fertility.

That kinship support of one's children provides a basis of a free-rider problem (yet another externality), leading to too many children being born, has been noted in one strand of the demographic literature (see e.g. Cain, 1984). But I have not seen it recognized that this is so only if the benefits of having children are not equally diffused across the kinship. An excessive number of children is the outcome only when parents appropriate a greater proportion of the benefits their children provide than the proportion they incur of the cost of rearing them. Professor John Caldwell has told me that this would appear to be the normal case in sub-Saharan Africa.[28]

---

[27] For the formal model being sketched here, see Becker (1960, 1981), Becker and Lewis (1973), Easterlin, Pollak and Wachter (1980), Nerlove, Razin and Sadka (1987a), and Cigno (1991). Birdsall (1988) provides a fine, non-technical account.

[28] To see that there is no distortion if the proportions were the same, suppose c is the cost of rearing a child and N the number of couples within a kinship. For simplicity let us assume that each child makes available y units of output (this is the norm) to the entire kinship, which is then shared equally among all couples, say in their old age. Suppose also that the cost of rearing each child is shared equally by all couples. Let n^* be the number of children each couple other than the one under study chooses to have. (We will presently endogenize

Reproductive free-riding has not received attention in what is often called the 'new economic demography', whose hallmark is the assumption that fertility and family specialization between market and non-market productive activities can be modelled as outcomes of optimizing behaviour on the part of the household. Surveying the field, T. P. Schultz (1988b: 417) writes: 'Consequences of individual fertility decisions that bear on persons outside of the family have proved difficult to quantify, as in many cases where social external diseconomies are thought to be important'. Given the ingenuity economic demographers have displayed in estimating household demand functions for children, goods and services, it is hard to imagine that reproductive free-riding has been particularly difficult to quantify. One suspects, rather, that quantification hasn't been attempted.

Matters are different in societies where the conjugal bond is powerful. This is the case in most of Asia. Parents together bear the bulk of the cost of raising their children, even though the sexes typically do so unevenly. The extent of economic dependency of women on men now assumes a central role. As we observed in the previous chapter, this dependency is enormous in the Indian sub-continent, especially in the North. In these types of patriarchal societies women rightly perceive sons as having especially high value as insurance against personal calamities, such as widowhood and abandonment. But sons can't be guaranteed. So one has to keep trying. In east and south-east Asia (and also southern India and Sri Lanka) women's economic dependency is less. Among those that were the world's poorest countries in the early 1970s, fertility rates have fallen most dramatically in this part of the world. In a wide-ranging essay on the old-age security hypothesis, Cain (1984) used the median age difference between spouses as an index of female economic dependence in patriarchal societies to demonstrate a remarkably high correlation between this and the total fertility rate in a cross-sectional study of nations.

These are thus forces at work which move the fertility goals of women relative to men in opposite directions. In poor societies marked by gender-based asymmetry in employment opportunities and power, women's reproductive goals don't differ noticeably from those of men (see Mason and Taj, 1987). But professed desires are sensitive to the extent to which women are educated: educated women tend to desire smaller families than

---

this.) If n were to be the number of children this couple produces, it would incur the resource cost $C = [nc + (N–1) n^*c]/N$, and eventually the couple would receive an income from the next generation equalling $Y = [ny + (N–1)n^*y]/N$. Denote the couple's aggregate utility function by the form $U(Y)–K(C)$, where both $U(\cdot)$ and $K(\cdot)$ are increasing and strictly concave functions. Letting n be a continuous variable for simplicity, it is easy to confirm that the couple in question will choose the value of n at which $yU'(Y) = cK'(C)$. The choice sustains a social equilibrium when $n = n^*$. (This is the symmetric non-cooperative Nash equilibrium of the social system.) It is easy to check that this is also the condition that is met in a society where there is no reproductive free-riding.

illiterate ones (although in sub-Saharan Africa the difference appears to be small). A preference for sons is nearly universal in the Indian subcontinent. In sub-Saharan Africa this isn't so (see N. E. Williamson, 1976). Indeed, in parts of Africa for which data on uterine sibling groups have been obtained, there is no evidence of stopping rules which would reveal an implicit sex-preference (see Goody et al., 1981a, b).[29]

12.9 Allocation Failure and Public Policy

A good bit of the motivation underlying analytical work on fertility behaviour has been in identifying circumstances where there is no allocation failure, that is, situations in which individual household decisions unencumbered by any public population policy yield Pareto-efficient outcomes.[30] The literature depicts economists busily burying any 'distortion' they can imagine, and heaving a sigh of relief when they have fashioned a world in which none is visible. This is customarily achieved by the simple expedient of studying economies that comprise a single household, or dynasty (see Chapter *12, Section *12.1). In this chapter I have identified reasons for rejecting this point of view. Nevertheless, for the moment let us ignore social externalities. Let us ignore as well the fact that a person's utility function doesn't necessarily correspond to the function that reflects her well-being. I want to argue that even then there is a need for public policy. Throughout this book I have stressed repeatedly that public policy does not end when well-being efficiency is in sight. The distribution of benefits and burdens can be unjust. We have noted the importance of children as producer and insurance goods in poor households. The availability of household infrastructure in the form of cheap fuel and potable water makes children less important as income-earning assets. By a similar token, availability of credit and access to the capital market lowers the importance of children as insurance goods.

Children as producer goods and children as old-age security yield somewhat different implications for public policy. But they do both entail public policy. The provision of such patterns of household infrastructure

---

[29] Stopping rules based on sex preference provide a different type of information regarding sex preference than sex ratios within a population. The reason is that in a steady state stopping rules have no effect on the sex ratio. To see this, suppose that, in a society where sons are preferred, parents continue to have children until a son is born, at which point they stop. Assume for simplicity that at each try there is a 50% chance of a son being conceived. Now imagine a large population of parents, all starting from scratch. In the first round 50% of the parents will have sons and 50% will have daughters. The first group will now stop and the second group will try again. Of this second group, 50% will have sons and 50% will have daughters. The first sub-group will now stop and the second sub-group will have another try. And so on. But at each round the number of boys born equals the number of girls. The sex ratio is 1.

[30] See e.g. Becker and Barro (1986), and Becker, Murphy and Tamura (1990). For a critique of this, see David (1986).

as we have identified requires resources, and in Chapters 6–7 I offered reasons why it is the State's obligation in poor countries to make attempts to ensure their supply. The aim should not be to force people to change their reproductive behaviour.[31] Rather, it should be to identify policies that would so change the options men and women face that their reasoned choices would involve a lowering of their fertility rates to replacement levels. The evidence, some of which I have put together here, tells us that poor parents in poor countries *do* calculate when making such decisions as those that bear on household size and assets, even though what emerges at the end is a greater number of yet another cohort of poor, illiterate people. It would certainly be unjust of governments to insist on parents sending their children to schools for so many years if this requirement further impoverished poor households. But it would not be unjust if the complementary household production inputs were made available through the provision of family-planning and public health services, and infrastructural investment, and for governments then to make free school attendance compulsory.[32] Reasoned choice at the household level would be expected to respond to this through an alteration in fertility goals.

In the absence of such public provisions, the dynamics of a social system can be horrifying. For reasons I have identified, the bulk of the very poor in poor countries have continually to aim at large household sizes, making it in turn much more difficult for them to lift themselves out of the grip of poverty: household labour productivity remains abysmally low, investment credit is for the most part unavailable to them, and the avenue of savings is consequently that much constrained for them. The matter is different for those with a greater access to resources. They are, as always, in a position to limit their household size and increase the chance of propelling themselves into still higher income levels. I have not been able to locate published data on the matter, but my impression is that among the urban middle clases in India the demographic transition has already been achieved. This doesn't mean there is an inexorable 'vicious circle of poverty', however. People from the poorest of backgrounds have been known to lift themselves out of the mire. Nevertheless, there are forces at work which pull rich and poor groups away from one another in terms of the quality of life. The Matthew Effect ('For unto everyone that hath shall be given, and he shall have abundance; but from him that hath not shall be taken away even that which he hath') works relentlessly in poor countries.

I am putting matters in stark terms so as to focus only on the idea that

---

[31] The draconian measures employed in India during the Emergency period 1975–7 concerning sterilization are an example of the kinds of activities governments must avoid.

[32] The school-year in rural USA until the beginning of this century was shorter than in urban areas, to take account of seasonal labour requirements. I am grateful to Professor Gary Becker for giving me an account of this.

parents would have a different set of fertility goals were the relative prices of environmental and infrastructure goods different, and were the economic dependency of women on men less. As regards the latter, female education is now widely recognized to be a key propellent. But increased employment opportunities for females are also a route to greater autonomy.

There are, of course, other measures which should be thought about in parallel. Compulsory schooling, for example, makes children prohibitively expensive as assets for generating current income, so it reduces their attractiveness as a commodity. Making available alternative sources of basic household needs improves the well-being of poor households via an altered set of fertility goals.

Let me sum up. I have identified three broad categories of policies for alleviating the population problem: (i) increasing the costs of having children, (ii) reducing the benefits of reproduction, and (iii) improving the information base concerning the technology of reproduction, and affecting the locus of household decision-making. Categories (i) and (iii) have found much expression in the demographic literature, but unhappily, at the expense of (ii). However, it is (ii) that raises the most interesting economic issues; it tells us that among the most potent avenues open for easing the population problem may well be those that involve social co-ordination (see Chapter *12), the provision of infrastructural goods, and measures of social security. But these services are desirable in themselves, and commend themselves even when we don't have the population problem in mind. It seems to me that this consonance among desirable social policies is a most agreeable fact.

Admittedly, in saying all this we are looking at matters wholly from the perspective of the parents. This is limiting.[33] In the following chapter we will explore the right basis for population policies. These are extremely difficult matters, and our examination will be very incomplete. What I have tried to argue in this chapter is that there is much we can establish even were we to leave such conceptual difficulties as we will discover aside. Population policy involves a good deal more than making family planning centres available to the rural poor. It also involves more than a recognition that poverty is a root cause of high fertility rates in a number of societies. The problem is deeper, but it is identifiable.

---

[33] Enke (1966) is a notable exploration in the value of prevented births when the worth of additional lives is based entirely on their effect on the current generation. As a simplification, he took the value of a prevented birth to be the discounted sum of the differences between an additional person's consumption and output over the person's lifetime.

Strategic Complementarities in Fertility Decisions

★12.1 *Atmospheric Externalities*

In Section 12.3 I identified the social milieu as something that influences fertility decisions. It is a source of externality. We will call it an *atmospheric externality* (see Meade, 1952). Here I will formalize a simple version of the idea. But it is as well to note that the formulation has wide applicability, and is not restricted to fertility behaviour. My purpose here will be to demonstrate that social externalities often lead to multiple Nash equilibria. This means that history matters, and that societies that are similar in terms of technology and utility functions may gravitate in the long term to quite dissimilar states of affairs. I have used this idea a number of times in this book to explain observed phenomena (Chapters 8, 9, and 12).

There is a wide variety of actions that we all regularly engage in which are numerical; that is, they are scalar in dimension. (The analysis can be generalized to the case where decision variables are vectors.) They also share the feature that any given individual's goal-maximizing choice of action is an increasing function of the choice of action of any other individual. This isn't quite the primitive one wants (choice is to be explained, not assumed), and we look for properties of utility functions that will yield this. So, supposing there are M people ($k, n = 1, \ldots, M$), let X_k (a real number) be individual k's action. Assume too that k's utility function is of the form $U_k(X_1, \ldots, X_M)$; which we also write as $U_k(X_k, \mathbf{X}_{-k})$.[1] The primitive that will do the job is that k's marginal utility of her *own* action is an increasing function of the choice of action by any other person. Formally, this means:

$$\partial^2 U_k(X_k, \mathbf{X}_{-k})/\partial X_k \partial X_n > 0, \qquad \text{for all } k \neq n. \qquad (\star 12.1)$$

When individual utility functions satisfy ($\star$12.1), we will say that the social system involves *strategic complementaries* among individuals' motivations (see Cooper and John, 1988). In game theory it would be to say that payoff functions are *supermodular* (see e.g. Milgrom and Roberts, 1990a, b).[2]

---

[1] $\mathbf{X}_{-k} = (X_1, \ldots, X_{k-1}, X_{k+1}, \ldots, X_M)$. We used this notation in Ch. 3.
[2] This isn't strictly correct. The inequality in ($\star$12.1) is taken to be weak in the definition of supermodularity. We lose nothing here by assuming strict inequality.

We will find it useful to appeal to a specification that is somewhat sharper than (*12.1). It will be assumed that a person's utility is a function of her own action and of the *average* action of all others (hence the term 'atmospheric externality'); and that the marginal utility of her own action is an increasing function of the average action of all others.

Examples abound. They include how hard we work at our tasks, what wage rate we accept as reasonable (Chapter 9), how much we spend on a particular type of consumer durable (through, for example, what Duesenbery, 1949, christened the 'demonstration effect', or through what in modern industrial organization literature are called 'network externalities'—see Farrell and Saloner, 1986), how much education we allow our daughters to attain, at what age they get married, how many children we aim for (albeit this only allows for non-integer values), and so forth. In sociological parlance, these examples reflect peer-group emulation and norm-guided behaviour, and in economics they are often called *atmospheric external economies.*[3]

Earlier, we discussed household reproductive decisions, and the concomitant private costs and benefits of having children. These decisions are also influenced by aspects of shared values within a community. A woman on her own will not find it desirable to break out and assert her autonomy when no one else is doing so. (Among other things, the psychic costs may be too high.) But she may find it permissible to do so if all others (or at least most others) are doing so. Both are self-enforcing situations, and they sustain quite different behaviour. We often refer to this as a society's *custom* or *practice* (e.g. 'The custom in rural India is to have many children'). Of course, there may well be several self-enforcing levels of activity, not just two; that is to say, there may be several (non-cooperative) Nash equilibria, with their associated practices. That we find ourselves at one equilibrium reflecting a particular custom is no reason for insisting there isn't another equilibrium (reflecting a different custom) at which individual well-being would be higher.

To see this, imagine a number of identical households, each of whose strategy (say, the level of some activity) is, without loss of generality, a number between 0 and 1 (see Fig. *12.1). I denote the representative household's activity level by Z, and the average value of the activity level chosen by all other households by $\hat{Z}$. Let $U(Z,\hat{Z})$ denote the typical household's utility function, net of costs of choosing Z. For each possible value of $\hat{Z}$ there is a corresponding value of Z, say Z^*, at which $U(\cdot)$ is maximized. (We ignore multiple household optima for simplicity.) We

---

[3] It is also on occasion called *Marshallian external economies.* The idea has a long and distinguished pedigree (see Rosenstein-Rodin, 1943; Scitovsky, 1954), and it has found rich expression in recent years (see e.g. Schelling, 1978; David, 1985, 1987; Stiglitz, 1987a; Cooper and John, 1988; Murphy, Shleifer and Vishny, 1989a; Durlauf, 1990, 1991; Hahn, 1990; Matsuyama, 1991). An underlying idea is to find a general condition (e.g. condition (*12.1)) under which a social system can possess several non-cooperative (Nash) equilibria, at least two of which can be ranked on the basis of the Pareto criterion.

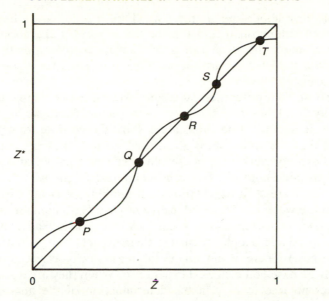

Fig. *12.1   Desired family size as a function of average family size

write this as $Z^*(\hat{Z})$. It is the household's *reaction curve*, and is drawn in Fig. *12.1. We are assuming that $\partial^2 U(Z,\hat{Z})/\partial Z\partial\hat{Z} > 0$. This means $Z^*(\hat{Z})$ is upward-sloping, as in Fig. *12.1.

Since households are identical, the household whose reaction curve we have drawn is a representative one. We now simplify for expositional ease and pick a representative household from all the remaining households. This would be anchored most firmly were we to assume that when the average choice of all other households is Z, it is a consequence of each of them having chosen this average. So we do so. We are now interested in points at which $Z^*(Z)$ intersects with the 45° line. Each intersection is a non-cooperative Nash equilibrium point of the social system. Each household's level of activity at an intersection is utility-maximizing on the assumption that all other households choose this same level. The intersections are social equilibrium points. In Fig. *12.1 there are five equilibrium points, P, Q, R, S, and T. Notice that I have not assumed utility functions to be concave. Equilibrium is guaranteed by virtue of the assumption of strategic complementaries.

Because households behave identically at equilibria, the latter can be ranked by the Pareto criterion. Equilibria can also be ranked in terms of household well-being. So there is a best and a worst equilibrium, and there are equilibria of intermediate goodness.

The question arises as to which equilibrium point gets selected. The answer depends on the relative importance of a number of things, all of which can be succinctly captured by two notions: that of the *expectations* individuals have about one another (which have on occasion been called 'eductive' considerations), and that of the *history* of the social system (which has frequently been called the 'evolutive' consideration). The former is the stuff of the pure theory of games, the latter is the material of social sciences.[4]

To illustrate their differences, it is simplest to think of a situation where the activity level has to be chosen each period (day, week, year, or whatever). Imagine that decisions are costlessly reversible from period to period, so that everything starts afresh each period. If in any period each household expects every other household to choose a particular equilibrium action, each household will find it in its interest to choose this action as well. Not only are such expectations self-fulfilling, it is the expectations that do all the work. Under an educative mode a Nash equilibrium is held up by its own bootstraps, so to speak. (A charismatic leader may come along and persuade people to change their expectations to a set of self-fulfilling ones.) There is no analytical reason why expectations must necessarily be based on historical experience. When they are not so based, history has no role to play in the determination of the final outcome, although of course it is special contingencies (e.g. the emergence of a charismatic leader) that do the picking from the set of equilibria. On the other hand, expectations are typically influenced by history. In this case history has a strong role to play even under an eductive mode.[5]

An extreme alternative has history assuming the dominant role. Suppose, for example, that in each period households base their expectations of what others will do on what was done on average in the previous period. This is sometimes called the Marshallian *tâtonnement*. Its rationale is provided by substantial sunk costs incurred in each period's decisions, so that from period to period only marginal changes in individual decisions are undertaken, if they are undertaken at all. Consider the simplest form of this: each household in each period expects the average level of activity to be equal to the average level of activity during the previous period. (Easterlin, Pollak and Wachter (1980) have analysed US data to show that a person's fertility goals are influenced positively by the size of the household in which the person was raised.) It is now an easy matter to check that, under the dynamics generated by such adjustments in behaviour, P, R, and T are stable equilibrium points, while Q and S are unstable.

To illustrate, imagine that, through a sequence of chance events, households find themselves at R (where, say, the average age of marriage for girls is low) and that households' well-being would be greater at P (where the average age of marriage for girls is somewhat higher). There is then a precise sense in which households are engaged in an excessive

---

[4] See Krugman, 1991 for an elaboration of this distinction.
[5] Note that individuals in the society we are studying in the text are not locked in a Prisoners' Dilemma. There are multiple equilibria here, and no dominant strategy for any household.

level of activity at R (i.e. a rapid turnover of daughters in households). It is possible that each household knows this. But no household on its own has an incentive to deviate from its chosen pattern of behaviour. This is a social dilemma, and only a co-ordinated policy can overcome it.

This is an extreme example. I don't mean the example's technical features, for example that households are identical—this can be relaxed easily without our losing anything other than simplicity. I mean something else. Habitual behaviour is internalized, and so breaking out of established patterns of behaviour even when others are doing so can prove hard for an individual. This gives a certain additional stickiness to established equilibrium behaviour. Social equilibria are yet more history-dependent. In Section 12.3 it was argued that the structure of relative prices of non-traded goods is dependent on the economy's history. Our present example has not reckoned with these additional reasons why history matters. It has been designed only to explore the possible multiplicity of Nash equilibria.

Becker, Murphy and Tamura (1990) have analysed the fertility behaviour and human capital acquisition over time in an economy comprising a single, optimizing dynastic household. They built in scale economies in production possibilities by assuming that the rate of return on human capital is up to a point an increasing function of the stock of human capital. They found that the Euler equation associated with the dynasty's optimization exercise can have multiple stationary states. This means that the dynasty's long run behaviour, and thus fortune, depends on the state of affairs in which it finds itself to begin with. Put more generally, the dynasty's optimal long run behaviour depends on chance events that occur in the short run. (See Arrow and Kurz, 1970; Keeler, Spence and Zeckhauser, 1972; Dasgupta, 1982a, for earlier examples of this phenomenon.) Becker, Murphy and Tamura use this contrivance to explain why some countries (e.g. advanced industrial ones) enjoy low fertility rates and a large human capital base, while others (e.g. sub-Saharan Africa) suffer from high fertility rates and a small human capital base. The authors suggest that this sort of history dependence is akin to that which is associated with multiple Nash equilibria of social systems. But it isn't. History dependence in their model has no policy implications: the economy consists of a single dynasty, and it acts as an optimization agent; so there is no role for public policy. In contrast, the multiplicity of Nash equilibria in the model of this chapter arises from the presence of atmospheric externalities. The externalities *per se* provide a ground for State involvement, while the multiplicity of Nash equilibria offers a role for history. Taken together, they suggest that it may indeed be desirable for governments in sub-Saharan Africa to initiate policies that will encourage households to move towards low fertility and high human capital acquisition. The Becker–Murphy–Tamura analysis is incapable of offering us any such conclusion.

*12.2   *Why Nash Equilibria?*

In this book we are for the most part studying societies consisting of a large number of agents. (An exception has been the household in Chapter 11.) Provided each agent is small relative to society, no agent can influence societal outcome. There is no role for strategic behaviour. In these circumstances Nash equilibria are compelling objects. Where the number of agents is small, the study of Nash equilibria requires justification. It will not be possible for us to probe into the circumstances in which Nash equilibria are the natural objects of study even here. To do so would take us somewhat afield. But I should remark briefly on that set of circumstances most commonly alluded to in game theory, which is based on eductive reasoning. This consists of those situations where agents know one another's utility functions and beliefs, where they know the rules governing the social system, and where there is perfect recall by all of all that has taken place in the past. A central further hypothesis is that all this is 'commonly known'; that is, not only does each agent know it, but also, each agent knows that each agent knows it, each agent knows that each agent knows that each agent knows it, and so on, *ad infinitum*. Myerson (1984), Mertens and Zamir (1985), Binmore and Dasgupta (1986), Aumann (1987a), and Brandenberger and Dekel (1989) offer accounts of how, taken together, these assumptions (allied to a few other technical requirements) imply that, *if* there is a rational outcome in a given social system, it has to be a Nash equilibrium. (Note that this is a conditional support of the idea that Nash equilibria are the natural objects to study. It is not axiomatic that a game must have a solution.) However, Aumann and Brandenburger (1991) have shown that this is overly strong. That players are rational needs only to be mutually known in two-person games (i.e. each knows that the others are rational), not commonly known.

If the assumption of common knowledge of beliefs is dropped, as is done by Bernheim (1984) and Pearce (1984) in their development of the idea of 'rationalizable strategies', other consequences (or outcomes) in a social environment acquire as much claim on our attention as do Nash equilibrium outcomes. Neither Bernheim nor Pearce allows learning to take place. Matters would be different were people to learn about one another and the social structure by observing one another's choice of actions in a stationary environment. (By a 'stationary environment' I mean one that repeats itself indefinitely.) We may expect learning over time to take place in such a way that agents' choices converge to a set of Nash equilibrium strategies. For example, Bayesian learning should be expected to converge to the statistical truth, and thereby to provide a justification for our interest in Nash equilibria. The vital papers on this evolutive approach are Crawford (1988), Fudenberg and Kreps (1988), and Canning (1989, 1990).

13

Population and Savings: Normative Considerations

13.1 *Parental Concerns*

In developing his contractual theory of justice among generations, Rawls (1972: 284–94) writes:

The parties do not know to which generation they belong or, what comes to the same thing, the stage of civilization of their society . . . Thus the persons in the original position are to ask themselves how much they would be willing to save . . . at any given phase of civilization with the understanding that the rates they propose are to regulate the whole span of accumulation . . . Since no one knows to which generation he belongs, the question is viewed from the standpoint of each and a fair accommodation is expressed by the principle adopted. All generations are virtually represented in the original position, since the same principle would always be chosen . . . Moreover, it is immediately obvious that every generation, except possibly the first, gains when a reasonable rate of saving is maintained . . . The process of accumulation, once it is begun, and carried through, is to the good of all subsequent generations. Each passes on to the next a fair equivalent in real capital as defined by a just savings principle . . . Only those in the first generation do not benefit . . . for while they begin the whole process, they do not share in the fruits of their provision. Nevertheless, since it is assumed that a generation cares for its immediate descendants, *as fathers say care for their sons*, a just savings principle . . . would be acknowledged. (Italics mine)

In this passage Rawls is concerned with intergenerational savings, not population policies. There is no suggestion in his book that he regards unalloyed contractualism to be capable of providing a basis for the latter. One may doubt that it is.[1] But public policies bearing on fertility and savings decisions can't be kept independent of each other: desirable investment policies are a function of demographic profiles, and defendable population policies depend upon investment rates. The two need to be discussed simultaneously.[2]

---

[1] See Dasgupta (1974c, 1988c) and Barry (1977).
[2] Dasgupta (1969), Lane (1977), and Gigliotti (1983) have applied the classical utilitarian calculus to address this joint exercise. See also Meade (1955), who noted the connection but did not analyse it.

A number of authors have expressed the thought that, external effects aside, population and savings decisions don't involve social ethics. They have argued that considerate parents take into account the well-being of their children when choosing their family size and deciding how much to save. If they are in addition thoughtful parents, they would know that the welfare of their children will depend upon the well-being of their grand-children, that the welfare of their grandchildren will in turn depend upon the well-being of *their* children, and so on, down the generations. In short, there is a natural recursion of well-being interests along a family line. Thoughtful parents could be expected to take account of their distant descendants, even when they are directly interested only in their own children. A variety of such recursive formulae have been put to work in economic models for the purposes of studying their implied investment rates (see Phelps and Pollak, 1968; Arrow, 1973b; Dasgupta, 1974a,b; Calvo, 1978; Rodriguez, 1981). Recursive formulae have also been used for a combined study of their implied fertility and investment rates (see Dasgupta, 1969, 1974c; Barro and Becker, 1989). It will prove useful to see what the argument amounts to.

Earlier, we took parental utility to depend upon parental consumption (c), the number of children (n), and the average quality of their children (z). We now reinterpret z to be the average welfare of the children, and for simplicity we identify welfare with well-being. Consider generation t (≥ 0) of a family line. We assume there are N_t members. Each person is to be thought of as a completely autonomous agent. I denote the representative member's welfare by W_t. Writings by c_t generation t's average 'consumption' stream, and by n_t the number of children each member of this generation has, we can write

$$W_t = W_t(c_t, n_t, W_{t+1}). \tag{13.1}$$

It makes obvious sense to simplify and assume that W_t doesn't depend explicitly on t. We can then simplify further by supposing that parents keep the worth of their consumption distinct from the other determinants of their welfare. An obvious form of this is

$$W_t = U(c_t) + \delta n_t L(n_t) W_{t+1}, \qquad \text{where } 1 \geq \delta > 0. \tag{13.2}$$

In this expression δ, a constant, is a time discount factor, and $L(n_t)$ is a (concave) function of n_t, given to assuming positive values only.

Repeated use of expression (13.2) implies that

$$W_0 = \Sigma \delta^t N_t Q_t U(c_t) \tag{13.3}$$

where $Q_t = \Pi L(n_\tau)$, and N_t is the size of generation t of this dynasty.[3]

---

[3] That is, $N_t = N_0 n_0 n_1, \ldots, n_{t-1}$. As an example, suppose $L(n_t) = 1$. Then $Q_t = 1$, and we are left with a well-being function which is a pristine form of classical utilitarianism. See Dasgupta (1969).

There is a problem with this though. Even when parents admit to a concern with the well-being of their descendants through such a recursive formula, it doesn't follow that they award the right weights to the well-being of their descendants. We began with thoughtful parents. Such folk ask themselves what are the correct arguments to use when choosing family size and the amount to save or dissave. That they are thoughtful means only that they will ask the question, it doesn't imply they will have an answer 'wired' into them. This is one weakness with Professor Rawls's theory of intergenerational justice, a weakness embedded in the concluding sentences of the passage with which we began. It is a theory concerning how generations might be *expected* to save, not about how they *ought* to save. Theories of optimum population and saving address this latter question. But as we will see, we are nowhere near to having a persuasive answer.[4] Of course, in situations of severe economic stress there may not be an ethically right answer.

13.2 *The Genesis Problem and the Repugnant Conclusion*[5]

'Utilitarian' theories of optimum population and savings have broadly speaking been of two kinds, based on aggregate utility functions reflecting *average* and *total* utility.

The average view (attributable to Mill, Cannan, Wicksell, Robbins, and

---

[4] See Meade (1966) and Phelps and Pollak (1968) for theories of savings based, respectively, on complete and incomplete impartiality across generations. Dasgupta (1974b) was an attempt at interpreting Rawls literally and exploring the idea that his theory requires parental preferences to be taken as the sole basis for intergenerational justice. The article was an exercise in intergenerational (non-cooperative) Nash equilibrium savings rules. It was shown that, unless parental preferences extend sufficiently into the future, Nash equilibrium savings rules yield consumption programmes that are Pareto-inefficient across generations. As a basis for justice among generations, this will not do. Arrow (1973b) and Solow (1974), on the other hand, interpreted Rawls's theory to be the intergenerational extension of his lexicographic maxi-min principle. They and Dasgupta (1974b) proved that, unless parental preferences extend sufficiently into the future, the principle implies either a stagnant economy, or a programme of savings and dissavings which would be revoked by the generation following any that were to pursue it. The programme is therefore intergenerationally 'incoherent'. One should contrast this with the corresponding implications of classical utilitarianism, which are (i) that it is coherent, and (ii) that in plausible economies the optimum rate of savings is of the order of 40–5% of national income (see Mirrlees, 1967). A third possible interpretation of Rawls's principle of just savings is intergenerational bargaining behind a 'veil of ignorance'. This was explored by Dasgupta (1974b). The problem with this route is that a number of well-known bargaining solutions admit to far too many outcomes in plausible economies. The principle therefore has no cutting power. For a substantive theory of justice, this matters. For example, it was shown that both the intergenerational α-core and β-core are to all intents and purposes as large as the set of all intergenerationally Pareto-efficient consumption programmes. This is hardly a guiding principle: there is usually an infinity of Pareto-efficient consumption programmes.

[5] The remainder of this chapter is based on Dasgupta (1974c, 1988c, 1989c), which were in turn much influenced by the many discussions I had in the early 1970s with Simon Blackburn.

Wolfe; see Gottlieb, 1945) is at once problematic, in that it does not specify if we are to maximize the intertemporal sum of each generation's average level of utility, or if we are to maximize the ratio of the intertemporal sum of each generation's total utility to the total number of all who are ever born.[6] The former has been explored by Pitchford (1974); so we know theoretically what it implies in the way of policy. The problem is that the principle lacks philosophical foundations: it is *ad hoc*, and it does not reduce to a defendable theory of just savings in those situations where population is not subject to choice.[7]

The latter interpretation, of maximizing the ratio of the intertemporal sum of each generation's total utility to the total number of all who are ever born, can be given a rationale. (Which island would you choose among islands of varying population sizes and levels of individual utility, if you were not to know which person's shoes you would occupy in any island, and were to attribute 'equi-probability' to each such position?)[8] However, programmes that maximize such an objective are intergenerationally incoherent (see fn. 4 above). This means that, if any generation were to set such a programme into motion, it would be revoked by the next generation. As the earlier generation would know this in advance, it would hardly wish to set the programme into motion.

But this is only one difficulty; there is a prior problem with the formulation. It is questionable whether the thought-experiment of choosing among islands has much to do with the problem in hand, which is to determine a defendable future population size (see Dasgupta, 1988c). Average utilitarianism, whichever way we define 'average', would seem to have fundamental problems with it.

Unlike the 'average' view, the 'total' view isn't so readily vulnerable to scrutiny. It has in any case an impeccable pedigree, namely classical utilitarianism:

For if we take Utilitarianism to prescribe, as the ultimate end of action, happiness as a whole, and not any individual's happiness, unless considered as an element of the whole, it would follow that, if the additional population enjoy on the whole positive happiness, we ought to weigh the amount of happiness gained by the extra number against the amount lost by the remainder. So that, strictly conceived, the

---

[6] Letting N_t denote the size of generation t and W_t the average level of its well-being (alternatively, welfare), the former takes the form $\Sigma \delta^t W_t$, and the latter takes the form $\Sigma \delta^t N_t W_t / \Sigma \delta^t N_t$; where δ, a constant ($0 < \delta \leq 1$), reflects a simplified view of the conditional probability rate of extinction.

[7] I am grateful to Professor Kenneth Arrow for this last observation.

[8] See Harsanyi (1955) and Vickrey (1960). I have qualified equi-probability in the text because it makes no sense when the future has no termination. To give it sense we must suppose that the probability of extinction over the indefinite future is unity. We may then talk of equi-probability of the conditionals. See Dasgupta and Heal (1979, ch. 9) for elaboration of this.

point up to which, on Utilitarian principles, population ought to be encouraged to increase, is not that at which average happiness is the greatest possible . . . but that at which the product formed by multiplying the number of persons living into the amount of average happiness reaches its maximum. (Sidgwick, 1907: 415–16)

This formulation was revived in the important work of Meade (1955). It was subsequently developed for an intertemporal economy in Dasgupta (1969), Lane (1977), and Gigliotti (1983), among others.[9] As an exploration into a deep and difficult set of issues, this literature has something to commend it, but not much. The theory's weakness is its insistence on casting the problem of optimum population and savings as a Genesis Problem, not as an actual problem. This has been the source of a number of seeming paradoxes, much discussed in the recent philosophical literature.[10] It will pay to look at the more striking ones.

In the Genesis Problem there are no actual people. All persons are potential. In its purest form, the Genesis Problem asks how many lives there should be, enjoying what living standards. Now the application of classical utilitarianism to the Genesis Problem in a world with finite resources can imply a 'large' population size. By this I mean that optimum average welfare, even though positive, can be 'low'. So long as average welfare falls slowly enough when the number of individuals increases, population size under classical utilitarianism is encouraged to grow indefinitely no matter how low the average has fallen (see Dasgupta, 1969: 307; Rawls, 1972: 162–3). Parfit (1982, 1984) finds this repugnant. So he has a term for it: the Repugnant Conclusion.

Personal identities ought not to matter in the Genesis Problem. One may argue that they cannot matter, since in the Genesis Problem all persons are potential. In a comparison of possible worlds there *is* no privileged position; no particular agent's point of view, no family's point of view, no generation's point of view. Consider a possible world of M persons which, if created, would be one where each person enjoys a welfare (or well-being; I will use these terms synonymously in this chapter) level equal to W^*. Using the notation developed in Chapter 3, we may express aggregate well-being in this possible world as $W(W^*, M)$, where the second argument has been introduced to indicate that there is to be a comparison of possible worlds of different population sizes. Now imagine another possible world, of $M + 1$ persons, in which if created each person would enjoy the same welfare level, W^*. Aggregate well-being in this world is then $W(W^*, M + 1)$. I shall now confine myself to that class of

[9] Blackorby and Donaldson (1985) and Hammond (1988) have offered axiomatic bases for the classical utilitarian view of population and savings.

[10] Parfit (1976, 1982, 1984, 1987, 1990) is the source. See also Bayles (1976), Sikora and Barry (1978), McMahan (1981), Hurka (1983), Blackorby and Donaldson (1985), Sterba (1987), Temkin (1987), Cowen (1989), Ng (1989), Hauser (1990), and Heyd (1992).

ethical theories in which there is a unique value of W^*, such that, for all $M \geq 0$, $W(W^*, M) = W(W^*, M + 1)$. I calibrate this W^* as *zero*. This defines the zero level of welfare.[11] Levels of well-being in excess of this reflect good states of affairs, and such theories as I am discussing here state that it is good that people enjoy a good quality of life. Contrariwise, levels falling short of this (i.e. negative levels of well-being) reflect bad states of affairs, and such theories as I am discussing here will also hold that it is an undesirable world wherein the quality of lives is bad.

Consider two possible worlds, $(W_1, \ldots, W_M)$ and $(W_1, \ldots, W_M, W_{M+1})$. Call them X and Y respectively. They differ solely in the feature that Y would have an additional person (labelled $M + 1$), with well-being W_{M+1}. The identities of the first M labels (e.g. their genetic makeup) in the two worlds may not correspond, but within the class of theories we are restricting ourselves to here it is of no consequence in the Genesis Problem (X and Y are only possible worlds.) The question is: how should X and Y be ranked?

One can argue that X is the better world if W_{M+1} is negative, a guiding principle in such theories as we are discussing being that, *ceteris paribus*, it would be wrong to bring into existence a person whose life is to be bad. But if W_{M+1} is positive, what then?

In a thoughtful essay, Sikora (1978: 42) has reasserted the classical thesis that 'it is *prima facie* wrong to prevent the existence of anyone with reasonable prospects of happiness', the implication being that, in the event W_{M+1} is positive, Y is a better possible world than X. Sikora calls theories based on this thesis Obligation Theories. His wording is curious; I mean the idea of preventing the existence of *someone*. It suggests an image of potential immigrants to a place of reasonable plenty condemned instead to suspension in an eternal limbo. It would be an error to regard potential persons as a special sort of people. The recognition that W_{M+1} is positive involves no more than a comparison of the level of well-being of person $M + 1$ in Y with the worst state such that it is not a positively bad thing that a person should live in such a state. It would be an odd thing to say that, were Y instead of X to come about, person $M + 1$ would be benefited. Certainly, it would not convey the sense we usually impute to the term 'benefiting'. Above all, we must avoid the error of regarding zero well-being as the point at which a person is indifferent between dying and continuing to live. Subsequently we will need to come back to this point.

Ethically, the only relevant difference between X and Y in the Genesis Problem is that Y would have an additional person enjoying a positive level

---

[11] Theories in this class will of course differ as to the *kind* of life at which the level of welfare is zero. I shall return to this important point later. We should note that classical utilitarianism, in which the W function is additive in individual welfares, belongs to this class of theories.

of well-being. Call the conception that says that therefore *Y* is the better world the *Pareto-plus Principle*. The principle is so appealing that many philosophers have felt no need to justify it (see e.g. Sikora, 1978). But there would seem to be a problem with it: under fairly weak conditions the Pareto-plus Principle implies the Repugnant Conclusion. Parfit (1984) calls this implication the Mere Addition Paradox.[12]

I will argue in the next section that this is no paradox: there is nothing *repugnant* about the Repugnant Conclusion. I will then argue (Section 13.4) that the Genesis Problem is in any case a wrong problem for us. Even if the Mere Addition Paradox were a paradox, nothing of consequence to ethics would have followed from it.

13.3 Is the Repugnant Conclusion Repugnant?

Recall our definition of the zero level of well-being. This isn't a standard arrived at through a comparison with 'non-existence'. Such comparisons can't be made. The 'unborn' aren't a class of people. It makes no sense to attribute a degree of well-being, low or high or nil, to the 'state of not being born'. Non-existence is like nothing for us, not even a very long night, because there is no *us* to imagine upon. One can't be asked what it would be like to experience one's own non-existence, for there is no *subject* of experience in non-existence.[13] The impossibility of imagining our own non-existence gives spurious credence to the view that non-existence must be a long dismal night from which we must try to rescue people. We can, of course, feel grateful to the persons who created us for doing just that,

---

[12] See also Parfit (1982) and Blackorby and Donaldson (1985). The reasoning is as follows. Suppose X_0 is a potential world with M persons, each enjoying a level of well-being equal to W_0, where W_0 is positive. Assuming that $W(W_0,M)$ is continuous, the Pareto-plus Principle implies that X_0 is exactly as good a world as X_1, where X_1 is a potential world with M persons, each enjoying W_0, and an additional person whose level of well-being is nil. But then there is a positive level of well-being, say W_1, such that X_1 would be exactly as good as a potential world in which *each* of the $M + 1$ persons would enjoy a level of well-being equal to W_1. Now, any conception of aggregate well-being for a fixed number of people which is 'more egalitarian' than the lexicographic maxi-*max* will have it that $W_1 < W_0$. Let us assume this. Next, construct X_2 from X_1 in the same way as X_1 was constructed from X_0, and define W_2 analogously. Then $W_2 < W_1$, and so $W_2 < W_1 < W_0$. Proceeding in this way, we can create more and more populous worlds. In particular, for the kth extension, $0 < W_k < W_{k-1} < \ldots < W_2 < W_1 < W_0$. This means that W_k tends to a limit as k tends to infinity. If the limit is zero we have the Repugnant Conclusion; if not, we don't. We finally note that, if the aggregate well-being function for each given number of people is *additive* over individual well-beings, or is a function more equality-conscious, then $W_0 \geq (M + k)W_k/M$. This means that W_k tends to zero as k tends to infinity, which is the Repugnant Conclusion.

[13] I am talking of non-existence in the text, not death, which is a different matter altogether. In talking of death we talk of some existing person's death. Thus T. Nagel's (1986a) claim that imagining one's death is no different from imagining oneself unconscious isn't directly relevant to our discussion.

not because they rescued us from anything, but because they are responsible for all this experience. To say that a person has a wretched life, a dismally low standard of living, is not at all to say that the person would have been better off unborn. It is to say only that it is *bad* that her standard of living is what it is. No doubt it is enormously difficult to make such an assessment (e.g. where are we to draw the line separating positive and negative levels of well-being?). This does not mean we can avoid making it, nor that we ought to even if we could. Possible people aren't actual (or future) people, any more than clay by the river bank is a mud hut. It is actual persons who have feelings, aspirations, needs, claims, projects, and a sense of justice. In short, it is actual persons who are moral agents. When we revere the memory of deceased persons it is to their memory that we show reverence, not to 'them'. When we debate at what stage in the development of a foetus we ought to regard the foetus a person, we recognize that there is something akin to a discontinuity in the process of each person's creation. The debate no doubt shows the notion to be fuzzy, even more than, and intrinsically a good deal more important than, the notion of a heap of stones (how many stones are needed to form a heap?), but this doesn't mean that the notion is spurious, nor that it depends upon mere convention. Social convention, possibly backed by formal legislation, dictates how in fact we resolve the issue of when a foetus becomes a person. This does not mean the resolution is right, it only means we think there is something to resolve. In this we *are* right.

It is for these reasons permissible to say that a person has a wretched existence (or, to put it sharply, a low, negative level of well-being), and that it is bad that she should be in such a state, and yet to insist that the person has moral worth, that her life has value, that her existence has value, because, if nothing else, it is *her* life. 'Better if *you* hadn't existed' is a different judgement from 'better if an additional life isn't created'. This delinking of the notion of zero well-being from the worth of an actual person's life implies that the quality of life at which well-being is zero isn't what is conventionally urged upon us by philosophers working on normative population theory. Consider, for example, Parfit's framing of the Repugnant Conclusion: 'For any possible population of at least ten billion people, all with a very high quality of life, there must be some larger imaginable population whose existence, if other things are equal, would be better, even though its members have lives that are barely worth living' (Parfit, 1984: 388).

One would not deny that this is repugnant, but then one should not contest that it is rigged. We are first tempted with a population size about twice the world's current population, a figure almost certainly to be reached by the middle of the next century, and a figure that, given current and expected future technology and resources, many think can in principle be sustained at reasonable material comfort.[14] This is at once followed by a picture of a vastly overcrowded earth, where people scramble for resources so as to eke out an existence, leading lives 'barely worth living'. But the underlying logic in zero well-being is a far cry from this. A person whose life is barely worth living has a *very low*, *negative* living standard. She is one of the wretched of the earth, and there are hundreds of millions of such people alive today, disfranchised, malnourished, prone to illness— but surviving, and tenaciously displaying that their lives are worth living by the persistence with which they continue to wish to live. When the Conclusion is stated as Parfit states it, it *is* repugnant. But it is not a conclusion to which the Pareto-plus Principle leads us if the principle is applied to comparisons of well-being in the Genesis Problem. There is nothing repugnant about a very large imaginable population, all enjoying positive well-being. As well-being would be positive, their lives would be good; they would be more than just worth living. There is nothing morally repugnant in judging that in the Genesis Problem sufficient numbers can compensate for average well-being, so long as average well-being is positive; that is, so long as lives are good.

13.4 *Actual Problems and an Underlying Asymmetry*

We have seen that the Pareto-plus Principle, when applied to the Genesis Problem, does not imply a large population suffering lives not worth living. The Mere Addition Paradox is therefore no paradox within the confines of the Genesis Problem. It is not even a problem. But this provides no excuse for studying the Genesis Problem. The Genesis Problem is the wrong problem to investigate. We should instead be studying actual problems.

In an actual problem there are actual people, real persons whom I shall for simplicity call the current generation, who deliberate over future population sizes and future living standards. They are by the nature of things the decision-makers. Actual parents are members of the current generation, and as thoughtful parents they grapple with actual problems, not with the Genesis Problem. This leads us back full circle to fertility decisions, the subject of the previous chapter. The size of the current generation is given, it is a datum.

Consider the following problem. A couple have a newly born daughter, whose well-being over her entire life is firmly expected to be nil unless additional resources (for example, additional health care and education in her early years) are diverted to her needs. Option X is to make available such resources as will raise her well-being level to W^{**}. Option Y is for

---

[14] Many experts, on the other hand, do not: see e.g. Ehrlich and Ehrlich (1990).

the couple to create an additional child, with the understanding that resources will be diverted to this new child sufficient to enable it to enjoy a lifetime standard of living equal to W^{**}; however, under Y the little girl's well-being over her entire life will be nil. What should the couple do?

If, as Sidgwick (1907) would have it, pleasure or agreeable consciousness is the sole good, and if the fact that something good would be the result of one's action is the basic reason for doing anything (the ground of binding reasons), then the couple in question should be indifferent between X and Y.[15] But classical utilitarianism presupposes a conception of persons quite unsuitable for analysing so personal a problem as this. As a model for obtaining the ends of personal action, the theory won't do.[16]

There are many considerations the parents can legitimately bring to bear in choosing between X and Y. How many children do they already have? What is the source of the additional resources under the two options? What are the implications of their decisions on the family? What is their motivation in having children? And so on. It is thus tempting to insert a *ceteris paribus* clause in the example, so as to let it pose the problem of choice in a sharp way. In the Genesis Problem it is possible to do this; so the literature on optimum population is littered with the *ceterus paribus* clause (see e.g. Parfit, 1982, 1984, 1990). In actual problems it isn't possible to do so.

One reason (there are others) why it isn't possible is that the newly born daughter is part of what constitutes the couple's *family*, whereas the possible further child under option Y is not. A theory of obligation which invites the idea of a family, and more generally of a *community*, to play a role will provide a reason to the couple for choosing X over Y. This reason does not of course settle the matter. (The little girl may be their only child; this may be the last opportunity for having another child; three may not conform to the couple's conception of a family; and so forth). What it does do is expose the fact that family members have a special claim upon one another.[17] Potential persons don't have this claim. 'They' are not members of the community.

Each of us, to be sure, belongs simultaneously to many communities, involving varying strengths of ties and commitments; and in Chapter 5 I invoked the idea of a wide community when appealing to the differing

---

[15] For this example I am assuming implicitly that well-being is a measure of 'agreeable consciousness'.

[16] We need not rehearse the reasons why it is so; the literature identifying classical utilitarianism's weaknesses is now vast. See e.g. Williams (1985). It is a striking feature of procreation that as an activity it is at once intensely personal and social.

[17] I am grateful to Paul Seabright for discussions on this point. In Seabright (1989) he has, by showing how potent is the idea of a community in population policy, provided a non-rights-based rationale for the argument I used in Dasgupta (1982b, 1989c) when developing this example. In the earlier work I appealed to the *rights* of the existing child.

spheres of citizenship and their implied obligations on the part of the State towards its citizens. Here I am thinking of the family as a nuclear community. But it is a community with so very many special properties that it is unlike any other community we belong to.[18] Among other things, it is special in that a child is never a party to the decision that leads to her birth. It is also special in that, assuming happy circumstances, her creation is the decision of a loving couple. Parents, by virtue of their act, acquire an obligation towards their offspring that no others have. People of course don't have an obligation to become parents, but they acquire an obligation if they do choose to become parents. By the same token, children have a type of claim on their parents which no one else has.

In the example with which we started, this special claim of the little girl on her parents has a number of implications. From our perspective here, one such implication is that thoughful parents will not, and should not, attach the same weight to the little girl's well-being as to the potential well-being of an additional child. The special claim provides a prima facie case for choosing X over Y. The case is, of course, not decisive. But it must play a role in the couple's decision.[19] The problem is, this asymmetry leads to a seeming paradox: an intransitivity of ethical relations. I turn to this and its resolution.

Consider now a couple with three children. Option A facing them is not to have any more children and to enjoy a lifetime living standard equal to 10 units for each of the five members of the family (see Table 13.1).[20] Options B and C are to have yet another child, followed by two different resource allocations. Under B the existing members of the family would still enjoy lifetime living standards equal to 10 units, and the new child would enjoy 3 units. Under C each of the six members would enjoy 9 units. We take it that the couple cannot pre-commit, in that both B and C remain viable options even after the third is born. (Of course, once the third child is born option A is no longer available.) What should the couple do?

[18] These properties include the fact of close genetic linkage between members of the nuclear community. I am stressing the special nature of the family so as not to give any suggestion that the modern State with its attendant parts is merely a large family. It is so far from it that it can do no useful work for the purposes of developing just rules governing the basic structure of society. There is no inconsistency in our appealing to what is an explicit communitarian consideration here when peering inside the household's reproductive decisions, and in avoiding it when developing the ends of public policy.

[19] Neo-Utilitarians too have reached this conclusion of asymmetric treatment, but by a different route: 'We are in favour of making people happy, but neutral about making happy people' (Narveson, 1973: 73). The pioneering paper on what I call actual problems is Narveson (1967). He labelled the version of utilitarianism that accommodates this asymmetry 'person-affecting utilitarianism'. See also Narveson (1978) and Warren (1978). For a far-reaching critique of classical utilitarianism when applied to reproductive decisions, see Heyd (1992).

[20] I revert to living standards rather than the more comprehensive well-being (or welfare), because it has greater immediacy when discussing the problem in hand.

Table 13.1   Fertility choice of a five-member family

	A	B	C
Father	10	10	9
Mother	10	10	9
First child	10	10	9
Second child	10	10	9
Third child	10	10	9
Fourth child	—	3	9

Notice first that the group comprising the family on whose behalf the couple chooses among these three options is different from the group comprising this same family on whose behalf the couple would choose among B and C were the fourth child to be born. This matters. But first we will see how the desired asymmetry leads to a seeming intransitivity of the underlying moral relation.

We will assume for concreteness that the living standards of actual people count for thrice the living standards of possible people. This isn't of course how thoughtful parents reason; they reason more qualitatively. The way a moral dilemma is *framed* can matter, and in any case not everything of moral significance can be articulated. There is more than mere vulgarity in attaching explicit weights to the well-being of different people. But our purpose here isn't to resolve a dilemma, it is to illustrate a point. So we imagine that it is possible to use quantitative weights in making fertility decisions.

We will assume next for simplicity that the couple in our example evaluate alternatives on the basis of the weighted sum of living standards, the weights applied to actual persons being always equal. Notice that this implies they subscribe to the Pareto-plus Principle. We will see though that in spite of this there is no whiff of the Mere Addition Paradox. Consider then how the couple might reason. Take first the initial evaluation of A, B, and C. As there are five actual members and one possible addition, aggregate living standard under A is $3(10 + 10 + 10 + 10 + 10) = 150$; under B it is $3(10 + 10 + 10 + 10 + 10) + 3 = 153$; and under C it is $3(9 + 9 + 9 + 9 + 9) + 9 = 144$. From the point of vew of the five-membered family, the ranking is therefore 'B over A over C'. The couple would now be well-advised to have a fourth child, but for one thing: it knows in advance that once the new child is born the ranking of B relative to C will reverse itself. (What kind of family are we that allows our littlest to enjoy a living standard of only 3 while each of the rest of us enjoys 10 each?) In reality, this is what happens: Once the fourth child is born, the composition of the family changes, and there are six actual people. The couple now assesses aggregate living standards under B and C to be

$3(10 + 10 + 10 + 10 + 10) + 3 \times 3 = 159$ and $3(9 + 9 + 9 + 9 + 9 + 9) = 162$, respectively. This reversal of ranking violates the well-known 'independence of irrelevant alternatives' axiom in social choice theory.[21] The axiom may have ethical bite when population size is not subject to choice, but it has no bite in the present context (see below). When A, B, and C are all feasible options, the fourth child is only a potential child. But when B and C are the only alternatives, the fourth child is an actual child; option A is not an 'irrelevant' alternative.

As the couple can't pre-commit (and it is important to recognize that they will desire *not* to pre-commit), they will know in advance when faced with A, B, and C that after the birth of the fourth child they will reverse their decision and opt for C, the least desirable option from the point of view of the existing five-membered family.

This looks incoherent (it looks as though the couple suffers from intransitive moral preferences), and in an influential paper it has in effect been used by Parfit (1976) as an argument for rejecting the distinction between actual and possible people.[22] But there is no incoherence here. It would have been an incoherent state of affairs were arguments provided to demonstrate that the ranking of options ought to be independent of the family's composition (which is the case in the Genesis Problem). But I have seen none provided by anyone, at least none that is itself coherent. When family size is the object of choice there can be no overall moral ordering of options, and it is a mistake to search for one. Moral perspective has to be from somewhere, it can't be from absolutely nowhere. This is why the Genesis Problem offers such a very misleading substitute framework for thinking about actual problems. It explains why so much of the literature on normative population theory is divorced from life. That the ranking of options based on a family's well-being changes when its membership increases is no paradox. With the addition of the fourth child the family's perspective changes. There is a new member now, and *she* must count.

The notion of impartiality in social ethics, the idea that we should seek to peer at matters from no one particular person's viewpoint (as in Harsanyi's notion of impartial preferences (Harsanyi, 1955), and Rawls's reasoning behind the veil of ignorance), has force when future numbers are not subject to choice. In such situations we, the actual people, can deliberate over options affecting ourselves and future people. We can look at the world not only from our perspective, but also from the perspective

---

[21] I am grateful to John Broome for drawing my attention to this.

[22] I say 'in effect' only because Parfit's objective was to reject Narveson's person-affecting utilitarianism.

of future people as and when they appear. The veil of ignorance provides us with a reason for doing so.

The problem here is different. Future numbers are a matter of decision. Neither Harsanyi's nor Rawls's construct can get a grip on the matter here. It isn't possible to assume the perspective of possible people. The veil can be worn for a pure savings problem, where future numbers are given. It can do no work for the joint savings and population problem. For the joint problem an overall ordering can only be conceived for each generation of actual people. The moral viewpoint is thereby *generation-relative*.[23] As generations change with the appearance of newer and newer people, the point of view changes. This means that the ordering itself changes. What appears to be intransitivity isn't intransitivity because the perspective changes.[24]

How then ought the couple to reason? Rationality dictates the familiar backward-induction reasoning. The couple have a reason for choosing A, the second-ranked option among A, B, and C. This is because the couple knows that were it to have a fourth child it would be guided by a different ordering, which would result in the eventual choice of C.

Earlier I argued that the Repugnant Conclusion is not repugnant once we recognize that a life involving zero well-being ought not to be equated to a life barely worth living. From this we concluded that the Pareto-Plus Principle when applied to the Genesis Problem does not imply a vast population. The distinction between the Genesis Problem and actual problems reduces even further the possibility that desirable population sizes are 'large'. In an actual problem Parfit's Mere Addition Paradox cannot be constructed out of the Pareto-Plus Principle. Redefine A to be the option, open to the current generation, of enjoying a moderately high standard of living and of *not* adding to its numbers; redefine B to be the option where the current generation maintains its moderately high living standard and adds a number of new persons with a low but positive

[23] Compare this with the agent-relativity of ethical reasoning demonstrated by Bernard Williams in his essay in Smart and Williams (1973), and by Nagel (1986b), among others. For convenience I am now identifying generations with actual people. In this account generations change every time a person is born. For convenience of exposition, I am also assuming that future numbers are totally subject to choice, so that there are no exogenously given number of future people to reckon with.

[24] Taken on their own, contractual theories cannot get off the ground when fertility is subject to choice. They need to be embedded within a larger theory embracing reproductive choice. For every possible population profile one can develop a contractual theory of intergenerational justice; but across different profiles it makes no sense to try and do so. (Who are the contractees?) This is one reason why Hare's criticism of Rawls's theory, that it has embarrassing consequences when possible people are included among parties in the Rawlsian 'original position', is off the mark (see Hare, 1973: 245–6). For an attempt at constructing a method of making fertility decisions consistent with a contractual view of intergenerational savings, see Dasgupta (1974c, 1988c).

standard of living; and, finally, redefine C to be the option where these new people are created and everyone shares the earth's resources, so that the current generation's living standard, though it remains positive, is much reduced. It is perfectly coherent for the current generation to maintain that, while it recognizes C to be a better world than B were the additional people to be born, and while from *its* ethical perspective B would be a better world than A, it will nevertheless choose A because, from *its* perspective again, A is a better world than C.[25] There is nothing in ethical reasoning which requires of us to create a world with large numbers of people, all having a very low standard of living.

These ideas extend themselves to the more complex question of savings and fertility decisions across the whole sequence of generations. As I have argued, the question can only be seen from the perspective of actual and future people. With the passage of time *some* potential lives become actual lives as the world unfolds along a path determined by choices made by Mother Nature and actual people of the past. No doubt the present generation plays God in choosing the next generation's size and its resource and capital base. But there is no unique present generation. Each future generation in turn becomes the present and has to choose. So long as there are future generations, no generation is privileged in this sense. Just as *we* have to peer into the future, each generation in turn peers into future possibilities having accepted the resource and capital base it has inherited from the past. Given the asymmetry we have identified for fertility decisions, each generation awards a higher weight to its own living standard when proposing the sizes of all future generations and choosing the size of the next generation.

This isn't the place to develop the formal argument. (For this see Dasgupta, 1974c.) The numerical example we have just studied indicates a way we might proceed. For each decision-maker (I have been calling them 'generations' here) fertility and savings decisions need to be made sequentially, not simultaneously. Corresponding to each possible demographic profile, the present generation deliberates over alternative savings programmes. For our purposes here it doesn't matter how choice over these programmes is arrived at. It could be based on contractarian notions, or utilitarian notions, or whatever. What is obtained is a savings *rule*, a mapping from demographic profiles into savings programmes.[26] Given its

<hr/>

[25] A number of additional paradoxes of population have been presented in the recent literature. See especially Parfit (1984, 1990) and Temkin (1987). Each of them can be resolved in much the same way as the Mere Addition Paradox, provided of course that we address actual problems.

[26] For an account of optimal utilitarian savings rates in aggregative models of economics, see Cass (1965), Koopmans (1965, 1967), Mirrlees (1967), Chakravatry (1969), and Arrow and Kurz (1970). In each of these works, population size is assumed to be given.

own perspective, the choice of future numbers is then made by the present generation, they having kept in mind that the programme must be acceptable to all who are born in the course of its duration. This is, of course, hopelessly non-substantive. But it seems to offer the right grammar for constructing a substantive theory of optimal population and savings. For the moment it would seem to be the most we may expect.

13.5 *Rational Ends*

Population ethics has for long been an underdeveloped branch of moral philosophy. That it has remained backward has much to do with the insistence of philosophers writing on the subject on ignoring the ethical relevance of parental desires, and the related question of what gives meaning to us concerning our own lives. That my neighbour is not as close to me as are my daughters and son is a genetic fact, but that isn't quite the point here. More to the mark is that my children provide me with a means of self-transcendence, the widest avenue open to me of living *through* time. Mortality is necessary if we are to imbue life with a sense of urgency. Without it time would be costless, and so life would be shorn of one essential value. But life's achievements are rendered durable by the possibility of procreation. The ability to leave descendants enables us to invest in projects that will not cease to have value once we are gone, projects that *justify* life rather than merely serve it. These projects include not only the creation of ideas and artefacts; more pervasively, they include the formation of personal values. Thus the questions, 'what kind of person ought I to try and be; what should I value?' do not presume the questioner to own a specific set of talents, abilities, or resources (anyone can, and must, ask them); they presume only that they play a role in any reasoned answer.

Procreation is a means of making one's values durable. We imbue our children with values we cherish not merely because we think it is good for *them*, but also because we desire to see our values survive. It seems to me that our descendants do something supremely important for us here: they add a certain value to our lives which our mortality would otherwise deprive them of. Alexander Herzen's remark, that human development is a kind of chronological unfairness, since those who live later profit from the labour of their predecessors without paying the same price, and Kant's view, that it is disconcerting that earlier generations should carry their burdens only for the sake of the later ones, and that only the last should have the good fortune to dwell in the completed building, or in other words, the thought that we can do something for posterity but it can do nothing for us (see Rawls, 1972: 291), is a reflection of an extreme form of alienation—alienation from one's own life.

This viewpoint, of seeing ourselves as part of a delegation of generations, has roots reaching far back, in many cultures; and in recent years it has found its deepest expression in Schell (1982) and Heyd (1992). We act upon this perspective most often with no explicit verbalization to accompany it. We assume parenthood quite naturally; we don't make a big intellectual meal of it. It's the sort of thing we take responsibility for in the normal course of events. Of course, special circumstances may deflect us; we may have more urgent projects and purposes. Here, the fact of a general assumption of parenthood is of importance. An artist, for example, may regard his work as more important than parenting; but he is able to do so only because others are assuring him by their actions that there will be a next generation to bestow durability to the value of his work. The springs that motivate the general run of humankind to assume parenthood are deep and abiding. The genetic basis of the matter merely explains the existence of this motivation, it doesn't justify it. Justification has to be sought elsewhere, and any reasonable answer must come allied to the viewpoint that every generation is a trustee of the wide range of capital stocks (be it cultural or moral, manufactured or natural) it has inherited from the past. Looking backward, it acknowledges an implicit contract with the previous generation, of receiving the capital in return for its transmission, modified suitably in the light of changing circumstances and of increasing knowledge. Looking forward, it offers an implicit contract to the next generation, of bequeathing its stocks of capital in return that they be modified suitably by it and then passed on to the following generation. The idea of intergenerational exchange is embedded in the perspective of eternity. But the intellectual source of such exchange is a far cry from the conception that balked Herzen in his effort at locating mutually beneficial terms of trade.

Recent attempts by social thinkers in Western industrial countries at creating an *environmental ethic* draw their strength from something like this conception (see e.g. Schell, 1982). But it does not provide enough of an apparatus for them to succeed. Finally, there is no avoiding the question, 'what should I value?' if we are to see ourselves living through time, rather than in time. It is, for example, a mistake to try to justify the protection of the giant redwoods—or of a seemingly trivial species such as the hawksbill turtles—or, more widely, the preservation of ecological diversity solely on instrumental grounds; on the grounds that we know they are useful to us, or that they may prove useful to our descendants. Such arguments have a role, but they are not all. Nor can the argument rely on the 'welfare' of the members of such species (it doesn't account for the special role that *species* preservation plays in the argument); or indeed on the 'rights' of animals. A full justification must base itself also on how we see ourselves, on what kind of people we ought to try to be, on what our rational desires are. In examining our values, and thus our lives, we have to ask if the destruction of an entire species-habitat for some immediate gratification is something we can live with comfortably. The mistake is to see procreation and ecological preservation as matters of personal and political morality. It is as much a matter of ethics.

Population ethics is rightly regarded a difficult field of inquiry. In this chapter I have tried to argue that the kinds of difficulty that have intrigued philosophers in recent years are insubstantial. Real difficulties lie elsewhere. They lie in deep conceptual problems actual people are faced with when they contemplate the desirable size of their family and the amount of savings that should accompany it. They lie in particular in the problems that poor households in poor countries repeatedly face when deliberating on this.

Classical Utilitarianism in a Limited World

★13.1 *The Model*

In this chapter I put classical utilitarianism to work in a world with limited resources, and check the implications of this. By 'limited resources' I mean that production possibilities are constrained by some fixed factor, such as land, whose limitations aren't expected to be overcome through indefinite technological progress. As noted in Chapter 13, classical utilitarianism views the matter as a Genesis Problem. There are only possible people to consider; there aren't any actual people when the analysis is conducted. A full intertemporal solution to such a problem was given in Dasgupta (1969). Here I simplify the model so as to expose the essentials of the argument. It transpires that little of analytical importance is lost by this move.

It is simplest to think of a timeless world. I take it that there is a given quantity, K, of an all-purpose consumption good lying around in the world. There is no production possibility open to any who may inhabit it. If C is a person's consumption level, his *utility* index is $U(C)$, where U is a numerical function, increasing in C (i.e. $U'(C) > 0$), with diminishing returns (i.e. $U''(C) < 0$).[1] Let C_0 denote the level of consumption at which utility is nil; that is, $U(C_0) = 0$. We will refer to C_0 as the *utility subsistence level of consumption*. I assume that C_0 is positive (see Fig. ★13.1; see also Section 13.2).

Let N denote the number of people created, and for ease of computation let N be a continuous variable.[2] I assume that the same utility function can be attributed to all potential persons. Now marginal utility is a decreasing function of consumption. We can then conclude from classical utilitariansism that an equal distribution of K among all who are created is the optimum distribution. If N people are created, each should receive K/N units of the consumption good. Total utility is then $NU(K/N)$, and in the Genesis Problem we search for that value of N which maximizes this.

---

[1] Here I will use the word 'utility' in a generic sense, being a numerical measure of the quality of life. One may think of it as 'well-being'.
[2] This is a perfectly good assumption if K is large.

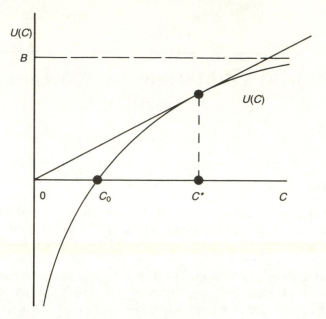

Fig. *13.1   Sidgwick–Meade optimum population size

*13.2   *The Solution*

So we differentiate $NU(K/N)$ with respect to N, which yields the derivative $U(K/N) - (K/N)U'(K/N)$. This we equate to zero. The optimum population size is the solution of this equation. Write $C \equiv K/N$. Since we know K, locating the optimum N is the same as locating the optimum C. The condition which yields optimum C is therefore

$$U'(C) = U(C)/C; \qquad\qquad (*13.1)$$

that is, the value of C at which *marginal* utility of consumption equals *average* utility per unit of consumption.

   Equation (*13.1) is fundamental to classical utilitarianism. (See Meade, 1955, and Dasgupta, 1969, for successive generalizations of this.) I shall call it the Sidgwick–Meade Rule here. Its intuitive basis is simple. Suppose we have located the optimum population. Neither a marginal increase in population size, nor a marginal decrease, should change total utility. So suppose we were to contemplate a marginal increase. (The argument associated with a marginal decrease is analogous.) Then this additional person would share K equally with the 'original' population. The gain in introducing this additional person is his utility, which is $U(C)$. But there is also a loss, which is that each of the remaining persons has slightly less consumption. This utility loss is $CU'(C)$. At the optimum population size this gain and loss must equal. The Sidgwick–Meade Rule asserts this equality. Figure *13.1 shows how we may locate the optimum consumption level per head with the help of the Sidgwick–Meade Rule. I denote the solution by C^*.

We now consider a special class of utility functions to obtain quantitative results. Consider the following class:

$$U(C) = B - C^{-\alpha},   (*13.2)$$

where B and α are positive constants. Equation (*13.2) is useful because it is defined by two parameters, B and α. Frank Ramsey (1928) called B the 'bliss level', for obvious reasons: B can be approached, but never attained.

With (*13.2) as the utility function, it is an easy matter to check that C_0 is given by the expression

$$C_0 = (1/B)^{1/\alpha}.   (*13.3)$$

Now use (*13.2) in the Sidgwick–Meade Rule (*13.1) to obtain the optimum per capita consumption level as

$$C^* = [(1 + \alpha)/B]^{1/\alpha}.   (*13.4)$$

Finally, use (*13.3) in (*13.4) to re-express (*13.4) as

$$C^*/C_0 = (1 + \alpha)^{1/\alpha}.   (*13.5)$$

Now α is a positive number, and it is a well-known mathematical fact that when α is positive $(1 + \alpha)^{1/\alpha}$ is less than e (the base of natural logarithms), which in turn is approximately 2.74 . . . I conclude therefore that

$$C^*/C_0 = (1 + \alpha)^{1/\alpha} < e \approx 2.74 . . .   (*13.6)$$

Taking exact figures, suppose $\alpha = 1$. Then $C^*/C_0 = 2$, which is to say that optimum consumption per person is only twice as large as the utility subsistence consumption level. Quite obviously, the larger is α, the closer is C^*/C_0 to *unity*. This is the precise sense in which classical utilitarianism can advocate 'overly large' population sizes, which Parfit (1982, 1984) has reiterated and christened the Repugnant Conclusion. In Chapter 13 I argued that non-existence is not a state of existence. We concluded from this that the utility subsistence rate has to be given an interpretation altogether different from the one given to it by Parfit. When this is done, (*13.6) is not at all repugnant. Thus, even were we to see the problem of population and savings through classical utilitarian spectacles and see it as the Genesis Problem, we would not subscribe to huge populations leading lives barely worth living.

PART IV

Undernourishment and Destitution

Food Needs and Work Capacity

14.1 *Complementarities among Nutrients*

The nutrients we consume are conventionally divided into five categories: proteins, carbohydrates, fats, vitamins, and minerals. For this reason, in estimating the prevalence of malnourishment in a region, or country, it is common practice to choose benchmarks (or, as some would say, critical limits) which reflect nutrient requirements for representative members of various categories of people (e.g. children, male adults, pregnant and lactating women), and then to calculate the percentage of each population falling below these benchmarks. These are *headcount indices*. In Chaper 4 we studied the headcount index of poverty in the three continents where poverty is widespread: Asia, Africa, and Latin America. Poverty there was defined by low income. But in poor countries poverty lines are often based on nutrition intakes, and, while nutrition requirements may be stated in terms of foods of different kinds (e.g. the balanced-diet lists issued by the Indian Council for Medical Research), or nutrients of various types (e.g. the illustrations in S. Davidson *et al.*, 1975; Chapter 13), in population-wide studies the index most often chosen is *food energy*.[1] There is a reason for this, and it will be useful to identify it before we study the link between nutrition and the capacity for work. This is what we shall do in this section.

Nutrients to an extent display complementarities among themselves, just as they do with sanitation and personal hygiene (see Chapter 4 and Section 14.2 below), in that a person can't make up for deficiencies in one by consuming a lot of another. For example, supplementation of dietary energy does not improve children's health if their diets continue to have insufficient quantities of minerals and essential amino acids (see e.g. Golden and Golden, 1990).[2] Moreover, if the quantities were reduced

---

[1] The classic economy-wide estimation (it was for India) is Dandekar and Rath (1971). For subsequent estimates of the magnitude of undernourishment in India, see Bardhan (1973), and Sukhatme (1977, 1978, 1981a, b, 1982a). For the headcount index of the world's undernourished, see Reutlinger and Selowsky (1976), Reutlinger and Alderman (1980), Reutlinger and Pellekaan (1986), FAO (1987), and United Nations (1987). I will discuss the FAO methodology for making such calculations in the following chapter.

[2] Pollitt (1991) has demonstrated how diverse are the functional effects of iron deficiency in children from different communities. It was his point that these communities differ widely in the character of their nutritional deficiencies.

even while proportions were maintained, a person would reach a point where his health was at risk. A diet is *balanced* if the various nutrients appear in it in their required quantities. To be sure, diets in most poor countries are often quite unbalanced, so that, for example, adequate supplies of vitamin A, iron, iodine, and the B-group vitamins are not assured even if, say, protein needs are met. But, *very broadly speaking*, those suffering from a deficiency in any one nutrient on a periodic basis should be suspected of suffering from a deficiency in another. In poor countries nutritional deficiencies are today mostly an outcome of poverty.[3]

The implications for policy of deficiencies in proteins or carbohydrates or fats (the macro-nutrients) are different from those arising from short-falls in minerals and vitamins (the micro-nutrients). Thus, the most common form of anaemia is iron deficiency. The condition refers to a situation where the concentration of haemoglobin in the blood is below the requirements of the person in question.[4] Haemoglobin provides the mechanism for carrying oxygen to muscles and other tissues of the body. At low levels of concentration the body's ability to produce energy and meet other functional needs is impaired. The person feels weak and listless, and his capacity for undertaking both physical and mental activities is affected. He also becomes more susceptible to infections. Popkin (1978), for example, found in a study undertaken in the Philippines that haemo-globin concentration was a good predictor of average daily output among workers engaged in loading, unloading, and working the soil. Anaemic workers were also more frequently absent from work than their non-anaemic counterparts. In a double-blind intervention trial among tappers and weeders in an Indonesian rubber plantation, Basta *et al.* (1979) found anaemic latex workers to be producing on average 80 per cent of the amount produced by non-anaemic workers.[5] In Chapter 4 we noted that the condition is prevalent in poor countries, most especially among pregnant and lactating women. The reason women are especially prone to anaemia is their increased need for iron when in these conditions. (Iron requirements increase during menstruation as well, because iron is expelled during the process.)

Anti-anaemia programmes can take two forms: *supplementation* and *fortification*. Supplementation involves providing a person with extra iron

---

[3] On protein–calorie malnutrition (or PCM), see the remarkable synthesis by Waterlow (1992a). This book not only reports on the epidemiological literature (which is what I shall be reporting for the most part here), but also probes the physiological and biochemical bases of the phenomenon.

[4] Davidson *et al.* (1975) is a classic on dietetics. I am drawing on material from this, and also from WHO (1985) and Scrimshaw (1991).

[5] For additional studies, see Gardner *et al.* (1975) on Sri Lankan workers, and Viteri and Torun (1974) on Guatemalan sugarcane cutters. Useful reviews of the literature are in Spurr (1983) and Martorell and Arroyave (1988).

in medicinal form. This can be done either orally or by injection. Fortification, on the other hand, involves adding iron to a diet, say in salt, sugar, and infant foods. It can also mean making available ascorbic acid, which aids the absorption of iron from food. The magnitude of public health measures involving either is different from (and less extensive than) the measures that would be required were severe deficiencies in macro-nutrients to manifest themselves within a population. I elaborated on this in Chapter 4.[6] Admittedly, it is possible to imagine populations being given supplements of macro-nutrients orally. But it is a massive undertaking, and one's thought quite naturally turns to devising ways of altering the prevailing resource allocation mechanism, which is the source of the problem in the first place.

The link between consumption and production is at its most vivid when we think of the transformation of calorie intake into work. It heightens our sense of the circularity involved in living, something we touched upon in Chapter 1. Humans, like all animals, obtain their energy from their food in a chemical form, derived directly or indirectly from plants.[7] But the human body does not take energy directly from food. Such energy is bound temporarily in molecules of carbohydrates, fats, and proteins. Oxidation of food generates high-energy bonds in substances such as adenosine triphosphate (ATP), which could be regarded as units of currency, transferring the energy to reactions that involve work. There are thus intermediate stores of energy along the process that transforms the energy in ingested food into work. At each stage of conversion there is dissipation of energy. It is still customary to measure energy in *kilo-calorie* units (or *kcal*), and this is what we will do here. (The preferred alternative for some are *kilo-joule* units. See Chapter 10.)

There is a not-so-very-subtle reason why social scientists are especially interested in calorie consumption. The body requires energy not only for internal functions (for example tissue repairs, beating of the heart, digestion, lactation, and growth during childhood), but also in order to do work. The conversion of chemical energy into mechanical energy (or work) is not very efficient. Most of it is dissipated in heat, which in turn regulates the temperature of the body and maintains it at an approximately constant level. Total energy expenditure is the sum of the heat produced and the

[6] Scrimshaw and Wallerstein (1982) is a valuable collection of essays on food fortification and supplementary feeding. See also Baker and De Maeyer (1979), Pollitt *et al.* (1982), C.E. Taylor (1983), Underwood (1983), Scrimshaw (1984), and Levin (1986).

[7] Green plants have evolved a way of preventing electrons in chlorophyll molecules that have been excited by solar photons from instantly re-emitting them, and thereby losing the added energy. These energized electrons in turn are used to charge sub-cellular batteries. The energy stored in these batteries is then transported within the cell via chemicals specially adapted for this to provide the power necessary for chemical synthesis of inorganic materials, such as CO_2, H_2O, NH_3, and SO_4, into proteins, fats, and carbohydrates.

work done. The proportion of consumed energy that is converted into the energy manifesting itself in both internal and external work is called the *efficiency of energy metabolism*. It is the ratio of the mechanical-plus-chemical work performed to the energy expended in performing it. It differs across people, but, contrary to what is frequently asserted (see Chapter 15 for references), there is virtually no physiological evidence that the human body can operate with variable efficiency of energy metabolism as a way of stabilizing the metabolic process. (There is one well-established exception: so-called 'slow' muscle fibres are more efficient *sensu stricto* than fast ones.) We will be particularly careful to distinguish short-term adjustments from long-term adaptation. We will also see later in this and the following chapter that there are mechanisms at work, not so benign among those at risk from malnutrition, which act as stabilizers. They involve loss of active tissue mass and alteration in the composition of active tissues. The efficiency of energy metabolism is to be contrasted with a sharper notion, *mechanical efficiency*, which is the ratio of the external work done to the (chemical) energy expended in doing it. The order of magnitude of the latter is 25–30 per cent, not too different from that of an internal combustion engine (see e.g. Waterlow, 1986).

Proteins are a source of energy, but their contribution seldom exceeds 20 per cent of the total energy in a balanced diet. The form in which energy is stored varies among people, but it is predominantly (of the order of 80–85 per cent) fat. Dugdale and Payne (1977) classify people as 'metabolically fat' or 'metabolically lean', depending on their genetic predisposition as regards the ratio of fat to protein as stores of energy. The real importance of proteins lies in the fact that every cell in the body is partly composed of protein molecules, and they are continually subject to wear and tear. In earlier days, by undernourishment in poor countries nutritionists typically meant the whole spectrum of protein–calorie malnutrition (PCM). In recent years the focus of undernourishment has on the whole been on one end of PCM's spectrum, namely, calorie deficiency. (See Beaton, 1983, for reflections on this.) This is not because protein deficiency has been eliminated; it is that in large parts of the world (for example, the northern parts of the Indian sub-continent) diets are such that protein requirements could be expected to be met if calorie needs were met. This isn't so in parts of sub-Saharan Africa, where diets draw heavily on (low-protein) tubers, such as cassava and yam; and it used not to be so in south India, where the staple food is rice, which is low in protein. There, the meeting of calorie requirements says little about the fulfilment of protein needs. For this reason *kwashiorkor* (a clinical disorder arising from a deficiency of protein) is a prevalent condition among children in parts of sub-Saharan Africa, whereas the chief manifestation of childhood malnourishment in the Indian sub-continent today is *marasmus* (a clinical disorder arising from persistent deprivation of both dietary energy and protein).

Nutrition on its own isn't enough for survival, let alone good health. Freedom from infections and general health care are complementary needs. In Chapter 4 I touched upon the link between nutrition and disease. I shall now elaborate on this link.

14.2 *Nutrition and Infection*

As nutrition isn't the sole determinant of health, food adequacy standards depend upon other factors as well, including potable water, immunization and general medical care, sanitation, and personal hygiene. Water-borne and water-based diseases, such as cholera, typhoid, and hepatitis on the one hand, and guinea worm on the other, are immediate examples of why nutrition isn't sufficient for good health. While diarrhoeal infections (a central cause of infant and child deaths in poor countries) are not usually transmitted by contaminated water, they are spread by contact, and can be contained by washing in clean water. Unhappily, over 1 billion people in Africa, Asia, and Latin America have no reliable access to drinking water (see Feacham, McGarry and Mara, 1977; World Bank, 1992). It is thus not unusual for children in poor countries to suffer between six and eight episodes of diarrhoea per year on average, all adding up to some two months' diarrhoeal illness each year (see e.g. Elliot and Cutting, 1983). This retards growth, and it retards growth systematically. In a celebrated set of publications, Mata *et al.* (1972) and Mata (1978b, 1988) compared weight as a function of an infant's age in weeks with frequency of illness. The two graphs, based on longitudinal studies, showed that there is a direct, negative relationship between the number of days an infant suffers from diarrhoeal illness and the infant's growth. But although infections produce short-term faltering in growth, they cannot explain the long-term deficits in growth observed among the poor in poor countries. A diet has to be very marginal if it cannot cover the relatively modest quantities of additional nutrients required for catching up during childhood and adolescence (see Waterlow, 1992a; and Section 14.6 below). This is a prime reason we are concentrating on food needs when developing the notions of nutritional status and work capacity.[8]

There is synergism among diseases, in that reducing deaths from one disease helps reduce deaths due to other forms of illnesses. In a wide-ranging empirical study on infant and child mortality rates in poor

---

[8] Air-borne diseases, such as influenza, pneumonia, and the whooping cough, continue to be prominent causes of infant and child deaths in poor countries, being responsible for a quarter to a third of child mortalities there. I noted aspects of this when developing the idea of an epidemiological transition in Ch. 4 (see also Morley, 1973).

countries, K. Hill and Pebley (1989) have found that there is a threshold level for the under-five mortality rate (about 150 per 1000) such that progress in reducing the rate is slow when the number is above it, but fairly rapid when the number falls below it.

There is a similar link between malnutrition and diarrhoeal infection. Fauveau *et al.* (1990), in their study of data on children in the age group 6–36 months in the Matlab Thana experiment in Bangladesh, report that the relative risk of death from diarrhoea among the severely malnourished, as compared with those who were not suffering from severe malnutrition, was 17 times as great. About 60 per cent of all deaths in this age range occurred in the 5 months following the monsoons, when infections are rampant. Children with no previous diarrhoea indicated a positive association between malnutrition and subsequent diarrhoea. Furthermore, diarrhoeal illness in one period was found to increase the likelihood of its occurring in some subsequent period. In short, diarrhoea begets diarrhoea (Chowdhury *et al.*, 1990).

The complementary needs of nutrition and freedom from infections are also synergistic in a number of cases. This is so in the case of tuberculosis, measles, the diarrhoeas, cholera, and most respiratory infections. It means that a person's nutrition requirements up to a point diminish as her environment improves. This in turn implies that there is some possibility of substitution among them (see Crompton and Nesheim, 1982; Taylor, 1983; FAO, 1987; Tomkins and Watson, 1989; Ulijaszek, 1990). Severe or repeated infections are a common cause of malnutrition, and there are several paths along which this happens, including as they do both 'supply' and 'demand' factors. It will prove instructive to see what they are (see also Waterlow, 1992a).

On the demand side, infections create an additional need for nutrients, by increasing a person's metabolic rate and the rate of breakdown of tissues (Beisel, 1977). Indirectly, they also reduce the supply of nutrients. This they do for a variety of reasons. First, infections often reduce a person's appetite. (For the case of children, see Mata, 1978a, b; Martorell *et al.*, 1980). Second, they lower a person's ability to absorb nutrients, by affecting the functioning of the gastro-intestinal tract. Third, there is increased loss of major macro-nutrients, vitamins, and minerals through the faeces because of the increased speed of transit of the food that is eaten. And fourth, infections result in the direct loss of nutrients in the gut (see Mola *et al.*, 1983; Martorell and Habicht, 1986). Malnutrition is frequently precipitated by outbreaks of infectious diseases, such as gastroenteritis.

The debilitating effects of infectious diseases go beyond undernourishment. Infections can lead to an increase in the excretion of micro-nutrients. And deficiencies in any of these is damaging. For example, in Asia some 5 million suffer from non-corneal xerophthalmias, a disease people are vulnerable to when suffering from vitamin A deficiency. In sub-Saharan Africa, over 30 million people are estimated to suffer from goitre, caused by iodine deficiency, and half of all children under 12 years are judged to suffer from iron-deficiency anaemia.

The relationship between nutrition and infection would seem to work the other way as well. Reviewing an extensive literature, Briend (1990) has concluded that malnutrition predisposes one to diarrhoea. Moreover, a person's ability to fight an infection once she has caught it is reduced under conditions of moderate to severe malnutrition: her immune system is affected (see Scrimshaw, Taylor and Gordon, 1968; Scrimshaw, 1970, 1983; Mata, Urrutia and Lechtig, 1971; Chowdhury and Chen, 1977; Rowland, Cole and Whitehead, 1977; Mata, 1978b; Chandra, 1983; Ulijaszek, 1990). But there are exceptions, and nutritional status has negligible influence on the impact on morbidity and mortality of the plague, smallpox, typhoid, yellow fever, tetanus, and AIDS. It is even possible that mildly undernourished hosts enjoy survival advantages over their well-fed counterparts for some of these infectious diseases. For example, people suffering from iron-deficiency anaemia would enjoy this perverse effect were the invading pathogen unable to obtain enough free iron to multiply as rapidly in their bloodstream as it could in well-nourished people.[9] This is still a matter of speculation, but historically it could have been important. Of the infectious diseases that have been identified as leading causes of deaths during the eighteenth and nineteenth centuries, those whose relationship with nutritional status could be 'perverse' accounted for about one-third of the number of deaths.[10] Fortunately, so far as public policy goes, it isn't a matter of any great moment that we do not know if such 'perverse' effects are at all significant. Today it is possible to have our food and eat it too: modern public health measures can prevent the spread of a number of such life-threatening pathogens as those we are identifying here.

The difficulties in disentangling the effects of malnutrition from those of infection do not prevent one from investigating the best predictors of ill-health and death; or indeed, their proximate causes. Table 14.1, taken from Briend, Wojtyniak and Rowland (1987), gives the relative risk of death associated with various factors in the rural district of Matlab,

[9] However, this must be balanced against the detrimental effect of malnutrition on the host's immune system. See Weinberg (1978) and, on a related matter, Sugarman (1983). Among pathogens that are equivocal or variable with respect to the nutritional status of the host are typhus, diphtheria, syphilis, and systematic worm infections. See Tomkins and Watson (1989), Ulijaszek (1990), and the *Journal of Interdisciplinary History*, 14 (2) (1983): 503–6.

[10] See Carmichael (1983), Livi-Bacci (1983), and Tomkins and Watson (1989) for questioning a *carte blanche* use of the synergistic model of nutrition and infection. I am grateful to Sheila Johansson for drawing my attention to them.

Table 14.1   Relative risks of death in Matlab, Bangladesh

Risk factor	Relative risk
Female gender	2.6
No breast-feeding	2.1
Any diarrhoea	4.8
Diarrhoea > 7 days	7.6
Bloody diarrhoea	11.3
Acute respiratory infection	11.6
Oedema	84.1
Mid-upper arm circumference $\leq$ 10 cm	48.0
Mid-upper arm circumference $\leq$ 11 cm	20.1
Mid-upper arm circumference $\leq$ 12 cm	11.1
Mid-upper arm circumference $\leq$ 13 cm	6.3

Source: Briend, Wojtyniak and Rowland (1987).

Bangladesh. Notice that diarrhoea imposes a rather low risk when compared with the presence of oedema. In an earlier article, L.C. Chen (1986) calculated that in this district about forty-five percent of deaths are related to nutritional deficiencies.

We will study the functional impairments of calorie deficiency in the remainder of this and the following chapter. So as to concentrate on food needs, we will take as given the background infrastructure defining public health service and hygiene. We will see that despite this the matter is complex, and that as a consequence it has generated much discussion among nutritionists and development economists. There is a great deal that is not well understood. Nevertheless, the literature is rich, and the social scientist can imbibe from it much of profound importance to any inquiry into well-being and destitution.

14.3   *Energy Conservation*

Energy requirements vary among people. Even for a given individual they are not fixed. As requirements can never be measured directly (they can only be inferred; see below), it is often suggested that the notion be dispensed with. This is a mistake. Motor cars of the same make differ in their need for lubrication, and the same car displays different lubricant efficiencies over time, and over differences in the treatment meted out to it. Despite this, car owners find it imperative to ask how often oil ought to be changed, and what quality of oil should be used.

It should not be doubted that the human body is more complex than an internal combustion engine, if only because it is capable of adapting in a number of ways. But the general point remains: requirements are a meaningful (and, as we will confirm, useful) notion, even though it may be hard to pin them down quantitatively. Figures for energy requirements among people of a certain type, engaged in a given set of activities, and living in a particular environment are more like signposts. They provide information on groups of people likely to be operating near the margin, and who are, therefore, in danger of becoming subject to nutritional stress. Since the margin is not an 'edge' but a 'band', we should ideally use the language of probabilities if we are to be precise about matters concerning undernourishment (see below and Chapters 15 and *16). But the presence of a band isn't a reason either for abandoning the concept of requirements or for doing away with the notion of undernourishment.

Despite this stricture, I shall begin by idealizing matters and eschew uncertainty. My aim, first of all, will be to use the law of energy conservation (here it means calories marshalled equalling calories expended; see below) as an introduction to the study of the nutritional status of a person. In this section we will consider an adult male, or an adult female who is neither pregnant not lactating.[11] Children and pregnant and lactating women require additional considerations, and we will touch upon them subsequently (Sections 14.6–14.7).

We divide time into discrete periods ($t = 1,2. . .$). It is safest to regard a period as a day, even though nutritionists often like to think of longer periods (e.g. a week, or even a year) when studying a person's energy balance. It makes sense to hold the climate fixed, and so we won't need a symbol for it.[12] We now partition an individual's characteristics into those that are unalterable (e.g. his genotype, and in an approximate sense his height), and those that can alter over time (e.g. his weight and body composition). The former is a parameter, the latter a variable, but we bring them together and we label them all as H_t in period t. H_t represents the person's *state*.[13] It is a state variable, and a vector, although we will later think of it as a composite index. H_t incorporates within it the person's *nutritional status*, as measured by height, weight, lean body mass (see below), various skinfold-thicknesses, and so forth. We also denote by s_t an index of the individual's stores of energy (mainly adipose tissues), which are typically measured in units of mass, or weight (e.g. kilograms). As H_t is the individual's state, it encompasses s_t. When we come to study changes in a person's nutritional status we will, for expositional simplicity, look only at changes in s_t. We next denote by x_t the energy content of the food

---

[11] The formulation here generalizes the one in Dasgupta and Ray (1990).

[12] Climate quite obviously matters. Energy requirements in the tropics are a shade lower; but there is uncertainty about the extent to which corrections need to be made for the higher mean ambient temperature. For this reason WHO (1985) does not refer to climate when providing estimates of requirements.

[13] The idea of a state here is the same as the one we made use of in Ch. 3.

the individual eats (expressed in kcal) during period t. This will sometimes be called his *energy intake*, and at other times his *energy ingestion*. It is a flow variable.

Let δs_t be the change in the individual's stock of energy stores. We will find it useful to regard it as negative if he *accumulates* fats and proteins, and positive if he *decumulates* them. Thus, $\delta s_t = s_t - s_{t+1}$. Often, it will help to simplify and to think of δs_t as a change in the person's body weight, and we will do so, always keeping in mind our sign convention. We can now denote by M_t the amount of energy *marshalled* by the individual at t. In the obvious functional notation, we then have $M_t(\cdot) = M_t(H_t, x_t, \delta s_t)$.

We now suppose that the person is engaged daily in a specific set of activities, for example walking, running, sleeping, playing, gossiping, bathing, eating, maintaining hygiene; farming or cutting sugarcane or pulling a rickshaw or working at a construction site or felling trees or carrying loads or cooking and cleaning; and so forth. Some amount to recreation (and are therefore called *discretionary activities* in the nutrition literature), while the others can only be called *work*. We next simplify by assuming that the individual undertakes these activities at the same pace in each period. In so doing we are supposing not only that activities have been specified, but even that their pace and duration have been specified in advance. We are thinking here of a supremely routinized being. However, the level of activity of even a routinized person registers daily fluctuations around some mean. Furthermore, no one's body weight remains absolutely constant. Even when a person is in energy balance (see below) his weight varies around some mean. In Chapter 15 we will assume that the daily energy such a person marshalls and the daily energy he expends (see below) can both be represented by stationary stochastic processes.

Let the person's activities be labelled by the vector $\boldsymbol{\alpha}$, and the levels at which the activities are undertaken by the vector $\boldsymbol{\beta}$. Each component of $\boldsymbol{\alpha}$ is an activity, which we will regard for simplicity as a specific sort of *task*. So each component of $\boldsymbol{\beta}$ is the number of units of the corresponding task the person completes in each period. (The pace at which tasks are undertaken are by implication included in $\boldsymbol{\beta}$.) Thus, for example, the component of $\boldsymbol{\beta}$ which corresponds to the task of cutting sugarcane reflects the amount of sugarcane cut by the person during the period, measured in tons, say; and so forth.

We denote by E_t the amount of energy *expended* by the person at t. Then in the obvious notation, we have $E_t(\cdot) = E_t(\boldsymbol{\alpha}, \boldsymbol{\beta}, H_t, \delta s_t, x_t, \delta x_t)$, where $\delta x_t = x_t - x_{t-1}$. The inclusion of the first four arguments in $E_t(\cdot)$ is obvious enough; it is inclusion of the last two, x_t and δx_t, that requires explanation. They reflect the energy expended in the process by which food energy is converted into work and bodily stores of energy, including the energy spent in metabolizing food. (We also include in this the energy excreted as bodily wastes). The *thermic effect of food* (see Section 14.5) reflects this inclusion, as does the idea of *homeostasis*, which we will investigate in Chapter 15.

We can now express as an identity the conservation of energy, which says that in each period the energy marshalled must equal the energy expended. Thus,

$$M_t(H_t, x_t, \delta s_t) \equiv E_t(\alpha, \beta, H_t, \delta s_t, x_t, \delta x_t) \quad \text{for } t \geq 1, \text{ where } x_0 \text{ is given.}^{14} \quad (14.1)$$

This is far too general a form, in that it isn't useful for applied work on nutrition. We need to iron out some of the non-linearities in each of the functions, $M_t(\cdot)$ and $E_t(\cdot)$. So we simplify by assuming that they are to some extent decomposable. The most common method of decomposing $E_t(\cdot)$ is to break it up into two composite parts: (i) the basal metabolic rate and the energy spent on food digestion and essential physical activities, such as washing, eating, dressing, and so forth; and (ii) the energy expended in all other activities, such as work and play. We let r_t denote the former, and q_t the latter. (We will ignore energy lost in the faeces and urine, which is only a small fraction of total expenditure for human beings.) Thus, $r_t = r(\alpha, \beta, H_t, x_t, \delta x_t)$ and, as a simplification, $q_t = q(\alpha, \beta, H_t)$. We will refer to $r(\cdot)$ as the *maintenance requirement*. Its dependence on α and β is not significant, but it is there. Its dependence on H is substantial, and we will explore it in Section 14.4. I have already commented on its assumed dependence on x and δx.

That q is a function of α and β should be obvious (q is the energy expended in physical activities); its dependence on H may be less obvious. But we should note, for example, that a well-built person is capable of wielding a pick at a pace a small, skinny person is not capable of. At the same time, however, a larger body expends greater energy in the sheer act of moving around, and so for non-sedentary occupations we should expect q to depend on H.

As with $E_t(\cdot)$, it is customary to decompose $M_t(\cdot)$ into two categories: *metabolizable energy* obtained from the energy intake (which we will at times call *energy consumption*), and the energy released from bodily stores (or used and congealed in accumulating bodily stores). As an approximation, we express the former as $\mu_t x_t$, and the latter as $\sigma_t \delta s_t$. In words, the underlying assumption is that each is a proportional transformation. μ_t is a composite of what are known as Atwater factors (see Chapter 15). We will see later that $\mu_t = \mu(H_t)$ and, more interestingly, $\sigma_t = \sigma(H_t, \text{sign}[\delta s_t])$, the second dependence of $\sigma(\cdot, \cdot)$ signifying that the amount of energy used in laying down a kilogram of, say, fat is different from the amount used

---

[14] We will not explore the equation which describes the intertemporal behaviour of H_t and s_t. But see Chapter 16.

in coverting body-stores of a kilogram of this same fat into work. (As it happens, it exceeds it.) We will also see that μ_t depends on the diet. This dependence will be ignored for the moment. As we are introducing specific functional forms into identity (14.1), what was an energy-conservation *identity* becomes an energy-conservation *equation*:

$$\mu_t x_t + \sigma_t \delta s_t = r_t + q_t, \qquad \text{for } t \geq 0,$$

which, upon rearrangement, assumes the more intuitive form:

$$\mu_t x_t = r_t + q_t - \sigma_t \delta s_t, \qquad \text{for } t \geq 0. \tag{14.2}$$

The left-hand-side of the equation represents metabolized energy, and the right-hand-side energy expenditure. In subsequent sections we will study each of the terms in equation (14.2). But before doing this it will prove fruitful to use the equation to illustrate a few ideas, and to offer some overall orders for magnitude.

14.4 *Energy Requirements, Nutritional Status, and Productivity*

The fundamental question in the economics of nutrition will be explored in this and the following chapter: how does nutrition affect the capacity for physical activity? Although there is much we don't know about these matters, enough is known to make it a reasonable question to ask. The place to start is the notion of *energy requirements*.

In its illuminating and influential report by an expert group on calorie and protein needs, WHO (1985: 12) defines energy requirements in terms of energy intakes as follows:[15]

The energy requirement of an individual is the level of energy intake from food that will balance energy expenditure when the individual has a body size and composition, and level of physical activity, consistent with long-term good health; and that will allow for the maintenance of economically necessary and socially desirable physical activity. In children and pregnant or lactating women the energy requirement includes the energy needs associated with the deposition of tissues or the secretion of milk at rates consistent with good health.

Using this definition, we may say that *undernourishment* is a state in which the physical functioning of a person is impaired to the point where she cannot maintain an adequate level of performance at physical work, or at resisting or recovering from the effects of any of a garden variety of diseases. It is also a state in which individuals are unable to maintain an adequate rate of growth and the processes of pregnancy and lactation. I had much to say about this state in Chapter 4.

---

[15] The report was sponsored jointly by the Food and Agriculture Organization (FAO), the World Health Organization (WHO), and the United Nations University (UNU). It was published by WHO. Beaton (1985) contains a fine discussion of the idea of energy requirements.

Admittedly, these definitions do not enable one easily to ascertain if an individual is undernourished, nor therefore to estimate the magnitude of undernourishment in the world (see Chapter 15). But the ideas they express are clear enough. WHO (1985: 13) suggests that, once the person's body weight and composition and her activities have all been fixed (and for children an appropriate growth rate defined), there is only a narrow band of energy for which equation (14.2) can be satisfied. This band can therefore be presumed to define the person's energy requirements (but see below). Formally, this is to say that, given s_t (more accurately, H_t), none of the relevant terms in equation (14.2), namely, μ, r, q, and σ, permits much leeway; none is capable of adjusting sufficiently to allow the person to make do under a wide range of energy intake levels while maintaining α, β, and body weight indefinitely. The dependence of r on x and δx is judged by WHO (1985) to be very limited.

Now, the claim that the band is narrow in the short run has been contested by Sukhatme (1977, 1978, 1981a, b; 1982a, b) and Sukhatme and Margen (1982), and in the long run on the basis of primary field data by Edmundson (1977, 1979), Adair (1984), Prentice (1984), Stein, Johnston and Greiner (1988), and Edmundson and Sukhatme (1990), among others. We will study both sets of critiques in Chapter 15 (Sections 15.3–15.7). Here, we do not need to take a position on either set, one way or the other. For each possible body weight, we could estimate the width of the permissible band on intakes and then call the lower bound a person's energy requirement at that body weight. For every individual there is also a range of acceptable body weights and compositions. It follows that there is a maximum quantity of stored energy in the form of adipose tissues and protein upon which a healthy person can draw while maintaining her activity levels without precipitating a breakdown. As this is a finite amount, weight must be maintained over the long run.

We will see below (equation 14.7)) that the energy requirements of a person in good health can in principle be measured either by her habitual intake or by her expenditure. But energy intakes of free-living people are fiendishly difficult to measure (see Chapter 15). With advances in ways of measuring energy expenditure (the doubly labelled water method is currently the best-practice technique; see James, Haggarty and McGaw, 1988; Waterlow, 1992a), the latter has become the object of study in the nutrition literature, and the basis on which energy requirements are assessed. The following account will reflect this.

It has taken long to arrive at a useful, simple indicator of *nutritional status*. For any given adult height, there is a range of body weights and compositions consistent with good health. As an index, weight is no good unless it is normalized for height. The most commonly used measure today is the *body mass index* (BMI), which is the ratio of a person's weight (w)

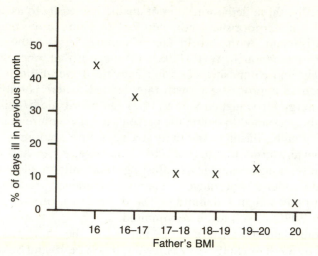

Fig. 14.1   Morbidity as a function of BMI
Source: Waterlow (1992b).

to the square of her height (h), or in other words w/h^2. It is also called the Quetelet index. In adults of either sex BMI has been found to be an index of both the principal stores of energy (i.e. fats) and the active tissue mass (see below). To a reasonable approximation, BMI is independent of height. This makes it a good measure of adult nutritional status and, more generally, of health. It is a measure of *current* nutritional status.[16] If weight is measured in kilograms and height in metres, the acceptable range for BMI is something like 18.5–25 for both men and women. A value in excess of 25 is an almost sure sign of being overweight. However, a value below 18.5 does not imply that a person is wasted. For example, Shetty (1984) found a sample of poor Indian labourers who performed well in physical fitness tests even though their BMIs were in the range 15–16. This may suggest that we should enlarge the acceptable range to something like 15–25. But to do so on the basis of only a few studies would be to display an obsession with avoiding type −1 errors (calling someone malnourished when she is not). A BMI value less than 15 is an almost sure sign of chronic energy deficiency (the person is *wasted*; see Chapter 4), and a value of around 12 is probably the lower limit of survival. But a figure of 15–18.5 or so is an indication that the person is at risk. Indeed, below 17 a person should be regarded as frankly undernourished (see Waterlow, 1986, 1990,

[16] J. Lee. Kolonel and Hinds (1981) provided an early overview of the subject. The authors argued that the more general measure, w/h^p, where p is derived from the set of weight–height measurements, is a more suitable index for the population under review. But see below.

1992a, b; James, Ferro-Luzzi and Waterlow, 1988; C.J.K. Henry, 1990; Ferro-Luzzi *et al.*, 1992; James *et al.*, 1992). Fig. 14.1 (attributed to J. Pryer) explains one sense in which the body mass index is an indicator of health; with but little exception, the percentage of days in a given month in which individuals in a sample of adult males in Bangladesh were ill was found to be a declining function of BMI. Fig. 14.2, taken from a study in Hyderabad, by Naidu, Neela, and Rao (1991), is more dramatic. It shows that the chance of a baby being born with low birth weight (under 2.5 kg) is a declining function of the body mass index of its mother. For the under-nourished mother, low birth weight is a beneficial form of adaptation (it reduces obstetric risks); but not for the baby. In two wide-ranging searches for a reliable and usable indicator of nutritional status, James, Ferro-Luzzi and Waterlow (1988) and James *et al.* (1992) have argued in favour of the body mass index. These are considered judgements, and I will base my discussion on their reckonings.

We depict the findings in a stylized form in Fig. 14.3, which presents the probability (π) of a person *not* experiencing a breakdown in health as a function of the body mass index (m). It is zero until m reaches the value 12 or thereabouts, rises slowly until m reaches 15 or so, then rises rapidly until $m \approx 18.5$, then flattens in the interval 18.5–25. The value of π falls beyond $m = 25$, when obesity sets in. All this is stylized, but only to a small extent. In any event, the analytical point of interest in nutritional

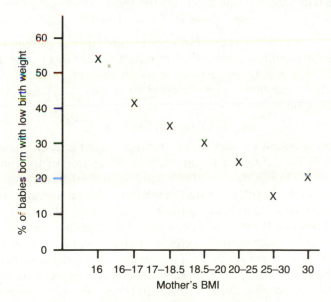

Fig. 14.2   Women's health status as a function of BMI
Source: Waterlow (1992b). Original source: Naidu *et al.* (1991).

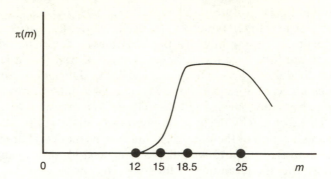

Fig. 14.3   One minus the probability of health breakdown as a function of BMI

economics is that $\pi(m)$ is *non-concave* in the interval $12 \leq m \leq 18.5$; that is, $\pi''(m) > 0$.[17] This is the (probabilistic) generalization of the fact that there is a large maintenance (i.e. fixed) cost involved in the process of living. We will study the implication of this in Chapter 16.

Let us assume that the person under observation is in good health, and that she maintains her activity levels. Bearing in mind all the caveats we have noted so far, let S (≥ 0) be the outer limit of the amount of body mass she can decumulate without endangering her health. If she is to maintain her health, then, in addition to satisfying equation (14.2), her intakes and expenditures must respect the sequence of further constraints:

$$\Sigma_{t=1}^{T} \delta s_t \leq S, \qquad \text{for } T \geq 1. \tag{14.3}$$

Suppose, for simplicity, that both her maintenance requirement (r) and her energy expenditure on physical activities (q) are given. We may then regard $E^* = q + r$ to be her energy requirement. Assume that μ is approximately constant. Then, on using equations (14.2) and (14.3), it is easy to show that

$$[(\mu\Sigma_1^{T}x_t)/T] - E^* \geq - S/T. \tag{14.4}$$

This places a bound on how far her time-averaged energy intake can be permitted to fall below her requirement as a function of the time-period of averaging. The longer is the period over which the averaging is done, the smaller is the permitted deviation between average intake and requirement. This is intuitively obvious.

Inequalities (14.3) allow for fluctuations in weight over, say, the annual cycle. For poor people, body reserves (S) are small even in the most bountiful times. I have yet to see a fat person among the poor in any poor country. So the idea that a person should maintain her recommended body weight and composition even over the short run, and not merely over the

---

[17] $\pi''(m)$ is the second derivative of π with respect to m.

long haul, should be central to the concept of energy requirements in poor countries. This ought to be borne in mind, even although substantial weight fluctuations over the agricultural cycle among poor farmers in West Africa (where there is a single rainy season) are a routine matter. Adults lose up to 10 per cent of their body weight during the pre-harvest period, making it up during the dry season, when food is available and agricultural work is at a minimum. Reserves of fat are of use as a buffer against the effects of seasonal food shortages or increases in agricultural work (Dugdale and Payne, 1987; Ferro-Luzzi, Pastore and Sette, 1987; Ferro-Luzzi *et al.*, 1990). Of course, if the stored energy is large enough (e.g. if the body mass index is 22 or so), there need be no health risks even during the deficit season.

How much energy does a peasant woman obtain from decumulating her adipose tissues over the annual cycle? Here is a very rough calculation. Estimates suggest that about 9000 kcal of energy can be obtained from 1 kg of adipose tissues.[18] If a rural woman weighing 50 kg in the dry season were to lose 10 per cent of her weight during the wet season, this would make available 45 000 kcal of energy. Were the lean season to last 6 months, she could 'afford' a deficit (calorie intake less expenditure) of something like 250 kcal per day during these 6 months. Even though over the long run weight may be maintained by those who survive, such wide fluctuations as have been observed in West Africa and elsewhere are not symptomatic of good health (see Chambers, Longhurst and Pacey 1981; Adair and Pollitt, 1983; Adair, 1984; Sahn, 1987; Whitehead, 1989; Chapter 4): poor people in those parts don't live very long. Moreover, the child mortality rate has been found to peak during the lean season, and birth weight has been observed to dip. To rest contented with the fact that weight is maintained over the annual cycle is to disregard these costs.

We now come to a central conception in nutritional economics, that of a *stationary state* (or *steady state*). This is a state of affairs where a person's weight fluctuates round a constant figure. On average, energy intake equals energy expenditure. Assume now for simplicity of exposition (but see Chapter 15) that the process is deterministic. In this special case there are no fluctuations in weight, and no fluctuations in intakes of expenditures. Thus, by setting $\delta s_t = 0$ in (14.2), we obtain what is widely referred to as the *energy balance condition*:

$$\mu_t x_t = r_t + q_t, \qquad \text{for } t \geq 1. \tag{14.5}$$

(setting $\delta s_t = 0$ implies trivially that the constraints embodied in (14.3) are all satisfied.) Since we are studying a stationary state in a deterministic model, we may as well drop all time subscripts, and write (14.5) as

[18] 1 kg of fat stores about 9000 kcal. About 2000 kcal is lost in the process of converting this into usable energy. So 7000 kcal are available for 'use'. These are rough and ready figures.

$$\mu x = r(\alpha,\beta,H) + q(\alpha,\beta,H). \tag{14.6}$$

Equation (14.6) is fundamental. We will make repeated use of it and its different versions.[19]

We wish first of all to see how calorie intake affects productivity. Equation (14.6) enables us to do that in a simple class of situations. What we will do is to vary the extent to which a single, given activity is undertaken by the person, and relate it to variations in energy intake. The activity could, for example, consist in moving earth and rubble at a construction site. We will vary the number of units of this composite task she performs while holding all her other activities at fixed levels. Let β denote the number of units of this composite task she completes in each period. The individual can choose the level of β by choosing the pace at which she undertakes the overall activity. The energy expenditure in all her other activities is a constant, and we write this as θ. As a reasonable approximation, we may assume that her overall state (H) is independent of the choice of β, and therefore that her resting metabolic rate is also independent of it. Finally, by choosing units appropriately, we can set $\mu = 1$. Equation (14.6) then reduces to the form

$$x = r + \theta + q(\beta), \tag{14.7}$$

where $q(\cdot)$ is an increasing function of β; that is, the greater the number of units of the composite task she performs, the more energy she has to expend. In short, $q'(\beta) > 0$. Quite obviously, also, $q(0) = 0$. We thus see that when in energy balance the individual's calorie expenditure consists of a *fixed* component (the maintenance requirement, r) and a *variable* one representing external work ($\theta + q(\beta)$).

We will come to their orders of magnitude shortly. Now, in our example, the energy expenditure (θ) involved in all the person's other activities is a constant term. We may then ignore it and drop the term, so as to contrast the energy expended in maintenance with the energy spent in the variable, external work. Paradoxically, the simplest way of doing this is to incorporate it in r. So we re-express (14.6) as

$$q(\beta) = x - r, \qquad \text{for } x \ge r,$$

which can be reassembled yet again as

$$\beta = q^{-1}(x - r) \equiv \phi(x - r), \qquad \text{for } x \ge r, \tag{14.8}$$

where $q^{-1}(\cdot)$, which I denote by $\phi(\cdot)$, is the inverse function of $q(\cdot)$.[20] Since $q'(\cdot) > 0$, it follows that $\phi'(\cdot) > 0$. Furthermore, $\phi(0) = 0$. The idea now is to see how ϕ varies with x.

---

[19] I have dropped the dependence of r on x as a simplification. I will confirm subsequently that this is a good move.

[20] The dimension of ϕ is, therefore, the number of units of the composite task.

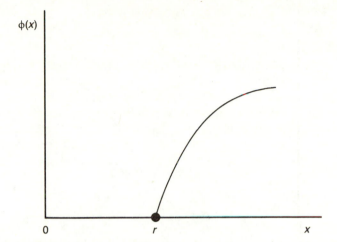

Fig. 14.4   Nutrition productivity curve

In Fig. 14.4 I have drawn a prototypical function form for $\phi(\cdot)$. As a matter of convention, I have also set $\phi = 0$ for $x < r$. It bears emphasis that it *is* merely a convention I am following here, nothing more, and there will be nothing amiss in my doing so. The reason this should be regarded a mere convention is that, in contrast to Fig. 14.3, we are assuming here that the individual maintains her energy balance. (She remains in a stationary state, and her body weight remains constant). So we are not entitled to study the region $x < r$ in Fig. 14.4. Were $x < r$, the individual would not be in energy balance (no matter what is her choice of β), and something would have to give: she would either lose weight, or she would have to cut down on some other activity; and we have assumed she does not experience either sort of loss.

Fig. 14.4 is a particular idealization, in that I have assumed $\phi(x)$ to be a strictly concave function of x for $x \geq r$; that is, $\phi''(x) < 0$. Nothing will hang on this, so long as $\phi''(x) < 0$ for large enough x. which is patently the correct assumption to make. For there is a limit to the pace at which a person can work at a task no matter what her energy intake (see Sections 14.6 and 14.7). Of course, we are entitled to consider only a limited range of values for x here: between maintenance requirement, r, and some upper limit. At large levels of daily intake the person's health suffers. As she overeats, she is unable to maintain energy balance, and so equation (14.8) becomes inappropriate.[21] Subject to the restriction that x lies in a limited

[21] In contrast to energy, when more protein is ingested than is required for metabolic purposes, all the excess is metabolized and the end-products are excreted. Protein is not stored in the body in the way energy is stored in adipose tissues. Furthermore, and again in contrast to energy, no detrimental effect has been noted when protein intake exceeds requirements in moderate amounts.

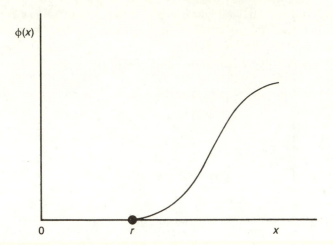

Fig. 14.5 Nutrition productivity curve

interval (say, in the region 2000–3500 kcal per day for an adult male), $\phi(x)$ can be thought of as the *nutrition–productivity curve*. We will have much to do with that curve in this and the following chapters.

Now, it cannot be emphasized strongly enough that the nutrition–productivity curve drawn in Fig. 14.4 is an idealization. The functional relationship is certainly not deterministic (see Chapters 15–16), and in all probability is not of uniform curvature either. Bliss and Stern (1978b) explored the then existing literature to see what one could say about the slope of $\phi(x)$ slightly to the right of $x = r$. They collated some limited evidence to suggest that the curve is a straight line in this region. Fig. 14.5, which displays 'increasing returns' to energy intake immediately to the right of $x = r$, is yet another possibility, and we could easily work with this in what follows, even if at the expense of some expositional ease. But none of these finer details is a matter of any significance to the theory we will develop.

It is important to distinguish critical from inessential assumptions. In extending resource allocation theory by taking the nutrition–productivity link into account in Chapter 16, we will for the most part make use of Fig. 14.4. But the theory does not rest on the special properties of the figure, and we should bear this in mind when we come to develop it. What is critical for the theory are two assumptions: (i) that maintenance require-ment is a significant fraction of total energy expenditure, and (ii) that, at levels of intake somewhat in excess of maintenance requirement, there are diminishing gains in productivity from further increases in consumption (i.e. $\phi''(x) < 0$). As both are incontrovertible, we are on firm ground.

I should reiterate that we are considering an adult here. Her past nutritional status (reflected in H) is a parameter, and so $\phi(x)$ reflects the effect on her productivity of her stationary-state nutritional intake. Looking ahead, though, we would be interested in the future productivity of her current children. (Martorell, 1985, and Spurr, 1988, 1990, have good discussions of this.) Their long-run nutritional status can be influenced by policy, both in the public and household spheres. In Section 14.6 we will study the effect on productivity of past nutrition. This breakdown of nutritional status into long- and short-run components has much to commend it. As I observed in Chapter 4, height is a useful measure of past nutrition, and weight (relative to height, namely the body mass index) is a good measure of current nutritional status.

There have now been a number of field studies whose findings provide empirical support for the model I have just constructed, but they do so only indirectly. Consider a population that is only moderately deficient in calories. The problem for the analyst is that in long-run equilibrium the better-fed within such a population would be expected to spread the expenditure of their greater energy intake over a number of activities (including leisure activities); they wouldn't put it all into a single activity. This has been confirmed in a well-known series of longitudinal studies conducted among Guatemalan sugarcane cutters and loaders. Viteri (1974), Immink and Viteri (1981), Immink, Viteri and Helms (1981, 1982), and Immink *et al.*, 1984a, b), found caloric supplementation to be positively related to energy expenditure, but the additional expenditure was diffused. Supplemented workers completed their tasks faster, spent less time travelling back home after a day's work, and slept less during their leisure hours. Their productivity at work (as measured by the number of tons of sugarcane delivered) was not significantly greater than the unsupplemented workers. On the other hand, neither group had suffered from any serious energy deficiency prior to the introduction of the supplementation programme: these were not undernourished people. Workers receiving energy supplements adapted by extending their leisure activities, and not by producing more at work. Immink and Viteri (1981) inferred from this that strong diminishing returns appear in the nutrition–productivity function at moderate levels of nutrition intake. They recognized that it is the workers' behavioural patterns that account for it. Their study cannot, therefore, reveal whether such workers would have been able to maintain their productivity had nutrition intake among them been *reduced*. That this is the correct way to read the Immink–Viteri findings is supported by the work of Wolgemuth *et al.* (1982), who found a fairly strong effect on productivity of energy supplementation among Kenyan construction workers whose previous energy consumption was low. It is also supported by Strauss (1986), who found a positive link between agricultural labour productivity and calorie availability per equivalent-consumer in a sample of farm households in Sierra Leone.

From the perspective of the economics of destitution, it is possible to level a general criticism at many of the investigations that have studied the effect of energy supplementation on productivity: the people chosen for supplementation have been employed workers; they have not been chosen from the frankly malnourished and disfranchised.[22] As our aim is to explain the analytical link between undernourishment and destitution, this is a serious drawback. We will see why in greater detail when in Chaper 16 we construct a theory of the labour market based partly on the nutritional status of potential workers.

Table 14.2   Energy requirement of subsistence farmer in the tropics doing moderate activity work[a]

	Hours	kcal
In bed, at 1.0 × BMR	8	520
Occupational activities, at 2.7 × BMR	7	1230
Discretionary activities: socially desirable and household tasks, at 3.0 × BMR	2	390
Residual activities, at 1.4 × BMR	7	640
Total = 1.78 × BMR	24	2780

[a] Age: 25; weight: 58 kg; height: 1.61 m; basal metabolic rate (BMR, defined in the text): 65 kcal per hour, or 1560 kcal per day.

Source: WHO (1985, table 10).

What are the orders of magnitude of calorie requirements? They depend on the person's state (her genetic traits, height, weight, body composition, disease state, and so forth) and the activities she is engaged in. Tables 14.2 and 14.3 provide estimates of energy requirements of two representative persons, one a male subsistence farmer engaged in moderate activity, the other a female peasant. Both are assumed to live in the tropics. The figures are taken from WHO (1985). We will find it useful to refer to these tables as we go along.

In population-wide studies the maintenance requirement (r) of a representative person is taken by nutritionists to be approximately 1.4 times the basal metabolic rate (to be defined below). From Table 14.2 we can infer that for the male subsistence farmer $r = 2184$ kcal per day. The farmer's daily energy requirement for physical activities is, therefore, (2780 − 2184) or 596 kcal. In other words, the *fixed* part of the farmer's energy

---

[22] An exception is the work of Prof. Spurr and his colleagues, which I report below and in Ch. 15.

Table 14.3 Energy requirement of a rural woman in a developing country[a]

	Hours	kcal
In bed, at 1.0 × BMR	8	425
Occupational activities:		
housework, preparing food, etc., at 2.7 × BMR	3	430
working in fields, at 2.8 × BMR	4	595
Discretionary activities, at 2.5 × BMR	2	265
Energy expenditure over residual time, at 1.4 × BMR	7	520
Total = 1.76 × BMR	24	2235

[a] Age: 35; weight: 50 kg; height: 1.6 m; basal metabolic rate (BMR, defined in the text): 53 kcal per hour, or 1272 kcal per day.

Source: WHO (1985, table 14).

requirements adds up to just over 72 per cent of the total. For the rural woman, $r = 1795$ kcal per day (see Table 14.3). Her daily energy requirements for physical activities amount to 440 kcal. This means that the fixed part of her energy requirements $(2235 - 440)$ adds up to just over 75 per cent of the total.

Admittedly, neither individual is engaged in heavy manual work, which is what is involved when a person cuts earth, or fells trees, or saws wood, or cuts sugarcane, or pedals a rickshaw, or picks in a mine, or loads sacks, or digs holes at a construction site, or ploughs a field. Daily energy requirements for a male engaged in such work in the tropics are in the order of 3550 kcal. The maintenance requirement, as a proportion of the total energy requirements of such a person, is a bit lower, in the order of 65 per cent. This is still a large fraction though. We will see that this large fixed cost has substantial implications for the economics of living.[23]

14.5 *Basal Metabolic Rates and Maintenance Requirements*

The maintenance requirement (r) of a person is his daily calorie requirement when engaged in the most minimal of activities, such as eating and maintaining essential hygiene. Energy requirements for work and play and for preparing food are not included. Energy intake equalling the

[23] On estimates of protein and energy requirements for different categories of persons, see Durnin and Passmore (1967), Viteri *et al.* (1971), Torun, Young and Rand (1981), Spurr (1983, 1984), Rand, Uauy and Scrimshaw (1984), and WHO (1985).

maintenance requirement would not allow a person to enjoy long-run health were he to do anything over and above this minimum of physical activities; it is the intake that sustains an inactive, dependent person. We can divide it into three components.

The first, which is called the *basal metabolic rate* (BMR), is the energy expenditure of an individual who is at complete rest in a thermo-neutral environment, and who has fasted for a period of at least 13 hours.[24] It is the energy required to maintain body temperature, to sustain heart and respiratory action, to replace tissues, to support ionic gradients across cell membranes, and so forth (see Chapter 15). BMR therefore represents the cost of maintaining various fluxes in the body. This is not always an easy thing to measure. And so when conditions of measurement are not adequately fulfilled, the term *resting metabolic rate* is used as a proxy for BMR. It is slightly in excess of BMR because it includes the small, additional energy expended by postural movements. To all intents and purposes, the basal and the resting metabolic rates are the same.

The second component consists of the energy expended in the minimum of physical activities postulated in sitting, eating, and maintaining personal hygiene. And the third component is the *thermic effect of food* (alternatively, *dietary thermogenesis*), which is the increase in the metabolic rate, lasting several hours, following the consumption of carbohydrates, fats, and proteins.[25] The thermic effect of food varies, and by far the greatest number of studies have explored it among obese people, not among people who habitually eat little. Very roughly speaking, it accounts for a bit over 10 per cent of ingested calories (x) (see e.g. Horton, 1984; Waterlow, 1986). In the case of the subsistence farmer in Table 14.2, the thermic effect of food amounts to no more than 300 kcal per day.

When an organic substance is combusted in the human body, oxygen is consumed in amounts directly related to the energy released as heat. In this way the energy expenditure of a person is related quantitatively to his oxygen consumption. *Indirect calorimetry* is the measurement of this oxygen consumption. It provides the basic means by which an individual's expenditure of energy is measured.[26] Literally thousands of such measurements have been conducted, and the basal metabolic rate has been

---

[24] By a thermo-neutral environment I mean a range of ambient temperatures within which the person is in thermal balance, at a constant body temperature, experiencing no net heat loss or production.

[25] This is also often called the 'specific dynamic action of food' (Davidson *et al.*, 1975; WHO, 1985), sometimes 'diet-induced thermogenesis' (Waterlow, 1986), and on occasion 'postprandial increase in metabolic rate' (Prentice, 1984).

[26] *Direct calorimetry*, in contrast, measures the heat produced while someone engages in mechanical work. It is difficult and costly, and so indirect calorimetry is the method in use. Davidson *et al.* (1975, Ch. 3) and Horton (1984) have good accounts of the variety of laboratory techniques in use for measuring oxygen consumption, and Brun (1984) provides a commentary of techniques for measuring energy expenditure under free-living conditions.

regressed against a number of characteristics embodied in our all-purpose notion of a person's state. BMR is a function of the mass of metabolically active tissues, otherwise called the *active cell mass*. Because it is relatively simple to estimate, the *lean body mass* (the difference between weight and the mass of adipose tissues) is often taken to be a surrogate for this. But BMR depends on the composition of lean body mass. For example, the visceral component of lean body mass (e.g. the liver, heart, kidney) utilizes nearly 45 per cent of the total oxygen consumption under resting conditions, while the skeletal muscle, which comprises about 50 per cent of an adult's body weight, contributes just under 20 per cent to the resting metabolic rate. Thus, visceral tissues have a higher rate of metabolic activity. Recent studies have shown that the basal metabolic rate per kilogram of lean body mass is significantly higher among subjects of low nutritional status than among well-nourished controls.[27] This is currently best explained by the finding that mild to moderate undernourishment results in a reduction of skeletal muscle mass, but not in the visceral mass (Soares *et al.*, 1991). Severe undernourishment tells on the visceral mass as well, and the composition of lean body mass can change sufficiently to result in a decline in the basal metabolic rate per kilogram of metabolically active tissues (see e.g. Shetty, 1984). This latter observation has often been interpreted to mean that undernourished people adapt by an 'improvement' in metabolic efficiency (see Chapter 15). But this is to misunderstand the physiological basis of adaptation.[28]

The basal metabolic rate is thus dependent on body size and body composition. It depends also on the person's disease status (Chapter 4 and Section 14.2). Age affects it, primarily because age is related to body composition. The reason body composition matters is that some organs and some tissues are metabolically more active than others. For example, the brain comprises about 10 per cent of a newborn's weight, and so can account for some 44 per cent of the baby's BMR. The latter percentage drops to 19 per cent in the adult. The neonate has relatively small *muscle cell mass* (the difference between weight and the sum of the masses of the person's adipose tissues, bone cells, and extracellular water), which accounts for only 5 per cent of BMR, in contrast to an adult, whose muscle cell mass accounts for something like 18 per cent (see WHO, 1985, table 1). The basal metabolic rate is dependent on gender, inasmuch as male–female body size and composition differ: adult males are on average larger than adult females, and have a smaller percentage of their body weight in the form of adipose tissues.

---

[27] See e.g. Kurpad, Kulkarni and Shetty (1989). The 'chronically energy-deficient' subjects were stunted (< 165 cm), wasted (body mass index less than 18), and had low lean body mass.

[28] Shetty (1990a) has a fine discussion of this point.

It transpires that, for each gender, within every age-range a good and *easily measurable* predictor of the basal metabolic rate is *weight* (see WHO, 1985: 37, 71).[29] But the relationship is not proportional, and so BMR per unit weight is a function of weight. If W denotes the body weight of a representative person at age i (years), the function currently in use is of the form

$$BMR = a_iW + b_i, \tag{14.9}$$

where $a_i > 0$ for all i, $b_i < 0$ for $i \leq 3$, and $b_i > 0$ for $i > 3$. It is customary to estimate (14.9) for different age ranges; for example, 0–3, 3–10, 10–18, and so forth. It transpires that $b_i \approx 0$ at age less than 3 years. On the whole, the functional relationship between W and BMR gets flatter and the intercept larger with increasing age. Furthermore, BMR per unit weight, when evaluated at the mean weight at any age range, varies with age, being highest for young children and lowest for the elderly. Of course, (14.9) is a crude approximation. It assumes a linear form for a relationship that is almost certainly non-linear, most assuredly at extreme values for body weight.[30] The linear form (equation (14.9)) is currently the best on offer, discriminating as it does different age groups. So use is made of it.

14.6 *Special Requirements, 1: Growth and Development*

In Chapter 4 I had much to say about early growth among members of poor households in poor countries. I noted there that, unless the circumstances of life improve, the first three years of life appear to have a pronounced effect on a person's mature body stature. Early nutrition and the extent of freedom from infections have a lasting effect. Why this should be so isn't understood at the physiological level; it is a finding of epidemiological studies. Admittedly, the studies referred to did not explore the extent to which it is possible for a person to catch up in height during her adolescence if she had suffered from deprivation when young. It was noted that there is scope for making up past deficits, even though the process is slow (Eveleth, 1985; Waterlow, 1985, 1992a). In order to catch up, a stunted adolescent needs more protein and energy than would be required by a normal adolescent. But if the person has been deprived

[29] Schofield, Schofield and James (1985) conclude, from reviewing a large literature from both poor countries and advanced industrial nations, that the BMR among Indians is about 10 per cent less than the expected rate, based on weight and height, of Europeans and North Americans. It isn't known if this reflects racial differences. Other sources of difference are climate, diet, and adaptation to habitual lower rates of energy intakes. See also McNeill *et al.* (1987) and Henry and Rees (1988) for reviews of a wider range of studies. We will explore possible sources of adaptation in Ch. 15.

[30] Payne and Waterlow (1971) found that the daily energy expended for maintenance (BMR) is remarkably similar in a wide variety of species, including humans, when expressed per kg of body weight (W) to the power 0.75. Specifically, they found that BMR $= 70W^{0.75}$

when young, the reason presumably was poverty, in which case she will hardly be in a position to command more than is required for normal growth during adolescence.

There are usually two periods of rapid growth in a normal individual free from infections: early infancy and adolescence. They are super-imposed on what is, roughly speaking, a regular pattern of growth. Of course, when we speak of a 'regular' pattern, we are using a thick temporal lens for viewing things; for growth occurs in spurts, it does not happen in a continuous fashion. The variability in weight gains over short periods, such as a month, can be considerable. As earlier, I shall glide over protein requirements, and requirements for other nutrients. I shall instead con-centrate on energy needs. Along the way we will study how children adapt when energy needs are not met.

The energy cost of growth has two components: the energy stored, and the energy used in the chemical reactions in storage. The amount stored depends on the composition of the tissues laid down. If it were adipose tissues containing 80 per cent fat, the energy stored would be about 7.5 kcal per gram. If it were lean tissues, containing 20 per cent protein, the corresponding figure would be about 1.1 kcal/g. In large-scale studies one has to aggregate over types of tissues. For infants, the energy required for laying down additional tissues is something like 4.4–6 kcal/g.[31] This yields a rounded figure of 5 kcal/g, of which 4 kcal/g could be identified as representing the energy stored, the remaining 1 kcal/g being the energy used in the chemical reactions in storage. (The latter is part of maintenance costs.) For an infant of 4 months, maintenance expenditure is something like 1.34 × BMR, which for a representative infant is approximately 71 kcal/g/day. If the infant gains 3 g/kg/day, this yields a total energy requirement of (71 + 12) = 83 kcal/kg/day.

By the end of the first year a child's growth rate becomes quite small. It is less than 1 g/kg/day, and falls to about 0.35 g/kg/day at age 3 years. These correspond to energy costs of 4 and 1.4 kcal/kg, respectively. The basal metabolic rate per unit body weight remains constant at about 45–55 kcal/kg. So the energy cost of growth accounts for about 5 per cent of requirement at 1 year, falling to less than 2 per cent at 3 years. They are small figures, but they are vital. Moreover, by year 1 physical activities assume great importance (see below). Similar calculations have been undertaken for subsequent stages of growth (see Waterlow, 1992a; Chapter 15). Failure in growth amounts to wasting and stunting, and earlier (Chapter 4) we saw its implications for morbidity and mortality.

Because there are two identifiable periods of rapid growth among

[31] For infants recovering from malnutrition, the figure has varied from study to study. WHO (1985, Annex 4: 185) records figures ranging from 3.5 to 7.1 kcal/g.

children in normal health, the body mass index (BMI) is not as useful a measure of nutritional status for the young as it is for adults. Up to the age of 10 years or so, an individual's nutritional status is usually measured by weight-for-age (the Gomez scale). It has serious limitations (the measure does not distinguish between a short but tubby child and a tall and skinny one), but it is a single index and easy to measure. BMI becomes a useful measure from about age 10 years. These are aggregate indicators, and if resources permit one may obtain a battery of relevant indicators, such as measures of skinfold thickness from various parts of the body. These measures reflect current nutritional status. Other commonly used measures, such as hip, thigh, arm, calf, and waist circumferences, sitting height, breadth of the hip, elbow, knee, and wrist, and grip strengths, reflect past (or long-term) nutritional status.[32]

One way a person can economize on energy expenditure is by reducing physical activities. Mild to moderately wasted pre-school children under free-living conditions have been observed to spend more time in sedentary and light activities than their healthy counterparts. They have been found to rest longer and to play more often in a horizontal position.[33] A Jamaican study found stunted children in the age group 12–24 months to be significantly less active than their non-stunted counterparts. The energy thus saved was comparable to the energy cost of growth at that age (Meeks Gardner *et al.*, 1990). At an extreme, when we observe little children in poor countries lying expressionless on roadsides and refraining from brushing the flies off their faces, we should infer that it is energy they are conserving. Among pre-school children, the first line of defence against low energy intake would appear to be reduced physical activity. Such behavioural modes of adaptation are not deliberately arrived at: we are 'wired' to so adapt. Little children by the wayside no more consciously husband their precarious hold on energy than bicyclists solve differential equations in order to maintain balance.

Chavez and Martinez (1979, 1948) have reported that, among a sample of infants from poor households in rural Mexico, differences in activity levels were marked from about 6 months of age onwards between those who received nutritional supplements and the control group. Supplemented children made greater contact with the 'floor', slept less during

---

[32] By using principal-components analysis, Chung (1991), in an interesting doctoral thesis, has summarized the anthropometric variation in 21 biological variables in a sample of Guatemalan people in the age range 12–26 years, to provide compact indicators of past and current nutritional status.

[33] See Rutihauser and Whitehead (1972), Chavez and Martinez (1979, 1984), Torun and Viteri (1981), and Torun (1984). Torun, Chew and Mendoza (1983) report on evidence that a moderate reduction in energy intake among pre-school children results in their economizing in physical activities; it has no effect on their growth.

the day, spent greater time outdoors, began playing almost 6 months earlier, and so forth. The thesis here is that low nutritional intake depresses activity, and this isolates the infant (or child) from contact with the environment, and from sources of stimuli of vital importance to both cognitive and motor development. It is of significance that the control group in the Chavez–Martinez study was not clearly under-nourished.[34]

Motor development is the process by which a child acquires basic movement patterns and skills, such as walking, running, jumping, hopping, throwing, kicking, and holding something in her grip. In normal circumstances children develop these fundamental motor patterns by the age of 6 or 7 years. It is through such movement patterns and skills that many childhood experiences, especially learning and interpersonal experiences, are mediated. During infancy and early childhood, interactions between the mother and child are of critical importance in this development (see, e.g. Malina, 1980a, b, 1984). This is a hidden cost of anaemia and low energy intake on the part of mothers. Since housework and production activity are mandatory, reductions in discretionary and child-rearing activities offer the mother a way of maintaining her energy balance. To be sure, societies differ in the way people other than the mother are involved in a child's upbringing. Nevertheless, the mother is an important figure in a child's cognitive and motor development in all societies.

Long-term malnutrition (e.g. stunting) would appear to be particularly associated with mental development, the presence or absence of oedema (i.e. current malnutrition) having a less pronounced effect.[35] Under conditions of severe undernourishment (e.g. marasmus or marasmic kwashiorkor) retardation of psycho-motor development in young children has physiological reasons as well. Some of the damage is extremely difficult to reverse and may indeed be irreversible. For example, even after 6 months of nutritional rehabilitation of a sample of infants hospitalized for severe malnutrition, Colombo and Lopez (1980) observed no recovery in their motor development (see also Celedon and de Andraca, 1979). It may be that severe malnutrition affects development of the brain, which experiences rapid growth starting round 10 weeks of pregnancy and continuing in spurts to about 3–4 years of age. (Foetal iodine deficiency is

[34] See Graves (1976) and Viteri and Torun (1981) for studies with a similar motivation in West Bengal and Guatemala, respectively. See also Monckeberg (1968), Rutihauser and Whitehead (1972), Pollitt *et al.* (1982), Popkin and Lian-Ybanez (1982), Reina and Spurr (1984), Powell and Grantham-McGregor (1985), Spurr and Reina (1988a, b) and Spurr (1990) for the effect of mild to moderate malnutrition on the behaviour of young children and adolescents.

[35] See Grantham-McGregor (1982) and Grantham-McGregor *et al.* (1990). Compare this with the finding in Meeks Gardner *et al.* (1990) mentioned earlier.

well know to damage the central nervous system.) However, there is evidence that malnutrition has an effect on brain development only when it coincides with a period of rapid growth and differentiation (Dobbing, 1990). Equilibrium reactions (otherwise called 'righting reflexes') are functions of the cerebellum and play an important role in the development of motor control (A. Kumar, Ghai and Singh, 1977; Falkner and Tanner, 1978). It is, of course, possible that even such anatomical changes as have been observed are retardation rather than permanent injury. But this is not known with any certainty.[36]

Among schoolchildren the matter is somewhat different, in that peer group pressure tends to counter the instinct for reducing physical activities. This is likely to be so especially among boys. To be sure, even for them decreased activity is a line of defence (Spurr and Reina, 1988a). However, studies by Barac-Neito, Spurr and Reina (1984), Spurr et al. (1988), and Spurr and Reina (1987, 1988b, c) indicate that in school-aged children the low energy expenditure associated with nutritional deficiency can be traced to low body weight: their basal metabolic rates are low. The development of lean body mass among undernourished children is retarded. This, as we will see, has a detrimental effect on their capacity to work when adults. Among marginally malnourished boys there does not appear to be reduced muscle function; their low capacity for work ($\dot{V}O_2$ max, see below) is due to their lean body mass being low.

On a wider front, malnutrition and infection have been found to have a pronounced detrimental effect among school children on such cognitive processes as attention and concentration. There is abundant evidence of children suffering from nutritional deficiencies and infections performing badly in aptitude tests (Pollitt, 1990). As we noted earlier, in extreme cases nutritional deficiencies affect the central nervous system. In less-than-extreme cases the matter isn't one of brain function; frequent absence and attrition affect learning as well.

Much international attention has been given to saving lives in times of collective crisis within poor countries. This is as it should be. Attention has also been paid by international agencies towards keeping children alive in normal times through public health measures, such as family planning counselling, immunization, and oral rehydration. This too is as it should be. That many poor countries fail to do either is not evidence of the problems being especially hard to solve. In fact, they are among the easier social problems: they can be fielded even while no major modification is made to the prevailing resource allocation mechanism. Much the harder

---

[36] The study of the effect of malnutrition on mental development is shot through with difficulties of interpretation. On this, see Grantham–McGregor, Powell, and Fletcher (1989), and the chapter by S. M. Grantham-McGregor in Waterlow (1992a).

problem, in intellectual design, political commitment, and administration, is to ensure that those who remain alive are healthy. It is also a problem whose solution brings no easily visible benefit. But the stunting of both cognitive and motor capacity is a prime hidden cost of energy deficiency and anaemia among children and, at one step removed, among mothers. It affects learning and skill formation, and thereby future productivity. The price is paid in later years, but it is paid.

14.7 *Special Requirements, 2: Pregnancy and Lactation*

Earlier, we observed how maternal malnutrition results in low birth weight and high prenatal and neonatal mortality. During pregnancy well-nourished women in Western industrial societies acquire something like 7.5 kg of extra weight. (The median infant birth weight there is 3.3 kg.) This translates into an energy cost of a bit more than 80 000 kcal over the 9-month period. The cost is not distributed evenly over the three trimesters of pregnancy. Nevertheless, for practical purposes it makes sense to recommend a uniform addition to energy intake for the duration. It works out to something like 285 kcal per day (see WHO, 1985: 85; see also Harmish and Munroe, 1981).

The energy cost of lactation is the energy content of the milk secreted plus the energy required in converting food intake into milk. For healthy women in Western industrial societies this additional energy requirement is something like 700 kcal per day. If requirements during pregnancy have been met, a woman will start lactating with about 36 000 kcal of additional reserves of fat. This is a source of approximately 200 kcal per day if the reserve is to be drawn over 6 months. It follows that she needs an additional 500 kcal per day (see WHO, 1985: 87–9). Women in poor countries have been known to get by with less. From this it is perhaps tempting to conclude that they get by with far, far less. A well-known study of pregnant and lactating women in Keneba (the Gambia) and Cambridge (England) conducted at the Dunn Nutrition Unit in Cambridge (see Prentice *et al.*, 1981; Whitehead *et al.*, 1981; Prentice, 1984) has claimed that energy intakes of Keneba women fall short of their counterparts in Cambridge by some 30 per cent. This is so low that it borders on the unimaginable.[37] In the following chapter we will analyse a few of the data in this study and argue that they are incoherent. But none of this detracts from the fact that poor women in poor countries routinely suffer from energy deficiency. Later we will look at various ways in which they adapt to low intakes.

[37] See James and Shetty (1982) for expressions of disquiet; and see Singh *et al.* (1989) for a retraction.

To what extent is the health cost of nutritional deprivation shared between a pregnant woman and her foetus? The evidence is mixed. The Gambian study has shown that it is shared during the lean season: the woman loses weight during pregnancy and the proportion of underweight births increases. This is a finding among people who would be presumed to have adapted to an annual food cycle. Nutritional supplementation programmes pick up something else, since they are not habitual. Prentice *et al.* (1980, 1983a, b) found energy supplementation to have no effect on lactation performance. On the other hand, average birth weight in the wet season responded to energy supplementation. (There was no response during the dry season).

A not-dissimilar finding has been reported from a field study of nutritional intervention among marginally undernourished women in west-central Taiwan (see Adair and Pollitt, 1983; Adair, 1984). While a combined energy–protein supplementation was found to have a significant effect on prenatal growth of the offspring, the study did not discover any effect on maternal anthropometry (e.g. skinfold thicknesses). Additional food was usurped by the foetus.

These special energy needs (for growth, pregnancy, and lactation) reflect additional terms which should enter equation (14.2). They make the equation a shade more complex, but they don't invalidate it. Having noted them, we will return to a study of adult men, and those adult women who are neither pregnant nor lactating. We will do this so as to focus attention on the determinants of a person's capacity to do work.

14.8 *Determinants of Work Capacity and Endurance*

In developing the nutrition–productivity curve ($\phi(x)$) of a person, we fixed his height and weight and varied his food intake. We now wish to compare the nutrition–productivity curves of different adult workers. We need to explore why they may differ. In order to do this we will peer into a few of the many characteristics summarized in our all-purpose notion of a person's state (H). Since several components of H (e.g. adult height and cognitive faculties) are influenced by early nutrition and freedom from infection, it will come as no surprise that among the kinds of public policy we will eventually arrive at are those affecting the young.

Earlier, we oberved that it is a reasonable approximation to associate with any task the work involved in completing it. The pace at which the task is performed can be varied, but this would be to vary the power (i.e. the rate at which work is performed), not the total work done in accomplishing it. Some tasks require a minimum flow of power (e.g. loading crates on to a truck). Slight people are incapable of lifting such weight. Muscular people are able to do things that slight people cannot.

This is a matter of casual observation; its recognition does not require knowledge of physiology or ergonomics. But it has often been overlooked in the recent development literature bearing on nutrition and productivity. Since the kinds of tasks unskilled labourers in poor countries perform are often strenuous, this lacuna should be kept in mind.

When nutritionists talk of *physical work capacity* (see Pollitt and Amante, 1984; Ferro-Luzzi, 1985; Collins and Roberts, 1988) they mean the maximum power (i.e. maximum work per unit of time) a person is capable of offering. Laboratory methods for estimating this in a person include getting him to run a treadmill, pedal a bicycle ergometer, and so forth. Here we are concerned with indirect measures, those that simultaneously reflect the determinants of physical work capacity. In this regard the most compelling index of a person's physical work capacity is his *maximal oxygen uptake*, usually denoted by the ungainly formula, $\dot{V}O_2$ max. It is the highest rate of oxygen uptake a person is capable of attaining while engaged in physical work at sea level. The reason maximal oxygen uptake provides us with the measure we need is that it is dependent on the body's capacity for a linked series of oxygen transfers (diffusion through tissues, circulation of haemoglobin, pulmonary ventilation, and so on). $\dot{V}O_2$ max measures cardio-respiratory fitness; the higher is its value, the greater is the capacity of the body to convert energy in the tissues into work. It thus measures the maximum energy output of the aerobic processes of the muscles involved in work and in the functional capacity of circulation.[38] Now this capacity itself depends on a person's (metabolically) active tissue mass, which is very nearly the same as his muscle mass (see Section 14.5). The latter is also on occasion called the *cell residue*. Clinical tests suggest that $\dot{V}O_2$ max per unit of muscle cell mass is approximately constant across well-nourished and marginally undernourished people (see Viteri, 1971). Even among undernourished persons the difference is not thought to be great. In one set of studies, over 80 per cent of the difference in $\dot{V}O_2$ max between mildly and severely malnourished people has been traced to differences in their muscle cell mass (Barac-Nieto *et al.*, 1980). To account for the remaining difference some have speculated that, among other things, the adenosine triphosphate (ATP) content of the skeletal mass tissue is reduced in severely malnourished people. It is, therefore, useful to have a measure of $\dot{V}O_2$ max per unit of muscle cell mass. A very rough approximation to this is provided by the *maximal aerobic power*, which is $\dot{V}O_2$ max per unit body weight. Moreover, since muscle cell mass and lean body mass (Section

---

[38] See Åstrand and Rodahl (1986). See also Patrick (1988) and Shephard (1988), which offer briefer accounts of this.

14.5) are related, we won't lose much in not being particular as to which we identify as the chief determinant of $\dot{V}O_2$ max.[39]

Earlier it was argued that the body mass index is the single most appropriate indicator of current nutritional status. The matter being discussed here is different: we are trying to identify the determinants of physical work capacity and endurance. Good nutritional status is necessary if one is to perform well at physical work, but it isn't sufficient. (One can be stunted but healthy.) Within a limited range, the body mass index of healthy people is approximately independent of height. But of two people with the same body mass index, the taller person typically possesses greater muscle cell mass; so his $\dot{V}O_2$ max is higher. Broadly speaking, then, taller and heavier non-obese people have greater physical work capacity (see equation (14.12) below). In addition, $\dot{V}O_2$ max depends on the level of habitual physical activity (what is called 'training' in sports parlance), but we will ignore this factor here. Unskilled labourers in poor countries may often be slight and weak, but they are never out of shape: it is sedentary workers who often are. Maximal oxygen uptake depends as well on the concentration of haemoglobin in the blood. I commented on this earlier. We shall ignore this too in what follows. $\dot{V}O_2$ max is usually expressed in litres per minute (l/min). To obtain a sense of orders of magnitude, we may note that 6 l/min is about as high as can be, while 2 l/min or a bit below is the sort of figure observed among chronically malnourished people (see below).

$\dot{V}O_2$ max, as the term suggests, measures the maximum volume of oxygen the body is capable of transferring per minute. Except for very short bursts, this maximum can't be reached. It transpires that the highest level of oxygen transfer a person is capable of sustaining over an extended period of 8 hours or so is of the order of 35–40 per cent of his $\dot{V}O_2$ max. More generally, there is a relationship between the rate at which a person works, expressed as a fraction of his $\dot{V}O_2$ max (which is sometimes also called the *relative work load*), and his endurance in maintaining this rate of work. The negative exponential function has been found to be a good approximation, even among undernourished subjects (Åstrand and Rodahl, 1986; Barac-Nieto, 1987), and so, writing endurance time by τ, we have

$$\% \text{ of } \dot{V}O_2 \text{ max} = e^{-b\tau} \qquad (14.10)$$

where b is a positive constant.

Barac-Nieto *et al.* (1978a, 1980) have found b not to be significantly different among people suffering from degrees of malnourishment ranging from mild to severe. The endurance time for 80 per cent of $\dot{V}O_2$ max in

---

[39] The mass of muscle tissue and muscle constitutes about 40% of body weight, and 50% of the lean body mass.

their sample was on average 97 minutes, with a coefficient of variation of 12 per cent. This means $b \approx 0.0023/\text{min}$. The suggestion isn't that this is a human constant; nor is it claimed that the energy cost of a task does not vary at all with the rate at which it is performed. All it means is that as a very rough approximation we may distinguish people's capacity for physical activities solely by their physical work capacity.

Let P denote physical work capacity, and V the maximal oxygen uptake ($\dot{V}O_2$ max). From (14.10), we conclude that

$$P = KVe^{-b\tau}, \tag{14.11}$$

where K is a positive constant. The total quantity of work a rested individual is capable of performing is then $P\tau = KV\tau e^{-b\tau}$, which attains its maximum value at $\tau = 1/b$. I conclude that, if it is aggregate work we are interested in (rather than relative work load), the duration of work should be $1/b$. If $b \approx 0.0023/\text{min}$, we have $1/b \approx 7.2$ hours. I do not know if, among healthy people in Western industrialized countries, an 8-hour day has been arrived at from such a consideration as this.

For strenous work, those with a low $\dot{V}O_2$ max need to be close to their physical work capacity. This means their hearts must beat at a fast rate. They are then overtaxed, and are incapable of maintaining the pace of work for long. This is reflected in (14.11). Consider as an example the well-known series of studies by Professor Spurr and his colleagues on chronically malnourished adult males from Colombia, and on nutritionally normal control subjects among sugarcane cutters, loaders, and agricultural workers.[40] Nutritional status was assessed on the basis of, among other things, weight-for-height, skinfold thicknesses, total body haemoglobin, and daily creatinine excretion (a measure of muscle cell mass). While, roughly speaking, the first three indices reflect current nutritional status, the fourth picks up nutritional history to an extent: *ceteris paribus*, taller people have greater muscle cell mass. A step-wise multiple-regression analysis with the data revealed that $\dot{V}O_2$ max is positively related to weight-for-height, total haemoglobin count, and daily creatinine excretion; and it is negatively related to skinfold thicknesses.[41] The chronically undernourished subjects ranged from 'mild' to 'intermediate' to 'severe'. Values of their $\dot{V}O_2$ max were, in turn, approximately 2.1, 1.7, and 1.0 l/min. The average $\dot{V}O_2$ max of the nutritionally normal sugarcane cutters was 2.6 l/min. As evidence in this field goes, this is about as clear

[40] See Spurr (1983, 1984, 1988, 1990) for a review of their work on the determinants of physical work capacity and endurance. The original publications are Spurr, Maksud and Barac-Nieto (1977), Spurr, Barac-Nieto and Maksud (1977), and Barac-Nieto *et al.* (1978a, b, 1980).

[41] Contrast this with the finding that, among nutritionally deprived adolescents, body weight is a central determinant of $\dot{V}O_2$ max (see Satyanaryana *et al.*, 1979; Spurr *et al.*, 1983a; Ch. 15).

as anyone could hope to find for the thesis that undernourished people suffer from depressed levels of $\dot{V}O_2$ max.

Consider an activity whose oxygen cost is 0.84 l/min. The nutritionally normal group could sustain it at 0.32 of $\dot{V}O_2$ max, whereas the remaining three groups would have to sustain it at 40, 50, and 80 per cent, respectively, of their $\dot{V}O_2$ max. At these paces, the nutritionally normal group could work for 8 hours, and the three malnourished groups for 6.5, 5, and 1.5 hours, respectively. That there is a positive link between nutritional status (e.g. height, muscle cell mass) and physical work capacity is not a subject of dispute today. But it is often overlooked. We will return to this theme in the next chapter.

All this has been on physical work capacity and endurance, not on *physical productivity*. One would expect though that they are closely related for unskilled manual work. And they are. For tasks such as sugarcane cutting, loading and unloading, and picking coffee, it is possible to measure physical productivity directly in terms of the amount done. Indeed, payment for such work is often at a piece rate (Chapter 16). There is now a wide range of evidence linking nutritional status to productivity in these occupations. In their work on Colombian sugarcane cutters and loaders, Spurr and his colleagues found height, weight, and lean body mass (i.e. $\dot{V}O_2$ max) to be significant determinants of productivity, as measured by daily tonnage of sugarcane delivered. Measuring productivity (ϕ) in units of tons-per-day, $\dot{V}O_2$ max (V in our notation) in litres per minute, and height (Ht) in centimetres, and denoting by F the percentage of body weight in fat, their most preferred specification was[42]

$$\phi = 0.81V - 0.14F + 0.03Ht - 1.962. \tag{14.12}$$

In their work, Immink *et al* (1984a) found the stature (and thus lean body mass and $\dot{V}O_2$ max) of Guatemalan labourers to be positively correlated with the quantity of coffee beans picked per day, the amount of sugarcane cut and loaded, and the inverse of the time taken to weed a given area. In a sample of factory workers (producing detonator fuses) in India, Satyanarayana *et al.* (1977) found weight-for-height to be the significant determinant of productivity. Strong effects of weight-for-height on both productivity and wages have been found among agricultural workers in south India by Deolalikar (1988). The elasticity of farm output with respect to weight-for-height was estimated as approximately two, and the elasticity of wages, in the region 0.3–0.7; the lower value reflects the effect in peak seasons, the higher value the effect in slack seasons, when the tasks are different. The link between nutritional status, physical work capacity, endurance, and physical productivity is an established fact.

---

[42] See Spurr (1984, 1988, 1990).

Adaptation to Undernourishment

15.1   *The International Incidence of Calorie Deficiency*

In estimating the magnitude of undernourishment in a population, two problems have to be resolved before anything else. First, we have to arrive at a method for determining individual nutritional status. Second, we need to find an acceptable index for aggregating the nutritional status of different people. The problem of aggregation has been explored in Chapters 2–5. So I shall bypass these issues here and simplify, by using the headcount index as our aggregate measure. This will allow us to concentrate on the first problem.

Earlier, we noted that anthropometric observations (for example, measuring the body mass index) are a reliable method for determining a person's nutritional status (Chapters 4 and 14). In a convincing sequence of publications, James, Ferro-Luzzi and Waterlow (1988), Ferro-Luzzi *et al.* (1992), and James *et al.* (1992) have shown that the distribution of body mass index in a population is relatively simple to ascertain. However, to date global estimates of the extent of malnourishment have invariably been based on indirect measures. The most popular route has been to assess individual nutrition intakes. (In Chapter 3 we called this an *input-based measure.*) There are a number of nutrients to reckon with though, and this creates yet another aggregation problem. In the previous chapter we saw how it can be at least partially circumvented by assessing calorie intakes only.[1] Recently, Reutlinger and Alderman (1980) and FAO (1987), among others, have used this approach in providing an estimate of the number of people in poor, non-communist countries who were undernourished in the decade of the 1970s. I shall review the FAO construction here, and sketch the approach of Reutlinger and Alderman.[2] They reflect alternative ways of going about the problem.

As in the previous chapter, I assume that each person has a fixed calorie requirement (but see below). Let x denote a person's energy intake and y

---

[1] United Nations (1987, 1988) contain the most complete set of estimates of worldwide undernourishment with which I am familiar, covering as they do a range of nutritional deficiencies, not merely deficiencies in calories.

[2] Beaton (1981, 1983) has a commentary on both. See also Waterlow (1989a).

his calorie requirement. x and y may differ, and so we let $M(x,y)$ denote the number of people whose intake is x and whose requirement is y. The headcount index, U, of those who are undernourished can then be expressed as

$$U = \Sigma_y \Sigma_{x<y} M(x, y). \qquad (15.1)$$

For each country in their list, Reutlinger and Alderman (1980) divided the population into income strata. Then, on the basis of an estimated relationship between income and mean intake, they calculated mean intake within each income stratum. The variability of intakes within each stratum was assumed to obey the normal distribution. The coefficient of variation was taken to be 15 per cent.

As regards requirements, people obviously differ. Within each income stratum this variability was also taken to be a normal distribution, with a coefficient of variation of 15 per cent. Reutlinger and Alderman assumed that the correlation coefficient between intakes and requirements is 0.7. Applying worldwide data to formula (15.1), and taking energy requirements to be 90 per cent of the figures suggested in FAO (1977), they found that the number of the world's undernourished in the early 1970s was about 600 million.

Estimating $M(x,y)$ in its entirety has a heroic air about it, and there are a number of steps at which significant errors can enter (see Beaton, 1983). It has been more common not to use formula (15.1), but instead to pursue the simpler route provided by the concept of a *reference person*. In applied studies this person has usually been taken to be an average adult male of a given age, occupation and desirable body weight, living in a particular environment. His calorie requirement is taken to be the norm, in that energy requirements of all other categories of people are obtained by the application of appropriate conversion factors to his requirement (see WHO, 1985: 15). We studied illustrations of this in the previous chapter. If this were done for each and every person, we would arrive at formula (15.1) for the headcount index. In practice it is not possible to do this except for a few categories of people (e.g. children, and pregnant and lactating women; see Chapter 14). What we therefore get is not formula (15.1), but something cruder. Assume that energy requirements of only a few categories of people have been normalized in terms of the reference person's calorie requirement, which I denote by y^*. Let $N(x)$ denote the number of people whose intake is x. The corresponding estimate of the headcount index is then U^*, where

$$U^* = \Sigma_{x<y^*} N(x). \qquad (15.2)$$

Most applied studies have used formula (15.2) as their basis for estimating the magnitude of undernourishment in a population (see e.g. Dandekar and Rath, 1971; FAO, 1987). As there are genotypic variations within any population, the standard deviation of requirements is positive even among a given category of people. We now simplify and suppose that the coefficient of variation is the same for all categories. Denote this by $\sigma_R/y^*.(\sigma_R$ is the standard deviation). As we are assuming that individuals have fixed requirements, σ_R/y^* reflects *inter*personal variations within each category, normalized in terms of the reference person. We will discuss *intra*personal variations presently.

There are immense problems in estimating $N(x)$ for any sizeable population. The main source of information on the distribution of house-hold food consumption within countries is sample surveys. For the overwhelming part, these do not record inequalities in intra-household food distributions, but only per capita household consumption (albeit, often in terms of adult-equivalent scales; see Chapters 3 and 4). So there is an error in the estimate right at this point.[3] Furthermore, survey techniques differ both in conception and competence across countries. To make their findings at least partially consistent requires ingenuity on the part of the analyst. It would take us far afield were we to study the technical difficulties posed by these and other problems, and the means that have been devised for circumventing them (for this see FAO, 1987: appendix). I shall focus instead on the choice of the reference person's energy requirement, y^*. FAO offers two estimates of the incidence of undernourishment in poor, non-communist countries. They are based on two alternative sets of assumptions regarding energy requirements within the population. The higher estimate is the more reasonable one. So I will discuss its basis.

FAO (1987) takes a person's maintenance requirement to be his total energy requirement. Energy needs for work and play are ignored. This at once introduces a conservative bias. But as the figure for the world's undernourished turns out to be large despite this assumption, it is a tactically shrewd move. The study follows WHO (1985) in regarding the maintenance requirement of a person to be approximately 1.4 times his basal metabolic rate (BMR). In short, FAO assumes that y^* equals 1.4 times the reference person's BMR. Let us call this $\hat{y}$. The estimate I am reporting here is based on the hypothesis that a person is undernourished if his calorie consumption falls short of $\hat{y}$. Using this construction on data from Asia, Africa, and Latin America (but excluding China, and other communist countries), FAO arrives at figures of 472 million under-nourished people for the period 1969–71, and of 494 million people for the period 1979–81; a significant increase.

Table 15.1 presents the data. Asia contains the bulk of the world's malnourished (compare Table 4.1 with this). It will be noticed that, except

---

[3] Haddad and Kanbur (1990) argue that this bias is unlikely to be negligible.

Table 15.1   The magnitude of calorie deficiency in poor market economies, 1969–71 and 1979–81

	Millions		Proportion	
	1969–71	1979–81	1969–71	1979–81
Africa	81	99	29	26
Asia (excluding Near East)	303	313	31	25
Latin America	53	56	19	16
Near East	34	25	22	12
Total	472	494	28	23

Source: FAO (1987, table 3.1).

in the Middle East, the number of undernourished people has increased in each region over the period in question. The proportion has declined everywhere, but only slightly. As noted in Chapter 12, both Asia and Latin America have enjoyed an increase in per capita food production and income during this period.

There are people whose basal metabolic rate falls short of the reference person even when they have been normalized in terms of the reference person, just as there are those whose basal metabolic rates are higher. We are thinking of genotypic differences here. This may suggest that we are counting as undernourished many who are not. But it would be wrong to conclude from this that 494 million is an overestimate. Quite the contrary: the figure is an underestimate. It will be instructive to see why.

FAO (1987) suggests that the coefficient of variation in the basal metabolic rate of adults of the same age and weight (which is $1.4\sigma_R/\hat{y}$) is about 6 per cent for males and 8 per cent for females (see also Schofield Schofield, and James, 1985). We may average the figure to 7 per cent. Assuming a normal distribution, this means that in judging if a person is undernourished we should see whether his intake falls short of $0.86\hat{y}$ (which is the mean minus twice the standard deviation), and not whether it falls short of $\hat{y}$. This is the source of the suggestion that 494 million is an overestimate. It is, however, only one side of the picture. The other side is that a person's total calorie requirement exceeds his maintenance requirement. A working person's maintenance requirement is in the region of 65–75 per cent of his total energy requirement. Let us assume the implausibly high figure of 80 per cent to illustrate matters. In this case the person's calorie requirement would be $0.86\hat{y}/0.80$, which is greater than $\hat{y}$. I conclude that the FAO's estimate of the world's undernourished is biased on the conservative side. The picture is even more horrifying than that portrayed by the figure of 494 million.

That this is a correct inference is also consistent with the findings in

United Nations (1987, 1988) and James *et al.* (1992). The former pair of studies bases its assessment of nutritional status in a population partly on anthropometric evidence (viz. children's weight). The latter study provides estimates of the proportion of people suffering from a low body mass index in samples from a number of countries. However, at present there is no worldwide estimate of the magnitude of undernourishment based on anthropometric data. It is time this was attempted. In the previous chapter we observed that nutritionists today like to infer calorie requirements from energy expenditure because the measurement of intakes is known to be quite unreliable. In the studies I have reviewed here there is a double confounding of measurement problems, since intakes are inferred from income. These have been pioneering studies, but there are compelling grounds for departing from their methodologies when the time comes for reassessing the magnitude of world undernourishment.

15.2 *Adaptation: Genetic, Physiological, and Behavioural*

Variations in the energy intake of people of similar size and stature, who maintain their body weight and who are engaged in similar activities, have usually been interpreted as a reflection of *inter*personal differences in the capacity for converting food energy into body maintenance and work.[4] The common assumption has been that individuals have approximately fixed energy requirements, and that requirements vary across otherwise similar people because of genetic differences. Our account of the nutritional status of poor people has so far been built on this presumption. It is a simplifying hypothesis, and has always been accepted as such. Recently, however, it has come under attack. The charge is that cross-sectional surveys of energy intakes among even poor people exaggerate differences in their well-being, because they neglect variability *within* each person. The thesis is that much of the variation observed in cross-sectional surveys of energy intake among people of a similar type, who on average maintain constant body weight, is occasioned by a short-term autoregulatory mechanism, or *homeostasis*, consisting of responses in the efficiency of energy metabolism.[5] There is more than a little irony in the fact that this thesis, which has had much influence among social scientists, is not based on any physiological evidence.[6] Going by the evidence as it now stands, short-term fluctuations

---

[4] Waterlow (1990) reports that, when conditions are rigidly standardized and results related to body composition, interpersonal variation in energy expenditure may be as low as 5%.

[5] See Sukhatme (1977, 1978, 1981a, b, c, 1982a, b, c, 1989), and Sukhatme and Margen (1978, 1982). For an explication of Sukhatme's thesis, see Srinivasan (1981, 1983a, b, c, 1993), and Payne (1993). For a critique, see Rand, Scrimshaw and Young (1985), among many others. See below in the text.

[6] I am most grateful to Professor John Waterlow for clarifying a great many points in the relevant physiology literature for me.

in the difference between energy intake and energy expenditure are mediated for the most part by adjustments in body weight, a relatively well-understood adaptive phenomenon (Section 15.3).

Far greater attention has been paid in the nutrition literature to regulatory processes operating over the long run.[7] In the previous chapter I identified a number of ways in which people adapt to permanently low levels of energy intakes. Here I will refer to them by the all-purpose name *long-term adaptation*. Among poor people in poor countries, these energy-sparing mechanisms are not costless. This was the principal conclusion in Chapters 4 and 14. In Section 15.5 I will try to codify such regulatory processes, and in Section 15.6 I will discuss a pair of studies which have looked at the process of transition from one long-term equilibrium to another.

Before I do this, however, it is as well to note three things. First, even if we were to regard homeostasis as a significant and costless regulatory mechanism, it would not have any bearing on the estimate reported in the previous section of the number of people in the world who are undernourished. We recognized that FAO's estimate would be conservative even if all forms of adjustment and adaptation were costless. Second, neither homeostasis nor long-term adaptation has any bearing on the analytical points developed in the previous chapter. For example, the fact that people are able to adapt over the long run to low energy intake doesn't imply there are no bounds on the process of adaptation. Significant fixed costs involved in repair and body maintenance remain, and no amount of adaptation can reduce maintenance requirements to zero. Third, we are studying poor people in poor countries in this book. As workers, they are typically engaged in strenuous work. They have little body weight to spare even in the best of times. So we should ask if such folk are capable of adjusting or adapting to reductions in their energy intakes costlessly. That both homeostasis and long-term adaptation may appear prima facie costless for people enjoying a high standard of living isn't the point here.

Gould and Lowentin (1979) observe that adaptation, which they define as a good fit of organisms to their environment, can occur at three hierarchical levels: genetic, physiological, and behavioural. The low average height of pygmies is a genetic disposition, whereas stunting among infants and children in poor households is an expression of physiological adaptation; on the other hand, economising on bodily movements in response to low energy intake is an instance of behavioural adaptation.

---

[7] See e.g. James and Shetty (1982), Adair (1984), Prentice (1984), Shetty (1984), Waterlow (1985, 1986, 1990), Blaxter and Waterlow (1985), WHO (1985), Martorell and Habicht (1986), Ferro-Luzzi (1988), Stein, Johnston and Greiner (1988), and Shetty (1990a, b). WHO (1985) and Waterlow (1986) also contain discussions of metabolic adaptation to low intakes of protein.

The levels are related, in that an organism's genetic make-up determines the extent to which it is capable of physiological adaptation, and the latter influences the necessary behavioural adaptations. There is influence running the other way as well. For example, behavioural adaptation can be a road to survival, and thereby reproduction.

The Darwinian mode operates at the genetic level, and is not the point of either homeostasis or long-term adaptation. Much of this book (Chapters 4, 14, 16–17) addresses behavioural adaptation to low intake. In this chapter our interest for the most part lies in physiological adaptation (but see Section 15.7), by which is meant the phenotypic plasticity that enables us to mould ourselves to meet prevailing circumstances, both in the short and the long run. It isn't a heritable characteristic, although the capacity to develop it is.

We begin by recalling the various forms of the energy conservation equation for an adult. We will find equation (14.2) to be the most suitable form here, and we rewrite it for convenience as

$$\mu(\alpha, \beta, H_t)x_t = r(\alpha, \beta, H_t, x_t) + q(\alpha, \beta, H_t, x_t) + \sigma(H_t, \text{sign}[\delta s_t])\delta s_t. \quad (15.3)$$

To recapitulate: x_t represents the energy value of food ingested in period t, which we will continue to call *energy intake*; $\mu(\cdot)x_t$ is the metabolizable energy intake, which we have been referring to as *energy consumption*; $r(\cdot)$ denotes maintenance requirements; $q(\cdot)$ the energy expended in external work (i.e. physical activity); δs_t is the change in body mass; and $\sigma(\cdot)\delta s_t$ the energy associated with this change.

We will often find it useful to refer explicitly to the subject whose regulatory mechanisms are being studied. We will also find it useful to simplify the notation. So we express (15.3) for person k in period t as

$$c_{kt} = r_{kt} + q_{kt} - \delta m_{kt}, \qquad k = 1, \dots, M. \quad (15.4)$$

Here, c_{kt} is k's energy consumption, r_{kt} her maintenance requirement, and q_{kt} her energy expenditure in physical activities. When positive, δm_{kt} denotes the energy released from reduced body mass; when negative, it represents the energy spent and stored in an increase in body mass.

15.3 *Short-Term Adjustment, or Homeostasis*

The modern debate on short-term adjustment (or homeostasis) was initiated by Professor P. V. Sukhatme. As it is frequently alluded to in the economics literature, it will be useful to present an account of it here.[8]

---

[8] I am not alone in having found Sukhatme's writings not very easy to follow. (See the commentaries on Sukhatme (1989) by J. C. Waterlow, W. P. T. James, and M. J. R. Healy in the *European Journal of Clinical Nutrition*, 1989: 43.) His views on short-term regulation have undergone change as his thoughts on these matters have progressed (see Osmani, 1990). I do not know if he has views on long-term adaptation (but see Gopalan, 1993). In any event,

Edholm *et al.* (1970) recorded energy intakes and expenditures among a group of British infantry recruits on a daily basis over a period of 3 weeks. Energy consumption was estimated from recruits' diets (i.e. intakes), and expenditure was assessed from published tables on maintenance requirements and energy costs associated with various physical activities. Consumption was taken to be a fixed fraction of intake (the Atwater factor; see below). Since for the purposes of my account here I will lose nothing by identifying consumption with intake, I shall do so. While the authors discovered a significant relationship between time averages of consumption and expenditure in each subject, they could find no relationship between daily consumption (c_{kt}) and daily expenditure ($r_{kt} + q_{kt}$). Now ($c_{kt} - r_{kt} - q_{kt}$) is subject k's daily *net energy consumption*. Edholm and his colleagues found this to be positively and significantly related to k's daily body weight. Because of its sharp findings, this study has become the basis of much of the debate on the source and extent of homeostasis. Let us look into it.

Reviewing the Edholm *et al.* data, Sukhatme and Margen (1982) observed that the coefficient of variation of average weekly energy intake by subjects was of the order of 15 per cent, and was greater than the coefficient of variation of average weekly energy intakes *between* subjects. Furthermore, they found the coefficient of variation of weekly energy expenditure to be about 8 per cent. Reasonably enough, they went on to argue that such large fluctuations in a subject's daily energy intake could not have been due to errors of measurement.

Sukhatme had earlier observed that in this same body of data a subject's intake did not equal his expenditure even when averaged over a week. He found that the data displayed substantial autocorrelation of the first order in a person's daily energy consumption. He also found that on any day a person's net energy consumption is regulated by its value on the preceding day (the autocorrelation of order 1), and that it varies between fixed limits, independent of the time period of observation. To Sukhatme this meant that, among people maintaining constant body weight over the long run, energy intake is used with variable efficiency by means of a homeostatic mechanism working for the good of the whole body. In this mechanism the composition of the body (influencing protein turnover, fluid pressure, chemical concentration, temperature, and so forth) is a control variable. The thesis is that dissipated heat is an increasing function of the difference

---

my intention here is not to provide an exegesis of his thoughts. Srinivasan (1981, 1993) are excellent guides. Here I shall be adopting the latter's formulation (Srinivasan, 1993) of the idea of homeostasis. The discussion that follows has been adapted from Dasgupta and Ray (1990).

between daily intake and daily expenditure. The mechanism stabilizes the system. I shall now formalize the notion.[9]

Let $\{c_{kt}\}$ and $\{q_{kt}\}$ be two exogenously given stationary stochastic processes in (15.4). It follows then that $\{r_{kt}\}$ and $\{\delta m_{kt}\}$ are endogenous stochastic processes, each adjusting in each period in such ways as to be consistent with the energy conservation equation. We say that k's metabolic process is *homeostatic*, and that the variances of $\{c_{kt}\}$ and $\{q_{kt}\}$ are within k's homeostatic range if $\{r_{kt}\}$ and $\{\delta m_{kt}\}$ are able to adjust to maintain $\{\delta m_{kt}\}$ stationary at mean value of zero. Homeostasis, as thus defined, involves daily adjustments in both body weight and the maintenance requirement, subject to the proviso that weight is maintained over the long run.[10] This means that, if the variances of $\{c_{kt}\}$ and $\{q_{kt}\}$ are within k's homeostatic range, he is in long-run energy balance; he is in a *stationary stochastic equilibrium*. In the previous chapter we learnt that maintenance requirements depend on both the mass of metabolically active tissues and their composition. Homeostasis, thus defined, is consistent with the thesis that short-term fluctuations in net energy consumption are mediated by adjustments in both mass and composition. At an aggregate level, it is in accordance with the idea that they are associated with changes in body weight. Homeostasis says nothing about variations in the 'efficiency of energy metabolism' at a cellular level. I shall come back to this point later.

Sukhatme observed in the Edholm *et al.* data that $\{c_{kt}\}$ obeys a first-order stationary Markov process for each k. To model this, we first normalize people in the sample for differences in their body stature, mean weight, and so forth. The observer can't, of course, tell normalized subjects apart; they all look the same. Thus, daily changes in c_{kt} within the sample reflect both interpersonal and intrapersonal variations. So the two need to be unscrambled. Towards this, let c^* denote the mean daily energy requirement of the overall population, of which the M subjects form a random sample.[11] Let γ ($0 \leq \gamma < 1$) be a constant, to be defined below. Denote by θ_k a normally distributed random variable with mean

---

[9] There are a number of metabolic reactions which produce no net chemical work, only heat. Appropriately enough, they are called 'futile cycles', some half-dozen of which are judged to account for 10–15% of the basal metabolic rate. It is thought that these cycles serve a regulatory function among well-nourished persons. From this it doesn't follow that they remain to serve poor people in poor countries. It is possible that even among marginally undernourished people the slack available from these cycles has been exhausted. See Waterlow (1990).

[10] An alternative formulation would have daily intake as exogenous, and allow the composite Atwater factors ($\mu(\cdot)$ in (15.3)) to be part of the adjustment mechanism controlling energy consumption. This would draw a wedge between intake and consumption. I ignore this formulation here, because the literature on homeostasis hasn't addressed it. I shall take it up when discussing long-term adaptation in the next section.

[11] 'Requirement' was defined in the previous chapter.

$(1 - \gamma)y^*$ and variance σ_0^2. Each subject is a draw from this distribution. So θ_k reflects interpersonal variations in energy requirements. Let ε_{kt} be independently and normally distributed random variables with zero mean and constant variance σ_ε^2. They reflect intrapersonal variations in energy requirements, in a sense to be made precise below.

Let us suppose that the M subjects are observed for T periods. The idea that c_{kt} obeys a first-order stationary Markov process for each k can then be expressed by means of the equation

$$c_{kt} = \gamma c_{kt-1} + \theta_k + \varepsilon_{kt}; \qquad k = 1, \ldots, M; t = 1, \ldots, T.[12] \qquad (15.5)$$

It will be noticed that α is the autocorrelation coefficient. Assume now that T is large. We may then define $\hat{x}_k = (\Sigma_1^T c_{kt})/T$ as the long-run average energy consumption by k. Repeated use of (15.5) allows us to confirm that $\hat{x}_k \approx \theta_k/(1 - \gamma)$. This is to say that, if k's daily energy consumption is subject to equation (15.5), it will move in a probabilistic sense to $\theta_k/(1 - \gamma)$. Therefore, the average daily intake over the entire population will move probabilistically to the value y^*, which is how we defined y^* to begin with.

Define $\phi^2 = \sigma_\theta^2/\sigma_\varepsilon^2$, and denote by μ_1 and μ_2 (with $\mu_1 + \mu_2 = 1$) the proportions of total variation due in turn to interpersonal and intrapersonal differences. It is a routine matter to confirm that

$$\mu_1 = \phi^2(1 + \gamma)/[(1 + \gamma)\phi^2 + (1 - \gamma)],$$

and[13]   (15.6)

$$\mu_2 = (1 - \gamma)/[(1 + \gamma)\phi^2 + (1 - \gamma)].$$

Equation (15.6) tells us that, the smaller is the value of ϕ^2, the more prominent are intrapersonal variations within total variations in daily energy consumption; also, the larger is the autocorrelation coefficient, γ, the more prominent are interpersonal variations.

Sukhatme (1977, 1978, 1982b, 1989) and Sukhatme and Margen (1982) emphasized the autocorrelation in daily energy intake in the Edholm *et al.* data-set when citing evidence for their belief that there are significant variations in the efficiency of energy metabolism (see also Srinivasan, 1981). But assessing habitual energy intake is known to be very difficult. One of the authors of Edholm *et al.* (1970) has argued that the techniques available more than two decades ago were such that the numerical findings were in all probability subject to considerable errors of measurement, both random and systematic (Healy, 1989: 209). In another study, Hallfrisch, Steele and Cohen (1982) have reported that of 24 subjects, only 4 were able to maintain their weight when fed the same amount of energy they

---

[12] See Bhargava (1992), from which this specification is taken.
[13] This follows from the relation: variance $(c_{kt}) = [\sigma_\theta^2/(1 - \gamma)^2] + [\sigma_\varepsilon^2/(1 - \gamma^2)]$.

had themselves reported having consumed during a week. Reviewing such studies as this, Ferro-Luzzi (1984) argued that fluctuations in weight, for example among the Gambian women mentioned earlier, indicate that energy intake when assessed over 7 days or so can't be guaranteed to represent 'habitual' intake. Weight fluctuation of 0.5 kg in a week can easily go undetected, and would account for an energy imbalance of 300–450 kcal per day. This is one danger with making sharp pronouncements on the character of homeostasis.

A second problem is that the autocorrelation observed in the Edholm *et al.* data tells us nothing about the physiological basis of homeostasis. In Chapters 9 and *9 I observed that poor households have limited access to the credit market. I also noted that storage facilities for such households are unreliable. Grain consumption by their members must, inevitably, follow food output. But this would show itself as autocorrelation in food intake; the poorer the household, the stronger the autocorrelation (see also Deaton, 1990; Morduch, 1990). Admittedly, the example is one of seasonal variation, and we are studying short-term adjustment here. The example nevertheless illustrates that daily autocorrelation says nothing about the nature of the energy-sparing mechanism coping with short-term fluctuations. Admittedly, also, the autocorrelation generated by credit constraints is irrelevant for British infantry recruits. But, by the same token, what are permissible adjustments for the British army may well be very costly for the poor in poor countries.

Bhargava (1992) has estimated the model in (15.5) for two sets of household data on daily energy intake: one from India (from the semi-arid areas covered by ICRISAT; see Chapter 9), the other from the Philippines. Average household income in the sample from the Philippines was higher. Moreover, in contrast to the Indian households, those in the Philippines don't face a dry season. This means that household income in the Philippines is likely to be smoother. We have argued that autocorrelation in food intake should be expected to be greater in the Indian sample. This is confirmed by the data. Table 15.2 presents the estimated values of α, ϕ^2, and μ_2. The proportion of total variation in daily energy intake attributable to intra-household variation is larger in India (0.650 as compared with 0.551), providing support for the thesis that μ_2 declines as

Table 15.2 Autocorrelation in energy intakes

Parameter	India	Philippines
γ	0.162	0.046
ϕ^2	0.387	0.744
μ_2	0.650	0.551

Source: Bhargava (1992).

income rises and becomes more smooth. This presumption is reinforced by Bhargava's finding that in the Indian sample μ_2 is lower for less poor households.

15.4 *Homeostasis and the Magnitude of Undernourishment*

What are the practical implications of all this? Consider the extreme case where interpersonal variations are negligible, so that we may set $\phi^2 = 0$. Suppose now that the entire burden of daily variations in energy intake is borne by adjustments in the efficiency of energy metabolism, and that body weight remains constant from day to day. Assume too that this imposes no additional risk on a subject's health. Then the spread in the intake of energy within any cross-sectional survey would reflect differences in intrapersonal variations occasioned by a benign homeostasis. All people would be well-nourished. Reliance on the energy requirement of the reference person (y^*) for arriving at the headcount index would be misleading. Use of formula (15.2) would exaggerate the incidence of undernourishment within the population.

What should one then do? Sukhatme (1977, 1978, 1981a, b, 1982a, b) suggested that we abandon the use of y^* in formula (15.2), and replace it by ($y^* - 2\sigma_\varepsilon$), which is a statistical cut-off point. Using this lower value on Indian data enabled him to argue that the proportion of India's undernourished population in the late 1960s was of the order of 20 per cent, and not the high figure of just over 40 per cent estimated by Dandekar and Rath (1971). This is at the operational heart of the controversy over estimates of the magnitude of undernourishment in poor countries.[14]

That energy intakes, energy expenditures, and net energy consumption vary daily for each one of us, rich or poor, is not under contention. It has been long noted by nutritionists. If a physiologist measures my energy intake and output over 24 hours, he will conclude that at no time am I in balance: after meals I am in 'positive balance' and at night I am in 'negative balance'. There are continuous changes in my energy stores, too small for him to detect (Waterlow, 1989b). The bone of contention lies elsewhere: in the statement that variation in energy balance is mediated by adjustments in the efficiency of energy metabolism. Sukhatme and Margen (1982) advance the thesis that it is. But they offer no physiological evidence. They claim, for example, that a person with an intake of 1900 kcal per day has an efficiency rate of 50 per cent, whereas someone ingesting 3200 kcal per day displays an efficiency rate of 30 per cent. They

---

[14] See Dasgupta and Ray (1990) for an account of the controversy.

also assert that someone with a daily intake at an intermediate level of 2550 kcal per day has an efficiency rate of 37 per cent. These numbers appear to have been plucked from the air; no evidence is provided by the authors. Moreover, when these rates of intake are multiplied by the respective efficiency rates, they yield approximately the same figure: 950 kcal. This coincidence in value reinforces one's suspicion that the Sukhatme–Margen thesis is based solely on a hunch.

Is there anything in the hunch? Rand, Scrimshaw and Young (1985) tested it on data from five sets of long-term metabolic studies. There were 42 subjects in all, and they were examined for periods of 63–90 days.[15] Crude estimates of energy intake required to maintain body weight for each subject were calculated. During each study the amounts of energy estimated were supplied at an unchanged level. The subjects were asked to maintain their usual level of physical activity in order to achieve a relatively constant rate of daily energy expenditure. The studies attempted to minimize daily variations in energy consumption (c_{kt}) and physical activity (q_{kt}). If energy metabolism adjusts to short-term fluctuations in needs (or intakes) while maintaining body weight, we would expect subjects to settle down quickly to a constant body weight. This did not happen: 19 of the 42 subjects experienced significant increases in weight, and 13 suffered significant declines. (Of these 32 individuals, 16 experienced a gain or loss throughout the length of the studies.) Of the remaining subjects, 8 experienced fluctuating weight with no apparent trend, and 2 maintained a stable weight. For the great majority of subjects, the apparently modest imbalance between daily energy intake and expenditure was not cushioned by changes in the efficiency of energy metabolism. Adjustments in body mass seem to have been the mediating mechanism.

Recall that the efficiency of energy metabolism is the proportion of consumed energy that is converted into the energy manifesting itself in both internal and external work (Chapter 14). It is the product of the ATP (adenosine triphosphate) formed per unit energy used and the work done per ATP used in doing it. As it happens, there is virtually no physiological evidence that the human body can operate with variable efficiency of energy metabolism. For one thing, with current techniques, internal work can't be measured. For another, even external work can't be measured very accurately: machines, like bicycle ergometers and treadmills, neglect movements of the upper body. Theoretically, there are possibilities for variations within a person in both the ATP formed per unit energy used and the work done per ATP used in doing it; but as far as internal,

---

[15] The five studies dealt with dietary nitrogen and energy intakes for 16, 8, 6, 6, and 6 subjects, for 63, 84, 82, 90, and 82 days, respectively.

chemical work goes, the considered judgement is that, if there are variations, they are in the quantities of energy flowing through the pathways (i.e. variations in flux rates, such as protein turnover), rather than in the efficiency with which the pathways operate.[16] There are also ways of economizing in the energy expended in carrying out tasks. (The subject of ergonomics is much concerned with this.) But this is quite different from the Sukhatme thesis.

Even were we to leave all this aside, there remains a vital reason for not lowering estimates of energy requirements when we come to assess the magnitude of undernourishment in a country. Sukhatme (1978) observed that in the Edholm et al. data-set intrapersonal variations in daily net energy consumption do not vanish even when they are averaged over a week. This does not affect estimates of headcount indices of undernourishment, which are often based on longer sample periods. For example, the Indian National Sample Survey data on expenditures and food consumption are *monthly* averages, and the estimate of the Indian headcount index by Dandekar and Rath (1971) relied on this. But the longer is the sample period, the closer the average energy intake of a person needs to be to her energy requirement if she is to maintain good health (inequality (14.4)). If average intake falls short of requirement, she will endanger her health.

There is a small additional cost attached to fluctuations in body weight which is worth mentioning. The major energy store is in the form of fat in the adipose tissue, followed by protein; roughly in the proportion 5:1.[17] Now storage isn't free. When formulating equation (14.2) in the previous chapter, we noted that the cost of storing energy per unit mass of fat (or protein) exceeds the cost of running down a unit mass of fat (or protein). Indeed, the latter is quite low.[18] To deposit a gram of protein requires 6 kcal of energy, while a gram of fat costs 9.3 kcal. Drawing down a gram of protein releases 4 kcal, while a gram of fat releases 9 kcal. These differences mean that a person with fluctuating intake will, on average, require a bit more energy than a person enjoying a fixed rate of intake. To get an order of magnitude of how much, assume that the resting metabolic rate is fixed at r and that the energy required for physical activity is fixed at q. We may then rewrite equation (15.3) as

---

[16] I am grateful to Professor John Waterlow for clarifying these points in correspondence.
[17] See e.g. Young and Scrimshaw (1970). There is also a very small store of energy (a few hundred kilo-calories) in the form of glycogen in the liver and muscle. The glycogen store is the first source of energy that is tapped when there is a drop in food intake, or a large gap between meals.
[18] In (15.3) this meant $\sigma(\cdot) = \sigma (H_t, \text{sign}[\delta s_t])$.

$$c_t = r + q + \sigma^-(s_{t+1} - s_t), \qquad \text{if } s_{t+1} < s_t,$$

and   (15.7)

$$c_t = r + q + \sigma^+(s_{t+1} - s_t), \qquad \text{if } s_{t+1} > s_t,$$

where $\sigma^+ > \sigma^- > 0$.[19] If body mass remains constant, energy requirement is simply $r + q$. But suppose body mass fluctuates because of fluctuating intake around requirement. Specifically, suppose that consumption fluctuates between a low (c') and a high (c''), with $c' < r + q < c''$. The long-term average intake is then $c^\circ = (c' + c'')/2$. From (15.7), it is now easy to show that, for body mass (s_t) to remain on average constant over time,

$$c^\circ = (r + q) + [(\sigma^+ - \sigma^-)(c'' - c')]/2(\sigma^+ + \sigma^-). \qquad (15.8)$$

As expected, $c^\circ > r + q$. To see what the order of magnitude is, consider the example from Sukhatme and Margen (1982). Using an average requirement of 2550 kcal as the daily energy requirement, $r + q$, of the reference Indian male, Sukhatme and Margen argued that the lower bound on energy intake (c') is 1900 kcal per day. If we were to assume that the energy released from fats and protein when body mass declines is in the same ratio as it is when body mass increases, then $\sigma^- \approx 8.0$ kcal/g and $\sigma^+ \approx 8.7$ kcal/g. Using these values in (15.8), we conclude that $c'' = 3262$ kcal and $c^\circ = 2581$ kcal, implying an average energy consumption 31 kcal per day higher than the one resulting from a fixed rate of consumption.

As matters are understood currently, it does not look as though short-term adjustments take place through hormonal changes and substrate alterations (see Section 15.6). At constant body weight the basal metabolic rate has in a large number of studies been found to be extremely stable (over days, weeks, even months), with coefficients of variation of merely 1–4 per cent (see e.g. Garby and Lammert, 1984; Soares and Shetty, 1987; Shetty and Soares, 1988; Henry, Heyter and Rees, 1989). BMR has also been found to respond slowly to the onset of energy deficiency. The time lag appears to be of the order of 48 hours.[20] So one looks to changes in body weight as a possible explanation of the Edholm et al. data. Our illustrative numbers are significant in that they are consistent with the thesis that the subjects adjusted for fluctuating net energy consumption by experiencing alterations in body mass. Daily weight changes of 0.05 kg in either direction are hardly uncommon, and can easily go undetected. Applying the figures for σ^- and σ^+ we have just used, we may conclude that depositing 0.05 kg uses up 435 kcal, whereas running it down releases 405 kcal. Average variation per day is 420 kcal ($= (435 + 405)/2$), which is about 15 per cent of the daily energy requirement of the subsistence

[19] I am simplifying the notation and writing $\sigma^- = \sigma(H_t, -)$ and $\sigma^+ = \sigma(H_t, +)$ in (15.3).
[20] Shetty (1990b) provides reasons for this.

452UNDERNOURISHMENT AND DESTITUTION

farmer in Table 14.2. It is also only a bit less than the coefficient of variation of daily calorie intakes in the Edholm *et al.* data-set.

Recommending a reduction in estimates of energy requirements of the poor in poor countries, as Sukhatme and Margen do, is easy. It is also very dangerous.

15.5 *Long-Term Adaptation*

In Chapter 4 we noted that stunting is a form of long-term adaptation to low food intake. In the previous chapter we observed how infants and children adapt behaviourally to food shortage. In this chapter we focus on adults. So we will think of a person, k, an *adult*, whose metabolic process is in stationary stochastic equilibrium, satisfying equation (15.4). We re-express this as

$$\mu_{kt}x_{kt} = r_{kt} + q_{kt} - \delta m_{kt}. \tag{15.9}$$

I shall assume that k's energy intake, $\{x_{kt}\}$, and his activity process, $\{q_{kt}\}$, are both exogenously given stationary stochastic processes. We now draw a distinction between intake (x_{kt}) and consumption (c_{kt}) and allow μ_{kt} to adjust. Therefore, we are to think that $\{\mu_{kt}x_{kt}\}$, $\{r_{kt}\}$, and $\{\delta m_{kt}\}$ are endogenous stochastic processes, adjusting in each period in such ways as to maintain the energy conservation identity. We will now say that k's metabolic process is homeostatic, and the variances of $\{\mu_{kt}x_{kt}\}$, $\{r_{kt}\}$, and $\{\delta m_{kt}\}$ are within k's homeostatic range if $\{\mu_{kt}x_{kt}\}$, $\{r_{kt}\}$, and $\{\delta m_{kt}\}$ are able to adjust to maintain $\{\delta m_{kt}\}$ stationary with mean zero. Within his homeostatic range k's metabolic process is stable, and on average he maintains weight.

Let us assume that at some date k's intake process, $\{x_{kt}\}$, is replaced by another stationary process, $\{\bar{x}_{kt}\}$, with a different mean, but the same variance. In the previous chapter we studied various forms of behavioural adaptation, among both adults and non-adults. In Sections 15.6 and 15.8 and Chapter 16 we will study it again. For the moment we will ignore it and assume that physical activities (α in our earlier notation) and the pace at which they are undertaken (β in our earlier notation) remain unchanged. We are interested in physiological adaptation here. So we will suppose that k's activity process, $\{q_{kt}\}$, remains unchanged. (There are ergonomic aspects of work and play which we are ignoring by this move.) *Long-term adaptation* is the process of achieving a new stationary stochastic equilibrium satisfying equation (15.9).[21] This form of adaptation involves changes in k's mean body mass (e.g. mean body mass index); it also

---

[21] Here I am adapting Srinivasan (1993). The discussion that follows is taken from Dasgupta and Ray (1990).

involves changes in the (endogenous) process governing the maintenance requirement, $\{r_{kt}\}$, and thereby changes in the process governing energy consumption, $\{\mu_{kt}x_{kt}\}$. Being in stationary stochastic equilibrium, the new body mass will obey a stationary stochastic process $\{\delta\bar{m}_{kt}\}$, with zero mean. As with homeostasis, there are limits (this time, to changes in the mean value of the energy intake process) for which the term 'long-term adaptation' is applicable. For example, if the mean of $\{\bar{x}_{kt}\}$ is very much lower than the mean of $\{x_{kt}\}$, a stationary stochastic equilibrium will not be feasible, in that the body mass index to be maintained in the new 'equilibrium' will be too low. Individual k's health will break down; he will suffer from acute nutritional stress. The extreme will be death. We formulated an expression of this in Fig. 14.3.

Among adults, long-term adaptation involves a move from one stationary stochastic equilibrium to another following a shift in the energy intake process.[22] As in every other field of inquiry, the move is ill-understood, since it involves disequilibrium behaviour. There have been two experiments, though, one by Keys et al. (1950) and another by Barac-Nieto et al. (1980), which tell us something about it. I will review a number of their findings presently (Section 15.6). But first, it is as well to identify the sources of long-term adaptation in adults. In doing this I will lean on equation (15.9). So our classification will be different from the one usually presented in the nutrition literature (e.g. Waterlow, 1990).

Imagine for concreteness that the mean of $\{\bar{x}_{kt}\}$ is lower than the mean of $\{x_{kt}\}$. There is little evidence that the mechanical efficiency of physical work (see Chapter 14) is greater among the poor in poor countries (Waterlow, 1986, 1990). As we are for the moment ignoring behavioural adaptation (including ergonomic variations), there remain three means of long-term adaptation: the Atwater factors (μ_{kt}), dietary thermogenesis, and the basal metabolic rate. (The latter two are a decomposition of the maintenance requirement, r_{kt}.) We will study these possibilities in turn.

1. *Atwater factors*. The energy value of a person's food intake (x_{kt}) is not fully transformed into metabolizable energy. There are inevitable losses of energy in the process of digestion (fecal losses) and in the process of oxidation of protein and other nitrogenous materials in the body. This means that the fraction of ingested energy that is retained, μ_{kt}, is less than 1. Energy consumption, c_{kt} ($= \mu_{kt}x_{kt}$), is less than energy intake.

In our formulation we have aggregated over different kinds of food, so that μ_{kt} has been taken to be a scalar. While μ_{kt} depends on the composition of the diet, it is fairly stable across individuals who have similar diets. In a disaggregated analysis, μ_{kt} would be a vector of fractions. These food-specific fractions are called *Atwater factors*. They are used

---

[22] Among infants and children, adaptation in growth rates must also be stipulated.

widely for the purposes of providing information about the calorie value of various types of food. The figures usually taken are in the range 90–95 per cent.

How reliable are these figures? In undernourished populations the answer appears to be: not very. Undernourishment (accompanied by episodes of acute diarrhoea) leads to an impaired ability to digest nutrients (Section 14.2). Figures for Atwater factors in such circumstances may be as low as 80 per cent (Mola, 1984). Since this says μ_{kt} declines as x_{kt} declines, however, it is adaptation in the wrong direction. In addition, food containing a high percentage of dietary fibre (that is, crude fibre exceeding 10 grams per day) is less easily digestible. Intakes of fibre exceeding 50 grams per day are not uncommon among rural populations in the tropics, and among vegetarians. This may reduce digestibility by a further 10 per cent (Prynne and Southgate, 1979; Uauy, 1985).

How important are these corrections? Consider an individual whose daily energy requirement is 2500 kcal. Dividing this by an average Atwater factor of 95 per cent yields a requirement of 2600 kcal of energy intake per day. If instead we were to take the figure to be 85 per cent, the intake requirement would be 2930 kcal, which is 330 kcal higher still per day. This is not negligible. It is only a bit under half of 596 kcal, the daily energy expenditure on physical activities we calculated for our male subsistence farmer in Table 14.2.

An Atwater factor of 85 per cent may well be overly low. Nevertheless, the order of magnitude predicted by the scanty evidence that exists is striking, and deserves more attention than it has received. Proponents of costless adaptation to low energy intake do not mention this issue. Work remains to be done on the problem.

2. *Dietary thermogenesis.* Little is known of the effect of habitually low energy intakes on the thermic effect of food. In commenting on possible pathways of adaptation among rural women in the Gambia (see Section 14.6, and below), Prentice (1984) observed that the frequency with which they eat meals is low, and they have few opportunities for snacks. Since the daily period over which the thermic effect of food operates is relatively short, some energy savings by Gambian women are probable here. Prentice also noted that protein intake among them is lower than among well nourished people, and protein is known to be particularly thermogenic. It is also possible that there has been genetic selection of lowered dietary thermogenesis. All in all, however, savings possibilities in the thermic effect of food can't be very significant. In the previous chapter we observed that dietary thermogenesis amounts to about 10 per cent of the energy value of meals. Even if women in the Gambia manage a 50 per cent reduction through long-term adaptation, it can't account for more than 70–80 kcal per day.

Table 15.3   Effect of body weight on energy expenditure

	Subject A	B
Weight (kg)	50	65
Height (m)	1.6	1.6
Body mass index (kg/m^2)	19.5	25.4
Basal metabolic rate (BMR) (kcal/day)	1445	1670
Maintenance requirement ($\approx$ 1.4 BMR)	2020	2340
Daily energy expenditure of moderately active man (1.8 BMR)	2600	3010

Source: Waterlow (1990, table 2.1).

3. *Basal metabolic rate (BMR)*. In the previous chapter we saw that body weight is a good predictor of the basal metabolic rate, and that within narrow limits a linear relationship (equation 14.9) is a reasonable approximation. This is a statistical finding, and it is a crude reflection of the fact that on average smaller people have smaller lean body mass. That losses in fat-free mass reduce the basal metabolic rate is incontrovertible, and it provides the connection between body weight and BMR. Table 15.3 offers an account of the sources of savings in daily energy expenditure by comparing two people of the same height (1.6 m) but different body weight (65 and 50 kg). The table thus compares energy expenditures associated with two long-term stationary metabolic processes. The basal metabolic rate has been calculated on the basis of its linear relationship with body weight, as provided in Schofield, Schofield and James (1985). The smaller person's BMR is lower by 225 kcal.[23]

Fat in the adipose tissues has a lower metabolic rate than lean tissues. When a person suffers from mild undernourishment it is the fat that is decumulated first. This may explain why the basal metabolic rate per unit of body weight is not significantly reduced under mild malnutrition. When the state of undernourishment is severe, the lean tissues alter in their composition, and the body suffers from an increase in intercellular water. The basal metabolic rate per unit of body weight declines significantly.

There is an additional pathway for reductions in the basal metabolic rate. It has been ascribed to improvements in the economy of energy metabolism mediated by hormonal changes and substrate alterations (e.g. protein turnover). The thought here is that BMR per unit of active tissue mass falls in response to reduced energy intake.[24] This compounds the fall

[23] A further 185 kcal is saved by him on account of a lower value of dietary thermogenesis and a smaller energy cost associated with body displacement, which we ignore here.
[24] Shetty (1990b) and Waterlow (1990) contain illuminating discussions of the biochemical mechanisms by which this can happen. The evidence is sufficiently confusing to allow one to question whether BMR per unit active tissue mass is a good index of metabolic efficiency.

Table 15.4   Adaptations in basal metabolic rate

	Normal person	Energy deficient person (adapted)
Height (m)	1.75	1.65
Weight (kg)	70	60
Body mass index	23	22
BMR (kcal per day)	1750	1341

Source: Ferro-Luzzi (1988, table 2).

in BMR due to a loss in lean body mass. In their work on semi-starved subjects (see Section 15.6), Keys *et al.* (1950) suggested that the fall in BMR per unit of active tissue mass could be as large at 16 per cent.[25] Table 15.4 presents hypothetical figures for the basal metabolic rates of two people differing in both height and weight. It is assumed that the smaller person has adapted by the full 16 per cent. The basal metabolic rate of the smaller person is 409 kcal lower than that of the larger person, accounting for a 25 per cent reduction.

Whether nutritionally deficient people can adapt even beyond the extent observed by Keys *et al.* (1950) in BMR per unit of active tissue mass has yet to be established. The study of women in Keneba, the Gambia, undertaken by the Dunn Nutrition Unit in Cambridge, England (see Chapter 14), is frequently cited as evidence that they can, and that they can do so at relatively little cost. But the evidence elsewhere doesn't support this conclusion.

One aspect of the study was a programme in which 156 lactating women were provided with energy supplementation to the extent of 723 kcal per day. Prentice *et al.* (1983b) report that supplemented women experienced an increase of 1.5 kg in body weight early in the programme (accounting for about 53 kcal per day of the supplemented energy), and that body weight then fluctuated over the annual cycle in much the way of unsupplemented women. This leaves 670 kcal per day unaccounted for. Unfortunately, neither the basal metabolic rates among subjects nor their activity levels were explicitly measured. If we assume that BMR per unit of active tissue mass increased by 16 per cent among supplemented women, it would account for an additional energy requirement of about 200 kcal per day. It can be argued that the remaining 470 kcal per day unaccounted for could

---

[25] See below in the text. (See also James and Shetty, 1982, for a review of the evidence on alterations in the basal metabolic rate due to changes in nutritional status.) The experiment of Keys and his colleagues is widely referred to as a study of 'semi-starvation'. Widdowson (1985: 98) thinks of the subjects in that experiment as suffering from only 'moderate malnutrition'. This is understandable. Immediately after the Second World War, Widdowson had observed the nutritional status of survivors of the Warsaw Ghetto.

easily have gone undetected were it to have been expended on additional physical activity.[26]

That women in Keneba suffer from deficient diets during the lean seasons and adapt to their deprivation is not in doubt. Nor can it be doubted that adaptation is often at the expense of both the mother's and the child's health. Thus, if a peasant woman in Keneba conceives in February and delivers in November, the second trimester of pregnancy and most of the third will fall within the hungry season. (From July onwards for 4 months or so there will be a particularly heavy agricultural workload, coupled with food shortage.) She will on average lose 3–5 kg of body fat, a complete reversal of what is desirable, i.e. a gain of 4 kg of fat during pregnancy.[27] The proportion of babies born weighing less than 2.5 kg (the cutoff figure in use for demarcating low-birth-weight babies) will rise to about 30 per cent, six times greater than the figure one expects in a healthy community. Milk output of lactating women reduces during the wet season, and the milk quality is compromised. In the dry season the volume of milk produced by the Keneba mother is about the same as that of a Cambridge (UK) mother, but its quality is inferior, in that it contains a smaller quantity of several vitamins.[28]

A most surprising conclusion of the Gambian study (see Prentice *et al.*, 1981; Whitehead *et al.*, 1981; Prentice, 1984) was that energy intakes of Keneba women during the lean season fall short of the intakes of their counterparts in Cambridge by some 30 per cent: 1300 kcal per day in Keneba as compared with 1980 kcal in Cambridge for pregnant women, and 1300 kcal per day in Keneba as compared with 2290 kcal in Cambridge for lactating women. The disparity has been claimed to be somewhat less during the dry season in the Gambia, when food is relatively plentiful and farm work is less intense.

Several other studies have recorded remarkably low energy intakes among the poor in poor countries, people who nevertheless have been observed to engage in strenuous physical activity (see e.g. Norgan, Ferro-Luzzi, and Durnin, 1984, and the references in Prentice, 1984). How may one account for this? Prentice *et al.* (1981) recorded fat losses up to 5 kg. But this amounts to something like 45 000 kcal of energy. Even were we

[26] See Ferro-Luzzi (1988). See also Durnin (1984).

[27] That in sub-Saharan Africa and the Indian sub-continent working adults use their reserves of fat to buffer the effects of seasonal food shortages or increases in agricultural work has been much noted. See Dugdale and Payne (1987), Ferro-Luzzi, Pastore and Sette (1987), Ferro-Luzzi *et al.* (1990), Norgan *et al.* (1992), and Pastore *et al.* (1992). We have made use of this finding earlier (Chapter 9).

[28] For reviews of this work, see Paul and Muller (1980), Prentice (1980, 1984), and Whitehead (1989). See also Chen, Chowdhury and Huffman (1979), and Chowdhury (1985) for a similar set of concerns in the context of Bangladesh; and Durnin (1980) for a corresponding study in New Guinea.

to assume conservatively that the loss occurs over a short, 4-month period, it would yield at most 375 kcal per day. This would then be the upper bound to any daily energy deficit (calorie intake less expenditure) a person could experience. But it falls far below the reported deficit of approximately 700 kcal per day, amounting to a straightforward violation of the law of energy conservation. It isn't believable. So it shouldn't be believed.

The measurement of energy intakes among free-living populations is fraught with difficulties. James and Shetty (1982) have argued that none of the published studies recording such low intakes as those reported in Prentice (1984) had been backed by proper measurement of the object of study. One should conclude that both short- and long-term adjustments in energy expenditure among the poor in poor countries are accompanied predominantly by alterations in spontaneous activity and changes in body weight, and not by metabolic adaptations in energy utilization. This is now a considered judgement. It has even been endorsed in a recent publication by the Keneba research unit (Singh *et al.*, 1989), in which the authors acknowledge that estimates of energy intake among free-living populations must have been wrong and conservative. As of now, there is no evidence that people are able costlessly to adapt beyond a limited extent to low nutrition intakes.

15.6   Metabolic Disequilibrium

The classic Minnesota experiment on the biology of semi-starvation among humans (Keys *et al.*, 1950) provides an account of the sequence of events

Table 15.5   Long-term adaptation to semi-starvation diet

	Before	After	Δ	Δ as	Δ as
	(kcal per day)			% of total Δ	% of control
Basal metabolism	1576	962	614	32[a]	39
Dietary					
thermogenesis	349	157	192	10	55
Physical activity	1567	451	1116	58[b]	71
Total	3492	1570	1922	100	

[a] 65% (i.e. 20.7% of total calories saved) savings due to reduced active tissue mass, and 35% (i.e. 11.2% of total calories saved) due to reduced tissue metabolism.
[b] 60% (i.e. 35% of total calories saved) due to reduced physical activities, and 40% (i.e. 23% of total calories saved) on account of reduced cost of body displacements.

Source: Taylor and Keys (1950).

constituting the move from one metabolic equilibrium to another.[29] In this experiment thirty-two men were investigated under laboratory conditions for a year. In the course of a 3-month control period they were in energy balance with an average daily intake of 3492 kcal. The semi-starvation diet was instituted at the end of this period and maintained for 6 months. It provided an average intake of 1570 kcal per day.[30] The effects were dramatic. Body weight fell (in accordance with the law of diminishing decrements), and stabilized by the end of the period of semi-starvation, when a new energy balance had more or less been established. The average weight loss was 24 per cent, and body fat decreased from 14 to 6 per cent of body weight. Maximal oxygen uptake ($\dot{V}O_2$ max) declined from approximately 3.5 1/min during the control period to about 1.9 1/min at the end of 24 weeks. $\dot{V}O_2$ max per unit of lean body mass also declined significantly. It was estimated that the subjects lost approximately 1990 g of protein during the first 12 weeks of dietary restriction, and a further 690 g during the final 12 weeks. The authors concluded that as protein was catabolized the reduction in $\dot{V}O_2$ max was probably due to a decline in muscle cell mass. Performance on the Harvard Fitness Test declined to about 30 per cent of control, and 'the subjects suffered a marked loss of strength and endurance as the starvation period progressed. The men commented that they felt as if they were rapidly growing old. They felt weak and they tired easily. They moved cautiously, climbing stairs one step at a time, and obviously reduced unnecessary movements to a minimum' (Taylor and Keys, 1950: 216).

Daily energy intake had been reduced by 1922 kcal per day. Table 15.5 provides a breakdown of the reduction in energy expenditure to match this. In comparison with the corresponding values in the control period, the basal metabolic rate declined by 39 per cent, the energy expended in physical activities by 71 per cent, and the thermic effect of food by about 55 per cent. As regards calorie expenditure, reduced physical activity was the largest contributor (58 per cent of total calories saved), with BMR a not-too-close second (32 per cent). Of the reduction in the basal metabolic rate, 65 per cent could be attributed to a decline in muscle cell mass. The remaining 35 per cent, therefore, is attributable to a decline in BMR per unit of active cell mass. James and Shetty (1982) computed from the data that the fall in BMR per unit of active cell mass was about 16 per cent. This decline occurred within the first 2 weeks, and remained unchanged

[29] See also Taylor and Keys (1950) and Young and Scrimshaw (1970). See also Grande, Anderson and Keys (1958) for an analysis of a different experiment on the effects of semi-starvation.

[30] The semi-starvation diet consisted of potatoes, cabbage, turnips, and cereals, with only a few grams of animal protein and fat per week. The protein and fat contents of the diet were 54.5 g and 27.1 g per day. Excepting for riboflavin and vitamin A, adequate allowances of minerals and vitamins were provided.

for the subsequent 22 weeks of semi-starvation. The conclusion should be, tentatively that reduction in the basal metabolic rate under long-term adaptation to low nutrition intake occurs in two stages. The first (lasting 2–3 weeks) is not attributable to changes in body weight or body composition. This decrease in BMR per unit active tissue mass is a measure of the increase in metabolic efficiency occasioned, possibly, by substrate alterations (e.g. protein catabolism and protein turnover) and hormonal changes. Under prolonged energy deficit (the second stage), the cellular metabolic rate remains approximately constant, and subsequent declines in BMR are a consequence of reduced active tissue mass. It follows that, the longer is the duration of low energy intake, the greater is the contribution of losses in active tissue mass to reductions in the basal metabolic rate (Shetty, 1990b).

The Minnesota experiment was not designed to answer the question we have been considering in this and the previous two sections, namely, long-term adaptation of low energy intake with unchanging physical activities. None the less, because it dramatizes the costs involved in physiological adaptation, it is a relevant experiment. Taylor and Keys (1950) noted that a part of the means by which subjects economized in their use of energy may have been a wastage of tissue rather than a depressed oxygen utilization of active tissue. There is evidence that the heart undergoes loss of muscle mass during prolonged periods of low food intake. The skeletal muscle loses weight as well, and it changes structure: the fibres lose protein and shrink, and the spaces between them become filled with intercellular material. There is also a thinning of the alimentary canal during prolonged undernutrition. Each is a mode of adaptation to malnutrition.[31] Children suffering from marasmus are known to adapt by lowering their basal metabolic rates. Marasmic infants discard their muscles in order to protect vital organs (such as the liver, pancreas, and intestines). Since each is a strategic response to a life-threatening situation, none should be acceptable. The Minnesota subjects experienced on average a 24 per cent loss in weight. Under really severe malnutrition (as with survivors of the Warsaw Ghetto) up to 50 per cent of body weight may be lost. Prolongation of this leads to the final stage, when no further adaptation is possible. The person dies.

The Minnesota experiment studied long-term adaptation to what was for its subjects a semi-starvation diet. By way of contrast, the experiment reported in Barac-Nieto et al. (1980) investigated long-term adaptation by severely malnourished subjects to food supplementation. In further contrast, the study focused on improvements in the physical capacity for work

---

[31] Widdowson (1985) and Waterlow (1992a: ch. 5) have excellent discussions of this.

as reflected by maximal oxygen uptake. It will pay us to review this aspect of the study.[32]

A group of severely undernourished subjects in Colombia was selected for observation under sedentary conditions in a hospital for a period of 124 days. Their nutritional status was assessed on the basis of the weight-for-height ratio (approximately 27 kg/m) and body consumption. The subjects' average maximal oxygen uptake was found to be approximately 1 1/min. This is to be contrasted with a group of nutritionally normal sugarcane cutters, loaders, and general farm labourers, with an average weight-for-height ratio of 36 kg/m, who served as controls and whose $\dot{V}O_2$ max was approximately 2.8 1/min. Upon entry into hospital, the under-nourished subjects were placed on a diet containing 2240 kcal of energy per day, judged suitable for levels of activity prevailing in the metabolic ward. Their protein intake was maintained at their pre-entry level, which was 27 g per day. The subjects' maximal oxygen uptake was measured at the end of 45 days (the basal period) on this diet. Protein intake was then increased to 100 g per day for a 79-day repletion regime, the increased calorie intake from proteins being balanced by a corresponding reduction in the carbohydrate content of their diet. Measurement of $\dot{V}O_2$ max was repeated at 90 and 124 days after admission to the hospital. Subjects enjoyed a slight gain in weight during the basal period, but there was no change in their $\dot{V}O_2$ max or their body compositions. There was a progressive gain in weight during the repletion regime, and $\dot{V}O_2$ max rose to nearly 1.5 1/min at the end of 90 days, and to approximately 1.7 1/min at the end of 124 days. We note in passing that even this terminal value fell short of the $\dot{V}O_2$ max of a group of mildly undernourished subjects (about 2.1 1/min) who were simultaneously under observation.

The experiment demonstrates neatly that the recovery process from severe malnourishment is slow. It also demonstrates the importance of proteins in body repair from the ravages of malnourishment, and it brings us back to our discussion in the previous chapter of the determinants of physical work capacity and endurance. $\dot{V}O_2$ max per unit of muscle cell mass does not seem to vary much with nutritional status. The chief determinant of maximal oxygen uptake is muscle cell mass. By extension, it is the chief determinant of the capacity to do physical work.

15.7 Food Intake, Efficient Productivity, and Stature

Earlier, we noted that muscle cell mass and lean body mass are functionally related to one another in an approximate sense. As a crude, aggregate measure of nutritional status, lean body mass and muscle cell mass can be

---

[32] For more detailed reviews of this experiment, see Spurr (1984, 1988, 1990).

used interchangeably. Other things being the same, taller people have greater lean body mass. They weigh more, and so we would expect their resting metabolic rates to be greater too. Such folk require more energy for maintenance, but they can produce more, both per unit of time and over time. In a stationary state, the nutrition–productivity curve takes the form $\phi(x, H)$, where x calorie intake, H is the person's nutritional status, and ϕ is the number of units of the composite task performed. So the question arises whether in manual work tall people are more productive than short people, net of their greater maintenance costs. We should also ask if, in view of the possibility that people can adapt to low intakes, the dependence of ϕ on calorie intake, x, has an operational content. This is another way of asking if equation (14.8) in Chapter 14 may have multiple solutions. The two questions are distinct, but it will pay to analyse them together.

A pair of studies that have been regarded significant by social scientists in showing that there is no operational content in the dependence of ϕ on x is Edmundson (1977, 1979).[33] The subjects were fifty-four East Javanese farmers. Each person was measured six times at 2-month intervals, for a total of 324 man-days of data. Food intake was measured, and its metabolizable energy content determined. Activities were recorded for each farmer, and *group mean* energy expenditures were estimated for ten basic activities on the basis of heat output as measured by indirect calorimetry. Work outputs for each person were then calculated by multiplying the mean energy expenditure per minute by the number of minutes each subject was engaged in that activity.

The results were putatively striking. While mean energy intake (2430 kcal per day) corresponded closely to mean energy expenditure (2443 kcal per day), there was no association between average intake and work output (more accurately, heat output) for individuals. The ratio of energy intake to work output (averaged over the six observations for each subject) ranged from a low of 0.59 to a high of 1.63.

In Edmundson (1979), eleven of the earlier fifty-four subjects were chosen for further observation. Most of them had unusually high or unusually low intakes in the earlier study, and the rest served as controls.[34] The subjects were so selected that average heights and weights in the high- and low-intake groups were similar. Basal metabolic rates of these subjects were measured, and a 6-day average of energy intakes was estimated for each farmer. The basal metabolic rate of the group enjoying high energy consumption was found to be twice as high as that of the group whose

[33] See also Edmundson (1980) and Edmundson and Sukhatme (1990).

[34] Of these farmers, 6 had intakes below 2000 kcal per day in the earlier study, 3 had intakes in excess of 3000 kcal per day, and 2 had intakes of about 2500 kcal per day.

energy consumption was low. Subjects enjoying high calorie consumption also expended greater energy in performing standard tasks, although the difference was not significant.[35] Edmundson concluded that the efficiency of energy metabolism adapts in response to a prolonged period of low consumption.

Let us study the studies. Consider the first experiment. While calorie intakes were measured individually, energy outputs for each subject were calculated by multiplying the number of minutes spent on a particular activity by the group-averaged energy expenditure per minute on that activity. Now this is something of an absurd thing to do, for there is no way to judge the work output for each individual per unit of time. Suppose you are ill-fed and hungry, and work at a lethargic pace for an hour. Your well-fed counterpart works for an hour too, but gets more done. Edmundson's technique of measuring energy outputs would attribute the same amount to both. Since this is the methodology, the claim that the 'most efficient' low-intake subject in the experiment released 1.63 times the energy he ingested does not mean anything. Moreover, there is no mention of subjects' body weights. We can't tell if they experienced weight changes. Furthermore, the experiment was designed to measure heat output, not mechanical work output. It is a seriously flawed piece of research.

Consider the second experiment. There, subjects with high energy intakes expended more energy per minute in performing standard tasks. It may then be argued that their greater efficiency permitted low-intake subjects to work just as hard, but required less energy. However, the argument is weak on two counts. First, of the two tasks, the lighter one did not exhibit differences in efficiency between the two groups that were significant at the 1 per cent level, although the heavier one did. Second, in measuring the basal metabolic rate and the energy expended per minute in performing standard tasks, the Edmundson experiments did not focus on quite the right objects. In the economics of nutrition in poor countries we should be interested in endurance and, more generally, in what we will call *efficient productivity*. Neither is captured by the Edmundson measures.

To illustrate this, consider the right-hand side of equation (14.1) in Chapter 14, which denotes energy expenditure. I have so far adopted the right-hand side of (14.6) as my approximation for energy expenditure in a stationary state. To interpret the Edmundson results, I have to adopt a slightly different approximation. Let α represent the standard tasks in the second experiment. Since subjects have similar heights and weights, we may as well ignore the parameter H. As the subjects are assumed to be in a

---

[35] Of the standard tasks, the light one involved pedalling a bicycle ergometer at a rate of 50 W/min, and the heavy task involved pedalling to produce power at the rate of 100 W/min.

stationary state, we may also drop the symbol for changes in weight. We may then express the right-hand side of (14.1) as $E(\alpha, x)$, which is the total energy expended by a person when his energy intake is x. This we decompose in our usual way as

$$E(\alpha, x) = r(\alpha, x) + q(\alpha, x). \tag{15.10}$$

Edmundson's assertion is that, for his two observed values of x (call them x_1 and x_2, with $x_1 > x_2$), $r(\alpha, x_1) > r(\alpha, x_2)$; and for two selected tasks of highly limited duration, $q(\alpha, x_1) > q(\alpha, x_2)$. In short, $E(\alpha, x_1) > E(\alpha, x_2)$. But this tells us nothing about endurance. Nor does it tell us anything about what one may call the 'productivity of work', something that can be inferred only from the entire nutrition–productivity curve, not from a pair of points on the curve, crudely measured. Moreover, the basal metabolic rates when expressed in kcal/kg/day among the subjects were claimed in Edmundson (1979, Table 1) to have ranged from 44 to 13. Judging by an extensive international literature (see Schofield, Schofield and James, 1985) such a wide range is so improbable as to be unbelievable. One can but conclude that the measurement techniques adopted were poor.

In the previous chapter I reported on studies that have uncovered a positive link between nutritional status, physical work capacity, and endurance. I will now formalize the notion of efficient productivity. It will emerge as central to the economics of destitution. In developing the notion, it will prove useful to move beyond the confines of the Edmundson experiments.

Consider two individuals (labelled 1 and 2), differing by way of, say, their lean body mass (or, alternatively, stature), which I will identify with nutritional status. We take it that individual 2 has the better build. His maintenance requirement is higher though, and at low levels of energy intake he can be out-performed by individual 1, in that he can't manage the number of units of the composite task individual 1 can manage to accomplish over a given period. But at high enough levels of energy intake, he is the more productive worker. This is shown in Fig. 15.1 in the form of their nutrition-productivitiy curves ($\phi_1(x_1)$ and $\phi_2(x_2)$) based on equation (15.10). As the figure is drawn, the curves cross.

Consider now two levels of work output, marked $\bar{\phi}$ and $\hat{\phi}$ in Fig. 15.1. The ratio of work output (not power, but total work done) to energy consumption at both $\bar{\phi}$ and $\hat{\phi}$ is higher for the person with the lower intake. That person is also the one with the 'inferior' nutritional status (individual 1). So we may think that person 1 is more efficient. But we would be wrong. At higher values of intake, the ratio of work output to energy consumption is higher for person 2. Of greater significance is the fact that, as a worker, person 2 is intrinsically more efficient, in that the *maximum* work output per unit of calorie consumption that person 2 can offer (at

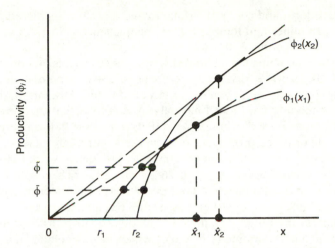

Fig. 15.1   Nutrition productivity curve as a function of nutritional status

consumption level $\hat{x}_2$ in the figure) exceeds the maximum individual 1 can offer (at consumption level $\hat{x}_1$). We will call the maximum ratio of work output to energy intake for a person his *efficient productivity*. This concept will prove potent when we come to study the workings of the labour market in Chapter 16. Here we note that it is injudicious to talk of the relative efficiency of different individuals by observing only a few neighbouring points on their nutrition–productivity curves. Efficient productivity is a global property of such curves. Even though the maintenance requirement of a better-built person is typically higher, he may none the less be a more efficient worker, in the strong sense that he produces more per unit of resource cost.

  People enjoying superior nutritional status enjoy a greater capacity for physical work. They are also able to endure longer hours (equations (14.10) and (14.11) of Chapter 14). At manual work they can perform a greater range of tasks (e.g. lift heavier loads) and accomplish them in less time. In short, they are capable of getting more done over a day. A person of low nutritional status suffers from the handicap that he has to work long hours if he is to earn his day's keep through manual work alone. His endurance being less than that of one enjoying superior nutritional status, he has to work at a slower pace, or take more frequent breaks, or both.[36] It is in this spirit we should interpret Edmundson and Sukhatme (1990: 264), when they write: 'Despite a low level of nutrition, the level of physical performance of the world's poor is high, not low. Within the port

---

[36] It is worth noting that to perform a task slowly may involve less expenditure of energy than to perform it fast. I am taking this into account in the text.

cities, stevedores and coolies work night and day carrying incredibly heavy loads . . . In mines and lumber camps, people start to work at sunrise and continue until evening.'

I have been at pains throughout this book to stress this fact of life among those of the world's disadvantaged who are nevertheless fortunate in obtaining manual employment. Edmundson and Sukhatme, however, don't draw the inference that I have about such folk: that their productivity is low, not high. They conclude instead that 'workers with low-energy intakes are often as or more productive than workers with high intakes', and that 'the poor expend more time on economically productive work than the rich' (Edmundson and Sukhatme, 1990: 264, 266). That rich people can afford more leisure *and* eat more than poor people has never been anything more than a banality. As in any other field of inquiry, a banality cannot be made to illuminate anything. But it can lead investigators astray, as it does Edmundson and Sukhatme (1990: 264), when they conclude: 'The conventional wisdom has stated that the chronic undernutrition thought to be widespread in low-income countries must result in low levels of human performance . . . that poorer people are environmentally determined by low food intake to be physiologically underproductive. This is not true.' The evidence I have brought together here says that it is very much true.

Our theoretical exploration has shown us how to formulate the idea of efficient productivity. But even this formulation is restrictive. In keeping with the nutrition literature, I have assumed that the subject is in a stationary state. So I have worked with nutrition–productivity curves implied at stationary states. A more general notion of efficient productivity would admit non-stationary states, and we would seek to determine productivity at each date as a function of calorie consumption in all previous dates. A suitable index of intertemporal productivity (viz. the present discounted value of the flow of output) should now be compared with an index of intertemporal energy consumption (viz. the present discounted value of the flow of energy intake). This way we may define efficient productivity in a fully dynamic setting. Ideally, the reckoning should start from the earliest stages of a person's life, for early nutrition and freedom from infections have a marked effect on adult height, and thus on adult productivity. While this extension is conceptually not a difficult matter, we will not pursue it here. It will not add anything to our analysis. Our conclusion that in poor countries individuals enjoying better nutritional status are also the more efficient manual workers is not easily resistible.

15.8 *Activity Possibility Sets*

In Chapter 3 we distinguished between the set of strategies (or plans) from which a person can in principle choose and the set of strategies from which he can actually choose. We called the latter his permissible set of strategies. We will now focus on those components of plans that cover consumption and physical activities. By this means we can give shape to the idea of *activity possibility sets*.

In the standard theory of resource allocation, different qualities of labour services are regarded as different commodities (see e.g. Koopmans, 1957; Debreu, 1959; Arrow and Hahn, 1971). You may be cutting sugarcane while I move earth. We would be producing different labour services. But you and I may differ in our capacity to cut sugarcane. If this is so, our labour services in sugarcane-cutting would be different goods, even though we might both be engaged in the same activity. This was given formal expression through the nutrition–productivity curves of Fig. 15.1. There, I froze all other activities (barring pure rest) and the pace at which they are undertaken, and depicted the functional relationship between nutrition intake and the maximum number of units of a given activity (or task) that each of two individuals is capable of accomplishing over a specified period of time. Activity possibility sets are a generalization of this. The *activity possibility set* of a person is the set of all combinations of nutrition intakes, activities, and their paces which the person is physically capable of engaging in. In the standard theory of resource allocation it is called the *consumption possibility set*. I have renamed it here so as to emphasize the fact that it is activities that are the source of human well-being. A person's activity possibility set is embedded in a space whose dimension is the sum of the number of all possible activities and the number of all possible nutrients and health-care services. In an intertemporal setting each of these components has an indefinite string of dates attached to it, so that for example, carrying a load today is a different activity from carrying a load tomorrow, and so forth. In an uncertain setting, each of *them* in turn has a string of possible events attached to it, so that for example ploughing the field tomorrow if it is dry is a different activity from ploughing that same field tomorrow if it is wet, and so on (see Chapters 6–8). A person's activity possibility set is thus embedded in a space of very many dimensions.

Inevitably, there are many activities a person is unequipped to undertake no matter what his health status is. Formally, this is to say that the number of units of each such activity he is capable of accomplishing is nil. His activity possibility set will be subject to these constraints. To be sure, there are activities he will be capable of undertaking at some future date if and only if he invests time, energy, resources, and care now. This is an expression of intellectual and physical capital formation. Such possibilities are part of the description of his activity possibility set. To be sure also, there are certain activities we all are capable of engaging in. Among them is the state of rest. Each individual's activity possibility set will have this as a possibility. In the previous chapter we observed why the state of rest is of especial interest in the economics of malnutrition.

The standard theory of resource allocation postulates an activity possibility set for each person. We have been denoting activities by the vector α, and the pace they are undertaken by the vector β. Rather than be altogether general, we will confine ourselves to the area circumscribed by the nutrition–productivity curve of a person. As earlier, we will also simplify by assuming that the person is in long-run energy balance. Consider a person's capacity for work in a given activity or task (sugarcane-cutting, load-carrying, and so on). Recall that the nutrition–productivity curve describes the number of units of a composite task (tons of sugarcane that are cut, hundredweights of earth removed, and so forth) a person is capable of accomplishing as a function of his nutrition intake. Recall also that in constructing the curve we are holding fixed his levels of effort in all other activities, including rest. It follows that a person's nutrition–productivity curve is itself dependent upon his other activities. Were his levels of effort in these other activities to be different, his nutrition-productivity curve would be different. By relaxing our assumptions ever so slightly, we now proceed to explore the choices he faces by virtue of this dependence.

Let us suppose that the person holds fixed his levels of effort in all activities other than leisure (e.g. the state of rest) and the one from which he earns his living. The latter may be sugarcane-cutting, load-carrying, or whatever. For any given level of nutrition intake, there are many possible combinations of work and leisure available to the person. As before, we must confine ourselves to a limited range of calorie intakes; otherwise the person would not be in long-run energy balance. For any level of intake

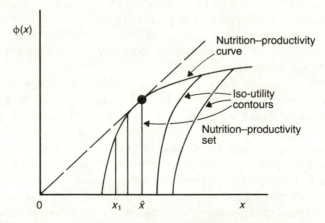

Fig. 15.2 Iso-utility contours and the nutrition–productivity set

in this range (say x_1 in Fig. 15.2), the corresponding point on his nutrition–productivity curve is the number of units of this work-task he would be capable of performing were he to reduce his leisure activity to a bare minimum. Naturally, points vertically below this would involve his enjoying greater leisure. We will call the set of points circumscribed by a person's nutrition–productivity curve his *nutrition–productivity set*, and in what follows we will assume that the nutrition–productivity set defines his feasible set of choices. This is of course a simplification, and a general account would have him select from feasible combinations of various activities (i.e. from his activity possibility set). But we would gain very little from the general formulation, and we would lose greatly as regards mathematical simplicity.

There is also an a priori justification for confining our analysis here to a person's nutrition–productivity set, and not working with the more general activity possibility set. Nutrition and health care, and rest and leisure are among what was referred to in Chapters 2 and 3 as the first tier of goods. They are basic needs. They make living possible. It could then be thought that a hungry person gives precedence to marginal quantities of food over all other things. Generalizing somewhat, it would seem plausible that the poorest of the poor economize on other consumptions and activities (including leisure activities), to the point where they are undertaken at something of an essential minimum level. The thought here is that very poor people can't allow for much substitution between these other things and food. Physical work being the means of obtaining food, it would then follow that an assetless person is forced by circumstances to confine his attention to his nutrition–productivity *curve*. Admittedly, this curve (and, therefore, the nutrition–productivity set as we have defined it) has been constructed for a person presumed to be in energy balance (see Chapter 14), and the poorest of people are often not in energy balance. But this move on our part has been a mere technical fix, to make the analysis simple, and earlier in this section we saw how to incorporate time, uncertainty, and thus non-stationary realizations of living into our account of activity possibility sets. We will elaborate on this in the following chapter.

The more interesting question is whether our presumption about the behaviour of poor people has any empirical grounding. *Do* poor people give precedence to food over all else? How persistently hungry do you have to be to have your eye only on food and the means of obtaining food? The evidence has narrowed down the zone in which the answer lies, but not by very much. In extreme situations, such as famines, the answer is clear. Food is of the greatest urgency, and victims act upon it. They travel in search of food, expending their precarious hold on energy in the

470 UNDERNOURISHMENT AND DESTITUTION

realization that all other courses of action guarantee starvation.[37] Under normal circumstances the matter is unclear. In the previous chapter we noted that, in their studies of caloric supplementation among Guatemalan sugarcane-cutters and loaders, Immink and Viteri (1981) found the additional energy to be diffused over a number of activities. Supplemented workers completed their tasks faster, spent less time travelling back home after a day's work, and slept less during their leisure hours. Their productivity at work (as measured by the number of tons of sugarcane delivered) was not significantly greater than that of unsupplemented workers (see also Immink, Viteri and Helms, 1981, 1982; Immink *et al.*, 1984a, b). But these subjects had not suffered from any serious energy deficiency prior to the introduction of the supplementation programme: they were not undernourished people. So the studies can't tell if workers would have cut down on their leisure activities had nutrition intake among them been *reduced* rather than supplemented. In a different vein, Wolgemuth *et al* (1982) and Strauss (1986) have provided evidence that poor households don't altogether substitute leisure activities for income-generating work when more food is available at the margin.

Behrman and Deolalikar (1987a) have reported a lack of significant correlation within a sample of households covered by the ICRISAT data (see Chapter 9) between calories on the one hand, and households' total expenditures and their expenditure on food on the other. The authors infer from this that the nutrient elasticity of household income may be close to zero. (See also Behrman, Deolalikar and Wolfe, 1988; and Ravallion, 1990, on a different data-set.) The thought here is that even poor households spend their marginal food expenditure on characteristics other than nutrition, such as taste (see also Shah, 1983), appearance, odour, and the extent to which it has been processed. One weakness of the underlying investigation is that the relationship tested between nutrient consumption and expenditure is taken to be linear, when the possibility exists that it is non-linear. A second weakness is that the ICRISAT data on calories, although obtained from the same households as data on expenditures, do not relate to the same food bundles. If the pattern of consumption of each household varies with time, nutrition measures will be divorced from measurement of expenditures.[38]

That these weaknesses may be telling is reinforced in Subramanian and Deaton (1992), where data on rural households from the 38th round of the National Sample Survey of India is studied. For the poorest households their estimate of the total expenditure elasticity of calories is 0.55. (In

---

[37] This was depicted most vividly in Satyajit Ray's 1975 film on the Great Bengal Famine, *Distant Thunder*.

[38] See Deaton (1988) for reflections on the Behrman–Deolalikar work.

other words, a 1 per cent increase in total expenditure is associated with a 0.55 per cent increase in expenditure on calories.) This isn't 1.00, but it isn't 0.00 either. This has implications for development policy (Chapter 17). The elasticity falls slowly with rising household expenditures, to a value of about 0.40 for the better-off households. The total expenditure elasticity of food demand is about 0.75, implying that households at a low threshold level of income begin switching away from coarse grains, paying more for their calories. (See also Bhargara, 1991.)

These studies have asked the question whether growth in income among poor households translates into an increase in calorie consumption. The Subramaniam–Deaton finding is that it does, but not fully. This latter feature may suggest that hungry people are not especially concerned with nutrition; that they don't give priority to it. It would be a wrong inference, though. First, it isn't calorie intake *per se* that are important, but intakes relative to requirements, and requirements differ among people. Ravallion (1992a) has exploited this fact to show on Indonesian data that *aggregate* undernourishment responds to growth in average income.

A second reason why the inference isn't correct is that such data are at the household, and not the individual, level. When intra-household allocation is discriminatory in favour of the decision-maker, and when his preferences prevail over food composition, the urgency of nutrients in a deprived member's reckoning does not get reflected. In Chapter 11 we noted that women often do not control cash income even when they control income from subsistence farming. This fact is relevant here. Survey data on family health and nutrition in Brazil points to the fact that unearned income in the hands of the mother has a bigger effect on her family's health (e.g. child survival rate) than income under the control of the father. (For child survival the effect is almost twenty times greater.) There is also evidence of gender preference: mothers prefer to devote resources to improving the nutritional status of their daughters, fathers for their sons (see Thomas, 1990). The share of the household budget allocated to food has been found to increase when the proportion of cash income accruing to women has increased; and, concurrently, the share allocated to alcohol and cigarettes has been observed to fall (Hoddinott and Haddad, 1991).

In her definitive work on the relationship between the sources of household income and the nutritional status of its members, Kennedy (1989) studied anthropometric data on Kenyan pre-school children from poor households enjoying varying sources of income. The data covered households involved in semi-subsistence (maize) farming, some of whom had moved a few years earlier to the production of sugarcane. Kennedy found no significant difference in the nutritional status of children from the two groups, even though incomes of households engaged in sugarcane were on average 25 per cent greater. (See also Kennedy and Oniang'o, 1990.) A move to cash crops also brings with it an accentuated seasonality in earnings. This tends to diffuse expenditure towards non-food items.

These observations are significant for delineating the way in which people locate themselves in their nutrition–productivity sets. Such studies as I have just referred to have addressed households, while nutrition-productivity sets pertain to individuals. And it is individuals we are concerned with here. Let us now define an *iso-utility contour* of a person to be a collection of points in his nutrition–productivity set at which his utility level is the same.[39] The person is 'indifferent' between points on an iso-utility contour. In Fig. 15.2 I have drawn a number of iso-utility contours for a person. Contours to the right are 'preferred'; they contain points involving greater nutrition intake for the same number of units of this work-task, implying therefore that there is more leisure. The figure depicts the case where at very low levels of nutrition intake the iso-utility contours are vertical. In that case, points on an individual's nutrition–productivity curve are monotonically ranked by him: the greater is the nutrition intake associated with a point, the higher is the point in the utility ordering (the more he prefers it). At higher intakes iso-utility contours cease to be vertical, and the individual trades off nutrition with labour effort. This too is depicted in Fig. 15.2.[40]

At what point do the contours cease to be vertical? As matters stand, we simply don't know. In the following chapter I shall assume that Fig. 15.2 is a reasonable description. In particular, I shall assume that the iso-utility contours are vertical up to a level of nutrition intake somewhat in excess of the level at which the person's productivity per unit of intake is at a maximum (i.e. his efficient productivity; $\hat{x}$ in Fig. 15.2). We will see that this has powerful implications for the economics of destitution.

---

[39] A person's utility function is a numerical representation of the ordering of points in his nutrition–productivity set on the basis of which he actually chooses.

[40] See Bliss and Stern (1978a) for a complete classification of cases.

16

Inequality, Malnutrition, and the Disfranchised

But it was only in the last generation that a careful study was begun to be made of the effects that high wages have in increasing the efficiency not only of those who receive them, but also of their children and grandchildren . . . the application of the comparative method of study to the industrial problems of different countries of the old and new worlds is forcing constantly more and more attention to the fact that highly paid labour is generally efficient and therefore not dear labour; a fact which, though it is more full of hope for the future of the human race than any other that is known to us, will be found to exercise a very complicating influence on the theory of distribution.

Alfred Marshall, *The Principles of Economics*

16.1 *Asset Ownership, Maintenance Costs, and Labour Power*

Activity possibility sets are non-convex.[1] Maintenance requirements make them so. Even though these costs are person-specific, the non-convexity appears in the same region in everyone's activity possibility set. In this crucial sense people are similar, not different. It means that large numbers of people taken together can't iron out the non-convexity, in a sense that will be made precise below.[2]

The standard theory of resource allocation assumes each person's activity possibility set to be convex. The theory therefore needs to be reconstructed with physiology taken into account. To do so in any generality requires formidable mathematical machinery (for confirmation of which, see Hammond, 1992). I want to avoid this here. So with one hand tied behind our backs we will proceed initially by considering a timeless model; that is, we will restrict ourselves to stationary nutritional states. Body weight and composition being given and fixed by assumption,

---

[1] Recall that a set is convex if the straight line joining any two points in the set lies entirely in the set.

[2] Contrast M. Farrell (1959), Aumann (1964, 1966), Starr (1969), and Arrow and Hahn (1971), who showed that non-convexities in utility orderings disappear in the aggregate when there are large numbers of diverse people. The non-convexity we are dealing with is different.

the model will be capable of linking a person's physical productivity to nutritional intakes when considered only as a *flow* (e.g. daily calorie intake). The previous two chapters have taught us that someone can be in long-term energy balance and yet can be undernourished. This means we won't lose much by our restriction. But we should bear in mind that it *is* a restriction. It doesn't leave room for an analysis of changes in a person's nutritional status over time. In Sections 16.8–16.9 and in Section *16.4 I will extend the model to incorporate non-stationary nutritional states. In this way we will be able to regard nutritional status (e.g. the body mass index, Fig. 15.1) as a *stock*, and to study variations in a person's nutritional status in response to her experience in the economic world she inhabits. We will discover that this extended theory is immune to a number of criticisms levelled recently against nutrition-based accounts of the conditions of living among the rural poor. These criticisms (e.g. Bliss and Stern, 1982; Rosenzweig, 1988c; Dreze and Mukherjee, 1989) have been prompted by too literal a reading of the simple, atemporal model. It will be confirmed that the substance of the intertemporal model is embedded in the one that is atemporal. Restriction to stationary nutritional states and a timeless framework may be draconian, but it isn't misleading. That is why we will study it in detail.

It is often said that even when a person owns no physical assets she owns one asset that is inalienable, namely *labour power*. The last two chapters have revealed the important truth that this is false. What an assetless person owns is *potential* labour power, nothing more. Conversion of potential into actual labour power can be realized if the person finds the means of making the conversion, not otherwise. Nutrition and health-care are the necessary means to this. Now, someone with an income that does not depend upon her doing work ('unearned income') is capable of bringing about at least a part of the conversion without having to work. In a poor economy she enjoys an advantage over her assetless counterpart, in that she can undercut the assetless in the labour market.[3] A theory of economic disfranchisement and undernourishment, which links their incidence and extent to the distribution of assets, can be fashioned out of these ingredients. The theory makes precise the intuitive idea we carry with us when we use the term *economic disfranchisement*; it also identifies the assetless as those who are particularly vulnerable. The economic outcasts are for the most part from this segment of the population.

A simple, stylized example may help. Suppose everyone needs 2000 kcal of energy per day to be able to function: anything less and a person's

---

[3] Whether she does undercut or whether social norms prevent her from doing so is a different matter and will not affect the thrust of what follows. Our main goal here is to demonstrate the existence of involuntary unemployment. Were undercutting socially not permitted, the volume of unemployment would be that much higher.

productivity is nil, anything more and her productivity is unaffected. (The nutrition–productivity curve is a step-function in this case. See Sections *16.2–*16.4.) Consider two people, one of whom has no non-wage income, while the other enjoys 1500 kcal per day of non-wage income. The first person needs a full 2000 kcal of wages per day to be employable, while the latter requires only 500 kcal per day. The former is prima facie disadvantaged, and she is the one who is assetless.

We will initially be studying a decentralized market economy. As we are interested in agrarian societies, it will be as well to aggregate and think only of markets for land, labour, and final output (e.g. food crops). Our aim is to explore the limits people face in their ability to convert potential labour power into actual labour power. So the market for labour will come up for scrutiny. Economic disfranchisement will be interpreted here as the inability to participate in the labour market. We will think of the outcasts as living on common-property resources (or alternatively, as beggars). They gradually waste away; their life expectancy is low even by the standards prevailing in poor countries. Such people exist in large numbers; they are the outsiders. Our analysis will provide an explanation of how this can come about.

The nutrition-based models I will develop here have very special structures; but they possess a number of general features. I shall be especially interested in those conclusions that are robust. This is a point of importance. In Chapter 9 we had a whiff of the fact that the institutional arrangements underlying agricultural work in poor countries are immeasurably complex and so specific to regions that no single model can be entirely applicable. One thing is certain though: models that are dissonant with physiological truths are hopelessly incomplete. In this chapter we will put the findings of the previous two chapters to work in extending the standard theory of resource allocation. A coherent account will be obtained of involuntary unemployment, an endemic phenomenon in the Indian sub-continent and Latin America.

In Chapters 9–*12 stress was laid on the fact that in rural communities of poor countries a great many markets of significance (e.g. credit, capital, and insurance) are missing, and a number of commodities of vital importance for household production (potable water, sources of fuel and fodder, and so forth) are available only at considerable time and labour cost. In order to concentrate on physiological matters, we will now go to the other extreme. We will postulate frictionless markets for land (more generally, all capital assets) and crops. In Chapter 9 it was observed that within villages in India the casual labour market is competitive, that if the market for land is dormant it is in great part because land offers a vital form of insurance to its owner, and not because the land market is absent. So we will postulate a flawless competitive spirit among employers and workers.

Even as a research strategy this makes sense, because at the level of theoretical discourse it doesn't do to explain malnutrition and disfranchisement by an appeal to monopsonistic landlords, or predatory capitalists, or a tradition-bound labouring class and to leave it at that. For one thing, this is far too easy a route. For another, to do so would leave us exposed to the argument that this merely proves that governments should concentrate their attention on freeing markets from restrictive practices. It does not provide an immediate instrumental reason why governments, if they are able to, should also intervene to ensure that people are not undernourished.

If an economy is vastly poor in assets, it is technologically not feasible for all citizens to enjoy adequate diet and health care. There has to be a sufficient accumulation of productive capability before this is possible. Thus, to say that an economy is 'vastly poor' is to say that its population size exceeds the land's carrying capacity. Consider then an economy that is neither rich in assets nor vastly poor. The theory to be developed will show that, were such an economy to rely on the market mechanism, the initial distribution of assets would play a crucial role in determining whether or not all citizens have their basic needs met. For example, we will confirm that, if a large fraction of the population were to be assetless, markets on their own would be incapable of enabling all to obtain an adequate diet (Result 5 below). On the other hand, were the distribution of assets sufficiently equal, the labour market would be capable of absorbing all, and no one would suffer from malnutrition (Result 9).

The formal construction of this chapter will be a classical one. Unlike a number of models explored in Chapters 9 and *9, the one I will develop in Sections 16.2–16.6 will have no missing markets. In particular, the involuntary unemployment to be shown to be a feature of our model economy will not be due to demand deficiency. To seal this point, we will note that all the equilibria in the timeless economy are Pareto-efficient (Result 6 below). This means, among other things, that there are no policies open to the government for alleviating the extent of undernourishment other than those that amount to consumption or asset transfers. A common wisdom is that such policies impede the growth of an economy's productive capacity because of their detrimental effect on saving and investment, incentives, and so forth. But this is only one side of the picture. Our model will stress the other side, which is that a transfer from the well-off to the undernourished can enhance output via the increased productivity of the impoverished (Results 7 and 8). We don't know in advance which is the greater effect, but to ignore the latter yields biased estimates of the effects of redistributive policies. One of my aims (Section *16.3) is to provide sample calculations which tell on the matter.

Asset transfers in a rural context suggest *agrarian reform*. This is what we will study here. But as always, it is good to rise beyond the immediate confines of a theoretical construct and seek the general message. Agrarian reform should be taken to be a metaphor here. This is only one route open to the State. There are other ways of redistributing benefits and burdens, and they include the provision of consumption transfers, public health care, education, and rural infrastructure, which are typically financed by taxes imposed on the relatively wealthy. Each of these types of redistribution should ideally be established in parallel. In earlier chapters (Chapters 2–4, 6, and 7) I had much to say about them. There I laid stress upon the fact that a number of basic needs are collective goods. Here I am concentrating on nutrition, which is a private good *par excellence*. By developing the economics of malnutrition, I will offer a final justification for the thesis that it is the singular responsibility of the State to be an active participant in the allocation mechanism guiding the production and distribution of positive and negative freedoms. This justification is built on the idea that in a poor economy markets on their own are incapable of empowering all people with the opportunity to convert their potential labour power into actual labour power. As a resource allocation mechanism, markets on their own simply aren't effective. The theory I will develop below also shows how a group of similar poor people can become fragmented over time into distinct classes, facing widely different opportunities. Risk and uncertainty will play no role in this. It is a pristine theory of class formation.

16.2   *The Labour Market and Involuntary Unemployment*[4]

We will be studying an economy capable of producing a single (composite) commodity called 'food crop'. (We could think of this commodity as a set of cash crops which are traded internationally at fixed prices.) For simplicity of exposition, I assume that only two inputs, land and labour power, are involved in the production of food crop. (Generalization to more inputs is a trivial matter.) Labour power is required to accomplish agricultural tasks. Again, for ease of exposition we will assume that agricultural work involves a single, composite task. In the notation of Chapter 14, α is to be thought of as a scalar. (See Section 16.7 for a generalization of the theory to accommodate more than one kind of task.) This means that we can identify the amount of labour a worker exerts with the amount of agricultural work he performs; in other words, we may identify the labour power a worker exerts in agriculture with the number of units of the composite task he accomplishes.[5] Let E denote the aggregate

---

[4] The analysis in Sects. 16.2–16.6 is taken from Dasgupta and Ray (1986, 1987).

[5] In Ch. 14 we denoted this by the vector β. This is a scalar here.

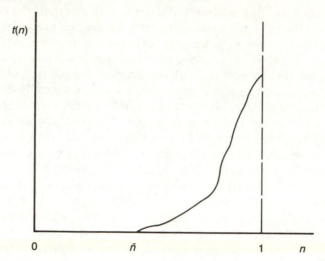

Fig. 16.1   Land distribution

amount of agricultural work performed. It is the sum of the amounts of work performed by all who are employed in agricultural production; in other words, it is the aggregate amount of labour power deployed. Let T denote the total quantity of land, and let $F(E,T)$ be the output of food crop, where $F(E,T)$ is assumed to be a concave function, displaying diminishing marginal products, and is both constant-returns-to-scale and increasing in each of E and T. The total quantity of land is assumed to be fixed, and is $\hat{T}$. Aggregate labour power deployed in agriculture is not given. It is endogenous to the construction.

The model is timeless. Total population, assumed without loss of generality to be equal to the potential workforce, is M, which is taken to be large. We can therefore approximate and consider a continuum of people. So we number people along the unit interval [0, 1]. Each person has a label, n, where n is a real number between 0 and 1. In this interval population density is constant, and is equal to M. We may then normalize and set $M = 1$, so as not to have to refer to the population size. A person with label n will often be called an n-person.

We are studying a private ownership economy. The proportion of land person n owns is $t(n)$, so that $\hat{T}t(n)$ is the total amount of land he possesses (i.e., $t(n)$ is a density function). Without loss of generality, we label people in such a way that $t(n)$ is non-decreasing in n. So $t(n)$ is the distribution of land, and we take it to be a continuous function. In Fig. 16.1 a typical distribution is drawn. Persons labelled 0 to $\bar{n}$ are landless, and $t(n)$ is an increasing function beyond $\bar{n}$. Thus, all persons numbered in excess of $\bar{n}$ own land, and the higher is the n-value of a person, the greater is the amount of land owned by him. $\bar{n}$ can be substantial. In the early 1970s the proportion of the rural populations of Brazil and Bangladesh that were landless or nearly landless was in the range of 70–75 per cent. In Bolivia and Guatemala the proportion is about 85 per cent, and in India it is something like 50 per cent (Sinha, 1984). A value of $\bar{n}$ in the region 0.5–0.7 does not appear to be uncommon.[6]

We will assume for simplicity that a person either does not work in the agricultural sector or works there for one unit of 'time'. Each person has a reservation wage which must as a minimum be offered if he is to accept a job in the labour market. For high n-persons this reservation wage will be high because their rental incomes are large. For low n-persons, most especially the landless, this reservation wage is low, but it isn't nil. The thought here is that if they find no employment they live on the fruits of local common-property resources (gathering, hunting, tapping, and so forth; see Chapter 10), or survive by begging. This involves work, but it doesn't require as much endurance as agricultural work. The landless don't starve when they fail to obtain jobs in agriculture. They are *destitutes* and become undernourished. We aren't modelling famines here, we are thinking of normal times. Subject to these considerations, an individual's iso-utility contours can be regarded as vertical under the nutrition–productivity curve, as drawn for low levels of nutrition intakes in Fig. 15.2.[7]

We wish to study the agricultural sector. It helps enormously to treat it in isolation, so we will assume that the goods and services obtainable from common-property resources are not exchangeable with food crops in the market. The cleanest way of formalizing this is to say that food crops are purchased by each person with only that part of his income that is derived from agriculture. Put another way, both wages and land rents are paid in terms of food crops.

Let us assume that there are competitive markets for both land and labour power (but see Section 16.7). Now let ρ denote the rent on land.

---

[6] Rudra and Chakraborty (1991) have found that for landholdings of size 2 h or more in India the Pareto curve fits nicely. It is a trivial matter to incorporate general distributions in the model being developed in the text. For example, were there to be a ceiling on landholdings, $t(n)$ would be flat for large n. And so on.

[7] Smoother labour–leisure choice can easily be built in, but it would violate the spirit of the exercise so much that I shall not introduce it.

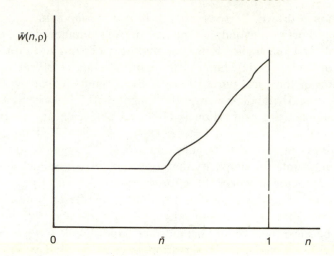

Fig. 16.2   The distribution of reservation wages

(As this is a timeless economy, ρ can also be thought of as the price of land.) Person n's rental income is therefore $\rho \hat{T} t(n)$.

The *reservation wage* is written as $\bar{w}(R)$, where R is non-wage income, including the value of leisure. $\bar{w}(R)$, although not R, is exogenously given in our timeless model. (But see Sections 16.8–16.9 and *16.4.) We take it that $\bar{w}(R)$ is continuous and increasing in R. For a landless person R is income from common-property resources. Should this person find and accept employment in agriculture, he has to forgo R. (He will have no time left for scavenging.) For a person owning a tiny piece of land, R is the sum of his rental income and income from common-property resources. If he finds and accepts employment in agriculture, he has to forgo his income from common-property resources, but not his rental income. Finally, someone owning a large piece of property can afford leisure. His non-wage income consists simply of rental income. He will not be involved in scavenging. It would be pedantic to model all this formally. So we construct a 'reduced form' of $\bar{w}(R)$, and write it as $\bar{w}(n,\rho)$. We assume it is non-decreasing as a function of n, non-decreasing as a function of ρ, and a positive constant in the interval $[0,\bar{n}]$. This means that the landless are identical. It also means that the commons provide a fixed quantity of sustenance per person no matter how many live on them. While it is hallowed by intellectual tradition (an exception is Guha, 1989), the assumption has little to commend it. For the moment we make do with it. (A typical form of $\bar{w}(n,\rho)$ is drawn in Fig. 16.2.) In Sections 16.8–16.9 and *16.4 we will dispense with it to fruitful effect.

Our first aim is to study the link between the distribution of physical assets and the incidence and extent of undernourishment and economic

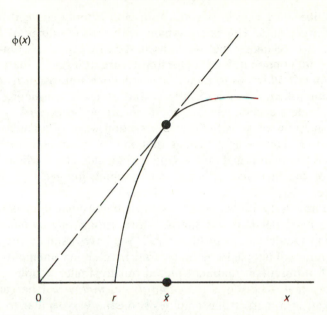

Fig. 16.3   The efficiency wage

disfranchisement. The analysis would be contaminated were we to suppose that people differ physiologically. Therefore, we take it that they differ only in terms of the quantity of land they own. The nutrition–productivity curve of the representative person is drawn in Fig. 16.3. We are to think of the ordinate of the curve as measuring the maximum labour power, ϕ, he is capable of offering in agricultural production. In keeping with our interpretation, we can also think of it as the maximum amount of agricultural work he is able to accomplish; in other words, the maximum number of units of the composite agricultural task he is capable of performing. We now make the crucial assumption that an employer can observe the amount of work done by a labourer. With our interpretation, this means that wages can be paid on a *piece-rate* basis. Now, labour time isn't a factor of production, but agricultural work is. It follows that labour will be remunerated on a piece-rate basis. To be sure, we can compute a worker's take-home pay (which we will denote by w). This we are able to do by multiplying the piece-rate by the amount of work accomplished (equation (16.6)). But the worker isn't paid for his time: he is paid on the basis of the amount of work he does.

The horizontal axis in Fig. 16.3 measures nutrition intake (or consumption), x, which we will henceforth identify with *income*. $\hat{x}$ denotes the level of nutrition intake at which marginal labour power equals average labour power. The person attains his *efficient productivity* at $\hat{x}$ (see Chapter 15).

I have deliberately chosen the nutrition–productivity curve to display a large curvature at $\hat{x}$. This is consonant with those findings of Professor Viteri and his colleagues that were discussed in Chapter 14. Our analysis is not dependent upon it, but it helps to interpret things in a sharp manner. For example, it allows us to regard $\hat{x}$ as someone's nutrition *requirement*. By the same token, it enables us to say that someone consuming less than $\hat{x}$ in this timeless economy is *undernourished* (see Section 14.4). The key assumption I now make is that the reservation wage of a landless person is less than $\hat{x}$. The thought here is that income from common-property resources is less than $\hat{x}$, and that it is quite inadequate even when allowance is made of the fact that gathering and tapping involve less work than agriculture.

We are now left with the concept of *involuntary unemployment*, which has yet to be defined. It is a sharper notion than *surplus labour*, much discussed in the development literature.[8] We have assumed the existence of a continuum of people for good reason. Involuntary unemployment has to do with differential treatment meted out to similar people. Formally, we will say that a person is *involuntarily unemployed* if he cannot find employment in a market that employs someone very similar to him, and if the latter person, by virtue of his employment in this market, is distinctly better off than him. Notice that this subsumes the situation where individuals are identical, in which case dissimilar treatment may arise because of rationing in the labour market (see Section 16.5). It is, however, frequently noted by thinkers that no two people are ever identical. Our definition accommodates this thought.

Earlier we noted that there is overwhelming evidence from village studies of involuntary unemployment in the Indian sub-continent. One way of measuring this is to ask for information on the number of days spent by a respondent in seeking employment at the prevailing wage and the number of days the respondent was successful. The ratio of the latter to the former would give the probability of employment in the casual labour market. One minus this ratio, when averaged over respondents, would then be a measure of involuntary unemployment.[9] The ICRISAT data on six central Indian villages revealed, for example, that in the mid-1970s average involuntary unemployment rates for males were about 12 and 39 per cent during the busy and slack season respectively. The corresponding estimates for females were 11 and 50 per cent (see Ryan and Ghodake,

[8] On surplus labour, see Leibenstein (1957a, b), D. Mazumdar (1959), Georgescu-Roegen (1960), T. W. Schultz (1964), Sen (1966), and Guha (1989). I will define the notion in Section 16.8 and will develop a model economy in which involuntary unemployment and surplus labour are simultaneously present.

[9] D. Mazumdar (1989) has a good discussion of this. See also Rudra (1982) and Bardhan (1984a).

1984). The seasonal nature of agricultural employment bears stressing, as does the extent of gender differences in the figures for the slack season. I shall deploy these observations later in this chapter.

The definition of involuntary unemployment has been cast within the context of markets only because we are studying the competitive market mechanism here. Moreover, it has been focused on unemployment only because we are studying labour allocation. But the underlying idea is of general significance. A weak ethical principle, much discussed in public economics, is that resource allocation mechanisms should be *horizontally equitable*, by which is meant that individuals who are the same in all relevant respects should be treated equally (Musgrave, 1959; Stiglitz, 1988a). Involuntary unemployment is an instance of horizontal *in*equity. We will discover that the involuntarily unemployed in our model economy are for the most part undernourished as well. The phenomenon is repugnant.

16.3 *Efficiency Wages and Piece-Rates*

Leibenstein (1957a, b), D. Mazumdar (1959), Prasad (1970), Mirrlees (1975), Rodgers (1975), Stiglitz (1976), and Bliss and Stern (1978a, b) have studied special cases of the construction we are developing here. Their analyses suggest that in our model economy the labour market does not necessarily clear. So I shall assume that there is a mechanism built into the market system which *rations* labour power if supply exceeds demand and if flexibility in the piece-rate is incapable of clearing the market. We don't need to be explicit about the mechanism, but some form of 'queueing' can be taken to be the process by which the rationing is realized. Queueing can vary in its mode of operation. Rudra (1982), for example, reports in his study of fifty-four villages in West Bengal that search on the casual labour market is undertaken by employers (and *not* by the workers), who typically visit labourers in their homes the evening before the day when work is to be undertaken. In the busy agricultural season employers aren't overly selective about the quality of workers they hire. In the slack season they are. There is overwhelming evidence there of labour rationing excepting for those few days of the year when agricultural activity is particularly intense.[10]

We begin with some technical preliminaries, involving no economics. They will prove essential when we come to the economics. Define w^* (n,ρ) as [11]

$$w^*(n, \rho) \equiv \arg\min \left[w/\phi(w + \rho\hat{T}t(n)), \text{ subject to } w \geq \bar{w}(n, \rho) \right]. \quad (16.1)$$

---

[10] See Bardhan and Rudra (1981) and Dreze and Mukherjee (1989) for additional village studies.

[11] 'arg min $[G(y)$, subject to $y \geq \bar{y}]$' is the value (or values) of y at which the real-valued function $G(y)$ is minimized subject to the constraint that y is at least at large as $\bar{y}$.

In words, $w^*(n, \rho)$ is that wage rate (i.e. wage paid to a labourer) which, at the land-rental rate ρ, minimizes the wage per unit of agricultural work that person n can accomplish, conditional on his being willing to work at this wage rate.[12] $w^*(n, \rho)$ is called the *efficiency wage* of person n. It is a function of n, not because people differ physiologically (in our model they don't), but because different people possess different landholdings. This explains why a person's efficiency wage depends in general on the rental rate on land. (A person's efficiency wage depends on his 'unearned' income.) By hypothesis, $\hat{x}$ exceeds the reservation wage of the landless. So $w^*(n, \rho) = \hat{x}$ for landless people. In words, the efficiency wage of a landless worker is his nutritional requirement. By continuity, we may conclude that, for someone who owns only a tiny piece of land, $\bar{w}(n, \rho) < w^*(n, \rho) < \hat{x}$.[13]

To fix ideas, let us suppose that the reservation wage schedule, $\bar{w}(n, \rho)$, is such that, for an individual who owns somewhat more than just a tiny plot of land, $\bar{w}(n, \rho) = w^*(n, \rho) < \hat{x}$. (His efficiency wage equals his reservation wage, which in turn is less than the nutritional requirement.) Let us also assume that the reservation wage schedule is such that, for someone who owns a vast amount of land, $\bar{w}(n, \rho) = w^*(n,\rho) > \hat{x}$. These latter two features aren't necessary for the analysis (see the example considered in Sections *16.2–*16.3), but they help to motivate it by bringing the model economy closer to the world as we know it. They stress that the efficiency wage of an individual can be high for one of two reasons: (i) he enjoys no unearned income, so that his entire labour power in agriculture has to be fuelled by wages; and (ii) his reservation wage is high. In an intertemporal economy (i) would encompass the case where the person's nutritional status is low. We will demonstrate that the economically disfranchised are in this state not because they don't wish to work, but because they are unable to offer the labour power the market demands. The rich are also too costly to hire as agricultural workers, but for reason (ii): they prefer to do other things.

In my exposition here I shall take it that labour is paid on a piece-rate basis. This means that an employer can observe the amount of work any given employee of his accomplishes. So the way the contract is agreed upon is a matter of no substance. For example, we could alternatively assume that payment is on a wage basis, but that there is agreement on what the job entails; that is, how many units of the composite task the worker

[12] If ϕ is of the form depicted in Fig. 16.3, the RHS of (16.1) has a unique value. If it isn't, then the RHS of the equation is not necessarily unique. When not, we should choose the largest solution and define $w^*(n,\rho)$ as the largest solution.

[13] To confirm this, transpose $\phi(\cdot)$ in Fig. 16.3 to the left by the tiny amount $\rho\hat{T}t(n)$, and then use (16.1).

is expected to accomplish. *The key assumption is that contracts are honoured*.

We may now define $\mu^*(n, \rho)$ as

$$\mu^*(n, \rho) \equiv w^*(n, \rho)/\phi(w^*(n, \rho) + \rho \hat{T}t(n)). \qquad (16.2)$$

For any given ρ, $\mu^*(n, \rho)$ is the minimum value of wage per unit of agricultural work to which person n can be forced. Now $\phi(x)$ is the maximum amount of agricultural work a worker can accomplish when his nutrition intake is x. Recall also that we are identifying a person's intake with his income. Therefore, $\mu^*(n, \rho)$ in equation (16.2) may be thought of as the *efficiency piece-rate* for person n. Since it is a function of n's non-wage income, it depends on ρ for those owning land. In Fig. 16.4 a typical shape of $\mu^*(n, \rho)$ has been drawn. It is relatively 'high' for the landless because they enjoy no rental income. For them $\mu^*(n, \rho) = \hat{x}/\phi(\hat{x})$. This is the nutrition intake per unit of agricultural work an individual is capable of performing when his intake equals his requirement. It is also the inverse of what in the previous chapter (Section 15.7) we called a person's efficient productivity. Thus, other things being the same, the efficiency piece-rate of a person with a high $\dot{V}O_2$ max (see Chapters 14–15) would be expected to be less than that of an individual with a low $\dot{V}O_2$ max (see Fig. 15.1). In Section 16.1 I provided an intuitive explanation for the fact that the landless are costly workers; they can be undercut by people having access to rental income. I will confirm this below.

Using the reservation wage function in Fig. 16.2, it is an easy matter to check from equation (16.2) that $\mu^*(n, \rho)$ is a shade lower than $\hat{x}/\phi(\hat{x})$ for 'small' landholders. To see why, recall that $\bar{w}(n, \rho)$ has been assumed to be a continuous function of n. This means that the reservation wage of a small landholder is lower than $\hat{x}$. As with landless people, the constraint in equation (16.1) does not bind for small landowners. Moreover, small landowners enjoy rental income. Taken together, these two facts imply that the efficiency piece-rate of a small landowner is lower than that of a landless individual.

I suggested earlier that we should think of the reservation wage schedule as rising steeply with n. It lends empirical credence to the model. It means that for large n the constraint in (16.1) binds when we compute n's efficiency wage: n's efficiency wage equals his reservation wage. It also means that $\mu^*(n, \rho)$ is large for large n. In Fig. 16.4 $\mu^*(n, \rho)$ has been drawn as something like a U-shaped curve. We will use this depiction to illustrate the outcome of the competitive market mechanism in our model economy. The figure is consonant with the assumptions we have so far made. But they don't guarantee the shape. In Sections 16.8 and *16.1 we will see that this shape isn't necessary for the analysis.

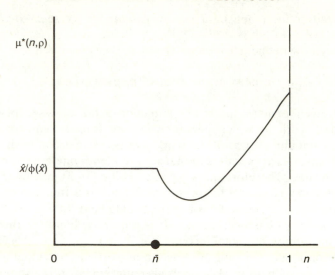

Fig. 16.4   Distribution of efficiency piece-rates

16.4   *Competitive Market Allocations*

As there are two factors of production (land and labour power), two factor markets have to be reckoned with. The market for food crops and the factor markets are all assumed to be competitive. By this we will mean that all decision units take prices as given. Our aim in this chapter is to extend the standard theory of resource allocation (Chapter 7) by acknowledging physiology. So it makes sense to stay close to the most pristine version of the theory (the Arrow–Debreu construct) in all other respects.

We will assume that market prices are public knowledge. Each 'agricultural enterprise' (we will often use the term 'employer') knows its own technology of production ($F(\cdot)$ is the aggregate technology), knows how much land it is operating, and can observe the amount of work accomplished by each worker employed by it. It does *not* need to know anything about the nutrition–productivity curves of workers.[14] Each individual knows how much land he owns (if any) and knows his capabilities, which in the context of our model means that he knows his

---

[14] This is often misunderstood. In commenting on models making use of the links between nutrition and productivity, Rosenzweig (1988c: 723) says: 'If the . . . model is modified to include alternative sources of consumption other than wage income for some workers, the model predicts diversity in time wages among workers, as long as employers have information about individual workers' circumstances (a likely scenario in the village economy).' Basu (1992: 109) makes the same mistake, but to worse effect, in that he builds an alternative construction so as to avoid this non-existent weakness of the theory.

nutrition–productivity curve (but see Section 16.7). He needs to know nothing about other people's capabilities, or about technological possibilities. As in the Arrow–Debreu theory, we assume that all contracts are honoured. In an intertemporal setting the corresponding assumption would be that there is a complete set of forward markets. We will drop this assumption in the last two sections.

The price of food crops can be set equal to unity by normalization. ρ is the rental rate on land. Let μ denote the price of a unit of labour power. We have been identifying a unit of labour power with a unit of agricultural work. Therefore, μ is the piece-rate. Employers (which may be households; see Chapter *9) are profit-maximizing and each individual aims to maximize his total income given the opportunities he faces.[15] In Chapter *16 I will provide a formal definition of competitive equilibrium allocations in our model economy. Here I will take the informal route when defining an equilibrium. Having done that, I shall characterize equilibrium allocations.[16]

We will use a tilde over economic variables to denote their values in equilibrium. Thus, $\tilde{\rho}$ and $\tilde{\mu}$ denote the rental rate on land and the piece-rate, respectively. Since prices are taken as given by all agents, $\tilde{\mu}$ must equal the marginal product of aggregate labour power ($\tilde{E}$), and $\tilde{\rho}$ the marginal product of land. In short,

$$\tilde{\mu} = \partial F(\tilde{E}, \hat{T})/\partial E \qquad (16.3)$$

and

$$\tilde{\rho} = \partial F(\tilde{E}, \hat{T})/\partial T. \qquad (16.4)$$

As $F(\cdot)$ is constant returns to scale, employers earn no profits after factor payments have been made or imputed. Formally,

$$F(\tilde{E}, \hat{T}) = \tilde{\mu}\tilde{E} + \tilde{\rho}\hat{T}. \qquad (16.5)$$

Equation (16.3) allows us to compute aggregate demand for labour power.[17] (We will come to the question of labour supply presently.) Land is supplied inelastically. The value of $\tilde{\rho}$ is such that at $\tilde{E}$ (16.4) holds. The land market clears. So does the market for food crops. By assumption, demand for agricultural produce is made by people with only that part of

[15] More precisely, he compares his maximal income if he works in agriculture to the sum of his reservation wage and maximal rental income if he is not working in agriculture.

[16] Rodgers (1975) and Stiglitz (1976) analysed an economy in which the landowners' reservation wage is in effect infinity. Thus, the only possible labourers are the landless. In this case it makes no difference whether there is a single employer (i.e. labour monopsony) or many: the outcome is the same. Because of this happy analytical coincidence Rodgers and Stiglitz did not need to develop the apparatus required to discuss non-monopsonistic markets, a need that can't be avoided if we wish to explore the implications of agrarian reform (Sect. 16.6); for after the reform the labour market can't be monopsonistic.

[17] The RHS of the equation is a declining function of E. Its intersection with $\tilde{\mu}$ yields $\tilde{E}$. See Fig. 16.8.

their income which comes from the agricultural sector. Aggregate demand equals aggregate supply. This is given by (16.5).

So far the description of an equilibrium has been conventional. The novel bit concerns the labour market. Labour is a differentiated commodity here: people differ in their efficiency wages. Let $D(n)$ be the market demand for the labour time of person n, and let his supply of labour time be $S(n)$. By assumption, $S(n)$ is either zero or unity. Let $\hat{G}$ denote the set of persons who are employed in agriculture, and let $\bar{w}(n)$ be the wage rate for every n-person in $\hat{G}$. Who belongs to $\hat{G}$?

To answer this, notice that the market demand for someone whose efficiency piece-rate exceeds $\bar{\mu}$ must be nil. Equally, this person cannot (or, given his reservation wage, will not) supply the labour quality the market can bear at the going rate $\bar{\mu}$.[18] Therefore, he supplies no labour time. For this n-person $S(n) = D(n)$. The labour market clears for all such people.

What of someone whose efficiency piece-rate is less than $\bar{\mu}$? Plainly, every employer desires his service. There is demand for his time. Speaking metaphorically, his wage $(w(n))$ is bid up to the point where the piece-rate he receives equals $\bar{\mu}$. Since for this n-person $\bar{\mu} > \mu^*(n, \bar{\rho})$, we may conclude that $\bar{w}(n) > w^*(n, \bar{\rho}) \geq \bar{w}(n, \bar{\rho})$. This means in turn that he supplies his unit of labour time (i.e. $S(n) = 1$) most willingly. Employers may as well demand this amount from him. (They make no profit from hiring him, so they are indifferent between hiring him and not hiring him.) Demand equals supply for any such individual's service. The labour market clears for this category of people as well.

We come finally to someone whose efficiency piece-rate equals $\bar{\mu}$. This category of people is of especial interest. Employers are indifferent between hiring someone in this category and not hiring him. Moreover, he is willing to supply his labour time: with eagerness if the wage he is to receive exceeds his reservation wage, and as a matter of indifference if it equals it.

How large is this class of people? The answer is: very large if $\bar{\mu} = \hat{x}/\phi(\hat{x})$, and infinitesimally small if $\bar{\mu} \neq \hat{x}/\phi(\hat{x})$ (see Section 16.5). If $\bar{\mu} = \hat{x}/\phi(\hat{x})$, all the landless fall into this category. Agricultural enterprises are indifferent between employing a landless person and not employing him, whereas every landless person is most eager to be hired.[19] The problem is that there are an awful lot of landless people (all n-persons in the range $[0, \bar{n}]$, to be precise), and if all were to be employed condition (16.3) would almost surely be violated. To confirm this, notice that when $\bar{\mu} = \hat{x}/\phi(\hat{x})$

---

[18] To confirm this, suppose the person were to be employed at a wage rate $w \geq \bar{w}(n, \bar{\rho})$. For this to be feasible, it must be that $w + \bar{\rho}\hat{T}t(n) \leq \bar{\mu}\phi(w + \bar{\rho}\hat{T}t(n)) + \bar{\rho}\hat{T}t(n)$; and so $w \leq \bar{\mu}\phi(w + \bar{\rho}\hat{T}t(n))$. This contradicts the fact that for this person $\mu^*(n, \bar{\rho}) > \bar{\mu}$.

[19] The latter follows from the fact that a landless person would earn $\bar{\mu}\phi(\hat{x}) = \hat{x}$ in wages, and by assumption, $\hat{x} > \bar{w}(n, \bar{\rho})$ for $n\varepsilon[0, \bar{n}]$.

the left-hand side of (16.3) gets fixed by physiology. Once we know what $\bar{\mu}$ is, we can determine $\bar{E}$ from the equation. Now recall that in equilibrium all n-persons whose efficiency piece-rates are less than $\bar{\mu}$ are employed. It is an easy matter to compute their supply of aggregate labour power in terms of $\bar{\mu}$ (see Chapter *16). Call this $\bar{E}_1$ and define $\bar{E}_2 = \bar{E} - \bar{E}_1$. In equilibrium just that mass of landless persons find employment as is needed to supply $\bar{E}_2$.[20] The remaining mass of the landless is rationed out of the labour market. It is forced to live on common-property resources. These people are involuntarily unemployed. The economy equilibrates by rationing the labour market.[21]

We have defined equilibrium allocations. But do they exist? Our first result affirms this.

RESULT 1. In the economy under review, a competitive equilibrium exists.[22]

Agricultural workers may as well be paid at a piece-rate. A person's wage equals the product of the piece-rate and the amount of work he performs. The problem is that this equality doesn't necessarily specify the wage: there may be more than one wage at which the equality holds.[23] Competition among employers drives the wage up to the largest solution. Formally, this is stated as:

RESULT 2. For all $n \varepsilon \bar{G}$, $\bar{w}(n)$ is the larger of the (possibly) two solutions of the equation

$$w/\phi(w + \bar{\rho}\hat{T}\iota(n)) = \bar{\mu}. \qquad (16.6)$$

Thus far a definition of equilibrium allocations; we have yet to characterize them. Before doing this it will prove useful to note that, among those

---

[20] Without loss of generality, suppose those who find employment in agriculture are in the interval $[0,\tilde{n}]$, with $\tilde{n} < \bar{n}$. Then $\bar{E}_2 = \tilde{n}\phi(\hat{x})$. $\tilde{n}$ gets determined from this equality.

[21] What we are calling a competitive equilibrium here is called a *quasi-equilibrium* in general equilibrium theory (Debreu, 1962) or, alternatively, a *compensated equilibrium* (Arrow and Hahn, 1971). The difference between an Arrow–Debreu equilibrium (Ch. 7) and a quasi-equilibrium lies in the way household demand is defined. (We will for simplicity think of demand as being uniquely given.) Let **p** be the price vector and **e** the vector of initial endowments of a household whose utility function of consumption is $u(\mathbf{x})$, where **x** is a consumption bundle. The demand vector, $\mathbf{x}^*(\mathbf{p}, \mathbf{e})$, in the Arrow–Debreu theory is defined as: $u(\mathbf{x}^*(\mathbf{p}, \mathbf{e})) \geq u(\mathbf{x})$ for all consumption bundles **x** such that $\mathbf{px} \leq \mathbf{px}^*$ $(\mathbf{p}, \mathbf{e}) = \mathbf{pe}$. In contrast, a commodity bundle $\bar{\mathbf{x}}(\mathbf{p}, \mathbf{e})$ is the household's *quasi-demand* if $\mathbf{px} \geq \mathbf{p}\bar{\mathbf{x}}(\mathbf{p}, \mathbf{e})$ for all consumption bundles **x** such that $u(\mathbf{x}) > u(\bar{\mathbf{x}}(\mathbf{p}, \mathbf{e}))$. Notice that there may be a consumption bundle costing the same as the one that is quasi-demanded and is strictly preferred. So at given prices a household may have a number of quasi-demands even when its demand is unique. Labour rationing is a way of splitting identical households into distinct groups, each group consuming different quasi-demand vectors. Rationing accomplishes this by getting identical people to face different budget constraints.

[22] I will not provide a formal proof of this (for which see Dasgupta and Ray, 1986). It will be simpler to study the matter diagrammatically.

[23] The reader can confirm that there can be at most two wages at which the equality holds.

who are employed in agriculture, larger landholders earn higher wages. Formally, this is stated as:

RESULT 3. For all n_1, $n_2 \varepsilon \tilde{G}$,

$$t(n_1) < t(n_2) \text{ implies } \bar{w}(n_1) < \bar{w}(n_2).[24] \tag{16.7}$$

This has proved to be a contested result (see Rosenzweig, 1988c). In a sample of rural households in India, Rosenzweig (1980) found no link between an agricultural worker's wage and the amount of land he owns. Notice that the finding would be consistent with Result 3 were household size an increasing function of the size of landholding. Unfortunately, the study did not investigate that question. In any event, since the model is timeless, landownership should be thought of as a surrogate for ownership of productive assets, in particular nutritional status. When this switch is made the matter is not so controversial. Deolalikar (1988) has found in his study of ICRISAT data that nutritional status is positively associated with wage.

If he is employed, an n-person's income (i.e. nutrition intake) is $\bar{x}(n) = \bar{w}(n) + \tilde{\rho}\hat{T}t(n)$. If he doesn't work as an agricultural labourer, his income is $\bar{x}(n) = \bar{w}(n, \tilde{\rho}) + \tilde{\rho}\hat{T}t(n)$.[25] Now $\bar{w}(n, \tilde{\rho})$ is an increasing function of n for $n \geq \bar{n}$. Moreover, Result 2 reflects the fact that competition bids up the wages of those with more land. Their rental incomes are, of course, greater. They are doubly fortunate. This is stated as:

RESULT 4. For all n_1, $n_2 \varepsilon [0, 1]$,

$$t(n_1) < t(n_2) \text{ implies } \bar{x}(n_1) < \bar{x}(n_2). \tag{16.8}$$

16.5 *Development Regimes*

Superimpose the horizontal curve $\mu = \bar{\mu}$ on to Fig. 16.4. There are three equilibrium regimes (Figs. 16.5–16.7). Population density and the distribution of landholdings together determine to which of the three the economy belongs. In this section we will hold fixed the distribution of land ($t(n)$). We will increase $\hat{T}$ and study its effect on equilibrium allocation. In the following section we will vary the distribution of land and then discuss the efficacy of economic growth with redistribution. The central result concerning growth is:

RESULT 5. For any given distribution of land, $t(n)$, a competitive equilibrium allocation exists, and is in one of three possible regimes:
(1) $\hat{T}$ is sufficiently small, $\bar{\mu} < \hat{x}/\phi(\hat{x})$, and the economy is characterized by malnutrition among all the landless and some of the near-landless (Fig. 16.5).

---

[24] This is proved in Sect. *16.1.
[25] $\bar{w}(n, \tilde{\rho})$ represents income from common-property resources for the rural poor. For the rich it reflects the income-equivalent of leisure.

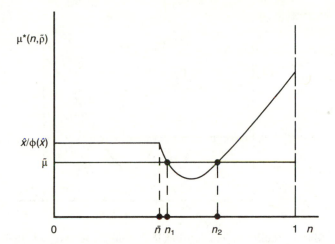

Fig. 16.5   Market equilibrium piece-rates in regime 1

(2) There are ranges of moderate values of $\hat{T}$ within which $\bar{\mu} = \hat{x}/\phi(\hat{x})$, and the economy is characterized by malnutrition and involuntary unemployment among a fraction of the landless (Fig. 16.6).
(3) $\hat{T}$ is sufficiently large, $\bar{\mu} > \hat{x}/\phi(\hat{x})$, and the economy is characterized by full employment and an absence of malnutrition (Fig. 16.7).

Let us study each regime in turn.

Regime 1. $\bar{\mu} < \hat{x}/\phi/(\hat{x})$. The regime is described in Fig. 16.5. All n-persons between n_1 and n_2 are employed in agriculture.[26] Unless $\hat{T}$ is exceptionally low, the borderline n_1-person is one for whom the market wage $\bar{w}(n_1)$ exceeds his reservation wage $\bar{w}(n_1,\bar{\rho})$. I shall assume this in the exposition. All n-persons below n_1 and above n_2 are out of the labour market: the former because their labour power is too expensive, the latter because their reservation wages are too high (they are rich).

All the landless are undernourished ($\bar{x}(n) < \hat{x}$). It can be verified that people between $\bar{n}$ and n_1 are also undernourished: their rental incomes are too meagre. Persons slightly to the right of n_1 consume less than $\hat{x}$. So some of the employed are undernourished as well.

Admittedly, there are no job queues in the labour market; nevertheless, the economy suffers from involuntary unemployment. To confirm this, note $\bar{w}(n_1) > \bar{w}(n_1,\bar{\rho})$. By continuity, we may infer that $\bar{w}(n) > \bar{w}(n,\bar{\rho})$ for

---

[26] I am assuming implicitly that the marginal product of labour power in agriculture is large when aggregate labour power employed in it is small. This means that agriculture is viable, and equilibrium $\bar{\mu}$ does not lie entirely below the curve $\mu^*(n,\bar{\rho})$.

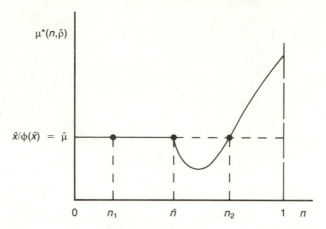

Fig. 16.6   Market equilibrium piece-rates in regime 2: the case of labour-rationing

all n in a neighbourhood to the right of n_1. These people are employed. They are distinctly better off than n-persons in a neighbourhood to the left of n_1, who suffer their reservation wages. The income schedule, $\bar{x}(n)$, is discontinuous at n_1. Persons with labels just to the left of n_1 are involuntarily unemployed.

Note finally that persons to the right of n_2 are voluntarily unemployed. Call them pure *rentiers* (or the *gentry*). They are capable of supplying productive labour power at the going piece-rate $\bar{\mu}$, but choose not to: their reservation wages are too high. They are to be contrasted with unemployed people to the left of n_1, who are incapable of supplying labour at $\bar{\mu}$. Despite the discontinuity of $\bar{x}(n)$, the economy in regime 1 is at an Arrow–Debreu equilibrium: all markets clear.

Regime 2. $\bar{\mu} = \hat{x}/\phi(\hat{x})$. The regime is described in Fig. 16.6. It was argued earlier that this isn't a fluke case: the economy is in this regime for certain intermediate ranges of $\hat{T}$. All persons betwen n_1 and n_2 are employed. Those to the right of n_2 remain out of agricultural work because their reservation wages are too high. The economy equilibrates by rationing landless people in the labour market. A fraction of the landless, $n_1/\bar{n}$, is involuntarily unemployed, and they live on common-property resources. They are the destitutes here, and they are undernourished. The remaining fraction, $1 - n_1/\bar{n}$, finds employment at the wage rate $\hat{x}$, which meets their nutritional requirements. It is also their efficiency wage. The unemployed and the malnourished are the same set of people. The proportion of the undernourished is a function of $\hat{T}$. The economy in regime 2 is not in an Arrow–Debreu equilibrium, it is in *quasi-equilibrium* (see fn. 21). Out of an originally homogeneous group of landless people two classes are created in the regime: one consists of the employed, the other the outcasts. Since

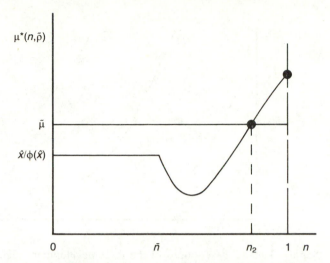

Fig. 16.7   Market equilibrium piece-rates in regime 3: full employment

those among the landless who are employed are paid their efficiency wage, this theory is often called an *efficiency-wage theory*.

Regime 3. $\bar{\mu} > \hat{x}/\phi(\hat{x})$. Fig. 16.7 depicts this regime. Persons from 0 to n_2 are employed, and those to the right of n_2 price themselves out of the labour market; their reservation wages are too high. $\bar{x}(n)$ is a continuous function. There is full employment. When in regime 3 the economy is in an Arrow–Debreu equilibrium.

A simple way of illustrating the regimes is to resort to a 'partial equilibrium' diagram, hold constant the rental on land, and study the aggregate supply and demand functions of labour power. In Fig. 16.8 aggregate labour power, E, has been plotted along the horizontal axis and the piece-rate is on the vertical axis. Aggregate demand is $\partial F(E, \hat{T})/\partial E$ and is downward-sloping. Aggregate supply is upward-sloping, but has a discontinuity at $\mu = \hat{x}/\phi(\hat{x})$, displaying a horizontal jump amounting to $\bar{n}\phi(\hat{x})$. (This is where having a mass of identical landless people plays its role.) If the aggregate demand curve goes through the gap (as does CD), the economy is in regime 2. If it cuts the supply curve beyond the gap on the right (as does $C'D'$), the economy is in regime 3; and if it cuts the supply curve before the gap on the left (as does $C''D''$), it is in regime 1.

Before discussing the menu of feasible public policies in this economy, it is important to note:

> RESULT 6. No matter which regime the economy is in, equilibrium allocations are Pareto-efficient. (For a proof, see Dasgupta and Ray, 1987).

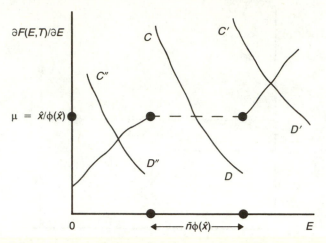

Fig. 16.8 'Supply–demand' descriptions of the three development regimes

This sets limits on the public agenda. Policies aiming at alleviating malnutrition in the short run simply have to involve a redistribution of benefits and burdens, in which some parties emerge worse off. Over the long run matters are different, of course, because there is the prospect that growth in net national product will trickle down to the poorest of the poor. So public policy needs to be founded on some combination of asset (or consumption) redistribution and income growth. We will study the two polar routes separately in the next section. In Section ★16.3 I shall present a sample calculation to illustrate how we may test their relative efficiency.

16.6 Growth with Redistribution

So as to provide a streamlined account, let us assume that for every possible $\hat{T}$ and $t(n)$ competitive equilibrium is uniquely given. This way we avoid having to select among equilibrium allocations.

We imagine a very poor economy ($\hat{T}$ is very small) and a given distribution of land, $t(n)$. Equilibrium allocation is in regime 1 (Fig. 16.5). If the gentry accumulates in land improvement, $\hat{T}$ increases. For ease of exposition, let us assume that the distribution of land remains approximately the same. With $\hat{T}$ increasing, the economy after some time enters regime 2 (Fig. 16.6), and eventually regime 3 (Fig. 16.7).[27] It is only in regime 3 that no one is malnourished. In the long run, growth in net national

---

[27] I do not have a proof that under general conditions the economy moves monotonically from regime 1 to 2 and then to 3 with increasing $\hat{T}$. The example we will study in Sect. ★16.2 displays this feature.

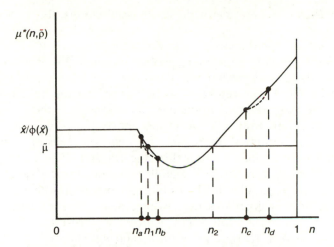

Fig. 16.9 Marginal redistribution of land

product trickles down even to the poorest of the poor. In Section *16.3 I shall estimate its speed with the help of a simple example; it will be found that the process is indeed slow.

As we have introduced time, we should think also of a credit market and allow people to borrow. That the ability of peasants to do so is severely restricted in poor countries (Chapter 9) only means that our account of the growth process passing through successive regimes is more than a metaphor. Nevertheless, assume now that there is a credit market where peasants can obtain consumption loans. As accumulation occurs in regime 1 the piece-rate increases. Thus, *ceteris paribus*, borrowing accelerates the transition from regime 1 to regime 2, because the peasant who obtains a consumption loan in effect has a non-wage income for that period. (He consumes in excess of his current income so as to raise his productivity.) On the other hand, if the economy is closed, this borrowing must be from the gentry, and making loans are an alternative to land improvement. This will retard the growth in $\hat{T}$. In regime 2 accumulation raises the volume of employment rather than the piece-rate. As the end of regime 2 approaches all landless people will wish to borrow. I conclude that a credit market will modify the 'trickle', but it will not eliminate any of the regimes.

Amiya Dasgupta (1975, 1976), ILO (1976), Adelman (1979), N. Hicks (1979), Sen (1981a), and Streeten *et al.* (1981) have made a plea for policies that seek redistribution with growth. They have suggested that certain patterns of egalitarian redistribution of benefits and burdens (e.g. agrarian reform, ensuring an economy-wide distribution of positive-rights goods, and so forth) enhance growth in net national product. At an extreme is the thought that some minimal redistributive measure is necessary even to generate growth. It is possible to test these ideas in our laboratory.

Begin with *marginal agrarian reforms*. Consider a transfer of a bit of land from the gentry to a group of involuntary unemployed people and to a group of those who are 'on the margin' of being unemployed. This is shown in Fig. 16.9. The reform is so fashioned that the new distribution of land is more egalitarian than the old, in the sense that the Lorenz curve of land distribution after the reform lies above that of the old one. The pre-reform equilibrium is in regime 1. Since the reform is marginal, equilibrium is in regime 1 even after the transfer. The figure displays changes evaluated at the original equilibrium pair of prices ($\bar{\mu}$, $\bar{\rho}$). People between n_a and n_b gain land. Their efficiency piece-rates decline, because their rental income increases even while their efficiency wages remain higher than their reservation wages. Efficiency piece-rates of those from whom land is taken (people between n_c and n_d) also decline, but for a different reason: their reservation wages are now slightly lower.

This pattern of redistribution has three effects. First, because their rental income increases, the unemployed become more attractive to employers. Second, those among the poor who are employed become more productive to the extent that they too receive land. And third, by taking land away from the gentry their reservation wages are lowered, and when this effect is strong enough it induces them to forsake leisure and enter the agricultural labour market. (However, this is not so in Fig. 16.9.) These three effects in combination ensure that aggregate output after the reform is higher. (For a proof, see Dasgupta and Ray, 1987). This gives us:

> RESULT 7. If the distribution of assets in a poor economy is very unequal, there are marginal agrarian reforms which are not only egalitarian, but result in an increase in the rate of growth of net national product.

Partial agrarian reforms of the kind just studied have a possible displacement effect, whereby 'newly' productive workers displace previously employed, less productive workers.[28] Even when aggregate agricultural output increases following a Lorenz-improving land redistribution, the mass of involuntarily unemployed people may increase. This is a shortcoming. Fortunately, there is no such effect in the case of *full agrarian reforms*, which we will now discuss.

In order to highlight the detrimental effects of unequal asset distribution on productivity and output, we will assume that there is enough land to feed everyone adequately. To make this notion precise, imagine that everyone consumes the same amount. If x is each person's nutrition

---

[28] In being 'less productive', I mean being associated with a higher efficiency piece-rate.

intake, aggregate output is $F(\phi(x), \hat{T})$.[29] For the allocation to be viable, x must be a solution of

$$x = F(\phi(x), \hat{T}). \tag{16.9}$$

If (16.9) has a solution, it typically has two solutions. We will concentrate on the larger of the two values and call it $x(\hat{T})$. Let $\hat{T}_1$ be the value of $\hat{T}$ for which $x(\hat{T}) = \hat{x}$, where $\hat{x}$, as before, is nutritional requirement. Equation (16.9) has a unique solution only in a fluke case. One can show that the smallest value of $\hat{T}$ for which a solution to (16.9) exists involves an $x(\hat{T}) < \hat{x}$. So $\hat{T}_1$ is uniquely defined.

At $\hat{T}_1$ the existing population size can be thought of as the land's *carrying capacity* (Chapter 10). If $\hat{T} < \hat{T}_1$, population size exceeds the carrying capacity. If $\hat{T} > \hat{T}_1$, the economy can in principle support more people. We may now state (see Dasgupta and Ray, 1987):

> RESULT 8. Consider an economy where $\hat{T} \geq \hat{T}_1$. Provided reservation wages are low enough, an equal division of consumption ($x(\hat{T}) \geq \hat{x}$) is achievable as a competitive equilibrium allocation if there is equality in landholdings.

This result, in alliance with the characteristics of regime 3, comes close to establishing that, if an economy is neither rich nor very poor in the aggregate, large inequalities in the distribution of assets are the cause of malnutrition and involuntary unemployment. Even so, they just miss the target. Fortunately, the next two results in conjunction with Result 8 nail the intuitive idea completely:[30]

> RESULT 9. There exists an interval $[\hat{T}_1, \hat{T}_2)$ such that, if $\hat{T}\varepsilon[\hat{T}_1, \hat{T}_2)$, there are unequal distributions of land for which competitive equilibrium allocation is in regime 2.

> RESULT 10. If $\hat{T} \geq \hat{T}_2$, no matter how unequal is the distribution of land, competitive equilibrium is in regime 3.

When discussing marginal agrarian reforms, we noted that they can have perverse effects on employment. Result 8 says that, if population is below the carrying capacity of land, a full agrarian reform eliminates unemployment and malnutrition. It follows that, unless an economy is well endowed (i.e. $\hat{T}$ is just short of $\hat{T}_2$), marginal reforms cannot accomplish what an aggressive reform can. Result 10 provides the link between our nutrition-based resource allocation theory and the now-standard Arrow–Debreu theory by implying that the chain connecting asset distribution and aggregate employment is snapped if the economy is richly endowed with assets. Now some of the most influential doctrines today concerning

---

[29] Recall that by normalization we have set the population size at unity.
[30] For proof, see Sect. *16.2. For a more wide-ranging analysis of land reform, see Moene (1992).

material prospects for poor countries are based on the efficacy of the market mechanism (see e.g. World Bank, 1986a). In earlier chapters (Chapters 6–7) I argued that 'getting prices right' is very much a desirable objective. I also argued that it is the singular responsibility of the State to ensure that positive-rights goods, such as health care and primary and secondary education, are within the reach of all; and it was shown that the market mechanism on its own is far from capable of ensuring this. It was also argued that natural monopolies, such as infrastructure, ought not to be left to the market mechanism. We are now going beyond this. Even if prices were to be got right in a poor economy, the market mechanism, unless acting upon a reasonable distribution of productive assets, can be relied upon to be an unmitigated disaster. The development of smoothly functioning anonymous markets are necessary, but by no means sufficient, for an immediate growth in general well-being in poor economies.

16.7   Robustness and Extensions

How robust are our general conclusions against relaxation of the underlying assumptions to meet observations from the world? Ten extensions suggest themselves. Eight can be discussed in a non-technical manner without loss, and we do so here. The remaining two are a shade more complex: they introduce new issues. We will discuss them in the next two sections.

1. *Heterogeneity of agricultural tasks*   Contrary to our assumption, there are many tasks involved in agricultural production. Let us take it that there are N tasks. They can be so measured that a unit task of each type involves a unit of labour power. The production function is now of the form $F(E_1, \ldots , E_N, \hat{T})$, where E_1 is aggregate labour power employed in the first task, and so forth. In competitive equilibrium the marginal product of labour power in each task equals its piece-rate. The analysis otherwise remains the same.

There are strong empirical correlates of this. In his surveys carried out in West Bengal villages, Rudra (1982) found wage rates to depend upon the nature of agricultural tasks. There are specific rates for male ploughmen in the busy season, female weeders in the slack season, and so forth. Significantly, wages attached to female tasks are lower (see also Bardhan, 1984a; and Chapters 9 and 11). The latter in itself doesn't imply taste discrimination by employers in a competitive market; for agricultural tasks are gender based, and wage variations could well be a symptom of statistical discrimination (Aigner and Cain, 1977), allied to differences in average productivity, both across tasks and the two genders. In the one study of which I am aware that has tested for employer discrimination in the casual agricultural labour market in a poor country (using time rate and piece rate data on agricultural wages from the Philippines), Foster and

Rosenzweig (1992b) have found that there is much ignorance on the part of employers about individual worker productivities. Thus, agricultural employers condition the expected productivity of a worker by gender, and this appears to reflect real differences in output. Gender-based wage differentials in the data reflect not only differences in the average productivities of males and females, but also statistical discrimination that favours males. Surprisingly, there is no evidence of taste discrimination.

2. *Heterogeneity of people*   People differ physiologically. So the nutrition–productivity curve should differ from person to person. As in Chapter 14, let H (for simplicity, a real number) denote a person's nutritional status. An individual is now defined by a pair of numbers (H, n), and using the earlier notation, we have $\phi(\cdot) = \phi(x_n, H)$. If no two people are physiologically the same, we can define the population spread as a uniform bivariate distribution on (H, n) pairs and reconstruct our analysis. This means there is no mass of people at any point on the space of (H, n) pairs. It also means there isn't a regime corresponding to regime 2. Aside from this, nothing in the analysis changes (see Section 16.8).

If innate skills for different tasks differ (some are more adept at weeding, some at threshing, and so forth), the same technique of labelling may be used. Once again, nothing in the analysis changes.

3. *Household decisions*   Notice that this device can also be used to distinguish people by their family size and thus their household commitments. A person with a family doesn't consume her entire income. She shares with her family. *Ceteris paribus*, the larger is her family, the less she consumes of her income. If it is a reasonable approximation to simplify and assume that members in a household share total income in some fixed manner, introducing an additional index to reflect family size suffices. If not, we need also specify how the allocation of food is reached within a household (via household welfare maximization, or bargaining, or whatever; see Chapters 11 and 12). The number of dependants (and this will be endogenous to the model, because the person in question may have a spouse or sibling who also is in search of a job outside) and the sharing rule will tell us how much of a person's income will be consumed by her. The rest of the argument is monumentally tedious, but routine.

It is often thought that the concept of involuntary unemployment is necessarily restricted to a wage economy. Recognition that people do household chores and cultivate family plots will spell ruin for the concept, or so it is argued; and I have heard it suggested that in extending the concept we will need to rethink the entire issue. This is not so. The term 'involuntary unemployment' has to do with work options open to a person and to those who are similar to her. It is a special case of a concern with her activity options and of the options facing those who are similar to her.

The concept has to do with horizontal inequity. The notion of involuntary unemployment can be extended in such a way as to be relevant for any resource allocation mechanism.

A family in abject poverty not only has to make do with little, it cannot even afford to share its poverty equally. In his highly original analytical work, Mirrlees (1975) pointed out that when a welfare-maximizing family is very poor it is forced to divide its consumption unequally among its members. The reason is the non-convexity of nutrition–productivity sets, the best-known and most extreme version of which is reflected by the problem of food allocation between two on a lifeboat with food enough for only one (Chapters 2, 11). Rich households don't face this dilemma; they can afford to provide all members with their nutritional requirements (see Mirrlees, 1975; Stiglitz, 1976; Martorell *et al.*, 1979; Payne, 1985a; Dasgupta, 1988e; Haddad and Kanbur, 1989). In Section *16.5 I will extend this analytical finding to a setting where the effect of low intake on health is uncertain, not deterministic.

Admittedly, non-convexity may not be the sole reason for unequal shares within poor, welfare-maximizing households. Pitt, Rosenzweig and Hassan (1990) have found evidence in Bangladesh that, despite considerable intra-household disparity in calorie intake, households are averse to inequality. They argue that both the higher level and greater variance in the calorie intake of men relative to women reflect in part the fact that men are engaged in activities where productivity is sensitive to a person's state of health.

There is, finally, the possibility that unequal shares are also an outcome of uneven bargaining powers among members of a household. In Chapters 11 and 12 we studied this and the related matter of gender bias in nutritional status. It seems plausible that all these sources of inequality are active in poor households. But, no matter what the process is by which intra-household allocations are reached, including it in our present analysis will not affect the general findings here, which have to do with inter-household transactions.

4. *Monopsony* The agricultural labour market in many poor regions is competitive. This was one of the most significant findings of the village studies in Chapter 9. It should nevertheless be asked how the theory we have developed here would change if the number of employers were small; in the extreme, if employers were to collude and form a cartel.

Bliss and Stern (1978a) have analysed a labour market not dissimilar to ours, except that there is a single employer, in other words a monopsonist. They assumed that the employer knows the nutrition–productivity curve of all potential workers, and so is able to compute a person's efficiency wage, which is then offered to the person. This is an unacceptably strong assumption, and it is necessary that we do away with it. In fact, if people are identical the Bliss-Stern analysis does not require the monopsonist to know the common nutrition curve: competition between workers could be expected to bid down the wage to its efficiency level.

But suppose workers are not identical. We need then to ask what the employer may be presumed to know. If he knows the distribution of workers according to different productivity 'types' (where a 'type' is defined, say, by a worker's nutritional status, which is unobservable to the employer), we are in an analytical terrain similar to the one made familiar in the literature on *screening* (Maskin and Riley, 1984a, b; Chapter 17). It would be in the interest of the employer to offer an entire wage schedule, where wage is a non-decreasing function of the amount of work that is accomplished. Each worker would be permitted to select her most preferred point on the schedule. (I am assuming workers know their own capabilities; but see point 6 below.) Depending upon the details of the model, either equilibrium has all employed workers 'pooling' (everyone but those remaining out chooses the same point), or it 'separates' (no two types choose the same point), or it is a mixture of the two (e.g., a mass of the employed choose the same point while others separate; and so forth). Non-convexity of the nutrition–productivity curve makes for complications; otherwise the analysis follows a path that is now routine.

5. *Moral hazard* How can an employer tell how much of her income a worker will herself consume? Should the employer not expect leakage? What guarantee is there that the worker will not waste her calories by spending more time on leisure activities? Neither matters for the theory if, as we have assumed so far, contracts are always honoured. An employer does not care what a worker does with her calories so long as the piece-rate she is paid does not exceed the market rate. (Of course, the employer must be able to observe the number of tasks she actually completes; otherwise piece-rates can't be implemented.) We have been developing a theory of competitive markets. A monopsonistic employer does care, and will take steps to see that wages are not thrown away in frivolous activities.[31] But that is a different matter.

6. *Noisy* φ People can't possibly know their own φ(·) function. So then how can a person commit herself to performing the amount of work she undertakes to accomplish? She can't of course. She, like the employer for whom she works, takes risks whenever agreeing on a contract. Attitudes towards risk, the availability of insurance, family support, and so forth, will influence the final outcome. These are familiar terrains, similar to the uncertainty one faces in production theory. We studied a number of these issues in Chapters 8–*9. They introduce additional complexities to the analysis here. However, they do not annul its central conclusions.

---

[31] An extreme case is slavery. On the constraints imposed on the activities of slaves, see Genovese (1974).

7. *Time and history*   Nutritional status is a capital asset. If we don't allow for the possibility of accumulation in other forms of capital, and if we allow for long-term contracts, competitive equilibrium in our timeless model can be viewed as a stationary equilibrium in an economy comprising dynasties (Ray and Streufert, 1992). However, if someone's nutritional status alters through time, intertemporal externalities rear their heads. Unless long-term contracts can be signed, employers will not be able to appropriate all the future benefits from employing a person now. (You hesitate to fatten a calf if you can't ensure it will not run away in the next period.) The problem has been avoided by our assuming in effect that all contracts are long-term. In the remaining two sections and in Section *16.3 I will develop an analysis of economies functioning through time, where nutritional status matters. It will be confirmed that the theory can easily account for the existence of the casual labour market. It can also account for the co-existence of casual and long-term employment contracts.

A person's history can be telling and very pernicious for her. It has been suggested to me by a number of colleagues that, if our model economy were to languish in a stationary state (no accumulation) in regime 2, the concept of involuntary unemployment would cease to have bite, because on average all the landless could be employed for the same number of periods. (This would be so if in each period a lottery were to be in use for rationing the labour market.) Over the long run, then, horizontal equity would be preserved.

This may well have some validity. Rudra (1982), Bardhan (1984a), and Ryan and Ghodake (1984), for example, have observed from village studies that the probability of being unemployed in a given season is not the same across people. However, they haven't collected longitudinal data to check whether people get shuffled around over time in such a way as to face the same probability of being employed over the long haul. One may doubt that they do so shuffle, since relatively unproductive agricultural workers in the Indian sub-continent would appear to be gradually weeded out of the casual labour market (see Mazumdar, 1989). Here is how this will work in the efficiency-wage theory.

When we introduce time into a model, we should introduce history as well. So we now introduce a tiny bit of history. Suppose the landless are all identical to begin with. Assume too that living on common-property resources involves an ever-so-slight deterioration in nutritional status, and therefore in their efficient productivity. In the first period a fraction of the landless are employed (regime 2). We can't tell in advance which particular fraction, because a lottery is in use. But in the next period the previously employed face an ever-so-slight advantage (because of their better nutritional history: Fig. 15.1). Subsequently most of the same people will find employment, and all who languished in the first period through bad luck will continue to languish—no longer through bad luck, but through *cumulative causation*.

Table 16.1 Food–feed shares of cereals

	Poor countries ($N = 40$)	Industrial market economies ($N = 26$)
Aggregate cereal demand (million metric tons)		
Food	208	104
Feed	5	288
Rate of growth of demand for cereals, 1966–80		
Food	2.9	1.0
Feed	3.8	1.3
Rate of growth of per capita demand for cereals, 1966–80		
Food	0.4	0.1
Feed	1.3	0.4
Income elasticity of demand for cereals		
Food	0.23	0.03
Feed	0.75	0.14

Source: Yotopoulos (1985, tables 1–2).

Long-term contracts in our model here have served the purpose of ensuring that in the future employers will be able to obtain the services of workers with better nutritional histories.[32] We have earlier encountered the phenomenon of cumulative causation (due to positive feedback) in economies with strong 'network externalities' (Chapters 12 and *12). We are now doing so again. It has appeared here because of the maintenance costs of living and not because of externalities. Thus, there are forces at work which pull poor people away from one another in the space that matters most: the space of well-being. Some propel themselves into higher income groups while others remain in the mire. A similar phenomenon has been noted in models of learning. The growing divergence can be between initially similar firms producing the same commodity (Dasgupta and Stiglitz, 1988b), or between the market shares enjoyed by rival products which were, to begin with, equally placed (Arthur, 1989; David, 1991). Here I am providing an account of the growing divergence in people's well-being. It is consistent with the positive association that has been observed between nutritional status and the ownership of land (see e.g. Valverde *et al.*, 1977; Bairagi, 1983). Admittedly, unless the size of the population gallops alongside, accumulation (e.g. improvement in land) should ensure that unemployment and malnutrition will disappear in time. The non-convexity of the nutrition–productivity set should cease to have

---

[32] In Ch. 9 we noted some of their other purposes.

a stranglehold over people's lives. We confirmed this in our basic model (Results 5 and 10). But it can be a long while before this happens. In the interim the State must be urged to consider redistributive policies. If they are judiciously chosen, they may even enhance economic growth.

8. *Food and feed*   Food has been aggregatd here into a single commodity. But there is no one thing called 'food'; there are various kinds of food, each possessing a different mix of characteristics. Cereals (wheat, rice, maize, millet, sorghum, rye, oats, barley) are a source of protein and energy, both directly (as food) and indirectly (e.g. as animal feed). Among the world's poor, cereals as food are the main source of nutrition, accounting for about 50 per cent of their total calorie intake (Valdes and Konandreas, 1981). As (non-vegetarian) people grow richer, their food basket changes from plant to animal protein. Income growth alters the composition of demand, from necessities to luxuries.[33] As Table 16.1 shows, in 1980 consumption of cereals in forty of the poorest countries was 208 million metric tons, whereas cereals as feed amounted to only 5 million tons. In contrast, the corresponding figures in twenty-six industrial market economies were 104 and 288 million metric tons. As the table also shows, income elasticities of demand for cereals as food and feed in the poorest countries are 0.23 and 0.75, respectively, and in industrial market economies they are 0.03 and 0.14. All this is in accordance with what one would expect.

The problem is, animal metabolism is not very efficient in the conversion of plant food. It requires 7 kcal of energy in grains in order to obtain 1 kcal of energy from grain-fed beef. (The corresponding ratio for poultry is 2:1.) Thus, growth in average income generates an incentive for farmers to shift land away from the production of food-grain towards that of cereals as feed-grain and grazing grounds. On the basis of calories, the shift is disproportionate because of the inefficient conversion process.[34] This goes to impoverish the poor further, either because grain prices rise to equilibrate the market (Yotopoulos, 1985), or because involuntary unemployment increases (as it would in the natural extension of our basic model here; see Baland and Ray, 1991), thereby reducing the demand for food grain.

In his work on Latin American poverty, E. Feder (1977, 1979) saw the process of rural impoverishment as being generated in great part by the rising international demand for meat products. In a notable article, Yotopoulos (1985) has argued that, when growth in national income in a poor country is unevenly shared, an additional source of the problem lies within the domestic economy itself: increases in the number of middle-income people exacerbate the incidence of malnutrition among those

---

[33] For an account of the effect of growing world income on the composition of demand for resources, see Keyfitz (1976).

[34] The world food crisis of 1972–4 involved a 3% shortfall in grain production accompanied by a 250% price increase.

without assets because the composition of demand shifts in an adverse way. There are indications that this is a potent force. For example, the annual rate of growth of cereal consumption in the poorest countries during 1966–80 was 2.9 per cent, whereas that of feed was 3.8 per cent. The introduction of necessities and luxuries into our basic model affects its detailed operations (e.g. it tends to retard the 'trickle-down effect'; see also Amiya Dasgupta, 1975); it doesn't alter its wider implications.

16.8 Involuntary Unemployment and Surplus Labour

The model economy studied formally so far in this chapter has been timeless. In the previous two chapters we learnt, however, that a person's physical productivity is a function of his nutritional status (e.g. body mass index; $\dot{V}O_2$ max), and that alterations in this take time to be realized. Nutritional status is a stock, not a flow. If employers are at all able to reap the benefits of paying high wages, they can do so in the future, not today. This means that they would have an incentive to pay efficiency-wages were the labour contract to cover a long period (say the agricultural cycle), but not otherwise. Taken at face value, the theory we have developed doesn't appear to speak to the operations of the casual labour market, which in many parts of the agrarian world is a daily happening, contributing as it does the bulk of the hired labour force (Chapter 9). For this reason the focus on permanent contracts has been seen to be a chief shortcoming of the efficiency-wage theory: 'the theory must be considered more plausible in the longer term than in the short run. The effects on strength and energy would be expected to show after weeks and months rather than a day or two. Thus one would, under the theory, expect permanent labour contracts to be rather common' (Bliss and Stern, 1982: 67). What then of our construct?

In an innovative work, Guha (1989) has used the fact of seasonality in labour requirements in agriculture to show how casual and permanent labour can co-exist in a world where the nutrition–productivity link makes itself felt. In hiring a permanent worker an employer can internalize the gains from paying him high wages. But the employee has to be paid even during the slack season, when there is little work to be done. In contrast, casual workers are paid only when they are hired, which is typically during the busy season. This suggests that they are cheaper. However, they may well be less productive because of the deprivation from which they suffer during the slack season. If their nutritional status were just that much worse, employers would be indifferent between hiring workers on a long-term basis and waiting to hire less productive casual labourers when the busy season arrives. This would mean also that in certain situations only short-term employment would prevail, while in others only permanent contracts would be found profitable.

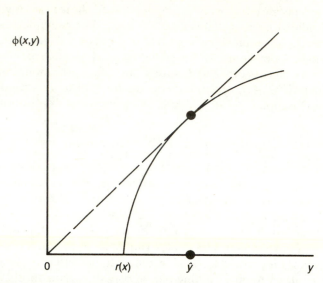

Fig. 16.10   Efficiency wages in the busy season as a function of slack-season consumption

In Section *16.4 I shall extend Guha's analysis in such a way as to absorb the nutritional model developed in the previous two chapters, and show that the central messages of our timeless construct carry over even when the model economy sustains both casual and permanent workers. Here I want to use a slightly different approach to meet two other criticisms, which together would appear to deliver a fatal blow to the efficiency-wage theory. The first is that there are seasonal variations in the daily wage of casual workers; and the second is that the daily wage varies across regions (indeed, across villages short distances apart: see Table 9.3). If the nutrition–productivity relationship is stable, based as it is on physiological grounds, one would expect the minimum of real wages across the year to be similar across regions. This is the criticism (Rosenzweig, 1988c: 726).

But it isn't quite on target. Consider a two-period world where nutrition intake in the first period (the slack season), x, affects a person's nutritional status in the second period (the busy season). I assume for simplicity that agricultural work is required only in the busy season, and that only casual labourers are hired. Formally, if y is consumption in the second period, let the person's second-period agricultural productivity be a continuous function $\phi(x,y)$ with the following properties (Fig. 16.10):

$$\phi(x,y) > 0 \qquad \text{if } y \geq r(x)$$

$$= 0 \qquad \text{if } y < r(x), \tag{16.10}$$

with $r(x)$, $r'(x) > 0$; $\partial\phi/\partial y > 0$; $\partial^2\phi/\partial^2 y < 0$. Notice that the maintenance requirement, $r(\cdot)$, of a person in the second period is an increasing function of first-period consumption, x.[35]

For simplicity of exposition, we will concentrate on the landless. We may as well then assume that the reservation wages of those who own land are so high that they don't work as labourers. This way we can ignore them. Let $\bar{M}$ be the population size of the landless. As before, we take $\bar{M}$ to be large and regard it a continuous variable.

If the population living on the commons in any season is M, their average consumption is given by the function $\gamma f(M)$, where γ is a scale factor, and f is a positive-valued, declining function of M. During the slack season all the landless live on the commons. So $x = \gamma f(\bar{M})$. Imagine that M_e people are employed as casual workers during the busy season. Their reservation wage is then $\gamma f(\bar{M} - M_e)$. As before, let us denote by $\hat{y}$ the efficiency wage of a worker; that is,

$$\hat{y} \equiv \arg\min\ [y/\phi(\gamma f(\bar{M}), y),\ \text{subject to}\ y \geq \gamma f(\bar{M} - M_e)].\ (16.11)$$

Assume that the reservation-wage constraint in (16.11) does not bind. Then $\hat{y} > \gamma f(\bar{M} - M_e)$. (I will justify this presently.) Clearly $\hat{y}$ is a function of x. When we need to, we will write this as $\hat{y}(x)$; or, alternatively, as $\hat{y}(\gamma, \bar{M})$. Now use (16.11) to define the efficiency piece-rate:

$$\mu^*(x) = \mu^*(\gamma f(\bar{M})) \equiv \hat{y}/\phi(\gamma f(\bar{M}), \hat{y}).\ (16.12)$$

The efficiency piece-rate of a person is the inverse of his efficient productivity (Chapter 15). Earlier, we observed that people enjoying superior nutritional status appear to be more productive. The way to formalize this here is to say that their efficient productivity is higher (Fig. 15.1). In short, $d\mu^*(x)/dx < 0$. This means:

$$\partial\mu^*(\gamma f(\bar{M}))/\partial\gamma < 0, \quad \text{and} \quad \partial\mu^*(\gamma f(\bar{M}))/\partial\bar{M} > 0.\ (16.13)$$

Inequalities (16.13) tell us nothing about the sign of $\hat{y}'(x)$. But one can show that, if $\phi(x, y)$ has a steep curvature in the neighbourhood of $\hat{y}$, then $\hat{y}'(x) > 0$ (see Section *16.3). We will assume this.

We seek equilibrium allocations in what corresponds to regime 2 in the timeless model (Section 16.5). This implies that we should study the class of situations where the equilibrium piece-rate, $\bar{\mu}$, equals the efficiency piece-rate of the landless. From our earlier discussion in this chapter, we know that they are equal when the total quantity of agricultural land, $\hat{T}$, is not too large. Let us assume this. As before, let agricultural output equal $F(E, \hat{T})$, where E is aggregate labour power deployed. Then $\bar{\mu}$ is given by the condition

---

[35] As always, the functional form makes sense only within the relevant range of intakes (e.g. the range that does not sustain obesity). The parameters of the model economy to be studied are so chosen that intakes will lie inside the range.

$$\bar{\mu} = \mu^*(\gamma f(\bar{M})) = \partial F(\bar{E},\hat{T})\partial E. \qquad (16.14)$$

Denote by $\bar{M}_e$ the number of employed people in equilibrium. Unless $f(\bar{M})$ is a steeply declining function, (16.14) holds with $\bar{M} > \bar{M}_e > 0$ and $\hat{y} > \gamma f(\bar{M} - \bar{M}_e)$. When this is so, the volume of involuntary unemployment amounts to $\bar{M} - \bar{M}_e$. The prevailing casual wage is $\hat{y} = \mu^*(\gamma f(\bar{M}))$ $\phi(\gamma f(\bar{M}), \hat{y}(\gamma, \bar{M}))$. It is a function of γ and $\bar{M}$. But $\hat{y}'(x) > 0$. So a marginal increase in the productivity of the commons, or a decline in the size of the population, leads to a rise in wages. In Chapter 9 we observed that in poor countries mobility costs are high, that even villages are often production enclaves. This being so, we should not expect population density $(\bar{M}/\hat{T})$ to be geographically uniform. Nor should we expect the local commons to provide a uniform source of sustenance across regions. Thus Bardhan's observation in West Bengal, that the casual wage rate is positively associated with normal rainfall (Bardhan, 1984a, : 53), is consistent with our model.

The model has generated testable propositions. Perhaps the most interesting is the one we have just deduced, that in any cross-section of villages those possessing a richer stock of common-property resources per person during the slack season are the ones that would be expected to sustain higher casual wages during the busy season. I do not know of any empirical study on this.

This is not to suggest that the generalized efficiency-wage model we have developed here can provide an adequate explanation for all that has been observed in agricultural labour markets in the Indian sub-continent or in Latin America. No single model can do that. For example, the persistent finding in Indian villages, that seasonal wages are remarkably uniform across labourers of a given sex, working at a given task, even when their productivities are known to differ, is belied by our model (or for that matter any simple model) and may have something to do with the difficulty of enforcing wage differentials on a fine-tuned basis. In any event, the link between nutrition and productivity should only be seen as providing an underlying structure of the conditions of living among the poorest of the poor. Superimposed on the theory lies a whole host of considerations shaping the detailed workings of the market for raw labour, a number of which we studied in Chapter 9. We should not expect any basic theory to do more.

The efficiency-wage theory, even in its general form, requires wages to depend on physiological considerations. But only in part. Current nutritional status is a function of past consumption, and among rural folk in poor countries nutrition intakes to a great extent are influenced by what the local commons have to offer. The hybrid model I have developed here is thus shaped by both physiology and ecological possibilities. To me, this is one of its attractions.

We now have at hand a theoretical explanation for involuntary unemployment even in the casual labour market. This is a central feature of our model. It also harbours an account of *surplus labour*, which is a different notion altogether. The agricultural sector is said to have surplus labour if a reduction in population leads to no decline in crop production (see Leibenstein, 1957a, b; D. Mazumdar, 1959; Sen, 1966; Guha, 1989). Suppose then that a few of the landless migrate out of the region under study. This amounts to a marginal decline in $\bar{M}$. From (16.13) we conclude that μ^* too declines marginally, and from (16.14) that $\bar{E}$ increases slightly. But this means F increases marginally. Thus, agricultural output would be expected to increase were population to decline in size. This is surplus labour with a vengeance.

16.9   *Who Resists Wage Cuts?*

Village surveys can be an intellectual minefield. The theory I have developed here sees competitive employers refusing to hire workers at a piece-rate in excess of that prevailing in the market. The theory also has it that workers would be *unable* to work at a lower wage were they required to provide comparable labour power.[36] This latter feature has often gone unnoticed by people writing on the subject. For example, in their survey of village studies of the labour market in India, Dreze and Mukherjee (1989) say that *all* efficiency-wage theories are doomed to failure. They do so because they attribute the resistance to wage cuts in these theories to employers rather than to workers. The authors cite their own observations in a north Indian village, which were consonant with the earlier findings of Bardhan and Rudra (1981) and Rudra (1982) in a sample of over 100 villages in West Bengal. When asked, employers said they did not pay less than the prevailing wage because of resistance from labourers. Workers in turn, when asked, responded by saying that they would indeed so resist, because earnings from lower wages would be insufficient.

But resist what? A wage cut accompanied by a reduction in the labour effort characterizing a day's work, or a cut *un*accompanied by any such decline? Field studies with which I am familiar do not distinguish the two. But the distinction is vital. In the model I have developed, a cut in wages *per se* would be attractive to employers, but workers would be unable to provide the labour power expected of them in the market. So they would be forced to resist the cut. On the other hand, workers would not necessarily object to a wage cut were it to be accompanied by a reduction in the supply of labour power commensurate with their physiological

---

[36] I am supposing that the worker's efficiency wage exceeds his reservation wage.

capabilities. However, employers would find any such alternative unattractive. (It would increase the piece-rate to a level in excess of the market equilibrium value.) The question that fieldworkers asked employers and workers did not pertain to this option, but rather, to a wage cut *per se*. The answers support the efficiency-wage theory, they don't contradict it.

To make the point more sharply than our timeless framework is capable of, we extend the model of the previous section.[37] Let s be a worker's body mass index at the beginning of the busy season and s' the index at the end of it. Let y denote the calorie-equivalent of the casual wage; $r(x)$ the maintenance requirement (where x is slack-season consumption); and $q(\phi)$ the energy expended in completing ϕ units of the composite agricultural task. Then the energy conservation equation (14.2) of Chapter 14 reads

$$y = r + q(\phi) - \sigma(s - s'), \qquad (16.15)$$

where σ is the coefficient of transformation of body mass into work. As before, let M_e be the number employed during the busy season. Now denote by m the representative person's body mass index at the end of the busy season were he to continue to live on the commons. As this is a function of $(\bar{M} - M_e)$, we write it as $m(\bar{M} - M_e)$. I take it that this is a decreasing function of its argument. Given his circumstances, nutritional status is of primary importance to this person; he cannot afford to accept employment if his body mass index is to fall below $m(\bar{M} - M_e)$. This we capture by the postulate that he will not accept a condition of employment involving $s' < m(\bar{M} - M_e)$. Assume, however, that subject to the condition $s' \geq m(\bar{M} - M_e)$, the individual prefers a higher income to a lower one. His 'preferences' are lexicographic. (See Section 2.4 above for a justification of this.)

We are now home. The analysis of the previous section can be repeated to show that, if $\hat{T}$ is not large and if average consumption from the commons, $f(M)$, doesn't decline too rapidly with M, competitive equilibrium in the casual labour market during the busy season sustains involuntary unemployment: people prefer to be employed in agriculture than to remain on the commons. In particular, the number employed, $\tilde{M}_e$, is such that $s' = m(\bar{M} - \tilde{M}_e)$. and the casual wage $\hat{y} > f(\bar{M} - \tilde{M}_e)$. Finally, equation (16.15) reads

$$\hat{y} = r(x) + q(\phi) - \sigma[s - m(\bar{M} - \tilde{M}_e)],$$

where ϕ is given by (16.10) and $x = f(\bar{M})$. The casual wage is rigid. Were any of the employed to be asked if they would be willing to work for less while performing the same tasks, they would say 'no'. Were any of the unemployed to be asked if they would be willing to work for something

---

[37] The analysis that follows is an extension of the one in sec. 7.4b in Dasgupta and Ray (1990).

less than the prevailing wage while performing the same number of tasks as the employed, they would say 'no'. Dreze and Mukherjee (1989) have merely misinterpreted the nutrition-based efficiency-wage theory. There is no contradiction here with the answers to their questionnaires.

16.10 *The Appeal of Nutrition-Based Theories of the Labour Market*

Why have we found it necessary to dig so deeply into the structure of those resource allocation mechanisms where the nutrition–productivity link plays a crucial role? Recall the answer we obtained in Chapters 14 and 15: the science of nutrition says it must play a role among the poorest of the poor. Moreover, we have found that resource allocation theory built on the link makes contact with a number of observed features of the labour market in the Indian sub-continent. It accounts for differences in wage rates in neighbouring villages; and it does so in a satisfying way, in that it provides an intimate connection between the availability of local common-property environmental resources and the seasonality of agriculture. The theory provides one explanation (there are others, which we studied in Chapter 9) for the coexistence of casual and permanent labour contracts; and it explains the empirical finding that it is the workers who resist cuts in wages even in the midst of involuntary unemployment. The theory furthermore provides a coherent explanation of the presence of surplus labour; and, most important of all, it offers a rigorous account of involuntary unemployment, a pervasive phenomenon not only in the Indian sub-continent, but in Latin America as well.

These are empirical observations of the broad brush. In Chapter 9 we learnt that the agricultural labour market is bewilderingly complex, that it has revealed any number of detailed features which no model should be required to explain. Here it is useful to recall the attitude we earlier found essential to any inquiry into well-being and destitution: that the institutional arrangements underlying agricultural work in poor countries are so complex, and so specific to regions, that no single model can entirely get off the ground. We can but nibble at an understanding. To do this, it is best to suspend disbelief and capture a few compelling features of the conditions of living among the rural poor in poor countries and see what they together tell us. We should not, of course, take any of the constructions literally, but we should take them seriously.

Analysis of Allocation Mechanisms when Nutrition Affects Productivity

*16.1 *Characteristics of Equilibrium Allocations in the Timeless World: Proofs*

In Sections 16.2–16.6 a resource allocation mechanism in which nutrition intake affects the capacity for work was analysed. The model developed was timeless. We began with the notion of efficiency wage ($w^*(n, \rho)$) and efficiency piece-rate ($\mu^*(n, \rho)$) for each person (equations (16.1) and (16.2)), and in our exposition we assumed for simplicity that $\mu^*(n, \rho)$ has the shape depicted in Fig. 16.4. However, the underlying assumptions of the model don't guarantee this shape. What they do imply more generally, is that, for any given ρ,

(a) $\mu^*(n, \rho)$ is constant in the interval $n\varepsilon[0, \bar{n}]$, and is a decreasing function of n in the region immediately to the right of $\bar{n}$.

(b) $\mu^*(n, \rho)$ is a decreasing function of n to the right of $\bar{n}$ so long as the reservation-wage constraint in (16.1) does not bind. (From this it follows that the reservation-wage constraint in (16.1) binds in any region of n where $\mu^*(n, \rho)$ is an increasing function of n.)

(c) If the reservation-wage constraint in (16.1) binds for some n-person, it binds for all persons who own more land.

(d) For large values of n, $\mu^*(n, \rho)$ is an increasing function of n, because the effect of a higher reservation wage ultimately outweighs the diminishing increments to labour power associated with larger income.

Recall that $S(n)$ is the supply of labour time by n (it can be either 0 or 1), and that $D(n)$ denotes market demand for n's labour time. Competitive equilibrium allocations were defined informally in the previous chapter. We now provide a formal definition:

DEFINITION. A rental rate $\bar{\rho}$, a piece-rate $\bar{\mu}$, a subset $\tilde{G}$ of the interval $[0,1]$, and the real-valued function $\bar{w}(n)$ on $\tilde{G}$ sustain a competitive equilibrium allocation if (and only if):

(1) for all n-persons for whom $\bar{\mu} > \mu^*(n, \bar{\rho})$, $S(n) = D(n) = 1$;

(2) for all n-persons for whom $\bar{\mu} < \mu^*(n, \bar{\rho})$, $S(n) = D(n) = 0$;

(3) for all n-persons for whom $\bar{\mu} = \mu^*(n, \bar{\rho})$, $S(n) \geq D(n)$, where $D(n)$ is either 0 or 1, and where $S(n) = 1$ if $\bar{w}(n) > \bar{w}(n, \bar{\rho})$;

(4) $\tilde{G} = [n|D(n) = 1]$, and $\bar{w}(n)$ is the larger of the (possibly) two solutions of $w/\phi(w + \tilde{\rho}\hat{T}t(n)) = \tilde{\mu}$ for all n with $D(n) = 1$;[1]

(5) $\tilde{\mu} = \partial F(\tilde{E},\hat{T})/\partial E$, where $\tilde{E}$ is aggregate labour power supplied by all who are employed in agriculture; that is,

$$\tilde{E} = \int \phi(\bar{w}(n) + \tilde{\rho}\hat{T}t(n))d\upsilon(n);$$

(6) $\tilde{\rho} = \partial F(\tilde{E},\hat{T})\partial T$.

Proofs of all results quoted in the previous chapter are in Dasgupta and Ray (1986, 1987). Here I offer proofs only of those that are distinctive of the theory being developed in this book.

Proof of Result 3. As before, write $\bar{x}(n) = \bar{w}(n) + \tilde{\rho}\hat{T}t(n)$ for $n \varepsilon \tilde{G}$. Clearly, $\phi(\bar{x}(n)) > 0$. Since $\phi(\bar{x})$ is strictly concave when $\phi(\bar{x}) > 0$ (Fig. 16.3), we have

$$\bar{w}(n_2) - \bar{w}(n_1) = \tilde{\mu}[\phi(\bar{x}(n_2)) - \phi(\bar{x}(n_1))] > \tilde{\mu}[\bar{x}(n_2) - \bar{x}(n_1)]\phi'(\bar{x}(n_2)),$$

which on rearrangement yields

$$[\bar{w}(n_2) - \bar{w}(n_1)][1 - \tilde{\mu}\phi'(\bar{x}(n_2))] = \hat{T}\tilde{\mu}\phi'(\bar{x}(n_2))[t(n_2) - t(n_1)]\tilde{\rho} > 0. \tag{$\star$16.1}$$

Now, the first-order condition for the maximization problem (16.1) is $\phi(w^* + \tilde{R})/w^* \geq \phi'(w^* + \tilde{R})$ for all $\tilde{R} \geq 0$. This and the fact that $\bar{w}(n_2) \geq w^*(n_2, \tilde{\rho})$ imply

$$\phi(\bar{x}(n_2)) \geq \bar{w}(n_2)\phi'(\bar{x}(n_2)). \tag{$\star$16.2}$$

It is simple to check from characteristics (b) and (c) of $\mu^*(n, \rho)$ that, if $n_1, n_2 \varepsilon \tilde{G}$ and $t(n_2) > t(n_1)$, then either $w^*(n_2,\tilde{\rho}) = \bar{w}(n_2, \tilde{\rho})$ or $\bar{w}(n_2) > w^*(n_2, \tilde{\rho})$. In either case ($\star$16.2) is a strict inequality. Using this and condition (4) of the definition of an equilibrium, it follows that $1 > \tilde{\mu}\phi(\bar{x}(n_2))$ in condition ($\star$16.1). $\square$

Proof of Result 8. Assume $\hat{T} \geq \hat{T}_1$, where $\hat{T}_1$ is the value of $\hat{T}$ at which the larger solution, $x(\hat{T})$, of equation (16.9) equals a person's nutritional requirement $\hat{x}$. Define $\hat{\mu} = F_E(\phi(x(\hat{T})), \hat{T})$ and $\hat{\rho} = F_T(\phi(x(\hat{T})), \hat{T})$.[2] Choose the reservation wages to be low enough so that $\bar{w}(\hat{\rho}\hat{T}) < \phi(x(\hat{T}))\hat{\mu}$, and let $\tilde{G} = [0,1]$, with $\hat{w}(n) \equiv \hat{w} \equiv \phi(x(\hat{T}))\hat{\mu}$ for all $n \varepsilon \tilde{G}$. (Recall that after the full agrarian reform $t(n) = 1$.) It remains to check that this allocation satisfies all the conditions met by an equilibrium allocation. $\square$

Proof of Result 9. Define $\hat{T}_0$ as the minimum value of $\hat{T}$ for which (16.9) has a positive solution. It follows immediately that

$$F_E(\phi(x(\hat{T}_0)),\hat{T}_0)/\phi'(x(\hat{T}_0)) = 1. \tag{$\star$16.3}$$

---

[1] I should add that all relevant functions, such as $D(n)$, are taken to be measurable. The Lebesgue measure is denoted by $\upsilon(\cdot)$. Observe that the two stated conditions regarding $\bar{w}(n)$ define it uniquely for each person in agriculture.

[2] For brevity, I write F's partial derivatives with respect to E and T as $F_E(\cdot)$ and $F_T(\cdot)$, respectively.

Using equations (16.9), (*16.3), and Euler's Theorem, we have

$$x(\hat{T}_0) = F(\phi(x(\hat{T}_0)), \hat{T}_0) = F_T \hat{T}_0 + F_E \phi(x(\hat{T}_0))$$
$$> F_E \phi(x(\hat{T}_0)) = \phi(x(\hat{T}_0))/\phi'(x(\hat{T}_0)). \qquad (*16.4)$$

From (*16.4) we conclude that $x(\hat{T}_0) < \hat{x}$, and since $x(\hat{T})$ is an increasing and unbounded function of $\hat{T}$, we have $\hat{T}_1$ well-defined and $\hat{T}_1 > \hat{T}_0$. Given this last, it follows from equation (*16.3) that, for all $\hat{T} \geq \hat{T}_1$,

$$F_E(\phi(x(\hat{T}), \hat{T})\phi'(x(\hat{T})) < 1. \qquad (*16.5)$$

(Indeed, (*16.5) is true for all $\hat{T} > \hat{T}_0$.) Moreover, $x(\hat{T}) > \hat{x}$ for $\hat{T} > \hat{T}_1$. Now define

$$\mu(\hat{T}) \equiv F_E(\phi(x(\hat{T}), \hat{T}). \qquad (*16.6)$$

Since $x(\hat{T}_1) = \hat{x}$, we may conclude from (*16.5) and (*16.6) that $\mu(\hat{T}_1) < \hat{x}/\phi(\hat{x})$. From (*16.6) it follows that $\mu(\hat{T})$ is an increasing and unbounded function of $\hat{T}$. Therefore, there exists $\hat{T}_2 > \hat{T}_1$ such that $\mu(\hat{T}_2) = \hat{x}/\phi(\hat{x})$.

What remains to be shown is that for $\hat{T} \in [\hat{T}_1, \hat{T}_2)$ an equal distribution of $\hat{T}$ sustains competitive equilibria in regime 3, whereas there are unequal distributions which sustain equilibria in either regime 2 (Fig. 16.6) or regime 1 (Fig. 16.5). The first part of the claim follows trivially from Result 8. What remains to be proved is the second part.

Consider an equilibrium resulting from an equal distribution of $\hat{T} \in [\hat{T}_1, \hat{T}_2)$. It is in regime 3. Let $\tilde{\rho}$, $\tilde{\mu}$, and $\tilde{w}$ be the rent on land, the piece-rate, and the wage rate, respectively. Then

$$\tilde{w}/\phi(\tilde{w} + \tilde{\rho}\hat{T}) = \tilde{\mu} > \min[w/\phi(w + \tilde{\rho}\hat{T})] \qquad \text{for } w \geq \tilde{w}(n, \tilde{\rho}). \qquad (*16.7)$$

(Notice that, because land is equally distributed, $\tilde{w}(n, \tilde{\rho})$ is independent of n.)

For each $\rho > 0$, define $E(\rho)$ by the condition

$$\rho \equiv F_T(E(\rho), \hat{T}).$$

It is easy to confirm that $E(\rho)$ is unique for each ρ, that $E(\rho) \to 0$ as $\rho \to 0$, and that $E(\rho) \to \infty$ as $\rho \to \infty$. Similarly, for each ρ define $\mu(\rho)$ by the condition

$$\mu(\rho) \equiv F_E(E(\rho), \hat{T}).$$

Notice that $\mu(\rho)$ is unique for each ρ, and that $\mu(\rho) \to \infty$ as $\rho \to 0$ and $\mu(\rho) \to 0$ as $\rho \to \infty$.

Now let $B(\rho) \equiv [n \mid \mu^*(n, \rho) < \mu(\rho)]$ and $G(\rho) \equiv [n \mid \mu^*(n, \rho) \leq \mu(\rho)]$. Notice that $G(\rho)$ is in general not the closure of $B(\rho)$. Define

$$K(\rho) \equiv \{G \subseteq [0,1] \mid G \text{ is closed and } B(\rho) \subseteq G \subseteq G(\rho)\}.$$

Now define the correspondence $M(\rho)$ as follows:

$$M(\rho) = \{E \in R^1 \mid E = \int \phi(w(n, \rho)$$
$$+ \rho \hat{T} t(n)) d\upsilon(n), G \varepsilon K(\rho)\} \text{ if } G(\rho) \text{ is not empty,}$$

$= \{0\}$ if $G(\rho)$ is empty. $\hfill$ (*16.8)

From (*16.7) we may confirm that $M(\rho)$ is a singleton at $\bar{\rho}$. It also follows that within a small neighbourhood of $\bar{\rho}$, say $[\rho_a, \rho_b]$, $M(\rho)$ remains a singleton. Since $\bar{\mu} = \bar{\mu}(\bar{\rho}) < \hat{x}/\phi(\hat{x})$, we can also ensure that $\mu(\rho_a) < \hat{x}/\phi(\hat{x})$.

Let δ be a small positive number, and define a 'slightly' unequal land distribution $t(n, \delta)$ as

$$
\begin{aligned}
t(n, \delta) &= 0 && \text{for } n\in [0,\delta] \\
&= 2(n{-}\delta)/(2{-}3\delta)\delta && \text{for } n\in [\delta,2\delta] \\
&= 2/(2{-}3\delta) && \text{for } n\in [2\delta,1]. \qquad (*16.9)
\end{aligned}
$$

Choose a small positive number δ_0 such that $t(n, \delta)$ in (*16.9) is well-defined for all $\delta\epsilon[0, \delta_0]$. We have chosen reservation wages to be sufficiently small. Choose δ_0 small enough so that reservation wages are non-binding for all $\rho\epsilon[\rho_a, \rho_b]$. Now define a correspondence $M(\rho, \delta)$ on $[\rho_a, \rho_b] \times [0, \delta_0]$ analogous to equation (*16.8) for the distribution of land given by (*16.9). Notice that $M(\rho, 0) = M(\rho)$. It is easy to verify that, if ρ_a, ρ_b, and δ_0 are chosen suitably, $M(\rho, \delta)$ is a function. It is also continuous in δ at $\delta = 0$. We conclude that, for δ close to zero but positive, there is $\bar{\rho}(\delta)\epsilon[\rho_a, \rho_b]$ such that $M(\bar{\rho}(\delta), \delta) = M(\bar{\rho}(\delta))$. It is a simple matter to check that this is an equilibrium. But because $\bar{\rho}(\delta) \geq \rho_a$ and $\mu(\rho_a) < \hat{x}/\phi(\hat{x})$, it must be true that the new equilibrium piece-rate, $\mu(\bar{\rho}(\delta))$, is less than $\hat{x}/\phi(\hat{x})$. $\square$

Proof of Result 10. Suppose it is not true. Then for some $\hat{T} \geq \hat{T}_2$ there exists a land distribution $t(n)$ such that $\bar{\mu} < \hat{x}/\phi(\hat{x})$. By definition of $\hat{T}_2$ and the fact that $\mu(\hat{T})$ is an increasing function for $\hat{T} > \hat{T}_1$ (see proof of Result 9 and equation (*16.6)), we have $\mu(\hat{T}) \geq \hat{x}/\phi(\hat{x})$ when $\hat{T} \geq \hat{T}_2$, so that, combining this with the strict concavity of F in E, we note:

$$\int_{[0,1]} \phi(\bar{x}(n)\mathrm{d}\upsilon(n) > \phi(x(\hat{T})). \qquad (*16.10)$$

Now consider the maximization problem:

Choose $\{x(n)\}$ so as to

maximize $\int_{[0,1]} \phi(x(n))\mathrm{d}\upsilon(n)$, subject to the feasibility constraint
$$\int_{[0,1]} x(n)\mathrm{d}\upsilon(n) = F(\int_{[0,1]} \phi(x(n))\mathrm{d}\upsilon(n), \hat{T}).$$
One can show that the solution, say $\bar{x}(n)$, is unique and equals $x(\hat{T})$ for n almost everywhere in $[0,1]$. But this contradicts (*16.10). $\square$

*16.2 A Two-Class Example

It will be illuminating to study an example in which equilibrium allocations can be solved for explicitly. I consider what is initially a two-class economy in which the aggregate production function is of the Cobb–Douglas form. The nutrition–productivity curve is taken to be a step function, and the reservation wage is assumed to be nil for all. Thus, assume:

$$\phi(x) = \bar{\phi} > 0 \qquad \text{if } x \geq \hat{x} > 0,$$
$$= 0 \qquad \text{if } x < \hat{x}, \qquad (\star 16.11)$$

$$t(n) = 1/(1-\bar{n}) \qquad \text{for } 1 \geq n \geq \bar{n} \geq 0,$$
$$= 0 \qquad \text{for } 0 \leq n < \bar{n}, \qquad (\star 16.12)$$

$$\bar{w}(R) = 0 \qquad \text{for all } R \geq 0, \qquad (\star 16.13)$$

$$F(E, T) = E^{\alpha} T^{(1-\alpha)} \qquad \text{where } 0 < \alpha < 1. \qquad (\star 16.14)$$

Using (16.1), we may confirm that the efficiency wage of n-person is

$$w^*(n, \rho) = \hat{x} \quad \text{for } 0 \leq n < \bar{n}$$
$$= \max \{0, \hat{x} - \rho \hat{T}/(1 - \bar{n})\} \qquad \text{for } \bar{n} \leq n \leq 1. \qquad (\star 16.15)$$

Similarly, on using (16.2) and ($\star$16.15), it is immediate that the efficiency piece-rate assumes the form

$$\mu^*(n, \rho) = \hat{x}/\bar{\phi} \quad \text{for } 0 \leq n < \bar{n}$$
$$= \max \{0, \hat{x} - \rho \hat{T}/(1 - \bar{n})\}/\bar{\phi} \quad \text{for } \bar{n} \leq n \leq 1. \qquad (\star 16.16)$$

I will keep fixed the distribution of land and vary $\hat{T}$ so as to illustrate Result 5. I will then illustrate Results 7–10. I will finally do a sample calculation to estimate the speed of the 'trickle-down' phenomenon.

Because $\bar{\mu}$ is anchored at $\hat{x}/\bar{\phi}$ in regime 2, we begin with it. The equilibrium conditions in this regime are:

$$\bar{E} = \bar{\phi}(1 - n_1) \qquad \text{where } 0 < n_1 < \bar{n} < 1 \qquad (\star 16.17)$$

$$\tilde{\rho} = \bar{\phi}^{\alpha}(1 - n_1)^{\alpha}(1 - \alpha)\hat{T}^{-\alpha} \qquad (\star 16.18)$$

$$\bar{\mu} = \alpha \bar{\phi}^{(\alpha-1)}(1 - n_1)^{(\alpha-1)}\hat{T}^{(1-\alpha)} \qquad (\star 16.19)$$

$$\bar{\mu} = \hat{x}/\bar{\phi}.^3 \qquad (\star 16.20)$$

Equations ($\star$16.17)–($\star$16.20) are four in number, and there are four unknowns, $\bar{E}$, $\tilde{\rho}$, $\bar{\mu}$, and n_1, to solve for. Using equations ($\star$16.19)–($\star$16.20), we find

$$n_1 = 1 - (\alpha \bar{\phi}^{\alpha} \hat{T}^{(1-\alpha)}/\hat{x})^{1/(1-\alpha)}. \qquad (\star 16.21)$$

Now $0 < n_1 < \bar{n} < 1$ in regime 2. Using this fact in ($\star$16.21), we may conclude that, given $\bar{n}$, if the economy is to be in regime 2, $\hat{T}$ must satisfy the inequalities

$$(1 - \bar{n})(\hat{x}/\alpha \bar{\phi}^{\alpha})^{1/(1-\alpha)} < \hat{T} < (\hat{x}/\alpha \bar{\phi}^{\alpha})^{1/(1-\alpha)}; \qquad (\star 16.22)$$

that is, $\hat{T}$ must be neither too small nor too large.

From ($\star$16.22) I conclude that the economy is in regime 3 if $\hat{T} \geq (\hat{x}/\alpha \bar{\phi}^{\alpha})^{1/(1-\alpha)}$, irrespective of the distribution of landholdings. In the language of Result 10,

$$\hat{T}_2 = (\hat{x}/\alpha \bar{\phi}^{\alpha})^{1/(1-\alpha)}. \qquad (\star 16.23)$$

Since $n_1 = 0$ in regime 3 (Fig. 16.7), equilibrium allocation can be computed explicitly as

---

[3] Notice that $\hat{G} = [n \mid D(n) = 1] = [n_1, 1]$.

$$\bar{E} = \bar{\phi}; \quad \tilde{\rho} = (1 - \alpha)\bar{\phi}^{\alpha}\hat{T}^{-\alpha}; \quad \text{and} \quad \tilde{\mu} = \alpha\phi^{(\alpha-1)}\hat{T}^{(1-\alpha)} > \hat{x}/\bar{\phi}. \tag{*16.24}$$

From (*16.22) we may conclude as well that the economy is in regime 1 (Fig. 16.5) if $\hat{T} \leq (1 - \bar{n})[\hat{x}/\alpha\bar{\phi}^{\alpha}]^{1/(1-\alpha)}$.

Equilibrium in regime 1 is a bit more complicated to solve for. It exhibits employment for all $n \in [\bar{n},1]$ so long as $\hat{T}$ is not too small. To calculate this bound, assume first that $\tilde{G} = [\bar{n},1]$. Then

$$\bar{E} = \bar{\phi}(1 - \bar{n}); \quad \tilde{\rho} = (1 - \alpha)\bar{\phi}^{\alpha}(1 - \bar{n})^{\alpha}\hat{T}^{-\alpha}$$
$$\text{and} \quad \tilde{\mu} = \alpha[\bar{\phi}(1 - \bar{n})]^{\alpha-1}\hat{T}^{-\alpha} < \hat{x}/\bar{\phi}. \tag{*16.25}$$

This is an equilibrium as long as $\tilde{\mu} \geq \mu^*(n,\tilde{\rho})$ for all $n \in [\bar{n},1]$; or in other words, if

$$\alpha[\bar{\phi}(1 - \bar{n})]^{\alpha-1}\hat{T}^{1-\alpha} \geq [x - \tilde{\rho}\hat{T}/(1 - \bar{n})]/\bar{\phi}. \tag{*16.26}$$

Since $\alpha < 1$, the right-hand side of (*16.26) is smaller than the left-hand side of (*16.22), which is the borderline for regime 1.

If $\hat{T}$ does not satisfy (*16.26), we are in regime 1 with only a subset of $[\bar{n}, 1]$ in employment. Without loss of generality, choose the subset to be $[n_1, 1]$, where $n_1 > \bar{n}$. For such an equilibrium, $\tilde{\mu} = \mu^*(n, \tilde{\rho})$ for $n \geq n_1$. So we define

$$\bar{E} = \bar{\phi}(1 - n_1); \quad \tilde{\rho} = (1 - \alpha)\bar{\phi}^{\alpha}(1 - n_1)^{\alpha}\hat{T}^{-a};$$
$$\text{and} \quad \tilde{\mu} = \alpha[\bar{\phi}(1 - n_1)]^{\alpha-1}\hat{T}^{1-\alpha} < \hat{x}/\bar{\phi} \tag{*16.27}$$

as the equilibrium values. Now solve for n_1 by using (*16.16) and (*16.27) to obtain

$$\alpha[\bar{\phi}(1 - n_1)]^{\alpha-1}\hat{T}^{1-\alpha} = [\hat{x} - \tilde{\rho}\hat{T}/(1 - \bar{n})]/\bar{\phi}.$$

Rearranging, we conclude that n_1 is the solution of

$$\alpha\bar{\phi}^{\alpha}(1 - n_1)^{\alpha-1}\hat{T}^{1-\alpha} + [(1 - \alpha)\bar{\phi}^{\alpha}(1 - n_1)^{\alpha}\hat{T}^{1-\alpha}]/(1 - \bar{n}) = \hat{x}.$$

This describes the regimes.

*16.3 The Speed of 'Trickle-Down'

In Section 16.6 we observed that asset or consumption redistribution is one route towards the alleviation of malnutrition and involuntary unemployment. Growth is another. The model I have developed here is a good laboratory in which to ask how long it takes for increases in aggregate wealth to trickle down to the poorest of the poor. To draw out the answer in a sharp form, I shall consider extreme circumstances. For example, when studying the efficacy of redistributive measures, I shall suppose that they can be implemented instantaneously and costlessly. When discussing the speed of the 'trickle-down' phenomenon, I shall take it that the distribution of land remains unchanged during the process of growth. So consider the economy modelled in equations (*16.11)–*16.14). Given that population by normalization is of size unity, the quantity of land capable in principle of meeting everyone's nutritional requirement can be calculated to be (see equation 16.9))

$$\hat{T}_1 = (\hat{x}/\bar{\phi}^\alpha)^{1/(1-\alpha)}.$$

Let $\hat{T} = \hat{T}_1$. Were land to be distributed equally, no one would be undernourished. Imagine instead that land is distributed according to equation (*16.12). Now use (*16.21) to show that $n_1 = 1 - \alpha^{1/(1-\alpha)}$. A plausible figure for α (the share of wages in agriculture in a poor country) is 0.8. This means $n_1 \approx 0.67$. Let us assume $\bar{n} > n_1 \approx 0.67$, so that the economy is in regime 2 to begin with. We have seen that the regime ends (and the economy enters regime 3) at the point when

$$\hat{T} = \hat{T}_2 = (\hat{x}/\alpha\bar{\phi}^\alpha)^{1/(1-\alpha)}.$$

Therefore

$$\hat{T}_2/\hat{T}_1 = \alpha^{-1/(1-\alpha)} \approx 3. \tag{*16.28}$$

Thus, if unassisted 'trickle-down' is to be relied upon, assets have to grow by a factor of 300 per cent in order that malnutrition is eliminated. This means that, were capital to grow at, say, 3 per cent per year, it would take about 37 years before destitution was a thing of the past. Now 3 per cent per year is a generous figure to assume for a typical poor country. I conclude that the fruits of economic growth trickle down slowly under the market mechanism.

Admittedly, the example is special. It has a number of unusual features, for example, that $\hat{T}_2/\hat{T}_1$ in (*16.28) is independent of $\bar{n}$ as long as $\bar{n} > 0.67$. But the moral, though banal, is important: there are redistributive measures on offer which enhance growth in output even while they alleviate the extent of undernourishment in the immediate future.

*16.4   The Coexistence of Casual and Permanent Labour

Guha (1989) has shown how the seasonality of agricultural work can be exploited to allow for the coexistence of casual and permanent labour in those resource allocation mechanisms in which the link between nutrition and productivity plays a crucial role. Unfortunately, the model of nutrition he deployed bore no resemblance to the world as we know it. But his insights remain valid. In this section I demonstrate this. (The analysis is based on Dasgupta, 1991d.)

There are two agricultural seasons: slack and busy. The analysis begins at the start of the slack season which lasts for, say, half a year. Solely for expositional ease, I shall assume that agricultural work needs to be done only during the busy season. The quantity of available agricultural land is $\hat{T}$. As before, I assume that this is privately owned by a large number of landholders. If E is aggregate labour power supplied in the busy season, agricultural output is $(F(E, \hat{T})$, where $F(\cdot)$ satisfies the same properties as in Section *16.1.

In order to focus on the temporal structure of things, I shall simplify and take it that there are only two classes of people: the landless and the gentry. The latter do no agricultural work (their reservation wage is very high). So we may as well ignore them henceforth and regard the landless as comprising a continuum of people in the unit interval [0,1]. As earlier, we label persons by the index n. The total number of landless people is M, assumed large. M is the density function over [0,1]. It will prove useful to see the effect of population growth (or decline) on equilibrium outcomes, and unlike with the timeless model it is not possible to do this here merely by reducing (or increasing) the size and quality of land. The latter has different implications. Presently, we will see why. So we will not normalize the population size.

Out of the landless, three classes can in principle emerge under the competitive market mechanism envisaged here: those who are unemployed involuntarily on a permanent basis; those who are unemployed during the slack season involuntarily, but who are employed during the busy season as casual labourers; and those who are employed as permanent workers for the entire agricultural cycle. The number of people permanently unemployed is denoted by M_u. Similarly, M_c and M_p denote the numbers who find casual and permanent employment, respectively. This means $M_u + M_c + M_p = M$. In the first period (the slack season) consumptions of representative members from the three groups are denoted by x_u, x_c, and x_p; their consumptions in the second period (the busy season) are expressed as y_u, y_c, and y_p, respectively.

During the slack season those who have not found permanent employment live by harvesting common-property resources (see Falconer and Arnold, 1989; World Bank, 1991b; Chapter 10). Consumption possibilities from the commons play a central role in the analysis to follow. In each season average consumption among those who live off the fruits of commons is a declining function of their total number. Following the notation introduced in Sections 16.9 and 16.10, we write this by the functional form $f(\cdot)$, where $f'(\cdot) < 0$. During the slack season, average consumption from the commons is $x_u = x_c = f(M - M_p)$. During the busy season only those who remain permanently unemployed live on common-property resources, and so $y_u = f(M - M_c - M_p) = f(M_u)$. For simplicity of notation, I take it that people discount future income and expenditure at a zero rate of interest. It makes sense to assume that agents entertain rational expectations. To suppose otherwise would be to provide a contrived explanation of endemic unemployment and destitution in rural communities.

People are physiologically identical to begin with. If x and y are the nutrition intakes of a person during the slack and busy seasons, respectively, then that person's productivity in agriculture during the busy season is given by the function

$$\phi(x, y) = \bar{\phi}(x) > 0 \qquad \text{if } y \geq r(x) \geq 0$$
$$\qquad\qquad = 0 \qquad\qquad \text{if } r(x) > y \geq 0, \qquad\qquad (\star 16.29)$$

where $\bar{\phi}'(x)$, $r'(x) > 0$, and $\bar{\phi}''(x)$, $r''(x) < 0$.

It will be noticed that nutritional status in the second period is being identified with food intake in the first period (x). For one thing, the second-period resting metabolic rate $(r(x))$ has been taken to be an increasing function of first-period nutrition intake. (We have seen a rationale for this hypothesis in Chapter 14.) For another, it has been assumed that, the better is the nutritional status of a person, the greater is his maximal productivity (Fig. 15.1). Notice also that, for every x, $\phi(x, y)$ has been taken to be a step-function of y. This is an idealization, and we are appealing to it only because the results we can obtain from the model are more transparent when we do so.[4] Fig. $\star 16.1$ depicts $\phi(x, y)$ as a function of y at two values of x.

We will now ensure that *efficient productivity* (see Section 15.7) is an increasing function of nutritional status, as was the case in Fig. 15.1. This we do by assuming

$$d[\bar{\phi}(x)/r(x)]/dx > 0 \qquad \text{for all } x. \qquad\qquad (\star 16.30)$$

The reservation wage of a casual worker at the start of the busy season is $f(M_u)$. I shall study those circumstances where this doesn't bind when we compute his efficiency piece-rate at the start of the busy season. Thus, I suppose that $r(x_c) = r[f(M_u + M_c)] > f(M_u)$. For the moment I simply assume this inequality. Later, we will identify the circumstances under which the supposition is correct. Given this, a casual worker's efficiency piece-rate is

$$\mu_c^*(x_c) \equiv \min [y_c/\bar{\phi}(x_c), \text{ subject to } y \geq r(x_c)] = r(x_c)/\bar{\phi}(x_c). \qquad (\star 16.31)$$

In the same way, I ignore the 'reservation utility' constraint of a permanent worker and compute his efficiency piece-rate as:[5]

$$\mu_p^* \equiv \min [(x_p + y_p)/\bar{\phi}(x_p)] = \min [\{x_p + r(x_p)\}/\bar{\phi}(x_p)]. (\star 16.32)$$

The first-order condition associated with problem $(\star 16.32)$ reads

---

[4] The nutrition–productivity curve in $(\star 16.29)$ is contrived. So it may make sense to the reader to regard $r(x)$ not as the maintenance requirement, but as something in excess of it to cover work in agriculture. The exact interpretation is unimportant, because the analysis readily goes through if we allow current nutrition intake to affect current productivity in the smooth manner postulated in Sects. 16.2–16.5, and in Sects. 16.8–16.9.

[5] I will confirm shortly that we may safely ignore the permanent worker's reservation-utility constraint.

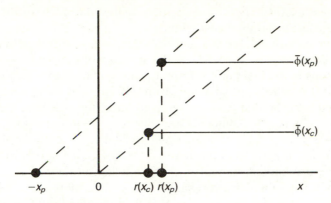

Fig. *16.1   Coexistence of casual and permanent workers

$$\bar{\phi}(x_p)/\bar{\phi}'(x_p) = [x_p + r(x_p)]/[1 + r'\ (x_p)]. \qquad (\star16.33)$$

Let $\hat{x}_p$ be the solution of equation ($\star$16.33). The pair of wages $(\hat{x}_p, r(\hat{x}_p))$ represents the efficiency-wage profile of a permanent worker. It is based exclusively on the two-period nutrition–productivity curve ($\star$16.29).[6] Substituting $\hat{x}_p$ in equation ($\star$16.32), we have

$$\mu_p^* = [\hat{x}_p + r(\hat{x}_p)]/\bar{\phi}(\hat{x}_p). \qquad (\star16.34)$$

As earlier, I denote equilibrium values by putting a tilde over variables. Thus, in particular,

$$\tilde{x}_u = \tilde{x}_c = f(M_c + M_u). \qquad (\star16.35)$$

Equations ($\star$16.31) and ($\star$16.35) tells us that the efficiency piece-rate of casual workers is not determined solely by the two-period nutrition–productivity curve; it is affected also by the number of workers in permanent employment. Let $\bar{\mu}$ denote the market piece-rate. If casual and permanent workers are to coexist (i.e. M_p, $M_c > 0$), it must be that

$$\bar{\mu} = r(\tilde{x}_c)/\bar{\phi}(\tilde{x}_c) = [\hat{x}_p + r(\hat{x}_p)]/\bar{\phi}(\hat{x}_p)$$
$$= \partial F(\bar{E}, \hat{T})/\partial E. \qquad (\star16.36)$$

We assume $\hat{T}$ to lie in that range of values for which equation ($\star$16.36) is satisfied. Fig. $\star$16.1 displays this situation. Using condition ($\star$16.30) in equation ($\star$16.36), we obtain $\tilde{x}_p > \tilde{x}_c$. But this means $\bar{y}_p = r(\tilde{x}_p) > \bar{y}_c = r$ $(\tilde{x}_c)$. So permanent workers are better off than casual ones in both periods. If they coexist, casual workers can be regarded as involuntarily unemployed over the agricultural cycle. Since $r(\tilde{x}_c) > f(\tilde{M}_u)$, their lot is in turn better than that of the permanently unemployed.

Under what circumstances will the competitive resource allocation mechanism support both casual and permanent workers? To answer this,

---

[6] This is similar to the efficiency wage of the landless in our timeless model.

it will prove useful first to explore the circumstances where the market mechanism sustains only casual labour.

Consider equations (*16.30) and (*16.31), which together imply $d\mu_c^*/dx_c < 0$. Write $M_{cu} = M_c + M_u$ as the number of people dependent on the commons in the first period. From equation (*16.35) we may conclude that $d\mu_c^*/dM_{cu} > 0$. So μ_c^* increases from a minimum value which would be attained were no one to be on the commons, towards an upper bound realized only when the commons are swamped by unlimited numbers of people. We now assume μ_p^* (equation *16.34)) to lie between these two bounds. This amounts to supposing that the commons have a lot to offer when there are limited numbers of people living on them, but have little to offer when numbers are very large. Given this, there exists a value of M_{cu} at which $\mu_p^* = \mu_c^*$. Denote it by $\bar{M}$. When the number of people living in the commons in the first period is $\bar{M}$, employers are indifferent at the margin between employing a casual and a permanent labourer. If $M_{cu} < \bar{M}$, we have $\mu_p^* > \mu_c^*$ for all $M_p \geq 0$, and so employers do not hire permanent workers. I conclude that if $M < \bar{M}$ there are only casual workers in agriculture; i.e. $M_{cu} = M$.

Let us begin by studying the economy when $M < \bar{M}$. Unless M is very small, we have

$$\mu_c^* = \bar{\mu} = \partial F(\bar{E}, \hat{T})/\partial E, \qquad (*16.37)$$

and so $\bar{M}_c$, $\bar{M}_u > 0$: there are casual workers and permanently unemployed people.[7] If a few people were to migrate out of the economy just before the beginning of the slack period, the number on the commons would decline, first-period consumption ($\bar{x}_c$) would increase, and so the productivity of casual workers ($\bar{\phi}(\bar{x}_c)$) would increase. This implies that their efficiency piece-rate (μ_c^*) would decline. In view of equation (*16.35), $\bar{E}$ would increase, and so $F(\bar{E}, \hat{T})$ would increase. I conclude that a slight decline in population under these circumstances would lead to a small increase in agricultural output. The economy contains surplus labour (see Section 16.8).

Let $M = \bar{M}$. Equation (*16.36) holds. There are no permanent workers in agriculture, and employers are indifferent at the margin between casual and permanent workers. As in Section 16.5, we shall conduct a sequence of exercises in 'comparative dynamics'. What we will do is to increase M gradually as a thought-experiment and track the resulting equilibrium allocations.

As M rises slightly beyond $\bar{M}$, equation (*16.36) continues to hold. Casual and permanent workers coexist (i.e. $\bar{M}_p$, $\bar{M}_c > 0$). As $\hat{T}$ is being held constant in our thought-experiment, $\bar{E}$ remains constant. (This is

---

[7] If M is sufficiently small $\bar{\mu} > \mu_c^*$, and there is full employment ($\bar{M}_u = 0$).

implied by the fact that μ_p^* is independent of market conditions.) There-fore, each increment in M raises $\tilde{M}_p$ by this same increment, while $\tilde{M}_c$ declines more than proportionately, so as to keep $\bar{E}$ constant.[8] This means that there exists a population size, say $\hat{M}$, at which equation (★16.36) holds, and there are no casual workers left to be replaced by additional permanent workers. Beyond $\hat{M}$, $\mu_c^* > \mu_p^*$, and there are only permanent workers in agriculture. When M is only slightly in excess of $\hat{M}$ involuntary unemploy-ment continues to exist: a fraction of the population remains permanently unemployed. This situation corresponds to regime 2 in our timeless model.

Our interest lies in situations where casual and permanent workers coexist; that is where $M\varepsilon[\bar{M}, \hat{M}]$. The economy sustains three classes of people. Consider what would happen if $\hat{T}$ were to increase slightly. (We will keep M constant now.) For equation (★16.36) to continue to hold, $\bar{E}$ would have to increase, and so $\tilde{M}_c$ would increase slightly, while $\tilde{M}_p$ would remain fixed.[9] I conclude that improvements in the productivity of land increase the share of casual labourers in the hired rural workforce. There is some evidence that this has been experienced in recent years (Singh, 1990). When $\hat{T}$ is large enough, $\bar{\mu} > \mu_c^* = \mu_p^*$, and agriculture mops up the entire population.

★16.5   Food Distribution within Poor Households

I have remarked on a number of occasions that extreme scarcity forces welfare-maximizing households to allocate food and healthcare unequally among its members. The reason for this is the non-convexity of activity possibility sets. I have heard it suggested that uncertainty in what consti-tutes a person's requirements makes this argument invalid. The thought is that requirements comprise a band, not a point. That matters are uncertain certainly smooth the maximization problem, but they don't invalidate the argument. A stylized example will make this clear.

For simplicity of exposition, consider two health states: good (S) and extreme stress (D). If x is the long-term calorie intake of a person, let $\pi(x)$ be the chance that her health will remain good. (Long-term calorie intake represents nutritional status, for example, the body mass index: see Chapter 14.) Personal welfare in S and D are $W(S)$ and $W(D)$, respectively. Obviously, $W(S) > W(D)$. Expected welfare is $\pi(x)U(S) + [1 - \pi(x)]U(D)$ $= \pi(x)[U(S) - U(D)] - U(D)$. I assume there exist values $\bar{x}$ and $\hat{x}$, with $\hat{x} > \bar{x}$, such that $\pi(x) = 0$ for $x\varepsilon[0, \bar{x}]$, $\pi'(x) > 0$ for $\hat{x} > x > \bar{x}$, and $\pi(x)$ $= 1$, for $x \geq \hat{x}$ (see Fig. 14.1). I am ignoring that $\pi(\cdot)$ declines for large values

---

[8] Notice that during this process the number living on the commons in the slack season remains the same. So $\bar{x}_c$ ($= \bar{x}_u$) remains constant.

[9] If $\tilde{M}_p$ were to increase $\bar{x}_c$ would increase, and so μ_c^* would decline, violating (★16.37).

of x. The sort of agent I am modelling here will not go beyond the point where $\pi(\cdot)$ starts declining, and will throw away any surplus calories.

If the household comprises two identical people, and the total quantity of calories available is K, its problem is:

Choose x and y so as to:

$$\text{maximize } [\pi(x) + \pi(y)][U(S) - U(D)], \text{ subject to } x + y \leq K. \qquad (\star 16.38)$$

Had $\pi(\cdot)$ been concave, problem $(\star 16.38)$ would have been concave, and its solution would have been equality of consumption: each would be awarded $K/2$. But $\pi(\cdot)$ is not concave. So unless K is large enough, or unless it is extremely low (so that π is relatively flat at the optimum and there are no substantial gains from inequality), the solution of problem $(\star 16.38)$ involves significant inequality (i.e. $x \neq y$). This is a generalization of the deterministic consideration I have alluded to before.

There is evidence that expremely poor households are less given to unequal allocations than merely poor households. Household inequality as a function of wealth is approximately $\cap$-shaped. Haddad and Kanbur (1989) have used the theory of bargaining to explain this. My point here is not that welfare maximization is a correct description of household behaviour. I argued that for certain purposes (e.g. explaining certain patterns of gender inequalities) the hypothesis simply won't do. I also suggested that for many purposes it is a useful tool for obtaining household response functions. My purpose in this section has been to suggest that problem $(\star 16.38)$ provides a convenient method for showing how acute are the stresses to which poor households are routinely subject—even when they are well-integrated households.

Incentives and Development Policies

17.1 *Agrarian Reform*

In the previous chapter it was shown how certain patterns of agrarian reform can lead to an increase in total output. Growth in national product and reduction in the extent of undernourishment are synergistic, the two being allied to improvements in labour productivity. This is an implication of any resource allocation theory that draws upon the link between nutritional status and productivity.

In Chapter 9 we studied a different reason why agrarian reform may be expected to increase agricultural output. The point there was that it is the small, family farms that are often the most intensively cultivated. Berry and Cline (1979), for example, have shown that in poor countries both yield per hectare and production of staple food decline with increasing farm size. They have argued that an equitable distribution of land could result in an increase of anything between 10 and 30 per cent in food production. This should be compared with the overall dietary energy gap reported for many poor countries, which is in the region 10–20 per cent of gross energy requirements (see FAO, 1982; Norse, 1985; see also Chapters 14–15). Such crude calculations do not rest on a mechanistic view of food allocation. A reduction in the proportion of landless households in an economy in which the distribution of land is overly concentrated to begin with increases the scope for family farming, and family farms have an easier access to food. For example, Bouis and Haddad (1989) have found in a study on the Philippines that a shift from corn (subsistence farming) to sugar (commercial farming) dislocated labour sufficiently to make the displaced bereft of resources; however, those who held on to land on average did a good deal better and recorded an improved nutritional status (see also Kennedy, 1989; Kennedy and Oniang'o, 1990). In a fine early paper, Gross and Underwood (1971) showed that, when agricultural development represents a shift from subsistence farming to the cultivation of cash crops, the nutritional status of non-earning members of households can deteriorate; and that this can happen even when the supply of food to households has increased. In Chapters 9 and 11 we studied reasons why we should not regard these findings as puzzling.

Localized learning-by-doing, by enabling family labour to become more efficient than hired labour (Chapter 9), could over time be expected to reinforce the productivity gains from agrarian reform. In principle, the overall increase in agricultural production should be sufficient to compensate the original landowners. Despite this, agrarian reform has remained the most explosive of political actions. It rarely enters the agenda of government, and its record in the Indian sub-continent, for example, has been dismal (see Singh, 1990).

Agricultural production, like its industrial counterpart, enjoys linkages with other sectors. A development strategy that is based on agrarian reform is not devoid of positive linkages. It can be presumed to yield geographically dispersed growth (and, thereby, somewhat equitable growth) because of linkages with the rest of the rural economy, for example through a demand for fertilizers, construction inputs, small-scale repair services, and basic consumer goods, activities that are intensive in the use of labour (see Thorbecke, 1969; Mellor and Lele, 1973; Johnston and Kilby, 1975; Mellor, 1976; Mellor and Johnston, 1984; Murphy, Shleifer and Vishny, 1989b; Tomich, Kilby and Johnston, 1991). Haggblade, Hazell, and Brown (1989) have estimated that in sub-Saharan Africa the multiplier associated with agricultural growth is of the order of 1.5; which is to say that a $1.00 increase in agricultural income can be expected to generate about $0.50 additional income, primarily among suppliers of non-farm goods and services. Estimates for India and Malaysia are higher, the growth multiplier being of the order of 2.5. Employment multipliers are also significant. Data from the Philippines and India suggest that agriculture–non-farm employment elasticities are between 1.0 and 1.3 (see Krishna, 1976).

Agrarian reform is a pristine form of asset redistribution, and the latter is prescribed by the Second Fundamental Theorem of Welfare Economics to be a focus of government activity in the socio-economic sphere of life (Chapter 7). In this connection, land taxes have often been seen as a substitute for land redistribution. The thought is that, since land is in fixed supply, its taxation is non-distortionary (see e.g. Newbery, 1987).[1] One obvious problem with this view is that the productivity of land can be affected by investment, and so the quality of a piece of land is not immutable (Chapter 10). Another, much less obvious, problem is that, unlike taxation of agricultural output, a land tax involves no sharing of agricultural risk between the government and the landowner: under a land tax, the landowner bears all the risk. In a world where insurance markets are sparse (see in particular Hazell, Pomereda and Valdes, 1986, on the difficulties of establishing crop insurance on account of the attendant moral

---

[1] Among economists this is often irreverently called the Henry George Theorem, the reference being to the 19th-c. American journalist and author who, in his famous 1879 treatise *Progress and Poverty*, advocated replacing all taxes by a tax on land.

hazard), this can matter, and it can mean that an excessive reliance on land taxes is undesirable (see Hoff, 1991; and Chapters 7–9). Agrarian reform and land taxes are not the same set of public instruments: they have different consequences.

We have been thinking of agrarian reform here, and this isn't the same as land reform.[2] It is useful to distinguish between ownership and control of so personalizable an asset as land, and between these in turn and the income a household can draw from it. You may own your land and may even be allowed full control over its use. But if the government's pricing policies are directed against agriculture, there isn't very much in cultivation for you. The income you can draw from it is low. Then again, land may have been redistributed, but if the farm you are part of is a collective, your incentives will be dulled, perhaps greatly so.

We have just noted that a well-designed reform could even prove to be self-financing, and so agrarian reform is not to be associated with out-and-out confiscation of land titles, which is plain robbery. However, for the reform to be successful, holdings need to be non-fragmented, and small farmers must have ready access to extension services and agricultural infrastructure, such as irrigation water and roads (Chapter 6). In those regions where agricultural mechanization has been made possible by the introduction of modern inputs, such as high-yielding seeds, pesticides and chemical fertilizers, access to formal credit has in some cases been found to increase not only with land size, but also with the amount of land under irrigation (e.g. tube wells) and with levels of household education. In short, access to formal credit can be expected to vary with the productivity of farm households, resulting in owners of large farms leasing in land from small farmers (Chapter 9; Kochar, 1992). As regards the distribution of farm sizes, there are thus unequalizing forces at work, a recurring theme of this book. Moreover, technological changes in agriculture have been known to come allied to increases in income inequality. But, as Quizon and Binswanger (1986) have shown in the context of the Green Revolution in northern India, it isn't technological change *per se*, but the eventual pricing of agricultural inputs and produce, that often prevents wages and employment from rising.

Admittedly, the postwar land reforms in Taiwan and South Korea were made possible in great part by the departure of Japanese landowners. Compensation was not required. But the success that followed had a great deal to do with the support their governments gave farmers.[3]

---

[2] I am taking it for granted that under the reform land titles have been issued. Siamwalla *et al.* (1990) have shown how important this can be if credit is to become available to farming households. We noted a rationale for this in Ch. 9.

[3] See Shen (1964), Ho (1966), Ranis (1975), Adelman (1979), Kuo, Ranis and Fei (1981), and Adelman and Robinson (1989). For an account of Japan's successful land reform, see

Contrast these Asian successes with the failure of land reforms in Latin America during the 1960s and 1970s. There, small farmers received little support in the form of credits and agricultural extension services. Governments for the most part helped modernize medium- to large-sized farms and ranches by awarding them tax advantages, selective price-support programmes, subsidized credits, and investments in infrastructure. For example, the largest 1 per cent of farmers received 50 per cent of public credits in Colombia, whereas the smallest 50 per cent of farmers received less than 4.2 per cent. The percentage of farm households receiving institutional credits amounted to only 27 per cent in Colombia, 22 per cent in Venezuala, 20 per cent in Honduras, 16 per cent in Mexico and 6 per cent in Peru (see de Janvry and Sadoulet, 1989). In post-1973 Chile water rights were reverted back to the original landowners. In a related context, E. Feder (1977, 1979), Mahar (1988), Repetto (1988) and Binswanger (1989) have noted the staggering environmental impact of government support for large-scale landholdings in Brazil. The link between environmental degradation and the incidence of destitution was studied in Chapters 10, 12, and 16.

17.2   Food Subsidies

Earlier (Chapter 7), I argued that the Second Fundamental Theorem of Welfare Economics has little operational appeal, beause much of the information it assumes the State to possess (personal characteristics, the level of effort an individual puts in at a task, and so forth) is private knowledge. This is a deep fact, not an incidental one, and is the source of adverse selection and moral hazard (Chapter 9) and, thereby, the problem of incentives. Thus, for example, in implementing an entitlement scheme for the needy (or for the poor), it is not enough to ask of a citizen if he has the relevant special needs (or if his income is low). The temptation to exaggerate (and thus 'free-ride') can be substantial, and while some may be immune to temptation, others can be relied upon not to be so. No government can possibly know such personal attributes as the degree of one's honesty. So, unless the entitlement scheme imposes an implicit cost on false declaration (or exaggeration), it will in general not be able to elicit the 'truth' about people. To be effective, public policy has to be compatible with incentives, a matter we discussed in Chapters 3, 7, and 9. By studying several types of policies, we will see below how this can be realized.

Dore (1959). No doubt there were other forces that made for the subsequent economic successes of these countries. A feature that has been much discussed in recent years is their cultural mores; Little (1979), Morishima (1981), and Scitovsky (1985), among others, have argued that variants of Confucian philosophy and the Chinese tradition of disciplined work ethic have contributed greatly.

Although quantitative estimates are sparse, civic responsibility probably differs enormously across societies. In poor countries, where the State (and thereby the public realm) is often viewed by communities as an alien fixture, the temptation to 'free-ride' on such State benefits as there are must be particularly strong. However, even in a 'well-ordered' society (I am using the term in the sense of Rawls, 1972) free-riding would not be uncommon: separation of the private and public spheres of life is not an easy matter (Chapter 5). Living off the State can become a way of life. The evidence with which I am familiar (mainly for the UK), however, makes interesting reading. Golding and Middleton (1983) have studied people's knowledge, attitudes and beliefs about the welfare-benefit system in the UK. Over 50 per cent of their working-class respondents found welfare benefits 'embarrassing'. However, the attitudes of potential claimants have been found to vary from one type of benefit to another. For example, prescription-charge exemptions seem to carry no stigma, but rent rebates do (see Taylor-Gooby, 1976). Why is this? One possible reason is that health problems are assessed by someone other than oneself (the doctor) and are either attributed to bad luck or acknowledged to be associated with certain verifiable states of affairs (e.g. childbirth, old age); but whether one's low earnings are due to bad luck, or lack of effort, or an absence of ability is not something that is easily detectable. In short, there are fewer problems of moral hazard and adverse selection associated with health than employment. This may be one reason why prescription-charge exemptions in the UK are seen as a 'right', whereas rent rebates are regarded as a 'benefit'.

Nutrition is a basic need, and in order to guarantee food security governments in several countries have in the past offered consumer subsidies on certain food items to the entire population (e.g. the much-discussed food subsidies in Egypt and Sri Lanka). Food subsidies (food stamps are only an extreme special case) are the means by which the price that consumers pay for staples can be reduced without bringing about a reduction in the price that producers receive. The theory of taxation (Chapter 7) enables us to discover how to regard the optimal design of commodity taxes and subsidies. At a more general level, the theory shows how taxes and subsidies, transfers and public expenditure ought simultaneously to be determined. Now in order that a policy is even viable (let alone optimal), taxes and subsidies have to be based on observable criteria; otherwise it will not be compatible with incentives. Thus, for example, if revenue is to be raised from a tax on income, the government must be in a position to assess at least a part of the income of some fraction of the population.

Food is a private good *par excellence*, and as such should belong to the private realm in resource allocation mechanisms (Chapter 6). But we observed in Chapters 7 and 16 that operations in the private realm on their own cannot be relied upon to distribute food to all: the assetless may not be able to command the required purchasing power. For this reason, food security has to be on the agenda of the public realm. The aim behind offering consumer subsidies on food is to ensure food security for the poor. The problem is that it is very difficult to assess household income in poor countries (Chapter 4, 9–12). So we have to look for some observable characteristic at the individual (or household) level that is sufficiently correlated with income. Consumer subsidies could then be targeted on those possessing this characteristic.

Why is targeting desirable? The reason is that if the coverage were universal those who can easily afford food would enjoy the same entitlements as those who cannot. As it reduces the need to work, universal coverage also reduces the supply of labour (see Reutlinger and Pellekaan, 1986). Thus, universal coverage has two weaknesses: first, it does not restrict the benefit to those who are truly needy (i.e. those who are poor for reasons beyond their control); second, it dulls the incentive to work. Besley and Coate (1992) label the first weakness as an inability to 'screen' the truly needy, and the second as the ability to 'deter' people from undertaking productive activity. Both are wasteful features and they are telling if those not in need of benefits are sufficiently large in number. To illustrate the first, it has been estimated that during the early 1980s poor households in Egypt enjoyed smaller absolute income transfers from food subsidies than those that were not poor, even though the total income of the poor was somewhat larger. Food subsidies in Egypt amounted to about 6 per cent of gross national product and some 16–18 per cent of annual government expenditure (see Scobie, 1983; Alderman and von Braun, 1984; World Bank, 1986a; Pinstrup-Andersen, 1989). The Sri Lankan experience was not dissimilar. Samarasinghe (1988) contains an account of the enormous budgetary problems faced by successive governments while attempting to maintain an extensive food subsidy programme. The problems became so acute that universal coverage had to be abandoned from about the middle of the second half of the 1970s (see also World Bank, 1986a; Pinstrup-Andersen, 1988a, b).

This waste is not inevitable. It can be avoided if the food subsidy is targeted in a reasonably accurate manner.[4] Here, two routes are available.

---

[4] See Reutlinger and Pellekaan (1986), World Bank (1986a), and Berg (1987) for assessments of a number of targeted food-subsidy schemes that have been established in poor countries over the past two decades. Diamond and Mirrlees (1971), Diamond (1975), Mirrlees (1976), Besley and Kanbur (1988), and Haddad and Kanbur (1991) contain formal analyses of the way such schemes ought to be designed. Besley and Coate (1991) have provided a definitive analytical account of the structure of optimal income maintenance programmes. In what follows, I will suppose that those in need of government assistance are sufficiently large in number to make universal coverage wasteful.

The first we have already noted. In it the subsidy is offered only to those who possess an observable attribute that is sufficiently correlated with income, and thereby with food needs. This is sometimes called 'tagging' (see Akerlof, 1978). Nutritional supplements for stunted and wasted people provide an obvious example. In the feeding programme of the Integrated Nutrition Project in Tamil Nadu (India), children are admitted when their growth falters, and are removed when their weight has increased satisfactorily. A weakness in the design of this programme is that it aims to cure: it doesn't try to prevent. Since prevention of malnutrition should also be a goal, a scheme that includes age (e.g. children in the range 6–36 months) as a 'tag' would be better. This is because age is a good indicator of those within a population who are particularly at risk from malnourishment.[5] Other than young children, those groups that are especially at risk are pregnant and lactating women, the elderly, and, in Asia, households that are headed by women (Chapters 4, 11, and 14). Thus, for example, food subsidy could be tagged to households with children under 5 years of age or pregnant or lactating women. This would be to make the subsidy a categorical benefit. To be sure, children of households that are not poor are typically not at risk either. Nor do all pregnant and lactating women fall prey to malnutrition in the absence of a food subsidy. Inevitably, also, there are people within groups not covered by a tagged subsidy who are at risk (e.g. adult males in poor households). In short, there are some in need who fall outside the net cast by a tagged subsidy, and there are beneficiaries who are not in need (an instance of what statisticians call the simultaneous occurrence of type 1 and type 2 errors). This price has to be paid when the tags are imperfectly correlated with the object of concern, namely, people at risk of malnutrition.[6]

Location provides another method of targeting food subsidies. The idea is to offer the subsidy only at publicly controlled stores located in neighbourhoods and regions suffering from a high incidence of poverty. As with any other characteristic, a problem with location as a criterion for tagging is the possibility of resale: unless the scheme is suitably designed, people who are entitled to the subsidy would be tempted to purchase food

[5] See Underwood (1983), Kennedy and Alderman (1987), Bell and Reich (1988), Alderman (1990), and Chs. 4 and 14. Knudsen (1981) and Kennedy and Knudsen (1985) contain useful discussions of different types of supplementary feeding programmes.

[6] Haddad and Kanbur (1991) provide an analytical account of the way tags ought to be chosen when the government has a specified budget for the programme and the social objective is the minimization of the value of some index of poverty. It transpires that minimizing any index of poverty subject to a government budget constraint can yield paradoxical results. (For example, if the needs of a deserving group increase, resources recommended to be targeted to it can decline: see Keen, 1992.) The Haddad–Kanbur analysis, however, covers a broader ground, and can be used for wider social objectives. It can also help ascertain the desirable level of public expenditure on the programme.

and sell it to those who are not entitled to it. Recall that this is not a problem with other basic needs, such as education and health care (Chapters 6 and 7): population-wide coverage of consumer subsidies in these goods *amounts* to tagging, and illegal side-markets do not flourish. With nutrition the matter is different. Everyone needs nutrition, and needs it every day.

Fortunately, illegal side-markets can be contained when food subsidies are tagged. The subsidies can take the form of food supplementation, administered at schools and health centres. The problem of resale does not arise when the supplements are required to be consumed at distribution centres. Nor does targeting the needy by locating publicly controlled food stores in poor geographical areas pose a problem of resale, so long as the magnitude of the subsidy (relative to transport costs) is not large enough to make it profitable for purchasers to transport food out of the region.

Supplementary feeding programmes for children may not be sufficient for meeting their nutrition requirements because of the possibility that their food intake at home would be fractionally reduced; the 'crowding out effect'. This is sometimes also called the 'knock-on effect'. Evidence of the magnitude of this phenomenon is mixed, because it varies across societies and with the design of programmes. For example, in the Integrated Nutrition Project in Tamil Nadu, mothers have not been found to reduce their children's food intake at home, apparently because of the sense of shame they would experience if their children were not to gain weight by the amount expected. That the project involved the active participation not only of mothers but, more broadly, of the community as well has been seen by many to be a key to the project's success (see e.g. Subbarao, 1989).[7] On the other hand, Cox and Jimenez (1992) have detected a significant crowding out of transfers from young adults to the old in response to the introduction of social security benefits in Peru.

A second method that is available for targeting lies in designing the subsidy in such a way that the needy 'self-select'. The scheme permits unlimited participation, but is so constructed that only members of the target group find it in their interest to participate.[8] This was the thrust of the work of Peter Diamond and James Mirrlees I have referred to earlier (although the social desirability of tagging by individual characteristics that are correlated with needs is also an immediate consequence of the Diamond–Mirrlees analysis; see Hahn, 1973b). Thus, a grain subsidy on only the coarsest varieties can be expected to be effective because on the

---

[7] That child benefit in the UK is paid to the mother and not to the father is a reflection of the finding that mothers can be relied upon more to use the resource for the beneficiary. I am grateful to Carol Dasgupta for pointing this out to me in 1974 when our first child was born.

[8] Akerlof (1978) includes this in his notion of 'tagging'.

whole those who are not poor will avoid eating coarse grain (Chapter 15). This is an extreme example, and the more general prescription is to subsidize those staples that, as a proportion of the population average, are consumed in the main by members of the target group.[9]

Self-selection is a natural means of targeting in other spheres of the public realm as well. For example, self-selection by the poor can be realized in the use of public health services if the rich are deterred from making use of government clinics. In poor countries, governments customarily achieve this by the simple expedient of offering public services of low quality (queues, uncomfortable furniture, aggressive medical staff, unhygienic environment in hospitals, and so forth). Sensibly, the rich stay away and use private medical facilities. Thus also for State education.

17.3 *Employment Guarantee Schemes and Rural Infrastructure*

Self-selection is a most effective method of screening the poor in a different kind of public food security scheme, namely, food-for-work (or cash-for-work) programmes. In the context of the formal model we studied in Chapters 16 and *16, establishing an employment guarantee scheme is tantamount to redistributing assets. A significant variant of this consists of food (or cash) transfers. Thus, cash transfers are on occasion made to deserving groups (e.g. UNICEF's cash transfer project in Ethiopia, which targeted some 7000 poor households), in return for which 'those who are able to' are expected to contribute labour to local investment projects aimed at producing certain types of collective goods (Chapter 6), such as roads, soil conservation, small-scale irrigation and drainage facilities, afforestation, and schools. The operative words are those in quotes, and we will return to their significance presently. (Berg, 1987, provides a good account of such schemes.) Except for situations where there is a severe shortage of food in a region, cash payment is the preferable mode of transfer to the poor. It generates demand in the region, and thereby prevents food from being transported away by wholesalers. It also saves on the transport costs the government would otherwise have to incur in bringing food into the region (see Reutlinger and Pellekaan, 1986; Dreze and Sen, 1990; World Bank, 1990). On the other hand, transfers in kind are obviously the preferable option when the government makes use of food aid as its source of fund.

---

[9] The precise statement is much more complicated, since, in order to calculate the poor's share of consumption, a set of social weights need to be used; see Diamond (1975), Mirrlees (1976), and Besley and Kanbur (1988). It is as well to note that substitution effects can be powerful. For example, one estimate for Bangladesh suggests that a small subsidy on pulses would result in a decline in protein intake by the poor because of cross-price effects (see Pitt, 1983). Note too that income supplements need not be as effective a way of improving nutrition as programmes that induce substitution for low-cost sources of nutrients.

The problem with both food and cash transfers is that they require the government not only to know who the needy are, but also to recognize those who are capable of offering work in return for welfare. To identify these features can be costly, unless the needy are visibly undernourished (as they would be during a famine). Food-for-work (or cash-for-work) programmes are superior on this count because they can be so designed that they entice the truly needy to the programme and simultaneously deter those who are able to earn their livelihood elsewhere. To be sure, there are people who are unable to work because of physical or mental ailments and are poor for this reason. The way to screen them is to offer as an additional option a benefit package consisting of both food and medical treatment. This would be a pure 'in-kind' transfer. If the food content of the benefit package were kept sufficiently low, or if the medical treatment were made sufficiently unenticing for those not in requirement of the treatment, the 'healthy but poor' would not wish to claim the package, but would rather opt for employment in the public project.[10]

We should observe first that the terms of employment (e.g. wages) in such an employment guarantee programme need to be worse than they are in the market, or else the unemployed would not be able to self-select. If they do not self-select, the purpose of the programme will have been vitiated, because public employment in the production of the collective good will have then to a large extent displaced private employment in the production of private goods. One of the reasons the Employment Guarantee Scheme in Maharashtra has been a success in reaching the poor, while not costing inordinate amounts, is that this self-selection constraint was built into its design, at least until recently (see Ravallion, 1991).

To fix ideas on how to compute costs and benefits of such schemes, let us assume that a public-works programme is to be initiated in a region in which the poorest of households (the target group) subsist on $1 a day, while other households earn in excess of $2 a day.[11] One way of thinking about this is to apply the ideas I developed in Chapter 16 and suppose that the people who are targeted are the involuntarily unemployed. The programme is designed to produce collective goods, say during the slack agricultural season, when unemployment is high. Working on the pro-gramme costs participants $0.40 (40 cents) a day for additional food, travel, and so forth. A wage of $2.40 would then be enough to attract the target population and deter those earning more than $2 a day. If the social value of a day's work on the public project is $3 and it costs $1.20 in materials to employ a person, the public cost of augmenting incomes is

---

[10] Blackorby and Donaldson (1988) provide an analysis of a similar problem.
[11] The example is taken from Reutlinger and Pellekaan (1986: 39). For a theoretical study of the relative merits of food-for-work programmes and food transfers with a universal reach, see Besley and Coate (1992).

$0.60 per person employed. Moreover, the target population's income increases by $1 for every $0.60 spent on the programme. This is plainly cost-effective. It is also compatible with incentives.

Employment guarantee schemes can be far-reaching, especially when they are financed by foreign aid. Costs borne by the domestic government can be kept low by the simple expedient of selling a part of the food aid to the rich and using the revenue for purchases of material inputs for the public works.[12] Srinivasan (1989) has argued on the basis of simulation studies that in India abject poverty can be eliminated quite promptly and at reasonable cost by means of public-works programmes.

Cash-for-work programmes not only offer employment to members of destitute households, they also improve the lives of vulnerable members of not-so-poor households. Guaranteed work provides them with an improved outside option, especially when wages are paid in cash. This increases their bargaining power within the household. Recall (Section 11.7) that the vulnerable party does not have to avail herself of the option: the mere presence of the option can improve her lot. Therein lies its subtlety.

17.4 Community Participation and Credit Facilities

Nothing is straightforward in the social sciences. Public works can be (and often have been) a potent route to the prevention of hunger and destitution, but they retard growth in net national product if the investments are unproductive. And all too often they have not been productive: the projects have been ill-conceived and badly managed, yielding little (see e.g. Basu, 1981; Dev, 1992). This is a constant problem in poor countries.

At first blush it is hard to imagine that investment projects in rural infrastructure could be anything but worth while. However, on reflection it is easy to so imagine. Project designers and managers are given State funds that have to be spent, and, unless they are given a stake in the project (e.g. through performance-related bonuses and promotions), they do not have the required incentives to realize productive investment, which involves not only identifying good projects, but also seeing them to fruition. Now the performance of public servants is hard to measure. One way of assessing it (good, fair, bad, or whatever) is to compare their achievements with those of others in their peer group (see Nalebuff and Stiglitz, 1983; Mookherjee, 1984). This involves doing an *ex post* social costing of comparable projects within neighbouring groups of villages (e.g. the number of months required to build a road, the number of labourers

---

[12] Since demand for food by the rich would be expected to be inelastic, this would be tantamount to applying discriminatory pricing. See Sec. 10.1 for an account of discriminatory pricing practised by farmers in response to the government food procurement scheme in India.

employed, the cost of material deployed). The problem is that, while such simulated competition among civil servants can be a way of getting *them* to work hard, it provides no incentives for the *labourers* to work hard. Therein lies an inherent weakness in cash-for-work programmes: as employment is guaranteed, labourers have every incentive to slack. This can pose an obstacle for project managers, especially when they are outsiders.

Community participation in the management of public works is a way of blunting this incentive problem: it is hard to slack if your neighbours are keeping an eye on your performance. Moreover, community involvement at the design stage (e.g. identifying sites) has informational advantages, since members of a community are likely to know about local matters relating to science and technology (e.g. soil quality, slope, drainage, precipitation, forest ecology), needs, and mores than outsiders (Chapter 10). User-oriented design and management is likely to be more responsive to the needs and demands of the intended beneficiaries than one imposed from outside.[13] The community is a residual claimant (Chapter 9) in any investment project that produces a local collective good. So it has every incentive to involve itself in the project's success. But it can't involve itself if it is not asked. The State can be an alien entity to rural folk even in democratic countries, let alone authoritarian ones. When the community is not asked, the economically advantaged often influence the design and operation to their further advantage.

The Rural Piped Water Programme in Malawi (cited in World Bank, 1989b: 85) is widely regarded as a successful instance of government and community involvement in the production of a basic need. Even though it isn't an employment guarantee scheme (and so isn't vulnerable to the particular moral hazard problem we are discussing here), it points in the right direction to such schemes. In the Malawi programme, local communities organize and manage the water facilities, identify sites, elect water committees and repair teams, organize the digging, raise funds for replacement parts, and enforce community rules for the use of water. The government, on the other hand, finances the initial capital investment,

---

[13] Here is an example: the Pathan tribeswomen of a particular village in the Northwest Frontier Province have traditionally walked some 8 km each way to a small aqueduct to wash clothes once a week. In order to ease the plight of these women, a foreign aid project built a traditional washing facility nearby. The project was a failure. While the women admired it, they refused to use it. A female anthropologist, employed to discover why the facility remained unused, discovered that the tribeswomen are rarely permitted to leave their homes. They spend most of their lives within the confines of the mud castles owned by each Pathan family. These weekly washing trips were their only chance to talk to the other women in the community, when they could laugh, gossip, and play. The event lasted the whole day, and was much looked forward to. The women also reasoned that if they were to complete the laundry in less time their husbands would merely find more things for them to do. (I am grateful to Andrew Feldman for this communication.)

adopts the technical responsibilities, and trains community members in water management. Financial responsibility on the part of the local community gives it just that much more of a stake in the project's success. There is no reason why this feature should not be introduced into employment guarantee schemes. If the local community (excluding the poor who would obtain employment, and thus benefit) were to recognize that it would benefit from a project, it would have an incentive to provide part of the required finance if it were made known that government funding was conditional on the local community so participating. Moreover, much like the building of trust, successful co-operation can be exected to breed further co-operation (Gambetta, 1988b; Seabright, 1990). The government's role would be to initiate and assist new areas and patterns of co-operation during changing circumstances (Chapters 6 and 8). This kind of service has the features of a public good, and is typically undersupplied in the market mechanism.

But public works are just that: public works. A significant failure of resource allocation mechanisms prevailing in poor countries is the inability of individuals to undertake productive investment in private goods because of a lack of working capital. Here, the fact that information about productive investment opportunities is most often known only privately is of paramount importance (Chapters 6 and 7). To identify and seize a profitable opportunity requires specialized knowledge, imagination, and a certain boldness. It also requires capital. Earlier, I argued that in poor countries the credit market is particularly ruthless towards the assetless (Chapters 9, 11, and Section 17.1). This means that such folk are especially constrained in their ability to undertake investment activity (in commercial undertaking, cottage industry, small-scale manufacture, agriculture, or whatever). Government credit schemes would seem to provide an answer, but for the fact that the operation of any credit market involves moral hazard and adverse selection. The government as creditor is subject to this problem just like any other credit agency.

Resource allocations under the market mechanism suffering from moral hazard and adverse selection are not, generally speaking, Pareto-efficient even in a constrained sense (see Greenwald and Stiglitz, 1986; Section 9.5). We conclude that there would be a role for government even if efficiency were the sole criterion for public intervention. But we have found compelling reasons for regarding aggregate well-being (and not Pareto efficiency) as the appropriate criterion for judging resource allocation mechanisms. From this it follows that the elimination of destitution should loom large on the State's agenda (Chapters 2, 3, and 6). Because loans offer a route by which the assetless can escape destitution's grip, the general non-availability of credit for them has been a recurring theme in this book. But loan applicants need to be screened, and, as we noted in

Chapter 9, the cost of screening can be high in rural parts of poor countries. As a general rule, governments have added to the inevitable moral hazard involved in loans by being lax in enforcing repayments. For example, Aleem (1990) has estimated that in the early 1980s the delinquency rate on non-institutional loans in Chambar (Pakistan) was approximately 15 per cent, but the mean cumulative rate of non-repayment was only 2.7 per cent; whereas the default rate in the formal sector was about 30 per cent. Government credit programmes (e.g. the Integrated Rural Development Programme in India) have proved to be among the worst in terms of the degree to which borrowers have defaulted on loans.

The importance of public expenditure on rural infrastructure has also been a recurrent theme of this book. The value of such investment lies in its reducing both agricultural risks and transportation costs. These in turn lower information asymmetries and widen the extent of the rural credit market. But in tandem with infrastructural investment, there is a need for improving the organization of government credit schemes. That 'politically motivated' debt-forgiveness should not be permitted is, of course, no more than a banality, and beyond noting the point there is not much to say about it here. Every agency, public or private, should be subject to scrutiny on a regular basis, and some form of autonomy on the part of the investigator is a minimal requirement if the scrutiny is to be effective. Let us recall also that to enshrine the scope of public activities by rules is a way of curbing malpractice. Rules smack of rigidity, but discretion has been known to open the door to public malfeasance (Section 3.1). In poor countries, public officials regularly take bribes, and show favouritism to the economically powerful, who often belong to their clan or caste. Earlier in this section we noted that instituting competition among officials is a way of improving their performance. As in any other area of activity, performance in the disbursement of credit cannot be judged on its own, but only in comparison with others. Rates of default on loans of particular types comprise one useful set of indices (there are others) with which to judge the performance of different lending units of a credit agency.

Over and above this, however, are residual amounts of moral hazard and adverse selection that public officials have to live with if they are to do the screening and monitoring of borrowers. The question arises if even this residual can be reduced by institutional reform. Joint participation in credit schemes (more generally, credit co-operatives) has been seen as a way of lowering screening, monitoring, and enforcement problems. Of the many rural credit programmes that have been studied (Aleem, 1990; Bell, 1990; Hoff and Stiglitz, 1990; Siamwalla et al., 1990; Besley, 1992, provide thoughtful commentaries), the one initiated by the Grameen Bank in Bangladesh has often been singled out for its success.[14] Members of the

---

[14] The word *grameen* means 'rural' in Bengali. Hossain (1984) provides an account of the Grameen Bank's activities.

target group (households owning less than 0.5 acres of land) of the bank have been offered loans (without collateral requirement) for the purposes of establishing very small-scale activities. Nearly half the beneficiaries so far have been destitute women. The default rate has been remarkably low, about 2–3 per cent. How was this managed? Here, we will consider one feature of the programme that has been recently discussed: peer monitoring. Thus, loan applicants have been required to form small groups, within each of which members are made jointly liable for each member's debt. (A group begins with a pair of members, rising to five in number eventually.) The scheme, therefore, provides an incentive to potential borrowers to seek out other potential borrowers with good prospects, to monitor each other's activities, and to enforce the terms of the loan contracts. The burden of screening and enforcement is thereby to a large extent transferred from the lending agent to the borrowers themselves. The social advantage of this is that the costs the latter incur in screening and enforcement are typically lower (Chapter 9). To be sure, there is a disadvantage also, in that small groups of poor borrowers are less capable of bearing risk than a credit institution. However, under certain circumstances the reduced moral hazard and adverse selection incurred under peer-monitoring override the social cost arising from the fact that the 'wrong' party bears the objective risks associated with investment projects.[15]

Innovations in the organization of production and exchange are public goods. We have seen that this feature provides a role for government in bringing about desirable organizational change (Chapter 6). Local participation is necessary for efficiency in the public realm, and we have studied reasons why this should be so (see also Chapter 10). But guidance from the State is necessary if the involvement of local people is to be facilitated. Neither the community nor the State can be effective on its own.

17.5 *Health and Education*

Throughout this book I have emphasized the productive value of expenditure in infrastructure, primary and secondary education, the production and spread of information, health care and potable water, and food and employment security. They are desirable in themselves, but in addition they add to the productivity of labour, and so have a derived value as well. Together with political and civil liberties, and the other services that have traditionally been expected of the Minimal State (see Nozick, 1974), they

[15] See Stiglitz (1990). See also Huppi and Feder (1990) and Bannerjee, Besley and Guinnane (1992) for analyses of more general forms of credit co-operative.

Table 17.1 Financial requirements for broadly based human resource development for sub-Saharan Africa (% of GNP)

Component of human resource development	1985 (actual)[a]	Required (immediately)	Required (2000)
Food security interventions	..	0.5	0.5
Nutrition	..	0.2	0.2
Universal primary education and quality improvement	1.3	1.5	2.2
Family planning	..	0.8	0.8
Water and sanitation	..	0.5	0.5
Primary health care	1.35[b]	2.0	2.5
Subtotal		5.5	6.7
Science and technology	..	0.5	0.8
Secondary and higher education	1.7	2.5	2.5
Total	4–5	8.5	10.0

[a] ..: negligible.
[b] Total health care, including primary and non-primary.
Source: World Bank (1989b, table 3.3).

provide the background environment within which citizens can go about their lives (Chapters 2–5). Striking the right balance between the public and private realms is the central problem of the social sciences.

The list of activities in the socio-economic sphere that I have identified as being on the agenda of responsible government is far-reaching. Governments in most poor countries don't do anything like enough in this respect: they are preoccupied with other things (Chapter 5–7 and 10). The question is, can they afford to do more? By this one usually means: will long-term growth in aggregate well-being be jeopardized if governments in poor countries are engaged in the activities we have identified for them? In Chapters 4 and 5 we found reasons for thinking that they can, and that it won't. But we didn't talk explicitly of the poorest of poor countries, those in sub-Saharan Africa. If sub-Saharan Africa can afford it, so can others.

Table 17.1 provides a set of World Bank estimates of financial requirements for a broadly based human resource development for sub-Saharan Africa, expressed as percentage of gross national product (GNP). Actual expenditure on basic needs at the time of the estimate (1985) amounted to less than 3 per cent (approximately 2.65 per cent) of GNP. It will be observed that public spending on such vital services as food security, nutrition, family planning, water, and sanitation was so small as to have been not worth recording. The World Bank's estimates of immediate requirements in expenditure amounted to 5.5 per cent of GNP. (If one were to include expenditure in science and technology and secondary and higher education to the list, the requirement came to 8.5 per cent of GNP.) This is a small amount, and it looks particularly affordable when we bear in mind that military expenditure as a percentage of GNP was at that time approximately 4.2 per cent.[16] Estimated requirements for the provision of basic needs for the year 2000 amount to 6.7 per cent of GNP. Since the projected gap is approximately 4 per cent (i.e. 6.7–2.65), even this would be affordable if the military budget were to be sufficiently pruned. There is no reason to think, therefore, that the poorest of poor countries cannot afford significant improvements in the availability of basic needs. And if *they* can afford it, so can countries in the Indian sub-continent. In poor countries as a whole, expenditure on the military, on health, and on education in the mid-1980s amounted to 4.3, 1.6, and 3.8 per cent of GNP, respectively. The continuing wastage of lives in the mere preparation of wars and strife is horrifyingly large. There is simply no excuse for it.

Repeatedly in this book I have mentioned that among the most potent of basic needs is female education (Chapters 4–5, 9–12). Its instrumental value would appear to be high. But the estimates I have so far offered have been in the main qualitative. At the quantitative level, one may ask if female education is socially cost-effective in poor countries. A rough calculation based on World Bank data on Pakistan (see L. Summers, 1992) indicates that it is an excellent form of social investment.

Educating an additional 1000 girls in Pakistan would have cost $40 000 in 1990. Each year of schooling in that country has been estimated to reduce the under-five mortality rate by about 10 per cent. The total fertility rate in Pakistan is a high 6.6. This translates to a saving of sixty deaths of children under five. The alternative of saving sixty lives with health-care interventions would have cost something like $48 000. But this isn't all. Educated women typically have fewer children (Chapters 4 and 12). An extra year of schooling in Pakistan reduces female fertility by 10 per cent. Thus, a $40 000 investment in educating 1000 women would avert 660 births. The alternative route of family planning expenditure for achieving the same result would have cost something like $43 000. Nor is *this* all. Increased female education has been found to lead to a reduction in maternal mortality. It has been calculated that in Pakistan an additional year of schooling for 1000 women would prevent the deaths of 4 women during childbirth. Achieving the same reduction through medical services would cost about $10 000.

Unfortunately, I am unable to provide figures for the instrumental worth of food security. I have not been able to find any quantitative estimate of the improvement in labour productivity that better nutrition would bring

[16] See McNamara (1992). The figure 4.2% was for Africa as a whole in 1988. But it transpires that sub-Saharan Africa's expenditure on the military, when expressed as a proportion of GNP, is about the same as that for the whole of Africa.

about in poor countries. The account of food needs and work capacity presented in Chapters 14 and 15 is an essential ingredient for any such exercise. But it is only an ingredient, and it doesn't tell us directly the things we would need to know if we were to try and conduct social 'cost–benefit analyses' of improved nutrition. Findings in nutrition science have told us a great deal; it is the final step that is missing, and it can only be achieved by economists working jointly with nutritionists.

This brings us back full circle to a point with which we began (Chapter 1), that the phenomenon of undernourishment has found little room in either modern resource allocation theory or the economics of poor countries. The latter has for the most part seen fit to identify the phenomenon with poverty. Replace 'undernourishment' by 'low income' in the recent literature on human development (e.g. UNDP, 1990, 1991; World Bank, 1990), and you will not detect any difference in the narratives. But the two belong to different categories of phenomena. Poverty is, of course, a central cause of undernourishment; but, as the analysis of Chapters 16 and *16 has shown, it is in turn perpetuated by undernourishment. We have seen that this two-way influence must be central to any account of destitution and its relief. To date I have seen no numerical model that is built on this fact. There is much that remains to be done.

17.6 *Envoi*

In great part this book has been about the conditions in which people are born and the manner in which they live and die in rural communities of poor countries. At the same time I have made an attempt to identify the kinds of things governments in these countries ought to be engaged in. The two together have comprised an inquiry into well-being and destitution. Thus, even while we have studied the workings of the private realm in detail (Chapters 4, 8–16), there has also been an attempt to identify the right balance between this and the public realm (Chapters 2, 3, 6, 7, 16, and the present chapter).

There were a number of routes we could have followed in exploring the role of the State, and I was in several minds about them when beginning this work. On reflection, it seemed sensible to start with the general (i.e. the goals that should motivate governments and the reasons why: Chapters 2–5) and then shift to the more specific (i.e. the locus of government activity and community participation: Chapters 6–7, 10–13, and 16–17). To have conducted the entire analysis within the context of resource allocation mechanisms, as I have done, was inevitable: the allocation of resources is central to the concerns of political philosophy and the social sciences.

I have argued that, broadly speaking, human interests in poor countries are best served and promoted in an environment where the public realm of the socio-economic sphere of life is limited to the production and allocation of collective goods, among which a number are basic needs. They include infrastructure (e.g. roads, cables, ports, canals, potable water, and irrigation facilities), public goods (e.g. security, the establishment and enforcement of laws of property and contracts, and public health), common-property resources (e.g. rivers and rivulets, forests, grazing lands, village ponds and water tanks), primary health care, and school education. Nutrition is also a basic need; but, as it is a private good and is easily marketable, it requires a somewhat different treatment. Targeted food subsidies (e.g. through nutrition supplementation), food- (or cash-) for-work programmes, agrarian reform, and credit facilities for the poor are ways of ensuring that people in need do not face destitution. They are a vital part of the locus of government activity in poor countries.

In its central guise, the standard theory of resource allocation outlined in Chapter 7 was codified within a decade after the last world war. The extensions studied in this book have been developed since then. Details apart, and leaving aside the nuances I have added to it and the package I have tried to create for it, the theory and its extensions have been in the public domain for a number of years. And yet it has been much neglected in the economics of poor countries. It isn't that planners, development economists, economic journalists, and concerned world citizens have taken resource allocation theory too seriously; it is rather, that they haven't taken it seriously enough. The idea that the abstract bits of reasoning that drive the theory could be about the world as we know it has proved easy enough to resist. A systematic use of modern resource allocation theory for the purposes of delineating the spheres within which individuals, agencies, communities, and collectivities in an economy ought to operate has been a rare occurrence.[17] Meanwhile, the cost has been gigantic. All too often, governments have been encouraged to spend time and resources on matters at which they have proved singularly inept and intrusive (e.g. in the production of private goods, such as steel, machinery, chemicals, and motor cars) and have not been charged with performing vital functions (e.g. supplying collective goods, health and food security). Phrases such as 'public ownership of the means of production', 'priority to manufacturing industries for economic development', and 'centralized command and control for the purposes of resource mobilization' have proved enduring even while people have remained uneducated, and have visibly gone malnourished and diseased. Background liberties in the civil and political spheres; an effective legal, judicial and regulatory system; basic needs in

---

[17] I am exaggerating somewhat to make the point as forcefully as I can. For example, World Bank (1991a) reflects a shift in the thinking of many development economists. However, the document did not attempt to found its arguments on an analytical framework. It relied on case-studies and international cross-section data, without much attention to theory to guide it.

the socio-economic sphere; and, more broadly, the motivational forces necessary for the promotion of well-being, including a conscious attempt to separate the private and public sides of life, have not exactly held sway in most poor countries; nor have they attained the high ground in the economics of poor countries. And yet, a wide battery of evidence and considerations inform us that they are indeed the key determinants of a population's well-being.

Admittedly, there are other spheres in which the State can be active, and on occasion has been known to be effective. That the State played a key role through its industrial and commercial policies in several East Asian countries has been reiterated over the years (e.g. Datta-Choudhuri, 1978; Kim and Roemer, 1979; Kuo, Ranis and Fei, 1981; Kim and Yun, 1988; Amsden, 1989; Wade, 1990). I mentioned this earlier even while observing that governments in these countries were also much engaged with human resource development. If I have subsequently underplayed the potential role of strategic industrial and trade policies, it is because I do not know what general morals emerge from the East Asian experience in this field of government activity, other than a banality: that, if the State is resolute and smart, it may indeed be able to detect potential winners among industries and help them along through temporary tax incentives, tariff protection, and so forth. Strategic trade with the rest of the world is easier to talk about than to practise.[18] A recent statistical analysis by Thomas and Wang (1992) on cross-country time series for nearly 70 countries (including those in East Asia) over 1960–87 provides us with no grounds for thinking otherwise. In any event, poor countries are littered with failed or ailing projects that were once thought to be potential winners by the State and are still kept alive by it. This alone tells us something.

In a characteristically reflective passage, Bauer (1971) expressed the thought that, if governments in poor countries were to restrict their engagements to those spheres that are set out under the terms and conditions of something like a Minimal State, and were to try and discharge their duties well, they would have no time or resources left for any other activity. I have found this thought illuminating; it seems to me both right and wrong, and I think it is instructive to see why.

The list of activities in the public realm arrived at in this book is substantially larger than the one to be found in a Minimal State. Experience does not suggest that they are beyond the financial reach of poor countries. So it remains to be confirmed that our list does not contain items that ought not be entrusted to the State by its citizens for reasons of moral hazard. Now, two things stand out about all the items in the list we have compiled:

---

[18] Little (1982), Bhagwati (1988b), and World Bank (1991a) contain especially good analyses of why.

first, the duties are easily codifiable; and second, it is not a difficult matter for the public to assess their government's performance in these tasks (see Chapters 2–5; the role of a free press is vital here). This means that citizens, as principals to a contract, would not experience undue moral hazard if the list under discussion were to comprise the duties of the State. Of course, it may be that the country does not possess an adequate civil service (or for that matter sufficient technical personnel) for the State to be able to perform well. But that would be a different matter; it would relfect a lack of human capital, a symptom of the poverty of the nation. The task of developing this capital base would then be a matter of the utmost urgency.

Contrast the tasks in our list with, for example, one that requires the government to identify productive industries and further them along through suitable measures (trade protection, credit facilities, input subsidies, and so forth—the exact mix of the means doesn't matter). Simulating competition among rival government agencies in this task is usually not feasible, not only because industries are typically interlinked, but also because in a (small) poor country a fledgling industry would typically have only one production unit. I conclude that, for the perspective of the citizens, this particular responsibility of the State would be shot through with moral hazard: subsequent to a failure, it would prove next to impossible for the public to confirm that it was due to a genuine mistake on the part of the government. It is also hard to see what penalty the public could impose in the event of failure. As a rule, it would seem to make sense to leave the burden of industry selection to the private realm, where much of the relevant information lies.

The problem of moral hazard has been a recurring theme here. I have argued (Chapters 2 and 3) that it should be central to any reasoned conception of political philosophy, and thereby to a defendable political economy. To ignore it is to build a conception of the organization of life that makes no contact with life. Early in this work I suggested that it is often easier to agree on 'values' than on 'facts'. But 'facts' are of profound importance for judging the instrumental worth of the various ways we can live. For far too long, the State in poor countries has been identified with the public. I have tried to show that a number of commonly held notions about human well-being, together with some incontrovertible features of life, provide considerable cutting power for identifying something that may be called 'a right balance' between the public and private realms of a poor society. If it finds resonance among readers, it is because they too will have arrived at a similar conception, possibly for the very same reasons that I have identified in this book. Admittedly, what I am calling a 'right balance' has only been sketched here. But it couldn't have been otherwise. There are few sharp truths in an area of discourse so immediate and vital to the way people are able to live.

REFERENCES

Abramovitz, M. (1956), 'Resource and Output Trends in the United States since 1870', *American Economic Review* (Papers and Proceedings), 46.

Abreu, D. (1988), 'On the Theory of Infinitely Repeated Games with Discounting', *Econometrica*, 56.

Abreu, D. and D. Pearce (1989) 'A Perspective on Renegotiation in Repeated Games', mimeo, Hoover Institution, Stanford.

Acharya, M. and L. Bennett (1983), 'Women and the Subsistence Sector: Economic Participation and Household Decision-making in Nepal', World Bank Working Paper No. 526.

Adair, L. S. (1984), 'Marginal Intake and Maternal Adaptation: The Case of Rural Taiwan', in Pollitt and Amante (1984).

—— and E. Pollitt (1983), 'Seasonal Variation in Maternal Body Dimensions and Infant Birthweights', *American Journal of Physical Anthropology*, 62.

Adelman, I. (1975a), 'Development Economics: A Reassessment of Goals', *American Economic Review* (Papers and Proceedings), 66.

—— (1975b), 'Growth, Income Distribution and Equity Oriented Development Strategies', *World Development*, 3.

—— (1979), *Redistribution before Growth* (Leiden University Press).

—— (1980), 'Income Distribution, Economic Development and Land Reform', *American Behavioural Scientist*, 23.

—— and C. T. Morris (1967), *Society, Politics and Economic Development* (Baltimore: Johns Hopkins University Press).

—— —— (1973), *Economic Growth and Social Equity in Developing Countries* (Stanford, Cal.: Stanford University Press).

—— and S. Robinson (1989), 'Income Distribution and Development: A Survey', in Chenery and Srinivasan (1989).

Aebi, H. and R. G. Whitehead (eds) (1980), *Maternal Nutrition during Pregnancy and Lactation*, (Bern: Hans Huber).

Agarwal, A. (1990) 'Human–Nature Interactions: A Case Study of a Central Himalayan Village', in Dasgupta and Mäler (1992).

—— and S. Narain (1989), *Towards Green Villages: A Strategy for Environmentally Sound and Participatory Rural Development* (New Delhi: Centre for Science and Environment).

—— et al. (1986), *The State of India's Environment* (New Delhi: Centre for Science and Environment), first published 1982.

Agarwal, B. (1985), 'Work Participation of Rural Women in the Third World', *Economic and Political Weekly*, 20.

—— (1986), *Cold Hearths and Barren Slopes: The Woodfuel Crisis in the Third World* (New Delhi: Allied Publishers).

—— (1989), 'Rural Women, Poverty and Natural Resources: Sustenance, Sustainability and Struggle for Change', *Economic and Political Weekly*, 24.

—— (1990), 'Social Security and the Family in Rural India: Coping with Seasonality and Calamity', *Journal of Peasant Studies*, 17.

Ahluwalia, M. S. (1976a), 'Inequality, Poverty and Development', *Journal of Development Economics*, 3.

—— (1976b), 'Income Distribution and Development: Some Stylized Facts', *American Economic Review* (Papers and Proceedings), 66.

Ahmad, A. (1991), *Women and Fertility in Bangladesh* (New Delhi: Sage).

Ahmad, E. and N. H. Stern (1984), 'The Theory of Tax Reform and Indian Indirect Taxes', *Journal of Public Economics*, 25.

—— —— (1989), 'Taxation for Developing Countries', in Chenery and Srinivasan (1989).

—— —— (1991), *The Theory and Practice of Tax Reform in Developing Countries* (Cambridge: Cambridge University Press).

Ahmad, Y.-J., S. El Sarafy, and E. Lutz (eds.) (1989), *Environmental Accounting for Sustainable Development* (Washington, DC: World Bank).

Ahmed, I. (ed.) (1985), *Technology and Rural Women: Conceptual and Empirical Issues* (London: Allen & Unwin).

Aigner, D. J. and G. G. Cain (1977), 'Statistical Theories of Discrimination in the Labor Market', *Industrial and Labor Relations Review*, 30.

Akerlof, G. (1976), 'The Economics of Caste and of the Rat Race and Other Woeful Tales', *Quarterly Journal of Economics*, 90.

—— (1978), 'The Economics of "Tagging" as Applied to the Optimal Income Tax, Welfare Programs, and Manpower Planning', *American Economic Review*, 68.

—— (1980), 'A Theory of Social Custom, of which Unemployment May Be One Consequence', *Quarterly Journal of Economics*, 94.

Alamgir, M. (1980), *Famine in South Asia: Political Economy of Mass Starvation* (Cambridge, Mass.: Oelgescher, Gunn & Hain).

—— and P. Arora (1991), *Providing Food Security for All* (London: International Fund for Agricultural Development).

Alchian, A. (1963), 'Reliability of Progress Curves in Airframe Production', *Econometrica*, 31.

—— and H. Demsetz (1972), 'Production, Information Costs, and Economic Organization', *American Economic Review*, 62.

Alderman, H. (1990), 'Food Subsidies and the Poor', in D. Lal and H. Myint (eds.), *Essays on Poverty, Equity and Growth* (Washington, DC: World Bank).

—— and J. von Braun (1984), 'The Effects of the Egyptian Food Ration and Subsidy System on Income Distribution and Consumption', Research Report No. 45, International Food Policy Research Institute, Washington, DC.

—— and C. H. Paxson (1992), 'Do the Poor Insure: A Synthesis of the Literature on Risk and Consumption in Developing Countries', Discussion Paper No. 164, Research Program in Development Studies, Woodrow Wilson School, Princeton University.

Aleem, I. (1990), 'Imperfect Information, Screening and the Costs of Informal Lending: A Study of a Rural Credit Market in Pakistan', *World Bank Economic Review*, 4.

Alexander, S. (1974), 'Rawls's *A Theory of Justice*: Social Evaluation through Notional Choice', *Quarterly Journal of Economics*, 88.

Alfin-Slater, R. B. and D. Kritchevsky (eds.) (1980) *Nutrition and the Adults: Macronutrients* (New York: Plenum Press).

Allen, F. (1985), 'On the Fixed Nature of Sharecropping Contracts', *Economic Journal*, 95.

Amsden, A. (1989), *Asia's Next Giant: South Korea and Late Industrialization* (New York: Oxford University Press).

Anand, S. and C. Harris (1990), 'Food and Standard of Living: An Analysis Based on Sri Lankan Data', in J. Dreze and A. Sen (eds.), *The Political Economy of Hunger*, i (Oxford: Clarendon Press).

—— and S. M. R. Kanbur (1989a), 'Inequality and Development: A Critique', *Journal of Development Economics*, 16.

—— —— (1989b), 'The Kuznets Process and the Inequality–Development Relationship', *Journal of Development Economics*, 16.

Anderson, D. (1987), *The Economics of Afforestation: A Case Study in Africa* (Baltimore: Johns Hopkins University Press).

Anderson, Jock (1979), 'Perspective on Models of Uncertain Decisions', in Roumasset, Boussard and Singh (1979).

Anderson, Julie (1990), 'Does Regulation Improve Small Farmers' Access to Brazilian Rural Credit?' *Journal of Development Economics*, 33.

Anderson, P. W., K. J. Arrow, and D. Pines (eds.) (1988), *The Economy as an Evolving System* (Reading, Mass.: Addison-Wesley).

Apffel Marglin, F. and S. A. Marglin (eds.) (1990), *Dominating Knowledge: Development, Culture, and Resistance* (Oxford: Clarendon Press).

Aristotle, *Nicomachean Ethics*, tr. by J. A. K. Thompson (London: Penguin Books, 1976).

—— *The Politics*, tr. by C. Lord (Chicago: University of Chicago Press, 1984).

Arora, A. (1990), 'The Transfer of Tacit Knowledge: How Can Intellectual Property-Rights Legislation Help?' mimeo, Department of Economics, Stanford University.

Arrow, K. J. (1951), *Social Choice and Individual Values* (New York: John Wiley).

—— (1962a), 'Economic Welfare and the Allocation of Resources for Inventions', in R. Nelson, (ed.), *The Rate and Direction of Inventive Activity* (Princeton, NJ: Princeton University Press).

—— (1962b), 'The Economic Implications for Learning by Doing', *Review of Economic Studies*, 29.

—— (1963), *Social Choice and Individual Values*, 2nd edn, (New York: John Wiley).

—— (1964), 'The Role of Securities in the Optimal Allocation of Risk-Bearing', *Review of Economic Studies*, 31.

—— (1965), *Aspects of the Theory of Risk-Bearing* (Helsinki: Yrjo Jahnssonin-saatio).

—— (1971a), 'Political and Economic Evaluation of Social Effects of Externalities', in M. Intriligator (ed.), *Frontiers of Quantitative Economics*, i (Amsterdam: North-Holland).

—— (1971b), *Essays in the Theory of Risk-Bearing* (Amsterdam: North-Holland).

—— (1972), 'Gifts and Exchanges', *Philosophy and Public Affairs*, 1.

—— (1973a), 'Some Ordinalist–Utilitarian Notes on Rawls's Theory of Justice', *Journal of Philosophy*, 70.

—— (1973b), 'Rawls's Principle of Just Savings', *Swedish Journal of Economics*, 75.

—— (1974), *The Limits of Organization* (New York: W. W. Norton).

—— (1977), 'Extended Sympathy and the Possibility of Social Choice', *American Economic Review* (Papers and Proceedings), 67.

—— (1985), 'The Economics of Agency', in J. Pratt and R. Zeckhauser (eds.), *Principals and Agents: The Structure of Business* (Cambridge, Mass.: Harvard Business School Press).

—— and G. Debreu (1954), 'Existence of Equilibrium for a Competitive Economy', *Econometrica*, 22.

—— and A. Fisher (1974), 'Preservation, Uncertainty and Irreversibility', *Quarterly Journal of Economics*, 88.

—— and F. H. Hahn (1971), *General Competitive Analysis* (San Francisco: Holden-Day).

—— and M. Kurz (1970), *Public Investment, the Rate of Return and Optimal Fiscal Policy* (Baltimore: Johns Hopkins University Press).

Arthur, W. B. (1988), 'Urban Systems and Historical Path Dependence', in J. S. Ausubel and R. Herman (eds.), *Cities and their Vital Systems* (Washington, DC: National Academy Press).

—— (1989), 'Competing Technologies, Increasing Returns, and Lock-In by Historical Events', *Economic Journal*, 99,

—— Yu M. Ermoliev, and Yu M. Kaniovski (1987), 'Path Dependent Processes and the Emergence of Macro-Structure', *European Journal of Operations Research*, 30.

Asheim, G. B. (1990), 'Unjust Intergenerational Allocations', mimeo, Norwegian School of Economics and Business Administration, Bergen.

Asher, H. (1956), *Cost–Quantity Relationships in the Airframe Industry* (Santa Monica, Cal.: Rand Corporation).

Åstrand, P. O. and K. Rodahl (1986), *Textbook of Work Physiology* (New York: McGraw-Hill).

Atkinson, A. B. (1970), 'On the Measurement of Inequality', *Journal of Economic Theory*, 2.

—— (1975), *The Economics of Inequality* (Oxford: Clarendon Press).

—— and N. H. Stern (1974), 'Pigou, Taxation and Public Goods', *Review of Economic Studies*, 41.

—— and J. E. Stiglitz (1980), *Lectures in Public Economics* (New York: McGraw-Hill)

Auerbach, A. J. and M. Feldstein (eds.) (1985, 1987): *Handbook of Public Economics*, i and ii (Amsterdam: North-Holland).

Aumann, R. (1964), 'Markets with a Continuum of Traders', *Econometrica*, 32.

—— (1966), 'Existence of Competitive Equilibria in Markets with a Continuum of Traders', *Econometrica*, 34.

—— (1981), 'Survey of Repeated Games', in M. Shubik (ed.), *Essays in Game Theory and Mathematical Economics: Essays in Honour of Oscar Morgenstern* (Mannheim: Wissenschaftsverlag, Bibliographisches Institut).

—— (1987a), 'Correlated Equilibrium as an Expression of Bayesian Rationality', *Econometrica*, 55.

—— (1987b), 'Game Theory' in J. Eatwell, M. Milgate, and P. Newman (eds.), *The New Palgrave* (London: Macmillan).

—— (1990), 'Nash Equilibria are not Self-Enforcing', in J. J. Gabszewicz, J.-F. Richard, and L. A. Wolsey (eds.), *Economic Decision-Making: Games, Econometrics and Optimization* (Amsterdam: North-Holland).

—— and A. Brandenburger (1991), 'Epistemic Conditions for Nash Equilibrium', Working Paper No. 91–042, Harvard Business School.

—— and L. Shapley (1976), 'Long-Term Competition: A Game-Theoretical Analysis', mimeo, Department of Mathematics, Hebrew University.

Axelrod, R. (1984), *The Evolution of Cooperation* (New York: Basic Books).

—— (1986), 'An Evolutionary Approach to Norms', *American Political Science Review*, 80.

Bahl, R., C. K. Kim, and C. K. Park (1986), *Public Finances during the Korean Modernization Process* (Cambridge, Mass.: Harvard University Press).

Bairagi, R. (1981), 'On the Validity of Some Anthropometric Indicators as Predictors of Mortality' (letter to the editor), *American Journal of Clinical Nutrition*, 34.

—— (1983), 'Dynamics of Child Nutrition in Rural Bangladesh', *Ecology of Food and Nutrition*, 13.

—— (1986), 'Food Crisis, Nutrition and Female Children in Rural Bangladesh', *Population and Development Review*, 12.

Baker, S. H. and E. M. De Maeyer (1979), 'Nutritional Anemia: Its Understanding and Control with Special Reference to the Work of the World Health Organization', *American Journal of Clinical Nutrition*, 32.

Baland, J.-M. and D. Ray (1991), 'Why Does Asset Inequality Affect Unemployment? A Study of the Demand Composition Problem', *Journal of Development Economics*, 35.

Balazs, R. *et al.* (1986), 'Undernutrition and Brain Development', in Falkner and Tanner (1986).

Baldwin, R. (1969), 'The Case Against Infant-Industry Tariff Protection', *Journal of Political Economy*, 77.

Banister, J. (1984), 'An Analysis of Recent Data on the Population of China', *Population and Development Review*, 10.

—— (1987), *China's Changing Population* (Stanford, Cal.: Stanford University Press).

Banks, D. L. (1989), 'Patterns of Oppression: An Exploratory Analysis of Human-Rights Data', *Journal of the American Statistical Association*, 84.

Bannerjee, A. V., T. Besley, and T. W. Guinnane (1992), 'Thy Neighbor's Keeper: The Design of a Credit Cooperative with Theory and Evidence', Discussion Paper No. 160, Research Program in Development Studies, Woodrow Wilson School, Princeton University.

Barac-Nieto, M. (1987), 'Physical Work Determinants and Undernutrition', *World Review of Nutrition and Dietetics*, 49.

—— G. B. Spurr, and J. C. Reina (1984), 'Marginal Malnutrition in School-Aged

Colombian Boys: Body Composition and Maximal O$_2$ Consumption', *American Journal of Clinical Nutrition*, 39.

—— *et al.* (1978a), 'Aerobic Work Capacity in Chronically Undernourished Adult Males', *Journal of Applied Physiology*, 44.

—— *et al.* (1978b), 'Body Composition in Chronic Undernutrition', *American Journal of Clinical Nutrition*, 31.

—— *et al.* (1980), 'Aerobic Work Capacity and Endurance during Nutritional Repletion of Severely Undernourished Men', *American Journal of Clinical Nutrition*, 33.

Bardhan, K. (1985), 'Women's Work, Welfare and Status: Forces of Tradition and Change in India', *Economic and Political Weekly*, 20.

Bardhan, P. K. (1973a), 'Size, Productivity, and Returns to Scale: An Analysis of Farm Level Data in Indian Agriculture', *Journal of Political Economy*, 81.

—— (1973b), 'On the Incidence of Poverty in Rural India in the Sixties', *Economic and Political Weekly*, 8.

—— (1974), 'On Life and Death Questions', *Economic and Political Weekly*, 9 (Special Number).

—— (1983), 'Labour-Tying in a Poor Agrarian Economy: A Theoretical and Empirical Analysis', *Quarterly Journal of Economics*, 98.

—— (1984a), *Land, Labor and Rural Poverty* (New York: Columbia University Press).

—— (1984b), 'Determinants of Supply and Demand for Labour in a Poor Agrarian Economy: An Analysis of Household Survey Data from Rural West Bengal', in Binswanger and Rosenzweig (1984).

—— (1988), 'On the Economic Geography of Sex Disparity in Child Survival in India: A Note', mimeo, Department of Economics, University of California, Berkeley.

—— (ed.) (1989), *The Economic Theory of Agrarian Institutions* (Oxford: Clarendon Press).

—— and A. Rudra (1978), 'Interlinkage of Land, Labour and Credit Relations: An Analysis of Village Survey Data in East India', *Economic and Political Weekly*, 13.

—— —— (1980), 'Terms and Conditions of Sharecropping Contracts: An Analysis of Village Data in India', *Journal of Development Studies*, 16.

—— —— (1981), 'Terms and Conditions of Labour Contracts in Agriculture, 1979', *Oxford Bulletin of Economics and Statistics*, 43.

—— —— (1986), 'Labour Mobility and the Boundaries of the Village Economy'', *Journal of Peasant Studies*, 13.

—— and T. N. Srinivasan (eds.) (1988), *Poverty in South Asia* (New York: Colombia University Press).

Barghouti, S. and D. Lallement (1988), 'Water Management: Problems and Potentials in the Sahelian and Sudanian Zones', in Falloux and Mukendi (1988).

Barr, N. (1987), *The Economics of the Welfare State* (London: Weidenfeld & Nicolson).

Barraclough, S. (1977), 'Agricultural Production Prospects in Latin America', *World Development*, 5.

Barro, R. (1991), 'Economic Growth in a Cross Section of Countries', *Quarterly Journal of Economics*, 106.

—— and G. Becker (1989), 'Fertility Choice in a Model of Economic Growth', *Econometrica*, 57.

Barry, B. (1965), *Political Argument* (London: Routledge & Kegan Paul).

—— (1977), 'Rawls on Average and Total Utility: A Comment', *Philosophical Studies*.

—— (1978), *Sociologists, Economists and Democracy* (Chicago: University of Chicago Press).

Basta, S. *et al.* (1979), 'Iron Deficiency Anaemia and the Productivity of Adult Males in Indonesia', *American Journal of Clinical Nutrition*, 32.

Basu, A. M. (1989), 'Is Discrimination in Food Really Necessary for Explaining Sex Differentials in Childhood Mortality?' *Population Studies*, 43.

Basu, K. (1981), 'Food for Work Programmes: Beyond Roads That Get Washed Away', *Economic and Political Weekly*, 16.

—— (1987), 'Disneyland Monopoly, Interlinkage and Usurious Interest Rates', *Journal of Public Economics*, 34.

—— (1990), *Agrarian Structure and Economic Development* (London: Harwood).

—— (1992), 'The Broth and the Cooks: A Theory of Surplus Labour', *World Development*, 20.

Bates, R. H. (1981), *Markets and States in Tropical Africa: The Political Basis of Agricultural Policies* (Berkeley, Cal.: University of California Press).

—— (1983), *Essays on the Political Economy of Rural Africa* (Cambridge: Cambridge University Press).

Bauer, P. T. (1946), 'The Economics of Planting Density in Rubber Growing', *Economica*, 13.

—— (1954), *West African Trade*, (Cambridge: Cambridge University Press).

—— (1957), *Economic Analysis and Policy in Underdeveloped Countries* (Durham, NC: Duke University Press).

—— (1971), *Dissent on Development* (London: Weidenfeld & Nicolson).

—— (1981), *Equality, the Third World and Economic Delusion* (London: Weidenfeld & Nicolson).

—— (1984), *Reality and Rhetoric* (London: Weidenfeld & Nicolson).

—— (1987), 'Marketing Boards', in J. Eatwell, M. Milgate, and P. Newman (eds.): *The New Palgrave: A Dictionary of Economics* (London: Macmillan).

—— (1991), *The Development Frontier: Essays in Applied Economics* (Cambridge, Mass.: Harvard University Press).

—— and B. Yamey (1968), *Markets, Market Control and Marketing Reform* (London: Weidenfeld & Nicolson).

Baumol, W. M. (1982), 'Contestable Markets: An Uprising in the Theory of Industry Structure', *American Economic Review*, 72.

—— and W. E. Oates (1975), *The Theory of Environmental Policy* (Englewood Cliffs, NJ: Prentice-Hall).

—— J. C. Panzar, and R. D. Willig (1982), *Contestable Markets and the Theory of Industrial Structure* (New York: Harcourt, Brace, Jovanovich).

Bayles, M. (ed.) (1976), *Ethics and Population* (Cambridge, Mass.: Schenkman).

Bayliss Smith, T. (1981), 'Seasonality and Labour in the Rural Energy Balance', in Chambers, Longhurst and Pacey (1981).

Beato, P. and A. Mas-Colell (1985), 'On Marginal Cost Pricing with Given Tax-Subsidy Rules', *Journal of Economic Theory*, 37.

Beaton, G. H. (1981), 'Numerical Descriptors of the Nutrition Problem: An Analytical Comparison of FAO and World Bank Approaches', mimeo, Department of Nutrition and Food Science, University of Toronto.

—— (1983), 'Energy in Human Nutrition: Perspectives and Problems', *Nutrition Review*, 41.

—— (1985), 'The Significance of Adaptation in the Definition of Nutrient Requirements and for Nutrition Policy', in Blaxter and Waterlow (1985).

—— (1989), 'Small but Healthy? Are We Asking the Right Questions?' *European Journal of Clinical Nutrition*, 43.

Becker, G. (1960), 'An Economic Analysis of Fertility', in G. Becker (ed.), *Demographic and Economic Change in Developed Countries* (Princeton, NJ: Princeton University Press).

—— (1964), *Human Capital* (New York: Columbia University Press).

—— (1965), 'A Theory of the Allocation of Time', *Economic Journal*, 75.

—— (1967), *Human Capital and the Personal Distribution of Income: An Analytical Approach* (Ann Arbor, Mich.: Institute of Public Administration).

—— (1981), *A Treatise on the Family* (Cambridge, Mass.: Harvard University Press).

—— (1983), *Human Capital: A Theoretical and Empirical Analysis, with Special Reference to Education* (Chicago: University of Chicago Press).

—— and R. Barro (1986), 'Altruism and the Economic Theory of Fertility', *Population and Development Review*, 12 (Supplement).

—— —— (1988), 'A Reformulation of the Economic Theory of Fertility', *Quarterly Journal of Economics*, 103.

—— and H. G. Lewis (1973), 'Interaction between Quantity and Quality of Children', *Journal of Political Economy*, 81.

——, K. Murphy, and R. Tamura (1990), 'Human Capital, Fertility, and Economic Growth', *Journal of Political Economy*, 98.

—— and N. Tomes (1976), 'Child Endowments and the Quantity and Quality of Children', *Journal of Political Economy*, 84 (Supplement).

Behrman, J. (1987), 'Intrahousehold Allocation of Nutrients and Gender Effects', mimeo, University of Pennsylvania.

—— (1988a), 'Intrahousehold Allocation of Nutrients in Rural India: Are Boys Favoured? Do Parents Exhibit Inequality Aversion?' *Oxford Economic Papers*, 40.

—— (1988b), 'Nutrition, Health, Birth Order and Seasonality: Intrahousehold Allocation Among Children in Rural India', *Journal of Development Economics*, 28.

—— and A. B. Deolalikar (1987a), 'Will Developing Country Nutrition Improve with Income? A Case Study from Rural South India', *Journal of Political Economy*, 95.

—— —— (1987b), 'Seasonal Demands for Nutrient Intakes and Health Status in Rural South India', in D. E. Sahn, (ed.), *Causes and Implications of Seasonal Variability in Household Food Security* (Washington, DC: International Food Policy Research Institute).

—— —— (1988), 'Health and Nutrition', in Chenery and Srinivasan (1988).

—— —— (1990), 'Intra-Household Resource Allocation: An Inferential Approach', *Journal of Human Resources*, 25.

—— —— and B. L. Wolfe (1988), 'Nutrients: Impacts and Determinants', *World Bank Economic Review*, 2.

—— R. A. Pollak, and P. Taubman (1982), 'Parental Preferences and Provision for Progeny', *Journal of Political Economy*, 90.

—— and B. L. Wolfe (1984a), 'The Socioeconomic Impact of Schooling in a Developing Country', *Review of Economics and Statistics*, 66.

—— —— (1984b), 'More Evidence on Nutrition Demand: Income Seems Over-rated and Women's Schooling Underemphasized', *Journal of Development Economics*, 14.

Beisel, W. R. (1977), 'Resumé of the Discussion Concerning the Nutritional Consequences of Infection', *American Journal of Clinical Nutrition*, 30.

Bell, C. (1988), 'Credit Markets and Interlinked Transactions', in Chenery and Srinivasan (1988).

—— (1990), 'Interactions between Institutional and Informal Credit Agencies in Rural India', *World Bank Economic Review*, 4.

—— and T. N. Srinivasan (1989), 'Interlinked Transactions in Rural Markets: An Empirical Study of Andhra Pradesh, Bihar, and Punjab', *Oxford Bulletin of Economics and Statistics*, 51.

Bell, David E., H. Raiffa, and A. Tversky (eds.) (1988), *Decision Making: Descriptive, Normative and Prescriptive Interactions* (Cambridge: Cambridge University Press).

Bell, D. and M. R. Reich (eds.) (1988), *Health, Nutrition and Economic Crises* (Dover, Mass.: Auburn House).

Benedict, F. *et al.* (1919), *Human Vitality and Efficiency under Prolonged Restricted Diet* (Washington, DC: Carnegie Institution).

Beneria, L. (1981), 'Conceptualising the Labour Force: The Underestimation of Women's Economic Activities', *Journal of Development Studies*, 17.

—— (ed.) (1983), *Women and Development: The Sexual Division of Labour in Rural Economies* (Geneva: International Labour Office).

Benn, S. and R. Peters (1959), *Social Principles and the Democratic State* (London: Allen & Unwin).

Bennett, L. (1989), 'The Role of Women in Income Production and Intra-Household Allocation of Resources as a Determinant of Child Nutrition and Health', *Food and Nutrition Bulletin*, 10.

Benoit, J.-P. and V. Krishna (1985), 'Finitely Repeated Games', *Econometrica*, 53.

Ben-Porath, Y. (1976), 'Fertility Response to Child Mortality: Micro Data from Israel', *Journal of Political Economy*, 84; reprinted in Preston (1978).

Berg, A. (1987), *Malnutrition: What Can be Done?* (Baltimore: Johns Hopkins University Press).

Bergson, A. (1938), 'A Reformulation of Certain Aspects of Welfare Economics', *Quarterly Journal of Economics*, 52.

Berlin, I. (1969), 'Two Concepts of Liberty', in *Four Essays on Liberty* (Oxford: Oxford University Press).

Bernheim, B. D. (1984), 'Rationalizable Strategic Behaviour', *Econometrica*, 52.

—— (1991), 'How Strong are Bequest Motives? Evidence Based on Estimates of the Demand for Life Insurance and Annuities', *Journal of Political Economy*, 99.

—— and D. Ray (1987a), 'Economic Growth with Intergenerational Altruism', *Review of Economic Studies*, 54.

—— —— (1987b), 'Collective Dynamic Consistency in Repeated Games', mimeo, Stanford University.

—— A. Shleifer, and L. H. Summers (1985), 'The Strategic Bequest Motive', *Journal of Political Economy*, 93.

Berreman, G. D. (1962), 'Village Exogamy in Northernmost India', *Southwestern Journal of Anthropology*, 18.

Berry, R. A. and W. Cline (1979), *Agrarian Structure and Productivity in Developing Countries* (Baltimore: Johns Hopkins University).

Besley, T. (1992), 'How Do Market Failures Justify Interventions in Rural Credit Markets?' Discussion Paper No. 162, Research Program in Development Studies, Woodrow Wilson School, Princeton University.

—— and S. Coate (1991), 'The Design of Income Maintenance Programs', Discussion Paper No. 74, John M. Olin Program for the Study of Economic Organization and Public Policy, Woodrow Wilson School, Princeton University.

—— —— (1992), 'Workfare vs. Welfare: Incentive Arguments for Work Requirements in Poverty Alleviation Programs', *American Economic Review*, 82.

—— —— and G. Loury (1992), 'The Economics of Rotating Savings and Credit Associations', *American Economic Review*, 82.

—— and R. Kanbur (1988), 'Food Subsidies and Poverty Alleviation', *Economic Journal*, 98.

Betancourt, R. (1971), 'The Normal Income Hypothesis in Chile', *Journal of the American Statistical Association*, 66.

Beteille, A. (ed.) (1983), *Equality and Inequality: Theory and Practice* (Delhi: Oxford University Press).

—— (1987), 'Equality as a Right and as a Policy', *LSE Quarterly*, 1.

Bewley, T. (1977), 'The Permanent Income Hypothesis: A Theoretical Formulation', *Journal of Economic Theory*, 16.

Bhagwati, J. (1973), 'Education, Class Structure, and Income Inequality', *World Development*, 1.

—— (1982), 'Directly Unproductive, Profit Seeking (DUP) Activities', *Journal of Political Economy*, 90.

—— (1988a) 'Poverty and Public Policy', *World Development*, 16.

—— (1988b), *Protectionism* (Cambridge, Mass.: MIT Press).

—— and P. Desai (1970), *India: Planning for Industrialization* (Oxford: Oxford University Press).

—— and T. N. Srinivasan (1983), *Lectures on International Trade* (Cambridge, Mass.: MIT Press).

Bhalla, S. (1986), 'Is Sri Lanka an Exception? A Comparative Study of Living Standards', in Bardhan and Srinivasan (1986).

—— and P. Glewwe (1986), 'Growth and Equity in Developing Countries: A Reinterpretation of the Sri Lankan Experience', *World Bank Economic Review*, 1.

Bharadwaj, K. (1974), *Production Conditions in Indian Agriculture* (Cambridge: Cambridge University Press).

Bhargava, A. (1991), 'Estimating Short and Long Run Income Elasticities of Foods and Nutrients for Rural South India', *Journal of the Royal Statistical Society* A, 154.

—— (1992), 'Malnutrition and the Role of Individual Variation with Evidence from India and the Philippines', *Journal of the Royal Statistical Society* A, 155.

Bhattacharji, S. (1991), 'Economic Rights of Ancient Indian Women', *Economic and Political Weekly*, 26.

Bhattacharya, N. *et al.* (1991), 'How Do the Poor Survive?' *Economic and Political Weekly*, 26.

Bhende, M. J. (1986), 'Credit Markets in Rural South India', *Economic and Political Weekly*, 21.

Bienen, H. (ed.) (1968), '*The Military Intervenes: Case Studies in Political Development* (New York: Russell Sage).

Bigsten, A. (1983), *Income Distribution and Development: Theory, Evidence and Policy* (London: Heinemann).

Binmore, K. (1987), 'Nash Bargaining Theory II', in K. Binmore and P. Dasgupta (eds.), *The Economics of Bargaining* (Oxford: Basil Blackwell).

—— (1989), 'Social Contract I: Harsanyi and Rawls', *Economic Journal*, 99 (Supplement).

—— and P. Dasgupta (1986), 'Game Theory: A Survey', in K. Binmore and P. Dasgupta (eds.), *Economic Organizations as Games* (Oxford: Basil Blackwell).

—— —— (1987), 'Nash Bargaining Theory: An Introduction', in K. Binmore and P. Dasgupta, (eds.), *The Economics of Bargaining* (Oxford: Basil Blackwell).

Binswanger, H. (1981), 'Attitudes towards Risk: Theoretical Implications of an Experiment in Rural India', *Economic Journal*, 91.

—— (1986), 'Risk Aversion, Collateral Requirements and the Markets for Credit and Insurance in Rural Areas', in P. Hazell, C. Pomareda, and A. Valdes (eds.), *Crop Insurance for Agricultural Development: Issues and Experiences* (Baltimore: Johns Hopkins University Press).

—— (1989), 'Brazilian Policies that Encourage Deforestation in the Amazon', World Bank Environment Department Paper No. 16.

—— *et al.* (1984), 'Common Features and Contrasts in Labour Relations in the Semiarid Tropics of India', in Binswanger and Rosenzweig (1984b).

—— *et al.* (1985), 'Credit Markets in Rural India: Theoretical Issues and Empirical Analysis', Report No. 45, Agriculture and Rural Development Department, World Bank.

—— and J. McIntire (1987), 'Behavioural and Material Determinants of Production Relations in Land-Abundant Tropical Agriculture', *Economic Development and Cultural Change*, 36.

—— —— and C. Udry (1989), 'Production Relations in Semi-arid African Agriculture', in Bardhan (1989).

—— and M. R. Rosenzweig (1984a), 'Contractual Arrangements, Employment and Wages in Rural Labor Markets: A Critical Review', in Binswanger and Rosenzweig (1984b).

—— —— (eds.) (1984b), *Contractual Arrangements, Employment and Wages in Rural Labor Markets in Asia* (New Haven, Conn.: Yale University Press).

—— —— (1986a), 'Behavioural and Material Determinants of Production Relations in Agriculture', *Journal of Development Studies*, 22.

—— —— (1986b), 'Credit Markets, Wealth and Endowments in Rural South India', Report No. 59, Agriculture and Rural Development Department, World Bank.

—— (1989), 'Wealth, Weather Risk and the Composition of Agricultural Investment', mimeo, World Bank.

Birdsall, N. (1977), 'Analytical Approaches to the Relationship of Population Growth and Devlopment', *Population and Development Review*, 3.

—— (1988), 'Economic Approaches to Population Growth', in H. Chenery and T. N. Srinivasan (eds.), *Handbook of Development Economics*, i (Amsterdam: North-Holland).

—— and D. Jamison (1983), 'Income and Other Factors Influencing Fertility in China', *Population and Development Review*, 9.

—— and W. P. McGreevey (1983), 'Women, Poverty and Development', in Buvinic, Lycette and McGreevey (1983).

Biswas, M. and P. Pinstrup-Andersen (eds.) (1985), *Nutrition and Development* (Oxford: Oxford University Press).

Black, F. and M. Scholes (1973), 'The Pricing of Options and Corporate Liabilities', *Journal of Political Economy*, 81.

Blackorby, C. and D. Donaldson (1985), 'Social Criteria for Evaluating Population Change', *Journal of Public Economics*, 28.

—— —— (1988), 'Cash versus Kind, Self Selection, and Efficient Transfers', *American Economic Review*, 78.

—— —— and J. Weymark (1984), 'Social Choice with Interpersonal Utility Comparisons', *International Economic Review*, 25.

Blaxter, K. and J. C. Waterlow (eds.) (1985), *Nutritional Adaptation in Man* (London: John Libbey).

Bleek, W. (1987), 'Family and Family Planning in Southern Ghana', in C. Oppong (ed.), *Sex Roles, Population and Development in West Africa* (Portsmouth, NH: Heinemann).

Bliss, C. (1975), *Capital Theory and the Distribution of Income* (Amsterdam: North-Holland).

—— and N. Stern (1978a), 'Productivity, Wages and Nutrition, 1: The Theory', *Journal of Development Economics*, 5.

—— —— (1978b), 'Productivity, Wages and Nutrition, 2: Some Observations', *Journal of Development Economics*, 5.

—— —— (1982), *Palanpur: The Economy of an Indian Village* (Oxford: Clarendon Press).

Blitzer, C., P. Dasgupta, and J. Stiglitz (1981), 'Project Appraisal and the Foreign Exchange Constraint', *Economic Journal*, 91.

Blurton Jones, N. G. and R. M. Sibly (1978), 'Testing Adaptiveness of Culturally Determined Behaviour: Do Bushmen Women Maximize their Reproductive Success by Spacing Births Widely and Foraging Seldom?' in N. G. Blurton Jones and V. Reynolds (eds.), *Human Behaviour and Adaptations* (London: Taylor & Francis).

Boadway, R. (1975), 'Cost Benefit Rules in General Equilibrium', *Review of Economic Studies*, 42.

—— and N. Bruce (1984), *Welfare Economics* (Oxford: Basil Blackwell).

Bongaarts, J. (1978), 'A Framework for Analyzing the Proximate Determinants of Fertility', *Population and Development Review*, 4.

—— (1980), 'Does Malnutrition Affect Fecundity? A Summary of the Evidence', *Science*, 208.

—— (1984), 'Implications of Future Fertility Trends for Contraceptive Practice', *Population and Development Review*, 10.

—— and M. Cain (1981), *Demographic Responses to Famine* (New York: Population Council).

—— and R. G. Potter (1983), *Fertility, Biology and Behavior: An Analysis of the Proximate Determinants* (New York: Academic Press).

Bonner, R. (1988), 'Famine in the Sudan', *The New Yorker*, 13 March.

Boserup, E. (1965), *The Conditions of Agricultural Growth* (London: Allen & Unwin).

—— (1970), *Women's Role in Economic Development* (London: St Martin's Press).

—— (1976), 'Environment, Population, and Technology in Primitive Societies', *Population and Development Review*, 2.

—— (1981), *Population Growth and Technological Change: A Study of Long-Term Trends* (Chicago: University of Chicago Press).

—— (1985), 'Economic and Demographic Interrelations in Sub-Saharan Africa', *Population and Development Review*, 11.

Boskin, M. and L. Lau (1990a), 'Capital Formation and Economic Growth', CEPR Publication No. 214, Stanford University.

—— —— (1990b), 'Post-War Economic Growth in the Group-of-Five Countries: A New Analysis', CEPR Publication No. 217, Stanford University.

Bouis, H. and L. Haddad (1989), 'The Tenure, Income, Consumption and Nutrition Effects of Agricultural Commercialization: A Philippines Case Study', Discussion Paper No. 93, Development Economics Research Centre, University of Warwick.

Bourne, K. L. and G. M. Walker Jr (1991), 'The Differential Effect of Mothers' Education on Mortality of Boys and Girls in India', *Population Studies*, 45.

Boussard, J.-M. (1979), 'Risk and Uncertainty in Programming Models: A Review', in Roumasset, Boussard and Singh (1979).

Bowes, P. (1978), *Hindu Intellectual Tradition* (New Delhi: Allied Publishers).

Boyd, R. and P. J. Richerson (1985), *Culture and the Evolutionary Process* (Chicago: University of Chicago Press).

Brandenberger, A. and E. Dekel (1989), 'The Role of Common Knowledge Assumptions in Game Theory', in F. Hahn (ed.), *The Economics of Missing Markets, Information and Games* (Oxford: Oxford University Press).

Braun, J. von and E. Kennedy (1986), *Commercialization of Subsistence Agriculture: Nutritional Effects in Developing Countries* (Washington DC: International Food Policy Research Institute).

Braverman, A. and L. Gausch (1984), 'Capital Requirements, Screening and Interlinked Sharecropping and Credit Contracts', *Journal of Development Economics*, 14.

—— and T. N. Srinivasan (1981), 'Credit and Sharecropping in Agrarian Societies', *Journal of Development Economics*, 9.

—— —— (1984), 'Agrarian Reforms in Developing Rural Economies Characterized by Interlinked Credit and Tenancy Markets', in Binswanger and Rosenzweig (1984b).

—— and J. E. Stiglitz (1982), 'Sharecropping and the Interlinking of Agrarian Markets', *American Economic Review*, 72.

—— —— (1986), 'Cost Sharing Arrangements under Sharecropping: Moral Hazard, Incentive Flexibility and Risk', *American Journal of Agricultural Economics*, 68.

Braybrooke, D. (1987), *Meeting Needs* (Princeton, NJ: Princeton University Press).

Breslin, P. and M. Chapin (1984), 'Conservation Kuna-Style', *Grassroots Development*, 8.

Briend, A. (1990), 'Is Diarrhoea a Major Cause of Malnutrition among the Under-Fives in Developing Countries? A Review of Available Evidence', *European Journal of Clinical Nutrition*, 44.

—— B. Wojtyniak, and M. G. M. Rowland (1987), 'Arm Circumference and Other Factors in Children at High Risk of Death in Rural Bangladesh', *Lancet*, 2.

—— *et al.* (1989), 'Nutritional Status, Age and Survival: The Muscle Mass Hypothesis', *European Journal of Clinical Nutrition*, 43.

Brockman, L. and H. Ricciuti (1971), 'Severe Protein-Calorie Malnutrition and Cognitive Development in Infancy and Early Childhood', *Development Psychology*, 4.

Broome, J. (1991), 'Utility', *Economics and Philosophy*, 7.

Brown, D. (1990), 'Equilibrium Analysis with Non-Convex Technologies', forthcoming in W. Hildenbrand and H. Sonnenschein (eds.), *Handbook of Mathematical Economics*, iv (Amsterdam: North-Holland).

—— and G. Heal (1979), 'Equity, Efficiency and Increasing Returns', *Review of Economic Studies*, 46.

—— —— (1983), 'The Optimality of Regulated Pricing: A General Equilibrium Analysis', in C. Aliprantis and A. Burkinshaw (eds.), *Advances in Equilibrium Theory* (Berlin: Springer-Verlag).

—— W. P. Heller, and R. M. Starr (1990), 'Two-Part Marginal Cost Pricing Equilibria: Existence and Efficiency', mimeo, Stanford University.

Brown, G. and C. B. McGuire (1967), 'A Socially Optimum Pricing Policy for a Public Water Agency', *Water Resources Research*, 3.

Brown, L. A. and B. Lentneck (1973), 'Innovation Diffusion in a Developing Country: A Mesoscale View', *Economic Development and Cultural Change*, 21.

Brown, L. R. *et al.* (1991), *State of the World* (New York: W. W. Norton).

Brown, W. N. (1970), *Man in the Universe: Some Cultural Continuities in Indian Thought* (Berkeley: University of California Press).

Brozek, J. (1982), 'The Impact of Malnutrition on Behaviour', in N. S. Scrimshaw and M. B. Wallerstein (eds.), *Nutrition Policy Implementation: Issues and Experience* (New York: Plenum Press).

Bruce, J. (1989), 'Homes Divided', *World Development*, 17.

Brun, T. (1984), 'Physiological Measurement of Activity among Adults under Free Living Conditions', in Pollitt and Amante (1984).

Brundtland, G. H. *et al.* (1987), *Our Common Future*, report by the World Commission on Environment and Development (New York: Oxford University Press).

Buchanan, J. (1975), *The Limits of Liberty: Between Anarchy and Leviathan* (Chicago: University of Chicago Press).

Bulatao, R. A. and R. D. Lee (eds.) (1983), *Determinants of Fertility in Developing Countries*, 2 vols. (New York: Academic Press).

Burgess, R. and N. Stern (1991), 'Taxation and Development', *Journal of Economic Literature*, 29.

Buskirk, E. R. and J. Mendez (1980), 'Energy: Caloric Requirements', in Alfin-Slater and Kritchevsky (1980).

Buvinic, M. (1983), 'Women's Issues in Third World Poverty: A Policy Analysis', in Buvinic, Lycette and McGreevey (1983).

—— M. A. Lycette, and W. P. McGreevey (eds.) (1983), *Women and Poverty in the Third World* (Baltimore: Johns Hopkins University Press).

Cain, M. (1977), 'The Economic Activities of Children in a Village in Bangladesh', *Population and Development Review*, 3.

—— (1978), 'The Household Life Cycle and Economic Mobility in Rural Bangladesh', *Population and Development Review*, 4.

—— (1981), 'Risk and Insurance: Perspectives on Fertility and Agrarian Change in India and Bangladesh', *Population and Development Review*, 7.

—— (1982), 'Perspectives on Family and Fertility in Developing Countries', *Population Studies*, 36.

—— (1983), 'Fertility as an Adjustment to Risk', *Population and Development Review*, 9.

—— (1984), 'Women's Status and Fertility in Developing Countries: Son Preference and Economic Security', World Bank Staff Working Paper No. 682.

—— S. R. Khanan, and S. Nahar (1979), 'Class, Patriarchy and Women's Work in Bangladesh', *Population and Development Review*, 5.

—— and A. B. Mozumder (1980), 'Labour Market Structure, Child Employment and Reproductive Behaviour in Rural South Asia', Working Paper No. 89, WEP 2–21, International Labour Organization.

Caldwell, J. C. (ed.) (1975), *Population Growth and Socioeconomic Change in West Africa* (New York: Columbia University Press).

—— (1976), 'Toward a Restatement of Demographic Theory', *Population and Development Review*, 2.

—— (1977a), 'The Economic Rationality of High Fertility: An Investigation Illustrated with Nigerian Data', *Population Studies*, 31.

—— (1977b), *The Persistence of High Fertility: Population Prospects in the Third World* (Canberra: Australian National University Press).

—— (1979), 'Education as a Factor in Mortality Decline: An Examination of Nigerian Data', *Population Studies*, 33.

—— (1981), 'The Mechanisms of Demographic Change in Historical Perspective', *Population Studies*, 35.

—— (1982), *Theory of Fertility Decline* (New York: Academic Press).

—— (1986), 'Routes to Low Mortality in Poor Countries', *Population and Development Review*, 12.

—— (1991), 'The Soft Underbelly of Development: Demographic Transition in Conditions of Limited Economic Change', *Proceedings of the World Bank Annual Conference on Development Economics, 1990*, (supplement to the *World Bank Economic Review* and the *World Bank Economic Observer*).

—— and P. Caldwell (1987), 'The Cultural Context of High Fertility in sub-Saharan Africa', *Population and Development Review*, 13.

—— —— (1990), 'High Fertility in Sub-Saharan Africa', *Scientific American*, 262 (May).

—— —— (1992), 'Population Growth, Physical Resources and Human Resources in sub-Saharan Africa', forthcoming in P. Dasgupta, K.-G. Mäler and A. Vercelli (eds.), *The Economics of Transnational Commons* (Oxford: Clarendon Press).

—— P. H. Reddy, and P. Caldwell (1986), 'Periodic High Risk as a Cause of Fertility Decline in a Changing Rural Environment: Survival Strategies in the 1980–1983 South Indian Drought', *Economic Development and Cultural Change*, 34.

—— —— —— (1988), *The Causes of Demographic Change* (Madison, Wis.: University of Wisconsin Press).

—— et al. (eds.) (1990), *Health Transition: The Cultural, Social and Behavioural Determinants of Health*, i and ii (Canberra: Australian National University Press).

Caliendo, M. A. (1979), *Nutrition and the World Food Crisis*, (New York: Macmillan).

Calvo, G. (1978), 'Some Notes on Time Inconsistency and Rawls's Maxi-Min Criterion', *Review of Economic Studies*, 45.

Canning, D. (1989), 'Convergence to Equilibrium in a Sequence of Games with Learning', ST/ICERD Economic Theory Discussion Paper No. 89/190, London School of Economics.

—— (1990), 'Social Equilibrium', Economic Theory Discussion Paper No. 150, Department of Applied Economics, University of Cambridge.

Caplin, A. and B. Nalebuff (1991), 'Aggregation and Imperfect Competition: On the Existence of Equilibrium', *Econometrica*, 59.

Carmichael, A. G. (1983), 'Infection, Hidden Hunger, and History', *Journal of Interdisciplinary History*, 14.

Carter, M. R. (1984), 'Identification of the Inverse Relationship between Farm Size and Productivity: An Empirical Analysis of Peasant Agricultural Production', *Oxford Economic Papers*, 36.

Cashdan, E. (1983), 'Territoriality among Human Foragers: Ecological Models and an Application to Four Bushman Groups', *Current Anthropology*, 24.

—— (1985), 'Coping with Risk: Reciprocity among the Basarwa of Northern Botswana', *Man*, 20.

—— (ed.) (1989), *Risk and Uncertainty in Tribal and Peasant Economies* (Boulder, Colo.: Westview Press).

Cass, D. (1965), 'Optimum Growth in an Aggregative Model of Capital Accumulation', *Review of Economic Studies*, 32.

Cassen, R. (1978), *India: Population, Economy, Society* (London: Macmillan).

Cecelski, E. (1987), 'Energy and Rural Women's Work: Crisis, Response and Policy Alternatives', *International Labour Review*, 126.

Celedon, J. M. and I. de Andraca (1979), 'Psychomotor Development during Treatment of Severely Marasmic Infants', *Early Human Development*, 3.

Chakravarty, S. (1969), *Capital and Development Planning* (Cambridge, Mass.: MIT Press).

Chambers, R., R. Longhurst, and A. Pacey (eds.) (1981), *Seasonal Dimensions to Rural Poverty* (London: Francis Pinter).

Chandra, R. (1983), 'Malnutrition and Immunocompetence: An Overview' in J. A. Bellanti (ed.), *Acute Diarrhoea: Its Nutritional Consequences* (New York: Raven Press).

Chatterjee, M. and J. Lambert (1989), 'Women and Nutrition: Reflections from India and Pakistan', *Food and Nutrition Bulletin*, 11.

Chatterjee, S. (1991), *Some Aspects of Economic Inequality in India*, Ph.D. dissertation, Department of Economics, Visva Bharati University, Santiniketan.

Chaudhuri, D. P. (1979), *Education, Innovation and Agricultural Development* (London: Croom Helm).

Chavez, A. and C. Martinez (1979), 'Consequences of Insufficient Nutrition in Child Character and Behaviour', in D. A. Levitsky (ed.), *Malnutrition, Environment and Behaviour* (Ithaca, NY: Cornell University Press).

—— —— (1984), 'Behavioural Measurements of Activity in Children and their Relation to Food Intake in a Poor Community', in Pollitt and Amante (1984).

Chen, L. C. (1982), 'Where Have the Women Gone? Insights from Bangladesh on the Low Sex Ratio of India's Population', *Economic and Political Weekly*, 17.

—— (1983), 'Evaluating the Health Benefits of Improved Water Supply through Assessment of Nutritional Status in Developing Countries', in Underwood (1983).

—— (1986), 'Primary Health Care in Developing Countries: Overcoming Operational, Technical and Social Barriers', *Lancet*, 2.

—— *et al.* (1974), 'Maternal Mortality in Rural Bangladesh', *Studies in Family Planning*, 5.

—— A. K. M. A. Chowdhury, and S. Huffman (1979), 'Seasonal Dimensions of Energy–Protein Malnutrition in Rural Bangladesh: The Role of Agriculture, Dietary Practices, and Infection', *Ecology of Food and Nutrition, 8.*

—— ——— (1980), 'Anthropometric Assessment of Energy–Protein Malnutrition and Subsequent Risk of Mortality among Preschool-Aged Children', *American Journal of Clinical Nutrition*, 33.

—— E. Huq, and S. D'Souza (1981), 'Sex Bias in the Family Allocation of Food and Health Care in Bangladesh', *Population and Development Review*, 7.

—— and N. S. Scrimshaw (eds.) (1983), *Diarrhea and Malnutrition: Interactions, Mechanisms and Interventions* (New York: Plenum Press).

Chen, M. A. (1989), 'Women's Work in Indian Agriculture by Agro-Ecologic Zones: Meeting Needs of Landless and Land-Poor Women', *Economic and Political Weekly*, 24.

Chenery, H., S. Robinson, and M. Syrquin (1986), *Industrialization and Growth* (New York: Oxford University Press).

—— and T. N. Srinivasan (eds) (1988, 1989), *Handbook of Development Economics*, i and ii (Amsterdam: North-Holland).

—— *et al.* (1974), *Redistribution with Growth* (New York: Oxford University Press).

Chiswick, B. (1974), *Income Inequality: Regional Analysis within a Human Capital Framework* (New York: National Bureau of Economic Research).

Chomitz, K. M. and N. Birdsall (1991), 'Incentives for Small Families: Concepts and Issues', *Proceedings of the World Bank Annual Conference on Development Economics 1990*, (Washington, DC: World Bank).

Chopra, K., G. K. Kadekodi, and M. N. Murty (1989), *Participatory Development: People and Common Property Resources* (New Delhi: Sage Publications).

Chowdhury, A. K. M. A. (1985), 'Maternal Nutrition in Rural Bangladesh', in Jain and Bannerjee (1985).

—— (1988), 'Child Mortality in Bangladesh: Food versus Health Care', *Food and Nutrition Bulletin*, 10.

—— and L. C. Chen (1977), 'The Interaction of Nutrition, Infection and Mortality during Recent Food Crises in Bangladesh', *Food Research Institute Studies*, 16.

—— A. R. Khan, and L. C. Chen (1978), 'Experience in Bangladesh and Pakistan', in Preston (1978).

—— *et al.* (1990) 'Does Malnutrition Predispose to Diarrhoea during Childhood? Evidence from a Longitudinal Study in Matlab, Bangladesh', *European Journal of Clinical Nutrition*, 44.

Christian, J. (1991), 'Liberalism and Individual Positive Freedom', *Ethics*, 101.

Christian, P. *et al.* (1988), 'The Role of Maternal Literacy and Nutrition Knowledge in Determining Children's Nutritional Status', *Food and Nutrition Bulletin*, 10.

Chung, K. R. (1991), 'A Bioeconomic Analysis of Wage and Human Capital Relationships: Evidence from Rural Guatemala', Ph.D. dissertation, Food Research Institute, Stanford University.

Cigno, A. (1991), *Economics of the Family* (Oxford: Clarendon Press).

Clark, C. W. (1976), *Mathematical Bioeconomics: The Optimal Management of Renewable Resources* (New York: John Wiley).

Clark, W. C. (1989), 'Managing Planet Earth', *Scientific American*, 261.

Cleland, J. and G. Rodriguez (1988), 'The Effect of Parental Education on Marital Fertility in Developing Countries', *Population Studies*, 42.

Cline, W. (1970), *Economic Consequences of Land Reform in Brazil* (Amsterdam: North-Holland).

—— (1975), 'Distribution and Development: A Survey of the Literature', *Journal of Development Economics*, 1.

Coale, A. J. and J. T. Trussell (1974), 'Model Fertility Schedules: Variations in the Age Structure of Childbearing in Human Populations', *Population Index*, 40.

—— and S. Watkins (eds.) (1984), *The Decline of Fertility in Europe* (Princeton, NJ: Princeton University Press).

Coase, R. (1960), 'The Problem of Social Cost', *Journal of Law and Economics*, 3.

Cochrane, S. H. (1979), *Fertility and Education: What Do We Really Know?* (Baltimore: Johns Hopkins University Press).

—— (1983), 'Effects of Education and Urbanization on Fertility', in R. Bulatao and R. Lee (eds.), *Determinants of Fertility in Developing Countries*, ii (New York: Academic Press).

—— (1991), 'Comments on "The Soft Underbelly of Development: Demographic Transition in Conditions of Limited Economic Change"', *Proceedings of the World Bank Annual Conference on Development Economics, 1990*, (Washington, DC: World Bank).

—— and S. M. Farid (1989), 'Fertility in Sub-Saharan Africa: Analysis and Explanation', World Bank Discussion Paper No. 43, Washington, DC.

—— J. Leslie, and D. O'Hara (1982), 'Parental Education and Health: Intracountry Evidence', *Health Policy and Education*, 2.

—— *et al*. (1980), 'Effects of Education on Health', World Bank Staff Working Paper No. 405.

Cohen, G. (1991), 'Incentives, Inequality and Community', Tanner Lectures in Human Values, Stanford University.

Cohen, J. (1980), 'Land Tenure and Rural Development in Africa', in R. H. Bates and M. F. Lofchie (eds.), *Agricultural Development in Africa: Issues of Public Policy* (New York: Praeger).

Cohen, J. S. and M. L. Weitzman (1975), 'A Marxian View of Enclosures', *Journal of Development Economics*, 1.

Collier, D. (ed.) (1979), *The New Authoritarianism in Latin America* (Princeton, NJ: Princeton University Press).

Collier, P. (1983), 'Malfunctioning of African Rural Factor Markets: Theory and a Kenyan Example', *Oxford Bulletin of Economics and Statistics*, 45.

Collins, K. J. and D. F. Roberts (eds.) (1988), *Capacity for Work in the Tropics* (Cambridge: Cambridge University Press).

Colombo, M. and I. Lopez (1980), 'Evolution of Psychomotor Development in Severely Undernourished Infants Submitted to an Integral Rehabilitation', *Pediatrics Research*, 14.

Colson, W. (1979), 'In Good Years and in Bad: Food Strategies of Self-Reliant Societies', *Journal of Anthropological Research*, 35.

Commander, S. (1983), 'The Jajmani System in North India: An Examination of its Logic and Status Across Two Centuries', *Modern Asian Studies*, 17.

Cooper, Richard (1975), 'An Economist's View of the Oceans', *Journal of World Trade Law*, 9.

Cooper, Russell and A. John (1988), 'Coordinating Coordination Failures in Keynesian Models', *Quarterly Journal of Economics*, 103.

Cotts Watkins, S. (1990), 'From Local to National Communities: The Transformation of Demographic Regions in Western Europe 1870–1960', *Population and Development Review*, 16.

Cowen, T. (1989), 'Normative Population Theory', *Social Choice and Welfare*, 6.

Cox, D. and E. Jimenez (1992), 'Social Security and Private Transfers in Developing Countries: The Case of Peru', *World Bank Economic Review*, 6.

Cox, J., S. Ross, and M. Rubinstein (1979), 'Option Pricing: A Simplified Approach', *Journal of Financial Economics*, 7.

Crafts, N. F. R. (1985), *British Economic Growth during the Industrial Revolution* (Oxford: Clarendon Press).

Cravioto, J. and R. Arrieto (1986), 'Nutrition, Mental Development and Learning', in Falkner and Tanner (1986).

Crawford, V. (1988), 'Learning and Mixed-Strategy Equilibria in Evolutionary Games', Department of Economics Discussion Paper 88–53, University of California, San Diego.

Cremer, H. and P. Pestieau (1991), 'Bequests, Filial Attention and Fertility', *Economica*, 58.

Crompton, D. W. T. and M. C. Nesheim (1982), 'Nutrition Science and Parasitology: A Case for Collaboration', *Bioscience*, 32.

CSE (1982, 1985), *The State of India's Environment: A Citizens' Report* (New Delhi: Centre for Science and Environment).

—— (1990), *Human–Nature Interactions in a Central Himalayan Village: A Case Study of Village Bemru* (New Delhi: Centre for Science and Environment).

Cubbin, J. S. (1988), *Market Structure and Performance: The Empirical Research* (London: Harwood).

Dahl, H. and P. Mitra (1989), 'Does Tax and Tariff Shifting Matter for Policy? An Application of General Equilibrium Incidence Analysis to Bangladesh', mimeo, Country Economics Department, World Bank.

Dandavate, P., R. Kumari, and J. Verghese (eds.) (1989), *Widows, Abandoned and Destitute Women in India* (New Delhi: Radiant Publishers).

Dandekar, K. (1975), 'Has the Proportion of Women in India's Population Been Declining?' *Economic and Political Weekly*, 10.

Dandekar, V. M. and N. R. Rath (1971), 'Poverty in India', *Economic and Political Weekly*, 6.

Dantwala, M. L. (1967), 'Incentives and Disincentives in Indian Agriculture', *Indian Journal of Agricultural Economics*, 22.

Dasgupta, Amiya (1975), *The Economics of Austerity* (Delhi: Oxford University Press).

—— (1976), *A Theory of Wage Policy* (Delhi: Oxford University Press).

—— (1985), *Epochs of Economic Theory* (Oxford: Basil Blackwell).

Das Gupta, M. (1987a), 'Selective Discrimination Against Female Children in India', *Population and Development Review*, 13.

—— (1987b), 'Informal Security Mechanisms and Population Retension in Rural India', *Economic Development and Cultural Change*, 35.

Dasgupta, P. (1969), 'On the Concept of Optimum Population', *Review of Economic Studies*, 36.

—— (1974a), 'On Some Problems arising from Professor Rawls's Conception of Distributive Justice', *Theory and Decision*, 4.

—— (1974b), 'Some Alternative Criteria for Justice between Generations', *Journal of Public Economics*, 3.

—— (1974c), 'On Optimum Population Size', in A. Mitra (ed.), *Economic Theory and Planning: Essays in Honour of A. K. Dasgupta* (New Delhi: Oxford University Press).

—— (1980), 'Decentralization and Rights', *Economica*, 47.

—— (1982a), 'Utilitarianism, Information and Rights', in Sen and Williams (1982).

—— (1982b), *The Control of Resources* (Oxford: Basil Blackwell).

—— (1982c), 'Resource Depletion, Research and Development and the Social Rate of Discount', in Lind (1982).

—— (1986a), 'Positive Freedom, Markets and the Welfare State', *Oxford Review of Economic Policy*, 2.

—— (1986b), 'The Theory of Technological Competition', in Stiglitz and Mathewson (1986).

—— (1988a), Patents, Priority and Imitation or, The Economics of Races and Waiting Games', *Economic Journal*, 98.

—— (1988b), 'The Welfare Economics of Knowledge Production', *Oxford Review of Economic Policy*, 4.

—— (1988c), 'Lives and Well-Being', *Social Choice and Welfare*, 5.

—— (1988d), 'Trust as a Commodity', in Gambetta (1988b).

—— (1988e), 'Poverty as a Determinant of Inequality', in W. M. Keynes, D. A. Coleman, and N. H. Dinsdale (eds.), *The Political Economy of Health and Welfare* (London: Macmillan).

—— (1989a), 'Power and Control in the Good Polity', in A. Hamlin and P. Pettit (eds.), *The Good Polity* (Oxford: Basil Blackwell).

—— (1989b), 'Exhaustible Resources', in Friday and Laskey (1989).

—— (1989c), 'Population Size and the Quality of Life', *Proceedings of the Aristotelian Society*, 63 (Supplementary Volume).

—— (1989d): 'Welfare, Positive Freedom and Economic Development', in I. Adelman and S. Lane (eds.), *The Balance between Industry and Agriculture in Economic Development: Social Effects* (London: Macmillan).

—— (1990a), 'Well-Being and the Extent of its Realization in Poor Countries', *Economic Journal*, 100 (Supplement).

—— (1990b), 'The Environment as a Commodity', *Oxford Review of Economic Policy*, 6.

—— (1991a), 'Poverty, Resources and Fertility: The Household as a Reproductive Partnership', in A. B. Atkinson (ed.), *Alternatives to Capitalism* (London: Macmillan), forthcoming.

—— (1991b), 'Savings and Population: Normative Issues', mimeo, Stanford University.

—— (1991c), 'Nutrition, Non-Convexities and Redistributive Policies', *Economic Journal* 101 (Special Number).

—— (1991d) 'The Allocation of Hunger', Walras–Bowley Lecture, Econometric Society.

—— (1992), 'Population, Resources and Poverty', *Ambio*, 21.

—— and P. David (1987), 'The Economics of Science and Technology', in G. Feiwel (ed.), *Arrow and the Ascent of Modern Economic Theory* (London: Macmillan).

—— —— (1991), 'Priority, Secrecy, Patents and the Economic Organization of Science and Technology', forthcoming in *Science in Context*.

—— and P. Hammond (1982), 'Fully Progressive Taxation', *Journal of Public Economics*, 11.

—— —— and E. Maskin (1979), 'The Implementation of Social Choice Rules: Some General Results in Incentive Compatibility', *Review of Economic Studies*, 46.

—— and G. Heal (1974), 'The Optimal Depletion of Exhaustible Resources',

Review of Economic Studies (Symposium of the Economics of Exhaustible Resources), 41.

—— —— (1979), *Economic Theory and Exhaustible Resources* (Cambridge: Cambridge University Press).

—— and K.-G. Mäler (1991), 'The Environment and Emerging Development Issues', *Proceedings of the Annual World Bank Conference on Development Economics* (Supplement to the *World Bank Economic Review* and the *World Bank Economic Observer*).

—— —— (eds.), *The Environment and Emerging Development Issues* (Oxford: Clarendon Press), forthcoming.

—— S. Marglin, and A. Sen (1972), *Guidelines for Project Evaluation* (New York: United Nations).

—— and E. Maskin (1986a), 'The Existence of Equilibrium in Discontinuous Economic Games, 1: Theory', *Review of Economic Studies*, 53.

—— —— (1986b) 'The Existence of Equilibrium in Discontinuous Economic Games, 2: Applications', *Review of Economic Studies*, 53.

—— and D. Ray (1986), 'Inequality as a Determinant of Malnutrition and Unemployment: Theory', *Economic Journal*, 96.

—— —— (1987), 'Inequality as Determinant of Malnutrition and Unemployment: Policy', *Economic Journal*, 97.

—— —— (1990), 'Adapting to Undernourishment: The Biological Evidence and Its Implications', in J. Dreze and A. Sen (eds.), *The Political Economy of Hunger: Entitlement and Well-Being* (Oxford: Clarendon Press).

—— A. Sen and D. Starrett, (1973), 'Notes on the Measurement of Inequality', *Journal of Economic Theory*, 6.

—— and J. Stiglitz (1972), 'On Optimal Taxation and Public Production', *Review of Economic Studies*, 39.

—— —— (1974), 'Benefit Cost Analysis and Trade Policies', *Journal of Political Economy*, 83.

—— —— (1980a), 'Market Structure and the Nature of Innovative Activity', *Economic Journal*, 90.

—— —— (1980b), 'Uncertainty, Industrial Structure and the Speed of R&D', *Bell Journal of Economics*, 8.

—— —— (1981), 'Resource Depletion under Technological Uncertainty', *Econometrica*, 49.

—— —— (1988a), 'Potential Competition, Actual Competition and Economic Welfare', *European Economic Review*, 32 (Supplement).

—— —— (1988b), 'Learning-by-Doing, Market Structure, and Industrial and Trade Policies', *Oxford Economic Papers*, 40.

—— and P. Stoneman (eds.) (1987), *Economic Policy and Technological Performance* (Cambridge: Cambridge University Press).

—— and Y. Ushio (1981), 'On the Rate of Convergence of Oligopoly Equilibria: An Example', *Economics Letters*, 8.

—— and M. Weale (1992), 'On Measuring the Quality of Life', *World Development*, 20.

d'Aspremont, C. and L. Gevers (1977), 'Equity and the Informational Basis of Collective Choice', *Review of Economic Studies*, 46.

Datta-Choudhuri, M. (1978), 'Industrialization and Foreign Trade: An Analysis Based on the Development Experience of the Republic of Korea and the Philippines', ILO Working Paper, WP II-4, Bangkok.

Da Vanzo, J. and D. Lee (1983), 'The Compatibility of Child Care with Market and Non-Market Activities: Preliminary Evidence from Malaysia', in Buvinic, Lycette and McGreevey (1983).

David, P. A. (1975), 'Transport Innovations and Economic Growth: Professor Fogel On and Off the Rails', in *Technical Choice, Innovation and Economic Growth: Essays on American and British Experience in the Nineteenth Century* (Cambridge: Cambridge University Press).

—— (1985), 'Cleo and the Economics of QWERTY', *American Economic Review* (Papers and Proceedings), 75.

—— (1986), 'Comment', *Population and Development Review* 12, (Supplement).

—— (1987), 'Some New Standards for the Economics of Standardization in the Information Age', in Dasgupta and Stoneman (1987).

—— (1988), 'Path-Dependence: Putting the Past into the Future of Economics', IMSSS Technical Report No. 533, Stanford University.

—— (1991), 'So, How Would It Matter if "History Mattered"? Path Dependence in Economics and its Long-run Implications', mimeo, Department of Economics, Stanford University.

—— (1992a), 'Path-Dependence and Predictability in Dynamic Systems with Local Network Externalities: A Paradigm for Historical Economics', forthcoming in C. Freeman and D. Foray (eds.), *Technology and the Wealth of Nations* (London: Frances Pinter).

—— (1992b), 'Knowledge, Property, and the System Dynamics of Technological Change'; forthcoming in *Proceedings of the Annual Conference on Development Economics 1992* (supplement to the *World Bank Economic Review* and the *World Bank Research Observer*).

Davidson, D. (1986), 'Judging Interpersonal Interests', in J. Elster and A. Hylland (eds.), *Foundation of Social Choice Theory* (Cambridge: Cambridge University Press).

Davidson, S. *et al.* (1975), *Human Nutrition and Dietetics*, 6th edn. (Edinburgh: Churchill Livingstone).

Davies, P. (1988), *The Cosmic Blueprint: New Discoveries in Nature's Creative Ability to Order the Universe* (New York: Simon & Schuster).

Deaton, A. (1988), 'Calories, Food and Expenditure: Notes on Behrman and Deolalikar', mimeo, Woodrow Wilson School, Princeton University.

—— (1989), 'Looking for Boy–Girl Discrimination in Household Expenditure', *World Bank Economic Review*, 3.

—— (1990), 'Saving in Developing Countries: Theory and Evidence', *Proceedings of the World Bank Annual Conference on Development Economics 1989* (supplement to the *World Bank Economic Review* and the *World Bank Research Observer*).

—— (1991), 'Household Saving in LDC's: Credit Markets, Insurance, and Welfare', Discussion Paper No. 153, Research Program in Development Studies, Woodrow Wilson School, Princeton University.

—— and J. Muellbauer (1986), 'On Measuring Child Costs: With Applications to Poor Countries', *Journal of Political Economy*, 94.

—— and C. H. Paxson (1990), 'Patterns of Aging in Thailand and Cote D'Ivoire', Discussion Paper No. 148, Research Program in Development Studies, Woodrow Wilson School of Public and International Affairs, Princeton University.

Debreu, G. (1952), 'A Social Equilibrium Existence Theorem', *Proceedings of the National Academy of Sciences*, 38.

—— (1954), 'Representation of a Preference Ordering by a Numerical Function', in R. Thrall, C. Coombs, and R. Davis (eds.), *Decision Processes* (New York: John Wiley).

—— (1958), 'Stochastic Choice and Cardinal Utility', *Econometrica*, 26.

—— (1959), *Theory of Value* (New York: John Wiley).

—— (1962), New Concepts and Techniques for Equilibrium Analysis', *International Economic Review*, 3.

—— (1975), 'The Rate of Convergence of an Economy', *Journal of Mathematical Economics*, 2.

—— and H. Scarf (1963), 'A Limit Theorem on the Core of an Economy', *International Economic Review*, 4.

Debysingh, M. (1980), 'The Cultural Geography of Poultry Keeping in India', in Sopher (1980c).

de Garine, I. and G. A. Harrison (eds.) (1988), *Coping with Uncertainty in Food Supply* (Oxford: Clarendon Press).

de Janvry, A. and E. Sadoulet (1989), 'A Study in Resistance to Institutional Change: The Lost Game of Latin American Land Reform', *World Development*, 17.

DeMeza, D. and D. Webb (1987), 'Too Much Investment: A Problem of Asymmetric Information', *Quarterly Journal of Economics*, 102.

Demsetz, H. (1966), 'Some Aspects of Property Rights', *Journal of Law and Economics*, 9.

—— (1967), 'Toward a Theory of Property Rights', *American Economic Review*, (Papers and Proceedings), 57.

—— (1972), 'Wealth Distribution and the Ownership of Rights', *Journal of Legal Studies*, 1.

Denison, E. F. (1962), *The Sources of Economic Growth in the United States and the Alternatives Before Us* (New York: Committee for Economic Development).

Deolalikar, A. B. (1988), 'Nutrition and Labor Productivity in Agriculture: Estimates for Rural South India', *Review of Economics and Statistics*, 70.

Deschamps, R. and L. Gevers (1978), 'Leximin and Utilitarian Rules: A Joint Characterization', *Journal of Economic Theory*, 17.

de Soto, H. (1989), *The Other Path: The Invisible Revolution in the Third World* (New York: Harper & Row).

Dev, S. M. (1992), 'Poverty Alleviation Programmes: A Case Study of Maharashtra with Emphasis on Employment Guarantee Schemes', mimeo., Indira Gandhi Institute of Development Research (Bombay).

Devarajan, S. and R. J. Weiner (1989), 'Natural Resources Depletion and National Income Accounts', mimeo, Kennedy School of Government, Harvard University.

de Waal, A. (1989), 'Famine Mortality: A Case Study of Dafur, Sudan 1984–85', *Population Studies*, 43.

Diamond, P. A. (1975), 'A Many Person Ramsey Tax Rule', *Journal of Public Economics*, 5.

—— (1982), 'Aggregate Demand Management in Search Equilibrium', *Journal of Political Economy*, 90.

—— and J. A. Mirrlees (1971), 'Optimal Taxation and Public Production: Parts 1 and 2', *American Economic Review*, 62.

Dierker, E. (1986), 'When Does Marginal Cost Pricing Lead to Pareto-Efficiency?' *Zeitschrift fur Nationaleconomie*, 5 (Supplement).

Dixon, J. A. (1992), 'Analysis and Management of Watersheds'; forthcoming in P. Dasgupta and K.-G. Maler (eds.).

—— D. E. James and P. B. Sherman (1989), *The Economics of Dryland Management* (London: Earthscan Publications).

—— —— —— (eds.) (1990), *Dryland Management: Economic Case Studies* (London: Earthscan Publications).

Dobbing, J. (1990), 'Early Nutrition and Later Achievement', *Proceedings of the Nutrition Society*, 49.

Dodge, P. R., A. L. Prensky, and R. D. Feigin (1975), *Nutrition and the Developing Nervous System* (St Louis, Mo.: C. V. Mosby).

Domenico, P. A. (1972), *Concepts and Models of Groundwater Hydrology* (New York: McGraw-Hill).

Dore, R. (1959), *Land Reform in Japan* (Oxford: Oxford University Press).

Dorner, P. (1972), *Land Reform and Economic Development* (Baltimore: Penguin Books).

Douglas, M. (1984), *Purity and Danger: An Analysis of the Concepts of Pollution and Taboo* (London: Ark Paperbacks).

Dow, T. (1971), 'Fertility and Family Planning in Africa', *Journal of Modern Studies*, 8.

Drewnowsky, J. and W. Scott (1966), *The Level of Living Index* (Geneva: UN Research Institute for Social Development).

Drèze, Jacques (ed.) (1974), *Allocation under Uncertainty: Equilibrium and Optimality* (London: Macmillan).

Drèze, J. (1990), 'Widows in Rural India', Development Economics Programme No. 26, London School of Economics.

—— and A. Mukherjee (1989), 'Labour Contracts in Rural India: Theories and Evidence', in S. Chakravarty (ed.), *The Balance between Industry and Agriculture in Economic Development iii, Manpower and Transfers* (London: Macmillan).

—— and A. Sen (1990), *Hunger and Public Action* (Oxford: Clarendon Press).

—— and N. Stern (1987), 'The Theory of Cost–Benefit Analysis', in A. J. Auerbach and M. Feldstein (eds.), *Handbook of Public Economics*, ii (Amsterdam: North-Holland).

D'Souza, S. and L. C. Chen (1980), 'Sex Differentials in Mortality in Rural Bangladesh', *Population and Development Review*, 6.

Duesenberry, J. S. (1949), *Income, Savings and the Theory of Consumer Behavior* (Cambridge, Mass.: Harvard University Press).

Dugdale, A. and P. Payne (1977), 'Patterns of Lean and Fat Depositions in Adults', *Nature*, 266.

—— —— (1987), 'A Model of Seasonal Changes in Energy Balance', *Ecology of Food and Nutrition*, 16.

Dupre, J. (ed.) (1987), *The Latest on the Best: Essays on Evolution and Optimality* (Cambridge, Mass.: MIT Press).

Durham, W. H. (1979), *Scarcity and Survival in Central America: Ecological Origins of the Soccer War* (Stanford, Cal.: Stanford University Press).

Durlauf, S. N. (1990), 'Nonergodic Economic Growth', mimeo, Department of Economics, Stanford University.

—— (1991), 'Multiple Equilibria and Persistence in Aggregate Fluctuations', *American Economic Review* (Papers and Proceedings), 56.

Durnin, J. V. G. A. (1980), 'Food Consumption and Energy Balance during Pregnancy and Lactation in New Guinea', in Aebi and Whitehead (1980).

—— (1984), 'Some Problems in Assessing the Role of Physical Activity in the Maintenance of Energy Balance', in Pollitt and Amante (1984).

—— and R. Passmore (1967), *Energy, Work and Leisure* (New York: John Wiley).

Dworkin, R. (1978), *Taking Rights Seriously* (London: Duckworth).

—— (1981), 'What is Equality? Part II: Equality of Resources', *Philosophy and Public Affairs*, 10.

—— (1984), 'Rights as Trumps', in J. Waldron (ed.), *Theories of Rights* (Oxford: Oxford University Press).

—— (1986), *Law's Empire* (London: Fontana Press).

Dwyer, D. and J. Bruce (eds.) (1988), *A Home Divided: Women and Income in the Third World* (Stanford: Stanford University Press).

Dyson, T. and M. Moore (1983), 'On Kinship Structure, Female Autonomy, and Demographic Behaviour in India', *Population and Development Review*, 9.

—— and M. Murphy (1985), 'The Onset of Fertility Transition', *Population and Development Review*, 11.

Dyson-Hudson, R. and E. A. Smith (1978), 'Human Territoriality: An Ecological Reassessment', *American Anthropologist*, 80.

Easter, K. W., J. A. Dixon and M. A. Hufschmidt (eds.) (1986), *Watershed Resources Management: An Integrated Framework with Studies from Asia and the Pacific* (Boulder, Col.: Westview Press).

Easterlin, R. A. (1964), 'Does Economic Growth Improve the Human Lot?' in P. A. David and M. W. Reder (eds.), *Nations and Households in Economic Growth: Essays in Honor of Moses Abramovitz* (New York: Academic Press).

—— (1975), 'An Economic Framework for Fertility Analysis', *Studies in Family Planning*, 6.

—— (1978), 'The Economics and Sociology of Fertility: A Synthesis', in C. Tilley (ed.), *Historical Studies of Changing Fertility* (Princeton, NJ: Princeton University Press).

—— (1980), *Population and Economic Change in Developing Countries* (Chicago: University of Chicago Press).

—— and E. Crimmins (1985), *The Fertility Revolution: A Supply–Demand Analysis* (Chicago: University of Chicago Press).

—— R. A. Pollak and M. L. Wachter (1980), 'Toward a More General Model of Fertility Determination: Endogenous Preferences and Natural Fertility', in Easterlin (1980).

Edholm, O. G. *et al.* (1970), 'Food Intake and Energy Expenditure of Army Recruits', *British Journal of Nutrition*, 24.

Edmundson, W. C. (1977), 'Individual Variations in Work Output per Unit Energy Intake in East Java', *Ecology of Food and Nutrition*, 6.

—— (1979), 'Individual Variations in Basal Metabolic Rate and Mechanical Work Efficiency in East Java', *Ecology of Food and Nutrition*, 8.

—— (1980), 'Adaptation to Undernourishment: How Much Food Does Man Need?' *Social Science and Medicine*, 14D.

—— and P. V. Sukhatme (1990), 'Food and Work: Poverty and Hunger?' *Economic Development and Cultural Change*, 38.

Ehrlich, P. and A. Ehrlich (1990), *The Population Explosion* (New York: Simon & Schuster).

—— —— (1991), 'The Value of Bio-Diversity', in P. Dasgupta, K.-G. Maler and A. Vercelli (eds). *The Economics of Transnational Commons* (Oxford: Oxford University Press), forthcoming.

—— —— and J. Holdren (1977), *Ecoscience: Population, Resources and the Environment* (San Francisco: W. H. Freeman).

El Badri, I. M. A. (1969), 'Higher Female than Male Mortality in Some Countries of South Asia', *Journal of the American Statistical Association*, 54.

Elliot, K. M. and W. A. M. Cutting (1983), 'Carry on Feeding', *Diarrhoea Dialogue*, 15.

Elster, J. (1989), *The Cement of Society: A Study of Social Order* (Cambridge: Cambridge University Press).

Enke, S. (1966), 'The Economic Aspects of Slowing Population Growth', *Economic Journal*, 76.

Ensminger, J. (1990), 'Co-opting the Elders: The Political Economy of State Incorporation in Africa', *American Anthropologist*, 92.

Epstein, S. (1967), 'Productive Efficiency and Customary Systems of Rewards in Rural South India', in R. Firth, (ed.), *Themes in Economic Anthropology* (New Haven, Conn.: Yale University Press).

Esman, M. J. and N. T. Uphoff (1984), *Local Organizations: Intermediaries in Rural Development* (Ithaca, NY: Cornell University Press).

Eswaran, M. and A. Kotwal (1985a), 'A Theory of Two-Tier Labour Markets in Agrarian Economies', *American Economic Review*, 75.

—— —— (1985b) 'A Theory of Contractual Structure in Agriculture', *American Economic Review*, 75.

—— —— (1986), 'Access to Capital and Agrarian Production Organization', *Economic Journal*, 96.

—— —— (1989), 'Credit as Insurance in Agrarian Economies', *Journal of Development Economics*, 31.

—— —— (1990), 'Implications of Credit Constraints for Risk Behaviour in Less Developed Economies', *Oxford Economic Papers*, 42.

Evans, R. and E. Maskin (1989), 'Efficient Renegotiation-Proof Equilibria in Repeated Games', *Games and Economic Behaviour*, 1.

Eveleth, P. B. (1985), 'Nutritional Implications of Differences in Adolescent Growth and Maturation in Adult Body Size', in Blaxter and Waterlow (1985).

—— (1986), 'Population Differences in Growth: Environmental and Genetic Factors' in Falkner and Tanner (1986).

—— and J. M. Tanner (1976), *Worldwide Variation in Human Growth* (Cambridge: Cambridge University Press).

Evenson, R. E. and Y. Kislev (1973), 'Research and Productivity in Wheat and Maize', *Journal of Political Economy*, 81.

—— —— (1975), 'Investment in Agricultural Research and Extensions: An International Survey', *Economic Development and Cultural Change*, 23.

Fagley, R. M. (1976), 'Easing the Burden of Women: A 16-Hour Workday', *Assignment Children* (UNICEF), 36.

Falconer, J. (1990), *The Major Significance of 'Minor' Forest Products* (Rome: Food and Agricultural Organization).

—— and J. E. M. Arnold (1989), *Household Food Security and Forestry: An Analysis of Socio-Economic Issues* (Rome: FAO).

Falkenmark, M. (1986), 'Fresh Water: Time for a Modified Approach', *Ambio*, 15.

—— (1989), 'The Massive Water Scarcity Now Threatening Africa: Why Isn't it Being Addressed?' *Ambio*, 18.

—— and T. Chapman (eds.) (1989), *Comparative Hydrology: An Ecological Approach to Land and Water Resources* (Paris: UNESCO).

Falkner, F. and J. M. Tanner (eds.) (1978), *Human Growth, ii: Postnatal Growth* (New York: Plenum Press).

—— —— (eds.) (1986), *Human Growth: A Comprehensive Treatise*, iii, 2nd edn. (New York: Plenum Press).

Falloux, F. and A. Mukendi (eds.) (1988), *Desertification Control and Renewable Resource Management in the Sahelian and Sudanian Zones of West Africa*, World Bank Technical Paper No. 70.

FAO (1977), *The Fourth World Food Survey* (Rome: FAO).

—— (1982, 1989), *The State of Food and Agriculture* (Rome: FAO).

—— (1985), *International Trade and World Food Security* (Rome: FAO).

—— (1986), *Food Outlook* (Rome: FAO).

—— (1987), *The Fifth World Food Survey* (Rome: FAO).

Fapohundra, E. R. and M. P. Todaro (1988), 'Family Structure and Demand for Children in Southern Nigeria', *Population and Development Review*, 14.

Farooq, G. M., I. I. Ekanem, and S. Ojelade (1987), 'Family Size Preferences and Fertility in South-Western Nigeria', in C. Oppong (ed.), *Sex Roles, Population and Development in West Africa* (Portsmouth, NH: Heinemann).

Farrell, J. (1986), 'How Effective is Potential Competition?' *Economics Letters*, 20.

—— (1987) 'Information and the Coase Theorem', *Journal of Economic Perspectives*, 1.

—— and E. Maskin (1989), 'Renegotiation in Repeated Games', *Games and Economic Behaviour*, 1.

—— and G. Saloner (1986), 'Installed Base and Compatibility: Innovation, Product Preannouncements and Predation', *American Economic Review*, 76.

Farrell, M. (1959), 'The Convexity Assumption in the Theory of Competitive Markets', *Journal of Political Economy*, 67.

—— (1970), 'The Magnitude of "Rate of Growth" Effects on Aggregate Savings', *Economic Journal*, 80.

Faruquee, R. and R. Gulhati (1983), 'Rapid Population Growth in Sub-Saharan Africa', World Bank Staff Working Paper No. 559.

Fauveau, V. *et al.* (1990), 'The Contribution of Severe Malnutrition to Child Mortality in Rural Bangladesh: Implications for Targeting Nutritional Interventions', *Food and Nutrition Bulletin*, 12.

Feacham, R., M. McGarry, and D. Mara (eds.), (1977) *Water, Wastes and Health in Hot Climates* (London: Heinemann).

Feder, E. (1977), 'Agribusiness and the Elimination of Latin America's Rural Proletariat', *World Development*, 5.

—— (1979), 'Agricultural Resources in Underdeveloped Countries: Competition between Man and Animal', *Economic and Political Weekly*, 14.

Feder, G. (1985), 'The Relation between Farm Size and Farm Productivity', *Journal of Development Economics*, 18.

—— and D. Feeny (1991), 'Land Tenure and Property Rights: Theory and Implications for Development Policy', *World Bank Economic Review*, 5.

—— R. Just, and D. Zilberman (1985), 'Adoption of Agricultural Innovations in Developing Countries: A Survey', *Economic Development and Cultural Change*, 33.

—— L. J. Lau, and R. H. Slade (1987), 'Does Agriculture Extension Pay? The Training and Visit System in Northwest India', *American Journal of Agricultural Economics*, 69.

—— and R. Noronha (1987), 'Land Rights and Agricultural Development in Sub-Saharan Africa', *World Bank Research Observer*, 2.

Fee T. (1976), 'Domestic Labour: An Analysis of Housework and its Relation to the Production Process', *Review of Radical Political Economy*, 8.

Feeny, D. *et al.* (1990), 'The Tragedy of the Commons: Twenty-two Years Later', *Human Ecology*, 18.

Feierman, S. (1985), 'Struggles for Control: The Social Roots of Health and Healing in Modern Africa', *African Studies Review*, 28.

Fernandes, W. and G. Menon (1987), *Tribal Women and the Forest Economy* (New Delhi: Indian Social Institute).

Fernandez, R. and J. Glazer (1991), 'Striking for a Bargain between Two Completely Informed Agents', *American Economic Review*, 82.

Ferro-Luzzi, A. (1984), 'Energy Intakes as Predictors of Energy Balance in Free-Living Populations', in Pollitt and Amante (1984).

—— (1985), 'Work Capacity and Productivity in Long-Term Adaptation to Low Energy Intakes', in Blaxter and Waterlow (1985).

—— (1988) 'Marginal Energy Malnutrition: Some Speculations on Primary Energy Sparing Mechanisms', in Collins and Roberts (1988).

—— N. G. Norgan and C. Paci (1981), 'An Evaluation of the Distribution of Protein and Energy Intakes in Some New Guinean Households', *Nutrition Report International*, 24.

—— G. Pastore, and S. Sette (1987), 'Seasonality in Energy Metabolism', in

B. Schurch and N. S. Scrimshaw (eds.), *Chronic Energy Deficiency: Consequences and Related Issues* (Lausanne: Nestlé Foundation).

—— *et al.* (1990), 'Seasonal Energy Deficiency in Ethiopian Rural Women', *European Journal of Clinical Nutrition*, 44.

—— *et al.* (1992), 'A Simplified Approach of Assessing Adult Chronic Energy Deficiency', *European Journal of Clinical Nutrition*, 46.

Fields, G. (1980), *Poverty, Inequality and Development* (Cambridge: Cambridge University Press).

Findley, R. (1989), 'The New Political Economy: Its Explanatory Power as Related to LDCs', forthcoming in G. M. Meier (ed.), *The New Political Economy and Development Policy-Making* (Oxford: Oxford University Press).

Fine, B. and K. Fine (1974), 'Social Choice and Individual Rankings, I and II', *Review of Economic Studies*, 44.

Fisher, A. and M. Hanemann (1986), 'Option Value and the Extinction of Species', *Advances in Applied Microeconomics*, 4.

Fishlow, A. (1972), 'Brazilian Size Distribution of Income', *American Economic Review* (Papers and Proceedings), 62.

Floud, R. (1987), 'Anthropometric Measures of Nutritional Status in Industrialising Societies: Europe and North America since 1750', mimeo, Department of History, Birkbeck College, London.

—— and K. Wachter (1982), 'Poverty and Physical Stature: Evidence on the Standard of Living of London Boys, 1770–1870', *Social Science History*, 6.

Fogel, R. W. (1964), *Railroads and American Economic Growth: Essays in Econometric History* (Baltimore: Johns Hopkins University Press).

—— (1987), 'Biomedical Approaches to the Estimation and Interpretation of Secular Trends in Equity, Morbidity, Mortality, and Labor Productivity in Europe, 1750–1980', mimeo, University of Chicago.

—— (1988), 'The Conquest of High Mortality and Hunger in Europe and America: Timing and Mechanics', mimeo, University of Chicago.

—— *et al.* (1983), 'Secular Changes in American and British Stature and Nutrition', *Journal of Interdisciplinary History*, 14.

Foldes, L. (1978), 'Optimal Savings and Risk in Continuous Time', *Review of Economic Studies*, 45.

Foster, A. and M. R. Rosenzweig (1992a), 'A Test for Moral Hazard in the Labour Market: Effort, Health and Calorie Consumption', mimeo. Department of Economics, University of Pennsylvania.

—— —— (1992b), 'Unequal Pay for Unequal Work: Asymetric Information, Sex Discrimination and the Efficiency of Casual Labor Markets', mimeo. Department of Economics, University of Pennsylvania.

Frank, C. and R. Webb (eds.) (1977), *Income Distribution: Policy Alternatives in Developing Countries* (Washington, DC: Brookings Institution).

Freedman, R. (1979), 'Theories of Fertility Decline: A Reappraisal', *Social Forces*, 58.

Friday, L. and R. Laskey (eds.) (1989), *The Fragile Environment* (Cambridge: Cambridge University Press).

Fried, C. (1977), 'Difficulties in the Economic Analysis of Rights', in G. Dworkin, G. Bermant, and P. Brown (eds.), *Markets and Morals* (Washington, DC.: Hemisphere Publishing Co.).

—— (1978), *Right and Wrong* (Cambridge, Mass.: Harvard University Press).

Friedman, J. (1971), 'A Non-Cooperative Equilibrium for Supergames', *Review of Economic Studies*, 38.

Friedman, M. (1957), *A Theory of the Consumption Function* (Princeton, NJ: Princeton University Press).

—— (1962), *Capitalism and Freedom* (Chicago: University of Chicago Press).

—— and R. Friedman (1980), *Free to Choose* (New York: Harcourt Brace Jovanovich).

—— and L. J. Savage (1948), 'The Utility Analysis of Choices Involving Risk', *Journal of Political Economy*, 56.

Fuchs, V. (1983), *How We Live* (Cambridge, Mass.: Harvard University Press).

—— (1986), *The Health Economy* (Cambridge, Mass.: Harvard University Press).

—— (1988), *Women's Quest for Economic Equality* (Cambridge, Mass.: Harvard University Press).

—— (1990), 'The Health Sector's Share of the Gross National Product', *Science*, 247.

—— and J. Hahn (1990), 'How Does Canada Do It? A Comparison of Expenditures for Physicians' Services in the United States and Canada', *New England Journal of Medicine*, 323.

Fudenberg, D. and D. Kreps (1988), 'A Theory of Learning, Experimentation, and Equilibrium in Games', mimeo, Graduate School of Business, Stanford University.

—— D. Levine, and E. Maskin (1986), 'The Folk Theorem with Imperfect Public Information', mimeo, University of California, Berkeley.

—— and E. Maskin (1986), 'The Folk Theorem in Repeated Games with Discounting and with Incomplete Information', *Econometrica*, 54.

—— —— (1990), 'Evolution and Cooperation in Noisy Repeated Games', *American Economic Review* (Papers and Proceedings), 80.

—— and J. Tirole (1991), *Game Theory* (Cambridge, Mass.: MIT Press).

Furubotn, E. and S. Pejovich (1972), 'Property Rights and Economic Theory: A Survey of Recent Literature', *Journal of Economic Literature*, 10.

—— —— (1974), *The Economics of Property Rights* (Cambridge, Mass.: Ballinger).

Gadgil, M. and K. C. Malhotra (1983), 'Adaptative Significance of the Indian Caste System: An Ecological Perspective', *Annals of Human Biology*, 10.

Gale, D. (1986a), 'Bargaining and Competition, 1: Characterization', *Econometrica*, 54.

—— (1986b), 'Bargaining and Competition', 2: Existence', *Econometrica*, 54.

Gambetta, D. (1988a), 'Mafia: The Price of Distrust', in Gambetta (1988b).

—— (ed.) (1988b), *Trust: Making and Breaking of Cooperative Agreements* (Oxford: Basil Blackwell).

—— (1992), *The Mafia: A Ruinous Rationality* (Cambridge, Mass.: Harvard University Press), forthcoming.

Gangrade, K. and S. Dhadda (1973), *Challenge and Responses: A Study of Famines in India* (Delhi: Rachana Publications).

Garby, L. and O. Lammert (1984), 'Within-Subjects Between-Days-and-Weeks Variation in Energy Expenditure at Rest', *Human Nutrition: Clinical Nutrition*, 38C.

Gardenfors, P. and N.-E. Sahlin (eds.) (1988), *Decision, Probability and Utility* (Cambridge: Cambridge University Press).

Gardner, G. W. *et al.* (1975), 'Cardiorespiratory, Hematological and Physical Performance Responses of Anemia Subjects to Iron Treatment', *American Journal of Clinical Nutrition*, 28.

Gastil, R. D. (1984), *Freedom in the World: Political Rights and Civil Liberties 1983–84*, (Westport, Conn.: Greenwood Press).

—— (1986), *Freedom in the World: Political Rights and Civil Liberties 1985–86* (Westport, Conn.: Greenwood Press).

Gauthier, D. (1986), *Morals by Agreement* (Oxford: Clarendon Press).

Geertz, C. (1962), 'The Rotating Credit Association: A "Middle Rung" in Development', *Economic Development and Cultural Change*, 1.

Genovese, E. D. (1974), *Plantation, Inequality, and Development: Essays on the Local History of American Slave Society*, ed. E. Miller and E. D. Genovese (Urbana, Ill.: University of Illinois Press).

George, V. (1988), *Wealth, Poverty and Starvation: An International Perspective* (Hemel Hempstead: Wheatsheaf).

Georgescu-Roegen, N. (1960), 'Economic Theory and Agrarian Reforms', *Oxford Economic Papers*, 12.

Gersovitz, M. (1983), 'Savings and Nutrition at Low Incomes', *Journal of Political Economy*, 91.

—— (1988), 'Saving and Development', in Chenery and Srinivasan (1988).

Gewirth, A. (1981), 'Are There any Absolute Rights?' *Philosophical Quarterly*, 31.

Ghai, D. and S. Radhwan (eds.), (1983), *Agrarian Policies and Rural Poverty in Africa* (Geneva: International Labour Organization).

Ghai, D. and Vivian, J. M. (eds.) (1992), *Grassroots Environmental Action: People's Participation in Sustainable Development* (London: Routledge).

Giddens, A. (1986), *Sociology: A Brief but Critical Introduction* (London: Macmillan Education).

Gigengack, A. R. *et al.* (1990), 'Global Modelling of Dryland Degradation', in Dixon, James and Sherman (1990).

Gigliotti, G. A. (1983), 'Total Utility, Overlapping Generations and Optimum Population', *Review of Economic Studies*, 50.

Gilbert, A. (1990), 'Natural Resource Accounting: A Case Study of Botswana', in Dixon, James and Sherman (1990).

Glewwe, P. (1986), 'The Distribution of Income in Sri Lanka in 1969–70 and 1980–81', *Journal of Development Economics*, 24.

Golden, B. E. and M. Golden (1990), 'Relationship among Dietary Quality, Children's Appetites, Growth Stunting, and Efficiency of Growth in Poor Populations', *Food and Nutrition Bulletin*, 12.

Golding, P. and S. Middleton (1983), *Images of Welfare* (Oxford: Basil Blackwell).

Goodin, R. (1988), *Reasons for Welfare* (Princeton, NJ: Princeton University Press).

Goodman, L. A. and H. Markowitz (1952), 'Social Welfare Functions Based on Individual Rankings', *American Journal of Sociology*, 58.

Goody, J. (ed.) (1973), *The Character of Kinship* (Cambridge: Cambridge University Press).

—— (1976), *Production and Reproduction: A Comparative Study of the Domestic Terrain* (Cambridge: Cambridge University Press).

—— (1986), *The Logic of Writing and the Organization of Society* (Cambridge: Cambridge University Press).

—— (1989), 'Family, Population and Development: Some Remarks on Recent Work', mimeo, St John's College, Cambridge.

—— (1990), 'Futures of the Family in Rural Africa', *Population and Development Review*, 16 (Supplement).

—— and S. J. Tambiah (1973), *Bridewealth and Dowry* (Cambridge: Cambridge University Press).

—— *et al.* (1981a), 'On the Absence of Implicit Sex-Preference in Ghana', *Journal of Biosocial Sciences*, 13.

—— *et al.* (1981b), 'Implicit Sex Preference: A Comparative Study', *Journal of Biosocial Sciences*, 13.

Gopalan, C. (1958), 'Studies on Lactation in Poor Indian Communities', *Journal of Tropical Paediatrics*, 4.

—— (1993), 'Undernutrition: Measurement and Implications', in S. Osmani (ed.), *Poverty, Undernutrition and Living Standards* (Oxford: Clarendon Press).

Gordon, H. Scott (1954), 'The Economic Theory of Common Property Resources', *Journal of Political Economy*, 62.

Gorman, W. M. (1968), 'The Structure of Utility Functions', *Review of Economic Studies*, 35.

Gottlieb, M. (1945), 'The Theory of Optimum Population for a Closed Economy', *Journal of Political Economy*, 53.

Gough, K. (1960/1), 'The Hindu Jajmani System', *Economic Development and Cultural Change*, 9.

Gould, S. J. and R. C. Lewontin (1979), 'The Spandrels of San Marco and the Panglossian Paradigm: A Critique of the Adaptationist Programme', in J. Maynard Smith and R. Holliday (eds.), *The Evolution of Adaptation by Natural Selection* (London: Royal Society).

Government of India (1986), *Statistical Abstract* (New Delhi: Ministry of Planning).

Graaff, J. de V. (1962), *Theoretical Welfare Economics* (Cambridge: Cambridge University Press).

Grande, F., J. T. Anderson, and A. Keys (1958), 'Changes of Basal Metabolic Rate in Man in Semi-Starvation and Refeeding', *Journal of Applied Physiology*, 12.

Grantham-McGregor, S. M. (1982), 'The Relationship between Development Level and Different Types of Malnutrition in Children', *Human Nutrition: Clinical Nutrition*, 36C.

—— C. Powell and P. Fletcher (1989), 'Stunting, Severe Malnutrition and Mental Development in Young Children', *European Journal of Clinical Nutrition*, 43.

—— *et al.* (1990), 'The Relationship between Undernutrition, Activity Levels and Development in Young Children', in B. Schurch and N.S. Scrimshaw (eds.), *Activity, Energy Expenditure and Energy Requirements in Young Children* (Lausanne: Nestlé Foundation).

Graves, P. L. (1976), 'Nutrition, Infant Behaviour and Maternal Characteristics: A Pilot Study in West Bengal, India', *American Journal of Clinical Nutrition*, 29.

Greenhough, P. R. (1982), *Prosperity and Misery in Modern Bengal: The Famine of 1943–1944* (Oxford: Oxford University Press).

Greenwald, B. C. and J. E. Stiglitz (1986), 'Externalties in Economies with Imperfect Information and Incomplete Markets', *Quarterly Journal of Economics*, 101.

Greif, A. (1989), 'Reputation and Coalitions in Medieval Trade: Maghribi Traders', *Journal of Economic History*, 59.

—— (1991), 'Cultural Beliefs as a Common Resource in an Integrating World: An Example from the Theory and History of Collective and Individualist Societies'; forthcoming in P. Dasgupta, K. -G. Maler and A. Vercelli (eds.), *The Economics of Transnational Commons* (Oxford: Clarendon Press).

—— P. Milgrom, and B. Weingast (1990), 'The Merchant Guild as a Nexus of Contracts', Working Paper No. E-90-23, Hoover Institution, Stanford University.

Griffin, J. (1986), *Well-Being: Its Meaning, Measurement and Moral Importance* (Oxford: Clarendon Press).

Griffin, K. (1976), *Land Concentration and Rural Poverty* (London: Macmillan).

—— (1978), *International Inequality and National Poverty*, (London: Macmillan).

—— and A. R. Khan (eds.) (1977), *Poverty and Landlessness in Rural Asia* (Geneva: International Labour Organization).

Griliches, Z. (1957), 'Hybrid Corn: An Exploration in the Economics of Technological Change', *Econometrica*, 25.

—— (1958), 'Research Costs and Social Returns: Hybrid Corn and Related Innovations', *Journal of Political Economy*, 66.

—— (1964), 'Research Expenditure, Education and the Aggregate Agricultural Production Function', *American Economic Review*, 54.

Gross, D. R. and B. A. Underwood (1971), 'Technological Change and Caloric Costs: Sisal Agriculture in North-Eastern Brazil', *American Anthropologist*, 73.

Grossman, S. and O. Hart (1983), 'An Analysis of the Principal-Agent Problem', *Econometrica*, 51.

Guesnerie, R. (1975), 'Pareto Optimality in Non-Convex Economies', *Econometrica*, 43.

—— and O. Hart (1985), 'Welfare Losses due to Imperfect Competition: Asymptotic Results for Cournot–Nash Equilibria with or without Free Entry', *International Economic Review*, 26.

Guha, A. (1989), 'Consumption, Efficiency, and Surplus Labour', *Journal of Development Economics*, 31.

Gulati, L. (1976), 'Unemployment among Female Agricultural Labourers', *Economic and Political Weekly*, 11.

Gurr, T. R. (1968), 'A Causal Model of Civil Strife', *American Political Science Review*, 63.

—— (1970), *Why Men Rebel* (Princeton, NJ: Princeton University Press).

Guth, W., R. Schmittberger, and B. Schwarze (1982), 'An Experimental Analysis of Ultimatum Bargaining', *Journal of Economic Behaviour and Organization*, 3.

Gutmann, A. (1980), *Liberal Equality* (Cambridge: Cambridge University Press).

Haas, J. D. and J.-P. Habicht (1990), 'Growth and Growth Charts in the Assessment of Pre-School Nutritional Status', in Harrison and Waterlow (1990).

Haddad, L. and R. Kanbur (1989), 'Are Better Off Households More Unequal or Less Unequal? A Bargaining Theoretic Approach to "Kuznets Effects" at the Micro Level', mimeo, World Bank.

—— —— (1990), 'How Serious is the Neglect of Intra-Household Inequality?' *Economic Journal*, 100.

—— —— (1991), 'Upper-Limit Indicator Targeting and Age-Based Nutritional Interventions: Optimality, Information and Leakage', Discussion Paper 107, Development Economics Research Centre, University of Warwick.

—— —— (1992), 'Intrahousehold Inequality and the Theory of Targeting', *European Economic Review* (Papers and Proceedings), 36.

Haggblade, S., P. Hazell, and J. Brown (1989), 'Farm–Nonfarm Linkages in Rural Sub-Saharan Africa', *World Development*, 17.

Hahn, F. (1970), 'Savings and Uncertainty', *Review of Economic Studies*, 37.

—— (1973a), 'On Transaction Costs, Inessential Sequence Economies and Money', *Review of Economic Studies*, 40.

—— (1973b), 'On Optimum Taxation', *Journal of Economic Theory*, 6.

—— (1990), 'Solowian Growth Models', in P. Diamond, (ed.), *Growth, Productivity, Unemployment* (Cambridge, Mass.: MIT Press).

Hallfrisch, J., P. Steele, and L. Cohen (1982), 'Comparison of Seven-Day Diet Record with Measured Food Intake of Twenty-Four Subjects', *Nutrition Research*, 2.

Hamilton, L. S. and P. N. King (1983), *Tropical Forested Watersheds: Hydrologic and Soils Response to Major Uses or Conversions* (Boulder, Colo.: Westview Press).

Hamlin, A. (1986), *Ethics, Economics and the State* (Brighton: Wheatsheaf).

Hammer, J. S. (1986), 'Population Growth and Savings in LDCs: A Survey Article', *World Development*, 14.

Hammond, P. (1976), 'Equity, Arrow's Conditions and Rawls's Difference Principle', *Econometrica*, 44.

—— (1979), 'Straightforward Incentive Compatibility in Large Economies', *Review of Economic Studies*, 46.

—— (1988), 'Consequentialist Demographic Norms and Parenting Rights', *Social Choice and Welfare*, 5.

—— (1991), 'Irreducibility, Resource Relatedness and Survival in Equilibrium with Individual Non-Convexities'; forthcoming in R. Becker *et al.*, *General Equilibrium and Growth: The Legacy of Lionel McKenzie* (New York: Academic Press).

—— (1992), 'Compensated Equilibria in Continuum Economies with Individual Non-Convexities', mimeo, Department of Economics, Stanford University.

Hampton, J. (1986), *Hobbes and the Social Contract Tradition* (Cambridge: Cambridge University Press).

Hancock, G. (1989), *Lords of Poverty* (New York: Atlantic Monthly Press).

Hardin, G. (1968), 'The Tragedy of the Commons', *Science*, 162.

Hardin, R. (1988), *Morality within the Limits of Reason* (Chicago: University of Chicago Press).

Hare, R. M. (1973), 'Rawls's Theory of Justice, Part II', *Philosophical Quarterly*, 23.

—— (1981), *Moral Thinking: Its Level, Method and Point* (Oxford: Clarendon Press).

Harmish, N. and M. B. Munroe (1981), 'Nutrient Requirements during Pregnancy', *American Journal of Clinical Nutrition*, 34.

Harrison, A. (1989), 'Environmental Issues and the SNA', *Review of Income and Wealth*, 35.

Harrison, G. A. and J. C. Waterlow (eds.) (1990), *Diet and Disease in Traditional and Developing Countries* (Cambridge: Cambridge University Press).

Harriss, B. (1990), 'The Intrafamily Distribution of Hunger in South Asia', in J. Drèze and A. Sen (eds.), *The Political Economy of Hunger,* i: *Entitlement and Well-Being* (Oxford: Clarendon Press).

Harrod, R. F. (1936), 'Utilitarianism Revised', *Mind*, 45.

Harsanyi, J. C. (1955), 'Cardinal Welfare, Individualistic Ethics and Interpersonal Comparisons of Utility', *Journal of Political Economy*, 63.

—— (1976), *Essays in Ethics, Social Behaviour and Scientific Explanation* (Dordrecht: Reidel).

—— (1977a), 'Rule Utilitarianism and Decision Theory', *Erkenntnis*, 11.

—— (1977b), *Rational Behaviour and Bargaining Equilibrium in Games and Social Situations* (Cambridge: Cambridge University Press).

—— (1982), 'Morality and the Theory of Rational Behaviour', in Sen and Williams (1982).

—— (1987), 'Morals by Agreement', *Economics and Philosophy*, 3.

Hart, O. (1975), 'On the Optimality of Equilibrium when the Market Structure is Incomplete', *Journal of Economic Theory*, 11.

—— and B. Holmstrom (1987), 'The Theory of Contracts', in T. Bewley, (ed.), *Advances in Economic Theory* (New York: Cambridge University Press).

Hartwick, J. (1990), 'Natural Resources, National Accounting and Economic Depreciation', *Journal of Public Economics*, 43.

—— and N. Olewiler (1986), *The Economics of Natural Resource Use* (New York: Harper & Row).

Hauser, M. (1990), 'Harming Future People', *Philosophy and Public Affairs*, 19.

Hay, M. J. and S. Stichter (eds.) (1984), *African Women: South of the Sahara* (London: Longman).

Hayami, Y. and M. Kikuchi (1981), *Asian Village Economy at the Crossroads: An Economic Approach to Institutional Change* (Tokyo: University of Tokyo Press).

—— and V. Ruttan (1970), 'Agricultural Productivity Differences among Countries', *American Economic Review*, 60.

—— K. Subbarao, and K. Otsuka (1982), 'Efficiency and Equity in Producer Levy of India', *American Journal of Agricultural Economics*, 64.

Hayek, F. (1945), 'The Use of Knowledge in Society', *American Economic Review*, 35.

—— (1960), *The Constitution of Liberty* (London: Routledge & Kegan Paul).

—— (1976), *The Mirage of Social Justice: Law, Legislation, Liberty*, ii (London: Routledge & Kegan Paul).

Hazell, P., C. Pomereda and A. Valdes (eds) (1986), *Crop Insurance for Agricultural Development: Issues and Experience* (Baltimore: Johns Hopkins University Press).

Heady, C. J. and P. K. Mitra (1986), 'Optimal Taxation and Public Production in an Open Dual Economy', *Journal of Public Economics*, 30.

—— —— (1987a), 'Optimal Taxation and Shadow Pricing in a Developing Economy', in Newbery and Stern (1987).

—— —— (1987b), 'Distributional and Revenue Raising Arguments for Tariffs', *Journal of Development Economics*, 26.

—— —— (1990), 'Commodity Taxation with Administered and Free Market Prices: Theory and an Application to China', mimeo, Country Economics Department, World Bank.

Healy, M. J. R. (1989), 'Comment on "Nutritional Adaptation and Variability"', *European Journal of Clinical Nutrition*, 43.

Hecht, S. (1985), 'Environment, Development and Politics: Capital Accumulation and the Livestock Sector in Eastern Amazonia', *World Development*, 13.

—— A. B. Anderson, and P. May (1988), 'The Subsidy from Nature: Shifting Cultivation, Successional Palm Forests and Rural Development', *Human Organization*, 47.

Heller, W. and D. Starrett (1976), 'On the Nature of Externalities' in S. Lin (ed.), *Theory and Measurement of Externalities* (New York: Academic Press).

Helmers, F. L. C. H. (1979), *Project Planning and Income Distribution* (London: Martinus Nijhoff).

Helpman, E. and P. Krugman (1989), *Trade Policy and Market Structure* (Cambridge, Mass.: MIT Press).

Henn, J. K. (1984), 'Women in the Rural Economy: Past, Present and Future', in Hay and Stichter (1984).

Henry, C. J. K. (1990), 'Body Mass Index and the Limits of Human Survival', *European Journal of Clinical Nutrition*, 44.

—— J. Heyter and D. G. Rees (1989), 'The Constancy of Basal Metabolic Rate in Free-Living Male Subjects', *European Journal of Clinical Nutrition*, 43.

—— and D. G. Rees (1988), 'A Preliminary Analysis of Basal Metabolic Rate and Race', in K. Blaxter and I. Macdonald (eds.), *Comparative Nutrition* (London: John Libbey).

Henry, C. (1974), 'Investment Decisions under Uncertainty: The Irreversibility Effect', *American Economic Review*, 64.

Herring, R. (1983), *Land to the Tiller: The Political Economy of Agrarian Reform in South Asia* (New Haven, Conn.: Yale University Press).

Hess, P. N. (1988), *Population Growth and Socioeconomic Progress in Less Developed Countries* (New York: Praeger).

Heyd, D. (1992), *Genethics: Moral Issues in the Creation of People* (Berkeley: University of California Press).

Hicks, J. R. (1939), *Value and Capital* (Oxford: Clarendon Press).

—— (1968), *A Theory of Economic History* (Oxford: Oxford University Press).

Hicks, N. (1979), 'Growth vs. Basic Needs: Is There a Trade-off?' *World Development*, 7.

—— and P. Streeten (1979), 'Indicators of Devlopment: The Search for a Basic Needs Yardstick', *World Development*, 7.

Higgins, G. M. *et al.* (1982), *Potential Population Supporting Capacities of Lands in the Developing World* (Rome: Food and Agriculture Organization).

Hildenbrand, W. (1974), *Core and Equilibria of a Large Economy* (Princeton, NJ: Princeton University Press).

—— and A. Kirman (1976), *Introduction to Equilibrium Analysis* (Amsterdam: North-Holland).

Hill, K. (1992), 'Fertility and Mortality Trends in the Developing World', *Ambio*, 21.

—— and A. R. Pebley (1989), 'Child Mortality in the Developing World', *Population and Development Review*, 15.

Hill, P. (1963), *The Migrant Cocoa-Farmers of Southern Ghana* (Cambridge: Cambridge University Press).

—— (1972), *Rural Hausa* (Cambridge: Cambridge University Press).

Ho, Y,-M. (1966), *Agricultural Development of Taiwan: 1903–1960* (Kingsport, Tenn.: Vanderbilt University Press).

Hobcraft, J. N., J. W. McDonald, and S. O. Rutstein (1984), 'Socio-Economic Factors in Infant and Child Mortality: A Cross-National Comparison', *Population Studies*, 38.

Hoddinott, J. and L. Haddad (1991), 'Household Expenditures, Child Anthropometric Status and the Intrahousehold Division of Income: Evidence from the Côte D'Ivoire', Discussion Paper No. 155, Research Program in Development Studies, Woodrow Wilson School, Princeton University.

Hodgson, G. and J. Dixon (1992), 'Sedimentation Damage to Marine Resources: Environmental and Economic Analysis', in J. B. Marsh (ed.), *Resources and Environment in Asia's Marine Sector* (London: Taylor & Francis).

Hoff, K. (1991), 'Land Taxes, Output Taxes, and Share-Cropping: Was Henry George Right?' *World Bank Economic Review*, 5.

—— A. Braverman, and J. E. Stiglitz (eds.) (1992), *The Economics of Rural Organizations* (Oxford: Oxford University Press).

—— and J. E. Stiglitz (1990), 'Introduction: Imperfect Information and Rural Credit Markets: Puzzles and Policy Perspectives', *World Bank Economic Review*, 4.

Hogarth, R. M. and M. W. Reder (eds.) (1986) *Rational Choice: The Contrast between Economics and Psychology* (Chicago: University of Chicago Press).

Hollander, S. (1965), *The Source of Increased Efficiency: A Study of Dupont Rayon Plants* (Cambridge, Mass.: MIT Press).

Holmstrom, B. (1982), 'Moral Hazard in Teams', *Bell Journal of Economics*, 10.

Horton, E. S. (1984), 'Appropriate Methodology for Assessing Physical Activity under Laboratory Conditions in Studies of Energy Balance in Adults', in Pollitt and Amante (1984).

Hossain, M. (1984), *Credit for the Rural Poor: The Experience of the Grameen Bank in Bangladesh* (Dhaka: Bangladesh Institute of Development Studies).

Howe, J. (1986), *The Kuna Gathering* (Austin, Tex.: University of Texas Press).

Hull, T. H. (1990), 'Recent Trends in Sex Ratios in China', *Population and Development Review*, 16.

Humana, C. (1983), *World Human Rights Guide* (London: Hutchinson).

—— (1986), *World Human Rights Guide* (London: Economist Publications).

Hume (1960), *A Treatise of Human Nature*, ed. by L. A. Selby-Bigge (Oxford: Clarendon Press).

Humphries, J. (1990), 'Enclosures, Common Rights, and Women: The Proletarian-ization of Families in the Late Eighteenth and Early Nineteenth Centuries', *Journal of Economic History*, 50.

Huppi, M. and G. Feder (1990), 'The Role of Groups and Credit Cooperatives in Rural Lending', *World Bank Research Observer*, 5.

Hurka, T. (1983), 'Value and Population Size', *Ethics*, 93.

Hurwicz, L. (1972), 'On Informationally Decentralized Systems', in C. B. McGuire and R. Radner (eds.), *Decision and Organization* (Amsterdam: North-Holland).

—— (1973), 'The Design of Mechanisms for Resource Allocation', *American Economic Review* (Papers and Proceedings), 63.

IIED/WRI (1987), *World Resources 1987* (New York: Basic Books).

Iliffe, J. (1984), 'Poverty in Nineteenth Century Yorubaland', *Journal of African History*, 25.

—— (1987), *The African Poor* (Cambridge: Cambridge University Press).

ILO (1976), *Employment, Growth and Basic Needs: A One-World Problem* (Geneva: International Labour Organization).

—— (1977), *Poverty and Landlessness in Rural Asia* (Geneva: International Labour Organization).

—— (1982), *Resolution Concerning Statistics of the Economically Active Population, Employment and Unemployment*, 13th International Conference of Labour Statisticians (Geneva: International Labour Organization).

Immink, M. D. C. and F. E. Viteri (1981), 'Energy Intake and Productivity of Guatemalan Sugarcane Cutters: An Empirical Test of the Efficiency Wage Hypothesis, Parts I and II', *Journal of Development Economics*, 9.

—— —— and R. W. Helms (1981), 'Food Substitution with Worker Feeding Programs: Energy Supplementation in Guatemalan Sugarcane Workers', *American Journal of Clinical Nutrition*, 34.

—— —— —— (1982), 'Energy Intake over the Life Cycle and Human Capital Formation in Guatemalan Sugarcane Cutters', *Economic Development and Cultural Change*. 30.

—— et al. (1984a), 'Microeconomic Consequences of Energy Deficiency in Rural Populations in Developing Countries', in Pollit and Amante (1984).

—— et al. (1984b), 'Functional Consequences of Marginal Malnutrition Among Agricultural Workers in Guatemala, II: Economics and Human Capital Formation', *Food and Nutrition Bulletin*, 6.

Intriligator, M. D. (1971), *Mathematical Optimization and Economic Theory* (Englewood Cliffs, NJ: Prentice-Hall).

Isenman, P. (1980), 'Basic Needs: The Case of Sri Lanka', *World Development*, 8.

—— (1987), 'A Comment on *Growth and Equity in Developing Countries: A Reinterpretation of the Sri Lankan Experience*, by Bhalla and Glewwe', *World Bank Economic Review*, 1.

Jacoby, H. and E. Skoufias (1992), 'Risk, Seasonality and School Attendance: Evidence from Rural India', mimeo. Department of Economics, University of Rochester.

Jain, D. and N. Bannerjee (eds.) (1985), *Tyranny of the Household: Investigative Essays on Women's Work* (New Delhi, Vikas).

Jain, S. (1975), *Size Distribution of Income: A Compilation of Data* (Washington, DC: World Bank).

James, W. F. T., A. Ferro-Luzzi, and J. C. Waterlow (1988), 'Definition of Chronic Energy Deficiency in Adults', *European Journal of Clinical Nutrition*, 42.

—— , P. Haggarty, and B. A. McGaw (1988), 'Recent Progress in Studies on Energy Expenditure: Are the New Methods Providing Answers to the Old Questions?' *Proceedings of the Nutrition Society*, 47.

—— and P. S. Shetty (1982), 'Metabolic Adaptations and Energy Requirements in Developing Countries', *Human Nutrition: Clinical Nutrition*, 36C.

—— et al. (1992), *Body Mass Index: An Objective Measure of Chronic Energy Deficiency in Adults* (Rome: FAO).

Jamison, D. T. (1986), 'Child Malnutrition and School Performance in China', *Journal of Development Economics*, 20.

—— and L. J. Lau (1982), *Farmer Education and Farm Efficiency* (Baltimore: Johns Hopkins University Press).

—— and J. Leslie (1990), 'Health and Nutrition Considerations in Education Planning, 2: The Cost and Effectiveness of School-Based Interventions', *Food and Nutrition Bulletin*, 12.

—— and P. R. Moock (1984), 'Farmer Education and Farm Efficiency In Nepal: The Role of Schooling, Extension Services and Cognitive Skills', *World Development*, 12.

—— and H. Mosley (1990), 'Selecting Disease Control Priorities in Developing Countries', in D. T. Jamison and H. Mosley (eds.), *Evolving Health Priorities in Developing Countries* (Washington, DC: World Bank).

Janowitz, M. (1964), *The Military in the Political Development of New Nations* (Chicago: University of Chicago Press).

Jazairy, I., M. Alamgir, and T. Panuccio (1992), *The State of World Poverty* (New York: New York University Press).

Jelliffe, D. B. and E. F. P. Jelliffe (1978), 'The Volume and Composition of Human Milk in Poorly Nourished Communities: A Review', *American Journal of Clinical Nutrition*, 31.

Jiggins, J. (1989), 'How Poor Women Earn Income in Sub-Saharan Africa and What Works Against Them', *World Development*, 17.

Jimenez, E. (1987), *Pricing Policy in the Social Sectors: Cost Recovery for Education and Health in Developing Countries* (Baltimore: Johns Hopkins University Press).

—— (1990), 'Social Sector Pricing Policy Revisited: A Survey of Some Recent Controversies', *Proceedings of the World Bank Annual Conference on Development Economics 1989* (Washington, DC: World Bank).

Jodha, N. S. (1980), 'The Process of Desertification and the Choice of Interventions', *Economic and Political Weekly*, 15.

—— (1981), 'Role of Credit in Farmers' Adjustment against Risk in Arid and Semi-Arid Tropical Areas in India', *Economic and Political Weekly*, 16.

—— (1984), 'Agricultural Tenancy in Semiarid Tropical India', in Binswanger and Rosenzweig (1984b).

—— (1986), 'Common Property Resources and the Rural Poor', *Economic and Political Weekly*, 21.

—— (1990), 'Rural Common Property Resources: Contributions and Crises', *Economic and Political Weekly*, 25.

Johansson, S. Ryan (1991a), 'The Health Transition: The Modernization of Morbidity during the Decline of Mortality', *Health Transition Review*, 1.

—— (1991b), 'Welfare, Mortality and Gender: Continuity and Change in the Explanation of Male/Female Mortality Differences over Three Centuries', *Continuity and Change*, 6.

Johnson, D. Gale and R. Lee (eds.) (1987), *Population Growth and Economic Development: Issues and Evidence* (Madison, Wis.: University of Wisconsin Press).

Johnston, B. F. (1989), 'The Political Economy of Agricultural Development in Kenya and Tanzania', *Food Research Institute Studies*, 21.

—— and P. Kilby (1975), *Agriculture and Structural Transformation: Economic Strategies in Late-Developing Countries* (Oxford: Oxford University Press).

Johnston, F. E. *et al.* (1976), 'Hereditary and Environmental Determinants of Growth in Height in a Longitudinal Sample of Children and Youth of Guatemalan and European Ancestry', *American Journal of Physical Anthropology*, 44.

—— *et al.* (1980), 'A Factor Analysis of Correlates of Nutritional Status of Mexican Children: Birth to 3 Years', in L. S. Greene and F. E. Johnston (eds.), *Social and Biological Predictors of Nutritional Status, Physical Growth and Neurological Development* (New York: Academic Press).

Joseph, K, and J. Sumption (1979), *Equality* (London: John Murray).

Kahneman, D., P. Slovic, and A. Tversky (eds.) (1982), *Judgment under Uncertainty: Heuristics and Biases* (Cambridge: Cambridge University Press).

Kakwani, N. (1980), *Income Inequality and Poverty: Methods of Estimation and Policy Applications* (New York: Oxford University Press).

—— (1981), 'Welfare Measures: An International Comparison', *Journal of Development Economics*, 8.

Kalai, E. and M. Smorodinsky (1975), 'Other Solutions to Nash's Bargaining Problem', *Econometrica*, 43.

Kaldor, N. and J. A. Mirrlees (1962), 'A New Model of Economic Growth', *Review of Economic Studies*, 29.

Kamarck, A. M. (1988) 'The Special Case of Africa', in Bell and Reich (1988).

Kaneko, Y. and K. Nidaira (1988), 'Towards Basic Human Needs in Relation to Public Health and Nutrition', in Bell and Reich (1988).

Karkaria, B. J. (1989), 'Prisoners of Gender', *Illustrated Weekly of India*, 111.

Katz, M. and C. Shapiro (1986), 'Technology Adoption in the Presence of Network Externalities', *Journal of Political Economy*, 94.

Kautilya (1967), *Arthasastra*, tr. by R. Shama Sastry under the title *Kautilya's Arthasastra* (Mysore: Mysore Publishing House).

Keeler, E., A. M. Spence, and R. Zeckhauser (1972), 'The Optimal Control of Pollution', *Journal of Economic Theory*, 4.

Keen, M. (1992), 'Needs and Targeting', *Economic Journal*, 102.

Kelley, A. C. (1988), 'Economic Consequences of Population Change in the Third World', *Journal of Economic Literature*, 26.

Kennedy, E. (1989), *The Effects of Sugarcane Production on Food Security, Health, and Nutrition in Kenya: A Longitudinal Analysis*, Research Report No. 78, International Food Policy Research Institute, Washington, DC.

—— and H. Alderman (1987), 'Comparative Analyses of Nutritional Effectiveness of Food Subsidies and other Food-Related Interventions', mimeo, International Food Policy Research Institute, Washington, DC.

—— and O. K. Knudsen (1985), 'A Review of Supplementary Feeding Programmes and Recommendations on Their Design', in Biswas and Pinstrup-Andersen (1985).

—— and R. Oniang'o (1990), 'Health and Nutrition Effects of Sugarcane Production in South-Western Kenya', *Food and Nutrition Bulletin*, 12.

Keyfitz, N. (1976), 'World Resources and the World Middle Class', *Scientific American*, 235.

—— and W. Flieger (1968), *World Population: An Analysis of Data* (Chicago: University of Chicago Press).

Keys, A. *et al.* (1950), *The Biology of Human Starvation* (Minneapolis, Minn.: University of Minnesota Press).

Kim, K. S. and M. Roemer (eds.) (1979), *Growth and Structural Transformation: Studies in the Modernization of the Republic of Korea: 1945–1975* (Cambridge, Mass.: Harvard University Press).

Kim, W. S. and K. Y. Yun (1988), 'Fiscal Policy and Development in Korea', *World Development*, 16.

King, E. (1987), 'The Effect of Family Size on Family Welfare: What Do We Know?' in Johnson and Lee (1987).

—— and R. E. Evenson (1983), 'Time Allocation and Home Production in Philippine Rural Households', in Buvinic, Lycette and McGreevey (1983).

King, M. (1990), 'Health is a Sustainable State', *Lancet*, 336.

King, T. (ed.) (1980), 'Education and Income', World Bank Staff Working Paper No. 402.

—— *et al.* (1974), *Population Policies and Economic Development* (Baltimore: Johns Hopkins University Press).

Klein, R. E. *et al.* (1976), 'Effects of Maternal Nutrition on Fetal Growth and Infant Development', *Bulletin of the Pan American Health Organisation*, 10.

Knudsen, O. K. (1981), 'Economics of Supplementary Feeding of Malnourished Children: Leakages, Costs and Benefits', World Bank Staff Working Paper No. 451, Washington, DC.

Kochar, A. (1991), 'An Empirical Investigation of Rationing Constraints in Rural Credit Markets in India', mimeo, Department of Economics, Stanford University.

—— (1992), 'Credit Constraints and Land Tenancy Markets in Rural India', mimeo, Institute for Policy Reform, Washington DC.

Kolm, S.-Ch. (1969), 'The Optimal Production of Social Justice', in J. Margolis and H. Guitton (eds.), *Public Economics* (London: Macmillan).

—— (1977), 'Multidimensional Egalitarianism', *Quarterly Journal of Economics*, 91.

Koopmans, T. C. (1957), 'The Price System and the Allocation of Resources', in *Three Essays on the State of Economic Science* (New York: McGraw-Hill).

—— (1964), 'On the Flexibility of Future Preferences', in M. W. Shelley and

G. L. Bryan (eds.), *Human Judgments and Optimality* (New York: John Wiley).

—— (1965), 'On the Concept of Optimal Economic Growth', *Pontificiae Academiae Scientiarum Scripta Varia*, 28; reprinted in *The Econometric Approach to Development Planning* (Amsterdam: North-Holland), 1966.

—— (1967), 'Objectives, Constraints and Outcomes in Optimal Growth Models', *Econometrica*, 35.

—— (1972a), 'Representation of Preference Orderings with Independent Components of Consumption', in C. B. McGuire and R. Radner (eds.), *Decision and Organization* (Amsterdam: North-Holland).

—— (1972b), 'Representation of Preference Orderings over Time', in C. B. McGuire and R. Radner (eds.), *Decision and Organization* (Amsterdam: North-Holland).

—— (1973), 'Some Observations on "Optimal" Economic Growth and Exhaustible Resources', in H. C. Bos, H. Linneman, and P. de Wolff (eds.), *Economic Structure and Development* (Amsterdam: North-Holland).

—— (1974), 'Proof for a Case where Discounting Advances the Doomsday', *Review of Economic Studies* (Symposium on the Economics of Exhaustible Resources), 41.

Kornai, J. (1986), 'The Soft-Budget Constraint', *Kyklos*, 39.

—— (1988), 'Individual Freedom and Reform of the Socialist Economy', *European Economic Review* (Papers and Proceedings), 32.

Kotlikoff, L. J. (1988), 'Intergenerational Transfers and Savings', *Journal of Economic Perspectives*, 2.

—— and A. Spivak (1981), 'The Family as an Incomplete Annuities Market', *Journal of Political Economy*, 89.

—— and L. Summers (1981), 'The Role of Intergenerational Transfers in Aggregate Capital Accumulation', *Journal of Political Economy*, 89.

Kreimer, A. and M. Munasinghe (eds.) (1991), *Managing Natural Disasters and the Environment* (Washington, DC: World Bank).

Kreps, D. (1979), 'A Representation Theorem for "Preference for Flexibility"', *Econometrica*, 47.

—— and R. Wilson (1982), 'Reputation and Incomplete Information', *Journal of Economic Theory*, 27.

—— et al. (1982), 'Rational Cooperation in the Finitely Repeated Prisoners' Dilemma', *Journal of Economic Theory*, 27.

Krishna, R. (1975), *Unemployment in India* (New York: Agricultural Development Council).

—— (1976), 'Rural Unemployment: A Survey of Concepts and Estimates for India', World Bank Staff Working Paper No. 234.

Krueger, A. O. (1974), 'The Political Economy of the Rent-Seeking Society', *American Economic Review*, 64.

—— (1990), 'Government Failures in Development', *Journal of Economic Perspectives*, 4.

—— M. Schiff, and A. Valdes (1988), 'Agricultural Incentives in Developing Countries: Measuring the Effect of Sectoral and Economywide Policy', *World Bank Economic Review*, 2.

Krugman, P. (1991), 'History versus Expectations', *Quarterly Journal of Economics*, 106.

Kumar, A., O. P. Ghai, and N. Singh (1977), 'Delayed Nerve Conduction Velocities in Children with Protein–Calorie Malnutrition', *Journal of Pediatrics*, 90.

Kumar, G. (1989), 'Gender, Differential Mortality and Development: A Perspective on the Experience of Kerala', *Cambridge Journal of Economics*, 13.

Kumar, S. K. and D. Hotchkiss (1988), 'Consequences of Deforestation for Women's Time Allocation, Agricultural Production, and Nutrition in Hill Areas of Nepal', Research Report 69, International Food Policy Research Institute.

Kunreuther, H. and G. Wright (1979), 'Safety-First, Gambling, and the Subsistence Farmer', in Roumasset, Boussard and Singh (1979).

Kuo, S. W. Y., G. Ranis, and J. C. H. Fei (1981), *The Taiwan Success Story: Rapid Growth with Improved Distribution in the Republic of China, 1952–1979* (Boulder, Colo.: Westview Press).

Kurpad, A. V., R. N. Kulkarni, and P. S. Shetty (1989), 'Reduced Thermoregulatory Thermogenesis in Undernutrition', *European Journal of Clinical Nutrition*, 43.

Kutcher, G. and P. Scandizzo (1981), *The Agricultural Economy of Northeast Brazil* (Baltimore: Johns Hopkins University Press).

Kuznets, S. (1955), 'Economic Growth and Income Inequality', *American Economic Review*, 65.

—— (1966), *Modern Economic Growth: Rate, Structure and Spread* (New Haven, Conn.: Yale University Press).

Kymlicka, W. (1990), *Contemporary Political Philosophy* (Oxford: Clarendon Press).

Kynch, J. and A. Sen (1983), 'Indian Women: Well-Being and Survival', *Cambridge Journal of Economics*, 7.

Lacville, R. (1991), 'A Sad Little-Girl', *Guardian Weekly* (9 June).

Laffont, J. -J. (ed.) (1979), *Aggregation and Revelation of Preferences* (Amsterdam: North-Holland).

—— and E. Maskin (1982), 'The Theory of Incentives: An Overview', in W. Hildenbrand (ed.), *Advances in Economic Theory* (Cambridge: Cambridge University Press).

Lal, D. (1983), *The Poverty of Development Economics* (London: Institute of Economic Affairs).

Lane, J. (1977), *On Optimum Population Paths* (Berlin: Springer-Verlag).

Lau, L. and P. A. Yotopoulos (1971), 'A Test for Relative Economic Efficiency and Application to Indian Agriculture', *American Economic Review*, 61.

Layard, R. and A. Walters (1978), *Microeconomic Theory* (New York: McGraw-Hill).

Leach, G. (1975), 'Energy and Food Production', *Food Policy*, 1.

Lear, J. (1988), *Aristotle: The Desire to Understand* (Cambridge: Cambridge University Press).

Lecaillon, J. *et al.* (eds.) (1984), *Income Distribution and Economic Development: An Analytical Survey* (Geneva: International Labour Organization).

Lechtig, A. *et al.* (1975), 'Influence of Maternal Nutrition on Birth Weight', *American Journal of Clinical Nutrition*, 28.

—— *et al.* (1978), 'Effect of Maternal Nutrition on Infant Mortality', in W. H. Mosley (ed.), *Nutrition and Human Reproduction* (New York: Plenum Press).

Lee, J., L. N. Kolonel, and M. W. Hinds (1981), 'Relative Merits of the Weight-Corrected-for-Height Indices', *American Journal of Clinical Nutrition*, 34.

Lee, R. B. (1972), 'Population Growth and the Beginnings of Sedentary Life among the !Kung Bushmen', in B. Spooner (ed.), *Population Growth: Anthropological Implications* (Cambridge, Mass.: MIT Press).

—— (1980), 'Lactation, Ovolution, Infanticide, and Women's Work: A Study of Hunter-Gatherer Population Regulation', in M. N. Cohen, R. S. Malpass and H. G. Klein (eds.), *Biosocial Mechanisms of Population Regulations* (New Haven, Conn.: Yale University Press).

Lee, R. D. and R. A. Bulatao (1983), 'The Demand for Children: A Critical Essay', in Bulatao and Lee (1983), Vol. 1.

—— and T. Miller (1991), 'Population Growth, Externalities to Childbearing, and Fertility Policy in Developing Countries', *Proceedings of the World Bank Annual Conference on Development Economics, 1990* (supplement to the *World Bank Economic Review* and the *World Bank Research Observer*).

Leibenstein, H. (1957a), 'The Theory of Underemployment in Backward Economies', *Journal of Political Economy*, 65.

—— (1957b), *Economic Backwardness and Economic Growth* (New York: John Wiley).

—— (1974), 'An Interpretation of the Economic Theory of Fertility: Promising Path or Blind Alley?' *Journal of Economic Literature*, 12.

—— (1975), 'The Economic Theory of Fertility Decline', *Quarterly Journal of Economics*, 89.

Leland, H. (1968), 'Savings and Uncertainty: The Precautionary Demand for Saving', *Quarterly Journal of Economics*, 82.

Leslie, J. (1988), 'Women's Work and Child Nutrition in the Third World', *World Development*, 16.

—— and D. T. Jamison (1990), 'Health and Nutrition Considerations in Education Planning, 1: Educational Consequences of Health Problems among School-Age Children', *Food and Nutrition Bulletin*, 12.

——, M. Lycette, and M. Buvinic (1988), 'Weathering Economic Crises: The Crucial Role of Women in Health', in Bell and Reich (1988).

—— and M. Paolisso (eds.) (1989), *Women's Work and Child Welfare in the Third World* (Boulder, Colo.: Westview Press).

Levhari, D. and T. N. Srinivasan (1969), 'Optimal Savings under Uncertainty', *Review of Economic Studies*, 36.

Levin, H. M. (1986), 'A Benefit–Cost Analysis of Nutritional Programs for Anemia Reducation', *World Bank Research Observer*, 1.

Levin, R. C. and P. C. Reiss (1984), 'Tests of a Schumpterian Model of R&D and Market Structure', in Z. Griliches (ed.), *R&D Patents and Productivity* (Chicago: University of Chicago Press).

Levy, S. and S. Nolan (1991), 'Trade and Foreign Investment Policies under

Imperfect Competition: Lessons for Developing Countries', *Journal of Development Economics*, 37.

Lewis, D. (1969), *Convention* (Cambridge, Mass.: Harvard University Press).

Lewis, W. A. (1954), 'Economic Development with Unlimited Supplies of Labour', *Manchester School of Economic and Social Studies*, 22.

Libbee, M. J. (1980), 'Territorial Endogamy and the Spatial Structure of Marriage in Rural India', in Sopher (1980c).

Lieberman, M. B. (1984), 'The Learning Curve and Pricing in the Chemical Processing Industries', *Rand Journal of Economics*, 15.

Lightfoot-Klein, H. (1989), *Prisoners of Ritual: An Odyssey into Female Genital Circumcision in Africa* (Binghamton, NY: Haworth Press).

Lim, E. and A. Wood (1985), *China: Long Term Development Issues and Options* (Baltimore: Johns Hopkins University Press).

Lim, Y. (1991), 'Disentangling Permanent Income and Risk Sharing: A General Equilibrium Perspective on Credit Markets in Rural South India', mimeo, Department of Economics, University of Chicago.

Lind, R. (ed.) (1982), *Discounting for Time and Risk in Energy Policy* (Baltimore: Johns Hopkins University Press).

Lindbeck, A. (1988), 'Individual Freedom and Welfare State Policy', *European Economic Review* (Papers and Proceedings), 32.

—— and D. Snower (1988), *The Insider–Outsider Theory of Employment and Unemployment* (Cambridge, Mass.: MIT Press).

Lindblom, C. (1977), *Politics and Markets* (New York: Basic Books).

Lindbert, P. (1980), 'Child Costs and Economic Development', in Easterlin (1980).

—— (1983), 'The Changing Economic Costs and Benefits of Having Children', in Bulatao and Lee (1983).

—— and J. Williamson (1985), 'Growth, Equality and History', *Explorations in Economic History*, 22.

Lipset, S. (1960), *Political Man* (Garden City, NY: Doubleday Anchor Books).

Lipton, M. (1976), *Why Poor People Stay Poor: Urban Bias in World Development* (London: Maurice Temple Smith).

—— (1983), 'Poverty, Undernourishment and Hunger', World Bank Staff Working Paper No. 597.

—— (1985), 'Land Assets and Rural Poverty', World Bank Staff Working Paper, No. 744.

Little, I. M. D. (1979), 'An Economic Reconnaissance', in W. Galenson (ed.) *Economic Growth and Structural Change in Taiwan* (Ithaca, NY: Cornell University Press).

—— (1982), *Economic Development: Theory, Policy and International Relations* (New York: Basic Books).

—— and J. A. Mirrlees (1969), *Manual of Industrial Project Analysis in Developing Countries: Social Cost Benefit Analysis* (Paris: OECD).

—— —— (1974), *Project Appraisal and Planning for Developing Countries* (London: Heinemann).

Livi-Bacci, M. (1983), 'The Nutrition–Mortality Link in Past Times: A Comment', *Journal of Interdisciplinary History*, 14.

Locay, L. (1990), 'Economic Development and the Division of Production between Households and Markets', *Journal of Political Economy*, 98.

Lockheed, M., D. Jamison, and L. Lau (1980), 'Farmer Education and Farm Efficiency: A Survey', *Economic Development and Cultural Change*, 29.

Loomes, G. and R. Sugden (1982), 'Regret Theory: An Alternative Theory of Rational Choice under Uncertainty', *Economic Journal*, 92.

—— —— (1986), 'Disappointment and Dynamic Consistency in Choice under Uncertainty', *Review of Economic Studies*, 53.

—— —— (1987), 'Some Implications of a More General Form of Regret Theory', *Journal of Economic Theory*, 41.

Lopez, A. D. (1984), 'Sex Differentials in Mortality', *WHO Chronicle*, 38.

Loury, G. (1979), 'Market Structure and Innovation', *Quarterly Journal of Economics*, 93.

Low, S. M. (1984), 'The Cultural Basis of Health, Illness and Disease', *Social Work in Health Care*, 9.

Lucas, R. (1988), 'On the Mechanics of Economic Development', *Journal of Monetary Economics*, 22.

—— (1991), 'Making a Miracle', Fisher-Schultz Lecture, Econometric Society; forthcoming in *Econometrica*.

Luce, R. D. and H. Raiffa (1957), *Games and Decisions* (New York: John Wiley).

Lunven, P. (1983), 'The Value of Time Use Data in Nutrition', *Food and Nutrition*, 9.

Lydall, H. (1979), *A Theory of Income Distribution* (Oxford: Clarendon Press).

Mabbut, J. (1984), 'A New Global Assessment of the Status and Trends of Desertification', *Environmental Conservation*, 11.

Machina, M. J. (1982), '"Expected Utility" Analysis without the Independence Axiom', *Econometrica*, 50.

—— (1987), 'Choice under Uncertainty: Problems Solved and Unsolved', *Journal of Economic Perspectives*, 1.

—— (1989), 'Dynamic Consistency and Non-Expected Utility Models of Choice under Uncertainty', *Journal of Economic Literature*, 27.

—— (1990), *The Economic Theory of Individual Behavior Toward Risk: Theory, Evidence and New Directions* (Cambridge: Cambridge University Press), forthcoming.

Mackie, J. L. (1978), 'Can There Be a Right-Based Moral Theory?' in P. A. French, T. E. Uehling, and H. K. Wettstein (eds.), *Studies in Ethical Theory* (Minneapolis, Minn.: University of Minnesota Press), reprinted in J. Waldron (ed.) *Theories of Rights* (Oxford: Oxford University Press), 1984.

Maddison, A. (1989), *The World Economy in the 20th Century* (Paris: OECD).

Magrath, W. and P. Arens (1989), 'The Costs of Soil Erosion in Java: A Natural Resource Accounting Approach', World Bank Environmental Department Working Paper No. 18.

Mahar, D. (1988), 'Government Policies and Deforestation in Brazil's Amazon Region', World Bank Environment Department Working Paper No. 7.

Majumdar, M. and R. Radner (1991), 'Linear Models of Economic Survival under Production Uncertainty', *Economic Theory*, 1.

Mäler, K. -G. (1974), *Environmental Economics: A Theoretical Enquiry* (Baltimore: Johns Hopkins University Press).

—— (1989), 'Environmental Resources, Risk and Bayesian Decision Rules', mimeo, Stockholm School of Economics.

—— (1991), 'National Accounting and Environmental Resources', *Journal of Environmental Economics and Resources*, 1.

—— (1992), 'Production Function Approach in Developing Countries', in J. R. Vincent, E. W. Crawford, and J. P. Hoehn (eds.), *Valuing Environmental Benefits in Developing Countries* (East Lansing: Michigan State University Press).

Malina, R. M. (1980a), 'Physical Activity, Growth, and Functional Capacity', in F. E. Johnston, A. F. Roche, and C. Susanne (eds.), *Human Physical Growth and Maturation: Methodologies and Factors* (New York: Plenum Press).

—— (1980b), 'Biosocial Correlates of Motor Development during Infancy and Early Childhood', in L. S. Greene and F. E. Johnston (eds.), *Social and Biological Predictors of Nutritional Status, Physical Growth and Neurological Development* (New York: Academic Press).

—— (1984), 'Physical Activity and Motor Development/Performance in Populations Nutritionally at Risk', in Pollitt and Amante (1984).

Malinowski, B. (1921), 'The Primitive Economics of the Trobriand Islanders', *Economic Journal*, 31.

—— (1960), *A Scientific Theory of Culture and Other Essays* (New York: Oxford University Press).

Malinvaud, E. (1972a), *Lectures on Microeconomic Theory* (Amsterdam: North-Holland).

—— (1972b), 'The Allocation of Individual Risks in Large Markets', *Journal of Economic Theory*, 4.

—— (1973), 'Markets for an Exchange Economy with Independent Risks', *Econometrica*, 41.

Manser, M. and M. Brown (1980), 'Marriage and Household Decision-Making: A Bargaining Analysis', *International Economic Review*, 21.

Mansfield, E. (1988), 'Social Rate of Return in Basic Science', in Z. Griliches (ed.), *R&D, Patents and Productivity* (Chicago: University of Chicago Press).

Marglin, S. A. (1976), *Value and Price in the Labour-Surplus Economy* (Oxford: Oxford University Press).

Marschak, J. (1950), 'Rational Behavior, Uncertain Prospects and Measurable Utility', *Econometrica*, 18.

—— and R. Radner (1972), *Economic Theory of Teams*, (New Haven, Conn: Yale University Press).

Marshall, A. (1920), *The Principles of Economics* (London: Macmillan).

Marshall, T. H. (1964), *Class, Citizenship and Social Development* (Garden City, NY: Doubleday).

—— (1981), *The Right to Welfare and Other Essays* (New York: Free Press).

Marsilius of Padua, *Defender of the Faith*, tr. by A. Gewirth (Chicago: University of Chicago Press, 1956).

Martorell, R. (1985), 'Child Growth Retardation: A Discussion of its Causes and Relationship to Health', in Blaxter and Waterlow (1985).

—— (1990), 'Body Size, Adaptation and Function', *Human Organization*, 48.

—— and G. Arroyave (1988), 'Malnutrition, Work Output and Energy Needs', in Collins and Roberts (1988).

—— and J.-P. Habicht (1986), 'Growth in Early Childhood in Developing Countries', in Falkner and Tanner (1986).

—— and T. J. Ho (1984), 'Malnutrition, Morbidity and Mortality', in Mosley and Chen (1984).

—— F. S. Mendoza, and R. O. Castillo (1989), 'Genetic and Environmental Determinants of Growth in Mexican–Americans', *Pediatrics*, 84.

—— J. Rivera, and H. Kaplowitz (1990), 'Consequences of Stunting in Early Childhood for Adult Body Size in Rural Guatemala', *Annales Nestle*, 48.

—— *et al.* (1975), 'Acute Morbidity and Physical Growth in Rural Guatemalan Children', *American Journal of Diseases of Children*, 129.

—— *et al.* (1979), 'Protein Energy Intakes in a Malnourished Population after Increasing the Supply of Dietary Staples', *Ecology of Food and Nutrition*, 8.

—— *et al.* (1980), 'The Impact of Ordinary Illnesses on the Dietary Intakes of Malnourished Children', *American Journal of Clinical Nutrition*, 33.

—— *et al.* (1981), 'Maternal Stature, Fertility, and Infant Mortality', *Human Biology*, 53.

—— *et al.* (1991), 'Long-Term Consequences of Growth Retardation during Early Childhood', mimeo, Cornell University.

Marx, K. (1970), *Capital*, i, (London: Lawrence & Wisehart), first published 1867.

Maskin, E. (1978), 'A Theorem on Utilitarianism', *Review of Economic Studies*, 45.

—— and J. Riley (1984a), 'Monopoly with Incomplete Information', *Rand Journal of Economics*, 15.

—— —— (1984b), 'Optimal Auctions with Risk Averse Buyers', *Econometrica*, 52.

Mason, K. O. and A. M. Taj (1987), 'Differences between Women's and Men's Reproductive Goals in Developing Countries', *Population and Development Review*, 13.

Mata, L. J. (1978a), 'Breast Feeding: Main Promoter of Infant Health', *American Journal of Clinical Nutrition*, 31.

—— (1978b), *The Children of Santa Maria Cauque: A Prospective Field Study of Health and Growth* (Cambridge, Mass.: MIT Press).

—— (1985), 'The Fight Against Diarrhoeal Diseases: The Case of Costa Rica', in Vallin and Lopez (1985).

—— (1988), 'A Public Health Approach to the "Food-Malnutrition-Economics Recession" Complex', in Bell and Reich (1988).

—— J. J. Urrutia, and A. Lechtig (1971), 'Infection and Nutrition of a Low Socioeconomic Rural Community', *American Journal of Clinical Nutrition*, 24.

—— *et al.* (1972), 'Influence of Recurrent Infections on Nutrition and Growth of Children in Guatemala', *American Journal of Clinical Nutrition*, 25.

Matsuyama, K. (1991), 'Increasing Returns, Industrialization, and Indeterminacy of Equilibrium', *Quarterly Journal of Economics*, 106.

May, D. A. and D. M. Heer (1968), 'Son Survivorship Motivation and Family Size in India: A Computer Simulation', *Population Studies*, 22.

Mayer, E. (1985), 'Production Zones', in S. Masuda, I. Shimada, and C. Morris (eds.), *Andean Ecology and Civilization* (Tokyo: Tokyo University Press).

Maynard Smith, J. (1982), *Evolution and Theory of Games* (Cambridge: Cambridge University Press).

Mazumdar, D. (1959), 'The Marginal Productivity Theory of Wages and Disguised Unemployment', *Review of Economic Studies*, 26.

—— (1965), 'Size of Farm and Productivity: A Problem of Indian Peasant Agriculture', *Economica*, 32.

—— (1989), 'Microeconomic Issues of Labour Markets in Developing Countries: Analysis and Policy Implications', EDI Seminar Paper No. 40, World Bank.

Mazumdar, V. (ed.) (1983), *Women and Rural Transformation* (Delhi: Concept).

McAlpin, M. B. (1983), *Subject to Famine* (Princeton, NJ: Princeton University Press).

McCamant, J. F. (1981), 'A Critique of Present Measures of Human Rights Development and an Alternative', in V. P. Nanda, J. R. Scarritt and G. W. Shepherd, Jr. (eds.), *Global Human Rights: Public Policies, Comparative Measures and NGO Strategies* (Boulder, Colo.: Westview Press).

McDowell, J. (1978), 'Are Moral Requirements Hypothetical Imperatives?' *Proceedings of the Aristotelian Society*, 52 (Supplement).

McElroy, M. (1990), 'The Empirical Content of Nash-Bargained Household Behaviour', *Journal of Human Resources*, 25.

—— and M. J. Horney (1981), 'Nash Bargained Household Decisions: Toward a Generalization of the Theory of Demand', *International Economic Review*, 22.

McGuire, J. and B. M. Popkin (1988), 'The Zero-Sum Game: A Framework for Examining Women and Nutrition', *Food and Nutrition Bulletin*, 10.

—— —— (1989), 'Beating the Zero-Sum Game: Women and Nutrition in the Third World: Part 1', *Food and Nutrition Bulletin*, 11.

McKay, H. *et al.* (1978), 'Improving Cognitive Ability in Chronically Deprived Children', *Science*, 200.

McKensie, L. (1981), 'The Classical Theorem on Existence of Competitive Equilibrium', *Econometrica*, 49.

McKeown, T. (1983), 'Food, Infection and Population', *Journal of Interdisciplinary History*, 14.

McMahan, J. A. (1981), 'Problems of Population Theory', *Ethics*, 91.

McNamara, R. S. (1992), 'The Post-Cold-War World: Implications for Military Expenditure in the Developing Countries', *Proceedings of the Annual Conference on Development Economics, 1991* (supplement to the *World Bank Economic Review* and the *World Bank Research Observer*).

McNeill, G. *et al.* (1987), 'Basal Metabolic Rate of Indian Men: No Evidence of Metabolic Adaptation to a Low Plane of Nutrition', *Human Nutrition: Clinical Nutrition*, 41C.

Meade, J. E. (1952), 'External Economies and Diseconomies in a Competitive Situation', *Economic Journal*, 62.

—— (1955), *Trade and Welfare* (Oxford: Oxford University Press).

—— (1964), *Efficiency, Equality and the Ownership of Property* (London: Allen & Unwin).

—— (1966), 'Life-Cycle Savings, Inheritance and Economic Growth', *Review of Economic Studies*, 33.

—— (1970), *The Theory of Indicative Planning* (Manchester: Manchester University Press).

—— (1973), *The Theory of Externalities* (Geneva: Institute Universitaire de Hautes Etudes Internationales).

—— (1976), *The Just Economy* (London: Allen & Unwin).

Meeks Gardner, J. M. *et al.* (1990), 'Dietary Intake and Observed Activity of Stunted and Non-Stunted Children in Kingston, Jamaica, Part II: Observed Activity', *European Journal of Clinical Nutrition*, 44.

Meillassoux, C. (1981), *Maidens, Meal and Money: Capitalism and the Domestic Community* (Cambridge: Cambridge University Press).

Mellor, J. W. (1968), 'Functions of Agricultural Prices in Economic Development', *Indian Journal of Agricultural Economics*, 23.

—— (1976), *The New Economics of Growth: A Strategy for India and the Developing World* (Ithaca, NY: Cornell University Press).

—— and R. Ahmed (eds.) (1988), *Agricultural Price Policy for Developing Countries* (Baltimore: Johns Hopkins University Press).

—— and G. M. Desai (1985), *Agricultural Change and Rural Poverty* (Baltimore: Johns Hopkins University Press).

—— and B. F. Johnston (1984), 'The World Food Equation: Interrelations among Development, Employment and Food Consumption', *Journal of Economic Literature*, 22.

—— and U. J. Lele (1973), 'Growth Linkages of the New Food Grain Technologies', *Indian Journal of Agricultural Economics*, 28.

Menken, J., J. Trussell, and S. Watkins (1981), 'The Nutrition Fertility Link: An Evaluation of the Evidence', *Journal of Interdisciplinary History*, 12.

Mensch, B., H. Lentzner and S. Preston (1986), *Socio-economic Differentials in Child Mortality in Developing Countries* (New York: United Nations).

Mertens, J. -F. and S. Zamir (1985), 'Formulations and Analysis for Games with Incomplete Information', *International Journal of Game Theory*, 14.

Merton, R. (1973), 'Theory of Rational Option Pricing', *Bell Journal of Economics and Management*, 4.

Messer, E. (1990), 'Social Science Perspectives on Primary Health Care Activities', *Food and Nutrition Bulletin*, 12.

Migot-Adholla, S. *et al.* (1991), 'Indigenous Land Rights Systems in Sub-Saharan Africa: A Constraint on Productivity?' *World Bank Economic Review*, 5.

Milgrom, P. (1987), 'Adverse Selection without Hidden Information', mimeo, University of California, Berkeley.

—— D. North and B. Weingast (1990), 'The Role of Institutions in the Revival of Trade: The Law Merchant, Private Judges and the Champagne Fairs', *Economics and Politics*, 2.

—— Y. Quian, and J. Roberts (1991), 'Complementarities, Momentum and the Evolution of Modern Technology', *American Economic Review* (Papers and Proceedings), 81.

—— and J. Roberts (1982), 'Predation, Reputation and Entry Deterrence', *Journal of Economic Theory*, 27.

—— —— (1990a), 'Rationalizability, Learning and Equilibrium in Games with Strategic Complementarities', *Econometrica*, 58.

—— —— (1990b), 'The Economics of Modern Manufacturing: Technology, Strategy and Organization', *American Economic Review*, 80.

Mill, J. S. (1975), *On Liberty*, ed. D. Spitz (New York: W. W. Norton).

Miller, B. (1981), *The Endangered Sex: Neglect of Female Children in Rural North India* (Ithaca, NY: Cornell University Press).

Milliman, J. W. (1956), 'Commodities and Price Systems and Use of Water Supplies', *Southern Economic Journal*, 22.

Mirrlees, J. A. (1965), 'Optimum Accumulation under Uncertainty', mimeo, Department of Economics, University of Cambridge.

—— (1967), 'Optimal Growth when Technology is Changing', *Review of Economic Studies*, 34.

—— (1969), 'The Evaluation of National Income in an Imperfect Economy', *Pakistan Development Review*, 9.

—— (1971), 'An Exploration in the Theory of Optimal Income Taxation', *Review of Economic Studies*, 38.

—— (1972), 'Population Policy and the Taxation of Family Size', *Journal of Public Economics*, 1.

—— (1974a), 'Notes on Welfare Economics, Information and Uncertainty', in M. Balch, D. McFadden and S. Wu (eds.), *Essays in Economic Behaviour under Uncertainty* (Amsterdam: North-Holland).

—— (1974b), 'Optimum Accumulation under Uncertainty: The Case of Stationary Returns on Investment', in Dreze (1974).

—— (1975), 'A Pure Theory of Underdeveloped Economies', in L. Reynolds (ed.), *Agriculture in Development Theory* (New Haven, Conn.: Yale University Press).

—— (1976), 'Optimal Tax Theory: A Synthesis', *Journal of Public Economies*, 6.

—— (1982), 'The Economic Uses of Utilitarianism', in A. Sen and B. Williams (eds.), *Utilitarianism and Beyond* (Cambridge: Cambridge University Press).

—— (1985), 'The Theory of Optimal Taxation', in K. J. Arrow and M. Intriligator (eds.), *Handbook of Mathematical Economics*, iii (Amsterdam: North-Holland).

Mitra, A. (1978), *India's Population: Aspects of Quality and Control* (New Delhi: Abhinar Publications).

—— (1979), *Implications of Declining Sex Ratio in India's Population* (Bombay: Allied Publishers).

Mitra, P. (1983), 'A Theory of Interlinked Rural Transactions', *Journal of Public Economics*, 20.

Modigliani, F. and R. E. Brumberg (1953), 'Utility Analysis and Aggregate Consumption Functions: An Attempt at Integration', mimeo, Department of Economics, University of Pennsylvania.

Moene, K. O. (1992), 'Poverty and Landownership', *American Economic Review*, 82.

Mola, A. (1984), 'Absorption of Macronutrients during the Cause Stage and after Recovery from Diarrhea of Different Aetiologies', *Food and Nutrition Bulletin*, 10 (Supplement).

—— *et al.* (1983), 'Effects of Acute Diarrhea on Absorption of Macronutrients during Disease and after Recovery', in Chen and Scrimshaw (1983).

Monckeberg, F. (1968), 'Effect of Early Marasmic Malnutrition on Subsequent Physical and Psychological Development', in Scrimshaw and Gordon (1968).

—— (1983), 'Socioeconomic Development and Nutritional Status: Efficiency of Intervention Programs', in Underwood (1983).

Montgomery, J. (ed.) (1984), *International Dimensions of Land Reform* (Boulder, Colo.: Westview Press).

Moock, P. M. and J. Leslie (1986), 'Childhood Malnutrition and Schooling in the Terai Region of Nepal', *Journal of Development Economics*, 20.

Mookherjee, D. (1984), 'Optimal Incentive Schemes with Many Agents', *Review of Economic Studies*, 51.

Mora, J. O. *et al.* (1981), 'The Impact of Supplementary Feeding and Home Education on Physical Growth of Disadvantaged Children', *Nutrition Review*, 1.

Moravcsik, J. (1988), 'Communal Ties', *Proceedings and Addresses of the American Philosophical Association*, 62.

Morduch, J. (1990), 'Risk, Production and Saving: Theory and Evidence from Indian Households', mimeo, Harvard University.

—— (1991), 'Consumption Smoothing Across Space: Tests for Village-Level Response to Risk', mimeo, Harvard University.

Morgan, L. H. (1963), *Ancient Society*, ed. E. B. Leacock (Cleveland, Ohio: World Publishing Company).

Morgane, P. J. *et al.* (1979), 'Maternal Protein Malnutrition and the Developing Nervous System', in D. A. Levisky (ed.), *Malnutrition, Environment and Behavior* (Ithaca, NY: Cornell University Press).

Morishima, M. (1981), *Why Has Japan Succeeded?* (Cambridge: Cambridge University Press).

Morley, D. (1973), *Paediatric Priorities in the Developing World* (London: Butterworth).

Morris, C. T. and I. Adelman (1987), *Patterns of Economic Growth: 1850–1914* (Baltimore: Johns Hopkins University Press).

Morris, M. D. (1979), *Measuring the Condition of the World's Poor: The Physical Quality of Life Index* (Oxford: Pergamon).

Morrison, D. G., R. C. Mitchell, and J. N. Paden (1989), *Black Africa: A Comparative Handbook* (New York: Paragon House and Irvington).

Moscardi, E. and A. de Janvry (1977), 'Attitudes towards Risk among Peasants: An Econometric Approach', *American Journal of Agricultural Economics*, 59.

Mosley, W. H. (1985), 'Will Primary Health Care Reduce Infant and Child Mortality? A Critique of Some Current Strategies, with Special Reference to Africa and Asia', in Vallin and Lopez (1985).

—— and L. C. Chen (eds.) (1984), *Child Survival Strategies for Research* (Cambridge: Cambridge University Press).

Mueller, E. (1976), 'The Economic Value of Children in Peasant Agriculture', in Ridker (1976).

—— (1983), 'Measuring Women's Poverty in Developing Countries', in Buvinic, Lycette and McGreevey (1983).

Mueller, W. H. and E. Pollitt (1982), 'The Bacon Chow Study: Effects of Nutrition

Supplementation on Sibling–Sibling Anthropometric Correlations', *Human Biology*, 54.

Mukherjee, A. and D. Ray (1992), 'Wages and Involuntary Unemployment in the Slack Season of a Village Economy', *Journal of Development Economics*, 37.

Murphy, K., A. Shleifer and R. Vishny (1989a), 'Industrialization and the Big Push', *Journal of Political Economy*, 97.

—— —— —— (1989b), 'Income Distribution, Market Size and Industrialization', *Quarterly Journal of Economics*, 104.

Murphy, Y. and R. Murphy (1985), *Women of the Forest* (New York: Columbia University Press).

Musgrave, R. (1959), *Theory of Public Finance* (New York: McGraw-Hill).

Myerson, R. (1984), 'An Introduction to Game Theory', Discussion Paper No. 623, Graduate School of Management, Northwestern University.

—— (1985), 'Bayesian Equilibrium and Incentive Compatibility: An Introduction', in L. Hurwicz, D. Schmeidler, and H. Sonneschein (eds.), *Social Goals and Social Organizations* (Cambridge: Cambridge University Press).

Myrdal, G. (1968), *Asian Drama* (London: Allen Lane the Penguin Press).

Nag, M., B. N. White, and A. C. Peet (1978), 'An Anthropological Approach to the Study of the Economic Value of Children in Java and Nepal', *Current Anthropology*, 19.

Nagel, J. (1974), 'Inequality and Discontent: A Nonlinear Hypothesis', *World Politics*, 26.

Nagel, T. (1978), 'Equality', in *Mortal Questions* (Cambridge: Cambridge University Press).

—— (1986a), 'Death', in P. Singer (ed.) *Applied Ethics* (Oxford: Oxford University Press).

—— (1986b), *The View from Nowhere* (New York: Oxford University Press).

Naidu, A. N., J. Neela, and N. P. Rao (1991), 'Maternal Body Mass Index and Birth Weight', *Nutrition News*, 12 (Hyderabad: National Institute of Nutrition).

Nalebuff, B. and Stiglitz (1983), 'Prizes and Incentives: Towards a General Theory of Compensation and Competition', *Bell Journal of Economics*, 11.

Narveson, J. (1967), 'Utilitarianism and New Generations', *Mind*, 76.

—— (1973), 'Moral Problems of Population', *Monist*, 57.

—— (1978), 'Future People and Us', in Sikora and Barry (1978).

Nash, J. (1950), 'The Bargaining Problem', *Econometrica*, 18.

—— (1951), 'Non-Cooperative Games', *Annals of Mathematics*, 54.

—— (1953), 'Two-Person Cooperative Games', *Econometrica*, 21.

Negishi, T. (1972), *General Equilibrium Theory and International Trade* (Amsterdam: North-Holland).

Neher, P. (1971), 'Peasants, Procreation and Pensions', *American Economic Review*, 61.

Nelson, R. (1959), 'The Simple Economics of Basic Scientific Research', *Journal of Political Economy*, 67.

—— (1982), 'The Role of Knowledge in R&D Efficiency', *Quarterly Journal of Economics*, 97.

Nelson, Ridley (1988), 'Dryland Management: The "Desertification" Problem', World Bank Environmental Paper No. 8.

Nerlove, M. and A. Meyer (1991), 'Endogenous Fertility and the Environment: A Parable of Firewood'; forthcoming in P. Dasgupta and K. G. Maler (eds.) (1992).

—— A. Razin, and E. Zadka (1985), 'The "Old Age" Security Hypothesis Reconsidered', *Journal of Development Economics*, 18.

—— —— —— (1986), 'Some Welfare Theoretic Implications of Endogenous Fertility', *International Economic Review*, 27.

—— —— —— (1987a), *Household and Economy: Welfare Economics of Endogenous Fertility* (New York: Academic Press).

—— —— —— (1987b), *Population Policy and Individual Choice: A Theoretical Investigation*, Research Report 60, International Food Policy Research Institute, Washington, DC.

Netting, R. (1985), *Hill Farmers of Nigeria: Cultural Ecology of the Kofyar of the Jos Plateau* (Seattle: Univerity of Washington Press).

Neumann, C. *et al.* (1989), 'Household Response to the Impact of Drought in Kenya', *Food and Nutrition Bulletin*, 11.

Newbery, D. (1987), 'Agricultural Taxation: the Main Issues', in Newbery and Stern (1987).

—— and N. Stern (eds.) (1987), *The Theory of Taxation for Developing Countries* (New York: Oxford University Press).

—— and J. Stiglitz (1979), 'Sharecropping, Risk Sharing and the Importance of Imperfect Information', in Roumasset, Boussard and Singh (1979).

—— —— (1981), *The Theory of Commodity Price Stabilization: A Study in the Economics of Risk* (Oxford: Clarendon Press).

Newcombe, K. (1984), 'An Economic Justification of Rural Afforestation: The Case of Ethiopia', Energy Department Paper No. 16, World Bank, Washington, DC.

Newman, L.F. (ed.) (1990), *Hunger in History: Food Shortage, Poverty and Deprivation* (Oxford: Basil Blackwell).

Ng, Y. -K. (1989), 'Hurka's Gamble and Methuselah's Paradox: A Response to Cowen on Normative Population Theory', *Social Choice and Welfare*, 6.

Nolan, P. (1988), *The Political Economy of Collective Farms: An Analysis of China's post-Mao Rural Reforms* (Boulder, Colo.: Westview Press).

Noor, A. (1981), 'Education and Basic Human Needs', World Bank Staff Working Paper No. 450.

Nordhaus, W. and J. Tobin (1972), 'Is Economic Growth Obsolete?' in *Economic Growth*, 5th Anniversary Colloquium of the NBER (New York: Columbian University Press).

Norgan, N. G., A. Ferro-Luzzi, and J. V. G. A. Durnin (1984), 'The Energy and Nutrient Intake and the Energy Expenditure of 204 New Guinean Adults', *Transactions of the Royal Society of London* B, 268.

—— *et al.* (1992), 'Determinants of Seasonality in Nutritional Status over a Rural South Indian Agricultural Cycle', *Ecology of Food and Nutrition*, 21.

Noronha, R. (1990), 'Common Property Resource Management in Traditional Societies', in P. Dasgupta and K. Mäler (eds.), 1992.

Norse, D. (1985), 'Nutritional Implications of Resource Policies and Technological Change', in Biswas and Pinstrup-Anderson (1985).

North, D. (1988a), 'Institutions, Transaction Costs and Economic Growth', *Economic Inquiry*, 25.

—— (1988b), 'Institutions, Economic Growth and Freedom: An Historical Introduction', in A. Walker (ed.), *Freedom, Democracy and Economic Welfare* (Vancouver: Frazer Institute).

—— (1989), 'Institutions and Economic Growth: An Historical Introduction', *World Development*, 17.

Novshek, W. (1980), 'Cournot Equilibrium with Free Entry', *Review of Economic Studies*, 47.

—— (1984), 'On the Existence of Cournot Equilibria', *Review of Economic Studies*, 51.

—— and H. Sonnenschein (1978), 'Cournot and Walras Equilibrium', *Journal of Economic Theory*, 19.

Nozick, R. (1974), *Anarchy, State and Utopia* (New York: Basic Books).

—— (1990), *The Examined Life* (New York: Simon & Schuster, Touchstone Books).

Nugent, J. (1985), 'The Old-Age Security Motive for Fertility', *Population and Development Review*, 11.

—— and T. Gillaspy (1983), 'Old Age Pension and Fertility in Rural Areas of Less Developed Countries: Some Evidence from Mexico', *Economic Development and Cultural Change*, 31.

Nussbaum, M. (1986), *The Fragility of Goodness* (Cambridge: Cambridge University Press).

Okin, S. M. (1989), *Justice, Gender, and the Family* (New York: Basic Books).

—— (1992), 'Gender Inequality and Cultural Differences', mimeo, Department of Political Science, Stanford University.

Olsen, W. K. (1987), 'Manmade "Drought" in Rayalaseema', *Economic and Political Weekly*, 22.

O'Neill, O. (1986), *Faces of Hunger: An Essay on Poverty, Justice and Development* (London: Allen & Unwin).

Osmani, S. R. (1990), 'Nutrition and the Economics of Food: Implications of Some Recent Controversies', in J. Drèze and A. Sen (eds.), *The Political Economy of Hunger: Entitlement and Well-Being* (Oxford: Clarendon Press).

Ostrom, E. (1990), *Governing the Commons: The Evolution of Institutions for Collective Action* (Cambridge: Cambridge University Press).

Page, H. J. and R. Lesthaeghe (eds.) (1981), *Child-Spacing in Tropical Africa: Tradition and Change* (London: Academic Press).

Pak, K. H. (1968), 'Economic Effects of Farmland Reform in the Republic of South Korea', in J. R. Brown and S. Lin (eds.), *Land Reform in Developing Countries* (Hartford, Conn.: University of Connecticut Press).

Palczynski, Z. and J. Gray (eds.) (1984), *Conceptions of Liberty in Political Philosophy* (New York: St Martin's Press).

Pant, P. *et al.* (1962), 'Perspectives of Development: 1961–1976, Implications of Planning for a Minimum Standard of Living' (New Delhi: Planning Commission of India).

Panzar, J. C. (1989), 'Technological Determinants of Firm and Industrial Structure', in R. Schmalensee and R. D. Willig (eds.), *Handbook of Industrial Organization*, i (Amsterdam: Elsevier).

Papanek, G. S. and O. Kyn (1986), 'The Effect of Income Distribution on Development, the Growth Rate and Economic Strategy', *Journal of Development Economics*, 23.

Parfit, D. (1976), 'On Doing the Best for our Children', in Bayles (1976).

—— (1982), 'Future Generations: Further Problems', *Philosophy and Public Affairs*, 11.

—— (1984), *Reasons and Persons* (Oxford: Oxford University Press).

—— (1987), 'A Reply to Sterba', *Philosophy and Public Affairs*, 16.

—— (1990), 'Overpopulation and the Quality of Life', in J. Glover (ed.), *Utilitarianism and its Critics* (London: Macmillan).

Pariser, E. R. (1982), 'Post-Harvest Food Losses in Developing Countries: A Survey', in Scrimshaw and Wallerstein (1982).

Pastore, G. *et al.* (1992), 'An Analysis of the Household Response to Seasonal Energy Stress in an Ethiopian Rural Community', *Ecology of Food and Nutrition*, 21.

Patrick, J. M. (1988), 'Ventilatory Capacity in Tropical Populations: Constitutional and Environmental Influences', in Collins and Roberts (1988).

Pattanaik, P. and Y. Xu (1990), 'On Ranking Opportunity Sets in Terms of Freedom of Choice', mimeo, Department of Economics, University of Birmingham.

Paukert, F. (1973), 'Income Distribution at Different Levels of Development: A Survey of Evidence', *International Labour Review*, 108.

Paul, A. A. and E. M. Muller (1980), 'Seasonal Variations in Dietary Intake in Pregnant and Lactating Women in a Rural Gambian Village', in Aebi and Whitehead (1980).

Payne, P. R. (1985a), 'The Nature of Malnutrition', in Biswas and Pinstrup-Anderson (1985).

—— (1985b), 'Nutritional Adaptation in Man: Social Adjustments and their Nutritional Implications', in Blaxter and Waterlow (1985).

—— (1993), 'Undernutrition: Measurement and Implications', in S. Osmani (ed.), *Poverty, Undernutrition and Living Standards* (Oxford: Clarendon Press).

—— and J. C. Waterlow (1971), 'Relative Energy Requirements for Maintenance, Growth and Physical Activity', *Lancet*, 2.

Pearce, D. (1984), 'Rationalizable Strategic Behaviour and the Problem of Perfection', *Econometrica*, 52.

Peffer, R. (1978), 'A Defense of Rights to Well-Being', *Philosophy and Public Affairs*, 8.

Pen, J. (1971), *Income Distribution: Facts, Theories, Policies* (New York: Praeger).

Perkins, D. H. (1988), 'Reforming China's Economic System', *Journal of Economic Literature*, 26.

Peskin, H. M. (1981), 'National Income Accounts and the Environment', *Natural Resources Journal*, 21.

Phelps, E. S. (1962), 'The Accumulation of Risky Capital: A Sequential Utility Analysis', *Econometrica*, 30.

—— and R. Pollak (1968), 'Second-Best National Savings and Game Equilibrium Growth', *Review of Economic Studies*, 35.

Phelps-Brown, H. (1988), *Egalitarianism and the Generation of Inequality* (Oxford: Clarendon Press).

Phillips, J. *et al.* (1988), 'Determinants of Reproductive Change in a Traditional Society: Evidence from Matlab, Bangladesh', *Studies in Family Planning*, 19.

Piddocke, S. (1965), 'The Potlatch System of the Southern Kwakiutl: A New Perspective', *Southwestern Journal of Anthropology*, 21.

Pierce, F. J. *et al.*, 'Productivity of Soils: Assessing Long Term Changes due to Erosion', *Journal of Soil and Water Conservation*, 38.

Pigou, A. C. (1920), *The Economics of Welfare* (London: Macmillan).

Pingali, P., Y. Bigot, and H. Binswanger (1987), *Agricultural Mechanization and the Evolution of Farming Systems in Sub-Saharan Africa* (Baltimore: Johns Hopkins University Press).

Pinstrup-Andersen, P. (1988a), 'Food Subsidies: Consumer Welfare and Producer Incentives', in Mellor and Ahmed (1988).

—— (ed.) (1988b), *Food Subsidies in Developing Countries: Costs, Benefits and Policy Options* (Baltimore: Johns Hopkins University Press).

—— (1989), 'Food Subsidies in Developing Countries', *Food and Nutrition Bulletin*, 11.

—— (1991), 'Government Policy, Food Security and Nutrition in Sub-Saharan Africa', in P. Dasgupta (ed.), *Issues in Contemporary Economics: Policy and Development* (London: Macmillan).

Pitchford, J. D. (1974), *Population in Economic Growth* (Amsterdam: North-Holland).

Pitt, M. M. (1983), 'Food Preferences and Nutrition in Rural Bangladesh', *Review of Economics and Statistics*, 65.

—— and M. Rosenzweig (1985), 'Health and Nutrient Consumption across and within Farm Households', *Review of Economics and Statistics*, 67.

—— —— and M. N. Hassan (1990), 'Productivity, Health and Inequality in the Intrahousehold Distribution of Food in Low-Income Countries', *American Economic Review*, 80.

Piwoz, E. G. and F. E. Viteri (1985), 'Studying Health and Nutrition Behaviour by Examining Household Decision-Making, Intra-Household Resource Distribution, and the Role of Women in these Processes', *Food and Nutrition Bulletin*, 7.

Platteau, J.-P. (1991), 'Traditional Systems of Social Security and Hunger Insurance: Past Achievements and Modern Challenges', in E. Ahmad *et al.*, (eds.), *Social Security in Developing Countries* (Oxford: Clarendon Press).

—— and A. Abraham (1987), 'An Inquiry into Quasi-Credit Contracts: The Role of Reciprocal Credits and Interlinked Deals in Small-Scale Fishing Communities', *Journal of Development Studies*, 23.

Polanyi, K. (1957a), 'The Economy as an Instituted Process', in K. Polanyi, C. W. Arensberg, and H. W. Pearson (eds.), *Trade and Market in the Early Empires* (London: Collier-Macmillan).

—— (1957b), *The Great Transformation: The Political and Economic Origins of Our Time* (Boston, Mass.: Beacon Press).

—— (1977), *The Livelihood of Man* (New York: Academic Press).

Polanyi, M. (1943–4), 'Patent Reform', *Review of Economic Studies*, 11.

—— (1962), 'The Republic of Science: Its Political and Economic Theory', *Minerva*, 1.

—— (1966), *The Tacit Dimension*, (London: Routledge & Kegan Paul).

Pollit, E. (1980), *Poverty and Malnutrition in Latin American Early Childhood Intervention Programs* (New York: Praeger).

—— (1990), *Malnutrition and Infection in the Classroom* (Paris: UNESCO).

—— (1991), 'Effects of a Diet Deficient in Iron on the Growth and Development of Pre-School and School-Age Children', *Food and Nutrition Bulletin*, 13.

—— and P. Amante (eds.) (1984), *Energy Intake and Activity* (New York: Alan R. Liss).

—— et al. (1982), 'Behavioral Effects of Iron Deficiency Anemia in Children', in E. Pollitt and R. L. Leibel (eds.), *Iron Deficiency: Brain Biochemistry and Behavior* (New York: Raven Press).

Popkin, B. M. (1978), 'Nutrition and Labor Productivity', *Social Science and Medicine*, 13C.

—— (1983), 'Rural Women, Work and Child Welfare in the Philippines', in Buvinic, Lycette and McGreevey (1983).

—— and M. Lian-Ybanez (1982), 'Nutrition and School Achievement', *Social Science and Medicine*, 16.

Popkin, S. L. (1979), *The Rational Peasant: The Political Economy of Rural Society in Vietnam* (Los Angeles: University of California Press).

Portes, R. (1971), 'Decentralised Planning Procedures and Centrally Planned Economies', *American Economic Review*, (Papers and Proceedings), 61.

Posner, R. A. (1974), *Economic Analysis of Law* (Boston: Little Brown).

—— (1979), 'Utilitarianism, Economics and Legal Theory', *Journal of Legal Studies*, 8.

Powell, C. A. and S. M. Grantham-McGregor (1985), 'The Ecology of Nutritional Status and Development in Young Children in Kingston, Jamaica', *American Journal of Clinical Nutrition*, 41.

Prasad, P. H. (1970), *Growth with Full Employment* (Bombay: Allied Publishers).

Pratt, J. A. (1964), 'Risk Aversion in the Small and in the Large', *Econometrica*, 32.

Prentice, A. M. (1980), 'Variations in Maternal Dietary Intake, Birthweight and Breast Milk Output in the Gambia', in Aebi and Whitehead (1980).

—— (1984), 'Adaptations to Long-Term Low Energy Intake', in Pollitt and Amante (1984).

—— et al. (1980), 'Dietary Supplementation of Gambian Nursing Mothers and Lactational Performance', *Lancet*, 2.

—— et al. (1981), 'Long Term Energy Balance in Child-Bearing Gambian Women', *American Journal of Clinical Nutrition*, 34.

—— et al. (1983a), 'Prenatal Dietary Supplementation of African Women and Birth Weight', *Lancet*, 1.

—— et al. (1983b), 'Dietary Supplementation of Lactating Gambian Women, II: Effect on Maternal Health, Nutritional Status and Biochemistry', *Human Nutrition: Clinical Nutrition*, 37C.

Preston, S. H. (ed.) (1978), *The Effects of Infant and Child Mortality on Fertility* (New York: Academic Press).

—— (1980), 'Causes and Consequences of Mortality Declines in Less Developed Countries during the Twentieth Century', in Easterlin (1980).

—— (1986), 'The Decline of Fertility in Non-European Industrialized Countries', *Population and Development Review* 12 (Supplement).

—— N. Keyfitz, and R. Schoen (1972), *Causes of Death: Life Tables for National Populations* (New York: Seminar Press).

—— and V. E. Nelson (1974), 'Structure and Change in Causes of Death: An International Summary', *Population Studies*, 28.

Provinse, J. H. (1955), 'Cooperative Ricefield Cultivation Among the Siang Dyaks of Central Borneo', in E. A. Hoebel (ed.), *Readings in Anthropology* (New York: McGraw-Hill).

Prynne, C. and D. Southgate (1979), 'The Effects of a Supplement of Dietary Fibre on Faecal Excretion by Human Subjects', *British Journal of Nutrition*, 41.

Pryor, E. (1977), *The Origins of the Economy* (New York: Academic Press).

Psacharopoulos, G. (1985), 'Returns to Education: A Further International Update and Implications', *Journal of Human Resources*, 20.

—— and M. Woodhall (1985), *Education for Development: An Analysis of Investment Choices* (Oxford: Oxford University Press).

Putnam, H. (1981), *Reason, Truth and History* (Cambridge: Cambridge University Press).

—— (1989), 'Objectivity and the Science/Ethics Distinction', WIDER Working Paper 70, (World Institute for Development Economics Research), Helsinki.

Pyatt, G. (1987), 'A Comment on *Growth and Equity in Developing Countries: A Reinterpretation of the Sri Lankan Experience*, by Bhalla and Glewwe', *World Bank Economic Review*, 1.

Qian, Y. (1988), 'Urban and Rural Household Saving in China', *International Monetary Fund Staff Papers*, 35.

—— (1990), 'A Theory of Shortage in Socialist Economies Based on the "Soft Budget Constraint"', mimeo, Department of Economics, Harvard University.

Quan, N. T. and A. Y. C. Koo (1985), 'Concentration of Landholdings: An Empirical Exploration of Kuznet's Conjecture', *Journal of Development Economics*, 18.

Quinzii, M. (1991), 'Efficiency of Marginal Cost Pricing Equilibria', in W. Brock and M. Majumdar (eds.), *Equilibrium and Dynamics: Essays in Honor of David Gale* (New York: Macmillan).

Quizon, J. and H. Binswanger (1986), 'Modeling the Impact of Agricultural Growth and Government Policy on Income Distribution in India', *World Bank Economic Review*, 1.

—— —— and M. J. Machina (1984), 'Attitudes towards Risk: Further Remarks', *Economic Journal*, 94.

Radner, R. (1981), 'Monitoring Cooperative Agreements in a Repeated Principal-Agent Relationship', *Econometrica*, 49.

—— (1985), 'Repeated Principal-Agent Games with Discounting', *Econometrica*, 53.

—— (1986), 'Repeated Partnership Games with Imperfect Monitoring and No Discounting', *Review of Economic Studies*, 53.

Raiffa, H. (1968), *Decision Analysis: Introductory Lectures on Choices under Uncertainty* (New York: Random House).

Raikes, P. (1986), 'Eating the Carrot and Wielding the Stick: The Agricultural Sector in Tanzania', in J. Boesen *et al.* (eds.), *Tanzania: Crisis and Struggle for Survival* (Uppsala: Scandinavian Institute of African Studies).

Ram, R. and T. Schultz (1979), 'Life Span, Health, Savings and Productivity', *Economic Development and Cultural Change*, 27.

Ramsey, F. (1928), 'A Mathematical Theory of Saving', *Economic Journal*, 38.

Rand, W. M. and N. S. Scrimshaw (1984), 'Protein and Energy Requirements: Insights from Long-Term Studies', *Bulletin of the Nutritional Foundation of India*, 5.

—— —— and V. Young (1985), 'Retrospective Analysis of Data from Five Long-Term Metabolic Balance Studies: Implications for Understanding Dietary Nitrogen and Energy Utilization', *American Journal of Clinical Nutrition*, 42.

—— R. Uauy, and N. S. Scrimshaw (eds.) (1984), 'Protein-Energy Requirement Studies in Developing Countries: Results of International Research', *Food and Nutrition Bulletin*, 10 (Supplement).

Ranis, G. (1975), 'Taiwan', in Chenery *et al.* (1975).

Rao, C. H. H. (1977), *Technological Change and Distribution of Gains in Indian Agriculture* (Delhi: Macmillan).

Rao, D. H. and J. G. Sastry (1977), 'Growth Pattern of Well-to-do Indian Adolescents and Young Adults', *Indian Journal of Medical Research*, 66.

Rasmussen, K. M. and J.-P. Habicht (1989), 'Malnutrition among Women: Indicators to Estimate Prevalence', *Food and Nutrition Bulletin*, 11.

Ravallion, M. (1987a), *Markets and Famines* (Oxford: Oxford University Press).

—— (1987b), 'Towards a Theory of Famine Relief Policy', *Journal of Public Economics*, 33.

—— (1990), 'Income Effects on Undernourishment', *Economic Development and Cultural Change*, 38.

—— (1991), 'Reaching the Rural Poor through Public Employment: Arguments, Evidence and Lessons from South India', *World Bank Research Observer*, 6.

—— (1992a), 'Does Undernutrition Respond to Incomes and Prices? Dominance Tests for Indonesia', *World Bank Economic Review*, 6.

—— (1992b), *Poverty Comparisons: A Guide to Concepts and Methods* (Washington, DC: World Bank).

Rawls, J. (1955), 'Two Concepts of Rules', *Philosophical Review*, 64.

—— (1972), *A Theory of Justice* (Oxford: Oxford University Press).

—— (1974), 'Reply to Alexander and Musgrave', *Quarterly Journal of Economics*, 88.

—— (1982a), 'The Basic Liberties and their Priority', *Tanner Lectures on Human Values*, iii (Salt Lake City, Utah: University of Utah).

—— (1982b), 'Social Unity and Primary Goods', in Sen and Williams (1982).

—— (1985), 'Justice as Fairness: Political not Metaphysical', *Philosophy and Public Affairs*, 14.

—— (1987), 'The Idea of an Overlapping Consensus', *Oxford Journal of Legal Studies*, 7.

—— (1988), 'The Priority of Right and Ideas of the Good', *Philosophy and Public Affairs*, 17.

Ray, D. (1984), 'Intertemporal Borrowing to Sustain Exogenous Consumption Standards under Uncertainty', *Journal of Economic Theory*, 33.

—— and P, Streufert (1992), 'Dynamic Equilibria with Unemployment due to Undernourishment', *Economic Theory*, 2.

Raz, J. (1986), *The Morality of Freedom* (Oxford: Clarendon Press).

Read, J. D. (1979), 'Sharecropping in American History', in Roumasset, Boussard and Singh (1979).

Read, M. S. (1977), 'Malnutrition and Human Performance', in L. S. Greene (ed.), *Malnutrition, Behaviour and Social Organization* (New York: Academic Press).

—— et al. (1975), 'Maternal Malnutrition, Birth Weight and Child Development', in C. Canova (ed.), *Nutrition, Growth and Development* (Basel: S. Karger).

Reij, C., P. Mulder, and L. Begemann (1988), 'Water Harvesting for Plant Production', World Bank Technical Paper No. 91.

Reina, J. C. and G. B. Spurr (1984), 'Daily Activity Level of Marginally Malnourished School-Aged Girls: A Preliminary Report', in Pollitt and Amante (1984).

Repetto, R. (1988), 'Economic Policy Reform for Natural Resource Conservation', World Bank Environment Department Working Paper No. 4.

—— et al. (1989), *Wasting Assets: Natural Resources and the National Income Accounts* (Washington, DC.: World Resources Institute).

Research Committee, Japan (1974), *Social Indicators of Japan* (Tokyo: Council of National Licensing, Japan).

Reutlinger, S. and H. Alderman (1980), 'The Prevalence of Calorie Deficient Diets in Developing Countries', *World Development*, 8.

—— and H. Pellekaan (1986), *Poverty and Hunger: Issues and Options for Food Security in Developing Countries* (Washington, DC: World Bank).

—— and M. Selowsky (1976), *Malnutrition and Poverty: Magnitude and Policy Options* (Baltimore: Johns Hopkins University Press).

Reynolds, S. (1984), *Kingdoms and Communities in Western Europe 900–1300* (Oxford: Clarendon Press).

Ricardo, D. (1911), *The Principles of Political Economy and Taxation* (London: Dent), first published 1817.

Richerson, P. J. and R. Boyd (1987), 'Simple Models of Complex Phenomena: The Case of Cultural Evolution', in Dupre (1987).

Ridker, R. G. (ed.) (1976), *Population and Development: The Search for Selective Interventions* (Baltimore: Johns Hopkins University Press).

Riley, J. (1987), 'Disease without Death: New Sources for a History of Sickness', *Journal of Interdisciplinary History*, 17.

Rimlinger, G. V. (1983), 'Capitalism and Human Rights', *Daedalus*, 112.

Riskin, C. (1987), *China's Political Economy* (Oxford: Clarendon Press).

Roberts, K. W. S. (1980a), 'Possibility Theorems with Interpersonally Comparable Welfare Levels', *Review of Economic Studies*, 47.

—— (1980b), 'Interpersonal Comparability and Social Choice Theory', *Review of Economic Studies*, 47.

—— (1984), 'The Theoretical Limits to Redistribution', *Review of Economic Studies*, 51.

Robinson, J. (1964), *Economic Philosophy* (Harmondsworth: Penguin Books).

Robinson, S. (1976), 'A Note on the U Hypothesis Relating Income Inequality and Economic Development', *American Economic Review*, 66.

Rodgers, G. (1975), 'Nutritionally Based Wage Determination in the Low-Income Labour Market', *Oxford Economic Papers*, 27.

Rodriguez, A. (1981), 'Rawls's Maxi-Min Criterion and Time Consistency: A Generalization', *Review of Economic Studies*, 48.

Rogers, E. M. and F. F. Shoemaker (1971), *Communication and Innovations* (New York: Free Press).

Rogerson, W. (1984), 'The First-Order Approach to Principal-Agent Problems', *Econometrica*, 53.

Romer, P. M. (1986), 'Increasing Returns and Long Run Growth', *Journal of Political Economy*, 94.

Rosenberg, N. (1988), 'Why Do Companies Do Basic Research (with their Own Money)?' mimeo, Department of Economics, Stanford University.

Rosenstein-Rodan, P. (1943), 'Problems of Industrialization in Eastern and Southeastern Europe', *Economic Journal*, 53.

Rosenzweig, M. R. (1980), 'Neoclassical Theory and the Optimizing Peasant: An Econometric Analysis of Market Family Labour Supply in a Developing Country', *Quarterly Journal of Economics*, 94.

—— (1988a), 'Risk, Implicit Contracts and the Family in Rural Areas of Low Income Countries', *Economic Journal*, 98.

—— (1988b), 'Risk, Private Information, and the Family', *American Economic Review* (Papers and Proceedings), 78.

—— (1988c), 'Labour Markets in Low Income Countries', in Chenery and Srinivasan (1988).

—— and R. Evenson (1977), 'Fertility, Schooling and the Economic Contribution of Children in Rural India: An Econometric Analysis', *Econometrica*, 45.

—— and T. P. Schultz (1982), 'Market Opportunities, Genetic Endowments and the Intrafamily Allocation of Resources: Child Survival in Rural India', *American Economic Review*, 72.

—— —— (1983), 'Consumer Demand and Household Production: The Relationship between Fertility and Child Mortality', *American Economic Review* (Papers and Proceedings), 73.

—— and O. Stark (1989), 'Consumption Smoothing, Migration, and Marriage: Evidence from Rural India', *Journal of Political Economy*, 97.

—— and K. I. Wolpin (1985), 'Specific Experience, Household Structure and Intergenerational Transfers: Farm Family Land and Labour Arrangements in Developing Countries', *Quarterly Journal of Economics*, 100.

—— —— (1989), 'Credit Market Constraints, Consumption Smoothing and the Accumulation of Durable Production Assets in Low-Income Countries: Investments in Bullocks in India', Bulletin No. 89–8, Economic Development Center, University of Minnesota.

Ross, W. D. (1930), *The Right and the Good* (Oxford: Oxford University Press).

Roth, A. (1979), *Axiomatic Models of Bargaining* (Berlin: Springer-Verlag).

Rothschild, M. and J. E. Stiglitz (1970), 'Increasing Risk, I: Definition', *Journal of Economic Theory*, 2.

—— —— (1971), 'Increasing Risk, II: Its Economic Consequences', *Journal of Economic Theory*, 3.

—— —— (1973), 'Some Further Results on the Measurement of Inequality', *Journal of Economic Theory*, 6.

Roumasset, J. A. (1976), *Rice and Risk: Decision Making among Low-Income Farmers* (Amsterdam: North-Holland).

—— J.-M. Boussard, and I. Singh (eds.) (1979), *Risk, Uncertainty and Agricultural Development* (New York: Agricultural Development Council).

Rowland, M. G. M., T. J. Cole, and R. G. Whitehead (1977), 'A Quantitative Study into the Role of Infection in Determining Nutritional Status in Gambian Village Children', *British Journal of Nutrition*, 37.

Royston, E. (1982), 'The Prevalence of Nutritional Anaemia among Women in Developing Countries: A Critical Review of Available Information', *World Health Statistics Quarterly*, 35.

Rubinstein, A. (1979), 'Equilibrium in Supergames with the Overtaking Criterion', *Journal of Economic Theory*, 21.

—— (1982), 'Perfect Equilibrium in a Bargaining Model', *Econometrica*, 50.

—— Z. Safra, and W. Thomson (1992), 'On the Interpretation of the Nash Bargaining Solution and its Extension to Non-Expected Utility Preferences', *Econometrica*, 60.

Rudra, A. (1982), *Indian Agricultural Economics: Myths and Realities* (New Delhi: Allied Publishers).

—— (1984), 'Local Power and Farm-Level Decision-Making', in M. Desai, S. H. Rudolph, and A. Rudra (eds.), *Agrarian Power and Agricultural Productivity in South Asia* (Berkeley, Cal.: University of California Press).

—— and U. Chakraborty (1991), 'Distribution of Landholdings in India: 1961–62 to 1982', *Journal of Indian School of Political Economy*, 3.

Runge, C. F. (1986), 'Common Property and Collective Action in Economic Development', *World Development*, 14.

Russett, B. M. (1964), 'Inequality and Instability: The Relation of Land Tenure to Politics', *World Politics*, 16.

Rutihauser, I. H. E. and R. G. Whitehead (1972), 'Energy Intake and Expenditure in 1–3-Year-Old Ugandan Children Living in a Rural Environment', *British Journal of Nutrition*, 28.

Ryan, G. and R. D. Ghodake (1984), 'Labour Market Behaviour in Rural Villages in South India: Effects of Season, Sex and Socioeconomic Status', in Binswanger and Rosenzweig (1984b).

Sabourian, H. (1988), 'Repeated Games: A Survey', in F. H. Hahn (ed.), *The Economic Theory of Missing Markets, Information and Games* (Oxford: Basil Blackwell).

Saflios-Rothschild, C. (1985), *The Status of Women and Fertility in the Third World in the 1970–80 Decade* (New York: Population Council).

Sah, R. K. (1991), 'The Effects of Mortality Changes on Fertility Choice and Parental Welfare', *Journal of Political Economy*, 99.

—— and T. N. Srinivasan (1988), 'Distributional Consequences of Rural Food Levy and Subsidized Urban Rations', *European Economic Review*, 32.

—— and J. E. Stiglitz (1987), 'The Taxation and Pricing of Agricultural and Industrial Goods in Developing Countries', in Newbery and Stern (1987).

Sahayam, M. (1988), 'Aged Females: The Most Deprived among the Deprived', *Indian Journal of Social Studies*, 49.

Sahlins, M. (1968) *Tribesmen* (Englewood Cliffs, NJ: Prentice-Hall).

—— (1976), *Culture and Practical Reason* (Chicago: University of Chicago Press).

Sahn, D. E. (ed.) (1987), *Causes and Implications of Seasonal Variability in Household Food Security* (Washington, DC: International Food Policy Research Institute).

Sahota, G. (1978), 'Theories of Personal Income Distribution: A Survey', *Journal of Economic Literature*, 16.

Samarasinghe, S. W. R. de A. (1988), 'Sri Lanka: A Case Study from the Third World', in Bell and Reich (1988).

Samuelson, P. A. (1947), *Foundations of Economic Analysis* (Cambridge, Mass.: Harvard University Press).

—— (1954), 'The Pure Theory of Public Expenditure', *Review of Economics and Statistics*, 36.

—— (1958), 'An Exact Consumption Loan Model of Interest with or without the Social Contrivance of Money', *Journal of Political Economy*, 66.

—— (1961), 'The Evaluation of "Social Income", Capital Formation and Wealth', in F. Lutz and D. Hague (eds.), *The Theory of Capital* (London: Macmillan).

Sandel, M. (1982), *Liberalism and the Limits of Justice* (Cambridge: Cambridge University Press).

Satahr, Z. and V. Chigambaram (1984), 'Differentials in Contraceptive Use', *World Fertility Survey Studies*, 36.

Satyanarayana, K. *et al.* (1977), 'Body Size and Work Output', *American Journal of Clinical Nutrition*, 30.

—— A. N. Naidu, and B. S. N. Rao (1979), 'Nutritional Deprivation in Childhood and the Body Size, Activity and Physical Work Capacity of Young Boys', *American Journal of Clinical Nutrition*, 32.

—— —— —— (1980), 'Adolescent Growth Spurt among Rural Indian Boys in Relation to their Nutritional Status in Early Childhood', *Annals of Human Biology*, 7.

Savage, L. (1954), *Foundations of Statistics* (New York: John Wiley).

Sax, J. (1990), 'Is Anyone Minding Stonehenge? The Origins of Cultural Protection in England', *California Law Review*, 78.

Scanlon, T. M. (1975), 'Preference and Urgency', *Journal of Philosophy*, 72.

—— (1978), 'Rights, Goals and Fairness', in S. Hampshire (ed.), *Public and Private Morality* (Cambridge: Cambridge University Press).

—— (1982), 'Contractualism and Utilitarianism', in Sen and Williams (1982).

—— (1992), 'The Moral Basis of Interpersonal Comparisons', in J. Elster and J. Romer (eds.), *Interpersonal Comparisons of Well-Being* (Cambridge: Cambridge University Press).

Schechtman, J. and V. Escudero (1977), 'Some Results on "An Income Fluctuation Problem"', *Journal of Economic Theory*, 16.

Schecter, M., M. Kim, and L. Golan (1989), 'Valuing a Public Good: Direct and Indirect Valuation Approaches to the Measurement of Benefits from Pollution

Abatement', in H. Folmer and E. van Ierland (eds.), *Valuation Methods and Policy Making in Environmental Economics* (Amsterdam: Elsevier).

Scheffler, S. (1976), 'Natural Rights, Equality, and the Minimal State', *Canadian Journal of Philosophy*, 6.

—— (ed.) (1988), *Consequentialism and its Critics* (Oxford: Oxford University Press).

Schell, J. (1982), *The Fate of the Earth* (New York: Avon).

Schelling, T. (1960), *The Strategy of Conflict* (Cambridge, Mass.: Harvard University Press).

—— (1978), *Micromotives and Macrobehavior* (New York: W. W. Norton).

Scherer, F. M. (1980), *Industrial Market Structure and Economic Performance* (Boston: Houghton Mifflin).

Schiff, M. and A. Valdes (1990), 'Nutrition: Alternative Definitions and Policy Implications', *Economic Development and Cultural Change*, 38.

Schofield, W. N., C. Schofield, and W. P. T. James (1985), 'Basal Metabolic Rate: Review and Prediction, together with an Annotated Bibliography of Source Material', *Human Nutrition: Clinical Nutrition*, 39C (Supplement 1).

Schultz, T. Paul (1988a), 'Education Investments and Returns', in Chenery and Srinivasan (1988).

—— (1988b), 'Economic Demography and Development', in G. Ranis and T. Paul Schultz (eds.), *The State of Development Economics* (Oxford: Basil Blackwell).

Schultz, T. W. (1964), *Transforming Traditional Agriculture* (New Haven, Conn.: Yale University Press).

—— (1974), *Economics of the Family: Marriage, Children and Human Capital* (Chicago: University of Chicago Press).

—— (ed.) (1978), *Distortions of Agricultural Incentives* (Bloomington, Ind.: Indiana University Press).

Scitovsky, T. (1954), 'Two Concepts of External Economies', *Journal of Political Economy*, 62.

—— (1976), *The Joyless Economy* (Oxford: Oxford University Press).

—— (1985), 'Economic Development in Taiwan and South Korea', *Food Research Institute Studies*, 19.

Scobie, G. (1983), 'Food Subsidies in Egypt: Their Impact on Foreign Exchange and Trade', Research Report No. 40, International Food Policy Research Institute, Washington, DC.

Scoble, H. M. and L. S. Wiseberg (1981), 'Problems of Comparative Research in Human Rights', in V. P. Nanda, J. R. Scarritt, and G. W. Shepherd, Jr. (eds.), *Global Human Rights: Public Policies, Comparative Measures and NGO Strategies* (Boulder, Colo.: Westview Press).

Scott, A. D. (1955), 'The Fishery: The Objectives of Sole Ownership', *Journal of Political Economy*, 63.

Scott, J. C. (1976), *The Moral Economy of the Peasant: Rebellion and Subsistence in Southeast Asia* (New Haven, Conn.: Yale University Press).

Scrimshaw, N. C. (1970), 'Synergism of Malnutrition and Infection: Evidence from Field Studies in Guatemala', *Journal of the American Medical Association*, 212.

—— (1983), 'Importance of Infection and Immunity in Nutrition Intervention Programs and Priorities for Interventions', in Underwood (1983).

—— (1984), 'Functional Consequences of Iron Deficiency in Human Populations', *Journal of Nutrition Science and Vitaminology*, 30.

—— (1991), 'Iron Deficiency', *Scientific American*, 265.

—— and J. E. Gordon (eds.) (1968), *Malnutrition, Learning and Behavior* (Cambridge, Mass.: MIT Press).

——, C. E. Taylor, and J. E. Gordon (1968), *Interactions of Nutrition and Infections* (Geneva: World Health Organization).

—— and M. B. Wallerstein (eds.) (1982), *Nutrition Policy Implementation: Issues and Experience* (New York: Plenum Press).

Seabright, P. (1988), 'Pluralism in Practice', mimeo, Faculty of Economics, University of Cambridge.

—— (1989), 'Creating Persons', *Proceedings of the Aristotelian Society*, 63 (Supplement).

—— (1990), 'Is Cooperation Habit-Forming?' forthcoming in P. Dasgupta and K. G. Mäler (eds.) (1992).

—— (1992), 'Quality of Livestock Assets under Selective Credit Schemes: Evidence from South Indian Data', *Journal of Development Economics*, 37.

Seckler, D. (1982), 'Small but Healthy: A Basic Hypothesis in the Theory, Measurement and Policy of Malnutrition', in P. V. Sukhatme (ed.), *Newer Concepts in Nutrition and their Implications for Policy* (Pune, India: Maharashtra Association for the Cultivation of Science).

—— (1984), 'The "Small but Healthy?" Hypothesis: A Reply to Critics', *Economic and Political Weekly*, 19.

Sefton, J. and M. Weale (1992), 'Natural Resources in the Net National Product: The Case of Foreign Trade', mimeo, Department of Applied Economics, University of Cambridge.

Selten, R. (1975), 'Re-examination of the Perfectness Concept for Equilibrium in Extensive Form Games', *International Journal of Game Theory*, 4.

Selznick, P. (1987), 'The Idea of Communitarian Morality', *California Law Review*, 75.

Sen, A. (1966), 'Peasants and Dualism: With or Without Surplus Labour', *Journal of Political Economy*, 74.

—— (1970), *Collective Choice and Social Welfare* (San Francisco: Holden Day).

—— (1973), *On Economic Inequality* (Oxford: Clarendon Press).

—— (1981a), 'Public Action and the Quality of Life in Developing Countries', *Oxford Bulletin of Economics and Statistics*, 43.

—— (1981b), *Poverty and Famines: An Essay on Entitlement and Deprivation* (Oxford: Oxford University Press).

—— (1982), 'Rights and Agency', *Philosophy and Public Affairs*, 11.

—— (1985), *Commodities and Capabilities* (Amsterdam: North-Holland).

—— (1987), 'Gender and Cooperative Conflicts', Discussion Paper No. 1342, Harvard Institute of Economic Research.

—— (1988a), 'Africa and India: What Do We Have to Learn from Each Other?' in K. Arrow (ed.), *The Balance between Industry and Agriculture in Economic Development* (London: Macmillan).

—— (1988b), 'Freedom of Choice: Concept and Content', *European Economic Review* (Papers and Proceedings), 32.

—— and S. Sengupta (1983), 'Malnutrition of Rural Children and the Sex Bias', *Economic and Political Weekly*, 18.

—— and B. Williams (eds.) (1982), *Utilitarianism and Beyond* (Cambridge: Cambridge University Press).

Sen, G. (1987), 'Women Agricultural Labourers: Regional Variations in Incidence and Employment', mimeo, Madras Institute of Economics.

—— and C. Sen (1985), 'Women's Domestic Work and Economic Activity: Results from a National Sample Survey', *Economic and Political Weekly*, 20.

Shaban, R. A. (1987), 'Testing between Competing Models of Sharecropping', *Journal of Political Economy*, 95.

Shafer, W. and H. Sonnenschein (1976), 'Equilibrium with Externalities, Commodity Taxation and Lump Sum Transfers', *International Economic Review*, 17.

Shah, C. H. (1983), 'Food Preference, Poverty and the Nutrition Gap', *Economic Development and Cultural Change*, 32.

Shaked, A. and J. Sutton (1984), 'The Semi-Walrasian Economy', ICERD Discussion Paper, London School of Economics.

Shapiro, C. and J. E. Stiglitz (1984), 'Equilibrium Unemployment as a Worker Discipline Device', *American Economic Review*, 74.

Shapley, L. and M. Shubik (1969), 'On the Core of an Economic System under Externalities', *American Economic Review*, 59.

Sharkey, W. (1982), *The Theory of Natural Monopoly* (Cambridge: Cambridge University Press).

Shen, T. H. (1964), *Agricultural Development on Taiwan since World War II* (Ithaca, NY: Comstock).

Shephard, R. J. (1988), 'Work Capacity: Methodology in a Tropical Environment', in Collins and Roberts (1988).

Shetty, P. S. (1984), 'Adaptive Changes in Basal Metabolic Rate and Lean Body Mass in Chronic Undernutrition', *Human Nutrition: Clinical Nutrition*, 38C.

—— (1990a), 'Energy Metabolism in Chronic Energy Deficiency', *Proceedings of the Nutrition Society of India*, 36.

—— (1990b), 'Physiological Mechanisms in the Adaptive Response of Metabolic Rates to Energy Restriction', *Nutrition Research Reviews*, 3.

—— and M. J. Soares (1988), 'Variability in Basal Metabolic Rates in Man', in K. Blaxter and I. Macdonald (eds.), *Comparative Nutrition* (London: John Libbey).

Siamwalla, A. *et al.* (1990), 'The Thai Rural Credit System: Public Subsidies, Private Information, and Segmented Markets', *World Bank Economic Review*, 4.

Sidgwick, H. (1907), *The Methods of Ethics* (London: Macmillan).

Siegelman, L. and M. Simpson (1977), 'A Cross-National Test of the Linkage Between Economic Inequality and Political Violence', *Journal of Conflict Resolution*, 21.

Sikora, R. I. (1978), 'Is it Wrong to Prevent the Existence of Future Generations?' in Sikora and Barry (1978).

—— and B. Barry (eds.) (1978), *Obligations to Future Generations* (Philadelphia: Temple University Press).

Silber, J. (1983), 'ELL (The Equivalent Length of Life), or Another Attempt at Measuring Development', *World Development*, 11.

Simon, J. L. (1974), 'Interpersonal Welfare Comparisons Can Be Made—And Used for Redistribution Decisions', *Kyklos*, 27.

—— (1977), *The Economics of Population Growth* (Princeton, NJ: Princeton University Press).

—— (1981), *The Ultimate Resource* (Princeton, NJ: Princeton University Press).

—— and H. Kahn (eds.) (1984), *The Resourceful Earth: A Response to Global 2000* (New York: Basil Blackwell).

Simon, L. K. (1987), 'Games with Discontinuous Payoffs', *Review of Economic Studies*, 54.

—— and W. R. Zame (1990), 'Discontinuous Games and Endogenous Sharing Rules', *Econometrica*, 58.

Simonson, E. (1971), 'Nutrition and Work Performance', in E. Simonson (ed.) *Physiology of Work Capacity and Fatigue* (Springfield, Ill.: Charles C. Thomas).

Singer, P. (1986), 'Animals and the Value of Life', in T. Regan (ed.), *Matters of Life and Death: New Introductory Essays in Moral Philosophy* (New York: Random House).

Singh, I. (1988a), 'Small Farmers in South Asia: Their Characteristics, Productivity and Efficiency', World Bank Discussion Paper 31.

—— (1988b), 'Tenancy in South Asia', World Bank Discussion Paper 32.

—— (1988c), 'Land and Labour in South Asia', World Bank Discussion Paper 33.

—— (1990), *The Great Ascent: The Rural Poor in South Asia* (Baltimore: Johns Hopkins University Press).

—— L. Squire, and J. Strauss (1986a), 'A Survey of Agricultural Household Models: Recent Findings and Policy Implications', *World Bank Economic Review*, 1.

—— —— —— (eds.) (1986b), *Agricultural Household Models: Extensions, Applications and Policy* (Baltimore: Johns Hopkins University Press).

Singh, J., *et al.* (1989), 'Energy Expenditure of Gambian Women during Peak Agricultural Activity Measured by the Doubly-Labelled Water Method', *British Journal of Nutrition*, 62.

Sinha, R. (1984), *Landlessness: A Growing Problem* (Rome: FAO).

Sivard, R. L. (1985), *World Military and Social Expenditures 1985* (Washington, DC: World Priorities).

Skeldon, R. (1986), 'On Migration Patterns in India During the 1970s', *Population and Development Review*, 12.

Smart, J. and B. Williams (1973), *Utilitarianism: For and Against* (Cambridge: Cambridge University Press).

Smith, E. A. (1987), 'Optimization Theory in Anthropology: Applications and Critiques', in Dupre (1987).

Smith, J. H. (1973), 'Aggregation of Preferences with Variable Electorate', *Econometrica*, 41.

Soares, M. J. and P. S. Shetty (1987), 'Long-Term Stability of Metabolic Rates in Young Adult Males', *Human Nutrition: Clinical Nutrition*, 41C.

—— *et al.* (1991), 'Basal Metabolic Rate, Body Composition and Whole-Body Protein Turnover in Indian Men with Differing Nutritional Status', *Clinical Science*, 81.

Solorzano, R. *et al.* (1991), *Accounts Overdue: Natural Resource Depreciation in Costa Rica* (Washington, DC: World Resources Institute).

Solow, R. M. (1957), 'Technical Change and the Aggregate Production Function', *Review of Economics and Statistics*, 39.

—— (1974), 'Intergenerational Equity and Exhaustible Resources', *Review of Economic Studies* (Symposium on the Economics of Exhaustible Resources).

—— (1986), 'On the Intergenerational Allocation of Natural Resources', *Scandinavian Journal of Economics*, 88.

Sommer, A. and M. S. Lowenstein (1975), 'Nutritional Status and Mortality: A Prospective Validation of the QUAC Stick', *American Journal of Clinical Nutrition*, 28.

Sonnenschein, H. (1974), 'An Axiomatic Characterization of the Price Mechanism', *Econometrica*, 42.

Sopher, D. E. (1980a), 'Sex Disparity in Indian Literacy', in Sopher (1980c).

—— (1980b), 'The Geographical Patterning of Culture in India', in Sopher (1980c).

—— (ed.) (1980c), *An Exploration of India: Geographical Perspectives on Society and Culture* (Ithaca, NY: Cornell University Press).

—— (1980d), 'Indian Civilization and the Tropical Savanna Environment', in O. R. Harris (ed.), *Human Ecology in Savanna Environments* (London: Academic Press).

Spence, A. M. (1986), 'Cost Reduction, Competition and Industry', in Stiglitz and Mathewson (1986).

Spurr, G. B. (1983), 'Nutritional Status and Physical Work Capacity', *Yearbook of Physical Anthropology*, 26.

—— (1984), 'Physical Activity, Nutritional Status, and Physical Work Capacity in Relation to Agricultural Productivity', in Pollitt and Amante (1984).

—— (1988), 'Marginal Malnutrition in Childhood: Implications for Adult Work Capacity and Productivity', in Collins and Roberts (1988).

—— (1990), 'The Impact of Chronic Undernutrition on Physical Work Capacity and Daily Energy Expenditure', in G. A. Harrison and Waterlow (1990).

—— M. Barac-Nieto, and M. G. Maksud (1977), 'Productivity and Maximal Oxygen Consumption in Sugar Cane Cutters', *American Journal of Clinical Nutrition*, 30.

—— —— —— (1978), 'Childhood Undernutrition: Implications for Adult Work Capacity and Productivity', in L. J. Folinsbee, *et al.* (eds.), *Environmental Stress: Individual Human Adaptations* (New York: Academic Press).

—— M. G. Maksud, and M. Barac-Nieto (1977), 'Energy Expenditure, Productivity, and Physical Work Capacity of Sugar Cane Loaders', *American Journal of Clinical Nutrition*, 30.

—— and J. C. Reina (1987), 'Marginal Malnutrition in School-Aged Girls: Dietary Intervention and Daily Energy Expenditure', *Human Nutrition: Clinical Nutrition*, 41C.

—— —— (1988a), 'Influence of Dietary Intervention on Artificially Increased Activity in Marginally Undernourished Colombian Boys', *European Journal of Clinical Nutrition*, 42.

—— —— (1988b), 'Patterns of Daily Energy Expenditure in Normal and Marginally

Undernourished School-Aged Colombian Children', *European Journal of Clinical Nutrition*, 42.

—— —— (1988c), 'Basal Metabolic Rate of Normal and Marginally Undernourished Mestizo Children in Colombia', *European Journal of Clinical Nutrition*, 42.

—— —— and M. Barac-Nieto (1983), 'Marginal Malnutrition in School-Aged Colombian Boys: Anthropometry and Maturation', *American Journal of Clinical Nutrition*, 37.

—— *et al.* (1983), 'Marginal Malnutrition in School-Aged Colombian Boys: Functional Consequences in Maximum Exercise', *American Journal of Clinical Nutrition*, 37.

—— *et al.* (1984), 'Marginal Malnutrition in School-Aged Colombian Boys: Efficiency of Treadmill Walking in Submaximal Exercise', *American Journal of Clinical Nutrition*, 39.

—— *et al.* (1988), 'Energy Expenditure using Minute-by-Minute Heart Rate Recording: Comparison with Indirect Calorimetry', *American Journal of Clinical Nutrition*, 48.

Squire, L. (1989), 'Project Evaluation in Theory and Practice', in Chenery and Srinivasan (1989).

—— and H. Van der Taak (1975), *Economic Analysis of Projects* (Baltimore: Johns Hopkins University Press).

Sraffa, P. (1960), *The Production of Commodities by Means of Commodities* (Cambridge: Cambridge University Press).

Srinivas, M. N. (1962), *Caste in Modern India and Other Essays* (Bombay: Asia Publishing House).

Srinivasan, T. N. (1981), 'Malnutrition: Some Measurement and Policy Issues', *Journal of Development Economics*, 8.

—— (1983a), 'Malnutrition in Developing Countries: The State of Knowledge of the Extent of its Prevalence, its Causes and its Consequences', mimeo, Department of Economics, Yale University.

—— (1983b), 'Measuring Malnutrition', *CERES*, 16 (March/April).

—— (1983c), 'Undernutrition: Extent and Distribution of its Incidence', mimeo, Department of Economics, Yale University.

—— (1989), 'Food Aid: A Cause of Development Failure or an Instrument of Success?' *World Bank Economic Review*, 3.

—— (1993), 'Undernutrition: Concepts, Measurement and Policy Implications', in S. Osmani (ed.), *Poverty, Undernutrition and Living Standards* (Oxford: Clarendon Press).

Stahl, I. (1972), *Bargaining Theory* (Stockholm: Economic Research Institute).

Starr, R. M. (1969), 'Quasi-Equilibria in Markets with Non-Convex Preferences', *Econometrica*, 37.

—— (1973), 'Optimal Production and Allocation under Uncertainty', *Quarterly Journal of Economics*, 82.

Starrett, D. (1972), 'Fundamental Non-Convexities in the Theory of Externalities', *Journal of Economic Theory*, 4.

—— (1973), 'A Note on Externalities and the Core', *Econometrica*, 41.

—— (1988), *Foundations of Public Economics*, (New York: Cambridge University Press).

Stein, T. P., F. E. Johnston, and L. Greiner (1988), 'Energy Expenditure and Socioeconomic Status in Guatemala as Measured by the Doubly Labelled Water Method', *American Journal of Clinical Nutrition*, 47.

Sterba, J. P. (1987), 'Explaining Asymmetry: A Problem for Parfit', *Philosophy and Public Affairs*, 16.

Stern, N. (1989), 'The Economics of Development: A Survey', *Economic Journal*, 99.

—— (1991), 'Comments', in Roundtable Discussion on 'Development Strategies: The Role of the State and the Private Sector', *Proceedings of the World Bank Annual Conference on Development Economics 1990* (supplement to the *World Bank Economic Review* and the *World Bank Economic Observer*).

—— and E. Ahmad (1989), 'Taxation for Developing Countries', in Chenery and Srinivasan (1989).

Steward, J. (1955), *Theory of Cultural Change* (Urbana, Ill.: University of Illinois Press).

Stewart, F. (1985), *Planning to Meet Basic Needs* (London: Macmillan).

—— and P. Streeten (1976), 'New Strategies for Development: Poverty, Income Distribution and Growth', *Oxford Economic Papers*, 28.

Stiglitz, J. E. (1974), 'Incentives and Risk Sharing in Sharecropping', *Review of Economic Studies*, 41.

—— (1976), 'The Efficiency Wage Hypothesis, Surplus Labour and the Distribution of Income in LDCs', *Oxford Economic Papers*, 28.

—— (1986), 'Introduction', in Stiglitz and Mathewson (1986).

—— (1987a), 'Learning to Learn, Localized Learning and Technological Progress', in Dasgupta and Stoneman (1987).

—— (1987b), 'The Causes and Consequences of the Dependence of Quality on Price', *Journal of Economic Literature*, 25.

—— (1988a), *Economics of the Public Sector*, 2nd edn. (New York: W. W. Norton).

—— (1988b), 'Economic Organization, Information and Development', in Chenery and Srinivasan (1988).

—— (1989), 'On the Economic Role of the State', in A. Heertje (ed.), *The Economic Role of the State* (Amsterdam: Bank Insinger de Beaufort NV).

—— (1990), 'Peer Monitoring and Credit Markets', *World Bank Economic Review*, 4.

—— and P. Dasgupta (1971), 'Differential Taxation, Public Goods and Economic Efficiency', *Review of Economic Studies*, 39.

—— and F. Mathewson (eds.) (1986), *New Developments in the Analysis of Market Structure* (London: Macmillan).

—— and A. Weiss (1981), 'Credit Rationing in Markets with Imperfect Information, Part 1', *American Economic Review*, 71.

—— —— (1983), 'Incentive Effects of Termination: Applications to the Credit and Labour Markets', *American Economic Review*, 73.

—— —— (1986), 'Credit Rationing and Collateral', in J. Edwards *et al.* (eds.), *Recent Developments in Corporate Finance* (New York: Cambridge University Press).

—— —— (1987), 'Credit Rationing with Many Borrowers', *American Economic Review* (Papers and Proceedings), 77.

Strauss, J. (1986), 'Does Better Nutrition Raise Farm Productivity?' *Journal of Political Economy*, 94.

—— (1990), 'Households, Communities, and Preschool Children's Nutrition Outcomes: Evidence from Rural Cote d'Ivoire', *Economic Development and Cultural Change*, 38.

Streeten, P. (1977), 'The Distinctive Features of a Basic Needs Approach to Development', *International Development Review*, 19.

—— (1981), *Development Perspectives* (London: Macmillan).

—— (1984), 'Basic Needs: Some Unsettled Questions', *World Development*, 12.

—— and S. J. Burki (1978), 'Basic Needs: Some Issues', *World Development*, 6.

—— *et al.* (1981), *First Things First: Meeting Basic Needs in Developing Countries* (Oxford: Oxford University Press).

Subbarao, K. (1989), 'Improving Nutrition in India: Policies and Programs and their Impact', World Bank Discussion Paper No. 49, Washington, DC.

Subramanian, S. and A. Deaton (1990), 'Gender Effects in Indian Consumption Patterns', Discussion Paper No. 147, Research Program in Development Studies, Woodrow Wilson School, Princeton University.

—— —— (1992), 'The Demand for Food and Calories: Further Evidence from India', mimeo, Woodrow Wilson School, Princeton University.

Sugarman, B. (1983), 'Zinc and Infection', *Review of Infectious Diseases*, 5.

Sukhatme, P. V. (1977), 'Incidence of Undernourishment', *Indian Journal of Agricultural Economics*, 32.

—— (1978), 'Assessment of Adequacy of Diets at Different Income Levels', *Economic and Political Weekly*, 13 (Special Number).

—— (1981a), 'On the Measurement of Poverty', *Economic and Political Weekly*, 16.

—— (1981b), 'On the Measurement of Poverty: A Comment', *Economic and Political Weekly*, 16.

—— (1982a), 'Measurement of Undernourishment', *Economic and Political Weekly*, 17.

—— (1982b), 'Poverty and Malnutrition', in Sukhatme (1982c).

—— (ed.) (1982c), *Newer Concepts in Nutrition and their Implications for Policy* (Pune: Maharashtra Association for the Cultivation of Science).

—— (1989), 'Nutritional Adaptation and Variability', *European Journal of Clinical Nutrition*, 43.

—— and S. Margen (1978), 'Models for Protein Deficiency', *American Journal of Clinical Nutrition*, 31.

—— —— (1982), 'Autoregulatory Homeostatic Nature of Energy Balance', *American Journal of Clinical Nutrition*, 35.

Summers, L. (1992), 'The Most Influential Investment', *Scientific American*, no. 267.

Summers, R. and A. Heston (1988), 'A New Set of International Comparisons of Real Product and Prices: Estimates for 130 Countries, 1950–1985', *Review of Income and Wealth*, 34.

Sundstrom, W. A. and P. A. David (1988), 'Old Age Security Motives, Labor Markets and Farm Family Fertility in Antebellum America', *Explorations in Economic History*, 25.

Suppes, P. (1987), 'Maximizing Freedom of Decision: An Axiomatic Analysis', in G. Feiwel (ed.), *Arrow and the Foundation of the Theory of Economic Policy* (London: Macmillan).

Sutton, J. (1986), 'Non-Cooperative Bargaining Theory', *Review of Economic Studies*, 53.

Svedberg, P. (1990), 'Undernourishment in Sub-Saharan Africa: Is There a Gender Bias?' *Journal of Development Studies*, 26.

Tandon, P. (1984), 'Innovation, Market Structure and Welfare', *American Economic Review*, 74.

Tanner, J. M. *et al.* (1982), 'Increase in Length of Leg Relative to Trunk in Japanese Children and Adults from 1957 to 1977: Comparisons with British and Japanese Americans', *Annals of Human Biology*, 9.

Taylor, C. E. (1983), 'Synergy among Mass Infections, Famines and Mortality', *Journal of Interdisciplinary History*, 14.

Taylor, C. L. and D. A. Jodice (1983), *World Handbook of Political and Social Indicators*, i (New Haven, Conn.: Yale University Press).

Taylor, H. and A. Keys (1950), 'Adaptation to Caloric Restriction', *Science*, 112.

Taylor-Gooby, P. (1976), 'Rent Benefits and Tenants' Attitudes', *Journal of Social Policy*, 5.

Temkin, L. S. (1987), 'Intransitivity and the Mere Addition Paradox', *Philosophy and Public Affairs*, 16.

Thomas, D. (1990), 'Intra-Household Resource Allocation', *Journal of Human Resources*, 25.

—— and J. Strauss (1992), 'Prices, Infrastructure, Household Characteristics and Child Height', *Journal of Development Economics*, 39.

—— ——, and M.-H. Henriques (1990), 'Child Survival, Height for Age and Household Characteristics in Brazil', *Journal of Developmental Economics*, 33.

—— —— —— (1991), 'How Does Mother's Education Affect Child Height?' *Journal of Human Resources*, 26.

Thomas, V. and Y. Wang (1992), 'Effects of Government Policies on Productivity Growth: Is East Asia an Exception?' mimeo, World Bank, Washington, DC.

Thorbecke, E. (ed.) (1969), *The Role of Agriculture in Economic Development* (New York: National Bureau of Economic Research).

Tietenberg, T. (1988), *Environmental and Natural Resource Economics*, 2nd edn. (Glenview, Ill.: Scott, Forsman).

Timmer, C. P. (1988), 'The Agricultural Transformation', in Chenery and Srinivasan (1988).

—— (1991), 'The Role of the State in Agricultural Development', forthcoming in C. P. Timmer (ed.), *Agriculture and the State: Growth, Employment and Poverty in Developing Countries* (Ithaca, NY: Cornell University Press).

—— W. P. Falcon, and S. R. Pearson (1983), *Food Policy Analysis* (Baltimore: Johns Hopkins University Press).

Tirole, J. (1988), *The Theory of Industrial Organization* (Cambridge, Mass.: MIT Press).

Tobin, J. (1970), 'On Limiting the Domain of Inequality', *Journal of Law and Economics*, 13.

Tomich, T. P., P. Kilby and B. F. Johnston (1991), *Agriculture and Structural Transformation: Opportunities Seized, Opportunities Missed*, mimeo, World Bank.

Tomkins, A. M. and F. Watson (1989), *Interaction of Nutrition and Infection* (Geneva: World Health Organization).

Topkis, D. M. (1979), 'Equilibrium Points in Nonzero-Sum *n*-Person Submodular Games', *Siam Journal of Control and Optimization*, 17.

Torun, B. (1984), 'Physiological Measurements of Physical Activity among Children under Free-Living Conditions', in Pollitt and Amante (1984).

—— F. Chew, and R. D. Mendoza (1983), 'Energy Costs of Activities of Pre-School Children', *Nutrition Research*, 3.

—— and F. Viteri (1981), 'Energy Requirements of Pre-School Children and Effects of Varying Energy Intakes on Protein Metabolism', in Torun, Young and Rand (1981).

—— V. R. Young, and W. M. Rand (eds.) (1981), 'Protein–Energy Requirements of Developing Countries: Evaluation of New Data', *Food and Nutrition Bulletin*, 5 (Supplement).

Townsend, R. M. (1989), 'Risk and Insurance in Village India', mimeo, Department of Economics, University of Chicago.

Trease, J. and B. Logue (1986), 'Economic Development and the Older Population', *Population and Development Review*, 12.

Turke, P. W. (1989), 'Evolution and the Demand for Children', *Population and Development Review*, 15.

Turnbull, C. (1972), *The Mountain People* (New York: Simon & Schuster).

Uauy, R. (1985), 'Commentary', in O. Brunser *et al.* (eds.), *Clinical Nutrition of the Child* (New York: Raven Press).

Udry, C. (1990), 'Credit Markets in Northern Nigeria: Credit as Insurance in a Rural Economy', *World Bank Economic Review*, 4.

Ulijaszek, S. J. (1990), 'Nutritional Status and Susceptibility to Infectious Disease', in Harrison and Waterlow (1990).

Ullmann-Margalit, E. (1977), *The Emergence of Norms* (Oxford: Oxford University Press).

Underwood, B. A. (ed.) (1983), *Nutrition Intervention Strategies in National Development* (New York: Academic Press).

UNDP (1990, 1991), *Human Development Report* (New York: United Nations Development Program).

UNEP (1984), *General Assessment of Progress in the Implementation of the Plan of Action to Combat Desertification 1978–1984*, Report of the Executive Director (Nairobi: United Nations Environment Program).

UNICEF (1987), *The State of the World's Children* (Oxford: Oxford University Press).

United Nations (1954), *International Definition and Measurement of Standards and Levels of Living* (New York: United Nations).

—— (1985), *Demographic Yearbook* (New York: United Nations).

—— (1987), *First Report on the World Nutrition Situation* (Rome: Food and Agricultural Organization).

—— (1988), *Supplement on Methods and Statistics to the First Report on the World Nutrition Situation* (Geneva: World Health Organization).

—— (1990), *Overall Socioeconomic Perspectives of the World Economy to the Year 2000* (New York: UN Department of International Economic and Social Affairs).

Usher, D. (1963), 'The Transport Bias in Comparisons of National Income', *Economica*, 30.

—— (1973), 'An Imputation to the Measure of Economic Growth for Change in Life Expectancy', in M. Moss (ed.), *The Measurement of Economic and Social Performance* (New York: National Bureau of Economic Research).

Ushio, Y. (1983), 'Cournot Equilibrium with Free Entry: The Case of Decreasing Average Cost Functions', *Review of Economic Studies*, 50.

—— (1985), 'Approximate Efficiency of Cournot Equilibria in Large Markets', *Review of Economic Studies*, 52.

Valdes, A. and P. Konandreas (1981), 'Assessing Food Insecurity Based on National Aggregates in Developing Countries', in A. Valdes (ed.), *Food Security in Developing Countries* (Boulder, Colo.: Westview Press).

Valverde, V. *et al.* (1977), 'Relationship between Family Land Availability and Nutritional Status', *Ecology of Food and Nutrition*, 6.

Vallin, J. and A. D. Lopez (eds.) (1985), *Health Policy, Social Policy and Mortality Prospects* (Paris: Institut National d'Études Demographiques).

Varian, H. (1984), *Microeconomic Analysis*, 2nd edn. (New York: W. W. Norton), first published 1978.

Vaughan, M. (1987), *The Story of an African Famine: Gender and Famine in Twentieth Century Malawi* (Cambridge: Cambridge University Press).

Vickrey, W. S. (1960), 'Utility, Strategy, and Social Decision Rules', *Quarterly Journal of Economics*, 74.

Victoria, C. G. *et al.* (1986), 'Risk Factors for Malnutrition in Brazilian Children: The Role of Social and Environmental Variables', *Bulletin WHO*, 64.

Visaria, P. (1967), 'The Sex Ratio of the Population of India and Pakistan and Regional Variations during 1901–61', in A. Bose (ed.), *Patterns of Population Change in India* (Bombay: Allied Publishers).

—— (1971), *The Sex Ratio of the Population of India*, Census of India, Monograph No. 10 (New Delhi: Manager of Publications).

—— (1980), 'Poverty and Unemployment in India: An Analysis of Recent Evidence', World Bank Staff Working Paper, No. 417.

—— and L. Visaria (1985), 'Indian Households with Female Heads: Their Incidence, Characteristics and Levels of Living', in D. Jain and Bannerjee (1985).

Viteri, F. E. (1971), 'Considerations on the Effect of Nutrition on the Body Composition and Physical Work Capacity of Young Guatemalan Adults', in N. S. Scrimshaw and A. M. Altshull (eds.), *Amino Acid Fortification of Protein Foods* (Cambridge, Mass.: MIT Press).

—— (1974), 'Definition of the Nutrition Problem in the Labor Force', in N. S. Scrimshaw and M. Behar (eds.), *Nutrition and Agricultural Development* (New York: Plenum Press).

—— (1982), 'Nutrition and Work Performance', in Scrimshaw and Wallerstein (1982).

—— and B. Torun (1974), 'Anemia and Work Capacity', *Clinics in Haematology*, 3.

—— —— (1981), 'Nutrition, Physical Activity and Growth', in M. Ritzen *et al.*, *The Biology of Normal Human Growth* (New York: Raven Press).

—— *et al.* (1971), 'Determining Energy Costs of Agricultural Activities by Respirometer and Energy Balance Techniques', *American Journal of Clinical Nutrition*, 24.

Vlassoff, C. (1990), 'The Value of Sons in an Indian Village: How Widows See It', *Population Studies*, 44.

Vlassoff, M. (1979), 'Labour Demand and Economic Utility of Children: A Case Study in Rural India', *Population Studies*, 33.

—— and C. Vlassoff (1980), 'Old-Age Security and the Utility of Children in Rural India', *Population Studies*, 34.

Vlastos, G. (1962), 'Justice and Equality', in R. Brandt (ed.), *Social Justice* (New York: Prentice-Hall).

Vogelsang, I. (1990), *Public Enterprise in Monopolistic Industries* (London: Harwood).

von Neumann, J. and O. Morgenstern (1944), *Theory of Games and Economic Behavior* (Princeton, NJ: Princeton University Press).

Waaler, H. T. (1984), 'Height, Weight and Mortality: The Norwegian Experience', *Acta Medica Scandinavia*, 679 (Supplement).

Wade, R. (1987), 'The Management of Common Property Resources: Finding a Cooperative Solution', *World Bank Research Observer*, 2.

—— (1988), *Village Republics: Economic Conditions for Collective Action in South India* (Cambridge: Cambridge University Press).

—— (1990), *Governing the Market: Economic Theory and the Role of Government in East Asian Industrialization* (Princeton, NJ: Princeton University Press).

Waldron, I. (1985), 'What Do We Know About the Causes of Sex Differences in Mortality? A Review of the Literature', *Population Bulletin of the United Nations*, 18.

Waldron, J. (ed.) (1984), 'Introduction', in *Theories of Rights* (Oxford: Oxford University Press).

Walker, T. S. and J. G. Ryan (1990), *Village and Household Economies in India's Semi-Arid Tropics* (Baltimore: Johns Hopkins University Press).

Wan, H. Y. and S. Clemhout (1970), 'Learning-by-Doing and Infant Industry Protection', *Review of Economic Studies*, 37.

Warneryd, K. (1990), *Economic Conventions: Essays in Institutional Evolution* (Stockholm: Economic Research Institute).

Warren, M. (1978), 'Do Potential People Have Moral Rights?' in Sikora and Barry (1978).

Waterlow, J. C. (1972), 'Classification and Definition of Protein–Calorie Malnutrition', *British Medical Journal*, 3.

—— (1985), 'What Do We Mean by Adaptation?' in Blaxter and Waterlow (1985).

—— (1986), 'Metabolic Adaptation to Low Intakes of Energy and Protein', *Annual Review of Nutrition*, 6.

—— (ed.) (1988), *Linear Growth Retardation in Less Developed Countries* (New York: Raven Press).

—— (1989a), 'Observations on the FAO's Methodology for Estimating the Incidence of Undernourishment', *Food and Nutrition Bulletin*, 11.

—— (1989b), 'Comment on "Nutritional Adaptation and Variability"', *European Journal of Clinical Nutrition*, 43.

—— (1990), 'Mechanisms of Adaptation to Low Energy Intakes', in G. A. Harrison and Waterlow (1990).

—— (with A. M. Tomkins and S. M. Grantham-McGregor) (1992a), *Protein Energy Malnutrition* (Sevenoaks, Kent: Edward Arnold).

—— (1992b), 'Nutritional Constraints on Human Resources', mimeo, London School of Hygiene and Tropical Medicine.

—— A. Ashworth, and M. G. Griffiths (1980), 'Faltering in Infant Growth in Less Developed Countries', *Lancet*, 2.

—— *et al.* (1977), 'The Presentation and Use of Height and Weight Data for Comparing the Nutritional Status of Groups of Children under the Age of 10 Yrs', *Bulletin of WHO*, 55.

Watts, H. (1968), 'An Economic Definition of Poverty', in D. P. Moynihan (ed.), *On Understanding Poverty* (New York: Basic Books).

Weinberg, E. D. (1978), 'Iron and Infection', *Microbiological Reviews*, 42.

Weiss, A. (1990), *Efficiency Wages: Models of Unemployment, Layoffs and Wage Dispersion* (Princeton, NJ: Princeton University Press).

Weitzman, M. (1970), 'Optimal Growth with Scale-Economies in the Creation of Overhead Capital', *Review of Economic Studies*, 37.

—— (1974), 'Prices vs. Quantities', *Review of Economic Studies*, 41.

—— (1976), 'Welfare Significance of National Product in a Dynamic Economy', *Quarterly Journal of Economics*, 90.

—— (1977), 'Is the Price System or Rationing More Effective in Getting a Commodity to Those Who Need It Most?' *Bell Journal of Economics*, 7.

White, G. F., D. J. Bradley, and A. V. White (1972), *Drawers of Water: Domestic Water Use in East Africa* (Chicago: University of Chicago Press).

Whitehead, R. G. (1989), 'Famine', in Friday and Laskey (1989).

—— *et al.* (1976), 'Factors Influencing Lactation Performance in Rural Gambian Mothers', *Lancet*, 2.

—— *et al.* (1981), 'Recommended Dietary Amounts of Energy for Pregnancy and Lactation in the United Kingdom', *Food and Nutrition Bulletin*, 5 (Supplement).

WHO (1983), *Measuring Change in Nutritional Status* (Geneva: World Health Organization).

—— (1985), *Energy and Protein Requirements*, Technical Report Series 724 (Geneva: World Health Organization).

—— (1990), *Global Estimates for Health Situation Assessment and Projections, 1990* (Geneva: World Health Organization).

Widdowson, E. M. (1985), 'Responses to Deficits in Dietary Energy', in Blaxter and Waterlow (1985).

Weissner, P. (1982), 'Risk, Reciprocity and Social Influences on !Kung San Economics', in E. Leacock and R. B. Lee (eds.), *Politics and History in Band Societies* (Cambridge: Cambridge University Press).

Wiggins, D. (1987), 'The Claims of Needs', in *Needs, Values and Truth* (Oxford, Basil Blackwell).

Wignaraja, P. (1990), *Women, Poverty and Resources* (New Delhi: Sage Publications).

Wilbanks, T. J. (1980), 'Accessibility and Social Change in Northern India', in Sopher (1980c).

Wilk, R. R. (ed.) (1989), *The Household Economy: Reconsidering the Domestic Role of Production* (Boulder, Colo.: Westview Press).

Williams, B. (1962), 'The Idea of Equality', in P. Laslett and W. G. Runciman (eds.), *Philosophy, Politics and Society* (Oxford: Basil Blackwell).

—— (1972), *Morality* (Cambridge: Cambridge University Press).

—— (1976), 'Moral Luck', *Proceedings of the Aristotelian Society* (Supplementary Volume); reprinted in Williams (1981b).

—— (1981a), 'Person, Character and Morality', in Williams (1981b).

—— (1981b), *Moral Luck* (Cambridge: Cambridge University Press).

—— (1985), *Ethics and the Limits of Philosophy* (London: Fontana/Collins).

Williamson, N. E. (1976), *Sons or Daughters? A Cross-Cultural Survey of Parental Preferences* (Beverly Hills, Cal.: Sage Publications).

Williamson, O. (1985), *The Economic Institutions of Capitalism* (New York: Free Press).

Willis, R. (1973), 'A New Approach to the Economic Theory of Fertility', *Journal of Political Economy*, 81 (Supplement).

—— (1980), 'The Old-Age Security Hypothesis and Population Growth', in T. Burch (ed.), *Demographic Behavior: Interdisciplinary Perspectives on Decision-Making* (Boulder, Colo.: Westview Press).

—— (1982), 'The Direction of Intergenerational Transfers and the Demographic Transition: The Caldwell Hypothesis Revisited', *Population and Development Review*, 8 (Supplement).

—— (1987), 'Externalities and Population', in Johnson and Lee (1987).

Winick, M. (1976), *Malnutrition and Brain Development* (New York: Oxford University Press).

Winter, J. M. (1988), 'Public Health and the Extension of Life Expectancy in England, 1901–60', in M. Keynes, D. A. Coleman, and N. H. Dimsdale (eds.), *The Political Economy of Health and Welfare* (London: Macmillan).

Wischmeier, W. H. (1976), 'Uses and Misuses of the Universal Soil Loss Equation', *Journal of Soil and Water Conservation*, 31.

Wiser, W. H. (1936), *The Hindu Jajmani System* (Lucknow, Uttar Pradesh: Lucknow Publishing House).

Wolfe, B. L. and J. R. Behrman (1982), 'Determinants of Child Mortality, Health and Nutrition in a Developing Country', *Journal of Development Economics*, 11.

—— —— (1987), 'How Does Mother's Schooling Affect Family Health, Nutrition, Medical Care Usage and Household Sanitation?' *Journal of Econometrics*, 16.

Wolgemuth, J. C. *et al.* (1982), 'Worker Productivity and the Nutritional Status of Kenyan Road Construction Labor', *American Journal of Clinical Literature*, 36.

Wong, J. (1977), 'Communization of Peasant Agriculture: China's Organizational Strategy for Agricultural Development', in P. Dorner (ed.), *Cooperative and Commune: Group Farming in the Economic Development of Agriculture* (Madison, Wis.: University of Wisconsin Press).

World Bank (1983, 1984, 1986a, 1988, 1990, 1991a, 1992), *World Development Report* (New York: Oxford University Press).

—— (1986b), *Population Growth and Policies in Sub-Saharan Africa* (Washington, DC: World Bank).

—— (1989a), *World Tables 1988–89* (Washington, DC: World Bank).

—— (1989b), *Sub-Saharan Africa: From Crisis to Sustainable Growth* (Washington, DC: World Bank).

—— (1991b), *The Population, Agriculture and Environment Nexus in Sub-Saharan Africa* (Washington, DC: World Bank).

Wynne, E. (1980), *Social Security: A Reciprocity System Under Pressure* (Boulder, Colo.: Westview Press).

Wyon, J. and J. Gordon (1971), *The Khanna Study* (Cambridge, Mass.: Cambridge University Press).

Yaari, M. (1985), 'On the Role of "Dutch Books" in the Theory of Choice under Risk', 1985 Nancy L. Schwartz Memorial Lecture, J. L. Kellog Graduate School of Management, Northwestern University.

—— (1987), 'The Dual Theory of Choice under Risk', *Econometrica*, 55.

Yotopoulos, P. (1985), 'Middle-Income Classes and Food Crises: The "New" Food-Feed Competition', *Economic Development and Cultural Change*, 33.

—— (1988), 'Distributions of Real Income: Within Countries and by World Income Classes', Occasional Paper No. 23, Development Research Institute, Tilburg University.

—— (1990), 'Exchange Rates and State-Led Capitalism: What Can the NICs Learn from Japan?' CEPR Policy Paper No. 212, Stanford University.

Young, V. and N. C. Scrimshaw (1970), 'The Physiology of Starvation', *Scientific American*, 225.

Zeldes, S. P. (1989a), 'Consumption and Liquidity Constraints: An Empirical Investigation', *Journal of Political Economy*, 97.

—— (1989b), 'Optimal Consumption with Stochastic Income: Deviations from Certainty Equivalence', *Quarterly Journal of Economics*, 103.

Zimmerman, M. B. (1982), 'Learning Effects and the Commercialization of New Energy Technologies: The Case of Nuclear Power', *Bell Journal of Economics*, 13.

INDEX OF NAMES

Abraham, A. 202 n.
Abramovitz, M. 153
Abreu, D. 215 n.
Adair, L. S. 12 n., 413, 417, 432, 442 n.
Adelman, I. xi, 16 n., 20, 25 n., 34 n., 97, 123, 126, 495, 527 n.
Agarwal, A. xi, 10 n., 80, 273, 281 n., 289, 290, 307 n.
Agarwal, B. 9 n., 13, 328 n., 329
Ahluwalia, M. S. 126
Ahmad, A. 306 n., 351
Ahmad, E. 174, 176 n., 185 n.
Ahmad, Y.-J. 281 n.
Aigner, D. J. 498
Akerlof, G. 211, 531, 532 n.
Alamgir, M. 10, 14 n., 20, 328 n., 362
Alchian, A. 178 n., 225
Alderman, H. 206, 254, 401 n., 437, 438, 530, 531 n.
Aleem, I. 202, 241 n., 250, 538
Alexander, S. 32 n.
Allen, F. 232
Amante, P. 433
Amsden, A. 107 n., 544
Anand, S. 81 n., 126 n.
Anderson, A. B. 291, 307 n.
Anderson, D. 282 n., 274, 277
Anderson, Jock 201 n.
Anderson, Julie xi, 237 n.
Anderson, J. T. 459 n.
Anderson, P. W. 142
Andraca, I. de 429
Apffel Marglin, F. 25 n.
Arens, P. 282 n.
Aristotle 23, 24, 43, 178 n.
Arnold, J. E. M. 10 n., 80, 291 n., 519
Arora, A. 153 n.
Arora, P. 10, 20
Arrieto, R. 12 n.
Arrow, K. J. xi, 10, 17, 22, 29, 31–2, 35 n., 52 n., 55, 69 n., 71, 105 n., 111, 112, 114, 138, 140 n., 142, 143, 145, 146 n., 168, 172 n., 178 n., 179, 189, 193 n., 196, 226 n., 283 n., 297 n., 298, 346, 375, 378, 379 n., 380 n., 391 n., 467, 473 n., 489 n.
Arroyave, G. 402 n.
Arthur, W. B. 142, 503
Asher, H. 178 n.

Ashworth, A. 90
d'Aspremont, C. 71
Åstrand, P. O. 433 n., 434
Atkinson, A. B. 3 n., 17, 35 n., 126, 146, 171 n.
Auerbach, A. J. 177 n.
Aumann, R. 66 n., 138 n., 210 n., 211, 215 n., 375, 376, 473 n.
Axelrod, R. 211

Bahl, R. 107 n.
Bairagi, R. 82 n., 503
Baker, S. H. 403 n.
Baland, J.-M. 504
Balazs, R. 12 n.
Baldwin, R. 179
Banister, J. 93, 270
Banks, D. L. 131
Bannerjee, A. V. 539 n.
Barac-Nieto, M. 12, 84, 430, 433, 434, 435 n., 453, 460
Bardhan, P. K. 139, 228, 229, 230 n., 233 n., 235, 239, 241 n., 242, 255, 314 n., 317 n., 318 n., 319, 401 n., 482 n., 483 n., 498, 508, 509
Barghouti, S. 279
Barr, N. 3 n., 35 n., 171 n.
Barraclough, S. 293
Barro, R. 179 n., 325, 356 n., 357 n., 368 n., 378
Barry, B. 28, 36, 288, 377 n., 381 n.
Basta, S. 13, 402
Basu, A. M. 309, 310
Basu, K. 241 n., 486 n., 535
Bates, R. H. 107, 122 n., 272 n.
Bauer, P. T. xi, 7, 16, 22, 25 n., 77 n., 106, 107, 167, 171 n., 228 n., 272 n., 350, 544
Baumol, W. M. 148, 284 n.
Bayles, M. 381 n.
Bayliss Smith, T. 278 n.
Beato, P. 148 n.
Beaton, G. H. 85 n., 87 n., 404, 412 n., 437 n., 438
Becker, G. 17 n., 98, 325, 356 n., 357 n., 364, 366 n., 368 n., 369 n., 375, 378
Begemann, L. 276 n.
Behrman, J. 17 n., 99, 100, 309, 310, 356 n., 470

Bell, C. 10, 20, 241 n., 242 n., 531 n., 538
Bell, D. E. 197 n.
Beneria, L. 80, 307 n.
Benn, S. 37
Bennett, L. 306 n., 341
Benoit, J.-P. 210 n.
Ben-Porath, Y. 364 n.
Bentham, J. 33, 47
Berg, A. 10, 20, 530 n.
Bergson, A. 22, 35 n.
Berlin, Sir Isaiah 40–1, 45
Bernheim, B. D. 48, 246, 376
Berreman, G. D. 320 n.
Berry, R. A. 139, 228 n., 525
Besley, T. 149, 176 n., 238, 530, 533, 534 n.,
    538, 539 n.
Beteille, A. 9, 106 n.
Bewley, T. 261 n.
Bhagwati, J. 16, 93, 101, 102, 107, 177 n.,
    179, 544 n.
Bhalla, S. xi, 113 n.
Bharadwaj, K. 228 n.
Bhargava, A. 446 n., 447, 448, 471
Bhattacharji, S. 321 n.
Bhattacharya, N. 80
Bhende, M. J. 242 n.
Bienen, H. 123
Bigot, Y. 244
Bigsten, A. 126 n.
Binmore, K. xi, 48, 210 n., 226 n., 326,
    330 n., 331 n., 337 n., 340 n., 376
Binswanger, H. 107, 196, 198, 202 n., 204,
    227 n., 229 n., 232, 233 n., 235, 238, 239,
    241 n., 242, 243 n., 244, 245, 254, 293,
    527, 528
Birdsall, N. 18, 59 n., 344 n., 345, 348 n.,
    354, 366 n.
Biswas, M. 10, 20
Black, F. 52 n.
Blackburn, S. 379 n.
Blackorby, C. 32, 71, 181, 381 n., 383 n.,
    534 n.
Blaxter, K. 12, 442 n.
Bleek, W. 362
Bliss, C. 11, 19 n., 138, 242, 420, 472 n.,
    474, 483, 500, 505
Blitzer, C. xi, 297 n.
Blurton Jones, N. G. 353 n.
Boadway, R. 3 n., 35 n., 171 n., 185 n.
Bongaarts, J. 353, 354, 364 n.
Bonner, R. 14 n., 147
Boserup, E. 18, 289 n., 307 n., 312, 321 n.,
    341, 361
Boskin, M. 153, 154, 156, 158 n.
Bouis, H. 525
Boussard, J.-M. 201 n.
Bowes, P. 236

Boyd, R. 208 n., 216 n.
Bradley, D. J. 13
Brandenberger, A. 375, 376
Braun, J. von 272 n., 275
Braverman, A. 241 n.
Braybrooke, D. 37 n., 40
Breslin, P. 288, 290
Briend, A. 82 n., 87, 407
Brockman, L. 12
Broome, J. 33, 389 n.
Brown, D. xi, 148 n.
Brown, G. 282 n.
Brown, J. 526
Brown, L. A. 147
Brown, L. R. 346
Brown, M. 325
Brown, W. N. 24 n.
Bruce, J. 307 n.
Bruce, N. 3 n., 35 n., 171 n.
Brumberg, R. E. 246 n.
Brun, T. 424 n.
Brundtland, G. H. 302
Buchanan, J. 22, 34, 42 n., 71
Bulatao, R. A. 354 n., 356 n.
Burki, S. J. 7
Buvinic, M. 59 n., 306, 307 n.
Byrne, P. xi

Cain, G. G. 498
Cain, M. 101, 201, 203, 320 n., 353, 354 n.,
    357, 360, 362, 364 n., 366, 367
Caldwell, J. C. 91 n., 100, 202 n., 246, 310,
    322, 355 n., 356 n., 357, 361, 362, 364 n., 366
Caldwell, P. 202 n., 310, 322, 356 n., 357,
    361 n., 362
Caliendo, M. A. 13
Calvo, G. 378
Cannan, E. 379
Canning, D. 376
Caplin, A. 66
Carmichael, A. G. 407 n.
Carter, M. R. 228 n.
Cashdan, E. 202 n., 288
Cass, D. 391 n.
Castillo, R. O. 84
Cecelski, E. 294 n.
Celedon, J. M. 429
Chakraborty, U. 479 n.
Chakravarty, S. 70 n., 391 n.
Chambers, R. 9 n., 254 n., 417
Chandra, R. 407
Chapin, M. 288, 290
Chapman, T. 276 n.
Chatterjee, M. 313 n.
Chatterjee, S. 80
Chaudhuri, D. P. 98
Chavez, A. 13, 90, 428, 429

Chen, L. C. 12, 13, 82, 95, 139, 254 n., 295, 309, 310, 311, 313 n., 364 n., 407, 408 n., 457 n.
Chen, M. A. 306, 319 n.
Chenery, H. 20, 97, 153, 273 n.
Chew, F. 428 n.
Chigambaram, V. 99
Chiswick, B. 98
Chomitz, K. M. 354
Chopra, K. 10 n., 209 n., 289, 290
Chowdhury, A. K. M. A. 82, 100, 254 n., 364 n., 406, 407, 457 n.
Christian, J. 42 n.
Christian, P. 100
Chung, K. R. 428 n.
Cigno, A. 325, 357 n., 366 n.
Clark, C. W. 277 n., 282 n.
Clark, W. C. 278 n.
Clemhout, S. 179
Cline, W. 126 n., 139, 228, 525
Coale, A. J. 353 n.
Coase, R. 142, 285 n.
Coate, S. 149, 530, 534 n.
Cochrane, S. H. xi, 99, 100, 307, 308, 349, 352, 354 n., 355, 361, 363
Cohen, G. 74
Cohen, J. 9 n., 294 n.
Cohen, L. 446
Cohon, R. xii
Cole, T. J. 407
Collier, D. 106
Collier, P. 243 n.
Collins, K. J. 433
Colombo, M. 13, 429
Colson, W. 141
Commander, S. 9
Cooper, Richard 282 n.
Cooper, Russell 371, 372 n.
Cotts Watkins, S. 351
Cowen, T. 381 n.
Cox, D. 532
Cox, J. 52 n.
Crafts, N. F. R. 153
Cravioto, J. 12 n.
Crawford, V. 376
Cremer, H. 246, 325, 357 n.
Crimmins, E. 354 n.
Crompton, D. W. T. 406
Cubbin, J. S. 148
Cutting, W. A. M. 405

Dandekar, K. 310
Dandekar, V. M. 126 n., 401 n., 438, 448, 450
Dantwala, M. L. 271
Dasgupta, A. 7, 11 n., 16, 20, 25 n., 73, 311 n., 495, 505
Dasgupta, C. xii, 532 n.

Das Gupta, M. 9 n., 291, 309, 310 n., 311, 314 n., 323 n.
Datta-Choudhuri, M. 107 n., 544
Da Vanzo, J. 309
David, P. A. xi, 142, 145 n., 152 n., 211 n., 320, 325, 352, 357 n., 365, 368 n., 372 n., 503
Davidson, D. 5 n.
Davidson, S. 54, 401, 402 n., 424 n.
Davies, P. 141 n.
Deaton, A. xii, 55, 240 n., 242 n., 253–4, 261 n., 262, 306, 309, 310, 447, 470, 471
Debreu, G. 10, 35, 58 n., 60 n., 62 n., 66, 138, 167 n., 168, 170, 467, 489 n.
Debysingh, M. 321
de Garine, I. 202 n., 254 n.
de Janvry, A. 253, 528
Dekel, E. 376
De Maeyer, E. M. 403 n.
DeMeza, D. 252 n.
Demsetz, H. 142, 225
Denison, E. F. 153
Deolalikar, A. B. 17 n., 310, 436, 470, 490
Desai, G. M. 272 n.
Desai, P. 107
Deschamps, R. 71
de Soto, H. 80, 107, 139
Dev, S. M. 535
Devarajan, S. 281 n.
de Waal, A. 14 n.
Dewey, J. 178 n.
Dhadda, S. 328 n.
Diamond, P. A. 176 n., 177 n., 186, 530 n., 532, 533 n.
Dierker, E. 148 n.
Dixon, J. A. 275 n., 279, 284 n., 285 n.
Dobbing, J. 430
Dodge, P. R. 12 n.
Domenico, P. A. 276 n.
Donaldson, D. 33, 71, 181, 381 n., 383 n., 534 n.
Dore, R. 528 n.
Douglas, M. 216
Dow, T. 362
Drewnowsky, J. 7, 34 n.
Dreze, J. 10, 14 n., 16, 20, 25 n., 171 n., 199, 205 n., 206, 242 n., 255 n., 273 n., 323 n., 474, 483 n., 509, 511, 533
D'Souza, S. 309, 310, 311, 313 n.
Duesenbery, J. S. 372
Dugdale, A. 404, 417, 457 n.
Durham, W. H. xii, 107, 293 n.
Durnin, J. V. G. A. 423 n., 457
Dworkin, R. 22, 26, 28 n., 29, 30 n., 34, 35 n., 37, 42 n., 43, 73
Dwyer, D. 307 n.
Dyson, T. 314 n., 320 n.

Dyson-Hudson, R. 288

Easter, K. W. 284 n.
Easterlin, R. A. 76 n., 349, 351, 354 n., 366 n., 374
Edholm, O. G. 444, 445, 446, 447, 450, 451, 452
Edmundson, W. C. 413, 462–4, 465, 466
Ehrlich, A. 274, 275, 346, 385 n.
Ehrlich, P. xii, 274, 275, 346, 385 n.
Ekanem, I. I. 351, 362
El Badri, I. M. A. 314 n.
Elliot, K. M. 405
El Sarafy, S. 281 n.
Elster, J. 208 n., 211, 212, 340 n.
Enke, S. 370 n.
Ensminger, J. 10 n., 142, 289, 292
Epstein, S. 9 n., 236
Escudero, V. 261 n.
Esman, M. J. 295 n.
Eswaran, M. 225 n., 227, 231 n., 242 n., 253, 257, 264
Evans, R. 215 n.
Eveleth, P. B. 83, 85 n., 426
Evenson, R. E. 59, 152 n., 308, 309, 365

Fagley, R. M. 307 n.
Falcon, W. P. xii, 272 n.
Falconer, J. 10 n., 80, 291, 519
Falkenmark, M. 276 n., 279, 280
Falkner, F. 12, 82, 86, 430
Falloux, F. 275 n.
Farid, S. M. 100, 308, 349, 352, 361 n., 363
Farooq, G. M. 351, 362
Farrell, J. 56, 137, 148, 215 n., 372
Farrell, M. 246 n., 473 n.
Faruqee, R. 309 n.
Fauveau, V. 87, 406
Feacham, R. 405
Feder, E. 106, 142, 243 n., 293, 504, 528
Feder, G. 101 n., 136, 228 n., 231, 242 n., 288, 289, 539 n.
Fee, T. 80
Feeny, D. 142, 243 n., 287 n., 289
Fei, J. C. H. 527 n.
Feierman, S. 309
Feigin, R. D. 12 n.
Feldman, A. xii, 536 n.
Feldman, M. xii
Feldstein, M. 177 n.
Fernandes, W. 294 n., 307 n.
Fernandez, R. 333 n.
Ferro-Luzzi, A. 254 n., 310 n., 415, 417, 433, 437, 415, 442 n., 447, 456 n., 457 n.
Fields, G. 126 n., 139
Findley, R. 107

Fine, B. 111, 113
Fine, K. 111, 113
Fisher, A. 52 n., 283 n., 346
Fishlow, A. 126 n.
Fletcher, P. 430 n.
Floud, R. 83
Fogel, R. W. 83, 352 n.
Foldes, L. 261 n.
Foster, A. 229, 230, 498
Frank, C. 126 n.
Freedman, R. 354 n.
Fried, C. 22, 28 n., 30 n., 34, 37, 40 n., 45
Friedman, J. 215 n.
Friedman, M. 71, 171 n., 202 n.
Friedman, R. 71, 171 n.
Fuchs, V. xii, 96
Fudenberg, D. 62 n., 210 n., 211, 215 n., 376
Furubotn, E. 142

Gadgil, M. xii, 290
Gale, D. 138 n.
Gambetta, D. xii, 142, 226, 537
Gangrade, K. 328 n.
Garby, L. 451
García Márquez, G. 321
Gardenfors, P. 197 n.
Gardner, G. W. 402 n.
Gastil, R. D. 131
Gausch, L. 241 n.
Gauthier, D. 22, 27 n., 47, 48, 340 n.
Geertz, C. 149
Genovese, E. D. 501 n.
George, V. 20
Georgescu-Roegen, N. 482 n.
Gersovitz, M. 242 n., 248
Gevers, L. 71
Ghai, D. 139, 295 n.
Ghai, O. P. 13, 430
Ghodake, R. D. 229 n., 255 n., 482, 502
Giddens, A. 208 n.
Gigliotti, G. A. 377 n., 381
Gilbert, A. 281 n.
Gillaspy, T. 358
Glazer, J. 333 n.
Glewwe, P. 113 n., 126 n.
Golan, L. 283
Golden, B. E. 401
Golden, M. 401
Golding, P. 529
Goodin, R. 40 n.
Goodman, L. A. 111, 113
Goody, J. xii, 9 n., 241 n., 312 n., 362, 368
Gopalan, C. 12, 443 n.
Gordon, H. S. 146 n., 282, 288
Gordon, J. E. 12, 13, 407
Gorman, W. M. 58 n.

Gottlieb, M. 380
Gough, K. 236
Gould, S. J. 442
Graaff, J. de V. 3 n., 6 n., 17, 22, 35 n.
Grande, F. 459 n.
Grantham-McGregor, S. M. 429 n., 430 n.
Graves, P. L. 13, 90, 429 n.
Gray, J. 42 n.
Greenough, P. R. 328 n.
Greenwald, B. C. 252, 537
Greif, A. xii, 210 n., 211, 214 n., 216 n.
Greiner, L. 413, 442 n.
Griffin, J. xii, 15 n., 23, 28 n., 30 n., 34 n., 37, 37 n., 40 n., 52
Griffin, K. 139
Griffiths, M. G. 90
Griliches, Z. 98 n., 152 n.
Gross, D. R. 335, 525
Grossman, S. 226 n., 233
Guesnerie, R. 148 n.
Guha, A. 480, 482 n., 505, 506, 509, 518
Gulati, L. 255 n.
Gulati, T. W. 539 n.
Gulhati, R. 309 n.
Gurr, T. R. 123
Gutmann, A. 4

Haas, J. D. 82 n.
Habicht, J.-P. 12, 82 n., 83, 84, 406, 442 n.
Haddad, L. 17, 310, 325, 439 n., 471, 500, 524, 525, 530 n., 531 n.
Haggarty, P. 413
Haggblade, S. 526
Hahn, F. xi, 10, 96, 138, 172 n., 197, 227, 261 n., 263, 372 n., 467, 473 n., 489 n., 532
Hall, B. xii
Hallfrisch, J. 446
Hamilton, L. S. 277
Hamlin, A. 22
Hammer, J. S. 308 n.
Hammond, P. xi, 71, 74 n., 170 n., 176 n., 381 n., 473
Hancock, G. 106
Hanemann, M. 283 n.
Hardin, G. 290
Hardin, R. 22–3, 26 n., 50 n.
Hare, R. M. 22, 47, 390 n.
Harmish, N. 12 n., 431
Harris, C. 81 n.
Harrison, A. 281 n.
Harrison, G. A. 202 n., 254 n.
Harriss, B. 310
Harrod, R. F. 50 n.
Harsanyi, J. C. xii, 22, 47, 48, 50 n., 58 n., 64, 330 n., 331 n., 380 n., 389, 390
Hart, O. 226 n., 233

Hartwick, J. 274 n., 297 n.
Hassan, M. N. 309, 334, 500
Hauser, M. 381 n.
Hawthorn, G. xii
Hay, M. J. 309
Hayami, Y. 202 n., 226, 271
Hayek, F. von 22, 26 n., 30
Hazell, P. 204, 526
Heady, C. J. 176 n.
Heal, G. xi, 9, 60 n., 70 n., 80, 148 n., 159 n., 161, 164, 190 n., 197, 203 n., 207, 274 n., 281 n., 284 n., 287, 294 n., 297 n., 303 n., 304, 375, 380 n.
Healy, M. J. R. 443 n., 446
Hecht, S. 291, 293, 307 n.
Heer, D. M. 357
Heller, W. P. 148 n.
Helmers, F. L. C. H. 184 n.
Helms, R. W. 421, 470
Helpman, E. 179
Henn, J. K. 308
Henriques, M.-H. 100
Henry, C. 52 n., 283 n., 346
Henry, C. J. K. 415, 426 n., 451
Herring, R. 139
Herzen, A. 392, 393
Hess, P. N. 356 n.
Heston, A. 79, 80, 108 n., 111 n., 117, 125 n.
Heyd, D. 357 n., 381 n., 387 n., 393
Hicks, J. R. 142
Hicks, N. 7, 20, 34 n., 495
Higgins, G. M. 278 n.
Hildenbrand, W. 138
Hill, K. 354, 406
Hill, P. 243 n.
Hinds, M. W. 414 n.
Ho, T. J. 82 n.
Ho, Y.-M. 527 n.
Hobcraft, J. N. 100
Hoddinott, J. 471
Hodgson, G. 285 n.
Hoff, K. 242 n., 527, 538
Hogarth, R. M. 197 n.
Holdren, J. 274, 275, 346
Hollander, S. 178 n.
Holmstrom, B. 226 n.
Horney, M. J. 325
Horton, E. S. 424
Hossain, M. 538 n.
Hotchkiss, D. 294 n., 306
Howe, J. 10 n., 211 n., 287 n., 290
Howes, S. xii
Huffman, S. 82, 139, 254 n., 457 n.
Hufschmidt, M. A. 284 n.
Hughes, S. xi
Hull, T. H. 93, 354 n.

Humana, C. 131
Hume, D. 50 n.
Humphries, J. 291 n.
Huppi, M. 539 n.
Huq, E. 309, 310, 311, 313 n.
Hurka, T. 381 n.

Iliffe, J. 9, 27 n.
Immink, M. D. C. 421, 470
Intriligator, M. D. 182
Isenman, P. 108 n., 113 n.
Iyer, R. xi

Jacoby, H, 253
Jain, S. 126 n.
James, D. E. 275 n., 279
James, W. F. T. 413, 426 n., 431 n., 440, 441, 442 n., 443 n., 455, 456 n., 458, 459, 464
Jamison, D. 13, 94 n., 95, 96, 98 n., 99 n., 100 n., 345
Janowitz, M. 123
Jaywardena, L. xii
Jazairy, I. 362
Jelliffe, D. B. 12, 90
Jelliffe, E. F. P. 12, 90
Jimenez, E. 176 n., 532
Jobling, R. xii
Jodha, N. S. 80, 229 n., 233 n., 242 n., 291, 292
Jodice, D. A. 108, 109, 111 n., 119, 130, 131
Johansson, S. R. xi, 88 n., 91 n., 313 n., 407 n.
John, A. 371, 372 n.
Johnson, D. G. 348 n.
Johnston, B. F. 93, 272 n., 354 n., 526
Johnston, F. E. 12 n., 84, 413, 442 n.
Joseph, K. 42 n.
Just, R. 231, 242 n.

Kadekodi, G. K. 10 n., 209 n., 289, 290
Kahn, H. 345
Kahneman, D. 197 n.
Kakwani, N. 34 n., 126 n.
Kalai, E. 333, 340
Kaldor, N. 179
Kamarck, A. M. 309 n., 362
Kanbur, R. 17, 176 n., 310, 325, 439 n., 500, 524, 530 n., 531 n., 533 n.
Kanbur, S. M. R. 126 n.
Kaneko, Y. 34 n., 115
Kant, I. 27 n., 392
Kaplowitz, H. 85 n.
Karkaria, B. J. 314 n.
Kautilya 24
Keeler, E. 375
Keen, M. 531 n.

Keliey, A. C. 346
Kennedy, E. 272 n., 275, 335, 471, 472, 525, 531 n.
Keyfitz, N. 94 n., 345 n., 504 n.
Keys, A. 453, 456, 458, 459, 460
Khan, A. R. 139, 364 n.
Khanam, S. R. 320 n.
Kikuchi, M. 202 n., 226
Kilby, P. 93, 272 n., 354 n., 526
Kill, K. 355
Kim, C. K. 107 n., 544
Kim, K. S. 107 n.
Kim, M. 283
Kim, W. S. 107 n., 544
King, E. 59, 100, 308, 309
King, M. 96
King, P. N. 277
King, T. 99 n.
Kirman, A. 138
Kislev, Y. 152 n.
Klein, R. E. 12 n.
Knudsen, O. K. 531 n.
Kochar, A. 254, 527
Kolm, S.-Ch. 22, 73, 126
Konandreas, P. 504
Koopmans, T. C. 22, 52 n., 58 n., 87 n., 138, 167 n., 170, 172 n., 227, 247, 257, 298, 391 n., 467
Kornai, J. 42 n., 179 n.
Kotlikoff, L. J. 246
Kotwal, A. 225 n., 227, 231 n., 242 n., 253, 257, 264
Kreimer, A. 287 n.
Kreps, D. 52 n., 210 n., 376
Krishna, R. 255 n., 526
Krishna, V. 210 n.
Krueger, A. O. 107, 177
Krugman, P. 179, 374 n.
Kulkarni, R. N. 425 n.
Kumar, A. 13, 430
Kumar, G. 313, 314 n., 319 n.
Kumar, S. K. 294 n., 306
Kunreuther, H. 201
Kuo, S. W. Y. 527 n., 544
Kurpad, A. V. 425 n.
Kurz, M. 297 n., 298, 375, 391 n.
Kutcher, G. 139, 228 n.
Kuznets, S. 126
Kymlicka, W. 22
Kyn, O. 126 n.
Kynch, J. 310

Lacville, R. 310
Laffont, J.-J. 74 n.
Lal, D. 25 n.
Lallement, D. 279
Lambert, J. 313 n.

Lammert, O. 451
Lane, J. 377 n., 381
Lau, L. xii, 98 n., 99 n., 101 n., 153, 154, 156, 158 n., 228
Layard, R. 11
Leach, G. 278 n.
Lear, J. 43 n.
Lecaillon, J. 126
Lechtig, A. 12 n., 86, 407
Lee, D. 309
Lee, J. 414 n.
Lee, R. 348 n.
Lee, R. B. 353
Lee, R. D. 325, 347, 354 n., 356 n., 357 n.
Leibenstein, H. 248, 354 n., 357 n., 482 n., 483, 509
Leland, H. 261 n., 262, 263
Lele, U. J. 526
Lentneck, B. 147
Lentzner, H. 100
Leslie, J. 13, 96, 100, 311 n.
Lesthaeghe, R. 353 n.
Levhari, D. 197, 261 n., 263
Levin, H. M. 12, 95, 403 n.
Levine, D. 210 n.
Levy, S. 179
Lewis, D. 208 n.
Lewis, H. G. 356 n., 364, 366 n.
Lewis, W. A. 248, 249
Lian-Ybanez, M. 429 n.
Libbee, M. J. 320
Lieberman, M. B. 178 n.
Lightfoot-Klein, H. 59
Lim, E. 247 n.
Lim, Y. xii, 202 n., 225 n., 239
Lindbeck, A. 42 n., 255 n.
Lindblom, C. 139
Lindert, P. 126 n., 356 n., 360
Lipset, S. 106, 123
Lipton, M. xii, 16, 139, 272 n.
Little, I. M. D. 16, 25 n., 174, 184 n., 297, 528 n., 544 n.
Livi-Bacci, M. 407 n.
Locay, L. 142 n.
Lockheed, M. 98 n., 99 n.
Loewenstein, M. S. 82 n.
Logue, B. 358
Longhurst, R. 9 n., 254 n., 417
Loomes, G. 32 n.
Lopez, A. D. 95, 313
Lopez, I. 13, 429
Loury, G. 149
Low, S. M. 59 n.
Lowentin, R. C. 442
Lucas, R. 157
Luce, R. D. 194, 330 n., 333, 340
Lunven, P. 307

Lutz, E. 281 n.
Lycette, M. A. 306, 307 n.
Lydall, H. 126

McAlpin, M. B. 14 n.
McCamant, J. F. 131
McDonald, J. W. 100
McDowell, J. 6 n.
McElroy, M. 325, 336 n.
McGarry, M. 405
McGaw, B. A. 413
McGreevey, W. P. 59 n., 306, 307 n.
McGuire, C. B. 282 n.
McGuire, J. 306 n., 307 n., 313 n., 348 n.
Machina, M. J. 197, 198, 199
McIntire, J. 243 n., 245
McKay, H. 13
McKensie, L. 170 n.
McKeown, T. 83
Mackie, J. L. 30 n.
McMahan, J. A. 381 n.
McNamara, R. S. 541 n.
McNeill, G. 426 n.
Maddison, A. 153, 273
Magrath, W. 282 n.
Mahar, D. 293, 528
Majumdar, M. 201 n.
Maksud, M. G. 12, 435 n.
Mäler, K.-G. xi, 80, 281 n., 283, 284 n., 290, 297 n., 348 n., 359 n.
Malhotra, K. C. 290
Malina, R. M. 13, 429
Malinowski, B. 141
Malinvaud, E. 11, 203 n.
Manser, M. 325
Mara, D. 405
Margen, S. 413, 441 n., 444, 446, 448, 449, 451, 452
Marglin, S. A. xi, 25 n., 174, 184 n., 185 n., 207 n., 248 n., 297
Markowitz, H. 111, 113
Marschak, J. 194, 325
Marshall, A. 248, 473
Marshall, T. H. 3 n., 22, 45 n., 104
Marsilius of Padua 23, 24
Martinez, C. 90, 428, 429
Martorell, R. xi, 12, 13 n., 82 n., 83, 84–5, 90, 402 n., 406, 421, 442 n., 500
Marx, K. 37
Mas-Colell, A. 148 n.
Maskin, E. xi, 66, 71, 74 n., 210 n., 211, 215 n., 501
Mason, K. O. 320 n., 367
Mata, L. J. 89, 90, 95, 405, 406, 407
Mathewson, F. 147
May, D. A. 357
May, P. 291, 307 n.

Mayer, E. 204
Mazumdar, D. 224, 228 n., 229 n., 239, 243 n., 482 n., 483, 502, 509
Mazumdar, V. 307 n.
Meade, J. E. 22, 145, 172 n., 172 n., 176, 185 n., 246 n., 284 n., 311 n., 371, 377 n., 379 n., 381, 396
Meeks Gardner, J. M. 428, 429 n.
Meillassoux, C. 221, 246, 307 n.
Mellor, J. W. 271, 526
Mendoza, F. S. 84
Mendoza, R. D. 428 n.
Menken, J. 353
Menon, G. 294 n., 307 n.
Mensch, B. 100
Mertens, J.-F. 376
Merton, R. 52 n.
Meyer, A. 348 n., 359 n.
Middleton, S. 529
Migot-Adholla, S. 142, 243 n., 289
Milgrom, P. xii, 66, 142, 211, 226 n., 371
Mill, J. S. 52, 70 n., 379
Miller, B. 310, 311
Miller, T. 325, 347, 357 n.
Milliman, J. W. 286
Mirrlees, J. A. xii, 22, 74 n., 174, 176 n., 177 n., 179, 184 n., 186, 197, 233, 261 n., 263, 297, 325, 334 n., 356 n., 379 n., 391 n., 483, 500, 530 n., 532, 533 n.
Mitchell, R. C. 106, 122 n., 123, 124
Mitra, A. 241 n., 313
Mitra, P. K. 176 n., 184 n.
Modigliani, F. 246 n.
Moene, K. A. 497 n.
Mola, A. 406, 454
Mönckeberg, F. 12, 90 n., 127, 429 n.
Montgomery, J. 173 n.
Moock, P. M. 13
Mookherjee, D. 535
Moore, M. 314 n., 320 n.
Mora, J. O. 84
Moravcsik, J. xii, 45 n.
Morduch, J. 206, 242 n., 254, 261 n., 264, 447
Morgan, L. H. 320
Morgane, P. J. 12 n.
Morgenstern, O. 194
Morishima, M. 528 n.
Morley, D. 405 n.
Morris, C. T. 25 n., 34 n., 97, 123, 126
Morris, M. D. 7, 34 n., 77
Morrison, D. G. 106, 122 n., 123, 124
Moscardi, E. 253
Mosley, H. 94 n., 95, 100 n.
Mosley, W. H. 95, 100
Mozumder, A. B. 101
Muelbauer, J. 55
Mueller, E. 26, 358, 360

Mueller, W. H. 12 n.
Mukendi, A. 275 n.
Mukherjee, A. 236, 242 n., 255 n., 474, 483 n., 509, 511
Mulder, P. 276 n.
Muller, E. M. 457 n.
Munasinghe, M. xii, 287 n.
Munro, M. B. 12 n., 431
Murphy, K. 368 n., 372 n., 375, 526
Murphy, R. 291
Murphy, Y. 291
Murty, M. N. 10 n., 209 n., 289, 290
Musgrave, R. 37, 146 n., 483
Myerson, R. 226 n., 376
Myrdal, G. 25 n., 248

Nag, M. 306
Nagel, J. 123
Nagel, T. 73, 383 n., 390 n.
Nahar, S. 320 n.
Naidu, A. N. 13, 83, 84, 415
Nalebuff, B. 66, 535
Narain, S. 10 n., 80, 281 n., 289, 290, 307 n.
Narveson, J. 387 n., 389 n.
Nash, J. 65, 66, 330, 337, 340
Naylor, R. xii
Neela, J. 415
Negishi, T. 179
Neher, 357 n.
Nelson, R. 94 n., 145 n., 276 n.
Nelson, V. E. 345 n.
Nerlove, M. 325, 348 n., 349, 357 n., 358, 359 n., 366 n.
Nesheim, M. C. 406
Neumann, C. 254 n.
Newbery, D. 207 n., 232 n., 526
Newcombe, K. 282 n.
Newman, L. F. 14 n.
Ng, Y.-K. 381 n.
Nidaira, K. 34 n., 115
Nolan, P. 270
Nolan, S. 179
Noor, A. 99 n.
Nordhaus, W. 34 n., 80, 81
Norgan, N. G. 254 n., 310 n., 457
Noronha, R. 136, 288, 289, 293, 294 n.
Norse, D. 272 n., 278 n., 525
North, D. 142, 143, 210 n., 211 n.
Nozick, R. 4 n., 22, 28, 30, 31, 34, 35, 37 n., 45 n., 53, 71, 138, 151, 174 n., 539
Nugent, J. 357 n., 358
Nussbaum, M. 32 n.

Oates, W. E. 284 n.
Ogilvie, S. xii, 360 n.
O'Hara, D. 100
Ojelade, S. 351, 362

Olewiler, N. 274 n.
Okin, S. 55
Oliver, R. xi
Olsen, W. K. 276 n.
O'Neill, O. 27 n., 29
Oniang'o, R. 472, 525
Osmani, S. R. 443 n.
Ostrom, E. 287 n.
Otsuka, K. 271

Pacey, A. 9 n., 254 n., 417
Paden, J. N. 106, 122 n., 123, 124
Page, H. J. 353 n.
Palczynski, Z. 42 n.
Pant, P. 34 n., 37
Panuccio, T. 362
Panzar, J. C. 147, 148
Papanek, G. S. 126 n.
Parfit, D. 18, 22, 381, 383, 384, 385, 386,
    389, 390, 391 n., 397
Pariser, E. R. 205 n.
Park, C. K. 107 n.
Passmore, R. 423 n.
Pastore, G. 254 n., 417, 457 n.
Patel, A. xii
Patrick, J. M. 433 n.
Pattanaik, P. 68 n.
Paukert, F. 126 n.
Paul, A. A. 457 n.
Paxson, C. H. 206, 254, 306
Payne, P. R. 254 n., 278 n., 310 n., 404,
    417, 426 n., 441 n., 457 n., 500
Pearce, D. 215 n., 376
Pearson, S. R. 272 n.
Pebley, A. R. 406
Peet, A. C. 306
Pejovich, S. 142
Pellekaan, H. 10, 20, 206, 401 n., 530, 533,
    534 n.
Pen, J. 126 n.
Perkins, D. H. 270
Peskin, H. M. 281 n.
Pestieau, P. 246, 325, 357 n.
Peters, R. 37
Pfeffer, R. 34
Phelps, E. S. 261 n., 263, 378, 379 n.
Phelps-Brown, H. 4
Phillips, J. 355
Piddocke, S. 202 n.
Pierce, F. J. 275 n.
Pigou, A. C. 145, 146, 284 n.
Pines, D. 142
Pingali, P. 244
Pinstrup-Anderson, P. 10, 20, 181, 310, 530
Pitchford, J. D. 380
Pitt, M. M. 17 n., 247, 309, 334, 500
Piwoz, E. G. 306 n.

Platteau, J.-P. 9 n., 202 n., 204, 208 n.
Polanyi, K. 9 n.
Polanyi, M. 145 n., 152 n.
Pollak, R. 349, 351, 356 n., 366 n., 374, 378,
    379 n.
Pollitt, E. 12, 96, 401 n., 403 n., 417,
    429 n., 430, 432, 433
Pomareda, C. 204, 526
Popkin, B. M. 59, 306 n., 307 n., 309,
    313 n., 348 n., 402, 429 n.
Popkin, S. L. 9
Portes, R. 281 n.
Posner, R. A. 22
Potter, R. G. 354 n.
Powell, C. A. 429 n., 430 n.
Prasad, P. H. 483
Pratt, J. A. 196
Prensky, A. L. 12 n.
Prentice, A. M. 12, 90, 254 n., 431, 432,
    442 n., 454, 456, 457, 458
Preston, S. H. 94 n., 100, 354 n.
Provinse, J. H. 202 n.
Pryer, J. 415
Prynne, C. 454
Pryor, E. 312
Psacharopoulous, G. 98, 99 n.
Putnam, H. 6, 25 n., 217
Pyatt, G. 113 n.

Qian, Y. 142, 179 n., 247 n.
Quizon, J. 198, 527

Radhwan, S. 139
Radner, R. 201 n., 203 n., 210 n., 325
Raiffa, H. 190 n., 194, 197, 330 n., 333, 340
Raikes, P. 272 n.
Ram, R. 365 n.
Ramsey, F. 70 n., 262, 397
Rand, W. M. 423 n., 441 n., 449
Ranis, G. 527 n.
Rao, B. S. N. 83, 84
Rao, C. H. H. 228 n.
Rao, D. H. 84
Rao, N. P. 13, 415
Rath, N. R. 126 n., 401 n., 438, 448, 450
Ravallion, M. 14 n., 139, 470, 471, 534
Rawls, A. xii
Rawls, J. xi, 17, 28 n., 23 n., 22, 25, 30,
    32 n., 34, 35, 37, 40 n., 42, 43, 45 n., 46,
    47, 48, 50 n., 53, 54, 64, 69 n., 71, 73, 74,
    105, 135 n., 140 n., 377, 379, 381, 389,
    390, 392, 529
Ray, D. xi, 48, 170 n., 236, 237, 409 n.,
    444 n., 448 n., 452 n., 477 n., 489 n., 493,
    496, 497, 502, 504, 510 n., 513
Ray, S. 309 n., 470 n.
Raz, J. 42 n.

Razin, A. 325, 349, 357 n., 358, 366 n.
Read, M. S. 12 n., 13
Reddy, P. H. 202 n., 322
Reder, M. W. 197 n.
Rees, D. G. 426 n., 451
Reich, M. R. 10, 20, 531 n.
Reij, C. 276 n.
Reina, J. C. 13, 84, 429 n., 430
Repetto, R. 80, 107, 272 n., 275, 281 n.,
   282 n., 287, 293, 528
Reutlinger, S. 10, 20, 206, 401 n., 437, 438,
   530, 533, 534 n.
Reynolds, S. 10 n.
Ricardo, D. 11
Ricciuti, H. 12
Richerson, P. J. 208 n.
Riley, J. 92, 501
Rimlinger, G. V. 3 n.
Riskin, C. 113 n., 270
Rivera, J. 85 n.
Robbins, L. 379
Roberts, D. F. 433
Roberts, J. 66, 142, 210 n., 371
Roberts, K. W. S. 32, 71, 74 n., 176 n.
Robinson, J. 6 n.
Robinson, S. 97, 126 n., 153, 527 n.
Rodahl, K. 433 n., 434
Rodgers, G. 483, 487 n.
Rodriguez, A. 378
Roemer, M. 107 n., 544
Rogers, E. M. 147
Rogerson, W. 233
Romer, P. M. 157
Ronald, M. G. M. 87
Rosenstein-Rodin, P. 372 n.
Rosenzweig, M. R. 17 n., 196, 202 n., 204,
   227, 229, 230, 232, 235, 238, 239, 240 n.,
   241 n., 242 n., 247, 254, 257, 261 n., 263,
   309, 311, 312, 319 n., 322, 334, 365, 474,
   486 n., 490, 498, 500, 506
Ross, S. 52 n.
Ross, W. D. 28 n.
Roth, A. 333, 340
Rothschild, M. 17, 126 n., 195, 260, 261 n.,
   262, 263
Rowland, M. G. M. 407, 408 n.
Royston, E. 12
Rubinstein, A. 211, 215 n., 327 n., 331 n.,
   340 n.
Rubinstein, M. 52 n.
Rudra, A. xii, 143, 152 n., 202 n., 229,
   230 n., 233, 235, 236 n., 238, 239, 241 n.,
   242, 249, 255 n., 479 n., 482 n., 483, 498,
   502, 509
Russett, B. M. 123
Rutihauser, I. H. E. 13, 428 n., 429 n.
Rutstein, S. O. 100

Ryan, G. 229 n., 255 n., 482, 502
Ryan, J. G. 204, 207, 229 n., 235, 238, 239,
   241, 242 n., 250, 254, 322
Ryan, T. S. 204, 207, 229 n., 235, 238, 239,
   241, 242 n., 250, 254
Ryder, H. E. 375

Sabourian, H. xii, 210 n.
Sadka, E. 325, 349, 357 n., 358, 366 n.,
   368 n.
Sadoulet, E. 528
Saflios-Rothschild, C. 307
Safra, Z. 327 n.
Sah, R. K. 176 n.
Sahayam, M. 323 n.
Sahlin, N. E. 197 n.
Sahlins, M. 141–2
Sahn, D. E. 417
Sahota, G. 126 n.
Saloner, G. 372
Samarasinghe, S. W. R. de A. 113 n., 530
Samuelson, P. A. 6 n., 22, 35 n., 146,
   213 n., 297 n.
Sandel, M. 23 n.
Sastry, J. G. 84
Satahr, Z. 99
Satyanarayana, K. 13, 83, 84, 435 n., 436
Savage, L. 58 n., 194, 202 n.
Scandizzo, P. 139, 228 n.
Scanlon, T. M. 5, 22, 26 n., 27 n., 33 n., 34,
   36, 40
Schechtman, J. 261 n.
Schecter, M. 283
Scheffler, S. 29, 43
Schell, J. 393
Schelling, T. 142, 351, 372 n.
Scherer, F. M. 147
Schiff, M. 177
Schoen, R. 94 n., 345 n.
Schofield, C. 426 n., 440, 455, 464
Schofield, W. N. 426 n., 440, 455, 464
Scholes, M. 52 n.
Schultz, T. P. 99 n., 311, 312, 319 n.,
   348 n., 349, 367
Schultz, T. W. 152 n., 272 n., 357 n., 482 n.
Scitovsky, T. 76 n., 251, 372 n., 528 n.
Scobie, G. 530
Scoble, H. M. 131
Scott, A. D. 286
Scott, J. C. 9 n., 208 n.
Scott, W. 7, 34 n.
Scrimshaw, N. C. 12, 13, 402 n., 403 n.,
   407, 423 n., 441 n., 449, 450 n., 459 n.
Seabright, P. xii, 31 n., 55 n., 209 n.,
   362 n., 386 n., 537
Seckler, D. 83
Sefton, J. 281 n., 298

Selowsky, M. 401 n.
Selznick, P. 45 n.
Sen, A. xi, 7, 10, 14 n., 16, 17, 20, 22, 25 n., 30 n., 34, 37, 42, 55, 59 n., 68 n., 71, 73, 78, 113 n., 117 n., 126 n., 139, 174, 184 n., 185 n., 205 n., 206, 207 n., 273 n., 301, 310, 325, 330 n., 340 n., 482 n., 495, 509, 533
Sen, C. 307 n., 319 n.
Sen, G. 307 n., 319 n.
Sen, P. xii
Sen, S. R. 270 n.
Sengupta, S. 310
Sette, S. 254 n., 417, 457 n.
Shaban, R. A. 229 n., 230
Shafer, W. 66
Shah, C. H. 470
Shah, S. xii
Shaked, A. 327 n.
Shapiro, C. 225 n.
Shapley, L. 211, 215 n., 285 n.
Shen, T. H. 527 n.
Shephard, R. J. 433 n.
Sherman, P. B. 275 n., 279
Shetty, P. S. xii, 414, 425, 431 n., 442 n., 451, 455 n., 456 n., 458, 459, 460
Shleifer, A. 372 n., 526
Shoemaker, F. F. 147
Shubik, M. 285 n.
Siamwalla, A. 538
Sibly, R. M. 353 n.
Sidgwick, H. 28, 47, 70 n., 381, 386
Siegelman, L. 123
Sikora, R. I. 381 n., 382, 383
Silber, J. 7, 34 n.
Simon, J. L. 18, 76 n., 345, 346, 361
Simon, L. K. 66
Simpson, M. 123
Singer, P. 37 n.
Singh, I. 10 n. 17 n., 98 n., 152 n., 222, 223 n., 224, 227, 228 n., 229 n., 230, 233, 238, 240, 247, 255, 257, 271, 324 n., 431 n., 458, 523, 526
Singh, N. 13, 430
Sinha, R. 139, 479
Sivard, R. L. 57
Skeldon, R. 323 n.
Skoufias, E. 253
Slade, R. H. 101 n.
Slovic, P. 197 n.
Smart, J. 390 n.
Smith, E. A. 288, 289 n.
Smith, J. H. 111, 113
Smorodinsky, M. 333, 340
Snower, D. 255 n.
Soares, M. J. 425, 451
Socrates 233 n.

Solórzano, R. 282 n.
Solow, R. M. xi, 153, 197, 297 n., 298, 379 n.
Sommer, A. 82 n.
Sonnenschein, H. 66, 168 n.
Sopher, D. E. 102, 103, 311, 317, 318–19, 321
Southgate, D. 454
Spence, A. M. 375
Spivak, A. 246
Spurr, G. B. 12, 13, 84, 402 n., 421, 422 n., 423 n., 429 n., 430, 435, 436 n., 461 n.
Squire, L. 17 n., 184 n., 222, 223 n., 224, 227, 247, 257, 324 n.
Sraffa, P. 38 n.
Srinivasan, T. N. 139, 176 n., 177 n., 197, 241 n., 261 n., 263, 273 n., 441 n., 444 n., 446, 452 n., 535
Stahl, I. 331 n.
Stark, O. 202 n., 322
Starr, R. M. 148 n., 199, 473 n.
Starrett, D. 3 n., 35 n., 126 n., 146 n., 185 n., 281 n., 285 n.
Steele, P. 446
Stein, T. P. 413, 442 n.
Sterba, J. P. 381 n.
Stern, N. xii, 19 n., 40 n., 127 n., 146, 171 n., 174, 176 n., 185 n. 242, 249, 273 n., 420, 472 n., 474, 483, 500, 505
Steward, J. 322 n.
Stewart, F. 16, 34 n.
Stichter, S. 309
Stiglitz, J. E. xi, 3 n., 17, 35 n., 56, 126 n., 142 n., 146, 147, 148, 159, 171 n., 175, 176 n., 177 n., 179, 186, 195, 207 n., 225 n., 226 n., 232, 233 n., 241 n., 242 n., 250 n., 252, 260, 261 n., 262, 263, 265, 297 n., 303 n., 325, 334 n., 372 n., 483, 487 n., 500, 503, 535, 537, 538, 539 n.
Strauss, J. 17 n., 85, 100, 222, 223 n., 224, 227, 247, 257, 324 n., 421, 470
Streeten, P. xii, 7, 16, 34 n., 20, 25 n., 37, 495
Streufert, P. 502
Subbarao, K. 271, 532
Subramanian, S. 310, 470, 471
Sugarman, B. 407 n.
Sukhatme, P. V. 401 n., 413, 441 n., 443, 444, 445, 446, 448, 449, 450, 451, 452, 462 n., 465, 466
Summers, L. 246, 541
Summers, R. 79, 80, 108 n., 111 n., 117, 125 n.
Sumption, J. 42 n.
Sundstrom, W. A. 325, 357 n., 365
Suppes, P. 68 n.
Sutton, J. 327 n.

Svedberg, P. 310
Syrquin, M. 97, 153

Taj, A. M. 320 n., 367
Tambiah, S. J. 312 n.
Tamura, R. 368 n., 375
Tanner, J. M. 12, 82, 83, 84, 86, 430
Taubman, P. 356 n.
Taylor, C. E. 12, 95, 403 n., 406, 407
Taylor, C. L. 108, 109, 111 n., 119, 130, 131
Taylor, H. 458 n., 459, 460
Taylor-Gooby, P. 529
Temkin, L. S. 381 n., 391 n.
Thomas, D. 85, 100, 470
Thomas, V. xii, 544
Thomson, W. 327 n.
Thorbecke, E. 526
Tietenberg, T. 274 n.
Timmer, C. P. 248 n., 272 n., 273
Tirole, J. 62 n., 147, 215 n.
Tobin, J. 34 n., 80, 81, 175
Tomes, N. 356 n., 364
Tomich, T. P. 93, 354 n., 526
Tomkins, A. M. 406, 407 n.
Topkis, D. M. 66
Torun, B. 13, 402 n., 423 n., 428 n., 429 n.
Townsend, R. M. 202 n., 225 n., 249
Trease, J. 358
Trussell, J. 353
Turnbull, C. 202 n.
Tversky, A. 197 n.

Uauy, R. 423 n., 454
Udry, C. 206, 225 n., 238, 241 n., 243 n., 245, 249
Ulijaszek, S. J. 406, 407
Ullmann-Margalit, E. 208 n.
Underwood, B. A. 10, 20, 127 n., 335, 403 n., 525, 531 n.
Uphoff, N. T. 295 n.
Urrutia, J. J. 407
Usher, D. 34 n., 81

Valdes, A. 177, 204, 504, 526
Valverde, V. 310 n., 503
Vallin, J. 95
Varian, H. 11, 58 n., 170 n.
Vaughan, M. 328 n.
Vickrey, W. S. 380 n.
Victoria, C. G. 100
Visaria, L. 323 n.
Visaria, P. 255, 313, 321 n., 323 n.
Vishny, R. 372 n., 526
Viteri, F. E. 13, 306 n., 402 n., 421, 423 n., 428 n., 429 n., 470, 482
Vivian, J. M. 295 n.
Vlastos, G. 43, 44

von Braun, J. 530
von Neumann, J. 194

Waaler, H. T. 83
Wachter, K. 83
Wachter, M. L. 349, 351, 366 n., 374
Wade, R. 10 n., 107 n., 209, 286, 290, 544
Waldron, I. 88 n., 313 n.
Waldron, J. 27 n., 29
Walker, T. S. 204, 322
Wallerstein, M. B. 12, 403 n.
Walters, A. 11
Wan, H. Y. 179
Wang, Y. 544
Warren, M. 387 n.
Waterlow, J. C. xi, 12, 82, 84, 85 n., 90, 402 n., 404, 405, 406, 413, 414–15, 424, 426, 427, 430 n., 437, 441 n., 442 n., 443 n., 445 n., 448, 450 n., 453, 455 n., 460 n.
Watkins, S. 353
Watson, F. 406, 407 n.
Watts, H. 78
Weale, M. xi, 108 n., 116 n., 281 n., 298
Webb, D. 252 n.
Webb, R. 126 n.
Weinberg, E. D. 407 n.
Weiner, R. J. 281 n.
Weingast, B. 210 n., 211
Weiss, A. 250 n., 265
Weissner, P. 202 n.
Weitzman, M. 37, 233 n., 281 n., 294 n., 297 n.
Weymark, J. 33, 71
White, A. V. 13
White, B. N. 306
White, G. F. 13
Whitehead, R. G. 12, 13, 90, 254 n., 407, 417, 428 n., 429 n. 431, 457
Wicksell, K. 379
Widdowson, E. M. 456 n., 460 n.
Wiggins, D. 37 n., 40
Wignaraja, P. 295 n.
Wilbanks, T. J. 147
Williams, B. 15 n., 23 n., 25 n., 32 n., 34 n., 37, 43, 68 n., 73, 151, 386 n., 390 n.
Williamson, J. 126 n.
Williamson, N. E. 368
Williamson, O. 142
Willig, R. D. 148
Willis, R. 356 n., 357 n., 361
Wilson, R. 210 n.
Winick, M. 12 n.
Winter, J. M. 54
Wischmeier, W. H. 275 n.
Wiseberg, L. S. 131
Wiser, W. H. 9 n., 236

Wojtyniak, B. 87, 407
Wolfe, A. B. 380
Wolfe, B. L. 99, 100, 470
Wolgemuth, J. C. 421, 470
Wolpin, K. I. 240 n., 261 n., 263, 322 n.
Wong, J. 270
Wood, A. 247 n.
Woodhall, M. 99 n.
Wright, G. 201
Wynne, E. 9 n., 202 n.

Xu, Y. 68 n.

Yaari, M. 194 n., 197
Yamey, B. 107, 272 n.

Yotopoulos, P. xii, 126, 179, 228, 503 n.,
    504
Young, V. 423 n., 441 n., 449, 450 n.,
    459 n.
Yun, K. Y. 107 n., 544

Zadka, E. 325, 349, 357 n., 358, 366 n.
Zamagni, S. xii
Zame, W. R. 66
Zamir, S. 376
Zeckhauser, R. 375
Zeldes, S. P. 240 n., 261 n.
Zimmerman, M. B. 178 n.

Index compiled by Frank Pert

INDEX OF SUBJECTS

abortion 89, 354
achievements 38, 54, 55, 113
  among middle-income countries 125
  freedom of 61
  lack of 124
  opportunities and 173
actions 29, 43, 72, 190, 205
  admissible sets 69
  choice of 65
  collective 25, 36, 163
  conditional 60, 61
  courses of 137
  freedom of 60
  hidden 226
  maximal sets 28
  permissible sets 62, 63, 69
  ultimate end of 380
active cell mass 425, 459–60
activity possibility sets 466–72
adipose tissues 417, 425, 450
Administrator, The 295 n.
'adult-equivalent scale' 55
adverse selection 226, 249, 251, 267, 322, 528
  regarding creditworthiness 241
  resource allocations suffering from 537
aerobic processes 84, 433
Africa, *see under various country names; also*
  North Africa; sub-Saharan Africa
agencies 15–19, 22–7, 68, 142, 286, 293
  moral 48, 51, 52
agents 48, 62, 65, 375
aggregation 29, 31, 32–6, 81
agrarian reforms 173, 476–7, 495, 525–8
  marginal 496, 497
agricultural cycle 519, 521
agricultural production 222, 225, 260, 478, 481
  allocation of 232
  diverse modes of 227
  features of 231
  household forced to refrain from investing in 262
  moral hazard in 230
  overall increase in 526
  perfect substitute for household labour in 257
  subject to punitive taxation 177

  two techniques of 264–5
AIDS (acquired immunity deficiency syndrome) 95 n., 355 n., 407
Alaknanda River 273
alienation point 327, 333, 337, 338, 340
Allais paradoxes 198 n.
allocations:
  among girls and boys 309–11
  analysis of mechanisms when nutrition affects productivity 512–24
  collective goods 542–3
  competitive market 486–90
  failure and public policy 368–70
  household, regional patterns 313
  just, implementation of 171–3
  Pareto-inefficient 181, 251
  unequal 524
  women's time 309
  work among women and children 294–6
  see also equilibrium allocations;
    Pareto-efficiency; resource allocation
anaemia 402–3, 429, 431
  iron-deficiency 407
  nutritional 12, 86, 348
  sickle-cell 94
Andes 204
Andhra Pradesh 229
Angola 122
aquifers 276, 279, 280, 286
arbitrage 301
arid regions 291
aristocracies 106, 292
Aristotelian Principle 43, 44
Arrow–Debreu theory 199, 486, 487, 497
  model 227, 229, 247, 252, 257
  see also equilibria; households; markets;
    prices; wages
ascorbic acid 403
Asia, *see under various country names*
Assam 317
assets 253, 260, 369, 473–7
  capital 242, 247, 276
  decumulating 261, 263
  distribution of 476, 480, 496–7, 498
  income-earning, children as 358
  indivisible 239
  physical, women's most valued 240
  productive 490, 498

redistribution of 173, 517, 533
safe 264
security on loans 241
associations 63, 105, 149
atmospheric stocks 300
ATP (adenosine triphosphate) 403, 433, 449
Atwater factors 411, 444, 445 n., 453–4
authoritarian regimes 57, 128, 140, 285
autonomy 27, 41, 74, 331, 355
female 96, 356
individual 35, 36, 68
Aztec belief 217

babassu 291
Bangladesh 101, 201, 254, 313, 364 n.,
    533 n.
children and food 310
children as producers 360
Grameen Bank 237, 538
households averse to inequality 500
ill adult males 415
landless populations 479
living standards 110, 112, 118
Matlab Thana 82, 87, 311, 355, 406, 407–8
purdah system 323
woman's reproductive life 348 n.
bankruptcy 266
banks 276
bargaining theory 324–9, 337–42
see also Kalai-Smorodinsky; Nash
basic needs 9, 37, 40, 51, 147, 180, 185, 477,
    543
availability of 53, 541
basic commodities 11
consumption of 248, 249
easy to market 150
goods that satisfy 54
government obligation and 46
lack of 42
modern concept of 44
not constant 39
social valuation of 175
beggars 255, 256, 475
Bergson–Samuelson social welfare
    functions 35 n.
biomass 273, 279, 280, 358
birth attendants 95
birth control 348, 353–6
birth intervals/spacing/order 100, 353, 357
birth weights, see body weight
black-markets 175, 181
BMI (body mass index) 413–16, 417, 428,
    434, 510
BMR (basal metabolic rate) 411, 422–7,
    439–40, 451, 455–6, 459–60, 462
body composition 413, 425, 461, 473
body mass 443, 452, 453, 456, 505

lean 425, 459, 461, 462
see also BMI
body weight 413, 419, 425–6, 449, 463, 473
birth 82, 85, 86, 431
fluctuations in 450
losing and making up 417
weight-for-age 84, 86, 311, 428
weight-for-height 82, 83, 84, 86, 461
Bolivia 110, 112, 114, 479
Bombay 125 n.
Borda Rule 109, 111, 113–14, 185
borrowing constraints 264, 265
Botswana 58, 109, 110, 113
brain development 429, 430
Brazil 291, 293, 471, 479, 528, 538
breast-feeding:
extended 308, 353
prolonged 354
bridewealth and dowry 311–13
Britain, see United Kingdom
Buddhism 103
budget constraints 160, 168, 227, 257, 258–9
Burundi 110, 111, 112

calories 11, 40, 403, 409, 417–18, 462–3, 466,
    468
costs 282
daily intake 452, 458, 459
deficiency 13, 408, 437–41
equivalent of casual wage 510
expenditure 459, 471
intra-household disparity 500
long-term 523
needs 282, 404
requirements 422, 423
supplementation 421, 470
surplus 524
transformation into work output 334
value 454
Cambridge 431, 456, 457
Cameroon 100
Canada 96
capital 154, 393
accumulation of 244, 248, 249, 302, 501
decumulating 263
fixed, depreciation of 281
human 302, 545
physical 248
working 228, 231, 259
capital gains/losses 302
capitalism 228, 231, 259
crony 139
predatory 476
State-led 179
carbohydrates 402, 403, 424
cardio-respiratory fitness 433
Caribbean 79, 98, 99, 347 n., 366

cartels 500
cash crops 201, 275, 472, 477
castes 106 n., 236–7, 290
casual workers 506, 518–23
  see also labour markets
cattle 239, 244, 245, 247, 287
  beef production 293
  extra, as insurance against droughts 276
  sales 240
cell residue 433
Central African Republic (CAR) 110, 111, 113
central nervous system 429–30
Chad 110, 111, 112
Champagne fairs 211 n.
children 213, 282, 352
  costs and benefits of having 366
  energy deficiency and anaemia among 431
  death rates 89, 123
  errant, disinheriting 246
  free mid-day school meals 54
  gender-based inequality among 335
  as goods 356–8, 365
  health/height 100
  maintenance costs 363
  malnutrition and 12–13
  mortality rates 405–6, 417
  not counted as capital assets 239
  as old-age security 363, 368
  opportunity cost of rearing 365
  prohibitively expensive as assets 370
  resources the responsibility of 291
  sold 240
  survival 100, 311, 353
  undernourished 84–5
  water, fuelwood, dung, and fodder
    collection 359
  welfare of 378
  work allocation among women and 294–6
  see also growth
Chile 125, 127, 528
China 87, 110, 113–14, 269, 313
  aggregate savings 247
  agricultural crash (1959–60) 178
  arable land per capita 278 n.
  barefoot doctors 93
  birthweight 86
  Great Leap Forward 205 n., 270
  life expectancy at birth 92
  magnitude of poverty 79
  male–female sex ratio 354 n.
  preference for sons 357
  total fertility rate 307, 345
choices 42, 61, 63, 65–6, 116
  collective 58
  ethical 28
  flexibility of 52, 233
  freedom of 60

government and 53
household 193; extent of 171
independent 67
individual 58, 60, 145; seeming oddities
  in 193
likely reflector of perception of good 70
motivation and 58–9
option value of permissible set of 69
rational 197
social 35, 199
under uncertainty 32 n., 193–9, 200, 201
well-being reduced by increasing 71
see also utilitarianism
Christianity 103, 321
citizenship 104–8, 166, 294
civil liberties 56–8, 107, 130, 139
  see also political and civil liberties
civil rights, *see* political and civil rights
claim-right 45
clean air 299
Cobb–Douglas production function 515
coercion 44, 53, 122, 124
cognitive development 429, 431
collateral 150, 243, 250, 265
  absence of 242, 244
  livestock as 239
collective farms 272
collectivization of agriculture 177–8
Colombia 84, 435, 461, 528
commercialization of agriculture 237
commodities 44, 53, 81, 180–1, 258, 282
  adult 310
  availability 54
  contingent 189, 194, 199
  converting, via household production and
    market exchange 171
  different 467
  durable 149
  future 189
  initial endowments of 184
  initial rights over sufficient amounts
    of 138
  perfectly perishable 213
  prized 239
  and services 14, 176, 182
  unknown 235
  see also basic needs; natural monopolies;
    public goods
common-property resources 80, 146, 147,
  288–93 *passim*, 508, 543
  access to 350
  breakdown of collective agreement
    between users of 360
  controlling 287
  foraging from 260
  harvesting 519
  income from 480, 482

landless forced to live on 479, 489, 502
local 511
management of 209
outcasts living on 475
commons 161–4, 286, 507, 510, 522
global 290
local 290–4, 295, 508
Communitarians 45 n.
communities 386–7
community-based controls 9–10
comparative dynamics 522
competition 148, 157, 178
competitive markets 202, 228, 479,
486–90
and efficiency 170–1
mechanism 138, 165–9
compulsory schooling 370
conflicts 15, 40
Confucianism 103, 528 n.
congenital disorders 88–9
Congo 122
conjugal bond 355, 366, 367
consequences 63, 190
acts and 27–32
utility 33, 34
woeful distributional 107
consequentialism 27, 28, 29, 30, 31, 32
consumption 144, 214, 215, 246, 378, 444
aggregate 300
alternative sources of 486 n.
average 451, 507, 510
basic needs 248, 249
behaviour over time 197
calorie 403, 439, 466, 471
carbohydrates, fats and proteins 424
cereal 505
competitive 146
current 247, 261, 263
decisions 257
dichotomy between saving and 249
energy 411, 443, 449, 451, 453, 464;
high 462–3; intertemporal 466
first-period 522
food crops 222–3
forgone 245
fuelwood 299
future possibilities 346
grain 447
household 260; elasticity of 223, 224
household food 439
insurance 246
as investment 245–9
lifetime profile 213
marginal utility of 262, 396
optimal 264
optimum per capita 397
oxygen 424, 425

possibility set 467
precautionary motive for 263
redistribution 517
renewable natural resources of direct use
in 280
slack-season 506 n.
smoothing 205, 240, 250, 252–4, 265
subsistence level of 395
total commodity 186
see also goods
contraception 99, 192–3, 225, 354
little reliance on 363
prevalence 355
contracts 485
contingent 193
desirability of different types of 67
efficient 232
ex ante 65–8
fixed-rental 229–30, 231
implicit 393
long-term 235, 236, 502
permanent 505
personalized 202
rational contractees 64–5
share 231, 232, 233
wage 229, 231
see also social contracts
co-operation 325, 329, 537
copyrights 145
corruption 140
cost-sharing 233
Costa Rica 125, 281, 313 n., 343
Côte d'Ivoire 91, 306–7, 309
credit 238, 264–5, 295, 322
access to 231, 237, 275, 328, 527
availability of 368
constraints 224–9, 257–68
facilities 204, 237, 535–9
formal 237, 527
investment 369
kinship a major source of 243
lack of, among the assetless 249–52
rationed 254, 265–8
subsidized 528
systematic dearth of 272
credit markets 202, 238–42, 244, 249, 251, 495
geographically segmented 202, 235
notoriously imperfect in poor
countries 148–9, 150
ruthless 250
Cuba 103, 127
culture 123, 140–3, 312, 324
cumulative causation 502, 503
custom or practice 372

Daedalus 113 n.
daughters 312, 322, 375, 471

deaths 123
  causes of 94, 407
  children 89, 96, 541
  incidence of 90
  income elasticity of 94
  infants 96
  risks of 83, 87
debt 237, 252, 261, 538
decentralization 52, 105, 165–83, 295
decision units 63
defensive expenditure 302
deforestation 274, 280, 284, 285, 293
degradation 293, 294, 348, 358–9
  and children as producer goods 358–61
  dangers of 346
Delhi 125 n.
demand 168, 471, 487–8, 488, 493, 504
demography 11
  applied 347
  economic 17, 349; 'new' 367
  transitions 345, 351, 360, 361, 364, 369
density and predictability 288, 289, 291
deontological reasoning 27, 28, 29, 30, 31, 34
dependence 63, 68, 273, 323, 367
depreciation 281
deprivation 10, 14, 109
descent 363
desert 33, 44, 46, 326
desertification 292
desertion of families 329
desire 36, 52, 87, 192, 209
  rational 61, 69, 70, 394
destitution 5–11, 21, 292, 323
  driven to a state of 170
  employment sole means of avoiding 41
  insurance against hunger and 207
  near-certain prospect of 358
  protection against 67, 205
  terminal 14
  women increasingly vulnerable to 27
deterministic functions 63
development regimes 490–4
Dharma 43
dictatorships 57, 106, 127, 140
dietary thermogenesis 424, 454, 458
disasters 199–201
discrimination 308, 310, 313
discriminatory pricing 270
diseases 123
  circulatory and degenerative 94
  communal-feeding-victimization 310
  communicable 92
  contagious, immunization against 144–5
  diarrhoeal 311
  heart 96
  infectious 84, 94, 406
  parasitic 92, 94

synergism among 405–6
  water-borne and water-based 405
distribution 26, 180
  asset 480, 496–7
  benefits and burdens 172
  food, within poor households 523–4
  goods and services 172
  in kind 42, 150, 181
  just 42, 52, 135, 172
  land 494–5, 496, 515
  landholdings 490
  purchasing power in the private realm 173
  reservation wages 480
  resources 52, 54, 55
  rights 135, 139
  states of mind 76
  utilities 172
  welfare 28
diversification 204
division of labour 142, 143, 362
domestic animals 276
dowry system 311–13, 362
drylands 272, 276, 279, 289, 292, 363
  fuelwood/water collection 13, 295
  management of 274
  reforestation 335
  rice cultivation 278
  topsoil loss 275
Dunn Nutrition Unit 431, 456
duties 48, 63–4, 106, 143, 545

ecological functionalism 141
economic growth 291
  education instrumental in generating 99
  efficacy of, with redistribution 490
  fruits of 518
  knowledge, organization and 151–8
  long-run 20, 21
economies of scale 222
economy-wide endowments 185
Ecuador 110, 111, 113, 114
education 152, 306, 345, 364, 498
  attainments 76, 102, 157–8
  difficult to resell 175, 181
  externalities 155
  fertility and 307
  gender bias 102
  health and 539–42
  improvements in 365
  increased 91
  indices 77
  instrumental in generating economic growth 99
  jobs that require little or no 309
  option of borrowing to buy 150
  positive effect on total factor productivity 158

state 533
see also female education; literacy;
    numeracy
efficiency 56, 72–4, 173, 448–9, 463
    competitive markets and 170–1
    mechanical 404
    metabolic 445, 460
    production 176, 177, 502
    relative 494
    well-being 177
    see also Pareto efficiency; piece-rates
efficiency wages 481, 500, 507
    theory 493, 502, 505, 506, 508, 510, 511
    see also piece-rates
Egypt 110, 112, 229, 529, 530
El Salvador 106, 293 n.
elderly people 213, 240, 241, 306, 531
Electricité de France 148
employment guarantee schemes 229, 533–5,
    537
employment opportunities 306, 312, 320,
    328, 351, 370
endogamy 320
ends 48, 53, 54, 67, 380
    rational 64–5, 392–4
endurance 432–6
energy 13, 85, 205, 278, 401–4, 408–32
    passim, 441–70 *passim*, 510
England 54, 431, 456
    eighteenth-century 291 n.
    nineteenth-century 88, 115 n., 144 n., 360
entitlements 44, 62, 69
environmental amenities 299, 300, 302
    see also degradation; regeneration;
    resources
epidemiological transition 94
equilibria:
    Arrow–Debreu 168, 489 n., 492, 493
    competitive 168, 169–70, 172, 199, 497,
    510, 514
    ex post 65–8
    multiple 234, 235, 236, 351, 352
    non-co-operative 331
    partial 493
    reflective 53
    stationary 445, 452, 453, 501
    stochastic 445, 452, 453
    strategies 65–6
    see also Nash equilibria
equilibrium allocations 487, 490, 493, 507,
    516
    competitive 497
    definition of 489
    in the timeless world 512–15
Equilibrium Existence Theorem 199
ethical theories 7, 25, 27 n., 30–6 *passim*,
    68, 382

Ethiopia 90 n., 254, 272, 289, 348, 533
    living standards 110, 111, 112, 118
    threats to government/civil war 106, 122,
    123
ethnic groups 83, 84, 121, 122
Euler's Theorem 514
Europe 67, 83, 88, 96, 115 n., 313 n.
    Eastern 179 n.
    eighteenth- and nineteenth-century 83
    medieval 210, 211
European Community 124
*European Journal of Clinical
    Nutrition* 443 n.
evaluative principles 53–6
evaporation 275, 276, 279
'evolutive' consideration 374
exchange:
    gift 140, 189, 202
    norms of behaviour pertaining to 166
    organization of 151, 157
    production and 142, 143, 151, 157
exchange rates 79, 177, 180, 181, 271,
    272
existence value 283
exit options 326, 327, 329
exogamy 320, 322
expectations 91, 194, 374
    firm 67
    rational 519
    self-fulfilling or equilibrium 65
    wrong 66
expected utility hypothesis 197, 198, 199,
    201
expediency 74
export crops 272, 275, 287
externalities:
    atmospheric 371–5
    cultural 324
    educational 155
    network 145, 352, 372, 503
    pecuniary 251
    population 349–53
    powerful 312
    public goods and common property
    resources 143–7
    reciprocal 284–8, 352
    reproductive 347–8
    unidirectional 284–8
extra-marital relationships 362

fair-price stores 271
fairness 22, 30–1, 43, 48, 64
false consciousness 41
Family Income Supplement 175
family labour 224–5
family planning 354, 355, 430, 541
famine 123, 205, 329, 335, 353

FAO (Food and Agricultural
    Organization) 412 n., 442, 525
  The Fourth World Food Survey (1977) 438
  *International Trade and World Food
    Security (1985)* 272 n.
  Food Outlook (1986) 272 n., 401 n.
  The Fifth World Food Survey (1987) 13,
    86 n., 139, 406, 437, 439, 440
farm servants 225, 242
fat 403, 412, 450, 457
  deficiencies in 402
  reserves of 417, 431
feasibility constraint 515
feed 504–5
female circumcision 59
female education 121, 351, 370, 541
  birth control and 353–6
  maternal 89, 99, 100, 101, 365
  rise in 308
fertility 100, 201, 276, 295, 308, 343–76, 541
  behaviour 17, 243
  education and 307
  savings and 246–7
fertilizers 243, 274–5, 526
first-best optimum 73
fisheries 281, 282
fixed costs 143, 221–2, 259, 334
  energy 19
  infrastructure and 147–9
fodder collection 273, 295, 306, 359
Fold Theorem 215 n.
folic acid 95
food 305–36, 469, 504–5
  distribution within poor households 523–4
  income, fertility and 343–6
  insecurity 20
  intake 461–6, 520
  limited aid 335
  low intake 460
  needs, and work capacity 401–36
  production 123, 178
  security 21, 529, 533
  subsidies 528–33, 543
  thermic effect of 411, 424
  total expenditure elasticity of demand 471
  transfers 534
food crops 222–3, 257–8, 477, 479, 486, 487
food-for-work (or cash-for-work)
    programmes 533, 534, 543
Food and Nutrition Bulletin 306 n.
foreign workers 235
forests 276–7, 281, 286, 291, 294, 299
  see also deforestation; reforestation
fortification 402, 402
France 156 n.
free-riding 287, 288, 350, 367, 529
freedom 38, 55, 60, 61, 129–31 *passim*, 139

basic 54, 78
concepts 43, 45
constraints on, imposed by the State 121
curtailment of 51
inputs necessary for the exercise of 53
link between commodity needs,
    claim-right and 45
measures of 68–70
negative 15, 40, 41, 51, 52, 53, 74
personal, indices of 71
positive 7, 15, 37, 40, 41, 43, 51, 76
socio-economic 42
welfare and 3–5
wider notions of 171
  see also rights
Freedom House 131
fuelwood 283, 299, 335, 359
  collection 13, 273, 295, 306
  consumption of 299
  output of 300
  resources 282
  sources 276
full optimum 73, 74
Fundamental Theorems of Welfare
    Economics 189, 190, 191–2, 225
  First 170, 171, 199
  Second 171, 172–6, 180, 182 n., 185, 186,
    199, 526, 528

Gambia 58, 109, 110, 112, 254
  Keneba women 431–2, 447, 454, 456, 457,
    458
game theory 70, 215 n., 375
games:
  bargaining 334, 341
  negotiation 330–1
  overlapping-generations 215 n.
  repeated 215 n.
  single-period 215 n.
  zero-sum 325
GDP (gross domestic product) 157, 181, 281
gender 89
  bias 7 n., 102
  BMR dependent on 425
  conflicts of interest between 356
  differentials 305–9, 311, 313, 321
  inequalities 311, 314, 318, 335
  preference 471
generation-relativity 390
Genesis Problem 381, 382–3, 385–6, 389,
    390, 395, 397
genetic differences 441
gentry 519
Germany 155, 156, 157
Ghana 91, 122, 363
Gini coefficient 126
girls 306, 312, 320, 357, 541

GNP (gross national product) 153, 154–5, 156, 158, 540–1
Goa 321
goal-based theories 28, 29
goals 6, 35 n., 36, 352, 367, 370
Gomez scale 84, 428
good:
  conceptions of 36, 37; pluralist 8, 34, 71, 73
  functional form of 69
  general 74
  maximum 69
  priority of, over rights 28
  range of what may constitute 69–70
  right over, priority of 27
  sense of 65
  undersupply of, in equilibrium 160
goods:
  basic-needs 45, 53, 54, 61, 62, 63, 68
  capital 298–9, 300
  children as 356–8
  claims of 36
  collective 149–51, 172, 173, 477, 536, 542–3
  commodity needs-based subsidies for 174
  consumer 223, 224, 356–8
  consumption 258
  date-contingent 192
  different categories of 76
  economic 140, 143, 144, 145–6
  first tier of 45, 51
  full equality in the distribution of 46
  higher-order 24
  insurance, children as 356–8
  less tangible 167
  literacy and other 121
  luxury 180
  manufactured 346
  marketed, extent of choice among 182
  merit 37
  natural-rights 37
  needs-based 37
  negative-rights 69
  non-farm, market-mediated transactions in 223
  pleasure or agreeable consciousness the sole 386
  positive-rights 63, 69, 495, 498
  primary 37, 42
  private 149–51, 173
  producer 178, 368
  resource-based 285
  rights-based 172
  scarce, positive rights asserted to 45
  tradable 173, 282
  see also public goods
goods and services:
  consumption of 80, 166
  contingent 203
  distribution of 172
  essential to basic liberties 144
  expenditure on 168
  final allocation of 136
  household, wrong relative prices of 348
  individual's command over 38
  initial endowment of 169–70, 171
  legitimately acquired 139
  marketed, widening in command over 78
  net outputs of 176
  non-traded 282
  not implementable 72
  price-contingent 193
  public realm 175
  two tiers of 40
governments 62, 179, 180, 295, 476, 533, 544
  democratically elected 139–40
  duties 63–4
  exercise of choice 53
  good 56, 57
  involvement 295–6
  land reform programmes 292
  militarily controlled 58, 123
  mismanagement 148
  obligation regarding basic needs 46
  performance 54, 55, 56, 545
  policies 68
  predatory 292
  pricing policies directed against agriculture 527
  private information and 74
  procurement policies on staple food 270–1
  responsibilities 15, 53
  responsible 540
  role 537; agency 15, 22–7
  supply of insurance 206
  violence against citizens 123
grandmothers 93, 356
greed 166
Green Revolution 10 n., 98, 527
greenhouse effect 277
growth (stature) 83–6 passim, 89, 405, 426–32
Guatemala 106, 310 n., 402 n., 421, 428 n., 429 n., 470
  differences in nutrition in early childhood 84–5, 90
  landless population 479
  stature of labourers 436
guilds 211, 212

haemoglobin 402, 433, 434, 435
Hamiltonian 298, 300, 301, 302–3
happiness 28, 43, 52, 380–1
Harvard 311, 459

Haryana 271, 319
HDI (human development index) 77–8
health 77, 127, 175, 539–42
  anthropometric measures 81–7
  children's 100
  current and future states of 76
  expenditure 96
  ill-, effects of 11–14
  insurance 150
  mother's 86, 89
  public, statistics 127
  risks to 85
  see also diseases; health care; illnesses;
    infections; morbidity; mortality
health care 100, 181, 354, 498
  interventions 541
  low levels 247
  nutrition and 474
  public 174
hedonistic theory 33
heights 82, 83, 84, 85, 86, 461
Henry George Theorem 526 n.
heterogeneity of people 498–9
Himalayas 204, 216, 273, 320 n., 359
hired labour 222, 224, 227
  supervising 225, 228, 231–2, 257–8
Holland 115 n.
homeostasis 411, 441, 442, 443–52, 453
Honduras 110, 112, 293 n., 528
Hong Kong 127, 157
honorabilitatem ('honourable class') 24
horizontal equity 502
horizontal inequity 483, 499
households 149, 175, 192, 204, 219–397
  as allocation mechanisms 305–36
  Arrow–Debreu 227, 259
  assetless 321
  autocratic 333
  bargaining v. well-being maximization
    within 333–6
  cash incomes 308
  credit constraints 257–68
  elasticity of labour supply 223, 224
  endowments 172
  expenditure 309–10
  headed by women 181, 308
  identical 159–60
  labourer-cultivator 228, 260
  peasant 221–4, 257–60
  poor food, distribution within 523–4
  power and control over own lives 173
  reasoning, versus societal reasoning 349–53
  as reproductive units 343–70
  self-cultivator 228
human resource development 544
hxaro system 202 n.
hybrid wheat/rice 271

Hyderabad 84, 229, 415
hygiene 89

ICRISAT (International Crops Research
    Institute for the Semi-Arid
    Tropics) 229–30, 239–42 passim, 254,
    264, 322, 447, 470, 482, 490
ideal-regarding theories 36
IIED/WRI 272 n., 281 n., 308 n.
illegal activities 80, 139, 532
illiterate societies 356
illnesses 90, 91, 94, 247
  diarrhoeal 93, 405, 406
ILO (International Labour Office) 25 n.,
    34 n., 37, 80, 495
IMF (International Monetary Fund) 27 n.
immunization 95, 144–5, 430
impartiality 22, 47, 48
impersonality 46–9, 64
imports 175, 178
incentives 181, 224, 231, 244, 271 n., 504,
    505
  developing the notion of 160
  and development policies 525–45
  devising 214
  full 232
  group 25
  income increase compatible with 535
  individual 25, 192, 193
  keeping the elderly 241
  lack of, for error-correction 57
  market, encouragement of 270
  private 26, 157, 272, 359
  problems of 72, 73, 74
  repaying loans 250
  stifling 178
  strong, for acquisition of forest lands 293
  worrying about 46
income 9, 70, 78–81, 206, 246, 265, 481, 501,
    510
  aggregate 291
  average 471
  cash, control of 308
  client's 237
  compatible with incentives 534–5
  dated-contingent commodity 192
  derived from agriculture 479
  distribution 126
  exogenous 260, 261, 263
  expected 266–7
  farmers', increasing 287
  female–male wage ratios 317, 319
  fertility and 343–6, 366
  four possible sources 222
  from the agricultural sector 488
  future 263, 519
  greater opportunities 341

growth in 116, 471, 504
household-specific 205
increasing function of 195
index of 37
inequalities 105, 126, 291, 527
lotteries 200, 201
low 78, 199, 200, 542
non-wage 475, 495
parental, increased 365, 366
per capita 111, 126, 182, 317
rental 480, 485, 490, 496
risky 195, 196, 197
sharing 499
sharp decline in 264
smoothing consumption over fluctuations
    in 240
threshold 200, 201
uncertain 195, 253, 261
unearned 471, 474
widening sources, in times of stress 322
women's 275
see also national income; real income
independence 67
Independence of Irrelevant Alternatives 338
India:
    agricultural labour market closed 234–5
    agricultural performance 269
    arable land per capita 278 n.
    Brahmanic land/culture 317, 321
    children 83, 101, 311
    Chipko Movement 285
    classical 24, 43
    common-property resources 209, 290,
        291, 292
    Council for Medical Research 401
    credit markets 225 n.
    CSE (Centre for Science and Environment)
        216, 273, 281 n., 289, 294 n., 359
    elderly who live with their children 358
    election results (1977) and basic
        liberties 47
    energy 295, 447–8
    fuelwood collection in drylands 13
    gender bias/inequalities 7 n., 314
    Government: expenditure (1988) 124;
        Household Survey 254; procurement
        policies 270–1; Statistical Abstract,
        1986 314 n., 317 n.
    Green Revolution 527
    Hindus/Hinduism 24, 236–7, 321, 322,
        323, 362
    household allocations 313–21
    human capital accumulation 365 n.
    industrial and landowning interests 106
    infrastructure 147
    Integrated Nutrition Project (Tamil
        Nadu) 531, 532, 538

involuntary unemployment 475
kinship support systems 291 n.
landless persons 479
life expectancy 88, 93
living standards 18, 109, 110, 112–14, 118,
    127
marasmus 404–5
marriage 312, 322–4
Muslims 321, 323
National Sample Survey 310, 450, 470
Population Census (1981) 323
population growth 347
poverty 79, 80
preference for sons 368
risk 198, 206
role of Christian Church 103
rural 102, 238–42, 254, 329
savings 247
self-contained enclaves of production 226
significant determinant of
    productivity 436
Succession Bill (1956) 323
total factor productivity 156
total fertility rate 343, 345, 357
undernourishment 86, 401 n.
urban middle classes, demographic
    transition 369
women 275, 328, 367
see also Andhra Pradesh; Delhi; Goa;
    Hyderabad; ICRISAT; Karnataka;
    Kashmir; Kerala; Maharashtra;
    Narangwal; Punjab; Rajasthan; Uttar
    Pradesh; West Bengal
India Today 323 n.
indirect calorimetry 424
Indo-Gangetic plain 122
Indonesia 110, 112, 247, 278 n., 343, 402
Indra 43
industrialization 248
inequality 17, 123, 125–6, 292, 335, 473–511
    access to medical care 96
    ex post 334
    gender 311, 314, 318, 335
    income 105, 126, 291, 527
    no substantial gains from 524
    social and economic 42
    strict 513
    wealth 105
inessential sequence economies 227
infant industry 178, 179
infant mortality 85–90 passim, 93, 95, 115,
    216, 348, 405–6
    decline in 119–20
    significant contributor to 82
infant survival 77, 93, 100, 117–21 passim, 124
    defined 89
    reduced rates 355

infanticide 89
infections 90, 95, 96, 402, 430
  ability to fight 407
  avoidable 216
  diarrhoeal, link between malnutrition
    and 40
  freedom from 83, 405, 406, 407, 426
  nutrition and 405–8
  severe or repeated 406
information 74, 191–3, 225, 301
  asymmetries in 226
infrastructure 147–9, 295, 498, 527, 543
  absence of 155
  availability of 142
  co-operative 326, 330
  household, availability of 368
  investment in 157, 528, 538
  lack of 361
  provision of 293
  rural: employment guarantee schemes
    and 533–5; importance of public
    expenditure on 538; systematic dearth
    of 272
inheritance 322–4
inputs 53, 180
  material 222, 223–4
insurance 189–217, 253, 264–5
  destitution 207
  drought, extra cattle as 276
  facilities 295
  government and supply of 206
  health 150
  hunger 202 n., 204, 207
  mutual 203, 205, 208
  premia 189, 192, 201
  self- 204
  trading in, of paramount importance
    202
interdependence 67
interest-groups 294
interest rates 242, 250, 251, 252, 267, 268
interests 5–6, 34, 36, 61–2, 208, 210
  individual/own 29, 41, 58
  vital 38–9
International Finance Corporation 179, 273
interventions 272
inventories 205
investment 253, 264–5, 272, 537
  infrastructural 157, 528, 538
  private, massive 293
  productive 535
  productivity of 179, 180, 262
involuntary unemployment 489, 491–2, 511,
    521, 534
  concept 499
  definition 483
  labour markets and 477–83

on a permanent basis 519
  surplus labour and 505–9
  theoretical explanation for 509
iodine deficiency 96, 407, 429
Iran 124–5
Iraq 106, 124–5
iron deficiency 95, 96, 294, 402, 407
irrigation 271, 275, 282, 527
  creation of facilities 289
  projects 207
  systems 277, 287
iso-utility contour 472
Israel 279

Jamaica 428
Japan 86, 92, 156 n., 157, 179, 527 n.
  children's heights 83 n., 84
  nineteenth-century 103
Java 306, 462
Jordan 110, 112, 114
judiciary 56 n., 57, 109
just society 53, 74, 105, 106
justice 22, 24, 46
  common conception of 74
  distributive 54
  right to 104
  theories of 30, 32 n., 34, 42, 43, 48

Kalahari region 353
Kalai–Smorodinsky bargaining solution 331,
    332, 333, 337, 340–2
karma 33
Karnataka 202
Kashmir 122
Kenya 122, 254, 275, 283, 292, 421, 471
  living standards 109, 111, 117
Kerala 92 n., 202, 317, 319–21 *passim*,
    354
kinship 59, 366
  control of women 362
  groups 67, 243, 249
  major source of credit 243
  networks 322
  support systems 26–7
knowledge 145, 151–8, 231, 240
  dissemination of 346
  hidden 226
Korea, *see* South Korea
Kuhn–Tucker theorem 186, 281 n.
!Kung San hunter-gatherers 202, 353
kwashiorkor 81, 404, 429

labour 154, 221–56, 530
  rationing 483, 492
  surplus 482, 509
labour effort 298–9, 300
labour markets 170, 238–42. 476, 488, 509

agricultural 496, 500, 508, 511;
  closed 234–5
capricious 260
casual 202, 255, 482, 483, 505, 509;
  competitive equilibrium in 510
geographically segmented 202, 235
and involuntary unemployment 477–83
married daughters' employment prospects
  in 312
nutrition-based theories of 511
rationing 482, 502
labour power 474, 477, 484, 487, 498, 509–10
  aggregate 478, 507
  aggregate supply and demand functions
    of 493
  asset ownership, maintenance costs,
    and 473–7
  competitive markets for 479
lactation 89, 402, 531
  see also Gambia (Keneba women)
Lagrange multipliers 160, 259, 262
land 154, 155, 221–56, 280, 527
  arable and grazing, quality of 274
  carrying capacity 278–80, 497
  competitive markets for 479
  distribution 478–9, 496, 515
  marginal product of 487
  nutritional status and the ownership of 503
  privatization of 292
  property rights on 288–9
  rental rate on 487, 479, 512, 514
  see also drylands
landlords 225, 230, 239
  absentee 241
  monopsonistic 476
Latin America 352, 356, 405, 504, 508
  average age of women at marriage 363
  calorie deficiency 440
  children's body size 83
  indicators of undernourishment 86
  involuntary unemployment 475, 511
  magnitude of poverty 79
  social rates of return on education 98, 99
  total factor productivity 155–6
  see also under various country names
Law of Large Numbers 203
Law of Single Price 168
learning by doing 157, 240, 525
Lebesgue integrals 288, 513
legislative and executive branches 56 n., 57
legitimacy 106, 123, 130, 326
leviratic unions 323
libertarian theories 71–2
liberties 15, 33, 35 n., 36, 72
  absence of 285
  basic 42, 47, 51, 52, 68, 76, 144
  curtailment of 16, 52

distribution of 172
indices of 193
negative 44, 63, 144, 172
positive 63
rights essential for 105
severe deprivation of 110
see also political and civil liberties
Libya 279
licensing agreements 153
life expectancy 77, 87–9, 108 n., 109–13
    passim, 115, 117–21 passim
  female 348, 358
  increasing 83, 92, 118–19, 306,
  low 13, 93
  male–female 313
  outcasts 475
literacy 77, 97–8, 108 n., 109–13 passim,
    115, 117–21 passim, 145, 317–18, 319, 356
  adult rate a rogue index 116
  essential for codifying information 152
  female 307
  low rate 359
  male–female 306, 314
livestock 239, 240, 244, 287
living standards 18, 77, 137, 271, 388
  dismally low 384
  future 385
  growth in 154
  higher 256
  increases in 142
  indicators, middle-income countries 125
  lifetime 386, 387
  long-run improvements 143
  low but positive 390–1
  moderately high 390
  world's poorest countries 109–14, 117–19
loans 237–8, 241, 242, 253, 322, 495
  ability to repay 251
  demand for 268
  from international agencies 293
  incentives for repaying 250
  Pareto-efficient allocation of 251–2
  price of 202
  riskiness of 267
  screening applicants 249–50, 500, 537,
    538, 539
  see also collateral
Lorenz curve 496
luxuries 504, 505

Mafia 142
Maghribi traders 211
Mahabharata 43
Maharashtra 229, 310, 319, 534
maintenance requirements 19, 439, 442,
    453, 507
Malawi 110, 111, 112, 328 n., 536

Malaysia 98 n., 222, 223, 224, 526
Mali 110, 111, 112
malnourishment 12, 90, 91, 434, 531
malnutrition 20, 96, 430, 473–511
  adaptation to 460
  chronic 12, 13
  infants recovering from 427 n.
  link between diarrhoeal infection and 406
  long-term 429
  maternal 431
  mild 455
  moderate to severe 407
  policies for alleviating 21, 494
  prevention of 531
  protein-calorie 402 n., 404
Malta 279
management 165, 167, 231–2
marasmus 404–5, 429, 460
marginal products 230, 232, 487
markets 16, 123, 137–40, 477
  annuity 246
  anonymous 245
  Arrow-Debreu 192
  capital 246, 275, 276, 358, 368
  clear 492
  contestable 56, 148
  contingent commodity 192, 199
  factor 221, 486
  and their failure 284–8
  formal 202
  forward 189, 487
  freeing, from restrictive practices 476
  illegal 532
  insurance 193, 244, 249, 250, 275
  land 238–42
  loan 250
  mediate inter-household transactions 17
  missing 476
  private 76
  rental 149
  risk 238
  rural, interlinked 241
  of significance 475
  smoothly functioning 498
  spot 235
  thin 234
  widening 18, 292, 295
  see also black-markets; competitive
    markets; credit markets; labour markets
Markov process 446
marriage 102, 312, 320, 322–4, 354
  average age of, for girls 375
  early and universal 363
  low age of, for women 307
Marshallian external economies 372 n.
Marshallian *tâtonnement* 374
Matthew Effect 369

Mauritania 91, 110, 112, 272, 289
Mauritius 58, 87, 109–14 *passim*
maximal aerobic power 84, 433
maximal oxygen uptake 433–6, 459, 461,
  485, 505
mechanization 225, 229, 232
medical attention 96
menstruation 402
Mere Addition Paradox 383, 385, 388, 390,
  391 n.
metabolic process 404, 406, 418, 433, 450,
  452, 458–61, 520
  see also BMR (basal metabolic rate)
Mexico 253, 358, 428, 528
microbes 276
Middle East 79, 106, 307, 352, 440
migration 234, 323, 509
milk 457
Minnesota experiment 460
minorities 57
mobility costs 234, 235, 508
monetary bets 197
money-lenders 238, 241, 242, 252, 322
monopsony 239, 476, 500–1
moral hazard 56, 149, 204, 226, 230–1, 249,
  251, 322, 501, 526–7, 528, 544–5
  granaries plagued by 244
  herding and 245
  involved in loans 538
  regarding creditworthiness 241
  rental market for draught animals and 242
  resource allocations suffering from 537
morbidity 38, 41, 83–4, 90–7, 407
  effective indicators of 82
  malnourishment and 39
  malnutrition and 12
Morocco 110, 112, 113
mortality 54, 92, 93, 343, 345, 351, 392, 407
  age-specific rates 88
  child rates 87, 101, 306, 317, 363
  declining 357, 364
  difference between rich and poor
    nations 90 n.
  effective indicators of 82
  female 313; maternal 216, 348, 541
  indices 87–90, 311
  livestock 287
  low rates 12, 345
  neonatal 89, 431
  perinatal 95
  prenatal 85, 431
  risks 82, 83
  see also infant mortality
mothers 58–9, 216
  education 89, 99, 365
  expectant 12
  health status 86

malnourished 90
 unearned income in hands of 471
motor development/control 429, 430, 431
mountain regions 291
muscle cell mass 425, 433–6 *passim*, 459,
 460, 461
Myanmar 106

Narangwal Rural Health Research
 Centre 95
Nash bargaining theory 327 n., 330–3,
 335 n., 337–40
Nash equilibria 66 n., 70, 72, 159, 209, 215,
 374, 375–6
 multiple 371
 non-co-operative 330, 372, 373
 savings rules 379 n.
 symmetric 160, 161, 162, 164
Nata River Bushmen 202
national income 108, 117, 118, 119, 181–3
 per head 87, 107, 114–15, 120, 182
 real 77, 81, 120, 184–8
national security 144, 146
natural monopolies 147, 151, 169, 237,
 498
 nationalized 148
needs 74, 278–80
 calorie 282, 404
 commodity 36–40, 45, 61, 187
 food 401–36
 individual 52
 nutritional 55, 61
 resource 277
 special 39, 175, 181
 see also basic needs
negative rights 7, 15, 40–6, 69, 73 n., 135
 equal 46
negotiation sets 327–30 *passim*, 333, 337,
 338, 340–1
Neo-Utilitarians 387 n.
Nepal 110, 112, 275, 306, 313 n.
nephews and nieces 363
New Guinea 457 n.
New York Times 355 n.
Niger 109, 111, 113
Nigeria 201, 206, 223, 249 n., 275, 289
 credit 225 n., 241 n.
 living standards 110, 112, 117
 violence 122
NNP (net national product) 281, 297–304,
 494, 495
non-corneal xerophthalmias 406–7
non-existence 383, 397
non-utilitarian theories 33
norms, *see* social norms
North American tribes 202
Norway 83

nuclear units 365
numeracy 97–103, 121, 145, 152, 356
nutrients 99, 437
 ability to absorb 406
 complementarities among 401–5
 depriving agriculture of 277
 household 310
 macro- 402, 403
 micro- 406
 soil 274–5
 urgency of 471
nutrition 13, 39, 82–7 *passim*, 89, 127, 254,
 275, 336, 429–46 *passim*, 441, 461, 484,
 485, 490, 498–502, 511, 529, 532, 542–43
 biases in allocation 309
 fecundity and 353
 and infection 405–8
 productivity and 247–8, 420, 462–75
 passim, 479, 481–2, 486–7, 499, 503,
 505–8, 512–25

obedience 50
obligation theories 382, 386
obligations 48, 50, 59, 74, 237, 387
 community contractual 291
 government/State 46, 53, 369, 387
 inter-household 202
 multiplicity of 105
 social or familial 242
oedema 408, 429
old-age security 357, 358, 361, 363, 368
oligopoly 179
Operation Barga 237
opportunism 122
opportunity costs 355, 365
optimal control 297–8, 301, 302
optimization 64–5, 298, 300
option value 283
oral rehydration 95, 430
outcasts 255, 256, 475
output 153, 156, 214, 299
 actual losses in 92
 agricultural 507, 509, 522
 annual percentage rates of growth 155
 cash crops 272
 equals its marginal cost of production 168
 farm, elasticity of household consumption
 of 224
 fuelwood 300
 grain 178
 gross 302
 indirect effect of reducing 91
 net, goods and services 176
 optimal level 148
 unequal asset distribution on 496–7
 work, transformation of calorie-intake
 into 334

ownership 241, 243, 288, 473–7, 503

Pakistan 241 n., 313, 348 n., 364 n., 541
  growth rate in income 80
  living standards 110, 112, 118
  non-institutional loans 250, 538
  pattern of government expenditure
    (1988) 124
  rural credit market 202
  tenancy 229
Panama 290
Panchayats 209
Papua New Guinea 310 n.
Paraguay 110, 113, 114
parenthood 393
parents 377–9, 385–6, 387
Pareto criterion 372 n., 373
Pareto-efficiency 73, 143, 174, 284, 328, 337,
    368, 476, 537
  equilibrium allocations 493;
    competitive 170, 172
  loan allocation 251–2
  resource allocation 138, 216
  risk-bearing allocation 199
  silent 171
  symmetric allocation 160
  two-person negotiations 333 n.
Pareto-inefficiency 379 n.
Pareto-plus Principle 383, 385, 388, 390
Partha 43
participation 238–9, 319–20, 535–9
patents 145, 153
paternalism 35, 36
path-dependent processes 142
Pathan tribeswomen 536
pathogens 95, 407
patriarchy 366, 367
patrilineal societies 102, 363
patron–client relationships 140, 208, 235, 236
peer group pressure 430
permissible sets 168
  of actions 62, 69
  of choices 69
  of plans 62, 63, 66–7
  of strategies 68, 467
personal life-style 96
personal service 143
Peru 139, 528
pharmaceuticals 277
phenotype plasticity 443
Philippines 157, 285 n., 402, 447, 525, 526
  living standards 110, 112, 113, 114, 118
piece-rates 229, 481, 498, 501, 514
  daily 233, 238
  efficiency 496, 512, 516, 520, 521
  efficiency wages and 483–6
  equilibrium 491, 492, 493, 507, 515
plans 61, 64

elementary 60
feasible set of 65, 72–3
permissible sets of 62, 63, 66–7
pluralism 56, 57–8, 123, 173–6
political and civil liberties 15, 37, 38, 42, 45,
    47, 55, 70, 107, 113–16 passim
  established 140
  guarantees of 56
  HDI oblivious of 78
  indices of 108, 123
  instrumental virtues, no reason to
    question 128
  lack of 52
  priority rule over 46
  protecting and promoting 57
  prototypical example of freedom 41
  severely restricted 127
  versus economic progress 116–21
political and civil rights 109, 115, 120, 182,
    185, 285
  freedoms used to assess 131
  indices 110–11, 112–13, 119, 129–31
  literacy and 116
poll tax 161, 165 n.
pollutants 274, 276, 284, 285, 299–300
polygyny 312, 355, 362
pooling workers 201–4, 205, 207, 244, 501
population ethics 392, 394
population growth 11, 17–19 passim, 270,
    280, 354–5
  macroeconomic consequences 346
  problem 346–9
positive rights 4, 7, 15, 40–6, 63, 69, 149
  asserted to scarce goods 45
  minimal 138
possible/potential people 384, 386, 389, 390
Potlatch system 202 n.
poverty 101, 116, 150, 269–95
  abject 499
  absolute 20, 21, 125
  alleviating malnutrition and 21
  and the environmental resource base
    269–96
  extreme 201, 347
  high incidence of 531
  illiteracy and 102
  magnitude of 79, 80
  synonymous with low income 78
  vicious circle of 369
poverty gap 78–9, 80
preferences:
  gender 357, 368, 471
  individual 180
  moral, intransitive 389
pregnancy 356, 402, 531
  see also Gambia (Keneba women)
prices 167, 168, 177, 496
  accounting 174, 182, 301

biased set of 281
competitive 172, 201, 202
constant relative, *see* shadow prices
contingent: absence of 202; goods and
    services 193
contingent-commodity 189;
    Arrow-Debreu 203 n., 304
differential 175
domestic: agricultural 272; tradable
    goods 173
food crop 487; elasticities with respect
    to 223
higher 180
household-specific 182, 186
import 175
international 173, 272
market 173, 174, 182, 285
producer, controls 272
relative 192; wrong 348
sectoral rigidities 173
sharpest and bluntest justification of
    mechanism 171
Prisoner's Dilemma 18 n., 163, 211, 347,
    348, 374 n.
privacy 73 n., 74, 225, 226
private medical facilities 533
private realm 149–51, 172, 174
    competitive mechanisms in 165–9
    distribution of purchasing power in
        173
privatization 164, 270, 292, 293
probability 30–1, 69, 201, 415
    distributions 288
    default 251
    employment 482
procreation 392, 394
production 140, 142, 143, 257
    basic goods and services 16
    beef-cattle 293
    capacity 156
    collective goods 542–3
    commodity 19, 345; single 168
    costs 258
    demand for material inputs in 223–4
    domestic, excessive protection of 179
    efficient 176, 177, 502
    enclaves 508
    factors of 155, 486; material 154
    firm's technologies 172
    food 123, 178
    household 170
    inefficient 178
    marginal cost of 148, 168
    mechanization of 225
    norms of behaviour pertaining to 166
    organization of 151, 152, 154, 155, 157;
        credit constraint and 224–9

possibilities 167, 184
price equal to average cost of 148
primitive 243
rice, technological practices in 319
rural, resource basis of 269–73
techniques 145, 233
uniform strategies 178
village enclaves as units of 234–8
see also agricultural production
production functions 161, 299, 515
productive capability 225
productivity 145, 475
    agricultural 506, 520
    efficient 463–5, 481, 485, 507, 520
    energy requirements and 412–23
    gains from agrarian reform 526
    growth in 142
    increased 476
    investment 179, 180, 262
    labour 98, 247, 248, 359, 365, 369
    marginal increase in 508
    maximal 520
    nutrition and 508, 512–24
    nutritional status and 412–23, 525
    physical 474, 505
    significant determinant of 436
    soil 243
    total factor 155, 156, 157, 158
    unequal asset distribution on 496–7
profits 163, 222, 223, 224
    maximizing 162, 164, 167
    super-normal 179
pro-natalism 357
property rights 284, 285 n., 288–9
    private 136, 138, 144, 286
    resources and 135–7
prospects 67–8
protectionism 178, 179, 180
protein 403, 424, 450, 459
    catabolism and turnover 460
    deficiencies in 402
    intake 461
    oxidation of 453
    requirements 404
psychic costs 105
public bads 145
public goods 51, 144, 537, 539
    and common-property resources 143–7,
        159–64
    providers of 24
public health services 533
public realm 149–51, 173, 174, 175
public supply 161
Punjab 98, 122, 271, 319, 321
purchasing power 173, 176, 177, 530
    parity 79
pygmies 442

quality of life 107, 125, 181, 384
  improvement in 170
  indicators for judging 183 n.
  indices 34
  inter-country comparison of 108–16
quantity control 163
Quetelet index 414
quotas 163, 178

R & D (research and development) 281–2,
  303 n.
rainfall 276, 279
Rajasthan 209, 292, 314 n., 320, 321
rates of return 98, 99
ration cards 271
rations 180
real income 77, 81, 184–8, 224
  current and prospective 76
  decline in per head 117
  growth in per head 120
  per head 121
reciprocity 208–12, 215, 322, 352
redistribution 20, 271
  asset 173, 517, 533
  benefits and burdens 494, 495
  efficacy of economic growth with 490
  egalitarian 495
  growth with 494–8
  purchasing power 176, 177
reforestation 335
regeneration 274, 277, 280, 299
religion 357
religious and ethnic groups 306
rentiers 492
rents 173, 179, 230, 231
  hidden, syphoning 140
  on land 479, 487, 512, 514
reproductive costs 356
repugnant conclusion 381, 383–5, 390, 397
reservation wages 484, 488, 491–3 passim,
  507
  casual workers 520
  constraint 512
  distribution of 480
  low 479, 485, 496, 497, 513, 515
reservoirs 277, 278, 279
residual claimants 225, 232
resource allocation 16, 55, 67, 537
  destitution as a problem 9–11
  equilibrium 234
  fundamental problem 73
  institutions which guide 41
  mechanisms 76, 135–58, 294, 477, 511,
    512, 542; changes in 57
  social organization as a basis for 44
resource allocation theory 347, 543
  modern 17, 542

nutrition-based 497
  standard 289, 305, 361, 467, 468, 475, 586;
    among households 133–217, 245, 249
resources 135–7
  availability of 63
  distribution of 54, 55, 63; just 52
  environmental 269–96, 302, 346
  exhaustible 280
  expenditure of 82, 225
  function of 61
  material 360
  natural 136, 155, 273, 274, 276, 280
  overlapping generations and the
    transmission of 212–17
  public 106
  right to a certain share of 104
  use of 55
  see also common-property resources;
    fuelwood; land; resource allocation;
    water
respect 73, 105
returns to scale 487
rice 271, 278, 319
rights 5
  absolute 35 n., 46
  accommodation and support 363
  animals 393
  background 26
  claims of 53
  distributional aspects of 137
  essential for basic liberties 104
  freedom and 40–6
  fundamental 34
  group 288
  immunization 150
  initial, over sufficient amounts of
    commodities 138
  instrumental worth of a wide variety of 26
  inviolable 35, 46, 72
  just distribution of 135
  natural 37, 43
  ownership 241
  pollutees' 284
  polluters' 284, 285
  priority of good over 28
  priority over utility or desert 44
  relatively few 58
  social contract 54
  socio-economic 3–5, 47, 116
  State 285
  theories of 29
  utility and 32–6
  violation of 25
  see also civil rights; negative rights;
    political rights; positive rights; property
    rights
rights-based theories 7, 30, 33, 34, 35, 36

absolutist 28–9
risk aversion 195–6, 198, 238, 250, 264
  absolute 240, 261
  choice under uncertainty and 193–9
  relative 263
risks 52, 57, 178, 234, 251, 253, 264–7
  agricultural 204–8, 244, 538
  attitudes to 65
  correlated 204–8
  death 83, 87
  health 85
  household's behaviour and revealed
    attitude towards 193
  household-specific 202
  idiosyncratic 203
  morbidity and mortality 82, 83
  obstetric 85
  pooling 203, 205, 207, 244; and
    spreading 201–4
  scope of transactions in 226
  trading in 201–4
rivers 279, 286
robustness and extensions 498–505
rules versus discretion 50–2
rural communities 149, 208
Rwanda 110, 111, 112, 118, 307

Sahel 274, 279, 289
salinization/saltwater intrusion 275, 276
sanctions 210–11, 212, 214
sanitation 92, 95
savings 221–56, 369
  collective associations 149
  dichotomy between consumption and 249
  formal facilities 237
  individual 245
  life-cycle 246, 253
  link between fertility and 246–7
  motive for 253, 260–4
  past 258
  precautionary 254, 260–4
Scandinavia 348 n.
schoolchildren 430
screening 249–50, 500, 537, 538, 539
seasonality 227, 483, 505, 511
second-best optima 176, 186
secrecy 145
self-interest 211
self-transcendence 356
semi-starvation 458–9, 460
sex ratio 313–14, 317–18, 319
sexual abstinence 308, 353, 354, 355–6
shadow prices 79, 174, 182, 183, 184
  environmental 280–3
  goods and services 280
  information for estimating 301
  non-negative 186

  not household-specific 187
  positive 186
sharecropping 229, 230, 232, 242
shifting cultivation 243, 244
shocks 205–6
short-term adjustment 443–8
Sicily 142
sick-leave 91
Sidgwick-Meade Rule 396, 397
Sierra Leone 110, 111, 112, 223, 422
Sikhs 321
Singapore 127, 157
single-party systems 57
skills 171, 184, 364, 499
social contracts 36, 46, 149–50
  Hobbsian 70
  hypothetical 27, 47, 207
  idea of 106
  implementation of 105
  objects of 50–74
  rights 54
  State role in 52
  theories 47, 48
social evaluation 175, 180, 182
social evaluation function 71, 73, 184, 185
social indicators 38–9
social mobilization 123
social norms 105, 234, 291–2, 328, 351, 355
  consistent with contingent goods and
    services 203
  cultural 312
  fertility 361
  internalization of 59
  mutual insurance codified through 207
  pertaining to production and
    exchange 166
  practice and enforcement 290
  reciprocity as, in stationary
    environments 208–12
  stringent 245
social security 67, 329, 358
social states, see states of affairs
social systems 66, 168
  dynamics of 369
  formulation 60–4
  history of 374
  stationary 65
social welfare function 71
soil 243, 274, 276, 277, 281, 282
  degradation/erosion 275
solidarity systems 9
Somalia 110, 111, 112, 122
sons 323, 357, 367, 368
South Korea, Republic of 90 n., 103, 107 n.,
  269 n.
  fertility rates 345
  land reforms 527

South Korea, Republic of (*cont.*):
   living standards 110, 111, 113, 114, 118
   total factor productivity 157
Spain 115 n.
Spearman correlation coefficients 114, 115, 120
species preservation 393
specific egalitarianism 175, 180, 181
Sri Lanka 81 n., 93, 103, 529, 530
   fertility rates 307, 345, 354, 367
   life expectancy 92
   living standards 87, 109, 110, 111, 113,
     118, 319
   violence 122
starvation 213, 470
State 144, 150, 177, 205, 238, 305, 335
   benefits 529
   bound by terms of social contract 139
   coercion 122, 124
   constraints on freedom imposed by 121
   duties 143, 545
   guarantees for medical care 151
   guarantees from 67
   imposition of lump-sum taxes 165
   information about needs, endowments and
     utilities 172, 176
   involvement 145
   is created 64
   markets for goods allied to explicit support
     by 76
   Minimal 138, 539, 544
   obligation 53, 369, 387
   political morality and 22–49, 123
   protection against destitution 67
   provisions 106, 146
   repression 58
   responsibility of 135, 477, 498
   rights 285
   roles: establishment of credit services 238;
     restricted, in socio-economic
     sphere 137–8; social contract 52, 207
   transactions need to be observable by 187
states of affairs 29–30, 35, 47, 185, 190 n.
   bad 382
   features of 53
   most desirable 72
   ranking of 58
   social ordering over 68
   utilitarian evaluations of 31
stationary outcome 168, 169
status quo point (threat point) 327
stochastic processes:
   endogenous 445, 452
   stationary, exogenously given 445, 452
strategies 60, 65–6, 68, 178
stress 91, 278–80
   nutritional, extreme 353
   resource 277

   undue 325
   water 279–80
   widening sources of income in times
     of 322
strong-neutrality axiom 71
stunting 83–6 *passim*, 361, 428, 429, 434, 442
   adolescent 426
   cognitive and motor capacity 431
sub-Saharan Africa 27 n., 209, 221, 540,
   541 n.
   agrarian relations 243–5
   agricultural production 269, 270, 271–2,
     526
   body weights 205
   child death rate 310
   child-spacing 353 n.
   consumption insurance for the young 346
   cost of rearing children 366
   diets 404
   droughts 190, 276
   energy expenditure 295
   fertility 307, 308, 345, 351–2, 355, 357,
     359 n., 360, 364 n.
   gender bias in survival chance 7 n.
   indicators of undernourishment 86
   iodine and iron deficiency 407
   land rights 288, 289
   life expectancy at birth 87–8
   living standards 18,
   magnitude of poverty 79, 80
   marriage 312, 362
   massive curtailment of liberties 16
   nutritional anaemia 12, 348
   population growth 347, 354–5, 359 n.
   sex-preference 368
   social rates of return on education 98, 99
   some special features 361–3
   total factor productivity 155, 156, 157, 158
   water collection 13
   see also under various country names
subsidies 181, 285, 528
   consumer goods 180
   consumer, cheap calls for 177
   export 179
   food 528–33; targeted 543
   household-specific 172, 175, 187
   needs-based goods 174
   optimum 175, 182
   person-specific 175
   Pigovian 146, 161
subsistence crops 223, 224
subsistence economies 273, 358
subsistence requirements 237
substitution 262, 346
Sudan 14 n., 106, 122, 123, 147
   living standards 110, 112, 118
Summers–Heston ranking 114 n.

sunk costs 148
supervision 225, 228, 231–2, 257–8
supplementations:
  calorie 421, 470
  diet 95, 401–2
  energy 401, 432
  nutritional 428, 432, 543; for stunted and
    wasted people 531
  programmes 470, 532
  women 456
surplus 163, 177
  labour 482, 509
survival 38
  chances of a newborn 100
  desire for 87
  instinct for 61
  long-term chances 335
  see also children; infant survival
sustainable development 302–3
Sweden 115 n.

taboos 355
tagging 181, 531, 532
Taiwan 103, 157, 432, 527
Tanzania 103, 178, 272, 287, 289
  living standards 110, 111, 112, 119
tariffs 178
taxation/taxes 163–4
  advantages 528
  border 178
  commodity 174, 175, 182, 529
  consumer goods 180
  consumption 180
  exemption from 293
  household-specific 161, 172, 174, 175, 187
  imports 178
  international-trade 178
  land 527
  lump-sum 165, 168, 172; optimal 175 n.
  person-specific 175
  producer versus consumer 176–81
  punitive 177, 272
  theory of 181
Taylor expansion 301
technological change 155, 527
technological innovations 157, 335
tenancy 229–33, 242
Thailand 103, 222–4 passim, 269 n., 306, 309
  fertility 343, 345
  infant mortality 100 n.
  living standards 110, 113, 114, 119
  population growth 354
time and history 501–3
time-rates 229, 233
Togo 122
topsoil 275
totalitarianism 74

trade:
  foreign/international 157, 172
  restrictions on 174, 180
  terms of 202, 272, 393
transaction costs 142, 287, 292
transfers 180, 476, 534
  lump-sum 172, 174, 186
transhumance 244
transport costs 202, 243, 282, 533, 538
trickle-down effect 20, 80, 494, 505, 516
  speed of 517–18
tuberculosis 83, 94
Tunisia 110, 112, 114
tyrannies 130

Uganda 111, 112, 119, 122
uncertainty 63, 230, 234, 235, 283
  choice under 32 n., 193–9, 200, 201
  environmental 189–93
  future 303–4
undernourishment 6–7, 12–14 passim, 20, 21,
  84–6 passim, 361
  adaptation to 39, 437–72
  and destitution 399–545
  effect on sexual reproduction 353
underpricing 285
UNDP (United Nations Development
  Programme) Human Development
  Reports: (1990) 7, 10, 16, 17, 20, 25 n.,
  34 n., 42, 77, 542; (1991) 77–8, 542
unemployment 254–6
  see also involuntary unemployment
UNEP (United Nations Environment
  Programme) 275 n.
unequal sharing 334
UNICEF (United Nations Children's
  Fund) 90, 306, 317 n., 533
United Kingdom 4, 156 n., 175, 529, 532 n.
United Nations 275, 313 n., 401 n., 437 n.,
  441
  see also FAO; UNDP; UNEP; UNICEF;
  UNU
United States 83, 152 n., 156 n., 352 n.,
  365, 369 n.
  aggregate savings 247
  arable land per capita 278 n.
  children's height 83 n.
  elderly who live with their children 358
  expenditure on defence 93
  female mortality rates 88
  health 96
  National Center for Health Statistics 84
  potential income losses due to illness 92
  regulation of private natural
    monopoly 148
  southern, nineteenth-century 201
unpaid family workers 307

untouchables 106 n.
UNU (United Nations University) 412 n.
urban middle class 369
urbanization 365
utilitarian theories 7, 28, 34, 47, 379
utilitarianism 31, 32, 35, 47
  average 380
  choice-theoretic 33, 35 n., 36, 48, 58, 171,
    172, 180
  classical 28, 33, 48, 378, 380–1, 386; in a
    limited world 395–7
  person-affecting 387 n., 389 n.
utility 3, 63, 65, 70, 71, 168, 185, 372
  average and total 379–80
  consequences 33, 34
  efficiency, see Pareto efficiency 73
  expected 265, 268, 327; see also expected
    utility hypothesis
  household 166, 222, 364
  improving/reducing 252
  major constituent of 87
  marginal 196, 263, 396
  parental 378
  and rights 32–6
  subsistence level of consumption 395
utility functions 58, 59, 62, 68, 136, 159, 187,
    193–7, 258–61, 325–8 passim, 337, 340,
    397
  aggregate 379
  altering 67
  borrower's 266
  iso-elastic 197, 263
  lender's 267
  reflection of ordering over actions 209
  State has full information about 172
  von Neumann–Morgenstern 194 n., 200,
    265, 267
  see also expected utility hypothesis
Uttar Pradesh 216

values 5–9, 106, 392, 394
vegetarianism 321
vegetation cover 275
Venezuela 528
Vietnam 103
violence 122, 123
von Neumann–Morgenstern theory 32 n.,
    193 n., 194 n., 197, 198, 200, 265, 267,
    364 n.
vulgaris ('common mass') 24

wages 302, 308, 328, 505, 508, 514
  Arrow–Debreu 227
  casual 508; calorie-equivalent of 510
  cuts 509–11
  daily rates 236
  female–male income ratios 317, 319

  market 491
  rise in 508
  see also efficiency wages; reservation
    wages
wars and strife 121–5
Warsaw Ghetto 456 n., 460
wastage/wasting 83, 86, 294, 361
water 279–80, 282, 358
  collecting 295, 306–7, 359
  drinking, access to 405
  evaporating 275, 276
  irrigation 271, 282, 527
  potable 95, 147
wealth 70, 166, 168, 196, 237
  growing 91
  household-specific lump-sum
    transfers 172
  index of 37
  inequalities in 105
  measure of 298
  optimal lump-sum transfers 174
  to obtain a bride 362
weaning foods 90
weight, see body weight
welfare-benefit system 529
welfarism 70
well-being:
  bargaining versus 333–6
  commodity basis of 3–21
  constituents and determinants 75–8
  efficiency 177
  from theory to measurement 75–103
  national income real as a measure of 184–8
  public judgements and aggregative
    evaluations of 32–6
  realization of 104–31
  social 81; functions 68, 70–2
  sustainable, Hamiltonian and 302–3
  theory of 1–131
  zero 384, 385, 390
West Bengal 59, 80, 233, 242, 429 n.
  casual workers 229, 255, 483, 508
  female participation rates 320
  tenancy 237
  wage rates 235, 236, 498, 508
Western socialist block 89
wheat 271, 319
WHO (World Health Organization) 86 n.
  Energy and Protein Requirements
    (1985) 83, 402 n., 409 n., 412, 413, 422,
    423, 424 n., 425, 426, 427 n., 431, 438,
    439, 442 n.
women 13, 91, 216, 282, 306, 335, 341, 355
  disproportionate portion of the casual
    workforce 239
  economic dependence on men 323, 367,
    370

employment opportunities 312, 351
farming by, viable 243
forgone work-capacity for 356
growing autonomy of 96
incomes 275
increasingly vulnerable to destitution 27
little control over cash income 309
longer hours of work 306–7
low age-of-marriage for 307
manual labourers in construction sites
  320
married 354
most valued physical asset 240
nomadic bush-dwelling 353
responsibility of 291
single 328
stunted 85
supplemented 456
time allocation 309
unemployment experienced
  disproportionately by 255
utility level 333
widowed 362
work allocation 294–5
young 59, 352
see also breast-feeding; lactation;
  mothers; pregnancy
work capacity 432–6
World Bank 27 n., 541
  *Population Growth and Policies in sub-
  Saharan Africa (1986b)* 272 n.

*Sub-Saharan Africa: From Crisis to
  Sustainable Growth (1989b)* 12, 99 n.,
  147, 243 n., 249 n., 269 n., 272,
  281 n.
*The Population, Agriculture and
  Environment Nexus in sub-Saharan
  Africa (1991b)* 348, 359 n.
World Development Reports: (1983) 93,
  108 n., 111 n., 119 n.; (*1984*) 18 n., 347,
  349, 354, 365; (*1986*) 16; (*1986a*) 21,
  25 n., 177, 179 n., 272 n., 498, 530;
  (*1988*) 89, 90 n., 92, 348 n.; (*1989b*) 536,
  540; (*1990*) 7, 10, 14 n., 16, 17, 20,
  25 n., 79 n., 80, 86, 124 n., 125 n., 139,
  269 n., 343 n., 533, 542; (*1990b*) 179 n.;
  (*1991*) 25 n.; (*1991a*) 92, 93, 94, 99, 107,
  122, 125, 157 n., 158, 180 n., 177,
  179 n., 273, 543 n., 544 n.; (*1991b*) 519;
  (*1992*) 276, 405
World Tables (1988–9) 108 n., 111 n.,
  118 n.
World Fertility Survey 308

Yemen 111, 112

Zaïre 111, 112, 122, 289
Zambia 111, 112, 289
zamindars 209
Zimbabwe 93, 111, 112

Index compiled by Frank Pert